Society today
FOURTH EDITION

Society

today

FOURTH EDITION

NORMAN GOODMAN
State University of New York
at Stony Brook

GARY T. MARX
Massachusetts Institute
of Technology

RANDOM HOUSE
NEW YORK

Fourth Edition

987654321

Copyright © 1971, 1973, 1978, 1982
by Random House, Inc.

Library of Congress Cataloging in Publication Data

Goodman, Norman.
  Society today.

  Bibliography: p. 541
  Includes index.
  1. Sociology. I. Marx, Gary T. II. Title.
HM51.G637   1982   301   81-8491
ISBN 0-394-32550-8   AACR2

Text design: Betty Binns Graphics/Martin Lubin

Cover art: *Flight* (48 inches by 60 inches), 1979. Bernard
Dreyfus. Courtesy Sutton Gallery, New York

Photo research: Cheryl Moch

Manufactured in the United States of America

ACKNOWLEDGMENTS FOR CROSS–CULTURAL
READINGS   **p. 36** From *Yanomamö: The Fierce People*
by Napoleon A. Chagnon. Copyright © 1968 by Holt, Rinehart
and Winston, Inc. Reprinted by permission of Holt, Rinehart
and Winston.   **p. 102** Reproduced by permission of the American Anthropological Association from *American Anthropologist*,
58 (1956), 503–507.   **p. 138** From *Tropical Childhood: Cultural Transmission and Learning in a Puerto Rican Village* by
David Landy. Copyright © 1959, the University of North Carolina
Press.   **p. 162** Abridgment of "Deviants from the Mundugumor
Ideal," in *Sex and Temperament in Three Primitive Societies* by
Margaret Mead. By permission of William Morrow & Company.
p. 232 From J. H. Hutton, *Caste in India* (1963), reprinted by
permission of Oxford University Press.   **p. 288** From Peter
Magubane, *Magubane's South Africa* (1978), reprinted by
permission of Alfred A. Knopf, Inc.   **p. 342** From Meyer F.
Nimkoff (ed.), *Comparative Family Systems*, Chapter 7.
Copyright © 1965 Houghton Mifflin Company. Reprinted by
permission.   **p. 364** From Joe Nicholson, Jr., *Inside Cuba*.
New York: Sheed & Ward, 1974, pp. 23–30.   **p. 386** From
Bernard Lewis, *Islam and the Arab World*. New York: Alfred A.
Knopf, 1976, pp. 25–40. Reprinted by permission.   **p. 432**
Copyright © 1966 by William Hinton. Reprinted by permission
of Monthly Review Press.   **p. 462** From Richard B. Lee and
Irven DeVere (eds.), *Kalahari Hunter-Gatherers: Studies of the
!Kung San and Their Neighbors*. Cambridge, Mass.: Harvard
University Press, 1976, pp. 138–151.   **p. 538** From *The New
York Review of Books*, May 15, 1980, pp. 23–24. Reprinted by
permission.

Preface

In this fourth edition of *Society Today*, we have striven to retain the major strengths of the earlier editions: comprehensive coverage of all the basic topics of sociology, including current research; clear, readable language; and lively graphic design. In addition, we have streamlined the text by reorganizing it into twenty-two chapters, grouped into seven units. This arrangement, we hope, will make the book a more flexible and manageable teaching tool. We have also added cross-cultural readings after a number of chapters; these explore some of the sociological issues discussed in the chapters they supplement and offer students the chance to develop a better understanding of both the nature and breadth of sociological inquiry. Here is a summary of the most important features of this new edition of *Society Today*.

Table of contents The book now consists of twenty-two chapters (instead of twenty-six) arranged into seven units (instead of eight). We have combined old Units Seven and Eight ("Demography and Urbanization" and "Social Instability and Change") into one unit, "Aspects of Modern Society." We have combined Chapters 7 and 8 of the third edition ("Childhood Socialization" and "Socialization in Adolescence and Adulthood") into a single chapter, 6, to remove extraneous material and to provide a better focus on the process of socialization. We have likewise joined what were formerly Chapters 13 and 14 ("The Class System in the United States" and "Status Attainment and Social Mobility") into one chapter, 11, which now is somewhat less encyclopedic yet provides a thorough discussion of current research. Finally, we have combined old Chapters 24 and 25 ("Collective Behavior" and "Social Movements") into one chapter, 21, that underscores the relationship between the two. Chapter 6 from the third edition, "Biology and Social Behavior," we chose to drop, integrating significant portions of it into other sections of the text.

Recognizing the crucial importance of the introductory chapters of any text, we have made a special effort to strengthen the first three chapters of this edition. In the interest of increased clarity, we have elaborated a number of the ideas considered in Chapter 1. The discussions of sociological research in Chapter 2 have been amplified, particularly the sections on other research methods. For example, discussions of trend studies, panel analysis, content analysis, secondary analysis, and comparative/historical analysis have been included. Because sociologists have often been criticized for influencing the responses of their subjects by their presence in research projects, a comprehensive discussion of unobtrusive research methods has been added. Most important is the inclusion in Chapter 2 of a section on ethics and the politics of sociological research. Chapter 3 has been enriched by a completely revised discussion on contemporary functional analysis and the controversy surrounding it. Moreover, the chapter has been expanded with the addition of a section on critical theory, which argues that, far from being a neutral science, sociology must take into consideration the impact of sociological research on social welfare.

Theory and research *Society Today* has always been known for its excellent coverage of current research. This high standard has been maintained in the fourth edition. For example, a discussion of Wallerstein's world systems has been included in Chapters 2 and 17. In addition to the improvements in the section on research methods in Chapter 2, the discussion of Lofland's study of the Divine Precepts group has been updated.

Cross-cultural readings Twelve of the chapters in this edition are followed by two-page cross-cultural readings, each of which is an excerpted article or chapter of a book introduced by a short headnote. These readings supplement the chapters they follow, and explore such varied subjects as childhood socialization in Puerto Rico, the caste system in India, marriage among the Bedouin, apartheid in South Africa, education in Cuba, the tenets of Islam, and modernization in the Arab states. We believe that instructors and students alike will find these readings helpful and instructive additions to the text.

Sociological controversy The fourth edition of *Society Today*, like its predecessor, challenges the reader to consider the major sociological questions under debate today. We introduce the arguments on the various sides of each issue, provide a wealth of relevant information—including the most recent data available—and invite the reader to form his or her own opinion.

Readability No text can be useful if students find it difficult to understand. We have edited this book to make it as logically organized, clear, and readable as possible, striving for a balance between thoroughness and conciseness.

Boxed features In the fourth edition, boxed features introduce a kaleidoscope of topics, from teenage drunkenness to urban gentrification, from the problems of working mothers to social status in a street gang. The primary aim of these features is to capture students' interest, but they also serve as supplements to the discussion of sociological topics in the text itself.

Pedagogical aids Each chapter is followed by a summary, a glossary, and an annotated list of recommended readings.

Illustrations The illustration program—always a strong feature of *Society Today*—has been updated as necessary, and we believe that its aesthetic and pedagogical quality is as high as ever. The photographs have been chosen for their inherent worth and their pertinence to the text. The charts and diagrams have been redesigned and simplified to make abstract concepts more accessible to students.

A great many people have helped in the preparation of this text. We are very much indebted to the critical readers who reviewed the chapters of the new edition and gave us detailed suggestions about their content: David Alcorn, Angelo State University; Margaret Anderson, University of Delaware; Edward Boldt, University of Manitoba; Richard Braungart, Syracuse University; M. Craig Brown, State University of New York at Albany; Richard Burkey, University of Denver; Michael Chernoff, Georgia State University; Robert E. Clark, Midwestern State University; Lawrence Clinton, East Texas State University; Janice Crumrine, University of Georgia; S. John Dackawich, California State University; Vasilikie Demos, University of Minnesota; Paula Dressel, Georgia State University; James Duke, Brigham Young University; Abbott Ferriss, Emory University; Harold Finestone, University of Minnesota; Francis D. Glamser, Northern Texas State University; Bennie Graves, Central Michigan University; Gary Hampe, University of Wyoming; Robert Hunter, University of Colorado; Charles Jaret, Georgia State University; Paul Kelly, University of Georgia; Ronald Knapp, Clemson University; Pat Lauderdale, University of Minnesota; Arnold Levine, West Virginia University; Richard Levinson, Emory University School of Medicine; Bill Mahoney, Western Washington University; Dave Marple, Loyola Marymount University; William Martin, Georgia State University; Fred Milan, Appalachian State University; David Miller, Western Illinois University; Jerry Miller, University of Arizona; Anthony Orum, University of Texas at Austin; Robert Perrin, University of Tennessee; Charles Perrow, State University of New York at Stony Brook; George Ritzer, University of Maryland; Brian Rowan, Texas Christian University; John Schorr, Stetson University; Anson D. Shupe, University of Texas at Arlington; Christopher Sieverdes, Clemson University; Connie Spreadbury, Stephen F. Austin State University; Jerry Talley, Stanford University; Ronald Turner, Colorado State University; John A. Vork, University of Northern Colorado; Frank Weed, University of Texas; Robert Whittenbarger, Eastern Illinois University; Anne S. Williams, Montana State University; and Ronald Wohlstein, Eastern Illinois University.

Random House staff members deserve special thanks for their help in planning and execution of the revision. Barry Fetterolf, acquiring editor, and Deborah Drier, project editor, worked closely with us to develop the manuscript in its final form; their good judgment and editorial skills are an asset to any project. Dorchen Leidholdt, manuscript editor, also deserves special thanks for overseeing the editing of the manuscript and for developing the illustration program. Other Random House staff members who contributed their skills to the book are photo editor R. Lynn Goldberg, assistant editors Ellen Fader and Sylvia Shepard, editorial assistants Susan Israel and Laurie Ottenstein, and production managers Barbara Lauster, Mary Kim, and Linda Goldfarb.

Finally, grateful mention should be made of the writers who helped to transform our ideas and initial drafts into even more readable prose—especially Jeannine Ciliotta, Betty Gatewood, Neil Gluckin, Helen Greer, and Saralyn Esh.

Norman Goodman and Gary T. Marx

CONTENTS

Unit four Primary components of social organization 164

Unit five Structures and processes of inequality 210

Unit six Social institutions 316

Unit seven *Aspects of modern society* 436

BOXED FEATURES

Introduction to sociology

CHAPTER ONE
WHAT IS SOCIOLOGY?

The social sciences study humans in their social relations. Because the various social science disciplines share a common subject matter—human social behavior—the dividing lines among them are not clear-cut and their activities often overlap. Nevertheless each discipline is quite distinct in its approach and each concentrates on different aspects of human behavior. An introductory course in sociology, for example, is very different from an introductory course in psychology, anthropology, economics, or political science. To illustrate these distinctions, we shall offer first a thumbnail sketch of the different social sciences and then briefly describe how they might approach a particular problem.

The social sciences

Sociology emphasizes human relationships within groups and interconnections among social institutions. Its primary subject matter is human societies—their patterns and arrangements, the processes through which they develop and change, and the interplay between these patterns and processes and the behavior of individuals and groups. This definition is very general because the studies done by persons who call themselves sociologists cover a wide range of topics. Thus, while the work of individual sociologists is often concentrated on a particular problem, the field itself is very broad. (In fact, many sociologists regard sociology as responsible for coordinating and synthesizing the work of the various social sciences.)

Psychology is mainly concerned with the bases of individual human behavior. Major areas of study include human development, behavior disorders, and learning; perception, sensation, and the biochemistry of the brain and nervous system; and individual emotions, motivation, personality, creativity, and the like. *Social psychologists* study the process of social interaction—the ways in which individuals and groups behave toward and influence one another.

Anthropology is partly a biological science, partly a social science; it deals with the origins, evolution, physical characteristics, and social customs and beliefs of human beings, usually through comparative study. *Physical anthropology* deals with the biological origins of the human species and biological variations within

The term "social science" encompasses many fields, including anthropology, the study of the origins and evolution of humans (top left), psychology, the study of individual behavior (top right), economics, the study of distribution of wealth within societies (middle right) and political science, the study of societal power structures (bottom right). (Jason Lauré/Woodfin Camp & Assoc.; Erich Hartmann/Magnum; Hazel Hankin; J. P. Lafont/Sygma)

it, including racial differences. Major attention is given to finding and classifying human fossils and artifacts. *Cultural anthropology* is devoted to observing or reconstructing the ways of life of preliterate societies and to studying human social relationships in general; in recent years it has turned its attention to the study of segments of modern industrial societies, such as neighborhoods and communities.

Economics is primarily concerned with the production, consumption, and distribution of wealth within societies. For example, in studying the gross national product, the unemployment rate, or the price of steel, economists are not simply studying statistics—these statistics reflect the behavior of individuals and the relationships among groups.

Political science specializes in the study of power. It specifically examines governments, the political processes by which social decisions are made, political parties and leadership, and individual and group political behavior.

Despite the obvious similarities, sociologists as a group can be distinguished from other groups of social scientists. Sociologists give much less attention to the individual and much more attention to groups than do psychologists. They are much more concerned with modern industrial societies and less concerned with preliterate societies than are most anthropologists. Although many sociologists study economic matters, they tend to give more attention to the relationship between the economy and other aspects of society than economists usually do. Similarly, although sociologists are very active in the study of politics, they are more inclined than political scientists to connect political behavior and institutions to nonpolitical areas of life.

To make these differences among the social sciences more concrete, consider how each might approach the question of how best to reform the present welfare system in the United States. *Psychologists* might examine how welfare programs influence the mental health of recipients, the extent to which different programs would increase the individual's sense of personal worth and competence, or how best to retrain the unemployed. *Anthropologists* might explore the patterns of self-help in isolated, impoverished communities, or they might report on how nonindustrialized societies deal with welfare problems. *Economists* might examine the impact of various welfare programs on taxation, on the unemployment rate, on consumer buying, or on inflation. *Political scientists* might study the legislative processes through which welfare policies are made or the operations through which government agencies administer welfare programs. *Sociologists* might examine the effects of welfare programs on family structure, public opinion, the birth rate, race relations, education, the formation of slums, or the distribution of power within society. They might also examine how each of these factors in turn influences welfare programs or creates the need for them. As can be seen from the breadth of the topics in this list, the concerns of sociology are extremely diverse. In fact, the American Sociological Association's official listing of subfields includes nearly fifty areas of specialization (see Table 1.1).

TABLE 1.1

THE MAJOR SUBFIELDS IN SOCIOLOGY*

Applied sociology/evaluation research, Bio-sociology, Collective behavior/social movements, Community, Comparative sociology/ macro-sociology, Criminal justice, Criminology/delinquency, Cultural sociology, Demography, Development/modernization, Deviant behavior/social disorganization, Economy in society, Environmental sociology, Ethnomethodology, History of sociology/social thought, Human ecology, Industrial sociology, Law and society, Leisure/sports/recreation, Marriage and the family, Mass communications/public opinion, Mathematical sociology, Medical sociology, Methodology: qualitative approaches, Methodology: quantitative approaches, Military sociology, Occupations/professions, Penology/corrections, Political sociology, Race/ethnic/minority relations, Religion, Rural sociology, Small groups, Social change, Social organizations/formal/complex, Social psychology, Socialization, Sociology of aging/social gerontology, Sociology of art/ literature, Sociology of knowledge, Sociology of language/social linguistics, Sociology of mental health, Sociology of science, Sociology of sex roles, Sociology of work, Sociology of world conflict, Stratification/mobility, Theory, Urban sociology

* As designated by the American Sociological Association.

The sociological perspective

One basic characteristic of the sociological approach is that it makes general statements about groups or categories of people. It produces propositions such as the following:

□ Regardless of their income, Catholics are more likely than Protestants to vote for the Democratic party.

□ Partners in second marriages are more likely to say they are happy than are partners in first marriages.

□ Americans are far more likely than people of other nationalities to mention freedom and "our system of government" when asked what they are proud of in their country.

These statements ignore the unique features of individual Catholics and Protestants, individual marriage partners, and individual Americans. Such propositions sum up the attitudes of categories or types of individuals;

they do not deal with Ms. Jones or Mr. Rodriguez specifically. Sociologists do consider Ms. Jones and Mr. Rodriguez, but only insofar as these individuals contribute to the categories in which they are observed, described, and classified. Sociology is interested not so much in particular people or events as in patterns and regularities in the social world. In fact, one distinguishing characteristic of sociology is its interest in producing broad, general propositions about larger elements of the social structure without regard to their individual members. For example, one sociologist has proposed that "the larger an organization, the more it is differentiated." Such a formulation essentially ignores the organization's individual members. The sociological emphasis on the group or aggregate sometimes leads one to believe that sociology is irrelevant to individual's personal experience. Yet nothing could be further from the truth. Understanding the social context of our experience can help us make sense of our own lives—as we shall see throughout this text.

Finally, it should be kept in mind that even though sociology can be distinguished from the other social sciences, there is not *one* sociological perspective. As we shall see in the chapters that follow, several schools within sociology view the social world in somewhat different ways, according to differing sociological theories.

THE VALIDITY OF THE SOCIOLOGICAL PERSPECTIVE

It is important to raise two questions about the sociological approach. The first question is, how valid is this approach? Obviously, no two people are identical, and each has had different experiences. So *can* people be

A sociologist, while not entirely ignoring this older woman, would be more likely to study the characteristics of the young crowd around her, of which she is not a typical member. (Dick Corten)

studied in terms of the various groups to which they belong—groups of Americans, students, farmers, women, and so on? This question is subject to *empirical investigation*—to proof or disproof by experiment or experience. And there is an answer to it. Sociologists have been able to produce accurate generalizations about groups and social categories. Such factors as shared religion, nationality, age, sex, marital status, and education have proved to be important determinants of what people believe, feel, and do. As Sherlock Holmes said—with some exaggeration—in Arthur Conan Doyle's *The Sign of Four:*

. . . while the individual man is an insoluble puzzle, in the aggregate he becomes a mathematical certainty. You can, for example, never foretell what any one man will do, but you can say with precision what an average number will be up to. Individuals vary, but percentages remain constant.

THE UTILITY OF THE SOCIOLOGICAL PERSPECTIVE

The second question that must be raised about the sociological approach is, what is the use of general statements about groups and social patterns? If we look at what sociologists term the *macro* level—the broad or large-scale social relations between groups or institutions—we find that such general statements can enable us to examine the ways in which the various groups in society overlap and interrelate. The sociologist C. Wright Mills demonstrates this point vividly in his book *The Sociological Imagination,* using as an example the area of social problems. Mills makes a clear distinction between the "troubles" an individual may encounter on the personal level and the "issues" which, while they may affect the individual very strongly, are nevertheless soluble only on the level of broad groups and structures in society:

In these terms, consider unemployment. When, in a city of 100,000, only one man is unemployed, that is his personal trouble, and for its relief we properly look to the character of the man, his skills, and his immediate opportunities. But when in a nation of 50 million employees, 15 million are unemployed, that is an issue, and we may not hope to find its solution within the range of opportunities open to any one individual. The very structure of opportunities has collapsed. Both the correct statement of the problem and the range of possible solutions require us to consider the economic and political institutions of the society, and not

Sociologist C. Wright Mills delineates micro-level social problems as the "troubles" of an individual and macro-level problems as "issues" that affect broad groups in a society. These men await emergency unemployment aid during the great depression of the nineteen thirties. Unemployment, though frequently thought of as an individual's misfortune, is a macro-level social issue. (UPI)

merely the personal situation and character of a scatter of individuals.

Consider war. The personal problem of war, when it occurs, may be how to survive it or how to die in it with honor; how to make money out of it; how to climb into the higher safety of the military apparatus; or how to contribute to the war's termination. In short, according to one's values, to find a set of milieux and within it to survive the war or make one's death in it meaningful. But the structural issues of war have to do with its causes; with what types of men it throws up into command; with its effects upon economic and political, family and religious institutions, with the unorganized irresponsibility of a world of nation-states.

Consider marriage. Inside a marriage a man and a woman may experience personal troubles, but when the divorce rate during the first four years of marriage is 250 out of every 1,000 attempts, this is an indication of a structural issue having to do with the institutions of marriage and the family and other institutions that bear upon them. (Mills, 1959, p. 9)

The general statements of sociology can also guide us at the *micro* level—that of local, day-to-day interaction and of individual behavior. Knowing about the groups and categories to which individuals belong can give us insight into their actions. In the sociological view, expectations for one's own behavior are learned from the groups one is in contact with, and thus the behavior of the individual—even when alone—is always guided by social forces. We can even gain some understanding of the individual's private feelings, attitudes, and ideas, for it is sociology's view that the process of thought itself has social determinants; we think by means of symbols—such as words—which are learned, in many cases early in life, from the people around us.

In short, macrosociology provides a bird's-eye view of broad social categories, structures, and patterns; microsociology gives us a close-up view of how individuals behave in a social setting. Both these aspects of the sociological perspective contribute valid and useful information about human social institutions and groups.

Sociology as a science

COMMON SENSE VERSUS SCIENCE

While you probably saw your first algebraic equation, your first molecule, or your first frog's heart in a classroom, in your introductory sociology class you will not come into contact with your subject matter for the first time. The topic of sociology is human societies, social institutions, and patterns of social interaction; thus much of what you will be exploring is already a part of your everyday experience. Likewise, the basic premises of sociology—that social life is patterned; that beliefs, values, and attitudes are learned; that we are as others see us—are statements that you probably assume intuitively. In short, the subject of sociology is people, and you already know quite a bit about people.

But let's test this idea. Here are some common-sense notions you may have about the world:

Violent crime is increasing at an alarmingly rapid rate (Chapter 7).

Kinship ties are being severed as the modern nuclear family becomes more geographically and socially mobile (Chapter 14).

The likelihood of divorce is much greater among middle- and upper-class couples than among lower-class couples (Chapter 14).

Revolutions are more likely to occur when living conditions continue to be very bad than when they are rapidly improving (Chapter 21).

If these statements seem like simple common sense to you—as they would to most Americans—then you can understand the surprise of many sociologists when systematic, empirical research showed that each of them is false! The things we "know" intuitively are sometimes true and sometimes not. In fact, many of the beliefs and preferences people hold are based not on fact but on conventional assumptions and other kinds of group-based prejudices. This is part of the challenge sociology faces. Nothing can be taken for granted; everything must be tested carefully against systematically selected and appropriate evidence.

The point we are making is that sociology is a science. It is a system of knowledge in which all statements about reality must be based on objectively and carefully collected observations. Like other scientists, sociologists work by forming hypotheses and subjecting them to empirical tests. Although sociologists lack many of the precise physical tools and laboratory methods of other sciences (a survey of public opinion is never as precise as a temperature reading, for example), they do have scientific techniques and instruments of their own. They use laboratories filled with recorders and equipped with one-way mirrors; they conduct interviews with large, randomly selected samples of the population; they seek out library data, including documents, historical accounts, and facts and figures; and they often carefully observe people in natural settings to see what they do in their everyday lives. Thus, sociology is not just a series of exercises in casual observation or "educated guessing," but a meticulous and objective science. Like other sciences, however, it can at times be incorrect. The history of every science consists of a process of revision and abandonment of old ideas, concepts, and "laws" for new ones. Initial research offered support for all of the "common sense" propositions listed above; only years of careful testing provided more complete and contrary data.

THE ORIGINS OF THE SCIENCE OF SOCIOLOGY

The systematic, scientific approach has not always been characteristic of social inquiry. Nor have people always been curious about the organization of social life.

In stable, traditional societies of the past, people tended not to question the social system; its workings seemed as inevitable as those of the natural environment. Such was the case, for example, in ancient Egypt and in the feudal societies of the European Middle Ages. But in times of social unrest, people become aware of their society as a human artifact—something created by people, which could be studied and analyzed. Political unrest was certainly typical of the first great period of social thought, the fifth and fourth centuries B.C. in Athens, when the world's first democracy was destroyed by war and replaced by a succession of rapacious and short-lived oligarchies. In this restless atmosphere Western philosophy was born, and the first item on its agenda was the study of society. How could the state be improved? What would be the ideal society? Who should rule and who should labor? Who should be educated and how? Where did the family fit into the system? These were the questions to which the Greek philosophers—Socrates, Plato, Aristotle—gave their intense scrutiny. The idea that society could be studied—and, simultaneously, the knowledge that it molded the lives of its members—was at last grasped by the human mind.

A second great age of social thought, from about 1600 to 1800, saw debate on the nature of the social order. During this period, in which strong national states developed in Europe, such thinkers as Thomas Hobbes (1588-1679), John Locke (1632-1704), and Jean-Jacques Rousseau (1712-1778) sought to explain how the state came to be. According to Hobbes, the state developed as people began to form groups for their own protection, realizing that surrendering some of their individual liberties to a ruler was better than living in an anarchic and brutal state of nature. This was the first statement of what has been called the "social contract theory." Locke, who differed sharply with Hobbes on the quality of the state of nature, elaborated the social-contract idea further. According to this theory, human beings formed the state because they had begun to accumulate private property and were concerned about its protection. Rousseau, also disagree-

ing with Hobbes, argued that the state of nature had been an ideal era of simplicity and freedom. Nevertheless, seeing the benefits that might come through cooperation, people did unite to form states, retaining the power to dissolve the contract if it violated their wishes—the influential idea of popular sovereignty.

During the late eighteenth and early nineteenth centuries, the rapidly rising natural sciences were beginning to eclipse religious faith. The social thought that grew out of the nineteenth century was therefore scientific in character. Whereas Plato and Aristotle had elaborated their visions of an ideal society, and the social-contract thinkers had speculated on how society might have come into existence, nineteenth-century social thinkers concentrated on scientific descriptions of actual societies. Thus, with the thought of such people as Auguste Comte, Emile Durkheim, Georg Simmel, and Max Weber, a tradition of social philosophy evolved into the scientific study of society, or sociology.

One pioneering work that exemplifies the shift from social philosophy to social science was Durkheim's 1897 study of suicide rates among members of various religions in Europe (1951), discussed in Chapter 3. As another example of this trend toward scientific study of social phenomena, let us briefly consider the method of inquiry used by Max Weber in his classic essay *The Protestant Ethic and the Spirit of Capitalism* (1930). Weber (1864-1920) rejected the view, then prevalent among German scholars, that the study of human interactions was necessarily very subjective, and that therefore theoretical models and statistical analysis were irrelevant to sociology. Weber believed that a model or framework must be devised to provide coherence for observations that would otherwise appear unrelated; moreover, such a framework had to be flexible enough to account for change. The framework Weber devised for this purpose was the *ideal type*—a "pure" model of a concept, against which the real world can be compared. In the case of this essay, the type was the Protestant as the embodiment of the Puritan ethic of salvation through hard work and denial of pleasure; for such a person, to work was to pray, and prosperity was a sign of God's favor. This stereotyped abstraction provided a useful general model for studying certain materialistic social patterns as they related to the development of modern capitalism. Moreover, the methodical approach made possible by this model gave Weber great flexibility; he could study the ideal type in various historical circumstances, and he could isolate and explain variations by comparing the ideal type with actual cases. (For further discussion of Weber's essay, see Chapter 16.)

What Weber had in effect done in devising his ideal type was to propose a general theory about the relationship between Protestantism and capitalism; this theory was then subject to modification and to proof. (Sociological theory is discussed in detail in Chapter 3.) As a result of the contributions of Weber and other pioneers, by the turn of the century sociology was on its way to becoming a science.

In the United States, sociology developed in close connection with various social-reform movements, beginning in the middle of the nineteenth century. Many of those concerned with "social questions" in America were allied with religiously oriented reform movements; a significant fraction were ministers, sons of ministers, or men who had trained for the ministry. Their efforts in behalf of the poor, convicts, immigrants, sweatshop laborers, and others included research into social conditions. The emphasis at that time was on gathering information to solve the nation's social problems. With the concomitant growth of institutions of higher education, sociology rapidly developed into an academic discipline. The nation's first sociology course was given at Yale in 1875, and thereafter the discipline gained wide acceptance. After the turn of the century, sociology began to differentiate into "pure," or theoret-ical, studies, and applied sociology, or the study of social problems. By the 1920s, with a journal of its own, sociology had become a full-fledged academic discipline.

SOCIOLOGY: HOW EXACT A SCIENCE?

The stature of sociology as a true science depends partly on what one means by the term *science*. If by science one means the testing of theories against appropriate evidence, then there is little controversy. Virtually all sociologists agree that they must use that standard to test their work, even if they battle mightily over what constitutes appropriate procedures for gathering evidence, what constitutes appropriate evidence, or even what it is that sociologists ought to be studying. If, however, one takes the more restrictive view that science is the formulation of powerful theories expressed mathematically and supported by evidence based on extremely precise measurements, then one would have to concede that not all sociology is scientific. It seems fair to point out, however, that sociology is a relatively new science, and few of today's most advanced sciences would have passed such a test at earlier stages in their histories.

This text uses the less restrictive definition of science. Sociology is a science to the extent that its practitioners scrupulously test what they suspect or believe

Harsh working conditions, like those in this early twentieth century "sweat shop," was one of the social problems that gave rise to the science of sociology. (UPI)

against observations of empirical reality. That is the common denominator of all sciences. But it is important to recognize that an extremely critical distinction between the physical and social sciences arises from differences in their subject matter. The social sciences face some unique difficulties because people are not simply aggregates of particles that consistently follow physical laws.

THE PROBLEMS OF STUDYING PEOPLE

People are involved in systems of relationships that are complex, overlapping, and mutually interrelated. Thus, predicting human behavior is quite difficult. Furthermore, unlike gases subjected to heat or chemicals mixed in a vat, people are self-aware and can to some extent choose their courses of action. As a result, the sociologist faces three major problems: (1) the fact of human choice makes it hard to predict what people will do (unlike chemicals, which can be counted on to explode when they are supposed to)—the more so because people are sometimes irrational and have only an imperfect knowledge of their own interests and relevant information; (2) because people are self-aware, the mere fact that they are being observed may change their behavior; and (3) because people may change their behavior, whether on the basis of social-science discoveries or for other reasons, these discoveries may become outmoded, which means that social science, unlike physical science, has uncovered few fixed and eternal laws.

Though these three problems may cause difficulties for the social scientist, they are also among the chief virtues of social-scientific inquiry, providing, in fact, a source of inspiration and hope to the researcher. First, the fact that people make conscious choices does not mean that explanations or predictions of human behavior are impossible. It simply means that human consciousness—and choice-making—must become an object of study. Frequently, it is not enough to look only at the external forces affecting humans; we must also understand how they perceive, respond to, and define their situations. Rather than making social science impossible, the existence of human choice makes the study of consciousness one of its most fascinating activities.

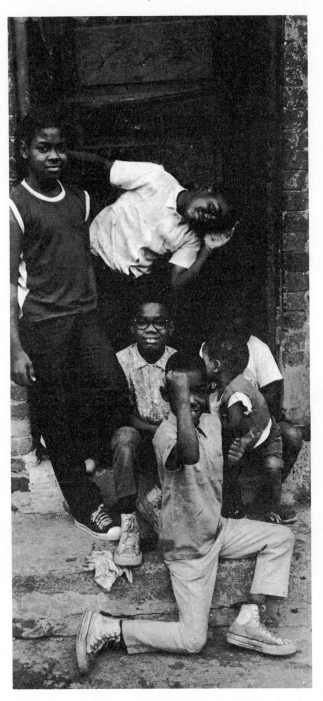

These children clowning for the camera illustrate one of the problems faced by sociologists: people often change their behavior when they are being observed. (Alan Mercer)

Second, it is true that because observation can change the behavior of those being observed, sociological research is made more difficult. For example, sociologists have ridden with police officers to see what they do during a normal day (Reiss, 1968); but on a *normal* day police officers are not being observed by sociologists—the presence of observers may change their behavior. Nevertheless, viewed more broadly, the fact that people *can* change their behavior, voluntarily, should give cause for hope. We are not eternally condemned to being bigoted, greedy, violent, and ignorant. If, in the process of studying people, social science can change its subjects' behavior in this sense—inspiring policemen to be on their "best behavior" to minorities and the poor, for example—then it is certainly worth pursuing.

Third, basic changes in human behavior can render any particular piece of social-science knowledge obsolete; but that too is a hidden virtue. If sociological observations about such problems as racism, poverty, crime, and mental illness can lead to even partial solutions, then the capacity of a sociological "law" to "self-destruct," far from being a drawback, provides one of the major justifications for sociological research.

These, then, are some of the general problems sociologists encounter and some of the reasons they continue their inquiries. In Chapter 2, we will discuss sociological research in more detail. However, we will not present sociological knowledge and research as if all the fundamental arguments had long been settled, for to do so would be to greatly distort reality. Sociology is an intense, ongoing quest; though much is known, much more is in dispute, and still more remains mysterious. The chapters that follow will try to report what sociologists know, what they argue about, and what they still need to understand.

Summary

Sociology is a social science that deals with the study of human behavior, emphasizing relationships within and between groups and institutions. The fundamental task of sociology is to establish valid statements about human social behavior in general.

By *empirical investigation*, sociologists determine the interrelationships of institutions at the *macro* level, and provide insight into small-group patterns and processes at the *micro* level. Since individual response is shaped by social determinants, sociologists can even gain knowledge of the individual's inner self, of thoughts and attitudes as they are shaped by the groups to which he or she belongs.

Through the efforts of such great scholars as Emile Durkheim and Max Weber, sociology has grown from a social philosophy to a rigorous social science, providing valid and useful observations and measurements of human social patterns and institutions.

In addition to the complexity of human relationships, some specific sociological investigation is made more difficult by three basic problems involved in studying people: (1) because they can make choices, their behavior can change "unpredictably"; (2) because they are self-aware, they may change their behavior when they are being observed; and (3) because they can change their behavior, observations of social science are always in danger of becoming obsolete. But each of these drawbacks contains a built-in advantage: (1) human unpredictability makes the study of choice-making both necessary and fascinating; (2) the fact that people can change their behavior gives hope that human problems can eventually be solved; and (3) the abrogation of particular sociological findings by alterations in human behavior is a sign of progress and, therefore, a major justification and motivation for sociological research.

Glossary

EMPIRICAL INVESTIGATION The method of acquiring primary knowledge by direct sensory observation, experimentation, and the testing of hypotheses.

IDEAL TYPE Weber's term for a contrived, exaggerated mental construct developed from scientific observation and used in comparative analysis of two or more social phenomena; it generates hypotheses and gives direction to empirical research not by reflecting reality, but by providing an abstract concept against which reality can be viewed.

MACRO THEORY The social-science perspective that deals with large-scale social relations, such as the influence of one social group or institution on another.

MICRO THEORY The social-science perspective that deals with small-scale social relations, such as the influence of day-to-day interaction on the behavior of individuals.

SOCIAL INTERACTION The mutual adjustment of individual action; the mutual or reciprocal influencing of the behavior of all persons involved in a social situation.

Recommended readings

Bates, Alan. *The Sociological Enterprise*. Boston: Houghton Mifflin, 1967. A brief introduction to sociology, less technical than Inkeles' book (below) and with somewhat more emphasis on the style and organization of sociologists as professionals.

Berger, Peter L. *Invitation to Sociology: A Humanistic Perspective*. Garden City, N. Y.: Doubleday, 1963. A well-written, easy to understand, brief introduction to sociology from a challenging but nontechnical perspective.

Bierstedt, Robert (ed.). *A Design for Sociology: Scope, Objectives and Methods*. Philadelphia: The American Academy of Political and Social Sciences, April 1969. The results of a conference involving a number of major figures in sociology convened to discuss the state of sociology as a discipline. Three major papers are presented (on the scope, objectives, and methods of sociology), along with a number of commentaries on each.

Inkeles, Alex. *What is Sociology? An Introduction to the Discipline and Profession*. Englewood Cliffs, N. J.: Prentice-Hall, 1964. A very brief introduction to sociology in fairly technical language. Chapters 1, 2, and 7 of Inkeles' book are related to Chapter 1 of this textbook.

Krause, Elliot. *Why Study Sociology?* New York: Random House, 1980. An informally written brief introduction to what sociology is and why it is of value to the student. Krause approaches the subject in a personal and nontechnical manner using frequent examples.

Sills, David E. (ed.). "Sociology," *International Encyclopedia of the Social Sciences*. New York: Macmillan and Free Press, 1968, Vol. 15, pp. 1–53. The article by Albert J. Reiss, Jr., "The Field," pp. 1–23, is an interesting statement on sociology as seen by one of its leading practitioners. The other two parts of the "Sociology" entry briefly scan the theoretical development of sociology (Shmuel Eisenstadt, pp. 23–36) and the early history of sociological research (Bernard Lecuyer and Anthony R. Oberschall, pp. 36–53).

Wilson, Everett K., and Hanan C. Selvin. *Why Study Sociology: A Note to Undergraduates*. Belmont, Calif.: Wadsworth, 1980. More a pamphlet than a book, this is a well-written statement by two respected sociologists who have devoted their considerable skills to the pedagogy as well as substance and methods of sociology.

CHAPTER TWO
DOING SOCIOLOGY

Although studying people presents special problems, as we saw in Chapter 1, sociologists have found ways to do it. One purpose of this chapter is to show how sociology is done by offering a behind-the-scenes view of sociologists going about their business, attempting to learn the answers to some important questions about people and society. But while the primary aim of the chapter is to illustrate some basic research procedures, it is not a manual of statistical or research techniques.

We begin with three studies that might be called sociological detective stories—descriptions of how four young sociologists went about solving some intriguing problems. We shall then consider some additional methods used by sociologists to find answers to the questions they are exploring.

An understanding of some of the methods of sociology is important for several reasons. First, some knowledge of method is vital to an understanding of what makes a study sound or unsound. A mistake in method can invalidate research findings, even if procedures are carefully followed. Second, the research design that is chosen will to some extent determine the findings of any study: certain methods yield certain kinds of information; other methods yield other kinds. Finally, method can help researchers avoid injecting their own biases into their research. Although sociologists, like all of us, frequently make mistakes, sound sociological method can help them avoid making the kinds of mistakes that might invalidate their research.

Field study: John Lofland

In the fall of 1960, John Lofland arrived at the University of California at Berkeley to study for a Ph.D. in sociology. He was determined to conduct close-up, face-to-face studies of social movements. Although there had long been active sociological study of such social movements as radical religious and political groups, these studies concentrated mainly on the social and economic conditions that allowed such movements to flourish and on their ideology. Their findings revealed little about how such groups operate on a day-to-day basis, how they recruit and keep their members, how they retain their commitment to their "unusual" beliefs in the face of a doubting world, or how they deal

	PARTICIPANT OBSERVATION	EXPERIMENT	SURVEY RESEARCH
Typical Cost	Inexpensive	Depends on equipment used	Depends on sample size and whether questionnaire or interview is used
Size of sample or group or number of subjects	Usually small	Limited by funds and time—usually small	Depends on size of population, funds, and time—can be very large
Type of interaction with subjects of study	Face to face—formal or informal	Face to face—formal	If questionnaire used, indirect (by mail). If interview used, face to face but formal.
Type of problem	Theory and variables generated in process of research—not controlled by researcher	Theory and variables known in advance and controlled in the lab	Theory and variables known in advance but not controlled by researcher
Can the independent variable be manipulated by the researcher? (Can events be timed?)	No	Yes	No
How are the variables controlled?	Through testing and revision of the theory	By random assignment to experiment and control groups	Through statistical analysis
Can the results be generalized to a larger universe (population)?	Yes (only if groups have been selected randomly)	No (sample not used)	Yes (by random selection of cases)
Must the theory be predictive?	Yes	Yes	Yes
Is it possible or likely that the act of doing the research will influence the results?	Yes: The researcher is a participant in the interaction to be studied	No	If questionnaire is used: No If interview is used: Yes
Can it be used to find out the distribution of a variable (for example, age) in a population	No	No	Yes
Where does the research take place?	In the field: In limited areas	In the lab	In the field: In extended area or several areas
Criteria for selection of groups, subjects, or cases	Nature of the study, availability	Convenience	Random selection from the population

with failure to transform society speedily or to convert a large number of persons.

These processes were precisely what Lofland wanted to understand. To analyze them, he first had to find a suitable group to study; this was not easy. At the time there were not a great many radical religious or political groups developing. Furthermore, the group had to be located in the San Francisco Bay area—Lofland had neither the freedom nor the funds to go elsewhere. Finally, the group had to be willing to let him study it. The notorious secretiveness of such groups explains why they had not been the subjects of much close sociological study.

FINDING A RADICAL RELIGIOUS GROUP

The group Lofland eventually found was the Unification Church, which at that time had about a dozen core members in the Bay area. It was part of a movement that had started in Korea when an engineer, Sun Myung Moon, announced that he was Christ returned

FIGURE 2.1
The table at left presents a summary of the uses and limitations of the three types of sociological research strategies discussed in this chapter.

to earth. He claimed that the world would soon end and that his followers would rule in heaven.

The San Francisco group had been formed by a convert to the movement. Sent as a missionary to America in 1959, she had settled first in a college town in the Pacific Northwest and gathered a small group of followers—all young people. When conflict developed between some of the members and their families and neighbors, the group moved to San Francisco. Several members left spouses and children behind.

When Lofland found them, the twelve or so followers of the Unification Church were living together and giving all their time to the group. They had been in the city for nearly a year and a half and had spent most of that period acquiring a large apartment house and a printing press, and printing an English translation of their holy book. Now they were beginning to look for new members.

From the beginning the group knew that Lofland was a sociologist interested in studying new religious movements. (Although he did not learn it until later, they also believed that God intended him to become a convert.) The group accepted Lofland, and he immedi-

ately began to spend all his available time with them, questioning the members closely about their past, their attachment to the group, and their everyday activities. Whenever he had the opportunity, he slipped away to make notes on what he was seeing and hearing. He also purchased a tape recorder and often sat in his car to record his observations after group meetings. Lofland's short handbook on conducting field research (1971) records in detail the techniques he began developing during this study. To check the validity of his observations and interpretations, he asked other sociologists to attend Unification Church meetings from time to time and make independent observations.

THEORY I: WHY PEOPLE CONVERT

As time passed, Lofland began to fashion a theory about certain factors that caused people to convert to the Unification Church. Initially, he based his theory on reconstructions of the life histories of those who had become proselytes. He searched out the common patterns that seemed to explain why these young Americans gave up their conventional life goals to become full-time missionaries for a Korea-based Christ.

The theory that Lofland developed contained the following sequence of seven steps by which a person became a convert to the new faith. The first four steps

To help determine why individuals like this young woman renounce conventional goals to become full-time missionaries, John Lofland conducted an intensive investigation of a San Francisco sect of the Rev. Moon's Unification Church.
(© Martin A. Levick 1978/ Black Star)

are *predispositional factors*, characteristics that the person brings to the conversion process before having any contact with the group:

1. The individual must experience an enduring, acutely felt tension or strain (for example, job failure or marital discord).

2. The person must hold a religiously oriented problem-solving perspective. He or she may well have rejected conventional faith, but must still view the world in religious terms—seeing problems as having religious, as opposed to political or psychiatric, solutions.

3. On the basis of the first two characteristics, the individual must define himself or herself as a religious seeker, open to new religious outlooks.

4. The encounter with the Unification Church must coincide with, or be very close to, a turning point in the individual's life. To convert, a person must be at a point when old lines of action and commitments are completed or have failed or been disrupted (or are about to be) and when the opportunity (or necessity) of doing something different in life arises. (For example, such a turning point may involve losing a job, being divorced, graduating, or recovering from a long illness.)

The last three steps are *situational factors*, characteristic of the interaction between the individual and the group:

5. The potential convert must form or already possess a close emotional tie with one or more Unification Church members. Many converts already had such ties—they were married to, closely related to, or long-time friends of a church member. Others failed to convert until they had formed such a tie. In a sense, conversion meant coming to accept the beliefs of one's spouse, sibling, or friends.

6. Ties with persons outside the Unification Church group must be nonexistent or neutralized. Some probable converts were held back by the unwillingness of spouses to convert or by the counterpersuasion and pressure of friends and families. Converts typically either lacked ties that could restrain them or had ties that were neutralized by absence.

7. To become an active Unification Church member, to move from verbal agreement to actually giving one's life to the movement, required intensive, day-to-day interaction with group members. Some verbal converts whose physical circumstances prevented such interaction never became full converts. Others did so only when their circumstances changed so that such interaction occurred.

After he had constructed his theory, Lofland began the long process of testing and revising it. Any theory built upon a set of data cannot be tested by the same data. It could have been mere coincidence, for example, that all the converts he had interviewed shared certain features: because these shared features were the source of his theory, the data and theory would automatically agree. Lofland could be confident that he had isolated the real causes of conversion only if he could successfully predict who would convert in the future. *Prediction* is one critical test of scientific propositions.

Lofland had to wait until the group secured a significant number of new converts who also exhibited the particular features that he had isolated in his theory. For example, before conversion each person should have bonds of close friendship or family ties with someone already a member. If a new convert lacked one of the features or elements in his theory, then Lofland would have to reconsider and change at least that part.

It was not enough just to keep track of new converts; Lofland also had to make a careful study of persons who attended meetings but failed to join the group. If the theory was valid, people who failed to become converts should *lack* at least one of the essential features. If anyone met all of the requirements of the theory but still failed to convert, then something important had to be missing from the theory.

For many months, Lofland investigated everyone who turned up at Unification Church activities. He moved in with the group for a few months to observe everyone closely, interviewed the former spouses of several early members, and talked with other people who were aware of the group's early activities. Lofland compiled hundreds of pages of field notes. At the same time he assisted by copyediting a new edition of the holy book—again printed on the group's own press.

As Lofland watched the group add more members and open two new headquarters, he became convinced that his theory of conversion was adequate: no one who met all its requirements failed to convert; no one converted who lacked any of the requirements. Colleagues who independently checked his observations and field notes agreed with his findings. In 1965 he published a paper, "On Becoming a World Saver: A Theory of Conversion to a Deviant Perspective," which he incorporated the following year in his book *Doomsday Cult*. Several years later he was able to revise and generalize his theory to make it apply more broadly to socialization into any kind of deviant role (*Deviance and Identity*, 1969). Since then, he has published a postscript to his research (1977) in which he looks back on his findings after the passage of more than a decade. In that article, he noted that as the Unification Church expanded, it began to draw converts from people who were not obviously "religious seekers." These, he observed, were often the alienated sons and daughters of the middle and upper classes who in one way or another had been associated with the youth counterculture of the late sixties and early seventies. This latest finding modified his profile of the probable convert somewhat.

Lofland's 1977 article also included further reflections on the church's methods of recruiting members. He found that as the church grew, it developed a well-organized and highly successful program of "processing" converts. He identified five stages in this process: picking up, hooking, encapsulating, loving, and committing. In the first stage, group members set up tables on college campuses and in various public places to "pick up," or make contact with, prospective converts. These people were then "hooked," or invited to a dinner during which they were greeted with great warmth, complimented, flattered, and invited to attend a weekend workshop run by the group in a country setting. During this workshop, guests were "encapsulated," that is, constantly surrounded by group members (including an assigned "buddy" who even accompanied the individual to the bathroom). Guests were expected to participate in a full schedule of group activities from 7:30 A.M. until 11:00 P.M. They were given no time to be alone or to reflect on their experience, and during the weekend there was virtually no opportunity for contact with the outside world—which contributed to the intensity of the experience. The church members' goal was to "drench prospects in approval and love," as Lofland put it (the members themselves called their method "love bombing"). After this "loving" stage, the "bombed" potential convert was invited to stay on for a week-long workshop—and if that went well, to stay longer. Thus did people form commitments to the group. Many found that after an extended stay in the superheated emotional atmosphere of the group they could no longer endure returning to their former lives. The group experience thus acted to produce an emotional "high" that could not be abandoned without some kind of withdrawal symptoms (Lofland, 1977).

THEORY II: THE CYCLE OF GROUP ACTIVITIES

From the beginning, Lofland was interested in more than the process and elements of conversion. He had begun with many other questions. For example, he wanted to know what kept the Unification Church going when it failed to win converts quickly. Lofland became convinced that the activities of the group had a cyclic pattern that enabled the members to overcome their disappointment at failing to convert more people in a short time. The cycle of activities helped to renew their hope.

Lofland noticed that people in the Unification Church alternated between highly energetic missionary activity and extremely vigorous internal projects. For example, when they suspended missionary projects, they would buy and completely refurbish a set of apartments or print a new edition of their book on their basement press. Lofland became convinced that they followed a three-phase cycle. First they would be very active outside the group, looking for potential converts. When they had succeeded in getting a number of new people (often about a dozen) to come to meetings, they would slow down external activity and concentrate all their energy on converting the new people they had gathered.

After a few months, as a rule, all of the new people would drop out of group activities; the group would suddenly find itself with nothing going on, usually with no new converts to show for its efforts, and with the high hopes of several months before dashed by failure. At these times, instead of going back into the streets to gather a new group, the members would invariably launch one of their internal projects, which would deeply engross them for several months, enabling them to gain new energy and confidence with the success of the project—a handsomely remodeled apartment, a newly printed book. After finishing a successful project, the group had enough motivation to renew missionary work.

How could Lofland be sure that this cycle was more than coincidence? First, by checking back on earlier group activity he was able to see what had gone on before he began his observations. From the guest book—in which all visiting potential converts recorded their names and date of entry—he reconstructed the patterns of past missionary activity. Lofland found in-

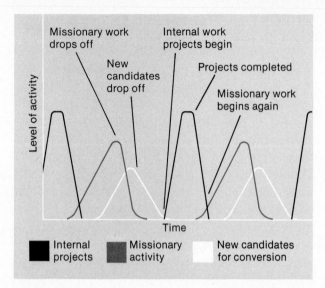

FIGURE 2.2

The three-phase cycle of activities of the Divine Precepts movement.

corded his observations. He had formulated specific questions, and he made efforts to locate and record specific kinds of information. For example, data about the background of everyone who attended group meetings were obviously critical for answering questions about the process of conversion.

Second, Lofland took many precautions to avoid deluding himself into seeing only what he expected or hoped to see. To guard against this he brought in outside observers several times during his study to judge independently the accuracy of his findings. Several of these colleagues periodically checked his methods and his data during the entire course of the study in order to evaluate long-term as well as specific or isolated observations. In fact, his objectivity and his precautions against bias helped him to understand the Unification Church movement better than did its members or leaders. As Chapter 1 indicated, it is precisely this painstaking attention to factual accuracy and to testing theories against facts that qualifies sociology as a science and distinguishes it from a common-sense understanding of social life.

A third important aspect of Lofland's method was his scrupulous preservation of the anonymity of the Unification Church and its members (calling it the "Divine Precepts" movement), even after the group had become nationally known. This began to happen in late 1971, when Moon himself came to live in the United States and galvanized his followers into a burst of reorganizing, fund raising, recruiting, and publicizing, culminating in his appearance at a series of huge rallies in 1974. In the next two years, however, a public reaction set in. The Unification Church came under attack for its deceptive practices, questionable goals and sources of income, involvement in politics, and alleged brainwashing of young recruits. Lofland reported in a follow-up study called "The Boom and Bust of a Millenarian Movement: Doomsday Cult Revisited" (1977) that by the end of 1976 membership in the United States had declined from a claimed maximum of 30,000 to about 2,000. Lofland predicted that the cyclical pattern of activity described above would gradually wind down, until by the early 1980s the Unification Church would lapse into quasi-obscurity, with a

tervals in which virtually no new persons were signed up interspersed with periods of very heavy sign-ups. He was also able to date various group projects, all of which occurred a few months after a heavy sign-up period and during a period when almost no new people signed up. Past patterns of group activity seemed to offer convincing support for his theory.

Lofland's theory of cyclic activity and its consequences, however, had yet to pass the test of prediction. He committed himself to predicting that at certain future times a group project would suddenly be proposed and carried out. In fact, he was able to tell in advance approximately when such projects would occur—well before any of the members had thought of them. As these predictions came true, Lofland gained considerable confidence that he had isolated a process or mechanism by which small social movements can maintain their hope in the face of discouraging circumstances.

METHOD: OVERVIEW

The method that Lofland used to collect his data is often called *participant observation*. The face-to-face interaction of the sociologist with those being studied makes possible direct observation of group processes as they unfold. For the kinds of questions with which Lofland was concerned, participant observation is undoubtedly the best method of research. What Lofland did differs sharply from everyday association with other people—for example, what you do when you are with your friends or in class. First, Lofland systematically re-

One of the problems faced by participant observers is that their presence affects the social processes they are studying. Would the Ghanaians shown here with anthropologist Michael Lowy interact as naturally in his presence as they would if he were not there? (Michael Lowy)

small, hardcore membership drawn together in enclaves.

Lofland's investigation exemplifies a research method known as the *field study*, in which the subjects are observed under their usual environmental conditions. In some field studies, as we have just seen, the participant-observation method is used; in others, researchers simply observe the subjects without forming relationships with them. In some cases the subjects may not even be aware that they are being observed. Such conditions are advantageous in helping to eliminate the effects of factors (such as nervousness or fear of the ex-

perimenter) that are extraneous to the social patterns being studied. But they can also present ethical dilemmas. In a classic early study (Hartshorne and May, 1928), children were exposed to various temptations to cheat, lie, and otherwise behave dishonestly without knowing that they were being observed. Was it fair or moral of the researchers to encourage immoral behavior in these children? On this point sociologists disagree, but concern about such ethical problems has been widespread enough to generate federal guidelines for research with human subjects; these guidelines permit government agencies through campus peer review to exercise some control over the funding of "deception" studies.

The field-study method is essential for approaching certain types of social phenomena, such as the formation and development of friendship groups over time (see Chapter 8). For other types of phenomena, a more suitable approach is one we turn to now: the study of social behavior under controlled experimental conditions.

Experiment: Karen Dion

We all know that we *ought* to value people for their inner rather than their outer selves; surely it is unfair and undemocratic if the accident of how one looks greatly affects how one fares in life. Until several years ago, even social scientists steadfastly ignored physical appearance as a significant factor in a person's social

life. But it is now clear that the extent to which people are judged by the way they look compels serious study. As George Herbert Mead (1934) and others have pointed out (see Chapter 6), we see ourselves as we believe others see us; in other words, our identities are socially constructed.

In the 1960s, studies published by Elaine Walster and others (1966) and Ellen Berscheid and others (1971) showed that dating choices among college students depend mostly on physical appearance. In 1967, Karen Dion decided to extend these studies to other kinds of social situations. The series of experiments that she conducted over the next several years dramatically revealed that physical appearance has a profound effect on the way people respond to and evaluate one another. As Dion found, the effect even extends to how young women respond to the misbehavior of children.

TESTING THE THEORY BY EXPERIMENT

Dion began with a hunch that a person's interpretation of a child's misbehavior as harmless, serious, or even pernicious might be influenced considerably by the child's physical appearance. She thought it likely that people would see pretty children as "little angels" and would find excuses for their misbehavior; similarly, they would see homely children as "little monsters" and would judge them harshly for exactly the same misbehavior.

Dion's next step was to devise a way to find out whether her suspicions were true. How could she determine whether beauty does in fact affect judgments this way? Her solution was to use an experiment. When it is possible to do so, many social scientists prefer to use experiments to test their theories because an experimental situation not only permits the manipulation of the factor believed to be the cause, but also allows the experimenter to isolate this factor from others that may also be operating. In a natural setting, for example, no two children ever commit the same act of misbehavior in the same way, and most children are average in appearance rather than unusually pretty or homely. In the laboratory, such complications can be eliminated.

THE EXPERIMENTAL DESIGN

Dion chose a simple and effective experimental design. To rule out variations in the misbehavior of children, she created several written descriptions of misbehavior allegedly committed by a seven-year-old in the school playground (see Figure 2.3). In this way, the *same*

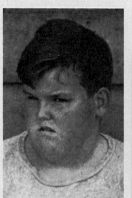

At one corner of the playground a dog was sleeping. Peter stood a short distance from the dog, picked up some sharp stones from the ground, and threw them at the animal. Two of the stones struck the dog and cut its leg. The animal jumped up yelping and limped away. Peter continued to throw rocks at the dog as it tried to move away from him. (Dion, 1972)

FIGURE 2.3

A hypothetical account of misbehavior used in Karen Dion's experiment on reactions to physical attractiveness, and photographs of children similar to those used in the research. (Left: Michael Alexander; right: Jason Lauré/Rapho/Photo Researchers, Inc.)

action could be attributed to a pretty or to a homely child simply by attaching different photographs to the written account. But how could Dion objectively determine who is good-looking when perceptions of beauty and ugliness are basically subjective?

By using a group of judges to rate a number of photographs as very attractive or very unattractive, she was able to choose photographs on which there was very substantial agreement; this procedure overcame idiosyncrasies of individual taste. Half of the pictures were girls, half were boys. The pictures and written accounts were the basic materials used in the experiment.

For subjects, Dion recruited 243 female undergraduate students. Each was presented with a series of accounts of misbehavior and, accompanying each account, a picture of the child who had allegedly committed the act. After reading a given account, each young woman had to rate the seriousness of the child's offense, the severity of punishment of the child should receive, and the likelihood that the child would commit such an act again. The women were asked to rate the child on a number of traits, including "good" or "bad," "kind" or "cruel," and others. Ideally, Dion would have liked each woman to rate the same incident for both an attractive and unattractive child to see whether she made a more positive judgment of the pretty one's behavior. But this procedure would have made it obvious that the picture was not that of the actual child who had committed the act. Instead, the experimenter showed half of the subjects a picture of a very pretty child and the other half a picture of a very homely child for each given act of misbehavior. To determine whether appearance influenced judgments, Dion then compared the ratings given to attractive children and those given to unatttractive children guilty of the same behavior.

The results of this comparison confirmed Dion's expectations that the influence of appearance was very strong (Dion 1972). Most of the women found excuses for the misbehavior of pretty children; they said that the acts were atypical and not a cause for serious concern. But when the same action was attributed to a homely child, the judgments were more often severe, and the women more frequently described the child as a chronic offender.

One young woman made this comment after reading about an attractive little girl who had supposedly thrown rocks at a sleeping dog:

She appears to be a perfectly charming little girl, well-mannered, basically unselfish. It seems that she can adapt well among children her age and make a good impression. . . . She plays well with everyone, but like anyone else, a bad day can occur. Her cruelty . . . need not be taken seriously.

All this woman had to go on was a description of cruelty to an animal and a pretty picture! When a picture of a homely little girl accompanied the same account of cruelty to a dog, another young woman concluded:

I think the child could be quite bratty and would be a problem to teachers. . . . She would be a brat at home. . . . All in all, she would be a real problem.

Clearly, beauty is not merely in the *eye* of the beholder; it also influences judgment.

With this general understanding of what Dion found and how she went about it, we can examine her experiment in greater detail. In it are all the critical elements of a proper experimental design (Figure 2.4).

The independent variable

All experiments include at least one independent variable over which the experimenter has control. It is called *independent* because it stands alone as the factor that is thought to be a cause of or to lead to changes in something. *Variable* means that this factor takes more than one value. If the independent variable were electrical current, for example, it would be necessary at least to be able to switch it on and off. The accounts of children's misbehavior in Dion's experiment did not vary; they were identical regardless of the picture attached to them and therefore were *not* the independent variable.

The independent variable in Dion's experiment was the attractiveness of the child that the young women saw, and it took two values: attractive and unattractive. The independent variable in an experiment is *manipulated*; that is, Dion could decide which subjects saw pretty or homely children when they read a given account of misbehavior.

FIGURE 2.4
Karen Dion's experimental design. The experimental method has the advantage of allowing the sociologist to manipulate the independent variable according to the purposes of the research and to control sources of error through random assignment (in this experiment, randomization of pictures of either pretty or homely children "assigned" to a given subject).

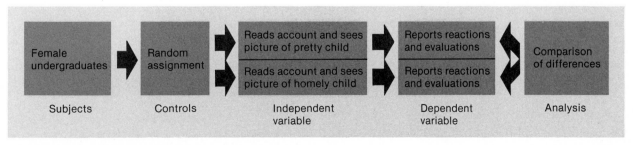

Subjects — Female undergraduates → Controls — Random assignment → Independent variable — Reads account and sees picture of pretty child / Reads account and sees picture of homely child → Dependent variable — Reports reactions and evaluations / Reports reactions and evaluations → Analysis — Comparison of differences

The dependent variable

The dependent variable is the factor that the independent variable is expected to affect; this factor is *dependent* on the independent variable. In Dion's experiment, the dependent variable was the degree of negative evaluation of children's actions. Dion found that it depended on the attractiveness of the child. The independent variable, then, produced the changes that occurred in the dependent variable.

Controls

In an experiment, to *control* means to exclude the possibility that some factor other than simple chance could be causing the changes in the dependent variable—in this experiment, the women's evaluations. Dion used *randomization* of the subjects to ensure against the operation of such other factors. Whether the subjects saw a picture of a pretty or a homely child with a given description of misbehavior was determined randomly. (A very simple way to randomize would have been to flip a coin to determine who saw what.) Had Dion not used randomization, she might—accidentally or through her own unconscious bias—have distributed the pictures of pretty children to subjects who were more than normally sympathetic toward all children and the pictures of homely children to subjects who were less than normally sympathetic, or vice versa. Differences in the subjects' sympathies for children—rather than in the children's appearance—could then have caused the differences found in the evaluations made by the two groups of subjects. She might also have selected more educated subjects for one of the groups, or subjects who had less experience with children. Using randomization, Dion had to worry only about simple chance differences that might occur—and these can be taken into account by standard statistical analysis.

Statistical analysis

How is it possible to compute the odds against the results on an experiment being due only to chance? The experimenter knows that the laws of probability account for the extent to which randomization makes all possible differences (such as greater or less than normal sympathy toward children) equal between the two groups (except, of course, for those resulting from ma-

TABLE 2.1

PERCEIVED LIKELIHOOD OF FUTURE TRANSGRESSIONS*

ATTRACTIVENESS OF CHILD	MEAN RATING	
Unattractive	13.12 }	
Attractive	10.70 }	$p < .001$

* Ratings range from 0 (very unlikely) to 17 (very likely).
SOURCE: Adapted from Karen Dion, 1972.

nipulation of the independent variable). There is a computable probability, for example, of tossing seven "heads" in a row. The odds against chance-produced findings in an experiment depend on the number of subjects used and on the size of the difference found between the two groups on the dependent variable (in Table 2.1, the difference between 13.12 and 10.70).

The usual way to compute these odds is to use a *test of statistical significance.** As a rule of thumb, experimenters usually require that the odds be at least 20 to 1 against chance findings before they call the results statistically significant or put any trust in their results. As shown in Table 2.1, the odds against Dion's main finding being the result of simple chance are at least 1,000 to 1. If she conducted this experiment 1,000 times, and if physical appearance actually *does not* influence judgments about the likelihood that a child will commit future transgressions, then she would get differences this great on the dependent variable only once. This probability is what is indicated by $p < .001$ in the table—the probability (p) that these findings are the result of chance is less than ($<$) one chance in 1,000 (.001). Clearly, Dion is betting on nearly a sure thing when she claims that appearance influenced the subjects' evaluations of children's misbehavior.

APPLICATIONS

Was all Dion's effort worth it? As we pointed out in Chapter 1, human behavior is not forever fixed. On the contrary, it can be changed. But it does not change as

* Even here there is disagreement among sociologists, though primarily in the context of experimental studies. Selvin (1957) has argued that "in design and in interpretation, in principle and in practice, tests of significance are inappropriate in nonexperimental research" (p. 527). A detailed discussion of this issue is the subject of Morrison and Henkel's (1970) volume, which concludes with a list of restrictions on the use of significance tests.

long as we remain unaware of why we think and behave the way we do. The results of this study and of others built upon its findings reveal that many children are probably being dealt with unfairly on the basis of their appearance. If such discrimination is objectionable and contrary to our ideals, we should find ways of alerting people to their unwitting biases. For example, it would seem reasonable to subject student teachers to such an experiment in order to demonstrate to them that they are influenced by outward appearances. Thus sensitized, they might guard against such biases in the classroom.

It should be noted, however, that Dion's study is not the last word on the subject of judging people by their appearance. Critics of the experiment have cautioned against drawing sweeping conclusions from it. For example, Dion's subjects were all young women (using older, more experienced classroom teachers as subjects might have produced different results). Moreover, the consensus procedure used to select "ugly" and "attractive" children produced a collection of extremes, while most real-life children are somewhere in between. It is also possible that one of the methods used to exclude variation from the experiment—presenting the descriptions of the misbehavior in writing—may have set up an overly artificial situation that "produced" the striking results. Although Dion's results should certainly be taken seriously, it is possible that the tendency to discriminate on the basis of appearance shows up more strongly in an experiment than in real life.

Survey research: Charles Y. Glock and Rodney Stark

On Christmas Eve, 1959, a gang of German youths desecrated a Jewish synagogue in Cologne. The swastikas they crudely smeared on the walls showed that anti-Semitism had not died with the Third Reich. Worse yet, within days the Cologne incident was repeated in many other German cities. But this was only the beginning. The wave rapidly spread beyond Germany, and then beyond Europe to the United States. By March 1960, barely two months after the first German occurrence, there had been at least 643 similar ones in America (Caplovitz and Rogers, 1960). They were a sensation in the news media for a while, but then the storm of incidents subsided as mysteriously as it had begun. Soon most people forgot about it. But one group did not.

The Anti-Defamation League (ADL) of B'nai B'rith, founded in 1912 to fight anti-Semitism in the United States, had faced an overwhelming task for many years. But times seemed to have changed, and by the late 1950s ADL leaders had come to believe that militant anti-Semitism had all but died out in America. They had then turned most of their attention to subtle problems of institutional discrimination and to the black civil-rights movement. The outbreak of vandalism against Jewish property, accompanied by occasional violence against Jews, shocked them deeply. They decided that their most pressing need was for basic research on the sources, persistence, and potentialities of American anti-Semitism and of prejudice in general. ADL leaders decided to seek the help of scholars at the University of California at Berkeley.

THE USES OF SURVEY RESEARCH

An interdisciplinary group of social scientists quickly assembled under the auspices of the Survey Research Center and divided the work into several independent but related studies; the ADL initially supplied $500,000 to fund the operation. Unlike the participant-observation field study done by John Lofland, large-scale *survey research*, the method generally employed by these scholars, is expensive. Lofland had to spend money only on his living expenses, a tape recorder, filing cabinets, and a lot of paper and typewriter ribbons. But conducting personal interviews with several thousand people randomly selected from the adult population in selected regions across the nation involves heavy costs in salaries and travel expenses. Coding these interviews for computer processing also requires a great deal of money and labor. One survey analyst can easily use up several thousand dollars each month for a year or two just to pay for computer time.

Survey research therefore requires extremely comprehensive and detailed planning. If you ask the wrong questions or fail to ask a significant one, you may have wasted the time and money allotted to you.

In spite of the difficulties involved, survey research is the most common research technique in sociology and the only reliable procedure for acquiring certain kinds of information. To establish the distribution of some trait—for example, anti-Semitism or political preference—in a population, no other method suffices. If a cheaper method existed for accurately forecasting elections, nobody would pay the Gallup or Harris organization tens of thousands of dollars to conduct a survey.

The study of anti-Semitism required survey research, not an experiment. People already are or are not anti-Semitic. One could not morally or practically find people who do not have attitudes about Jews and try to create positive or negative attitudes in them. Nor could the independent variables in which these social scientists were interested (such as level of education and religious preference) be manipulated in a laboratory: you cannot take people into a laboratory and create some of them as college graduates and some as high school dropouts. Nor could some of them be raised in a laboratory as religious conservatives and others as nonbelievers. The study on anti-Semitism had to take people as they were and try to determine why they were that way and what the consequences of their attitudes might be.

The group of social scientists disagreed strongly among themselves on the question of whether Christian teachings foster anti-Semitism. Charles Y. Glock, director of the Survey Research Center, and Rodney Stark, a graduate student in sociology, felt that this disagreement established the need for a separate study on the role of religion in American anti-Semitism. They decided to conduct such a study, and it is on their survey research that we shall concentrate.

THE METHOD AND MODEL

It was clear from history that the major source of anti-Semitism was religious conflict; religion was the only important way in which Jews had always differed from their neighbors. Ethnic differences among Christians had never resulted in the sustained conflict found between Christians and Jews. Furthermore, the develop-

FIGURE 2.5

A path-analysis diagram of Glock and Stark's survey research. The arrows linking the concepts show the direction of the relationships studied; for example, orthodoxy is seen to lead to religious hostility, which in turn leads to secular anti-Semitism. The thickness of the arrows represents the strength of these relationships; thus the strongest relationship was between orthodoxy and particularism. The white arrows represent potential relationships that were found not to exist; there was, for example, no relationship between particularism and seeing historical Jews as crucifiers. (Stark et al., 1971)

ment of laws curtailing Jewish freedoms and rights—for example, laws establishing ghettos within which Jews were forced to live—had been encouraged by various churches' decrees. The last legally enforced ghettoization of Jews in Europe before the rise of Nazism was in the Vatican State and was discontinued only in 1870.

Viewing this history, Glock and Stark developed a theory about the way in which commitment to traditional Christian doctrines and teachings about the religious status of Jews and their role in the crucifixion of Jesus Christ would continue to shape contemporary beliefs about Jews. This theory was a series of abstract concepts linked by propositions—statements about how these factors influenced one another in cause-and-effect relationships. Figure 2.5 shows the conceptual scheme of these factors in the form of a path-analysis diagram (one that shows the direction in which the factors are related so that it can be seen which is cause and which is effect). The diagram displays such concepts as *orthodoxy:* belief in the traditional teachings of Christianity; *particularism:* belief that Christianity is the only true religion and that salvation is open only to Christians; *negative religious images of the modern Jew:* belief that the Jews are still unforgiven for the crucifixion and therefore damned. Glock and Stark postulated a developing causal order, starting with orthodoxy and ending with a negative religious image of the modern Jew. They further postulated that these religious grounds for hostility would spill over into secular situations and make people especially susceptible to *secular anti-Semitism*—stereotyping Jews, mistrusting and resenting them, and discriminating against them.

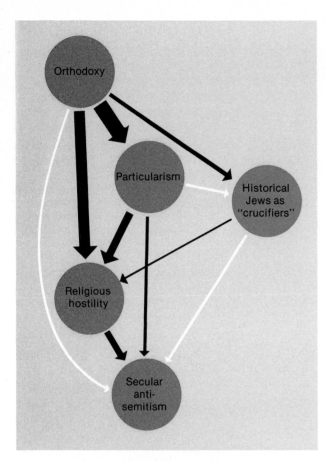

TESTING THE THEORY
BY SURVEY

To test their theory, Glock and Stark decided to send questionnaires to a small sample of church members in a single metropolitan area. Then they would *replicate*, or repeat, their study in an attempt to achieve the same results, using a different sample population, in a nation-wide interview survey to be conducted by Gertrude Selznick and Stephen Steinberg (1969). To begin, Glock and Stark chose four counties in the San Francisco Bay area and from them randomly selected 21 Catholic parishes and 97 Protestant congregations representing all major denominations.

About 70 percent of the church members who received the questionnaires filled them out and returned them. To guard against bias, Glock and Stark telephoned a sample of the nonrespondents and asked their age, sex, occupations, frequency of church attendance, level of education, and so forth. When the nonrespondents were compared with the respondents on each of these factors, the differences were very small; thus the findings were not badly biased in regard to these major social variables. Glock and Stark also knew that interview data from the national sample—in which there would be no appreciable bias—would constitute another check of their findings.

STATISTICAL ANALYSIS

What does it mean to say that religion and prejudice are or are not related? Now that the researchers had data on the beliefs, activities, and attitudes of more than 3,000 persons, how could they proceed? What they did is at the heart of virtually all science: they took the quantitative data—the bits of evidence gathered in their research, expressed in numbers—and did a statistical analysis of them.

To perform their analysis, Glock and Stark had to give each person a score on each of the concepts in their theory. They added up each person's answers to a set of questions designed to measure a particular concept or element in the theory. For example, orthodoxy was measured by responses to questions about belief in a personal God, in the divinity of Jesus, and in the existence of heaven and the devil. People who claimed firm belief in all four were given a score of four; those who rejected one belief were scored three, and so on down to a score of zero for those who rejected all four beliefs. In this way five groups were created for the concepts of orthodoxy, ranging from very orthodox down to very unorthodox believers. Other concepts were similarly measured and scored.

To see whether one set of scores is related to another set requires a simple comparison. The following example, taken from Glock and Stark's study, is based on two sets of scores. The first is a measure of what they called *religious dogmatism*—the independent variable. It combined the first three religious concepts in their theory into a single measure. The second is anti-Semitic belief—the dependent variable. To find out if religious dogmatism is in fact related to anti-Semitic beliefs, they first had to separate people into groups in accordance with their scores on religious dogmatism. Glock and Stark then condensed the original numerical scores into three different groups; the result is shown in Example A.

EXAMPLE A

RELIGIOUS DOGMATISM*

HIGH	MEDIUM	LOW
522 people	421 people	310 people

* Protestants only.

The next step was to see how each of these three groups was distributed on the measure of anti-Semitic beliefs. The results are shown in Example B.

EXAMPLE B

ANTI-SEMITIC BELIEFS	RELIGIOUS DOGMATISM		
	HIGH	MEDIUM	LOW
High	271	143	62
Medium	204	202	164
Low	47	76	84
Total	522	421	310

By converting the simple numbers into percentages, Glock and Stark then produced Example C, which enabled them to compare persons scoring high on religious dogmatism with those scoring lower to discover which group held more anti-Semitic beliefs.

EXAMPLE C

ANTI-SEMITIC BELIEFS	RELIGIOUS DOGMATISM		
	HIGH	MEDIUM	LOW
High	52%	34%	20%
Medium	39	48	53
Low	9	18	27
Total	100%	100%	100%

Reading across this table, you will see that the percentage scoring high on anti-Semitic beliefs falls as one moves from those high on religious dogmatism to those medium and low on this measure: 52–34–20. Or reading across the third row of the table, you can see that the percentage scoring low on anti-Semitic beliefs rises as religious dogmatism declines: 9–18–27. Thus, more than half of the persons in the high-dogmatism group scored high on anti-Semitism, but only one person in five among those in the low-dogmatism group scored high on anti-Semitism. This clearly shows a relationship

We turn now to relations between Christians and Jews. There is a great deal of disagreement about what Jews are like. Here are some things people have said at one time or another about Jews. For each statement, we would ask you to do two things:

First read the statement and decide whether you tend to think Jews are like this or not, and put your answer in Column A.

Then, whether or not you think Jews are like this or not, we would ask you to suppose that the statement actually were true. If the statement were true, how would it tend to make you feel toward Jews? Would you tend to feel friendly or unfriendly toward them because of this? Put your answer in Column B.

FIGURE 2.6

Sample questions from the questionnaire distributed by Glock and Stark in their survey research on the causes of anti-Semitism. (Glock and Stark, 1966)

between dogmatism and anti-Semitism, confirming Glock and Stark's theory that religion does play a role in contemporary American anti-Semitism.

Although such findings confirmed Glock and Stark's expectations, they still had much work to do to establish the accuracy of their findings. In survey research, investigators may find that an association between two factors is caused by a third factor. Thus it was possible that some factor other than dogmatism was responsible for the findings.

This problem, which Glock and Stark had to grapple with, is called *spuriousness.* When we can demonstrate that something other than dogmatism produced the findings, then we can say that the original relationship between dogmatism and anti-Semitism was spurious, not causal. Consider a silly, but apt, example of spuriousness: the more fire trucks present at a fire, the greater the fire damage will be. We can easily see that

| | COLUMN A | | | COLUMN B | | |
| | Do you feel Jews tend to be like this? | | | If Jews were like this would it tend to make you feel: | | |
	YES	SOMEWHAT	NO	FRIENDLY	UNFRIENDLY	NEITHER WAY
Jews are particularly generous and give a great deal of money to charity	☐	☐	☐	☐	☐	☐
On the average, Jews are wealthier than Christians	☐	☐	☐	☐	☐	☐
Jews are more likely than Christians to cheat in business	☐	☐	☐	☐	☐	☐
Jewish children tend to get better grades in school than Christian children do	☐	☐	☐	☐	☐	☐
Jews are less likely than Christians to oppose Communism	☐	☐	☐	☐	☐	☐
The movie and television industries are pretty much run by Jews	☐	☐	☐	☐	☐	☐
On the average, Jews tend to drink less than non-Jews	☐	☐	☐	☐	☐	☐
Because Jews are not bound by Christian ethics, they do things to get ahead that Christians generally will not do	☐	☐	☐	☐	☐	☐
While many Jews attend synagogues and worship God, most Jews are not very religious	☐	☐	☐	☐	☐	☐

although these two phenomena will occur together, their connection is spurious, not one of cause and effect; fire trucks are not causing the damage.

Similarly, some other factor could be making it appear that religious dogmatism is the cause of the anti-Semitic beliefs. Many sociologists would have a hunch that social class might be producing high scores on both measures (see Chapter 13). They would argue that poor people are both more religiously dogmatic *and* more anti-Semitic than are well-to-do people. They would therefore say that those who scored high on religious dogmatism typically are poor people and for this reason scored high on anti-Semitism; those who scored low on dogmatism typically are well-to-do people and therefore scored low on anti-Semitism. But would that hunch turn out to be spurious? Let's find out.

Figure 2.7 (p. 30) is a *hypothetical* illustration showing income as the cause of a spurious relationship between dogmatism and anti-Semitism. If variation in income produced the original connection between dogmatism and anti-Semitism, then when income is controlled for, the original relationship ought to *disappear*. Notice that it has disappeared in the hypothetical

table. For the group earning $7,000 or less, each level of dogmatism contains the same percentage of people who scored high on anti-Semitic beliefs; across the top row we read: 60–60–60. Similarly, for the group earning more than $7,000, the percentage of people who scored high on anti-Semitism is the same regardless of their score on dogmatism: 20–20–20. We can also see that regardless of the degree of dogmatism, people earning more than $7,000 are much less likely to score high on anti-Semitism than are those earning $7,000 or less: 60 percent versus 20 percent. We use such a control procedure to find out whether a relationship is spurious; we know that it is when the outcome is like the one in Figure 2.7—when the high, medium, and low correlations between dogmatism and anti-Semitism are all exactly the same in each income group.

However, this is *not* what happened when Glock and Stark controlled for income. They found that the original relationship between dogmatism and anti-Semitism *reappeared* in each of the income tables. Regardless of a person's income, religious views influenced judgments of Jews. Using similar procedures, Glock and Stark were also able to eliminate age, sex, education,

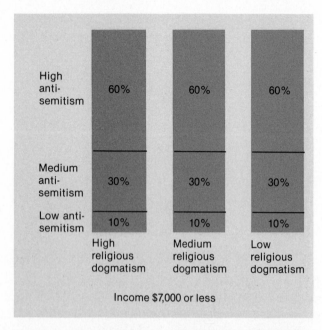

Income $7,000 or less

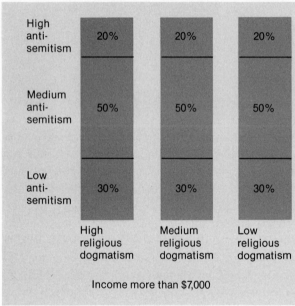

Income more than $7,000

FIGURE 2.7

A hypothetical chart presenting a *spurious* (false) relationship between the religious dogmatism and the anti-Semitic beliefs of two income groups. If income level were the cause of both dogmatism and anti-Semitism, then the correlation between dogmatism and anti-Semitism would disappear when income was controlled for—and, in this hypothetical chart, it does. But in actuality, when Glock and Stark controlled for income, dogmatism and anti-Semitism were found to be causally related and income level was found *not* to be a casual factor.

denomination, political affiliation, rural or urban origins, and a number of other potential sources of spuriousness. Such controls greatly increased the probability that religious dogmatism does in fact cause anti-Semitism.

APPLICATIONS

Recall why Glock and Stark had undertaken their study: to try to understand the causes of American anti-Semitism. Glock and Stark projected that perhaps as many as 17.5 million Americans at that time harbored ill-will toward Jews on the basis of their religious convictions.

The findings called for action. Glock and Stark believed that they were obligated to help find ways to change these pernicious patterns. Is this a violation of scientific neutrality? A proper scientist, whether sociologist or chemist, must be scrupulously impartial and careful in gathering and evaluating evidence. But once this has been done, the scientist is under no obligation to treat the findings neutrally or to do nothing about them. A chemist warns us that rising mercury levels in lakes and rivers endanger life. Glock and Stark believed that churches have an absolute obligation to undo what they have done, that is, to find ways to stop fostering prejudice.

They first acted on their findings when they supplied a preliminary report to the Vatican Council II, a worldwide meeting of Roman Catholic prelates that led to many changes in the church. The council issued a historic statement condemning the notion that the Jews bore the guilt of the crucifixion, and ADL leaders stated that Glock and Stark's report had been critical in prompting this action. Shortly thereafter Glock and Stark published their findings in *Christian Beliefs and Anti-Semitism* (1966). The book received considerable attention in the press; it was praised and damned, believed and denied. A number of Protestant churches made affirmations similar to the one made by the Vatican Council II (other churches had made such affirmations earlier). More important, church leaders generally agreed that positive action was necessary, that Sunday-school books and church literature needed considerable revision, and that educational campaigns at all levels were needed. For more than two years Glock and Stark toured the nation, meeting in seminars with church leaders, curriculum directors, and religious publishers, and they found that people listened to their results despite their misgivings. They were willing to listen because Glock and Stark had facts, not opinions.

Unfortunately, politicians and decision makers are not always so receptive to the implications of sociological research. The application of sociological knowledge is at least as complicated as is its acquisition. Nevertheless, courses and programs in applied sociology have proliferated over the last few years, reflecting an increasing interest in such concerns.

Other research methods

In this chapter we have discussed the use of surveys, questionnaires, field studies, and laboratory experiments in sociological research. While these methods are common, they are by no means the only approaches sociologists use for gathering data. A number of other methods are used for studying particular phenomena.

workings of an independent variable in an experiment by carefully controlling extraneous factors. Of course, given the nature of sociological inquiry—the fact that its objects are human beings—analytic studies often cannot be done. Sociologists have therefore sought other methods of gathering reliable data, many of them involving the sophisticated use of statistics.

RESEARCH STUDIES: GENERAL TYPES

The method a sociologist uses to examine a particular problem depends, as we have seen, on the nature of the problem. For example, if the object of research is a new phenomenon about which little is known, an *exploratory study* may be appropriate. In such a study, the sociologist seeks to gain new ideas and insights and to form hypotheses that can be the basis of further research. Lofland's study of the Unification Church, for example, was at least initially an exploratory study; eventually his observations led him to form hypotheses about what made people affiliate with the church. When he moved on to construct a careful description of church members, his work had become a *descriptive study*. This kind of study aims at compiling an accurate description of a group or other phenomenon by careful collection of reliable evidence. Finally, a third general type of study is the *analytic study*, such as Karen Dion's, in which the sociologist attempts to identify the

QUANTITATIVE METHODS

Sociologists can mine a good deal of quantitative (numerical) data from government and private sources, such as census reports and actuarial records. Often these collections of figures suggest sociological trends, such as changes in family life or age and population shifts. To obtain precise documentation of such ongoing changes, sociologists may devise *trend studies*.

The resurgence of anti-draft sentiment is one example of social phenomena measured by trend studies. These are used to determine if a pattern exists between a certain group and its feelings toward a particular issue. (© Jim Anderson 1980)

These are studies of the relationship between two variables at repeated points in time. Different (but comparable) samples are used each time the researcher questions the population. For example, a sociologist might design a trend study to identify changing attitudes among college students toward the military draft. In such a study, the researcher would ask the same series of questions to several groups of college students over a period of months or (more probably) years to determine how attitudes toward military service were changing. A study such as this should yield reliable information so long as the samples of students are comparable. (A sample that included a disproportionate number of older students or women, for example, might produce unwanted variation.)

A second technique used to measure changes in attitude is the *panel analysis.* In this kind of study, the *same* people are queried at different points in time, which yields evidence about the changing attitudes of particular people. If, for example, a given group of college students had been asked their opinion of the draft in the spring of 1979 (before the seizure of American hostages in Iran), in early December of that same year (just after the hostages were seized), in January 1980 (shortly after the Soviet Union invaded Afghanistan), and in May 1980 (after the failed attempt to rescue the hostages), we would have an indication of whether the events of international politics changed students' minds about the draft. Panel studies, then, can indicate the stability of people's attitudes—whether people change their minds; if so, which people do the changing; and what events had led to the change.

In addition to analyzing numerical data, sociologists study popular tastes and interests. The popularity of the film "Star Wars" could indicate a nation-wide interest in space, a need for imaginative release, a lack of anything better to do, or mere coincidence. (© Jim Anderson 1980)

QUALITATIVE METHODS: CONTENT ANALYSIS

In addition to making use of numerical data, sociologists also investigate phenomena by collecting qualitative data (expressed in language rather than in numbers) from sources such as newspapers, magazines, films, tapes, government and industry records, private diaries, and books of many kinds. One well-known investigation using qualitative data was Leo Lowenthal's (1956) content analysis of the biographical articles that had appeared in two magazines—*The Saturday Evening Post* and *Collier's*—between 1901 and 1941. The object of the study was to determine the extent to which the types of popular heroes described in these magazines changed from what Lowenthal called "idols of production" (such as political, professional, and business figures) to "idols of consumption" (such as entertainers). True to what one might expect (knowing how American values have shifted their focus from hard work to leisure—a shift we will explore in depth later in this book), there were declines in the percentages of business and professional people featured in the articles and a striking increase in the percentage of entertainers.

THE COMPARATIVE/HISTORICAL APPROACH

Sociological studies are not limited to contemporary data; a number of studies have examined other historical periods. An example from classic sociological literature is the series of studies done by Max Weber on Confucianism (1951), Hinduism (1958), Judaism (1952), and Protestantism (1930), in which Weber tried to show how these religions developed within their particular historical and social contexts, how they related to nonreligious social phenomena such as economic patterns, and how they contributed to social change (Weber's study of Protestantism was discussed briefly in Chapter 1). There are also many recent examples, such as the studies by Charles Tilly and his family (1975) of the riots, brawls, and other forms of mob action that occurred in France, Germany, and Italy in relation to the broad social changes in those countries from 1830 to 1930.

MODELS OF SOCIAL PROCESS

Although most sociological studies are concerned with "real" phenomena (the actions of real people, for example), that is not always the case. Some important relationships can be explored via models or simulations of social processes. Earl R. Babbie, in his book *The Practice of Social Research* (1975), gives an example: a sociologist might create a computer simulation of a human population with a particular "age-sex profile" (that is, a particular balance of young, middle-aged, and old people, and a particular balance of males and females), and then run tests to find out what would happen to that population if, for example, a war killed half the young men.

UNOBTRUSIVE METHODS

Sociologists have discovered that in certain contexts their very presence can have an influence on the data they collect; their entry into a situation can cause people to behave atypically. To avoid this problem, they have developed a number of methods of obtaining data either secretly or indirectly. These include *physical trace analysis*, in which the sociologist, somewhat in the manner of an archaeologist, seeks to identify patterns of behavior by observing what "tracks" people leave behind. For example, a researcher trying to identify changing trends in child rearing might survey all the public libraries in a city to see if manuals on baby care and child rearing were worn or rebound, indicating much use by library patrons. Other examples of trace analysis are more obvious: some sociologists have supplemented their studies of social class with analyses of people's garbage.

Archival record analysis is simply the use of public and private records (everything from census data to

Charles Tilly and his family studied the mob actions from 1830 to 1930 in France, Germany, and Italy. Their study explained the mob actions that occurred in that period, such as this looting of an Italian food store, in terms of broad social changes. (UPI)

newspapers) to gather information. Obviously, the reliability of these data depends on the accuracy of the source. Even the census, for example, had been faulted for undercounting certain groups within the population. However, analysis of census data is an extremely useful and frequently used technique of sociological investigation for studying such trends as the effects of population shifts, changes in marital forms and practices, and racial and ethnic integration of neighborhoods.

Another unobtrusive method used by sociologists is *simple observation*, or watching what people do. This may consist of merely observing people's appearance and clothing, or of watching how they move in their "territories," or of listening to what they say. Although this kind of observation may yield fascinating and suggestive results, its unsystematic nature cannot be denied; generalizations obtained on the basis of simple observation may be unreliable.

Unobtrusive analysis may be made even more unobtrusive by the use of hidden recording devices. Tape recorders, hidden microphones, one-way mirrors, cameras, and other devices can allow the observer to be completely invisible. Although these methods have their value, their use raises important ethical questions.

THE ETHICS AND POLITICS OF SOCIOLOGICAL RESEARCH

The use of hidden recording devices is but one of the ethical problems that sociological research presents. The sociologist commonly studies people, and the ultimate goal may be exposing attitudes and patterns of behavior that some subjects would rather not reveal.

The great question is, to whom does the sociologist owe the greatest obligation? To the subjects of the study, to the society at large, or to some abstract idea of the advance of knowledge? Should subjects always be protected with anonymity? Should there be some standard of privacy that the researcher should not cross? (In this respect, consider the sociologist who examines garbage in a "physical trace analysis.")

A broader problem is that of the sociologist's values. Most scientists today agree that perfect objectivity in any investigation is impossible. Sociologists, like all scientists, are human beings who have learned certain values from their culture and subculture. The sociologist must not only be aware of these views and prejudices but must attempt to acknowledge their effect on any research project. Finally, given the fact that many sociological studies are extremely expensive and are funded by groups with a special interest in the research results, the temptation to collect *particular* facts, or to interpret the data in accord with some particular theory must always be recognized.

In view of these ethical problems, sociologists today acknowledge the need to maintain a balance between the value of a particular investigation—its positive contribution to the society—and the inherent risk to participants. According to federal government rules, all subjects of a study must now give their informed consent before an investigation begins. Furthermore, each university in the United States must establish an internal committee to screen studies for their balance between value and risk before a go-ahead is given. Ultimately, sociologists have a primary responsibility to protect both the well-being and confidentiality of their respondents—only then will reliable and ethically responsible sociological research be produced.

Summary

The method of doing sociology—that is, the technique used to gather information—varies with the context of the sociological inquiry. *Field studies, experiments,* and *survey research:* each has unique contributions to make in the sociologists' quest for patterns in human behavior.

The *field study* provides the investigator with firsthand data on the day-to-day patterns of the subjects. One type of field study involves *participant observation,* in which the researcher takes part in a group's activities while observing the members' behavior.

In an *experiment,* the researcher investigates a phenomenon, called the *dependent variable,* by manipulating its pos-sible causes, called *independent variables.* By so doing, the causal relationship between the independent and dependent variables can be determined. The greatest advantage of the experiment is that the researcher controls the independent variables and can thus eliminate confusing or extraneous elements that might lead to *spurious* results.

Survey research is the best method for determining the distribution of a particular characteristic in a given *population.* Using personal or telephone interviews or mailed questionnaires, researchers can make a comprehensive and reliable appraisal of a large number of people.

Sociologists ensure the validity of their research by *con-*

trols, such as randomization and statistical manipulation. Results of research are tested for *statistical significance* to guarantee that the *theories* drawn from the investigation are, in fact, general statements that accurately describe patterns of human behavior.

Research methods in general can be classed as *exploratory, descriptive,* or *analytic.* Many sociological studies make use of *quantitative* methods. These include *trend studies* and *panel analysis*, both of which are frequently used to measure changes in people's attitudes over time. In addition to quantitative methods, sociologists make use of many kinds of *qualitative* data, which have even made possible sociological studies of eras in the distant past.

Since sociologists, like other scientists, hold values and prejudices, they must make efforts to ensure that their research results are not contaminated. They must also design their studies with a number of ethical considerations in mind, including subjects' rights to anonymity and privacy.

Glossary

CONTROL The statistical process of holding constant all factors other than the independent variable in order to see if a relationship between independent and dependent variables holds when all else is equal.

DEPENDENT VARIABLE The phenomenon under investigation that is believed to be caused or affected by another phenomenon (the independent variable).

EXPERIMENT In sociology, a research method in which subjects are exposed to an independent variable and observed for changes in behavior under carefully controlled conditions.

FIELD STUDY A research method in which subjects are observed in their usual environment, rather than in a laboratory.

HYPOTHETICAL Pertaining to a hypothesis, a proposition set forth as the explanation for the occurrence of a phenomenon, often asserted tentatively as a guide for research.

INDEPENDENT VARIABLE A phenomenon believed to cause or to affect another phenomenon (the dependent variable).

PANEL ANALYSIS A study of attitude change involving querying the same group of people at several points in time.

PARTICIPANT OBSERVATION An investigative technique in which the researcher takes part in the activities of his or her subject group while making an objective study of the group's behavior.

POPULATION The total aggregation of individuals who are subject to or included in a statistical study.

STATISTICAL SIGNIFICANCE The mathematical probability that a given research result was not produced by chance.

SURVEY RESEARCH An investigative technique that often uses interviews or questionnaires to determine the presence or distribution of a specific characteristic in a given large population.

THEORY A coherent group of principles proposed and at least partially verified or established as the explanation for a phenomenon.

TREND STUDY A study of the relationship between two variables at repeated points in time, in which comparable samples of the population are queried.

Recommended readings

Babbie, Earl R. *The Practice of Social Research.* 2nd ed. Belmont, Calif.: Wadsworth, 1979. A more detailed presentation than in Zito's book (below) of a broad range of current research methods, including various modes of analyzing quantitative data. Babbie provides a discussion of the logic as well as the tools of social research.

Cole, Stephen. *The Sociological Methods.* 3rd ed. Chicago: Rand McNally, 1980. An excellent introduction to *understanding* (as distinct from conducting) sociological research. This book is especially appropriate for students in introductory sociology courses.

Denzin, Norman K. *The Research Act: A Theoretical Introduction to Sociological Methods.* Chicago: Aldine, 1977. A unique attempt to blend an understanding of current research methods with an appreciation for their relevance to and ultimate utility in the explication and testing of sociological theory.

Hammond, Phillip E. (ed.). *Sociologists at Work: Essays on the Craft of Social Research.* New York: Basic Books, 1964. A fascinating book in which thirteen sociologists stand back from the important studies they have conducted and examine the personal and social factors involved in the process of their research.

Runcie, John F. *Experiencing Social Research.* Homewood, Ill.: Dorsey Press, 1976. A serious attempt to involve students in the process of social research using many of the major approaches to data collection. The book is written at a level appropriate for beginning as well as advanced undergraduate students of sociology.

Zito, George V. *Methodology and Meanings: Varieties of Sociological Inquiry.* New York: Praeger, 1975. A brief but useful introduction to a broad range of tools for conducting sociological research.

Doing fieldwork among the Yąnomamö

NAPOLEON A. CHAGNON

Napoleon A. Chagnon, a young anthropologist, describes the emotional and physical stress involved in fieldwork. His account of his experiences among the Yąnomamö Indians of the Amazon basin shows how difficult it is to divest oneself of cultural preconceptions and fully enter into the lives of people in an alien society.

The Yąnomamö Indians live in southern Venezuela and the adjacent portions of northern Brazil. . . . Some 125 widely scattered villages have populations ranging from 40 to 250 inhabitants, with 75 to 80 people the most usual number. In total numbers their population probably approaches 10,000 people, but this is merely a guess. . . .

But they have a significance apart from tribal size and cultural purity: the Yąnomamö are still actively conducting warfare. . . . I describe the Yąnomamö as "the fierce people" because that is the most accurate single phrase that describes them. That is how they conceive themselves to be, and that is how they would like others to think of them.

I spent nineteen months with the Yąnomamö, during which time I acquired some proficiency in their language and, up to a point, submerged myself in their culture and way of life. The thing that impressed me most was the importance of aggression in their culture. I had the opportunity to witness a good many incidents that expressed individual vindictiveness on the one hand and collective bellicosity on the other. . . .

My first day in the field illustrated to me what my teachers meant when they spoke of "culture shock . . ."

We arrived at the village, Bisaasi-teri, about 2:00 PM and docked the boat along the muddy bank at the terminus of the path used by the Indians to fetch their drinking water. It was hot and muggy, and my clothing was soaked with perspiration. It clung uncomfortably to my body, as it did thereafter for the remainder of the work. The small, biting gnats were out in astronomical numbers, for it was the beginning of the dry season. My face and hands were swollen from the venom of their numerous stings. In just a few moments I was to meet my first Yąnomamö, my first primitive man. What would it be like? I had visions of entering the village and seeing 125 social facts running about calling each other kinship terms and sharing food, each waiting and anxious to have me collect his genealogy. I would wear them out in turn. Would they like me? This was important to me; I wanted them to be so fond of me that they would adopt me into their kinship system and way of life, because I had heard that successful anthropologists always get adopted by their people. . . .

The entrance to the village was covered over with brush and dry palm leaves. We pushed them aside to expose the low opening to the village. The excitement of meeting my first Indians was almost unbearable as I duck-waddled through the low passage into the village clearing.

I looked up and gasped when I saw a dozen burly, naked, filthy, hideous men staring at us down the shafts of their drawn arrows! Immense wads of green tobacco were stuck between their lower teeth and lips making them look even more hideous, and strands of dark-green slime dripped or hung from their noses. We arrived at the village while the men were blowing a hallucinogenic drug up their noses. One of the side effects of the drug is a runny nose. The mucus is always saturated with the green powder and the Indians usually let it run freely from their nostrils. My next discovery was that there were a dozen or so vicious, underfed dogs snapping at my legs, circling me as if I were going to be their next meal. I just stood there holding my notebook, helpless and pathetic. Then the stench of the decaying vegetation and filth struck me and I almost got sick. I was horrified. What sort of a welcome was this for the person who came here to live with you and learn your way of life, to become friends with you?

. . . As we walked down the path to the boat, I pondered the wisdom of having decided to spend a year and a half with this tribe before I had even seen what they were like. I am not ashamed to admit, either, that had there been a diplomatic way out, I would have ended my fieldwork then and there. I did not look forward to the next day when I would be left alone with the Indians; I did not speak a word of their language, and they were decidedly different from what I had imagined them to be. The whole situation was depressing, and I wondered why I ever decided to switch from civil engineering to anthropology in the first place. I had not eaten all day, I was soaking wet from perspiration, the gnats were biting me, and I was covered with red pigment, the result of a dozen or so complete examinations I had been given by as many burly Indians. These examinations capped an otherwise grim day. The Indians would blow their noses into their hands, flick as much of the mucus off that would separate in a snap of the wrist, wipe the residue into their hair, and then carefully examine my face, arms, legs, hair, and the contents of my pockets. I asked Mr. Barker how to say "Your hands are dirty"; my comments were met by the Indians in the following way: They would "clean" their hands by spitting a quantity of slimy tobacco juice into them, rub them together and then proceed with the examination.

Mr. Barker and I crossed the river and slung our hammocks. When he pulled the hammock out of a rubber bag, a heavy, disagreeable odor of mildewed cotton came with it. "Even the missionaries are filthy," I thought to myself. Within two weeks, everything I owned smelled the same way, and I lived with that odor for the remainder of the fieldwork. My own habits of personal cleanliness reached such levels that I didn't even mind being examined by the Indians, as I was not much cleaner than they were after I had adjusted to the circumstances.

. . . Eating three meals a day was out of the question. I solved the problem by eating a single meal that could be prepared in a single container, or, at most, in two containers, washed my dishes only when there were no clean ones left, using cold river water, and wore each change of clothing at least a week to cut down on my laundry problem, a courageous undertaking in the tropics. I was also less concerned about sharing my provisions with the rats, insects, Indians, and the elements, thereby eliminating the need for my complicated storage process. I was able to last most of the day on *café con leche*, heavily sugared espresso coffee diluted about five to one with hot milk. I would prepare this in the evening and store it in a thermos. Frequently, my single meal was no more complicated than a can of sardines and a package of crackers. But at least two or three times a week I would do something sophisticated, like make oatmeal or boil rice and add a can of tuna fish or tomato paste to it. . . .

Meals were a problem in another way. Food sharing is important to the Yąnomamö in the context of displaying friendship. "I am hungry," is almost a form of greeting with them. I could not possibly have brought enough food with me to feed the entire village, yet they seemed not to understand this. All they could see was that I did not share my food with them at each and every meal. Nor could I enter into their system of reciprocities with respect to food; every time one of them gave me something "freely," he would dog me for months to pay him back, not with food, but with steel tools. . . .

Finally, there was the problem of being lonely and separated from your own kind, especially your family. I tried to overcome this by seeking personal friendships among the Indians. This only complicated the matter because all my friends simply used my confidence to gain privileged access to my cache of steel tools and trade goods, and looted me. I would be bitterly disappointed that my "friend" thought no more of me than to finesse our relationship exclusively with the intention of getting at my locked up possessions, and my depression would hit new lows every time I discovered this. . . .

The thing that bothered me most was the incessant, passioned, and aggressive demands the Indians made. It would become so unbearable that I would have to lock myself in my mud hut every once in a while just to escape from it: Privacy is one of Western culture's greatest achievements. But I did not want privacy for its own sake; rather, I simply had to get away from the begging. Day and night for the entire time I lived with the Yąnomamö I was plagued by such demands as: "Give me a knife, I am poor!" . . .

. . . Giving in to a demand always established a new threshold; the next demand would be for a bigger item or favor, and the anger of the Indians even greater if the demand was not met. I soon learned that I had to become very much like the Yąnomamö to be able to get along with them on their terms: sly, aggressive, and intimidating.

. . . For the most part, my own "fierceness" took the form of shouting back at the Yąnomamö as loudly and as passionately as they shouted at me, especially at first, when I did not know much of their language. As I became more proficient in their language and learned more about their political tactics, I became more sophisticated in the art of bluffing. . . .

Whenever I took such action and defended my rights, I got along much better with the Yąnomamö. A good deal of their behavior toward me was directed with the forethought of establishing the point at which I would react defensively. Many of them later reminisced about the early days . . . when I was "timid" and a little afraid of them, and they could bully me into giving goods away. . . .

With respect to collecting the data I sought, there was a very frustrating problem. Primitive social organization is kinship organization, and to understand the Yąnomamö way of life I had to collect extensive genealogies. I could not have deliberately picked a more difficult group to work with in this regard. . . .

I . . . went over the complete genealogical records with Rerebawä, genealogies I had presumed to be in final form. I had to revise them all because of the numerous lies and falsifications they contained. Thus, after five months of almost constant work on the genealogies of just one group, I had to begin almost from scratch!

Discouraging as it was to start over, it was still the first real turning point in my fieldwork. Thereafter, I began taking advantage of local arguments and animosities in selecting my informants, and used more extensively individuals who had married into the group. I began traveling to other villages to check the genealogies, picking villages that were on strained terms with the people about whom I wanted information. I would then return to my base camp and check with local informants the accuracy of the new information. If the informants became angry when I mentioned the new names I acquired from the unfriendly group, I was almost certain that the information was accurate. . . .

CHAPTER THREE
SOCIOLOGICAL THEORY

The social sciences, as noted in Chapter 1, are young in comparison with the natural and physical sciences. The ancient Egyptians observed the stars; the Greeks did experiments in physics and chemistry; physiologists began dissecting corpses centuries ago. But it was not until 1879 that Wilhelm Wundt founded the first psychological laboratory, and not until 1880 that Karl Marx devised one of the earliest questionnaires for workers. Sociology, therefore, has existed only for about the last seventy-five years, and only for the last generation or two have there been substantial numbers of practicing sociologists and major research programs.

Sociological theory, like other parts of the discipline, is still relatively new. In fact, much that has been given that name in sociology is not theory at all, but only preliminary work toward the construction of theories. This chapter will define and explore some of the major premises of current theoretical positions in the field of sociology. But first we will describe what theory is, and what part it plays in scientific research.

What is theory?

Theories are essentially scientific explanations. They are ways of linking *concepts*—ways of connecting the names scientists use to describe the objects, events, or processes they are studying. A theory states the logical relationships between a given set of concepts. For example, a theory of revolutions might make a statement about such concepts as *social class* and *intergroup conflict*; it might propose a logical relationship such as this:

"*If* persons in a deprived social class begin to make more money and gain more power and prestige, *if* these persons begin to expect that their lot will be even better in the future, and *if* these rising expectations are not satisfied, *then* intergroup conflict and perhaps a full-scale revolution are likely to occur."

The key terms are *if* and *then*—they serve to link antecedents to consequences.

THE RELATION BETWEEN THEORY AND RESEARCH

An essential characteristic of any *empirical* science—as distinguished from such purely formal sciences as logic or mathematics—is that establishing theories as "true"

One theory of revolution holds that "if people in a deprived social class begin to make more money and gain more power . . . and if they come to expect more . . . and if these rising expectations are not met, then a full scale revolution is likely to occur." This theory was verified by the Portugese revolution of 1975. Here, members of the revolutionary army are cheered in a Lisbon street. (Henri Bureau/Sygma)

or "false," "confirmed" or "refuted," or "sterile" or "fruitful" is contingent in some way upon what scientists call *evidence*, or *empirical data*. A scientific theory is always involved in an interaction with evidence. It is often said that the evidence comes first; if the theory does not fit the evidence, so much the worse for the theory. In practice it is not that simple. Often a conflict between a theory and evidence is resolved by collecting more evidence. Then, too, even when the evidence seems to refute one part of a theory, that part may still be regarded as "correct" or "true" if it has a logical connection with the other parts of the theory that do fit the evidence. In such cases a theory is more likely to

be modified or extended than rejected: a special axiom may be added to take care of the particular problem.

The history of science shows that in practice neither theory nor research inevitably comes first. A theory that is true or false without any relation at all to evidence is not a scientific theory; similarly, a description that is not related to any kind of theory is not scientific research. What happens, in fact, is that theory and research mutually guide and limit each other. Just as there is, in principle, no end to the number or kinds of theories that might be constructed, there is no end to the amount of evidence that might be collected. One important function of theory in science generally, and especially in sociology, is to guide the collection of evidence. A theory tells what data to collect—namely, those that are relevant to the confirmation or refutation of the theory. Otherwise we might go around studying and measuring everything, accumulating great mountains of data with no way of sorting them out or making sense out of what we have collected. Such nontheoretical sociology has often been called "outhouse counting," after the habit some researchers have of collecting great masses of information (usually from the United States Census, which surveys plumbing facilities, among other things), without ever interpreting the meaning of their research.

By the same token, an important function of research is to guide the building of theories. Research allows us to test and hence confirm, abandon, or modify our theories. In essence there is a dialectical relationship between theory and research. Plausible and highly logical interpretations of social life have existed at least since the time of Plato; but without the check of scientific evidence, they could, and did, go off in every direction. However, as the sociological theorist Kingsley Davis (1949) observed, "Fantastic schemes of reasoning have existed for centuries and have finally died through lack of interest rather than through disproof."

THE LANGUAGE OF SOCIOLOGICAL THEORY

Because of the relative newness of sociological theories, it has not often proved profitable to analyze them in the strict logical and mathematical way that works so well in the older, more developed sciences. Sociological theory is almost always presented as a verbal narrative, written in the ordinary language of the community in which the sociologist lives and works. It therefore has all the richness and subtlety of ordinary language. But it also retains the ambiguity and imprecision of that language. Unlike the specialized vocabulary of the natural sciences (which were forced to coin names for phenomena that had previously gone unnoticed—"quarks," for example), sociological terms must often struggle to retain their assigned definitions in the face of the less restrictive definitions of these same words in everyday language. All of us can define such terms as age, gender, role, race, unemployed, poor, or radical. But our definitions may give meanings to these terms that are quite different from those that a particular sociological theory intends. Such inconsistency leads to a great deal of confusion. Furthermore, use of everyday language in theories makes it hard to grasp the point that sociological concepts, like all scientific concepts, are *abstractions*. (An abstraction is more general than, and not fully represented by, any concrete instance of the class of objects or phenomena included in it: for example, an animal is not simply a dog or a horse—it is these and more.)

Because of all these problems, sociologists have become increasingly inclined to invent their own conceptual language. But when they do this—when they invent their own names for things that already have names in the common language—they are frequently ridiculed for the use of jargon and abominable prose. Since some specialized language is useful, there would seem to be no happy solution. Until sociologists develop enough theories that are sufficiently powerful to overcome this language problem, they will probably have to make do with terms taken from the everyday language and risk ambiguity and misunderstanding. Therefore, as the sociologist Philip Selznick once told a class of students in introductory sociology: "If you are planning to go on in sociology and can't tolerate a certain amount of vagueness and confusion in the concepts you use . . . well, let's face it, you're in the wrong field."

If sociological theory has its faults, however, it also has its virtues. Perhaps most important, theory concerns itself with questions that have proved to be of persistent interest to many people—sociologists and nonsociologists alike. Such questions include: How is society possible? What is the relationship between the individual and the various collectivities to which he or she belongs? What is the nature of the social hierarchy? These concerns have been of enduring interest to human beings; they have inspired philosophers, moralists, and political thinkers throughout world history. Sociological theory seeks to go beyond speculation and to address these questions with evidence.

NONEMPIRICAL ASPECTS OF THEORIES

The elements of a sociological theory that can be accepted or rejected by collecting evidence are its *empirical components*, or *testable propositions*; when these propositions are highly specific and refer to readily available data, they are usually called *hypotheses*. Some of these elements reappear so often that we can easily identify them. But we also need to be able to recognize the nonempirical, or nontestable, parts of a theory, so that we will not waste time or money trying to accept or reject them by amassing research results. The nonempirical elements of theories that we shall consider are: *definitions*—statements that are true by the nature of their constituent terms; the *classification scheme*—

the system of "pigeonholes" used for organizing concepts and events; and the qualification *other things being equal,*—a statement that is often attached to testable propositions but that severely restricts the kind of evidence that can be used to test them.

Definitions

We have pointed out that concepts are simply the names scientists give the objects they study. Obviously, it would be silly to ask whether such names are true or false. A rose by any other name still smells as sweet. It is only necessary that we agree on what group of objects is defined by the word rose. Similarly, definitions and, as we shall see, classification schemes do not raise the question of truth or falsity.

Definitions are statements that are always true by virtue of the meaning of their terms and the logical relations among them. When we assert that the concept of upward mobility means that persons end up higher in the stratification system than did their parents, we are not asserting something that could possibly be false. Instead we are saying what the term "upward mobility" means. There is complete identity of meaning between a term and its definition; they are the same thing. To say, "Boys will be boys" is certainly true (if vague), because the subject and the object are the same word. To say, "Boys will act like juvenile human males" is simply to put it another way. Trouble arises, however, when statements that appear to be theories, or are advanced as theories, turn out to be definitional.

The anthropologist Clyde Kluckhohn, in his classic work *Mirror for Man* (1949), claimed it was easy to explain why the Chinese dislike milk. He wrote that the Chinese do not like milk because of their culture. But as George Homans (1967) saw, this was not an explanation at all. For the fact is that Kluckhohn defined culture as the "total way of life of a people . . . [their] design for living." Part of the way of life of the Chinese is a dislike of milk. Thus, to say that they dislike milk *because* of their culture is simply to say that their culture is caused by their culture. It says nothing of the major point in question, which is *why* their culture is *this* way instead of some other way. Kluckhohn might as well have said the Chinese do as they do because they are Chinese. That is necessarily true. But it is not very interesting, and it is not an explanation. Had Kluckhohn used the case of the Chinese dislike of milk as an *example* of culture, all would have been well.

Definitions are vital to science: we must have them. But when they are mistaken for theories, definitions merely lead us to think we have gained understanding when we have not.

Classification schemes

Classification schemes are merely complex definitions. Frequently they are created by cross-classifying several concepts. Thus we may use the concepts of employment and sex to create a scheme into which all Americans can be placed—employed males, employed females, unemployed males, unemployed females. We can multiply these four types into eight by distinguishing between persons in the South and those not in the South. By further subdividing on the basis of those over and under thirty years old, we can create sixteen types.

Frequently in science it is very useful to construct elaborate classification schemes. For example, biology would be hopelessly confused without the Linnean system, which classifies all living organisms into kingdoms, orders, phyla, genera, species, and so on. Sociologists, too, find classification schemes useful.

One of the better-known classification schemes, created by Robert K. Merton (1967), is based on conformity to and deviance from social norms. Merton stated first that people can be divided into those who accept the goals of their society (for example, to get ahead in life) and those who do not. Second, those who use institutionalized (or legitimate) means for attaining goals can be distinguished from those who do not. Cross-classifying these two concepts yields four possible types. (Merton later added a fifth type, but that need not concern us.) The *conformist* accepts society's goals and uses institutionalized means to achieve them. The *ritualist* has given up on the goals but still goes through the motions of using the institutionalized means. The *retreatist* has rejected both goals and means. The *innovator* accepts the goals, but adopts noninstitutionalized means to achieve them. (Merton's scheme is discussed further in Chapter 7.)

Sociologists have frequently used Merton's classification scheme as the basis for statements such as "A person became an innovator *because* he accepted the goals of our culture (to be wealthy, for example) but rejected the means (for example, hard work as opposed to racketeering)." This seems a powerful explanation. In fact it is no explanation at all. Such a person is *by definition* an innovator, and the scheme will tell us nothing about who will become innovators. After the fact, a scheme such as Merton's can classify anyone—that is what it is supposed to do. Ahead of time, it can predict nothing—and prediction is precisely one of the things a theory *must* accomplish (explanation, understanding, and control of phenomena are the others).

"Other things being equal"

Sociologists often use the qualification "other things being equal" (sometimes indicated in Latin as *ceteris paribus*) in their explanations with very good reason. When a physicist declares in a theoretical statement that "X varies with Y, other things being equal," he or she does not stop at simply stating the theory but goes on to test it. Because of the vast knowledge and technique acquired in 400 years of research, the physicist is able to test the theory in an experiment in which other thing are literally *made* equal. Similarly, as we showed in describing Karen Dion's study in Chapter 2, the relation of X to Y is studied by causing X to vary while controlling or eliminating the effect of all known extraneous variables—while making "all other things equal"—and then measuring the concomitant variation in Y. Another method also used by Dion is "randomization."

Unfortunately, however, a great deal of sociological theory is concerned with events of such a character that little of the theory can be tested in rigorously controlled experiments. Sociologists test their theories principally by observation rather than by experimentation. Although observation can be subjected to some statistical controls, they are generally less effective than the direct control of variables used in the physical and biological sciences and to some extent in some branches of psychology. Sociologists must stress the "other things being equal" qualification in their theories partly because they cannot manipulate all the other variables that need to be made equal for the purposes of their research.

The "other things being equal" stipulation is also important because sociologists need to be able to construct relatively specific theories. One can imagine a sociological theory that is so comprehensive that no "other things being equal" clause is necessary because all the variation produced by the "other things" is accounted for by the propositions of the theory. Such theories have been attempted from time to time, but in practice they all have one fatal defect: the harder they try to explain everything in general, the less adequately they explain anything in particular. Using the "other things being equal" stipulation, however, the sociologist can depart from the general level and work at levels that are specific enough to be informative and useful.

Theoretical perspectives in sociology

Thus far we have concentrated on the logical structure of theories in general and on the problems connected with conceptual language in sociological theory. We can turn now to the substance of sociological theories. Most influential theories in sociology are addressed to one particular aspect of social life, such as prejudice, social inequality, or population growth. These specific theories will be discussed in later chapters that cover specific subjects. In this chapter we will cover the broad theoretical perspectives that have a strong influence on the formation of more specific theories.

Theoretical perspectives can be separated into two different levels of analysis. The first is small in scale and tries to understand social behavior at the small-group or face-to-face level of human interaction. Such theories are called *micro* theories. The second level is large in scale and tries to understand the links among large social units—the impact of economic institutions upon political and religious ones, for example. Theories at this level are called *macro* theories. John Lofland's study of the Divine Precepts movement (Chapter 2) is an example of a micro-level study; Norman Cohn's study (1961) of the effects of economic conditions on the creation of religious movements is an example of a macro-level study. Both are concerned with the same general subject matter but on a different scale.

It should be kept in mind, however, that the distinction between macro and micro is artificial. Some theories contain both large- and small-scale elements, and some sociologists do research on both levels. Nevertheless, most sociologists concentrate their work at one level or another. Despite the overlap, the distinction between micro and macro remains useful as a way of organizing the major approaches to sociological study.

Micro theoretical perspectives

Microsociology focuses on immediate, day-to-day interpersonal relationships. It takes into consideration factors such as the environment of a given face-to-face social situation, the number of people involved, the participants' short-term goals, and the resources at their disposal. It asks why in some circumstances individuals cooperate with each other, while in other circumstances they compete or come into conflict. It asks how and when small groups form, and how their inner structures develop; it also asks how small groups relate to one another and how they resolve potential conflicts.

Most of the members of this family group share a definition of a meal as an opportunity to converse—not just to eat and drink. The young woman at the right, however, shows signs of regarding the occasion as a boring ordeal, and is thus a potential source of conflict. (Sepp Seitz/Magnum)

SYMBOLIC INTERACTION

The microsociological view that is currently most prominent is the *symbolic-interactionist* perspective. Here the most important questions concern the *meanings* or definitions that people in a social relationship share—the way particular people in a relationship see each other, the relationship, and the world. For example, the partners in a marriage have a shared definition of the sexual aspect of their relationship. For both partners, sex may primarily represent an expression of love, a mode of physical pleasure, an assertion of marital rights, a mechanism by which one partner dominates the other, an opportunity for marital bargaining, or some or all of these. If the two partners agree on the meaning—the symbolism—of sex within their marriage, their interaction will be harmonious. But if they disagree—if, for example, sex means love to one partner and dominance to the other—conflict will result.

The fundamental insights of the symbolic-interactionist perspective are expressed in the name itself. First, social life requires communication, and human communication is highly *symbolic*. We communicate through symbols such as words and gestures and even through the symbols of music, paintings, sculpture, and billboards. Second, social life depends on *interaction*—the process in which the activity of one person affects the response of another person, which in turn, through various feedback mechanisms, affects the continuing activity of the first person.

The meaning of symbols

Symbolic interactionists stress that what is distinctive about human social behavior, setting it off from the intensive social behavior of lower animals such as baboons, ants, and many species of birds and fish, is the extent to which human interaction is *mediated* by symbols. Symbols almost always intervene between one person's action and another person's response to that action. The symbolic interactionists therefore argue that we must get at the *meaning* that symbols convey.

For most symbolic interactionists, the meaning of symbols is not considered to be an objective part of the relationship between symbols and the activities or events to which they refer. For them, meaning is subjective—a matter of the intentions and interpretations in the minds of actors. As one influential spokesman for symbolic interaction, Herbert Blumer, said, "Each individual aligns his actions to the actions of others by ascertaining what they are doing or what they intend to do—by getting the meaning of their acts" (Blumer, 1962). Many symbolic interactionists (including Blumer) go beyond this; the meaning of symbols and the interpretation of actions are not only subjective but are also at least in part indeterminate. Human response to and interpretation of action are held to involve a creative element; so no social scientific theory, including the sociological, can ever perfectly predict what a specific human being is going to do.

The social self

As will be considered in detail in Chapter 6, the central concept in symbolic-interaction theories of socialization is the *social self*. This concept was elaborated by the principal founder of the symbolic-interaction per-

spective, George Herbert Mead (1863–1931). Until Mead's time, it was widely thought that such human traits as *minds* and *selves* existed prior to any social process (such as socialization) in which people became engaged. Mead turned this conception around and argued that the social processes come first: from social interaction arise the traits of mind and selfhood. Because of their highly developed ability to use and manipulate symbols, humans have minds and selves, while lower animals, for all practical purposes, do not. In human communication, symbols come to be recognized as objects in themselves, independent, at least to a high degree, of the events and objects to which they refer.

For Mead, *mind* is a social process in which *significant symbols* evoke in the person who presents them the same response that they evoke in the person to whom they are presented. The *self* for Mead is likewise a social process; it is our learning or internalization of the general content of others' responses to our conduct. Through our self-conception each of us can do two things: we can see ourselves as others see us, and we can take on the role of others; in so doing, we learn to identify with the way other persons think of themselves and interpret social life. It is this ability to take on the role of others that makes it possible for persons to comprehend the meaning of their own and others' acts and for meaningful social interaction to occur.

Through taking the role of others, each of us learns how to behave appropriately in situations; we learn the norms, or standards of behavior (see Chapter 5), of the groups to which we belong; we understand the meanings attached by others to the physical and social environment; and we learn to shape our own actions and meanings to those of others. This process will be given more specific attention in Chapter 6.

The interactional situation

One major thrust of symbolic-interactionist research has been to understand how persons perceive and define reality in specific, day-to-day social situations. While it is true that people in any commonplace organized social situation will share and take for granted a large number of common-sense understandings, it is also true that this web of understandings is not totally fixed but emergent, shifting, and to some degree negotiable. Symbolic interactionists look closely at the way people entering a social situation—each with his or her own purposes, thoughts, and history—"feel out" the situation, make tentative definitions of it, check these definitions by interacting with one another, adjust them, and so on. For example, suppose a teenager in a leather jacket enters an elegant apartment house and approaches the doorman. The doorman has beliefs and predefinitions concerning teenagers in leather jackets. (He may *perceive* the teenager as a thief who is casing the place and *define* the look on his face as "shifty-eyed" or "suspicious.") These beliefs may be confirmed in the course of the interaction (if, for example, the teenager runs away or pulls a knife), or they may be set aside in favor of others (if, perhaps, the teenager looks the doorman in the eye and asks politely for Mrs. Chase in Apartment 3). What interests sociologists about this minor example is not only whether the teenager robs Mrs. Chase, but also whether the doorman's stereotyped beliefs about teenagers can be modified to any extent through interaction. Knowledge gained through investigation of such situations can shed light on more important social questions, such as those concerning intergroup prejudice.

Erving Goffman (1959), a theorist of the symbolic-interactionist school, looks at the social situation as a "drama." How those interacting play their parts in the drama and how "seriously" they take them depend greatly on specific situational factors such as time, place, and mood. For example, there are some respects in which all Episcopalian funerals are alike; but there

are some respects in which each one differs from all others. Some are large, some small, some expensive, some modest. In some the deceased was widely loved, in others barely tolerated or little known. In some the mourners are very much involved in the life of the church, in others they are once-a-year churchgoers. Thus the overall definition, "This religious service is an Episcopalian funeral," guides, but does not totally control, the participants' behavior. Goffman also points out that an *interactant* can attempt to *control* the shared definition of a situation, "managing" for his or her own personal ends the impressions the other participants get. (Anyone who has ever dressed up for a job interview knows how "managing impressions" works.)

ETHNOMETHODOLOGY

What compels people in an apartment-house lobby to behave according to "public-place" rules? They are merely conforming to some sort of unspoken agreement that they are in a public place. How such agreements develop is the subject of the school of microsociological research known as *ethnomethodology* (Garfinkel, 1967). What ethnomethodology studies is not shared meanings themselves, but the processes by which individuals come to realize and agree that shared meanings are developing. Ethnomethodologists point out that there is no orderly and connected social world, no

These people agree about and adhere to an unspoken rule governing behavior on a public bus. Ethnomethodology is the study of the processes by which individuals come to agree upon shared meanings. (Owen Franken/Stock, Boston)

"world taken for granted" (to use a phrase suggested by philosopher Alfred Schutz [1962, 1964]), until the participants agree that there is. Consider the following dialogue:

SUBJECT: I had a flat tire.

EXPERIMENTER: What do you mean, you had a flat tire?

Subject appears momentarily stunned and then replies in a hostile manner,

SUBJECT: What do you mean, "What do you mean?" A flat tire is a flat tire. That is what I meant. Nothing special. What a crazy question! (Adapted from Garfinkel, 1967, p. 42.)

In this example, the experimenter deliberately avoids acknowledging that a shared meaning (the understanding that he and the subject are having a casual conversation) exists; he deliberately avoids playing the social game of "casual conversation" according to the rules. This is done to expose more clearly the tiny, tentative cues and exploratory gestures made by the subject, which signal the question, "Are we developing a shared understanding or aren't we?" In a nonexperimental situation, however, both people would go through a series of tentative gestures—each cued by the other—which, if completed according to the expectations of both, would result in the development of the shared understanding. "This is a casual conversation in which suitable topics might include flat tires, the weather, and so on; the purpose of the conversation is not so much to convey information as to establish a friendly rapport between us."

Ethnomethodology is a developing perspective, so its adherents disagree as to the basic direction to follow. However, they are generally in agreement that one of their major contributions is to show that we cannot (and should not) take for granted what have come to be considered the "routine grounds" of everyday activities. It is precisely those underlying assumptions that ethnomethodologists take as the objects of their analyses.

EXCHANGE THEORY

The branch of micro theory known as *exchange theory* views social life as a process of bargaining or negotiation. According to this view, social relationships are established on the basis of mutual trust and interlocking self-interest (Warshay, 1975). The members of small groups thus exchange material and nonmaterial rewards, such as money, food, gratitude, and respect. This network of reciprocal rewards both constitutes and sustains the group's pattern of interaction.

For example, suppose that a woman takes a job as an account executive with a small advertising firm. By doing so, she agrees to perform certain tasks for a certain number of hours each week; in exchange, her employer agrees to pay her a certain salary. This reciprocal relationship continues for several months. Then the employer tells the woman that she must run the switchboard for two hours each day. The woman's duties increase, she must work more hours in order to keep up with her original tasks, and she loses some of her prestige; moreover, she receives no increase in salary. The pattern of exchange on which the relationship was formed and sustained has broken down. Exchange theorists would be interested in studying both aspects of this social relationship—the process by which the system of mutual rewards was established and maintained and the process by which it broke down.

POSITIVISM VERSUS VERSTEHEN

Not only do micro theories differ in their conceptual frameworks, but they also take somewhat different methodological stances. In general, the symbolic-interactionist and ethnomethodological perspectives stress the importance of using a phenomenological approach to obtaining knowledge about the social world, a view that is termed in German *verstehen*, or "understanding." *Verstehen*, an approach introduced into sociology in 1925 by Max Weber (1957), is a way of obtaining knowledge that relies on intuition or empathy—the ability of the sociologist to imagine the inner experience of the people being studied. There is no way of proving that what the sociologist *thinks* an individual feels or experiences is what that individual actually *does* feel or experience. From one point of view, then, the *verstehen* approach may be seen as taking an "educated guess." However, it has the virtue of using the insights derived from the similarities between the observer and the observed to help make sense of objectively derived data.

Not all sociologists have believed that such an ap-

Emile Durkheim believed that an individual's behavior is shaped, at least in part, by external social forces. While he could not predict which person in a given category will commit suicide, he asserted that all members of that category have a statistical likelihood of doing so. (© I. R. Sorgi)

proach is suitable for social science. At the level of macro theory (to be discussed in the next section), sociologists such as Auguste Comte (1896) and Emile Durkheim subscribed to the doctrine of scientific *positivism*—the doctrine that social science, like natural science, should study only those phenomena that can be objectively measured. For example, in a pioneering study in 1897, Durkheim (1951) focused on suicide rates in Europe. Suicide rates are *social facts*—facts concerning aggregates of people that can be studied with objective tools such as statistical analysis.

Unlike *verstehen*, which allows for a degree of indeterminacy and free will in the social world, positivism prescribes a search for objective causes. In his study of suicide, Durkheim showed that suicide rates varied with the religion of the persons being studied (among other factors); although he was able to show only a *correlation* between religion and the suicide rate, he believed that there were some *causal relationships* involved. (As was mentioned in Chapter 2 and earlier in this chapter, definite proof of the causal relationship would require removing the effects of all other factors that might be related.) Durkheim's point was that although behavior depends in part on individual psychological factors such as needs, drives, and emotions, it is also shaped, at least partially, by social forces outside the individual. While perhaps not being able to predict which individual in a given category of people would commit suicide, a sociologist could state that all members in the category had a certain statistical likelihood of doing so and could talk about the reasons why (Durkheim, 1951).

Although the macrosociological perspectives, which we will shortly explore, devote much of their attention to relatively objective, impersonal social factors such as economic and political patterns, and to nonhuman factors such as the effects of the physical or natural environment, they do not ignore subjective experience. Even large-scale social patterns such as a country's political order continue to exist only so long as the large numbers of people they involve continue to support them; and this support involves nontangible, nonobjective factors such as beliefs, ideas, and values. (For a discussion of these concepts, see Chapter 5.) Thus, as we survey the macro perspectives, we will find ourselves using both the *verstehen* and the positivistic approaches. In looking at macro perspectives, we will study the interplay between nonhuman factors, large-scale human factors, and the interpretations of reality that large numbers of people share.

CRITICAL THEORY

Another body of thought that departs from positivism has been called *critical theory*, which found its seedbed in the Frankfurt School (for example, see Horkheimer [1933]; Habermas [1970]). Whereas positivism draws a sharp line between the supposedly objective researcher and the social phenomenon being studied "scientifically," critical theory denies that division. Objectivity, according to this point of view, is an illusion, and to argue that society develops according to certain "laws" with which sociologists have no right to interfere is to offer an apology for the status quo. Moreover, when sociologists concentrate on gathering quantities of data according to some empirical standard, they are likely to produce studies describing the trees and not the forest; they inevitably miss the larger implications of their own findings. From the critical-theory point of view, the role of *verstehen* is an important one. Critical theory also argues that sociology is not and should not be a neutral science; researchers must always consider the impact of their studies on the social welfare. From this perspective, for example, a study of the flight of white families from the city to segregated suburbs would be inadequate if it did not include a discussion of ways to remedy the problem. Praxis and theory are inseparable.

Macro theoretical perspectives

Sociology has long been dominated by two powerful macro theoretical perspectives. Conflicts between them, on occasion extremely bitter, have reflected the differing political commitments of sociologists more than any irreconcilable differences between the two theoretical perspectives themselves. As we shall see, despite a fundamental difference in emphasis, the two perspectives have a great deal in common. Because they underlie much of what sociologists argue about, it is important to understand their basic similarities and differences. These matters are discussed frequently in later chapters, especially those in Units Five and Six.

Knowing that the founding father of one of these perspectives—conflict theory—was Karl Marx makes the political basis of dispute obvious. The other perspective—functionalism (or functional analysis)—in some ways reflects liberal opposition to Marxist analysis. The differences between liberal reformers and radicals in the political arena are often bitter indeed, but it does not necessarily follow that their theories of society are wholly different, even though it is often "good politics" for both sides to exaggerate and emphasize the differences. In any event, the disputes between functionalism and conflict theory today are not nearly as extreme as they once were. As will be demonstrated in later chapters, contemporary sociologists are attempting to build more powerful theories in a number of topic areas by combining elements of both functionalism and conflict theory.

FUNCTIONAL ANALYSIS

Functional analysis is not unique to sociology. In fact, its essential idea was borrowed from biology, where it originated. Its first application in the social sciences came in the field of anthropology, and some of those who articulated the first functionalist theories of social organization were actually anthropologists, such as Malinowski. The distinctive feature of most forms of functional analysis is that they *explain phenomena on the basis of their consequences*. The fundamental premise is that particular things happen or particular structures arise and are maintained because of their consequences. Malinowski, for example, observed that the Trobriand Islanders he studied had rich magical traditions (1948). He noted as well that magic was especially linked to certain kinds of activities. The islanders used a great deal of magic before they went on dangerous fishing expeditions on the high seas but little magic in preparing to fish in safe waters. His observations led Malinowski to suggest a functional explanation of magic in primitive societies. He proposed that magic was practiced because of its consequences: it gave the islanders a sense of control over the outcome of their activities. Malinowski theorized that magical rituals existed because of the function they served: if there were no anxiety connected with fishing expeditions, there would be no magic.

Systems and integration

In analyzing the functions that certain practices fulfill, functional theorists have emphasized the importance of the integration of social parts into wholes. In the case of Malinowski's fishermen, for example, we might observe that the roles given to certain men in the magical observances rewarded them with a special status. The practice of magic, therefore, was tied in with the social structure of the community. In a similar way, the rituals, in "protecting" the fishing parties, served to ensure the economic livelihood of the community. Practices and institutions thus touch on one another, forming social *systems* that by definition are *integrated*,

Malinowski suggested that magic rituals, such as this witch doctor attempting to drive "evil spirits" out of a sick man's body, give people a sense of control over their environment. (A. Maahs/Black Star)

consisting of many parts working together. According to the functional point of view, society works very much like a human body: all organs and systems act together to maintain life, and a change in one may have profound effects not only on other organs, but on the body as a whole. The task of sociology, then, is to determine what components of the system are influencing others, and how this process occurs.

Viewing society as a "social organism" in some ways analogous to the human body also illustrates two functionalist propositions. The first is that there are levels of functioning within the organism. A functional analysis may be done on several levels, just as a physiologist might study cells, tissues, organs, organ systems, or the interrelationship of all the organ systems. On the smallest scale, a functionalist might study an individual role; on the largest, the entire society. The second proposition is that for societies to operate as systems, some balance or equilibrium must be maintained among the various parts. When certain functional requisites are met—that is, if the social system meets the crucial needs of its human constituents—this state of equilibrium will be approached.

Functionalist theory: Robert Merton

Although functionalism has had many articulate spokesmen, including Talcott Parsons, who elaborated functionalist theory in a number of books and articles (1937, 1951), perhaps the most important functionalist theorist has been Robert Merton. Among his contributions has been a critical analysis of several basic functionalist concepts (1957). The first is the "functional unity postulate," the idea that social systems are necessarily tightly integrated. In place of this postulate, Merton argued, should be an emphasis on different forms and levels of integration in different aspects of the social system. Any integration must be empirically determined to exist, not simply presumed to inhere in the system. A second target of Merton's criticism was the idea of "functional universality," which held that any social item (such as Malinowski's magic) that existed in the social system must be an integral part of the system. Merton held that social items, like the appendix, might have no apparent function or even be dysfunctional. In addition, he distinguished between *manifest functions*, the recognized and intended consequences of a structure or activity, and *latent functions*, the unrecognized and unintended consequences (either functional or dysfunctional). For example, the manifest function of the public school system is to teach students reading, writing, and other basic skills; one latent function is to contribute to social order by inculcating certain values as well—"fair play," respect for the rights of others, avoidance of violence, and so on.

Finally, Merton questioned Malinowski's original idea that each cultural item fulfilled a vital and indispensable role. To the earlier functionalists, the very existence of a custom or institution was taken as evidence that it met an important need, and much of early func-

MAJOR SOCIOLOGICAL THEORIES		CONCERNS AND EMPHASES
MICROTHEORIES	Symbolic interactionism	The meanings people give to a social situation
		The importance of communication in symbols, especially language
		The significance of interaction in social life, especially in developing a definition of one's self
	Ethnomethodology	The processes by which people develop a shared definition of the situation
	Exchange theory	The bargaining or negotiation that underlies social life; patterns of exchange in social relationships
	Critical theory	The subjective relationship between the sociologist and the data gathered: the nonneutrality of sociology
		The importance of seeking out the larger implications of sociological research for public policy
MACROTHEORIES	Functional analysis	The explanation of phenomena on the basis of their consequences
		The integration of social parts into wholes
		The existence of levels of functioning within a social organism and equilibrium among parts of the social system
	Conflict theory	The opposition of various groups within society
		The significance of conflict among social groups as a force in history

FIGURE 3.1

This table presents the concerns and emphases of the major branches of sociological theory.

tionalist theory (such as the work of Parsons) was an attempt to identify exactly which institutions and customs were universal "functional requisites." In contrast, Merton stressed that the variety of structures that have developed in human society is more significant than any universals that might be hypothesized to exist.

Problems in functional analysis

Despite the prominence of the functional school in sociology, it must be admitted that functionalist theory presents a few problems. The first, which has been widely noted, is that of tautology, or circular statements. When we say, for example, that a certain social structure exists because it fills a need, and the cause of this structure is the need it fulfills, we have said very little. A second and related problem is that of "illegitimate teleologies," or assertions that something exists because a certain purpose or end state has "caused" it to exist, without being able to demonstrate the sequence of causation. Merton, for example, in a famous study of big-city political machines, argued that the needs of the new immigrant population caused the political machines to emerge. However, he offered no explanation of how this supposed causation actually operated. These logical problems make many propositions of functional analysis impossible to prove or disprove. In this sense, functionalists' arguments are similar to saying that something was inevitable after it has already happened: such a contention cannot easily be disputed.

Another problem with functional analysis is the vagueness of the terms it embraces: "equilibrium" and "integration," for example. Much functionalist vocabu-

The manifest function of the schools is to teach children reading, writing, and other basic skills; the latent functions include teaching certain values, such as cooperation, orderliness, and, as seen here, obedience to authority. (Inger McCabe/Photo Researchers)

lary is borrowed from the language of biology, but the analogy is an imperfect one. When the integration of body systems breaks down and their equilibrium is disturbed, there are measurable consequences: there may be a rise in temperature or an elevated blood count; the victim becomes ill or dies. In the case of a society, however, we do not have such an unambiguous state of affairs. Many of the functionalists' terms are approximate at best.

Finally, much of the controversy surrounding functionalism has had to do with the political implications of some of the basic notions. Critics have charged that functionalism boils down to a defense of the status quo, a sort of sociological version of "whatever is, is right." When functionalists analyze existing institutions and structures in terms of the ways they serve the vital needs of the social organism, this criticism is easy to understand. (Slavery, prejudice, war, and every other social evil, it might be argued, exist because they serve vital purposes in the social system. And if the social system is integrated with as much complexity as the human body, do we dare attempt social reform, which might involve the destruction of a vital organ?) However, functionalists have replied that nothing in their theory implies that there is only one way to fulfill necessary social functions. Although some form of government may be necessary, for example, it need not be a dictatorship or an absolute monarchy. Moreover, change is always possible; in fact, societies evolve and change as new human needs and social conditions arise.

CONFLICT THEORY

Most functional theorists would argue that some minimum degree of integration is necessary for a society to persist. Other functionalists would argue that a high degree of agreement or *consensus* among members on the society's major norms and institutions is economical because the cost of *social control* (maintenance of the normative order) is thus less than if the members disagreed. For example, societies such as Northern Ireland and Lebanon with two major competing religions, have more internal conflict than societies such as Spain, where one religion dominates; religion is a powerful agent in shaping norms and values.

However, most functionalists would not argue that a society *must have* a high degree of consensus on norms and institutions, for such an argument flies in the face of the facts: many societies around the world clearly exhibit a high level of *conflict*. Members of these societies disagree on norms and institutions, and groups and classes do not work together for any common interest so much as they compete for scarce resources.

Conflict has always been a topic of interest to classical sociologists, among them Georg Simmel (1858–1918). As Simmel (1950) pointed out, all social systems have divisive as well as associative forces operating within them. In any system, there will be an ebb and flow of both types of forces, the degree of cohesiveness depending on the type and structure of the social system. In Simmel's view, the more highly defined a social structure is, the less it will tolerate conflict; also, smaller social systems are less likely to absorb conflict than are larger ones. The massive, complex, and loosely organized modern state, for example, can tolerate much more internal conflict than a smaller state, such as the

French farmers riot in 1960 to protest the fact that low prices for their produce are keeping their standard of living below that of commercial and industrial workers. To conflict theorists, the farmers' demand that the government fix food prices would indicate competition among elements of a society for that society's limited resources. The Marxist view would be that artificially low food prices serve the ruling classes by enabling them both to buy food more cheaply themselves and to hold down the wages of their workers. (Roger Leclercq/Photo Researchers)

ancient Greek city-state. Lewis Coser (1956, 1967), a contemporary conflict theorist, elaborates on Simmel's argument, pointing out that some social structures have institutionalized means of handling conflict, such as "safety-value" mechanisms that provide substitute objects for the conflicting parties' hostilities. Coser also notes that in flexible social structures containing multiple group affiliations, "multiple conflicts crisscross each other and thereby prevent basic cleavages along one axis" (Coser, 1956).

Modern conflict theory also owes a debt to the work of the great nineteenth-century economist and social philosopher Karl Marx. Marx accepted certain functionalist assumptions; for example, he clearly assumed that societies are systems and that change in one aspect of society affects many other aspects. But an important difference between Marx and the functionalists lies in

their answers to the question, "functional for whom?" Most functionalists would answer "functional for the society as a whole." They stress the links among all parts of a society and use the whole social system as their basis for assessing costs and benefits. Most Marxists would answer "functional for the ruling class." They stress the way in which particular social arrangements—especially the economic arrangements—serve *particular groups within societies at the expense of other groups.* Marxists use class interest rather than the whole society as the basis for assessing costs and benefits, sometimes arguing that it is meaningless to speak of the interest of society as a whole in any sense that transcends the interests of particular classes. It is this emphasis on conflicts of group interest that gives rise to the label of conflict theory. Whereas functionalists stress the interdependence of all members of a society and their common interests, many conflict theorists emphasize exploitation of some members of society by others and their separate interests.

The starting point of Marx's analysis of social history stated that over the course of time social arrangements change, so that those that were good for one group tend to be replaced by arrangements that benefit another group. Marx charted the rise and fall of powerful or ruling groups in the history of societies. A fundamental thesis of conflict theory is that social arrangements are designed to give advantage to the most powerful groups in society. As Marx wrote in *The Communist Manifesto* in 1848, "The ruling ideas of any age are the ideas of its ruling class."

Details of Marx's argument about the dynamic behind the rise and fall of classes throughout history are presented in Chapter 13. What is important to recognize here is that Marx believed that changes in power in societies cause changes in major social arrangements. As Stinchcombe stated over one hundred years later (1968), *"The greater the power of a class, the more effective that class is as a cause of social structure."*

As we have mentioned, Marx believed that economic factors were primarily responsible for conflict between classes. Later conflict theorists have pointed out other factors that can also contribute to conflict. Ralf Dahrendorf (1958), for example, held that the unequal distribution of authority is the fundamental cause of social conflict. He noted that conflict is inherent in the manager-subordinate relationships found in any complex organization; it may be beneficial to the

Karl Marx (1818-1883), still the most influential of the early social scientists. (The Granger Collection)

organization for one person or a few people to be in charge, but the subordinates in this arrangement may not willingly accept such control.

THEORY AND IDEOLOGY

It has often been claimed that conflict theory is better able to account for changes in societies and that functionalism is better able to account for the persistent features of societies. Most sociologists now believe that this is too simple a distinction, and many attempts have been made to integrate the two perspectives. There are two major sources of change in societies (as we shall discuss in Unit Seven). One source is external pressures, such as wars or natural disasters; the other is internal imbalances (or dysfunctions) that result in conflicts and a need to establish a new balance. Coser (1956, 1967),

Whereas conflict theorists might point to these Maine farmers as victims of an affluent upper class, those who adhere to the functionalist perspective would counter that such poverty is an inevitable element of all social structures. (Arthur Grace/Stock, Boston)

for example, points out that if dysfunction leads to conflict, conflict can in turn lead to change, and change may well be functional, bringing the society to a new equilibrium. Robert Cole (1966), however, argues that it may not be necessary (or fruitful) to integrate the two perspectives on the broad level; instead, he suggests resolving the question empirically with regard to specific situations. In Cole's view, whether a conflict situation is to be seen in terms of an eventual re-equilibration in the social system—with good results for all—or whether it is to be seen in terms of a dialectic between classes whose interests are antithetical, depends on time and circumstances.

In any case, it is clear that both conflict theory and functionalism can accommodate both sources of change, although conflict theory may provide a clearer explanation of internal change. It is probably a safe generalization that many conflict theorists give greater emphasis to dysfunctions and social change because they are personally more likely to desire radical social change. Many functionalists give more attention to functions and to social stability because they are personally less likely to desire radical change and more likely to prefer change in terms of reform of present arrangements. Thus the ideological thrust of their theories reflects a desire on the one hand to know how to pull societies apart in order to restructure them and on the other hand to know how to prevent societies from being pulled apart so that necessary change can take place gradually.

In subsequent chapters you will find conflict and functionalist interpretations competing to explain many important social phenomena. Usually, the interpretations will be clearly identified. Nevertheless, it may be helpful to have some simple cues for recognizing each. When you read statements that emphasize the role of some social arrangements in serving the needs of a *society as a system*, that mention the needs of all the members of society, and that refer to shared values or a consensus over goals, you are most likely reading a functionalist interpretation. When you read statements that stress *inequalities of power within societies* and mention class conflict, special interests, coercion, or exploitation, you are most likely reading a conflict-theory interpretation.

This chapter has attempted to present enough discussion of the logical structure of contemporary sociological theories to enable you to distinguish theories from research results and to understand enough of the major assumptions of the various perspectives so that you may recognize their applications in later chapters. We have also tried to demonstrate here that no scientist can say anything about the world without making use of some kind of perspective as a device for interpretation, and no scientist can do much worthwhile research without a theory to guide his or her efforts.

Summary

Sociological theory explains, interprets, and predicts general social processes. Theory guides sociological investigation to relevant empirical data and, at the same time, depends on those data for its validity. No theory applies to everyone; rather, the sociologist offers a theory as a statement of statistical likelihood.

The component of theory that can be affirmed or refuted empirically by gathering evidence is a specific testable proposition, or *hypothesis*. Sociological theory also involves nontestable, conventional elements, including *definitions*—statements that are true by the meaning and arrangement of their terms; *classification schemes*—ways of organizing the subjects of study; and the qualification *"other things being equal"*—a signal that the observed changes are those which could be expected to take place if the effects of extraneous variables could be completely controlled or eliminated.

The two major theoretical perspectives in sociology are *micro theory*, which studies interaction between individuals and within small groups, and *macro theory*, which deals with large groups and social institutions. Although this distinction is somewhat artificial, it has been found to be of practical use.

Among the branches of micro theory are *symbolic interaction, ethnomethodology*, and *exchange theory*. The first two may involve *verstehen*, an approach involving the sociologist's "understanding" of subjects' attitudes and feelings. *Positivism*, however, maintains that only objectively measured phenomena should be used in sociological research. Positivism has been opposed by *critical theory*, which rejects the idea of objectivity and the claim that sociology is or should be a neutral science.

The fundamental difference in perspective at the macro level is between *functional analysis* and *conflict theory*. Two basic assumptions of functional analysis are that phenomena are parts of an interactive system and that each phenomenon is explained on the basis of its consequences. Functional analysis views society as a relatively stable system. Marx and other conflict theorists, however, maintain that society does not function as a whole, but rather functions for the ruling class at the expense of other social classes. The difference in power among groups is believed to cause conflict that will bring about social change.

Glossary

CONFLICT THEORY The macro theoretical perspective that views society as a collection of antagonistic groups, institutions, and classes, each contending for dominance.

CRITICAL THEORY A theoretical perspective that denies the existence of objectivity and rejects the contention that sociology is a neutral science.

CULTURE The set of artifacts, interaction patterns, beliefs, symbols, values, norms, and customs that distinguish one social group from another.

ETHNOMETHODOLOGY The micro theoretical perspective that examines the processes by which interactants realize and agree that shared meanings are developing.

EXCHANGE THEORY The micro theoretical perspective that views social life as a process of bargaining in which the participants in a relationship or the members of a small group negotiate for the material or nonmaterial rewards they will receive.

FUNCTIONAL ANALYSIS The macro theoretical perspective that views society as an interdependent set of institutions, each meeting a vital need for the maintenance of the social system.

LATENT FUNCTION The unintended, and often unnoticed, consequences of particular social arrangements.

MANIFEST FUNCTION The intended and recognized consequences of particular social arrangements.

NORMS Standards of correct, desirable, or appropriate behavior shared by members of a particular social group.

POSITIVISM The methodological view that stresses the importance of studying objective, measurable phenomena and excludes the subjective and the speculative.

SOCIAL SELF The idea that the self is formed and shaped through primary group interactions, so that the individual can view himself or herself from the standpoint of those around and can also take the role of and empathize with the other.

SYMBOL An object, idea, or event that represents something else and is given arbitrary meaning by social agreement.

SYMBOLIC INTERACTION The micro theoretical perspective that examines three elements of social phenomena: communication processes, interaction patterns, and the subjective meanings of social phenomena for people in a particular relationship. The individual assesses the meanings of these phenomena and acts accordingly.

VERSTEHEN Weber's term for the sociologist's subjective interpretation of the inner experience of the people being studied.

Recommended readings

Bottomore, Tom, and Robert Nisbet (eds.). *A History of Sociological Analysis.* New York: Basic Books, 1978. A collection of superb chapters, each written by a leading theorist on a particular facet or perspective of sociological theory. This is a well-crafted set of sociological and historical analyses.

Coser, Lewis A. *Masters of Sociological Thought: Ideas in Historical and Social Context.* 2nd ed. New York: Harcourt Brace Jovanovich, 1977. An extremely useful and interesting analysis of the lives, ideas, and intellectual context of fifteen major figures in the development of sociological theory. In addition, Coser discusses recent trends in sociological theory.

Kinloch, Graham C. *Sociological Theory: Its Development and Major Paradigms.* New York: McGraw-Hill, 1977. Kinloch delineates the emergence and the social and intellectual context of major types of traditional sociological theories. He then examines their present form and extrapolates major characteristics of types of explanations in sociological theories in general.

Tar, Zoltan. *The Frankfurt School: The Critical Theories of Max Horkheimer and Theodor W. Adorno.* New York: Wiley, 1977. A detailed exposition of the historical roots and analytical views of the Frankfurt School of philosophy and sociology. It is difficult but worthwhile reading.

Turner, Jonathan H. *The Structure of Sociological Theory.* Homewood, Ill.: Dorsey Press, 2nd ed. 1974, 1978. A detailed analysis of the historical roots and present state of four major theoretical perspectives in sociology (functionalism, conflict theory, interactionism, and exchange theory), plus a brief introduction to the recently developed perspective of ethnomethodology. Turner also discusses some major concerns that he believes are generally ignored in social theory.

Wallace, Walter L. (ed.). *Sociological Theory: An Introduction.* Chicago: Aldine, 1969. A basic overview of eleven perspectives in contemporary social theory is combined with selected readings that exemplify each perspective.

Warshay, Leon H. *The Current State of Sociological Theory: A Critical Interpretation.* New York: McKay, 1975. An ambitious attempt to examine the intricate relationships among various sociological theories. The specific theories themselves are described only briefly, but the ethical and political assumptions underlying them are examined in detail.

Basic sociological concepts

CHAPTER FOUR
SOCIAL STRUCTURE

Now that we have devoted three chapters to the methods and theory of sociology, it is time that we defined the underlying object of sociological thought. What is a society? The term *society* can be, and has been, defined in numerous ways by numerous sociologists. A fairly comprehensive and usable definition is as follows: *A society is a relatively large, relatively autonomous collection of people who have a common heritage that is transmitted from generation to generation and who interact with one another in socially structured relationships.*

Let us take a look at the components of this definition. First: a society is "relatively large." In theory, three people on a desert island constitute a society, and in fact the hunting and gathering societies of the Aborigines in Australia and of the Bushmen and Pygmies in Africa average only about fifty members (Pfeiffer, 1977, p. 155). However, today's societies tend to be considerably bigger than that. Technological advances have made it possible for a society to support large numbers of people; and modern travel and communication have virtually eliminated the isolation of small societies, so that they have tended to merge into increasingly large ones. Though not all societies are grounded in territories—nomadic societies, for example, move from one place to another—most are associated with specific geographical areas; modern societies are tied to political units known as states. (We will discuss the state in Chapter 17.)

Second: a society is "relatively autonomous." While New York City is many times more populous than most societies of the world, it cannot be called a society because it is not autonomous. It depends on a larger social system, the United States, for many of its laws, for its military defense, and for much of its food and raw materials. Sociologist Alex Inkeles has suggested a rather eerie test to determine whether a community is autonomous: imagine what would happen to that community if all the other communities of the world disappeared overnight. "If there were a good chance that the surviving community would go forward in substantially its present form through subsequent generations, then it qualifies as a society. Most simple tribes, however small, and virtually all nation-states clearly meet this requirement" (1964, p. 70). Nevertheless, in view of the increasingly large scale of international economic and political activity—in particular the predominance of multinational corporations—it is becoming inaccurate

These Amish men have formed a work group to raise a barn. Like all other groups within a society, their interactions are taking place within a pattern of social relationships. (UPI)

to call modern nation-states autonomous (Wallerstein, 1974). American society, for example, could hardly go on in its present form without imported oil; and substantial sectors of the economy depend on imports, from South American coffee beans to South African industrial diamonds. Hence the qualification "*relatively* autonomous."

Third: the people in a society "have a common heritage that is transmitted from generation to generation." This common heritage, called *culture*, includes all the values, customs, beliefs, and artifacts of the society. Because they share the same material and nonmaterial culture, the members of a society attach similar meanings to things and events. And this shared vocabulary of meanings forms one major basis for a society's cohesion. (We will discuss culture in more detail in Chapter 5.)

Fourth: the members of a society "interact with one another in socially structured relationships." A society's cohesion is based not only on its culture but also on the interaction among its members—their gift-giving, the way they say hello and goodbye, their quarrels, their financial transactions, their love-making, their tendency to butt into a line or to wait their turn. These interactions are in no way random. Nor are they entirely free of social influence. As our definition points out, relationships between members of the same society are generally *socially structured*; they follow a socially derived design.

How can we visualize this design? Society, the largest pattern of human social connection, contains many smaller patterns of social connection, which sociologists call *social relationships*. Every interaction that we have with another human being takes place within the context of such a relationship, and the nature of the relationship strongly influences the nature of the interaction. In other words, your response to the other person will vary depending, in large measure, on the social relationship that connects you to him or her—whether you live on the same block, belong to the same family, work for the same multinational corporation, attend the same sociology class, are both attempting to rob a bank or to get a driver's license at the motor vehicle bureau, are both Jewish, are both white, are both women, are both involved in education or in religion, or are both simply walking on the same sidewalk at the same moment. Whatever the link may be that connects you to the other person, it will carry with it a code of social behavior—that is, *norms*. And your dealings with the other person will generally conform to these norms. The concept of norms is an important tie between culture on the one hand and social structure on the other, since it expresses the content of the former within the

context of the latter. Because of its interconnection with both social structure *and* culture, we defer a more detailed discussion of norms until we take up culture in Chapter 5.

Together, the many relationships within which human beings interact in this organized fashion constitute the society's *social structure*, the subject of this chapter. First we will examine separately the major patterns within the social structure. Then we will discuss how the patterns relate to one another and how the structure itself changes over time. Finally, we will consider the thorny question of where the individual stands amid all these human groupings.

Types of social structure

As we saw in Chapter 1, a major effort of sociology has been to trace general laws of social relationships, applicable to all societies. But how is a sociologist to find laws that will apply equally, for example, to a wandering band of Aborigines and to a nation such as Great Britain? Given that they are both societies, what else could they possibly have in common? According to the early German sociologist Georg Simmel, a great deal. Simmel (1950) proposed that sociologists could get over the stumbling block of cultural diversity by keeping their eyes on units of social "connectedness," such as those we have just mentioned. For example, one social pattern would undoubtedly be found in both Great Britain and the Aborigine band—namely, the family. Thus, by comparing the Aborigine family with the British family, the sociologist could find out, from the similarities between the two families, something in general about families. And from the differences between the two families, he or she could find out something in general about hunting and gathering societies as opposed to industrial societies. Similar cross-cultural and historical comparisons could be made using groups larger than the family. For example, the sociologist could study a series of work groups, including a Samoan canoe-building party, a group of apprentices in the workshop of an Italian Renaissance painter, and a group of Japanese businessmen assembled around a conference table. Behind their differences, there might be discerned a pattern of the group in general and of the work group in particular.

Much sociological research has followed Simmel's lead. Indeed, a good deal of what sociologists have had to say about society in all its parts and aspects—the family, the group, education, religion, gender roles, race relations, and so on—has been learned by comparing similar social units cross-culturally and across historical periods and noting their similarities and differences. In the next sections we shall examine the two major units of social structure: the group (along with its subtypes) and the social category.

THE GROUP

A *group*, in sociological terms, is not just a collection of people. The passengers on a bus, for example, do not necessarily constitute a group. Rather, a group is a collection of people who have a sense of shared identity and who have a structured interaction pattern. When we analyze this structured pattern, we see that it consists of a set of interrelated *social positions*, also called *statuses*. Thus while the Jones family may regard itself as a group consisting of Harry and Sylvia Jones and little Cathy Jones, the unsentimental eye of the sociologist sees them as father, mother, and daughter—that is, as occupants of *formal* social positions. Likewise, if the bus mentioned above were stalled in a blizzard for twenty-four hours and the passengers began interacting on an intense level, suddenly becoming a group, a sociologist among them could probably pick out the

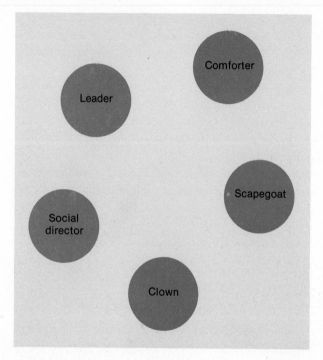
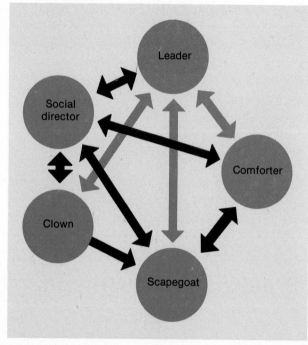

FIGURE 4.1

The diagram above shows some of the informal social positions, or statuses, possible within a small group. Note that *status* is a neutral term: it indicates nothing about a person's social ranking, or *prestige*, in the group. Only by enacting the *roles* associated with each status would each member become ranked; the Leader would then appear at the top of the diagram at right and the Scapegoat at the bottom. Also by enacting their roles, the members would form patterns of interaction, like those shown at right. (In some types of groups, a member's *formal* status does automatically convey rank. In a club, for example, the status of president confers prestige on the holder of that office.)

Leader, the Comforter, the Social Director, the Scapegoat, and other *informal* position holders of the new group (Figure 4.1). While the positions in a group often interlock reciprocally (for each daughter there is a parent), this is not true in all cases.

A member of a group, although he or she may not be aware of the sociological names of his or her social positions, is nevertheless aware of the behavior expected of him or her in that position—what sociologists term the individual's *role*. For example, in traditional families, Father may be expected to earn money, do dishes, take out the garbage, and discipline the child. Mother may be expected to make the meals, comfort the sick and the unhappy, and keep the house clean; she may also be expected to earn money. Daughter may be expected to do her homework, obey her parents, clean her plate, clear the table, and play. Each person's role may include behavior that helps further the interests or goals of the family as a whole, as well as those of the individual.

Once the importance of social positions and roles is understood, the term *group* can be defined, more precisely, as a pattern of social positions, the holders of which share a common goal or goals, a sense of group identity, and—most important—an interaction structured by the expectations attached to their positions. Precise and fussy as this definition may seem, it still covers a vast range of social configurations. The family, the street gang, the neighborhood community, the classroom, the university, the bowling team, the guerrilla band—each of these may be considered a group.

Because the term *group* is so inclusive, its usefulness in studying social behavior is somewhat limited. How much can be learned, after all, by comparing a bridge club with a corporation? They share the characteristics

The way people dress often indicates what social group they belong to. Similarly, people in a society come to expect certain roles to be fulfilled by individuals in particular types of attire. Here we can easily distinguish between the businessmen and the police. (Burt Glinn/Magnum; Lionel J. M. Delevingne/Stock, Boston)

of a group, as defined above, but not much else. Sociologists have solved this problem, to some extent, by delineating degrees of intimacy and more specific subtypes of the group.

The primary group and the secondary group

All groups, by definition, are characterized by a degree of intimacy shared by their members. Because the extent of this intimacy varies from group to group, many sociologists refer to this characteristic as the *primary-secondary dimension* of social relationships. Primary relationships denote a high degree of intimacy, deep involvement, and commitment among group members. Secondary relationships refer to less intimate, more seg-

mental involvement of group members. Although every group exhibits both primary and secondary relationships, sociologists traditionally label some groups as primary and others as secondary on the basis of the groups' closeness to one or the other of these two poles of social relations.

These Afghan guerillas constitute a *group*. They share common goals, a sense of collective identity, and an interaction based on the expectations connected with their roles. (© Joseph Murphy/Rapport 1980/Black Star)

The small group and the formal organization

In addition to establishing degree of intimacy as one means of analyzing groups, sociologists have classified groups into various types. Two important group sub-types, the *small group* and the *formal organization*, differ in several respects. First, as we saw just above, the small group is more likely to involve primary relationships; the formal organization, secondary relationships. Second, the two types of groups vary in size. A small group generally has no more than about twenty-five people, whereas a formal organization, such as General Motors or the United States government, may have thousands, even millions, of members.

Third, the two types vary in their degree of permanence. In part because of its size (and because of its complexity and its more rigid structure, matters that we will treat shortly), the formal organization is generally more permanent than the small group. If Pope John Paul II, the head of the Roman Catholic Church, and

Mrs. McGee, the head of a small and poor family, were both to die tomorrow, the machinery for replacing Pope John Paul II would go into action immediately, whereas there would be almost no chance of replacing Mrs. McGee quickly, if at all. With her death, the children might have to go to different relatives or foster homes, causing the group called the McGee family to disappear altogether. In short, a loss of personnel may wipe out the small group, whereas the formal organization can often absorb and survive this type of change.

A fourth dimension in which the two types of groups differ is structure—structural complexity and structural rigidity. The formal organization tends to have a large number of different positions, arranged in a hierarchy, or chain of command. Furthermore, each of these positions has a more or less explicitly defined role, negotiable only within relatively narrow limits. In the hospital, the surgeon and the nurse do not argue over who will do the heart transplant; in the United States government, the President and the Secretary of State do not flip a coin to see who will deliver the State of the Union address. By contrast, there are fewer positions in the small group, and these are often less rigidly defined and more negotiable. For example, in the family if Father decides that he wants to have a hand in decorating the house, he can easily do so. If Mother wants to share with Father both his role as breadwinner and her role as housekeeper, this too can be negotiated. In other words, the structure of the small group tends to be relatively loose.

This "pit-crew" has characteristics of both the formal organization and the small group. Like the former, the "pit-crew" has a rigid structure, with each member performing an explicit task, and a clearly defined goal—servicing the car as quickly as possible. Yet when its task is over, the "pit-crew" like other small groups, can easily disband. (Stephen J. Potter/Stock, Boston)

Fifth, the two types of groups differ in respect to their goals. In general, the formal organization tends to have clearly defined, specific goals, the achievement of which is central to its operations and necessary to its survival. The Acme Button Company, as its employees well know, *exists* in order to make buttons and profits; if it ceases to make either, it will probably cease to exist. In the small group, however, goals are usually less overt and more diffuse. Indeed, small groups, particularly friendship groups, sometimes seem just to "happen" rather than to be organized for the achievement of a goal. This is not to say that small groups do not have goals. By definition, all groups have goals. But in the small group goals are often changeable, diffuse, and only vaguely articulated. A neighborhood gang of boys may change its goals, over the years, from playing ball to playing cards to hanging out on a corner and looking at girls. If asked what the group's goals were, each member would probably have to think for a while before producing an answer, and his answer might well differ from those of the other members. Likewise, few people can quickly state the goals of their families. Some small groups—task groups—do have relatively explicit goals connected with accomplishing their task; but whether or not members are aware of it, these groups may have other, less explicit goals, such as providing companionship and mutual support.

Finally, the formal organization and the small group differ in the degree of accommodation that they are able to make to the individual. Social critics have argued repeatedly that formal organizations make no allowance whatsoever for individual preferences or individual strengths and weaknesses. Depending on the organization in question, this is certainly true to some degree. Newspaper reporters are not "supposed to" protest that deadlines cramp their style; a priest who is good at giving sermons but bad at handling confessions is not "supposed to" close down the confessional and concentrate on his sermons. Members of formal organizations are not there to exercise their individuality; they are there to fulfill relatively clearly defined functions so that the organization can achieve its goals. The further the individual deviates from the job description, the less likely he or she is to keep the job. In the small group, however, individuality fares somewhat better. In the family, the friendship group, or the hiking club, the person is often as important as the position and therefore is usually given some freedom in choosing a position and in tailoring the role to suit his or her needs. Furthermore, the individual who fails at his or her role is not necessarily excluded from the group. For example, if Sylvia Jones lapsed into alcoholism and began failing in many of her roles, her family and her friends would probably continue to look after her longer than the formal organization for which she worked.

There is considerable difference, then, between the formal organization and the small group. However, it should be clear that some of these differences are matters of degree. And not all groups fit neatly into one of these two categories. How, for example, would a sorority be classified? Ostensibly it is a friendship group, yet it has a board of elected officers and formal procedures for the admission and exclusion of members. And what about a rural post office that has had the same three employees for the last fifteen years? Though it is as permanent and as goal-oriented as any formal organization, the group is certainly not large or complex, and its structure may be quite loose and informal, even family-like. Actually, most groups fall somewhere between the two extremes that we have outlined. Thus the small group and the formal organization, as described above, are probably best seen not as two separate categories but rather as two ends of a continuum. The two categories also serve to define the concept of "social institution," an important idea that will be discussed in Chapter 5.

As research tools, however, these two group classifications have proved extremely useful, since they have allowed the sociologist to explore both the intimate and the formal spheres of social life. Sociologists have used small groups as convenient miniature laboratories for testing hypotheses about various facets of group interaction in general—leadership, conformity, friend selection, flow of communication, problem solving, rule making, and the like. (A more detailed discussion of small groups will be found in Chapter 8.)

Formal organizations, too, have been used as laboratories for the study of how the human personality manages to fit into the rigid structure of the organization, and how each attempts to bend the other to its needs. Largely through case studies of individual organizations, sociologists have explored the questions of how industry and bureaucracy reflect or violate social values (for example, egalitarianism); how organizations can attempt to increase efficiency and how workers can frus-

Perhaps the most important characteristic of a community is the fact that it exists in a particular geographic area. But other factors, such as shared values and a sense of common identity, are also significant, and can be seen reflected in the fronts of these San Francisco row houses. (© Peter Menzel/Stock, Boston)

trate these attempts; how an organization can transform an individual into an "organization man"; and how, in turn, workers can affect the operation of the formal organization through their own "informal organization," the network of standards, habits, and relationships that they establish among themselves. (These issues are explored further in Chapter 9.)

The community

So far, we have discussed groups largely in terms of the quality of the interaction that takes place among their members—intimacy or remoteness, formality or informality. The *community*, another type of group, is defined somewhat differently. According to Inkeles, "a community exists (1) when a set of households is relatively concentrated in a delimited geographical area; (2) their residents exhibit a substantial degree of inte-

grated social interaction; and (3) have a sense of common membership, of belonging together, which is not based exclusively on ties of consanguinity (kinship or 'blood ties')" (1964, p. 68). Thus a community is a group whose members not only share a pattern of interaction and a sense of group identity (as in all other groups) but also live in the same territory. Sometimes the term *community* is used without this geographical limitation. One hears, for example, of "the international community of scholars," the "worldwide community of Jews," or even "the intelligence community," denoting groups bound by a common interest, a common culture, or a common function. But, in general, *community* implies common residence as well.

In the strictest sense, a community is a small settlement. Indeed, the most common example of the community is the peasant village. Here we see the residential group in its purest form: all the residents know one another, live close together, interact with one another regularly, are subject to the same political and economic conditions, and are bound by the same culture. However, the term *community* has been broadened to include the town and the city as well—settlement areas that are much less closely knit and homogeneous than the village.

This looser definition raises certain questions. The

term *city*, for example, refers to a community that meets Inkeles' first criterion: a set of households concentrated in a geographical area. Yet the sheer *number* of those households leads one to ask whether a city is truly a community. How can the 8 million inhabitants of New York City share the kind of structured interaction and the sense of common identity that would qualify them for the label "community" or "group"? Can a group have 8 million members? In a sense, yes. New Yorkers, along with the residents of many other large cities, may share certain values (for example, cosmopolitanism and the love of heterogeneity and of urban excitement). They also share a sense of common identity, particularly in the face of the problems currently plaguing New York and other large cities. As for interaction, the 8 million New Yorkers certainly don't all interact with one another face to face, but they do interact symbolically, through their newspapers and newscasts. This widespread knowledge affects the residents' interactions with one another.

Another aspect of symbolic interaction on the urban scale is the integrated system of relationships among the smaller social units to which city dwellers belong—families, neighborhoods, schools, businesses, civic groups, cultural groups, religious organizations. Finally, it should be added that units of social interaction must not be defined too strictly. The phenomenon of social life, particularly in our own complex and heterogeneous society, includes a wide variety of human groupings; consequently, our terms also must be inclusive if they are to serve as useful tools in studying this phenomenon.

The idea of the community as a social unit has proved to be an extremely useful concept to sociologists. In the first place, because it is a relatively self-contained social unit, the community can serve as a kind of prototype of society, or mini-society, in which the sociologist can observe social processes and aspects of social structure that would be almost impossible to study in the society at large. In the 1920s and 1930s, for example, Robert and Helen Lynd (1929, 1937) conducted a painstaking investigation of a medium-sized town in Indiana, which they called Middletown. They studied its values, stratification system, customs and fashions, economics, politics, religion, and education, and they documented the changes in these areas of social life over the course of a decade. Similar studies have been conducted in a small New England town, in the German city of Darmstadt, and in many other communities. Of course, because they attempt to record the "typical," such studies are always vulnerable to the question of just how typical any one community can be of a large and complex society. But typical or not, the community studies are invaluable since, unlike studies of this or that small group or organization, they attempt to document the intricate linkage of an entire social structure, along with its cultural underpinnings, and they examine how that structure (and that culture) changes over time.

A second criterion for community that is important to sociologists is its spatial aspect. As we have seen, like a society but unlike any other group, a community by definition occupies a specific geographical area and is therefore affected by any changes in that area, such as population shifts. While the internal structure of a family, a friendship group, or a corporation is not as seriously affected by demographic shifts—increases, decreases, movements, and regroupings of population—a community is deeply affected by such changes, and so is a society. Indeed, it has been argued that the major social problems of contemporary societies are due to increases in population, the concentration of population in confined urban centers, and the value conflicts between different cultural groups as they crowd together in urban centers (Hauser, 1969). Such demographic changes cause changes in social life—racial conflict, for example. Demographic changes also cause ecological changes in the actual physical character of the area. The air and the water thicken with pollution; the streets become dirtier and noisier; neighborhoods disintegrate into slums. And these ecological changes in turn may affect social relations. The complex relationship of ecology and human behavior is considered in Chapter 20.

The study of the relationships among these three factors—population, ecology, and social relations—constitutes its own branch of sociology, *human ecology*, which is almost invariably based on research done on the community level. Indeed, human ecology began with an urban study. In the 1920s Robert Park and his associates left the classrooms of the University of Chicago, notebooks in hand, to immerse themselves in a study of life in the center of Chicago. Through firsthand observation they gathered an enormous amount of evidence on the way social relations were affected by the human and physical surroundings in which they took place. The result of this work was *The City* (1925), a pioneering community study and the model for many later studies in human ecology. This "Chicago Tradition" is still evident in the recent book, *Contemporary Urban Ecology,* by Brian J. L. Berry and John D. Kasarda (1977).

THE SOCIAL CATEGORY

People sometimes speak of Catholics, people in business, students, or the poor as social groups. In sociological terms, however, these sets of people are not groups because they are not routinely joined by a structured interaction, nor do they automatically define themselves in terms of a common identity. Rather, each is a *social category,* a set of people whom sociologists classify together because of a shared attribute (or cluster of attributes), but who do not necessarily have an established interaction pattern. Thus a black family, a black basketball team, or an association of black businesspeople is a group, but black people in general are a social category.

If social categories have no necessary internal interaction pattern or common identity, why are they important to the sociologist? Because, as we have seen,

FIGURE 4.2

Individuals in a society are placed in various social categories on the basis of attributes such as those shown in this diagram. In turn, individuals are located in a society's stratification system on the basis of the social categories to which they belong. That is, a society is stratified according to such social categories as class, sex, race, age, and so on, and membership in certain social categories enables some individuals to rank higher in the stratification system, and to receive more social rewards, than others.

the sociologist looks at society not as a haphazard collection of people but as a *structure*—an arrangement of social units engaged in a dynamic interrelationship—and it is clear that one important type of unit is based solely on sameness of attributes. A woman living in Milwaukee and a woman living in Sioux City may never meet and may have very different lives—one rich, the other poor; one Jewish, the other Baptist; one married, the other single—but together with all other American women they form a category that has a particular place and function within the structure of American society. (What these are have recently been subject to considerable debate.)

This point can be illustrated by looking at the stratification system. As we shall see in Chapter 10, it is through its stratification system that a society distributes rewards—namely power, prestige, and property—in unequal amounts to different collectivities of people. In the United States, the different reward levels are called classes. These classes themselves constitute social categories (for example, lower class, upper-middle class), but what is also interesting is that the process by which individuals are channeled into different classes is in part related to their membership in social categories other than class. It is certainly no secret, for example, that blacks, as a social category, are overrepresented in the lower class. How this happens is an enormously complex process, involving many factors. But one factor is that certain social categories are based on "markers"—clearly observable attributes such as speaking a foreign language or being of a particular skin color, sex, or age. The people in these "marked" categories tend

The elderly, members of a social category who share similar problems because of the often indifferent treatment of the aged in our society, have organized a political organization, the Gray Panthers, whose goal is to work for the rights of senior citizens. (© Jim Anderson 1980)

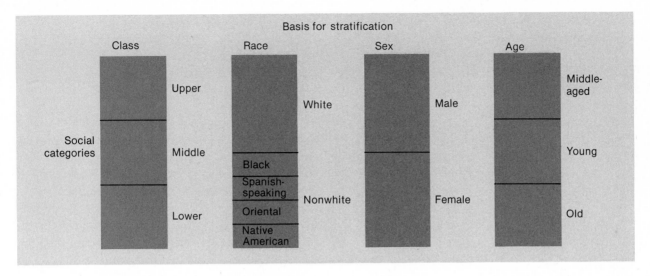

to be stereotyped; that is, other people automatically ascribe to them a cluster of attributes that presumably "go with" the marker attribute. For example, Hispanic Americans are often automatically classified as volatile, lazy, and violent. Because of this stereotyping and because of a host of large-scale societal factors—economic, political, and historical—the members of particular social categories (for example, Hispanic Americans and blacks) tend to be shunted into the lower levels of the stratification system.

Although social categories are not, strictly speaking, groups, they are related to groups in many ways. For one thing, groups may recruit new members from particular social categories. Families typically recruit, through marriage, members of their own race and class;

in recent years some colleges have energetically recruited black students (and such recruitment policies, of course, have their effect on the stratification system). Conversely, members of social categories may develop a common consciousness, partly on the basis of their common characteristics, which then leads them to form groups.

We have witnessed in the past decade the growth of organizations of blacks, women, youth, and senior citizens. The aim of organizations like the National Gay Task Force, the Gray Panthers, and the National Organization for Women is to promote the common awareness of members of their social category and to promote political and economic programs based on such heightened self-consciousness.

Process and change in the social structure

Having taken the social structure apart and examined its parts separately, we should now attempt to put it together again. How do the pieces fit? We said earlier that units of the social structure exist in a "dynamic interrelationship." What is the nature of this interrelationship?

TYPES OF RELATIONSHIPS BETWEEN SOCIAL UNITS

Social process, it is said, has three Cs and two As—cooperation, competition, conflict, accommodation,

and assimilation. *Cooperation* is the process whereby two or more units of social structure work together in an agreed-upon manner. They may be brought together by sharing the same goal, as in the case of organized crime and corrupt city officials, both intent on gaining money and power illegally. Or they may come together to fight a common enemy. An excellent example of the latter situation was the spirited cooperation of churches, schools, families, businesses, and ethnic groups—indeed, all groups—with the United States government and military during the American involvement in World War II. Families planted victory gardens; businesses converted to the production of war supplies; blacks, though faced with the insult of segregated barracks, enlisted in the armed forces as readily as whites.

Competition is the process whereby two or more social units work against each other for the same scarce rewards. In a relatively free society, such as the United States, competition can be seen everywhere. Law firms compete against one another to hire the best law school graduates; colleges compete for the best high school graduates; companies compete to induce the public to buy their soap powder. An important facet of competi-

tion is that it is regulated by social rules. The soap-powder companies may advertise vigorously against one another, but they may not hire gangsters to sabotage one another's delivery trucks.

When such rules are abandoned, the result is conflict. *Conflict* is the process whereby two social units not only compete against one another for the same scarce rewards but also do so by trying to injure or destroy each other. Conflict normally carries bitter associations. Yet, as Lewis Coser (1956, 1967) has pointed out, conflict often makes positive contributions to group life, increasing the group's cohesiveness and revitalizing its principles. Conflict can also benefit the entire society. Few people derived any pleasure from the American Civil War, but it did result in the formal abolition of slavery. Indeed, significant social change rarely occurs in the absence of conflict.

After or in place of conflict, opposing groups may achieve accommodation. *Accommodation* is the "work-

Conflict between two social units can lead to beneficial changes in the long run, but not without sacrifice. Ten steel workers were killed when this 1937 strike turned into a riot. Although many others were injured or killed in similar strikes, the workers eventually got better working conditions, high wages and union protection. (Wide World Photo)

Immigrants, like these turn of the century Jewish immigrants in New York City, have always had the difficult task of assimilating into a strange and sometimes hostile culture. (The Granger Collection)

ing together of individuals or groups in spite of differences or latent hostility" (Ogburn and Nimkoff, 1964, p. 148). For example, the Strategic Arms Limitation Talks (SALT) between the United States and the Soviet Union were undertaken as an attempt at accommodation. Likewise, different ethnic groups working in the same industry or occupying the same neighborhood may try to achieve accommodation in order to exert combined pressure on management or city hall. They cooperate, but without losing their sense of group identity or their sense of difference from the other group. Accommodation resembles cooperation, but the two differ in an important respect—the process of accom-

modation assumes underlying differences between the individuals or groups involved.

When the sense of difference among groups is wiped out, assimilation has taken place. *Assimilation* is the fusing of divergent groups. The term is often used in discussions of immigrants. For example, the German and Swedish immigrants who moved into the American Midwest in the nineteenth century were quickly assimilated into American society because their native culture was similar to the culture in which they settled. The Jewish and Italian immigrants who remained in the northeastern cities, however, became assimilated more slowly and with greater ambivalence. Because the culture of these immigrants was quite different from the Protestant culture in which they settled, native Americans accepted them less readily, and they themselves were less eager to embrace the new culture. Indeed, some sociologists question whether these immigrant groups in the Northeast ever were totally assimilated (Glazer and Moynihan, 1970). American blacks now face a similar dilemma. While many middle-class blacks quietly go about the process of seeking assimilation, some black radicals, fearing the loss of black culture, argue that the relationship between white and black should be limited to accommodation. This struggle is, of course, made more bitter by the fact that no matter what the blacks decide, many American whites still resist accommodation with, let alone assimilation of, blacks. (See Chapter 12.)

STRUCTURAL CHANGE AND DIFFERENTIATION

Change

Dynamic interrelationships such as cooperation, competition, conflict, accommodation, and assimilation often mark *change* in the social structure. Communities expand and subcommunities form within them; one group is assimilated by another; organizations proliferate. How does this change take place over the long run? Are there patterns behind the development of social structures?

In the nineteenth century, an era of ardent belief in "progress," a number of social thinkers—including Auguste Comte (1896) and, particularly, Herbert Spencer (1898)—developed evolutionary theories of social change. Human society was seen as progressing, through a predetermined sequence of stages, from barbarism and superstition to a luminous age of reason and science. Charles Darwin's treatise on the evolution of species (1859) was embraced by the evolutionary social thinkers as their scientific "proof." The fittest social arrangements, like the fittest organism, would survive and prosper, creating an ever more fit civilization. As Spencer proclaimed, "Evolution can only end in the establishment of the greatest perfection and the most complete happiness."

This dream has yet to come true. Though Darwin's specific theory of the evolution of species has been confirmed by science, the hopeful social theory of continued social progress through evolution, fostered by Darwin's discovery, has not found equal support. There is ample anthropological evidence that societies do *not* pass through a single, fixed sequence of stages. Further-

more, the historical developments of the twentieth century—the senseless slaughter of millions in World War I, the murder of almost 6 million Jews in the Holocaust of World War II, the ominous build-up of nuclear arms since the 1940s—do not suggest that human social arrangements are moving ever closer to perfection.

Nevertheless, the social evolutionists' claim that social development follows patterns has been borne out to a limited degree. *Some* patterns can be discerned. For example, there is a certain "directionality" to technological change. Societies tend to pass from a hunting and gathering technology to a horticultural technology to an agrarian technology to an industrial technology. (For a more detailed discussion of these types of technology, see Chapter 10.) This sequence is by no means an inexorable one to which all societies conform. We have no way of knowing, for instance, whether the hunting and gathering societies that exist today in Africa and Australia would, if left alone, eventually become horticultural, agrarian, and finally industrial societies. Yet in the history of certain other societies this pattern is apparent. And accompanying the pattern of technological change is a pattern of structural change characterized by increasing differentiation.

Differentiation

The process whereby a generalized structure develops into one characterized by many specialized parts is known as *differentiation*. A human embryo begins as a single fertilized egg, which in the course of nine months becomes differentiated into a baby—that is, a complex structure with many specialized parts: ten fingers to grasp with, two eyes to see with, two sets of eyelashes to protect those eyes, and so on. Likewise, as a society's technology becomes increasingly sophisticated, the social structure becomes increasingly differentiated. More and more *types* and more and more *numbers* of social units appear.

Let us look, for example, at the way societies become differentiated into a number of communities. A hunting and gathering society consists of only one community. Advanced horticultural societies, such as the Incas, had more communities, but of only two types: the capital and the outlying farm communities. By contrast, industrial societies typically have not only thousands of communities but also many special varieties of

The generalized structure of the early American one-room schoolhouse has given way to a complex system of multi-level schools, due to the increased demands of a highly differentiated society. (Daniel S. Brody/Stock, Boston)

community: communications capitals, manufacturing centers, government capitals, resort cities, suburbs, college towns, small towns, villages, farming communities, and so on.

Formal organizations and other groups also become differentiated as the technologies of societies change. In industrial societies, rising income and sophisticated communications lead to a demand for new products and services, which in turn leads to a proliferation of economic organizations—one company making one kind of cold cream, another company making another kind of cold cream. Since people must be trained to staff these economic organizations, new educational organizations spring up. At the same time, the increasing complexity of the society creates new social categories, and the different categories place their own de-

mands on the educational system. The result is a vast differentiation of educational organizations. America used to send its children to one-room schoolhouses (a fine example of the "generalized structure"), and from there certain privileged young people went on to college. Today the typical American city has schools that are differentiated not only by grade (nurseries and kindergartens, primary schools, middle schools, junior high schools, high schools, junior colleges, colleges, universities, graduate schools) but also by religion, sex, specialization, and educational philosophy: there are Jewish schools and Catholic schools, men's colleges and women's colleges, secretarial schools and medical schools, progressive schools and traditional schools.

As formal organizations become more numerous and more specialized within a society, so do other groups. A woman in a simple horticultural society may belong to three groups: her community, her family, and her combined work-and-friendship group. By contrast, a woman in an industrial society may belong to a multi-

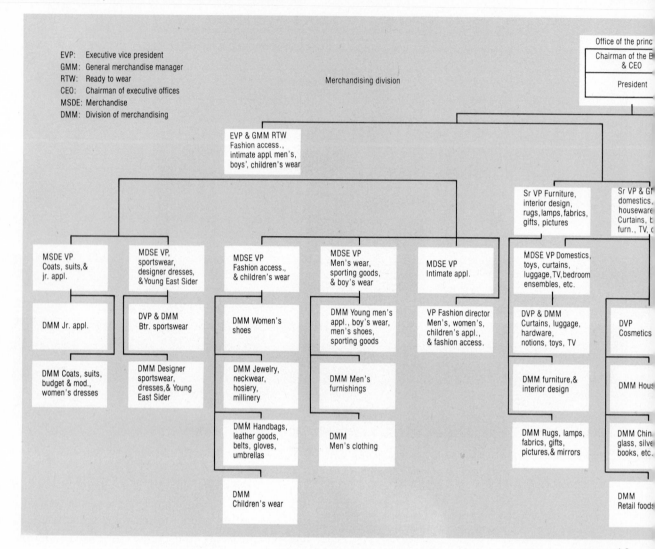

FIGURE 4.3

The nineteenth-century dry goods store, often owned, managed, and staffed by a few members of a single family, has given way to huge department stores with complex organizational structures such as the trendy and sophisticated Bloomingdale's. As technology becomes more and more advanced, organizations become increasingly differentiated.

tude of groups: her community, her neighborhood, the family into which she was born, the family into which she married, the family that she created through marriage, her work group, her professional association, her group of school friends, the PTA, her women's group, and her local drama group. To add to the complexity, the statuses and roles within these groups and organizations also become more differentiated and specialized. In a movie theater, for example, there is no longer just a manager, a projectionist, and perhaps an usher. There is now a person to sell tickets, another to take tickets from the customer, another (or even more) to sell refreshments, and so on.

In sum, technological change vastly increases the intricacy of the social structure. As a result, new problems of coordinating the multiplicity of units arise. What was once an easily comprehensible arrangement—generalized units of human association, each capable of fulfilling a variety of functions—becomes an immense network of specialized parts, dazzling in its variety and bewildering in its complexity. In the midst of this network stands the individual, who can be seen as a point at which a number of social units intersect. But what does it mean to the individual to be part of these patterned structures of meaning and behavior? This is the question we will examine next.

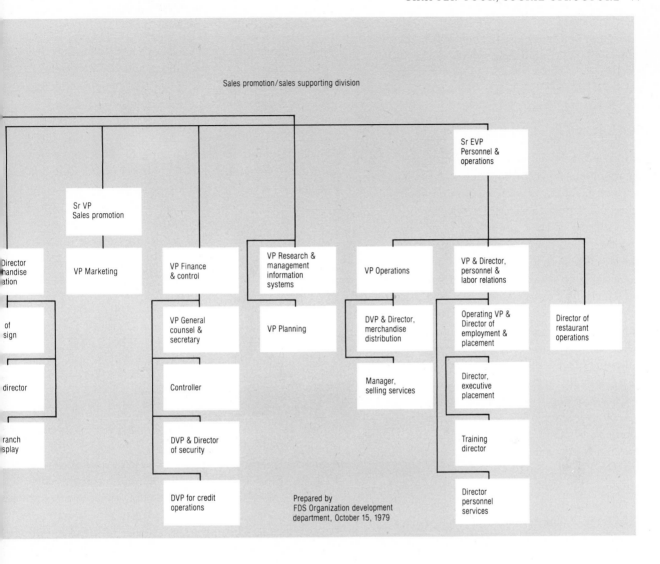

Sales promotion/sales supporting division

Sr EVP
Personnel &
operations

Sr VP
Sales promotion

Director
handise
ation

VP Marketing

VP Finance
& control

VP Research &
management
information
systems

VP Operations

VP & Director,
personnel &
labor relations

of
sign

VP General
counsel &
secretary

VP Planning

DVP & Director,
merchandise
distribution

Operating VP &
Director of
employment &
placement

Director of
restaurant
operations

director

Controller

Manager,
selling services

Director,
executive
placement

ranch
splay

DVP & Director
of security

Training
director

DVP for credit
operations

Prepared by
FDS Organization development
department, October 15, 1979

Director
personnel
services

The individual and the social structure

The social structure is influential in molding the individual's behavior. For an example, let us return to Harry Jones, whose social positions we discussed earlier, in the section on the group. Harry belongs to the Democratic party, the middle class, the black race, the Jones family, the poker group in his old neighborhood, the insurance company for which he works, and the suburban community in which he lives. All these units of the social structure (and probably several more besides) converge in him; in other words, the cluster of groups to which he belongs provides him with a cluster of social positions, a *status set*. And each of these positions, as

we have seen, carries with it a number of *roles*, or sets of behavioral expectations. In his status as the father of his family, Harry is expected to be affectionate toward his wife and daughter and to earn money. As an insurance adjuster for his company, he is expected to work seven hours a day, to adjust claims efficiently, and not to lose money for the company. As a member of his poker group, he is expected to be rowdy and fun-loving and to pay off on lost bets. As one of the few black residents of his suburban community, he is expected to be a model neighbor and to keep his lawn trimmed. Such expectations are usually unstated unless they have been violated. But they are clearly communicated through various cues, as we shall see in the next section, and they profoundly influence the individual's behavior.

SOCIAL CONTROL

What makes the individual think and behave in a role-appropriate manner? Groups and societies have various mechanisms for encouraging *conformity* to norms, rules, and expectations and for discouraging *deviance*, the violation of these norms, rules, and expectations. Together, such mechanisms constitute the group's or the society's method of *social control*.

Social control takes the form of positive and negative sanctions. *Positive sanctions* are the rewards that people give us for conforming to the norms and for fulfilling our roles. A job promotion, a nod of agreement, an invitation to a party, a box of candy on Valentine's Day—all these are positive sanctions. They let us know that we are behaving as we are "supposed" to behave, and, by reinforcing this behavior, they serve to keep us in line. When we step out of line, *negative sanctions*, or punishments, are applied. Negative sanctions range from a frown of disapproval to a prison sentence, depending on the seriousness of the deviance. Whatever the form of negative sanction, its purpose is to encourage us to step back into line. (For more on social control and deviance, see Chapter 7.)

However, most of the social controls to which we are subject are applied not by others but by ourselves. "Society," Peter L. Berger writes, "is not only something 'out there,' . . . but it is also 'in here,' part of our innermost being" (1963, p. 121). This is the result of *socialization*, the lifelong training that we receive in the culture of our society and in the roles that we must fill. As we move from position to position, we learn what is required of us in each of these positions, as well as what is required of the others in our groups. And what we learn, we internalize; society's rules become our rules. On the basis of these rules, we apply our own sanctions. We reward ourselves with self-approval when we do "right," and we punish ourselves with guilt when we do "wrong." Hence we become society's most powerful instrument of social control over ourselves; we keep ourselves in line. (Socialization is discussed in detail in Chapter 6.)

VARIABILITY IN BEHAVIOR

If all the members of a society are socialized within that society, internalizing its culture and its "conscience," how do we account for the fact that people think and behave so differently from one another? And how do we explain the fact that some people deviate from the rules? These questions arise only if we regard socialization as a uniform process, the same for all people reared in that society. But it is not a uniform process. Modern societies, as we have seen, generally contain many groups and subgroups, each of which has its own variation on that society's socialization program. One family disapproves when a child resorts to violence; another family feels that a child should fight it out and get it over with. The result is two different children and, eventually, two different adults. Another family may believe that people have the right to kill others in order to further their own interests. In our society, the result of such socialization would be an adult who was considered deviant. (Deviance can arise from causes other than differential socialization; we shall explore its various causes in Chapter 7.)

Two other sources of variation among individuals are *status conflict* and *role conflict*.* If in a given social position, or status, an individual's roles include contradictory expectations—as in the case of Father, who is expected to set limits for his children but at the same time be accepting of them and show them tenderness and affection—he may sense a degree of *role conflict*, which may in turn affect performance of the role. Furthermore, every individual, as we have seen, has a cluster of social positions, each of which may make different demands. When these demands do not agree, the individual suffers *status conflict*. Let us take the obvious example of the working mother. As a mother, she is expected to be available to her children in the evening; at the same time her job may demand that she often work late. Both kinds of conflict involve what William J. Goode (1960, p. 483) has termed *role strain*, "the felt difficulty in fulfilling role obligations" (see box). Role conflict and status conflict are usually resolved, or at least eased, through a sort of cost-reward calculation of compromise, often only dimly perceived. The person may take into account the costs and re-

---

* Some writers use *status conflict*, *role conflict*, and such terms as *role set conflict* interchangeably. The distinction between *status conflict* and *role conflict* is worth preserving, however, and we have done so here.

wards of fulfilling each of the conflicting roles and then devote herself or himself to the role that offers the greatest "profit," skimping on the opposing role. Or the individual may try to "split the difference" somehow. As a result, roles are seldom fulfilled in precise accordance with the societal "blueprint," or even the group "blueprint." The quality of a person's handling of a role depends on which other roles are competing for attention at the same time.

THE QUESTION OF FREEDOM

The social structure, then, functions in such a way that a degree of variability in people's behavior is inevitable. But does the social structure allow for freedom? Most people operate on the assumption that they have free will—that they *choose* how they will act. Yet sociology assumes that people think and act within units of the social structure and according to the demands made by

STATUS CONFLICT, ROLE STRAIN, AND THE WORKING MOTHER

As a result of what one manpower expert has called "the most outstanding phenomenon of our century," a new group of American workers may be experiencing unprecedented status conflict: women. Responding to a variety of factors in the last decade—a boom in white-collar jobs, the resurgence of feminism, and inflation—women have flooded the labor market to such an extent that for the first time more women work outside the home than as housewives. How have the institutions of American life moved to accommodate this phenomenon? Hardly at all. Women's new role as breadwinner has simply been tacked on to the traditional ones of housekeeper and child raiser, and an eighteen-hour day has become a grim but commonplace reality for many working mothers.

Of the several factors contributing to the situation, the basic one is that in American society, child care tends to be regarded as a woman's problem, not the concern of business, unions, government—or even husbands. Thus arrangements for the care of the 7 million small children whose mothers work outside the home are haphazard; with only 1.6 million licensed day-care openings (fewer than existed in 1945), 5.4 million children are left to be farmed out to relatives, neighbors, baby-sitters, and nursery schools. The United States is one of the few developed nations without a comprehensive child-care program.

Compounding the problem is the fact that working women lack the clout to make day care a major issue. Eighty percent of women still labor at such traditionally low-paying jobs as waitress, sales clerks, and secretary. One result is that the average woman earns only 59 percent of what a man earns, even though over 42 percent of working women are the sole support of their families. Only 17 percent of women workers belong to unions—whose male negotiators often do not see day care as a top priority. The women's movement, however, intends to make day care and other family-related issues major priorities for the eighties, hoping to change a system that it sees as preventing people from sharing parenthood.

For many working women—and an increasing number of men—more flexible work hours would go a long way toward ameliorating the problem. "Flextime" permits workers to pick their own starting and quitting times, as long as they work certain "core" hours and a required number of hours per week. But only 6 percent of all full-time workers in the United States now have flexible work hours, although additional companies and government agencies are experimenting with them. The benefits of flextime are known—it boosts morale, reduces lateness, and increases productivity by 5 to 15 percent—yet even optimistic supporters predict that by 1990 only 30 percent of American workers will be adjusting their own schedules.

Other countries take a much more organized approach to the problems of their working mothers. The Soviet Union's system serves 13 million children, and takes infants as young as two months; it has spent $1 billion on new day-care centers in the past two years. The French have an extensive *crèche* or nursery system, a free kindergarten service for children over three, and more than 200,000 professional nannies. In Sweden, comprehensive day care is part of a commitment to full employment and full equality of the sexes; day care is provided for children through ninth grade. The government will also pay 90 percent of either parent's salary so that a mother *or* father can stay at home. Only Japan has been as reluctant as the United States to create a national day-care system, which has resulted in the emergence of a private, unlicensed day-care industry that can charge as much as $40 per child per day.

Most analysts agree that if the institutional changes required to accommodate the surge of women into the labor market are to be effected, *men* must be committed to them. The bind in which many working mothers now find themselves illustrates that roles are interdependent—a change in one will change others. No "superwoman" can fairly be asked to play them all—alone. Otherwise, the effects are guilt, stress and neglect: role strain. In a time of inflation, two paychecks can be a necessity; in a time of recession, the government is not motivated to aid working mothers. This leaves the cutting edge of the "revolution" where it started—within the family. If both parents are breadwinners, can ways be found for both parents to share the responsibilities of parenthood too?

those units. Given this sociological assumption, is it ever possible for the individual to act outside the context of social demands?

Many sociologists have tackled this difficult question, but they have arrived at no single answer. Some believe, with Emile Durkheim (1950), that social facts represent an almost iron law and that, by comparison, individual intentions are negligible. Durkheim's contemporary, Max Weber (1947, 1949), however, felt that sociology must give attention not simply to the outer world, the world of social facts, but also to the inner world, the realm of individual intentions and interpretations of reality. Here, according to Weber, lay the source of certain freedom. By interpreting the social context somewhat differently from others, the individual could limit subservience to society and formulate his or her own unique intentions. Furthermore, by inducing enough people to accept that interpretation of reality, the individual could in fact change social reality—as did, for example, Moses, Jesus Christ, and Muhammad. In fact, neither pole of the free will–determinism dimension is likely to be the appropriate explanation of the shaping of human behavior. Social structure channels the options available to the individual, who then chooses (though not necessarily in deliberate fashion) from among these socially provided courses of action.

Regardless of whether or not Weber was correct, his analysis calls to our attention the fact that society exists not only around us but also in our minds. After all, as we have pointed out, it is the *expectations* for behavior that define the role; it is the *sense* of shared identity that shapes the group. In this chapter we have looked at social structure from an objective point of view—as a pattern that can be observed. But the ties that bind people together to form a society are not simply shared units of interaction, but also shared meanings, shared perceptions of reality. These cannot be directly observed by the sociologist; they can only be inferred.

Society, in other words, is composed of culture as well as social structure. The social structure, in a sense, is the mold of society; the culture is the content that fills the mold. The cultural content is the subject of the next chapter.

Summary

A *society* is a relatively large, relatively autonomous collection of people who share a common heritage handed down from generation to generation and who interact in socially structured relationships. The total set of these relationships defines a society's social structure.

Two major units of social structure are the *group* and the *social category*. A group is a set of interrelated *statuses*, or social positions, the holders of which share a common goal or goals, a sense of group identity, and a recurrent pattern of interaction. *Primary groups* are small and closely knit and *secondary groups* are large and more impersonal. *Small groups* and *formal organizations* differ on the bases of degree of intimacy (primary or secondary), size, permanence, structure, goals, and accommodation to the individual. The *community* is another type of group, distinguished by, among other things, the fact that its members are concentrated in a geographical area.

A *social category* is not a group; its members are classified together only on the basis of a shared attribute.

The various units of the social structure are interrelated through a number of processes: *cooperation, competition, conflict, accommodation,* and *assimilation*. These processes often signal *change* and *differentiation* in the social structure. As the technology of a society grows more sophisticated, the social structure becomes more differentiated, or specialized.

The social structure influences individual behavior through the *social controls* of *positive* and *negative sanctions*. Variations in individual behavior arise because *socialization* (the transmission of a society's heritage) and the application of sanctions are not uniform processes and because resolution of the *role strain* involved in *role conflict* and *status conflict* may affect the individual's role performance. Sociologists disagree about the extent to which the social structure allows freedom of individual behavior.

Glossary

ACCOMMODATION The process by which individuals or groups adjust their underlying differences in order to work together or to achieve an equilibrium.

ASSIMILATION The process by which members of a group adopt the behaviors and attitudes of the dominant group, leading eventually to the former group's disappearance as an independent, identifiable unit.

COMMUNITY A group whose members, in addition to exhibiting a sustained pattern of interaction and a sense of group identity, are concentrated in a geographical area.

COMPETITION The process by which social units, observing certain social rules, work against each other for the same scarce rewards.

CONFLICT The process by which social units, ignoring social rules, work against each other for the same scarce rewards by trying to injure or destory each other.

COOPERATION The process whereby two or more units of a social structure work together in an agreed-upon manner.

DIFFERENTIATION The process whereby a generalized structure develops into one characterized by many specialized parts, as when a society develops into a number and variety of social units.

GROUP A pattern of social positions, the holders of which share a common goal or goals, a sense of group identity, and an interaction structured by the expectations attached to their positions.

HUMAN ECOLOGY The branch of sociology that studies relationships among population, ecology, and social relations.

NEGATIVE SANCTION A mechanism of social control, consisting of a punishment given to an individual for failing to conform to the norms, rules, and expectations of a group or society.

POSITIVE SANCTION A mechanism of social control, consisting of a reward given to an individual for conforming to the norms, rules, and expectations of a group or society.

PRIMARY GROUP A group characterized by small size, a high degree of emotional intimacy, and (usually) physical proximity.

ROLE The set of behavioral expectations that accompanies a particular status.

SECONDARY GROUP A group characterized by relations that are more impersonal than in a primary group and by the instrumental rather than emotional significance it has for its members.

SOCIAL CATEGORY An aggregate of people classified together because they share some attribute, such as gender, race, income, or age.

SOCIAL CONTROL Regulation by a society of the behavior of its members to enforce conformity to norms and to curtail deviance through application of rewards and punishments.

SOCIALIZATION The process through which persons learn and internalize the culture and the social roles of their society and come to perform the roles expected of them.

SOCIETY A relatively large, relatively autonomous collection of people who have a common heritage that is transmitted from generation to generation and who interact with one another in socially structured relationships.

STATUS An individual's social position in relation to others within a group.

Recommended readings

Coser, Lewis A. (ed.). *Sociology Through Literature.* 2nd ed. Englewood Cliffs, N. J.: Prentice-Hall, 1972. An interesting approach to the explication of important sociological concepts by means of a judicious selection of appropriate nonsociological literature. Sections 2 and 6 are especially pertinent to this chapter.

Davis, Kingsley. *Human Society.* New York: Macmillan, 1948 and 1949. One of the finest advanced-level introductory texts from a structural-functional point of view. For further discussion of the topics covered in this chapter, see especially Chapters 4, 6, 11, and 12.

Kanter, Rosabeth Moss. *Commitment and Community: Communes and Utopias in a Sociological Perspective.* Cambridge, Mass.: Harvard University Press, 1972. An important and interesting analysis of the nature of community that focuses on historical and contemporary utopian communes. Kanter examines the underlying psychological and sociological mechanisms involved in the formation and maintenance of these social experiments, particularly the importance of commitment.

Parsons, Talcott, Edward Shils, Kaspar D. Naegeles, and Jesse R. Pitts (eds.). *Theories of Society: Foundations of Modern Sociological Theory.* 2 vols. New York: Free Press, 1961. A difficult and complex set of important selected readings. Volume I focuses on social structure.

Scott, W. Richard. *Social Processes and Social Structures: An Introduction to Sociology.* New York: Holt, Rinehart and Winston, 1970. A collection of classic short selections that elaborate several of the topics discussed in this chapter. See especially Part Two, Sections II and III.

Shils, Edward. *Center and Periphery: Essays in Macrosociology.* Chicago: University of Chicago Press, 1975. A collection of essays by an insightful sociologist that is difficult and complex, but worth the effort necessary to understand what is being said. Chapters 1-5, 13, 15, 19, and 20 are especially appropriate.

Wallerstein, Emmanuel. *The Modern World-System: Capitalist Agriculture and the Origins of the European World-Economy in the Sixteenth Century.* N. Y.: Academic Press, 1974. An extraordinary effort to look at development in terms of world economic history from a fresh viewpoint. Wallerstein takes the position that past efforts have been unsuccessful because they view the nation-state as the appropriate unit of analysis. He insists on taking a "world-systems" approach to the issue. It is a visionary work in the best sense of the term.

Williams, Robin. *American Society: A Sociological Interpretation.* 3rd ed. New York: Alfred A. Knopf, 1970. A detailed statement of basic sociological concepts in analyzing contemporary American society.

CHAPTER FIVE
THE CULTURAL DIMENSION OF SOCIETY

In 1972, news media around the world carried a bizarre story about a fifty-six-year-old Japanese soldier who was the lone holdout from a war that had ended a generation before. In 1941 Shoichi Yokoi had been a sergeant in the Japanese Imperial Army and one of 19,000 Japanese troops who occupied the South Pacific island of Guam during the war. When the American forces recaptured the island in 1944 and Japanese defeat was a certainty, hundreds of those Japanese soldiers escaped to the jungles rather than submit to capture. Over the years, some of them left the jungle; others died. Only Yokoi, who had been a tailor's apprentice in Nagoya before the war, remained. He had read the leaflets that had been dropped, announcing that the Japanese had lost the war, but he considered it shameful to surrender. And so he fashioned a solitary existence in the jungle, living in an underground cave, subsisting on fruit and nuts, and going out only at night. After twenty-eight years, some fishermen spotted and captured this twentieth-century Rip Van Winkle. Yokoi returned to his native land, which had been transformed in the thirty years he had been away, and was given a hero's welcome.

Very few people ever have the experience of being cut off from human society for such a long time, and one might expect that Yokoi's long exile would have worked some deep change in him. And yet, even after his decades of self-imposed isolation in the jungle, Yokoi was still very much a member of society. He had subsisted not because of any "survival instinct," but rather because he had learned and modified certain socially-transmitted skills for coping with the environment. He made buttons out of wood and sandals out of coconut shells, and he employed his skills as a tailor in fashioning suits from tree bark. Such socially-developed, learned solutions to recurrent problems of survival are an important part of what sociologists refer to as *culture*.

Most certainly this Japanese hermit living in the jungles of Guam did not have "culture" in the sense commonly meant by that word. In normal usage, one who prefers Bach to the Beatles, reads Homer's *Iliad* rather than *True Confessions* magazine, and eats caviar rather than peanut butter is thought to have culture. As social scientists use the word, however, culture is something that everyone has, and no distinction is implied between those with "good taste" and those with

After twenty-eight years of solitary life in the jungles of Guam, Shoichi Yokoi, age fifty-six, visits his family's tomb in Nagoya, Japan. His survival in the jungles of Guam was due to socially acquired skills and values rather than a "survival instinct." (UPI)

more commonplace preferences. In the words of the anthropologist Ralph Linton, the term *culture*

refers to the total way of life of any society, not simply to those parts of this way of life which the society regards as higher or more desirable. . . . It follows that for the social scientist there are no uncultured societies or even individuals. Every society has a culture, no matter how simple it may be, and every human being is cultured, in the sense of participating in some culture on another (1945, p. 30).

Shoichi Yokoi adapted to his environment in a way that was distinctly determined by his cultural background. The manufacture of buttons and sandals and the making of fires are examples of learned, socially-transmitted skills and knowledge useful in performing the tasks of providing shelter, clothing, and food. But there is another respect, more subtle but equally important, in which his behavior was influenced by culture. A culture consists not only of technological skills but also of a set of shared ideas, values, beliefs, and norms that perform the indispensable task of making its members' lives meaningful. (These concepts will be discussed in more detail in the course of this chapter.) As Yokoi explained to reporters, "I kept my determination alive by thinking, 'I am living for the Emperor and for the spirit of Japan.'" Throughout his decades of solitude, he justified his behavior by recalling the distinctly Japanese symbols and values that gave it significance and allowed him to sustain a sense of pride for not giving in to the enemy. In this sense, the culture in which he participated was like a shared story, which had the ef-

fect of reminding him what it meant to be a human being—specifically, a Japanese human being.

In this chapter we will explore the components of culture, the importance of language and its relationship to culture, and the nature and extent of cultural patterning. But first, let us examine what culture is as well as its significance.

What is culture?

Since culture is a broad topic, its basic characteristics have been the subject of a good deal of social-scientific debate. Edward B. Tylor's definition (1871), now a century-old antique, sounds like a laundry list: "Culture is that complex whole which includes knowledge, belief,

art, morals, law, custom, and other capabilities acquired by man as a member of society." One of the most frequently repeated definitions, suggested by Ralph Linton (1945), states that culture consists of everything that is learned and repeated in a given society, "the social heredity of a society's members" (p. 32). Clyde Kluckhohn emphasizes a slightly different aspect of culture, defining it as "the distinctive way of life" of a group of people, their complete *"design for living"* (1949; italics added).

Let us put together a comprehensive definition of the concept of culture, combining the most significant elements of each of these ideas:

Culture is a learned, socially-transmitted heritage of artifacts, knowledge, beliefs, values, and normative expectations that provides the members of a particular society with tools for coping with recurrent problems.

Examining in turn each of the major elements in this definition, we note first that culture is *learned*—that is, not instinctive. Unlike the behavior patterns of other animal species, which involve some learning but are also heavily determined by inborn patterns and capabilities, almost all human behavior is guided by what is learned—even those kinds of behavior that we might intuitively sense as instinctive, such as habits of pos-

ture, how we make love, how we play, and what we find entertaining.

Second, culture is a pattern of living *shared* among a certain group of people. Although there is never in any group a complete consensus about such components of culture as values, beliefs, or norms, a group's way of life depends on a general agreement in such matters. Take, for example, a college or university: without some measure of agreement on the goals of higher education, the courses students should take, and how students and professors should behave in class, the social order of this organization would collapse. (Such a collapse did occur, in fact, during the student rebellions of the late 1960s and early 1970s precisely because earlier "agreement" about goals was challenged.) Some measure of agreement is likewise essential in the society as a whole: if half of our population decided to drive on the left side of the street, our social order would dissolve into chaos.

Third, culture represents a *legacy from the past*. It reflects the collective experience of our ancestors in meeting certain recurrent problems. Because of culture, none of us has to depend completely on individual ingenuity in responding to each new situation. Every time we depend on an invention for which we are not personally responsible—such as geometry, language, or the internal combustion engine—we are "standing on the shoulders of giants."

Of course, just as culture enables us to benefit from

For a spider, spinning a web is an instinctive activity with no cultural component. For humans, however, the analogous activity of weaving is cultural: it is learned rather than instinctive; awareness of its practical and aesthetic purpose is shared by members of a society, and its techniques are transmitted from one generation to another. (Richard R. Hoit/Photo Researchers, Inc.; Roger Malloch/Magnum)

what our ancestors learned, it also means that we are influenced by their superstitions, their foibles, their sense of human limitations. But people are not prisoners of culture. Though it was "invented" by our ancestors, it is constantly being changed by us and by our contemporaries. Those changes will be passed on to the next generation, who will in turn modify it further. True, most of the time we experience culture as something external to ourselves, a tradition to be learned and obeyed; only rarely are we aware of making or modifying that tradition. Nonetheless, this process of change does take place. Anyone who invents a new recipe that others share, coins a new phrase that is then used by others, helps to bring about a change in the laws, or performs music in a new style that influences others is in some sense modifying the cultural tradition.

Culture—whatever its expressions—is an achievement that is distinctly human. It is made possible by the uniquely human ability to use *symbols* (words, ges-

tures, objects, or visual images which represent other ideas or objects). Without the set of symbols we call language, we would not be able to transmit culture from one generation to the next. But, as we have noted, culture is not merely passed on; it is revised and reconstructed by every new generation. As human beings, we are surrounded by a "created" environment quite different from that of other forms of life. Unlike animals, we have no instinct to tell us, for example, what kind of shelter to construct for ourselves. Instead, our culture tells us to build a boxy structure of wood or bricks: what we know as a house. Another culture might guide us to build a teepee or a yurt instead. Thus, culture imposes some order on the possible chaos of human capabilities. Yet it does not bind us to the past. We need only compare a modern house, with its geometric shape and large expanses of glass, with a gingerbread "cottage" built a hundred years ago to see the dynamic nature of culture.

WHAT'S IN A FLAG?

Flags are simple pieces of colored cloth, yet they have the power to rouse our deepest feelings—of love, pride, fear, or hatred. As befits their significance and power, they are treated with solemn ritual and revered as if sacred.

Every nation flies a unique flag—a simple fact, but one that intrigued sociologist Sasha R. Weitman (1973). Weitman believed that, like other symbols, flags could be decoded to reveal insights about the phenomena they represent.

To go about his "decoding," Weitman first identified the 137 sovereign nations of the world. Then he recorded specific information about each flag: its proportions, its colors, its field design (for example, all-over stripes, plain field with emblem at the upper right corner, and the like), and the type of emblem it carried. His strategy was to record information about each nation's flag in as much detail as possible; a hammer, pickaxe, or sickle appearing on a flag's emblem was recorded specifically as a hammer, a pickaxe, or a sickle, not abstractly as a "work tool." This kind of coding gave Weitman great flexibility in analyzing his data, enabling him to return to the data long after they had been collected and combine them into whatever categories seemed appropriate. "Work tools," for example, might later be interpreted as "potentially lethal weapons."

When he analyzed his data, Weitman discovered that flags—ostensibly just pieces of cloth—are also complex symbols, which communicate to each nation's citizens the kind of relationship they are to have with the state. The bright colors of flags invite people to keep the nation in mind, and their toughness (official flags are made of highly resilient fabrics) and even the way they fly freely in

the wind enable them to symbolize a "living," ongoing, perhaps even indestructible state. Likewise, rituals of "flag etiquette" tell citizens that flags are sacred objects; violations of the flag code amount to crimes against the state. One is not permitted to bury a flag (symbolic meaning: the nation is immortal). The flag flies high in the air, and one is required to salute and pledge allegiance to it (symbolic meaning: the nation has highest authority). All these codes make the flag a powerful agent for mobilizing people's emotions. One need only recall the uproar that resulted when flags were burned in protest against the Vietnam War to understand how closely people identify a flag with the nation it represents.

Furthermore, flags say much about each nation's place in the world community. For example, though each is unique, almost all flags are similar in size and shape. This tells a nation's citizens that their state, though distinct, belongs in the international community. Nations are wary of appearing *too* distinct; 80 percent use red in their flags and 70 percent use white. Nations in the same geocultural bloc have very similar flags, displaying their unity to one another and to the world. Scandinavian flags, for example, are differently colored but use the same basic design, and Arab nations express their unity with the Pan-Arabic colors—red, black, white, and green.

Color, in addition to representing political-cultural links, also tells us how nations identify their attributes and aspirations. Struck by his findings about the popularity of red and white, Weitman examined the meanings that nations assign to these colors. He found that "the vast majority of nations use . . . red to symbolize . . . 'wars fought against aggressors,' 'military valor,' 'courage,'

The components of culture

Culture is a tool for adapting to our physical *and* social environment. We can understand this most clearly if we separate it (for purposes of this analysis) into two components—material and monmaterial culture.

MATERIAL CULTURE

Material culture is perhaps the most obvious part of the legacy we receive from previous generations. It consists of the things that we make or use—everything from birch-bark canoes to Boeing 747s, from fireworks to freeways, from paintings to paper-hanging equipment. The thousands of technological items in use every day

'blood shed in battle,' . . . etc." (pp. 349–350). In short, red represents aggressive self-defense and tells its citizens and the world that "the nation is dauntless and indomitable" (p. 350).

Pictures on flags broadcast the same message. Eighty percent of the animals on flags are predators, such as lions, eagles, and cavalry horses, and a majority of the artifacts shown are symbols of war, including spears, bayoneted rifles, shields, swords, and cannons. In Weitman's view, the theme of aggression is "addressed as much to the nation's own nationals as it is to outsiders" (p. 351). The flag tells each new generation that it must be prepared to defend the country as bravely as its predecessors did.

As for the color white (used in conjunction with red in 50 percent of the flags in which it appears), the meanings nations most often attribute to it are purity and peace (p. 353). "It is as though," Weitman observes, "having rattled their sabres . . . , nations now hasten to let it be known that they really are . . . peaceful, friendly, oozing with good will" (p. 353). The same message goes out to their own citizens, Weitman continues:

Each nation must endeavor to convince its nationals that IT is committed to Peace, to the highest and purest ideals (Justice, Brotherhood, Liberty, etc.), and to the innocent pursuit of the level of material well-being to which they are entitled. That, I should like to propose, is why national flags present, alongside their primary image of aggressiveness, and almost as prominently, complementary images of peace-lovingness, virtuousness, and idealism. (p. 362)

have an obvious survival value: they help us to cope with the natural environment, to farm more efficiently, to get from one place to another, and to manufacture the products we consume. Some also have esthetic value, and some have value as aids to play and recreation. Material culture becomes part of the totality of a society's physical environment; members of the society must interact with it as they interact with the natural world. It is tangible—unlike nonmaterial culture.

NONMATERIAL CULTURE

Nonmaterial culture consists of those abstractions that are shared and transmitted across generations by human beings organized into social groups. These abstractions may be in the form of a system of symbols, such as language, mathematics, or musical notation. Or they may be knowledge, beliefs, and values, as well as the shared rules of appropriate conduct known as norms.

Knowledge and beliefs

Knowledge involves those ideas for which we have reasonable empirical support (for example, "Smoking by women hastens the onset of menopause"). *Beliefs*, by contrast, are those ideas that have not as yet been adequately tested (for example, "There is intelligent life in other places in the universe") or which are untestable (for example, "I believe our corn is flourishing because the spirits are looking upon it with favor").

What are some of the areas about which we have knowledge or hold beliefs? Obviously, the natural environment is one. Another is that part of our environment which has been created by humans—in other words, our material culture. Knowledge and beliefs in this area might include blueprints, designs, instructions for operation of mechanical devices, ideas about their best use, and so on. A third has to do with the intangible—what happens after death, how the earth was created and continues to exist, the meaning of human joy and suffering, the significance of life in a community, and so on. All societies have knowledge and beliefs concerning this intangible sphere.

Values

Not all of our shared thoughts are rational or objective. *Values*, for example, are somewhat like beliefs, but they are tinged with socially-learned judgments. They can be defined as shared standards of desirability—criteria for distinguishing good from bad, acceptable from unacceptable. Values are not matters that can be settled by scientific experiment; rather, they are matters of collective preference, expressing the criteria according to which the members of any culture make crucial choices of behavior. Linton reports, for example, that among the Comanche Indians, when an enemy group raided a man's camp, he was expected to save his mother-in-law before attempting to save his own life or property (1936, p. 260).

Such shared values as respect for one's parents or an emphasis upon honesty, efficiency, or obedience to the gods all serve the same purpose: they help to coordinate the activities of a society, enabling its members to choose certain behaviors from the vast range of ways in which they might act. We often attach strong feelings to values precisely *because* they are not necessarily tied to belief or objective knowledge, and hence concern matters in which choice is difficult. Many are connected with intense sensations of attraction or repulsion, approval or disapproval, which we have learned to feel in connection with them.

Shared, intensely felt values are therefore a fundamental part of the more or less orderly interactions that take place in any society. If one knows a society's values, one can make certain predictions concerning the way its members will behave. Values seem to be the link between the cognitive aspects of culture (knowledge and beliefs) and another facet of culture: its structure of rules for behavior, or *norms*.

Norms

Norms are shared rules of conduct, directing what should and should not be done by certain individuals under certain specified circumstances. A norm is an obligatory standard for behavior in a specific situation. It is through norms that values are put into action; thus, norms are essentially tools for accomplishing group goals.

Some norms, like the norm that prohibits incest, apply to everyone in the society. Some apply only to certain categories of people (all taxpayers are supposed to report all sources of income). And some apply only to certain people at certain times (some three-year-olds are permitted to draw pictures on *some* walls, for example, in a specified place in a particular day-care center).

FIGURE 5.1

The dramatic changes in the values of entering college students in the 1970s reflect, in part, the political and economic changes taking place in the United States during this time. The end of the Vietnam War and growing inflation and unemployment contributed to greater interest in individual achievement and affluence and a lessening interest in social and political change. (American Council on Education, *National Norms for Entering Freshmen,* Fall 1970, pp. 42–43, and *The American Freshman National Norms* for Fall 1976 [pp. 56 and 60] and Fall 1979 [pp. 55 and 56])

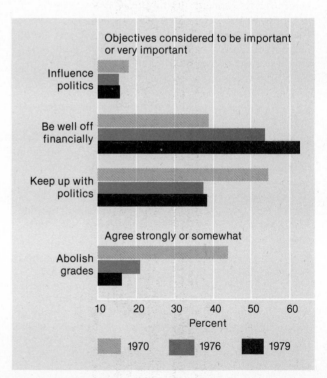

These people are aware that the sanctions for being on the grass are not particularly harsh. The importance of certain norms varies, as does the severity of sanctions imposed for violating these norms. (Patricia Hollander Gross/Stock, Boston)

Any norm, however, no matter how general or specific its application, can be thought of as part of a *role*. (We discussed roles in Chapter 4.) The norm prohibiting incest is part of the role of "family member." The norm requiring honest reporting of income is part of the role of "taxpayer." And it is possible that a norm permitting some three-year-olds to write on some walls may be part of the role of "three-year-old in the Main Street day-care center." Norms may be thought of as the building blocks of which roles are constructed. The relative importance of a given norm may vary from one era to the next; consider, for example, the now-faded taboo on the smoking of cigarettes by women which was once a very widespread and strongly upheld norm.

The severity of sanctions

As is clear from our examples, certain norms are more important than others from a societal point of view. The incest taboo is extremely important, as are norms pertaining to citizens' duties; but most norms regarding children's play activities are not quite so important. Sociologists often make distinctions among norms, based on the intensity and importance of the behavioral expectations involved and on the severity of the *sanctions* considered appropriate if a norm is violated. (Sanctions were also discussed in Chapter 4.) On one end of the scale are *customs* and *fashions*. These are norms governing activities not generally considered crucial to society's existence or functioning and whose violation is not associated with severe sanctions. (Sumner, 1906, called these folkways.) For example, it is a rule of etiquette in our society (though not in many other societies) that one should never belch in "polite" company. A person who repeatedly violates this rule may face social ostracism (a mild sanction) but is unlikely to be given a jail term (a severe sanction).

At the other end of the scale are those more important norms whose violation is likely to cause strong indignation or moral outrage. (Sumner, 1906, called these

mores.) A person who willfully injures another, a woman who beats her child, or a man who has sexual intercourse with his daughter would almost certainly be examples of persons in violation of such norms. *Laws* represent norms that have been codified in written form by the state; the sanctions appropriate to transgression of the law—whether murder or grand larceny—are established by statute and imposed by representatives of the society: in our case, by judges and juries. (For further discussion of the relativity and variability of what is considered a serious transgression, see Chapter 7.)

Institutions

Every society has certain needs: to provide food, clothing, and shelter for its members; to bring up and educate children; to defend itself against its enemies; and so on. Most sociologists would identify at least five major areas of societal functioning that serve these needs. The *political* sector's public goal is to govern and protect us; the *economic* sector's is to provide us with goods and services; the *religious* sector's is to minister to our spiritual needs; the *educational* sector's is to teach us skills to prepare us for life and work; and the *family's* is to produce and socialize children and provide its members with companionship.

Obviously, these activities are not carried out by individuals working in isolation. The economy does not run by one person's pouring cement, another person's mining coal, and so on, in an unorganized way. Instead, society's needs are met by the interaction of people in groups. Social institutions develop around each sector of social functioning. Sociologists define *institution* as *a relatively stable configuration of values, norms, statuses, roles, groups, and organizations that provides a structure for patterning human behavior to meet the social needs that exist in a particular area of activity.* The institution of the economy in American society, for example, includes norms such as the one that directs us to use U.S. currency rather than Monopoly money; it also encompasses groups and organizations such as those we know as the "bank," the "labor union," the "corporation," and so on. The *form* that an institution takes may vary from society. For example, some societies have a capitalist economy, some a socialist economy,

and some a mixed economy. But all have some arrangement for producing and distributing necessary goods and resources for their members, in other words, an economy. Each institution also has an underpinning of values. The family, for example, is a vehicle for expressing some of the most intensely held values in our society, such as the belief that the young deserve care and protection.

Because the institution, as defined here, includes both social-structural phenomena (statuses, groups, and organizations) and cultural phenomena (norms and values), it is debatable whether institutions should be considered part of culture—as they are here—or part of social structure. It should be recognized that culture and social structure are always closely intertwined. Each reflects the other, and it is not always possible—or even necessary—to separate them.

The analysis of a society's institutions is an important sociological tool to discover how that society "works" (or fails to "work," as the case may be). A broad overview of each of the major American institutions is given in Chapters 14 through 18.

Language and symbolic communication

Long before social scientists began to explore the basis of human nature, preliterate people acknowledged the importance of language, considering it a gift from the gods which set human beings apart from the animal kingdom. What is the most important difference between human communication and that of animals? Essentially, the difference is this: animals use *signs*, and we use *symbols*. (We use signs also, but most of our communication is symbolic. For further discussion of this difference, see the box on pages 91–92.)

Signs are representational; they are sounds, smells, gestures, and so on that may have to be learned but that do not require social agreement on their meanings. There is a direct and inherent connection between the sign and the reality to which it refers. (If your dog growls, it intends to bite; if you see smoke, you can assume there is a fire or some other form of combustion.) Symbols, by contrast, have arbitrary meanings; at some time their meanings were agreed on by members of the group, and they may vary from group to group. (An open raised hand, for example, may be a friendly

greeting in one society and a warning in another.) Signs generally have direct reference to something that is actually present or will be present in the immediate future. (Putting on your coat, for example, can be a sign to your dog that it is about to be taken out for a walk.) Symbols, however, do not necessarily refer to present, tangible reality.

Through symbols, we can think logically, relive the past and speculate on the future, reformulate our thoughts, come up with entirely new ideas, and engage in fantasy. Furthermore, through symbols we can amass and recall the experience of all the members of our cultural tradition.

Symbolic communication, or language, is as much a human tool as a screwdriver or a wrench, and more useful by far than either. With language, humans have built symbolic structures of religion and myth, science and superstition, that loom much larger in their significance than any physical structure. And language does something that makes us quite different from any other species: it allows us to get outside of ourselves in such a

HUMAN AND ANIMAL COMMUNICATION—DIFFERENCES AND SIMILARITIES

There is no fundamental difference between man and the higher mammals in their mental faculties. [The difference between them consists] solely in man's almost infinitely larger power of associating together the most diversified sounds and ideas. . . . The mental powers of higher animals do not differ in kind, though greatly in degree, from the corresponding powers of man.

CHARLES DARWIN, *The Descent of Man* (1871)

One way of understanding what is distinctive about the human capacity for symbols is to compare our communications with those of monkeys, apes, and other primates. It has often been assumed that since we share the globe with a great variety of species that shriek, growl, hoot, burble, and beat their chests, we might teach them our language or learn theirs. It sounds suspiciously arrogant to assert that all humans, even those living in the most primitive cultures, have fully developed languages, while no chimp—not even a "genius" chimp—has developed a language that is remotely comparable to our own. Isn't it possible that other species might be taught to use human language? Recent research allows us to see the difference between our communications and those of such species as chimps, and thus to understand more about symbolic communication.

Verbal versus nonverbal communication

Human speech, like animal communication, employs a relatively small number of basic sounds, often no more various than those emitted by certain birds or baboons. In nonverbal communications, many species seem to be more skillful than we are. Watch a dog proceed from tree to tree, marking each one with urine, and you are witnessing a signal system that works quite effectively. Because we humans are more of an eye species than a nose species, we tend to overlook the importance of olfactory signals among other species. Also, you don't need to look very closely at the behavior of the short-tailed monkeys called macaques to notice the special significance of neck-biting, by which they maintain their dominance hierarchy. That most species depend on an intricate combination of body postures and tactile, olfactory, and auditory signals for their communications proves that complex messages need not be verbalized or vocalized. (The "sign language" of the deaf, after all, depends not on vocalized sounds, but on symbols conveyed by hand and facial gestures.) But humans share with the other primates a gift for vocalization, which is a particularly efficient means of communication. It allows us to produce a wide range of combinations, each different from all the others, without expending much energy. The great advantage of verbal symbols is that they can easily be combined. Because each

word can be produced quickly, we can efficiently string together a series of words and thoughts and construct a complex statement.

Stereotyped communication versus flexible communication

To understand the difference between our symbolic communication and the communications of other species, it is useful to examine one of the most sophisticated of all nonhuman communication systems, that of the honeybee, whose celebrated "waggle dance" was first decoded by biologist Karl von Frisch (1967). When a worker bee returns from the field to the hive, it can tell other worker bees both the direction and the approximate distance of a food source by performing this dance in a figure-eight movement. The most important part of the dance is the straight run (or the middle of the figure eight), which is given a particular emphasis by a rapid lateral vibration of the body (the waggle). The straight run represents the direction of flight from the hive to the target. The distance is indicated by the frequency of the waggles.

In what ways is this different from the abstractions we convey in language? Like the communications of most other species, the waggle dance is highly stereotyped. The explorer bee cannot return with the message, "I didn't find any pollen out there, but you should see the sunset!" It is limited to a message with only two components, distance and direction. Furthermore, like most animal communications, the behavior of the honeybee, as well as the responses of other bees to that signal, is nearly constant throughout all members of the species. By human standards, the number of signals employed by most animal species is quite limited. Even the rhesus monkey, which is a virtuoso in this respect when compared with other species, has only thirty-seven separate signals in its repertoire. In contrast, human beings by combining nouns, verbs, and other speech parts, can produce an infinite number of sentences for use in communication.

Symbols versus signs

Communication takes place only when the sender and the receiver of certain signals or symbols agree upon their meaning. The worker bee, for example, clearly understands the meaning of the waggle dance. The advantage we have as humans is that as members of a certain culture, we share a language. The language consists of a very large number of words, all of which have a certain shared meaning, and a structure for combining them, a grammar.

In order to distinguish clearly between human communications and those of other species, we need to understand what it means to say that only humans use symbols in their communications, while other species use signs. Obviously, you can teach dogs, horses, apes, and many other species to respond to specific commands. As a matter of fact, most species would not be able to survive without this ability to learn, by trial and error, that certain phenomena are signs of certain others, existing or about to exist. For example, many cats connect the sound of a can being opened with the expectation of being fed, and run into the kitchen. A sign is something to act upon; it is a physical event or thing that indicates the presence of some other thing or event, as smoke indicates the presence of fire. The important thing to remember about signs is that their meaning can be established by sensory rather than intellectual means. Once the relationship has been established between a certain sound and response, the meaning of the stimulus becomes identified with its physical form and is perceivable with the senses.

Humans differ from animals of other species in that they play an active role in determining the meaning of a certain sound, making it a symbol. That meaning cannot be perceived by the senses; it has to be taught. At some moment in the past, some human bestowed the meaning of a word upon a certain sound; it then became part of the language tradition that each new generation learns. The connection between any word and its meaning is arbitrary. Unless you learn the English language, the word *desk*—and all the other words in that language—will be meaningless to you. By contrast, the "meaning" contained in the warning signal of a rhesus monkey, for example, is not something that has to be learned in the same way that language does, and it is not so arbitrary as the connection between a word and what it stands for.

Conversations with a chimp

Most of the attempts to teach language to animals have been performed with chimpanzees, who would seem to be ideal students. Biologically, the structure of the chimp's blood protein and even the circuitry of its brain are remarkably similar to our own. The chimp hears as well as we do, and its vision is about as sharp. Chimps are intelligent, too. Equally important, they are highly sociable, which is a very useful trait if you are trying to teach language through extended interaction.

In one experiment, two psychologists, Allan and Beatrice Gardner, decided to try to teach a chimp named Washoe the American Sign Language, chosen because they knew that chimps frequently manipulate objects with their hands. The experiment set up by the Gardners involved a great deal of social interaction between the chimp and human companions, to simulate as closely as possible the conditions in which a human infant learns language. After two years, Washoe could make certain demands and answer questions by using certain noun "signs." At last report, Washoe had thirty or so "words"

in her vocabulary and was combining them to make short sentences.

Another chimpanzee, Lana, has been taught to communicate through pictographs. According to Duane Rumbaugh and Timothy Gill, her teachers, Lana has not only responded to humans who "converse" with her via the pictograph machine, but she has also initiated some of the conversations. When confronted with an object for which she has not been taught a word, Lana has been known to create one. For example, when she was shown a ring for the first time, Lana identified it—using terms that she already knew—as a finger-bracelet. Rumbaugh maintains that the studies on apes have not taught them to think. "There is no doubt among those working with them that apes have cognition. . . . All we do . . . is to agree with them upon a vocabulary" (quoted in Hayes, 1977, p. 76).

Francine Patterson, another psychologist, is conducting the first language research on a gorilla. In five years Patterson's subject, a female gorilla named Koko, has amassed a vocabulary of 300 words. She has even been known to react to conversations going on around her.

These studies, understandably, have attracted a good deal of interest and publicity. But what can we conclude from them? Do some animals actually have the ability to use language in a human way? The answer is apparently a qualified no. Although these apes can use and respond to words similar to our own, they are hardly using language as human beings do. The vocabulary and in particular the grammar possessed by a young child far surpass those of any ape, even after years of determined training. Like the dancing honeybee, the apes still cannot combine words grammatically to produce the infinite number of spontaneous utterances of which human beings are capable. Dr. Herbert S. Terrace of Columbia University has gone even further, asserting that much of the apes' behavior is simply drill. In other words, they have learned words or signs by being prompted and rewarded by their trainers, much in the manner of trained dogs or circus animals. Dr. Terrace, who trained a chimp of his own (called "Nim Chimpsky" after the linguist Noam Chomsky), found that the animal rarely initiated "speech" on its own. Moreover, it seemed merely to string words together, not to form real sentences ("Give orange me give eat orange me eat orange give me eat orange give me you," for example).

These qualifications do not diminish the remarkable findings of the Gardners and other researchers, however; the studies of Washoe and the other apes have extended our understanding of animal communications. Nevertheless, the extraordinary efforts necessary to teach even the simplest bits of "language" to the apes, in contrast with the seemingly automatic way in which children absorb an intricate grammar, highlight human beings' astonishing ability to communicate in symbols.

In our culture a flexed muscle is a sign of physical strength and, to some, a symbol of masculinity. This linking of a gesture with an abstract concept is a purely human phenomenon.
(© Hazel Hankin)

way that we become objects to ourselves. This ability is implicated in our development of identity (see Chapter 7). In fact, much of what we experience is symbolic; this includes not just words, but many gestures (such as holding one's fingers in a "V" shape) and even things (like the "holy water" of the Ganges, which is important not because of what it is chemically, but because of what it symbolizes).

As Edmund Carpenter expresses it:

Language is a storage system for the collective experience of the tribe. Every time a speaker plays back that language, he releases a whole charge of ancient perceptions and memories. This involves him in the reality of the whole tribe. Language is a kind of corporate dream; it involves every member of the tribe all of the time in a great echo chamber (p. 139, 1970).

Language enables each of us to be related to all other members of our cultural tradition in a very different way from that in which an animal is related to others of its species.

LINGUISTIC RELATIVITY: THE SAPIR-WHORF HYPOTHESIS

Language does far more than provide us with a means of communicating with one another. We use language even when we are by ourselves: most of what we mean by "thinking" is a verbal process—a more or less elaborate conversation with ourselves. Thus, it is largely through language that we experience our culture. The pictures in our heads (of ourselves or of the world around us) are not just mental snapshots, the same as those of everyone else who has had "the same experience." Rather, what we experience is to a considerable degree what the peculiarities of our language have taught us to notice. Experiencing is an active process: we are alert to certain things while we ignore others.

FIGURE 5.2
The linguistic relativity hypothesis postulates that culture influences language, which, in turn, greatly influences thinking. The way we view reality, Sapir and Whorf maintain, depends largely on the language we use. (Adapted from Albrecht et al., p. 74)

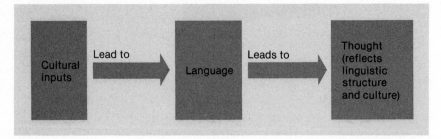

And we tend to pay attention to what we have words for.

This perspective, which has been argued most strongly by two American linguists, Edward Sapir (1929) and Benjamin Lee Whorf (1956), is referred to as the *linguistic relativity hypothesis*. Essentially, Sapir and Whorf maintain that we all interpret the world through the grammatical forms and categories supplied by the languages we learn (see Figure 5.2).

What exactly do we mean when we say that the way we view reality depends largely on the language we use to interpret experience? Let us look at this hypothesis in more detail.

THE CONNECTIONS BETWEEN WORDS AND PERCEPTIONS

Vocabulary

One element of every language is vocabulary. Some languages provide an elaborate and highly specific vocabulary for objects or concepts that other languages gloss over with vague words, or for which (in some cases) they have no words at all. Generally, the more elaborate and precise the vocabulary connected with a class of things, the more important is that class to the members of the culture. For example, Eskimos live in an environment where snow is much more important than it is to most other North Americans. The Eskimo language has no generic word for snow, but it has more than twenty specific words for different types of snow—fluffy snow, hard-packed snow, drifting snow, and so on. The fact that we can express these distinctions about snow in our own language suggests that we are aware of them, but we have to combine an adjective and a noun to express what Eskimos need only one word for. In our own culture, if we were asked about the weather, it would be sufficient to say, "It's snowing." The fact

that the Eskimos have twenty words to choose from reflects the importance that observation of the weather has in their environment. As Eskimo children learn the language, they also learn to look closely at snow. Sapir and Whorf would argue that when vocabulary is elaborate and precise, observations are precise as well.

Grammar

Language consists of grammatical constructions as well as a specific vocabulary. Just as the vocabulary influences us to pay attention to certain things and to ignore others, so does the grammatical structure of the language. For example, many European languages impose a distinction between two forms of address, the formal and the familiar. The French use the formal *vous* where the relationship is one of respect or deference, and the familiar *tu* to address equals or intimates. In English, of course, we make no such distinction. The all-purpose *you* glosses over status distinctions that some other languages emphasize.

LANGUAGE AS A COGNITIVE MAP

The main point of the Sapir-Whorf hypothesis is that a language is more than a specific vocabulary and grammar. It embodies a special way of looking at the world and interpreting experience. In the course of its development (which parallels the development of the society itself), it is shaped to some extent by the constraints of the environment. And it in turn shapes the concept of reality that each individual acquires through the process of socialization into the society (Krech, Crutchfield, and Ballachey, 1962, p. 303). Karl Mannheim wrote that "the most important thing to know about a man is what he takes for granted." A good deal of what each of us takes for granted can be understood by examining the fine print of the cultural contract we signed (without being given any choice) when we were taught one language rather than some other.

It is as important for individuals who share a cultural tradition to accept a common language (already developed) as it is for a group of people playing baseball to accept the rules that have already been established, and for the same reasons. Language provides a map of the "real" world that members of one's cultural tradition have explored. Think of what a map does for you: it draws your attention to certain points by providing labels for them. Many things that exist in that territory are disregarded—are not labeled. (A road map, for example, tells you nothing about local vegetation.) At the perimeters of the map are regions that are not well marked. In effect, as the philosopher Ludwig Wittgenstein once said, "The limits of your language mean the limits of your world." Just as some of the old maps seen in museums bear the warning that beyond their perimeters "There be monsters," language encourages us to think that its limits are the limits of reality itself.

Whoever ventures into those areas that are poorly represented—or not mentioned at all—in our linguistic tradition has to manufacture new words to express new experiences. In fact, one common feature of periods of rapid social change is that language changes more rapidly as well. Just as maps must be revised to make them correspond more closely to the terrain they represent, language changes to reflect new discoveries or preoccupations (for example, the words "charm" and "quarks" designate new discoveries in physics and astronomy).

EVALUATING THE SAPIR-WHORF HYPOTHESIS

The fact that our language expands to meet new social needs suggests that our perceptions may shape our language as much as our language shapes our perceptions—perhaps even more so. Many scholars have criticized the Sapir-Whorf hypothesis for just this reason. Although a few empirical studies have supported the idea that speakers of different languages perceive the world differently, the actual discrepancies have been found to be slight. Languages surely *do* reflect the cultural preoccupations of the societies in which they exist. Consider the number of colors that an English-speaking American can identify: coral, cinnamon, burgundy, brick, and magenta are all reds, but the fashion industry has taught us to discriminate among them. We may be more conscious of these variations in color than would members of a society less preoccupied with fashion. Yet most people could identify the actual variation in color, even if they lacked names for the different shades. Similarly, Americans could probably perceive many of the differences Eskimos see in snow even without twenty different words. Having names for things probably does heighten our perception of them, however: things we can name may "stand out" for us while unnamed things remain in the background. In other words, language may direct our attention to some things rather than others; but those other things are still there and can be perceived. Language thus may affect what we notice more than what we can see.

Cultural diversity

Just as the most striking feature of human languages is their variety, the very different ways in which they convey perceptions and interpretations of reality, a striking feature of human cultures is their staggering diversity. Every culture is in many ways unique, different from all others. Whether the topic is food preferences or fashions in dress and self-adornment, sexual standards or attitudes toward the accumulation of goods, the only reliable generalization seems to be that "human nature" is almost infinitely variable.

Take, for example, some of the behavioral patterns that to us seem so "natural" that we regard them as

inevitable—for example, the nodding and head-shaking gestures we use to indicate yes and no. The Ainu of northern Japan use their hands—not their heads—to indicate yes and no. In Delhi, Moslems indicate assent by throwing their necks diagonally backward, with a slight turn of the neck. The Semang of Malaya thrust their heads forward (much as we might do if our collars were too tight) to say yes, and cast their eyes down to say no (LaBarre, 1947).

Or, for example, take the various meanings given to the biological fact of puberty. As Ruth Benedict pointed out years ago, the *rites of passage*—the ceremonies associated with the transition from childhood to adulthood—make sense mainly as a form of basic training for the adult roles required in any culture. Since these roles are almost unimaginably varied, rites of passage are strikingly varied too. Among the preliterate peoples of Australia, for example, where male adulthood means participation in an exclusively male cult, puberty ceremonies for boys stress the severing of bonds with women. Among native American tribes in the interior of British Columbia, where the rites serve as a form of occupational training for both sexes, young boys and girls are expected to prove their competence in such practical tasks as carrying water or running swiftly. While from the point of view of an outsider these rituals may seem bizarre, each in its own way provides an apprenticeship for the adult characteristics desired in those societies.

Rites of passage, the ceremonies associated with the transition from childhood to adulthood, vary from culture to culture. These girls await the Catholic communion ceremony which will make them full members of the church. (George Cohen/Stock, Boston)

CULTURAL RELATIVISM

Benedict observed in her classic book *Patterns of Culture* (1934) that it is just this staggering diversity among cultures that makes comparisons so difficult. Most cultures, she wrote, "are traveling along different roads in pursuit of different goals, and those ends and those means in one society cannot be judged in terms of another society" (p. 206). As her words suggest, social science must be conducted with an eye focused on the *relativism* of cultures. That is, each society's culture must be understood in terms of the meanings, attitudes, and values shared by the members of that society. If our vision is distorted by our own beliefs and values, we will inevitably see something different from what is actually there.

It is no easy task to suspend one's own beliefs and values long enough to describe and analyze another culture from the perspective of its members. For example, in our culture we value generosity, mutual trust, respect for the elderly, and sympathy for those who cannot take care of themselves. The Yanomamo of Brazil, however, seem to have discarded much of what we might

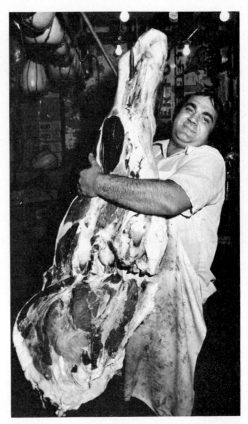

Each society's culture must be understood in terms of the meanings, attitudes, and values shared by the members of that society. According to the religion of Hinduism, the predominant religion in India, the cow is sacred and never killed, while beef is one of the staples of the American diet. (George Daniell/Photo Researchers, Inc.; David A. Krathwohl/Stock, Boston)

think of as "natural" humanitarianism: they are at war almost continually (about 33 percent of adult male deaths result from sneak raids and ambushes), and female infanticide is common. What the social scientist must realize in studying such practices is that the outsider's response to them, particularly a negative one, is likely to have been shaped by the needs of that person's own society. For example, during the past fifty to one hundred years, the survival of our society has depended (at least to some degree) on our efforts to safeguard individual lives. In the environment the Yanomamo inhabit, by contrast, food-supply limitations require that the population be kept down to a certain level; in the absence of effective methods of contraception, it periodically becomes necessary to eliminate a certain percentage of the population if the society as a whole is to survive (Harris, 1975).

The inability to transcend one's own perspectives, the tendency to view one's own set of practices as natural and right and to judge all others on this basis, is called *ethnocentrism*. An ethnocentric perspective is almost universally condemned in scientific circles because it erroneously grants little or no validity to alternative values or modes of behavior and recognizes little or no difference in the social, historical, or geographical conditions that may have given rise to the different practices we see among cultures.

CULTURAL UNIVERSALS

Despite the vast differences among the cultures of the world, all of them share certain practices known as *cultural universals*. The anthropologist George P. Murdock (1945) has identified more than sixty of these, including fire making, cooking, cooperative labor, kinship nomenclature, the use of tools, and religious rituals. These universal practices reflect the tasks shared by all socie-

This Mexican Indian woman exhibits a few of the cultural universals—cooking food, the use of fire, and the use of tools. Cultural universals are practices which are found in all cultures. (Mark L. Rosenberg/Stock, Boston)

ties: members must be fed, clothed, and sheltered; children must be cared for and taught; the sick must be tended; the bodies of the dead must be disposed of, and so on. These universal activities are brought about by the demands both of human biology and of the environment, although the mode of these activities may vary from one society to the next. It is environment that is most important in determining how a particular cultural universal will be expressed.

CULTURAL PATTERNING

Another attribute of every culture that can help guide the social scientist is the connectedness, or patterning, of its various aspects. Cultures are not crazy quilts made up of a thousand unrelated elements stitched together. They are carefully woven tapestries. The various customs, rituals, and values of any culture tend to form a more or less integrated pattern. Therefore, a change

that takes place in one part of a cultural system can have many (often unanticipated, sometimes undesirable) effects on other parts of that system.

As just one apparently minor example of an element in the patterning of a culture, let us consider games. It might be assumed—as most social scientists have in the past—that the games played in any society are not particularly important in understanding basic cultural patterns. Play and games, after all, are regarded as "time out" from the serious activities of life. But recent research indicates that there are as many patterns of play as there are languages, and that the lessons conveyed by many games are well integrated into the culture of which they form a part (Melville, 1974).

One researcher studied the games played by the Inuits (Eskimos) of Canada and noticed that they were essentially cooperative and noncompetitive, as was Inuit culture in general. When softball was introduced to this group by whalers, the Inuits quickly rewrote the rules of the game. They played with two teams, as we do, but those teams typically consisted of members ranging from the very young to the elderly. They did not observe the rules that distinguish beween winners and losers. Because there was no emphasis on winning, novices and highly skilled players could enjoy the game together. One team would bat until all of its members had had a chance. No one kept score. But when the Canadian government planned a new town near the Inuit settlement that brought many southern Canadians—who have values much like our own—to the area, the young Inuits started to play baseball according to the newcomers' rules. The culture changed when the value of competition began to predominate over cooperation. No part of the pattern—not even the game preferences—was left undisturbed (Melville, 1974).

Subcultures and countercultures

The cultures of modern industrial societies tend to be increasingly heterogeneous, for two reasons. First, whereas the institutions of small-scale societies are not highly differentiated from one another, modern industrial societies have markedly differentiated and separate institutions, the guiding values of which do not always agree. Consider, for example, the altruistic values taught by most of the established religions in the United States compared with the "anything to make a buck" or "dog eat dog" tradition of American business.

Second, complex societies include a variety of groups that do not fully share the dominant culture. The world *subculture* refers to groups within a society whose members share certain values and practices that differ from those of the larger culture (even though they may adhere to some values or practices that do characterize the entire culture). In New York City's Puerto Rican community, for example, there are certain food preferences and religious observances, as well as attitudes toward family obligations and child rearing, that are not characteristic of American culture in general. More recently, in addition, we have witnessed the growth of *countercultures*, embodying the values and practices of subgroups, which are in active opposition to those of the larger society. Examples of countercultures in our society are the militant groups at both extremes of the political spectrum. Countercultures tend to generate strong reactions—often of repression by societal representatives (for example, the police). But often there is reasonable tolerance for subcultural differences, sometimes manifested in cooptation by the general public (witness the change in hair and clothing styles over the last decade or two).

Many subcultures and countercultures have their own peculiar jargon, which serves as a badge of membership in a given group. Subcultural jargon—whether of an ethnic minority, a juvenile street gang, or a scientific discipline—not only identifies those who are part of a dissenting group but offers them a distinctive shorthand way of expressing their point of view. Some student radicals, for example, expressed their scorn for policemen by calling them "pigs"; more conservative students were sometimes referred to as "boy scouts" or "straight arrows." This kind of abusive language reflects the extreme polarization of the campus in those days, and the students' preoccupation with dividing the world into those who were "part of the problem" as opposed to "part of the solution."

These children and their teacher belong to a community of Hasidic Jews in Brooklyn, New York. They are members of a subculture which has different customs, dress, and values from, yet which is still a part of, the larger American society. (Leonard Freed/Magnum)

American cultural themes

If, in general, the cultural themes of complex, industrial societies are more heterogeneous than are those of small-scale, preliterate societies, perhaps one of the most heterogeneous cultures of all is our own. The United States is basically a nation of immigrants, all of whom brought customs, traditions, and values from other places. In addition, it has a great variety of religious traditions and environmental conditions. Despite our society's heterogeneity, however, social scientists have identified certain predominant values—observed by foreign visitors who remark about "characteristically American" traits, and confirmed by polls and opinion surveys.

One analyst, Robin Williams (1970), compiled a list of fifteen basic value orientations in American culture. Among these are:

1. *Achievement and success.* We stress personal achievement, especially as expressed in occupational success.

2. *Activity and work.* As Williams comments, "It is no accident that the business so characteristic of the culture can also be spelled 'busyness'" (1970, p. 458). Foreign observers have frequently commented on the American inclination toward ceaseless activity, our devotion to regular, disciplined work.

3. *Moral orientation.* Americans tend to judge behavior consistently in terms of right and wrong, to test individual conduct against some shared ethical standards.

4. *Humanitarianism.* This refers to the American ideal of disinterested concern and helpfulness, expressed in the form of personal kindness as well as organized philanthropies.

5. *Efficiency and practicality.* Americans are intensely practical, assuming that where there is a problem, there must be a solution.

Williams' list also includes such traits as a belief in equality, freedom, conformity, democracy, science and rationality, and patriotism. It is evident that some of these values—such as the belief in progress, science and rationality, and patriotism—have been widely challenged, if not partially rejected, in the years since Williams compiled this list. Moreover, as Daniel Yankelovich (1978) has pointed out, further changes are on the way, particularly in our attitudes toward work. (See Chapter 18.) Noting Americans' increasing "preoccupation with self," he suggests that the values of hard work and the traditional drive toward success may be fading. More people than ever are finding their greatest satisfaction in leisure rather than work, withdrawing from their work emotionally, and seeking some other identity than that of "employee." It will be interesting to observe the impact of these changing views on "characteristically American" traits in the years to come.

Summary

Culture may be defined as a learned, socially transmitted heritage of artifacts, knowledge, beliefs, values, and normative expectations that provides the members of a particular society with tools for coping with recurrent problems. Culture is a pattern of living shared among a certain group of people; each culture teaches its members distinctive ways of life, depending on the past experience of that society. Although culture is a legacy from the past, it is constantly changing with the actions of each new generation. It is a distinctly human achievement, made possible by human beings' ability to manipulate complex systems of symbols, the most important of which is *language.*

Culture is a tool for adapting to our physical and social environment. It is compounded of *material culture* (things that are made or used) and *nonmaterial culture* (those abstractions that are shared and transmitted across generations, such as language, knowledge, beliefs, and norms). Both material and nonmaterial culture are involved in the makeup of *institutions.*

Language is basic to the formation of culture. Animals can communicate through *signs*, but humans communicate primarily through *symbols*. According to the linguistic-relativity or "Sapir-Whorf" hypothesis, different languages—because they are symbolic—convey different views of reality. Thus, while every language is characterized by a specific vocabulary and a specific grammar, it is also marked by the ways of perceiving reality and interpreting experience that it conveys.

Cultures are as diverse as languages, which makes comparisons among them difficult. Certain general types of behavior, however, may be regarded as virtually universal—for example, fire making and cooking. Also universal is the patterning of the various elements of a culture into a relatively coherent, balanced whole.

Complex modern societies do not possess only one culture; usually they include a number of *subcultures* (groups that share values and practices that differ from those of the larger society) and *countercultures* (groups opposed to the culture of the larger society). Although American culture has historically been based on certain shared values (for instance, an emphasis on work, achievement, and practicality), the universality of these beliefs has recently been questioned.

Glossary

BELIEF An idea that has not been or cannot be adequately tested empirically.

COUNTERCULTURE The values and practices of a group within a society that are in active opposition to those of the larger society.

CULTURAL RELATIVISM The view that each society's culture must be understood in terms of the meanings, attitudes, and values shared by the members of that society.

CULTURE A learned, socially-transmitted heritage of artifacts, knowledge, beliefs, values, and normative expectations that provides the members of a particular society with tools for coping with recurrent problems.

ETHNOCENTRISM The tendency to view one's own culture as natural and right and to judge all other cultures on that basis, granting them little or no validity of their own.

INSTITUTION A relatively stable configuration of norms, statuses, roles, groups, organizations, and values that provides a structure for patterning human behavior to meet the social needs that exist in a particular area of activity.

KNOWLEDGE Ideas for which empirical proof exists.

LANGUAGE A set of verbal symbols used to facilitate communication.

LAW A norm that has been codified in written form by officials of the state.

NORM A shared rule of conduct, directing what should and should not be done by certain individuals under certain specified circumstances.

SIGN A word, gesture, object, or visual image that directly rather than arbitrarily represents another idea or object that is, or is about to be, tangible or present.

SUBCULTURE The values and practices of a group within a society that differ from those of the larger culture.

SYMBOL A word, gesture, object, or visual image that is arbitrarily agreed on by the members of a group to represent another idea or object that is not necessarily tangible or present.

VALUE A particular culture's shared standard of what is good or bad, acceptable or unacceptable; a conception of the desirable.

Recommended readings

Benedict, Ruth. *Patterns of Culture*. Boston: Houghton Mifflin, 1934. A classic illustration of the relative coherence of culture within three "primitive" societies. This paperback book is rich in description and analysis of the concept of culture and of its impact on individual lives.

Harris, Marvin. *Cows, Pigs, Wars, and Witches: The Riddles of Culture*. New York: Random House/Vintage, 1975. A fascinating description of what are seen as irrational, unusual, and enigmatic customs among modern as well as preliterate peoples. Harris, following Benedict's *Patterns of Culture* (above), attempts to make sense of apparently "bizarre" practices.

Hershovits, Melville J. *Cultural Relativism: Perspectives in Cultural Pluralism*. Frances Hershovits (ed.). New York: Random House/Vintage, 1973. A paperback collection of a leading anthropologist's essays on the issue of cultural pluralism and its relationship to developments in history and in the philosophy of science.

Kroeber, A. L., and Clyde Kluckhohn. *Culture: A Critical Review of Concepts and Definitions*. New York: Random House/Vintage, 1952. A major review by two outstanding anthropologists of the history of the concept of culture, various definitions of culture, and the components of culture.

The authors end the book with an overview of the conceptual problems involved and a statement of their own position.

Linton, Ralph. *The Cultural Background of Personality*. New York: Appleton-Century-Crofts, 1945. A very useful and easy-to-read paperback that contains five lectures by an eminent anthropologist on the interrelationships of culture, society, and the individual. Chapter 2 is especially relevant to the material in this chapter.

Peterson, Richard A. "Revitalizing the Culture Concept," in Alex Inkeles, James Coleman, and Ralph H. Turner (eds.), *Annual Review of Sociology*, Vol. 5, 1979, 137–166. A systematic attempt to revitalize the concept of culture in sociology by focusing on expressive symbols. Attention is given to language, the mass media, and the "production" of culture.

White, Leslie A. *The Concept of Cultural System: A Key to Understanding Tribes and Nations*. New York: Columbia University Press, 1977. A short but important last statement by one of the deans of American anthropology. In this volume, White continues his argument for examining culture at its own level of analysis and for avoiding reductionist explanations.

Body ritual among the Nacirema

HORACE MINER

Americans, like most other people, are ethnocentric. We tend to regard the norms and values of our own culture as the only right way to live. The reading below, by anthropologist Horace Miner, should convince most of us that the customs we take for granted are no less strange than any ever practiced by the remotest tribe.

. . . Professor Linton first brought the ritual of the Nacirema to the attention of anthropologists twenty years ago, but the culture of this people is still very poorly understood. They are a North American group living in the territory between the Canadian Cree, the Yaqui and Tarahumare of Mexico, and the Carib and Arawak of the Antilles. Little is known of their origin, although tradition states that they came from the east. According to Nacirema mythology, their nation was originated by a culture hero, Notgnihsaw, who is otherwise known for two great feats of strength—the throwing of a piece of wampum across the river Pa-To-Mac and the chopping down of a cherry tree in which the Spirit of Truth resided.

Nacirema culture is characterized by a highly developed market economy which has evolved in a rich natural habitat. While much of the people's time is devoted to economic pursuits, a large part of the fruits of these labors and a considerable portion of the day are spent in ritual activity. The focus of this activity is the human body, the appearance and health of which loom as a dominant concern in the ethos of the people. While such a concern is certainly not unusual, its ceremonial aspects and associated philosophy are unique.

The fundamental belief underlying the whole system appears to be that the human body is ugly and that its natural tendency is to debility and disease. Incarcerated in such a body, man's only hope is to avert these characteristics through the use of the powerful influences of ritual and ceremony. Every household has one or more shrines devoted to this purpose. The more powerful individuals in the society have several shrines in their houses and, in fact, the opulence of a house is often referred to in terms of the number of such ritual centers it possesses. Most houses are of wattle and daub construction, but the shrine rooms of the more wealthy are walled with stone. Poorer families imitate the rich by applying pottery plaques to their shrine walls. . . .

The focal point of the shrine is a box or chest which is built into the wall. In this chest are kept the many charms and magical potions without which no native believes he could live. These preparations are secured from a variety of specialized practitioners. The most powerful of these are the medicine men, whose assistance must be rewarded with substantial gifts. However, the medicine men do not provide the curative potions for their clients, but decide what the ingredients should be and then write them down in an ancient and secret language. This writing is understood only by the medicine men and by the herbalists who, for another gift, provide the required charm.

The charm is not disposed of after it has served its purpose, but is placed in the charm-box of the household shrine. As these magical materials are specific for certain ills, and the real or imagined maladies of the people are many, the charm-box is usually full to overflowing. The magical packets are so numerous that people forget what their purposes were and fear to use them again. While the natives are very vague on this point, we can only assume that the idea in retaining all the old magical materials is that their presence in the charm-box, before which the body rituals are conducted, will in some way protect the worshipper.

Beneath the charm-box is a small font. Each day every member of the family, in succession, enters the shrine room, bows his head before the charm-box, mingles different sorts of holy water in the font, and proceeds with a brief rite of ablution. The holy waters are secured from the Water Temple of the community, where the priests conduct elaborate ceremonies to make the liquid ritually pure.

In the hierarchy of magical practitioners, and below the medicine men in prestige, are specialists whose designation is best translated "holy-mouth-men." The Nacirema have an almost pathological horror of and fascination with the mouth, the condition of which is believed to have a supernatural influence on all social relationships. Were it not for the rituals of the mouth, they believe that their teeth would fall out, their gums bleed, their jaws shrink, their friends desert them, and their lovers reject them. . . .

The daily body ritual performed by everyone includes a mouth-rite. Despite the fact that these people are so punctilious about care of the mouth, this rite involves a practice which strikes the uninitiated stranger as revolting. It was reported to me that the ritual consists of inserting a small bundle of hog hairs into the mouth, along with certain magical powders, and then moving the bundle in a highly formalized series of gestures.

In addition to the private mouth-rite, the people seek out a holy-mouth-man once or twice a year. These practitioners have an impressive set of paraphernalia, consisting of a variety of augers, awls, probes, and prods. The use of these objects in the exorcism of the evils of the mouth involves almost unbelievable ritual torture of the client. The holy-mouth-man opens the client's mouth and, using the above mentioned tools, enlarges any holes which decay may have created in the teeth. Magical materials are put into these holes. If there are no naturally occurring holes in the teeth, large sections of one or more teeth are gouged out so that the supernatural substance can be applied. In the client's view, the purpose of these ministrations is to arrest decay and to draw friends. The extremely sacred and traditional character of the rite is evident in the fact that the natives return to the holy-mouth-men year after year, despite the fact that their teeth continue to decay. . . .

The medicine men have an imposing temple, or *latipso*, in every community of any size. The more elaborate ceremonies required to treat very sick patients can only be performed at this temple. These ceremonies involve not only the thaumaturge but a permanent group of vestal maidens who move sedately about the temple chambers in distinctive costume and headdress. . . .

No matter how ill the supplicant or how grave the emergency, the guardians of many temples will not admit a client if he cannot give a rich gift to the custodian. Even after one has gained admission and survived the ceremonies, the guardians will not permit the neophyte to leave until he makes still another gift.

The supplicant entering the temple is first stripped of all his or her clothes. In every-day life the Nacirema avoids exposure of his body and its natural functions. Bathing and excretory acts are performed only in the secrecy of the household shrine, where they are ritualized as part of the body-rites. Psychological shock results from the fact that body secrecy is suddenly lost upon entry into the *latipso*. A man, whose own wife has never seen him in an excretory act, suddenly finds himself naked and assisted by a vestal maiden while he performs his natural functions into a sacred vessel. This sort of ceremonial treatment is necessitated by the fact that the excreta are used by a diviner to ascertain the course and nature of the client's sickness. Female clients, on the other hand, find their naked bodies are subjected to the scrutiny, manipulation and prodding of the medicine men.

Few supplicants in the temple are well enough to do anything but lie on their hard beds. The daily ceremonies, like the rites of the holy-mouth-men, involve discomfort and torture. With ritual precision, the vestals awaken their miserable charges each dawn and roll them about on their beds of pain while performing ablutions, in the formal movements of which the maidens are highly trained. At other times they insert magic wands in the supplicant's mouth or force him to eat substances which are supposed to be healing. From time to time the medicine men come to their clients and jab magically treated needles into their flesh. The fact that these temple ceremonies may not cure, and may even kill the neophyte in no way decreases the people's faith in the medicine men.

There remains one other kind of practitioner, known as a "listener." This witch-doctor has the power to exorcise the devils that lodge in the heads of people who have been bewitched. The Nacirema believe that parents bewitch their own children. Mothers are particularly suspected of putting a curse on children while teaching them the secret body rituals. The counter-magic of the witch-doctor is unusual in its lack of ritual. The patient simply tells the "listener" all his troubles and fears, beginning with the earliest difficulties he can remember. The memory displayed by the Nacirema in these exorcism sessions is truly remarkable. It is not uncommon for the patient to bemoan the rejection he felt upon being weaned as a babe, and a few individuals even see their troubles going back to the traumatic effects of their own birth. . . .

Reference has already been made to the fact that excretory functions are ritualized, routinized, and relegated to secrecy. Natural reproductive functions are similarly distorted. Intercourse is taboo as a topic and scheduled as an act. Efforts are made to avoid pregnancy by the use of magical materials or by limiting intercourse to certain phases of the moon. Conception is actually very infrequent. When pregnant, women dress so as to hide their condition. Parturition takes place in secret, without friends or relatives to assist, and the majority of women do not nurse their infants. . . .

Becoming a social being

CHAPTER SIX
SOCIALIZATION

From time to time the media report tragic cases of children found in solitary confinement in attics, basements, or closets after years of imprisonment by deranged parents or guardians. These *feral* children (literally: "untamed") are of special importance to sociology because they provide a basis for judging the importance of learning through social interaction in the process of becoming human. Deprived of all but the most trivial and fleeting contact with others, extremely neglected children have only their genetic resources to draw upon in order to develop. When found, they show only superficial signs of belonging to the human species. Although some have been in their late teens when discovered, they can merely grunt, are indifferent to their surroundings, make no effort to control bowel and bladder functions, and frequently spend their time rocking rhythmically back and forth on their heels. Attempts to treat these children have had just enough success to show that their condition is not the result of mental deficiency, but of isolation. Not one has ever become normal, but those who survive have shown considerable ability to learn (Davis, 1940, 1947, 1948–1949).

What is socialization?

In the past, many social scientists believed that much of human behavior could be attributed to inherited traits. Even today, when sociologists are generally opposed to seeing behavior as genetically determined and emphasize the influence of *environment*, there are those who give *heredity* the larger role in shaping our behavior. Depending on one's stance in this "nature-versus-nurture" controversy—that is, whether human behavior is seen as relatively fixed or as open to change—certain political actions taken to equalize opportunity in jobs, education, and so on may seem more or less worthwhile.

This chapter will emphasize the part played by the environment. What the unfortunate children in the opening example demonstrate is that *humans learn to be human.* Biological factors set important limits and provide certain initial capacities. But becoming a human being requires a social and cultural process of intensive communication and interaction between the developing child and others—a process of emotional, physical, and cognitive stimulation (Goodman, 1981).

The process through which human beings learn to be human is called *socialization*. Through it, a society teaches its children very early what to respect and what to scorn, how to use tools such as eating utensils and pencils, when it is acceptable to be aggressive or submissive, and countless other role behaviors. Thus the social script and its meanings are passed along from one generation to the next, allowing new members to take their parts in the drama of social life and ensuring the continuation of the society as a whole—a mechanism known as *social reproduction*.

Socialization thus ensures the continuation of the class structure and of subcultures within the larger society. In any society, and especially in a large, heterogeneous one like that of the United States, there is not one social script but many. The norms and values to which a particular child is socialized depend on the family's socioeconomic status, religious affiliation, and ethnic identity. In a working-class family, for example, a child may be expected to be neat, obedient, and respectful; transgressions are likely to meet with physical punishment. A middle-class family may concentrate instead on inculcating self-control and initiative by means of verbal and psychological punishments (Belkin and Goodman, 1980, pp. 88–89).

As we learn proper role behavior, we also internalize society's norms and values so thoroughly that they become *our* norms and values; we feel guilty when we violate them. Through *internalization*, we learn to regulate our own behavior. Thus, from the point of view of the society, socialization is an important means of *social control* (see Chapter 4). Society could not possibly police all its members to secure adherence to its standards. (And who would police the police?) One solution to this problem is socialization; by internalizing society's standards, individuals come to conform most of the time and more or less willingly and automatically to societal norms.

Yet another aspect of socialization—and a rather far-reaching one—is the creation of the individual *self*. It is through our social interaction, guided by the roles into which we are socialized, that we develop and maintain a coherent sense of our inner being—of who and what we are. As Murry Webster writes, "Man creates culture. . . . But culture also creates man" (1975, p. 187)—and, we might add, woman.

Theoretical perspectives

There are several perspectives on the dynamic process by which childhood socialization takes place and shapes the developing person. One perspective, the psychoanalytic view first put forward by Sigmund Freud, sees socialization as a constant struggle between society, demanding "civilized" behavior, and the child, dominated by strong, asocial sexual and aggressive drives. As these conflicts are resolved in early childhood, personality characteristics or *traits* are formed that endure throughout life. Erik Erikson's neo-Freudian perspective combines psychoanalytic and anthropological views in a theory that focuses on the *self* or *ego* as a mediator between the individual and society.

A second perspective is that of Jean Piaget, whose discovery that mental development takes place in stages led to the realization that socialization, which depends on the ability to learn and understand, must be related to a child's level of cognitive development in order to be successful. A third perspective, in contrast, envisions a self that is the product of social interaction and that may change throughout life as the social context changes. This is the sociological view put forward by George Herbert Mead.

FREUD: THE PSYCHOANALYTIC VIEW

Sigmund Freud (1856–1939), who developed the first systematic psychoanalytic theory, argued that the individual personality develops in a fixed series of psychosexual stages. In the first or *oral* stage, the child seeks satisfaction in oral gratifications such as sucking and biting. In the second or *anal* stage, the familiar battles over toilet training occur. And in the third or *phallic* stage, what Freud called the *oedipal* struggle occurs: the child enters into a hostile rivalry with the same-sex parent for the sexual attentions of the opposite-sex parent. How well the child internalizes social norms and controls (that is, incorporates them as part of his or her own value system) depends in part on the severity with which parents repress attempts at gratification. Much

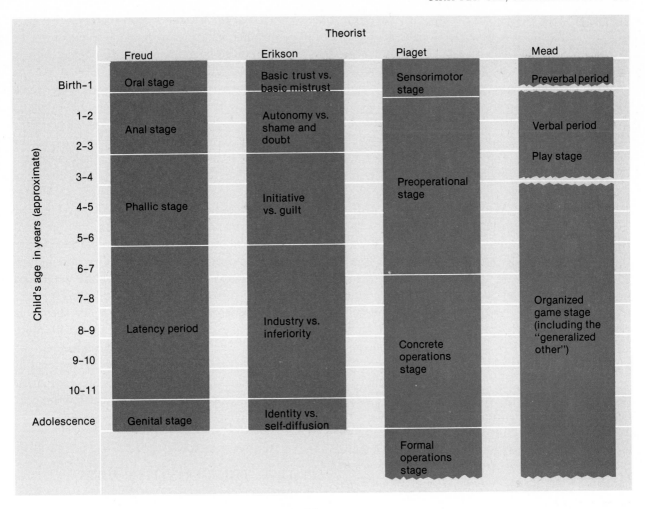

Theorist

	Freud	Erikson	Piaget	Mead
Birth–1	Oral stage	Basic trust vs. basic mistrust	Sensorimotor stage	Preverbal period
1–2	Anal stage	Autonomy vs. shame and doubt		Verbal period
2–3				Play stage
3–4	Phallic stage	Initiative vs. guilt	Preoperational stage	
4–5				
5–6				
6–7	Latency period	Industry vs. inferiority		Organized game stage (including the "generalized other")
7–8				
8–9			Concrete operations stage	
9–10				
10–11				
Adolescence	Genital stage	Identity vs. self-diffusion		
			Formal operations stage	

(left axis label: Child's age in years (approximate))

FIGURE 6.1

This table summarizes the various stages of childhood personality development formulated by four major theorists whose work is discussed in this chapter. The label given to each stage and the approximate age at which each stage occurs are shown for quick reference and comparison. (Note that the divisions between Mead's stages are especially flexible.)

that guide the parent. During the *latency* stage, which begins at about age five, sexual desires recede in importance as the child strives to learn about the world and to acquire new skills. When sexual interest reappears in adolescence and beyond, the individual has reached the *genital* stage and, ideally, the capacity for a mature sharing of sexual pleasure.

In Freud's view, the child's personality is like a battleground: the *superego*, or conscience (which represents an internalization of societal standards through the parents, often in crude, oversimplified form), strives to quell the *id*—the innate part of the personality dominated by the drive for pleasure and by inborn sexual and aggressive urges. Between these antagonists stands the *ego*, the rational part of the personality, processing information obtained from the outside world and attempting to satisfy the id in ways acceptable to society. How successfully the ego performs its task of mediation, and what behavioral traits develop in conse-

also depends on the degree to which the child is able to identify successfully with the same-sex parent in the phallic stage. In normal development, the child gives up the idea of actually possessing the opposite-sex parent, eventually choosing the next best thing to winning—namely, identifying with the winner. The child is then in a position to internalize the norms and values

quence, may depend in part on the ways parents deal with the child in the various developmental stages—whether, for example, they encourage or punish aggression; demand high achievement or accept the child unquestioningly; punish overt sexual behavior or deal with it in a relaxed way.

Much in Freud's theory has been of interest to sociologists: it highlights the importance of the social context—particularly the family—on the development of the individual. Since it offers insight into some possible causes of such behavior as violence, delinquency, and achievement striving, it has sparked sociological research into the child-rearing practices of various classes, religious groups, and ethnic groups. But Freud's belief that the psychosexual stages and the oedipal crisis are universals—fixed, inborn developmental patterns—has been questioned. Most modern approaches acknowledge that there is no single, inevitable, quasi-genetic sequence in child development. Nor are the basic factors that Freud assumed to be operating comparable from society to society, as anthropological data show.

Societies vary widely in their ways of dealing with such child-rearing issues as feeding (on schedule? on demand? when parent prefers?), weaning (sudden or gradual? at six months or four years?), obedience and independence training, and toilet training. Moreover, the family constellation itself varies. Not all societies have the authoritarian *paterfamilias* of Freud's mid-Victorian Europe. In fact, there are cultures in which the father is not directly responsible for control and punishment at all; these tasks are carried out by other relatives. Even *modal personality* (the ideal and to some extent typical personality) varies among societies, from the rather tightly controlled, high-achieving, authority-respecting middle-class male of Freud's society to the suspicious, maritally untrustworthy, dour, jealous, resentful Doebu of New Guinea (Benedict, 1934).

Erikson's adaptation

Erik Erikson, a neo-Freudian who was influenced by the anthropological perspective on socialization, developed a theory that was general enough to allow for a great variety of socialization patterns. His view is partly psychoanalytic; like the Freudian view, it is based on quasi-genetic unfolding of the personality through a series of fixed stages. But it also reflects sociological concerns in its focus on the ego as a mediator *between the individual and the society*. Erikson believed that part of normal personality growth is "a readiness to be driven toward, to be aware of, and to interact with, a widening social radius."

In each stage of life the ego is required to develop a new capacity in its interpersonal dealings. For example, the infant must develop the capacity for "basic trust" before moving on to the next stage in the sequence of development; if the infant does not, "basic mistrust" will prevent mastering the central task of the next stage, "autonomy versus shame and doubt" (see Figure 6.1). Erikson also believed that the larger social order is framed to harmonize with the individual developmental stages: it has a tendency to "meet and invite" the ego's developmental outreaching and to attempt to "safeguard and to encourage the proper rate and proper sequence of" the ego's unfolding (1968, p. 270).

Finally, Erikson differed with Freud's theory in emphasizing the continuing nature of socialization. Unlike Freud, who believed that most of the important turning points for the personality were encountered in childhood, Erikson saw such crises as continuing through life. According to his theory, socialization goes on even in old age.

PIAGET: THE COGNITIVE VIEW

Years of research demonstrated to the Swiss psychologist Jean Piaget (1950, 1962, 1968) that intellectual growth is, in part, a programmed process that occurs in a series of distinct stages. Since successful socialization depends on a child's ability to understand, the kind of socialization that can take effect at any given age will depend on the stage of cognitive maturation.

Piaget has identified four stages of human cognitive development. During the *sensorimotor stage* (birth to about eighteen months), children practice perfecting their contact with the objects around them. For example, an infant will bounce in her crib in order to move a toy that is attached. During the *preoperational stage* (about eighteen months to seven years), developing language abilities permit the child to communicate with others and to engage in representational thought. Children also demonstrate *egocentrism* early in this period: that is, they do not make a distinction between their own perceptions, thoughts, needs, and feelings and those of others; they do not realize there are points of view different from their own. This may account for some of the difficulty parents have trying to teach a small child to share toys or to allow another child to "go first."

When children reach the stage of *concrete operations* (from about seven years to about twelve years of age), they are able to take other people's points of view into consideration. They also begin to understand the complex relationships among concrete objects. At this stage, they can understand the principle of conservation: that is, they recognize that liquids and solids can change in shape without changing volume and mass.

In the stage of *formal operations* (from about twelve on), adolescents begin to think abstractly. They are now capable of considering all the possible ways a particular problem might be solved and the possible forms a particular solution might assume.

It is in these last two stages—concrete and formal operations—that Piaget emphasizes the importance of inner maturational factors as distinct from the influence of the environment. In his view, although the exact age at which the individual traverses these stages varies from child to child and from society to society, the maturational *sequence* itself is universal and invariant: children cannot be taught formal logic or formal cognitive techniques until they have developed the necessary mental structures.

Piaget's approach focuses primarily on mental processes as they relate to the physical world; but it also sheds light on social dealings. For example, during the preoperational stage the child learns to use language and thus to communicate with others, discovering what they approve and disapprove of. During the stage of concrete operations, the child learns that there are viewpoints other than his or her own. Thus, some of Piaget's insights into cognitive development complement the sociological insights of Cooley and Mead.

MEAD: A SOCIOLOGICAL VIEW

A fully sociological view of childhood socialization was developed by the social philosopher George Herbert Mead. He took as a point of departure the idea of his predecessor Charles Horton Cooley that the self is not conceived in isolation and then guided out into social interaction; rather, it is a product of social interaction to begin with. According to Cooley (1902), the image one has of oneself is a view of the combined reflections of a number of mirrors, and these mirrors are the eyes of other people. Hence, we have what Cooley called a *looking-glass self*: we see ourselves as we think others see us. Cooley divided the looking-glass self into three components: (1) our notion of how we appear to others; (2) our notion of how others judge that appearance; and (3) some sort of self-judgment, which again is derived from the presumed judgments of others. These others who are important to us have been called variously *reference groups* or *reference others*. They are individuals and groups (even, on occasion, abstract ideas, such as justice, liberty, freedom, and so on), taken into account in our thinking and acting. This concept is more fully explicated in Chapter 8. The important point here is that these others permit us to view ourselves from the "outside." They allow us to "take the role of the other" and to reflect on our own behavior—the essence of the looking-glass self. What Mead added to Cooley's basic perspective was an insight into the actual development of the social self, which begins in childhood.

Developing the social self

In Mead's view (1934), the child's development can be divided into two general periods: *preverbal* and *verbal*. (Though Mead himself did not make this division explicit, it is consistent with his view and provides a useful basis for discussion.) In the preverbal period, the child begins to interact with others. The first step is to differentiate between the self and what is not the self (for example, crib, father, rattle). Though his or her ability to use language is still rudimentary, the child begins to communicate with others, primarily through gestures such as smiles and scowls; from the reactions of others, the child begins to learn what wins approval and what does not. This early communication makes it possible for the child to begin to internalize the parents' standards and consequently to begin to make self-evaluations.

Gradually the child learns to speak and enters the verbal stage. In this period, not only a vocabulary and grammar, but also a whole new dimension of social meaning, are mastered. (We discussed the importance of language as a conveyor of culture in Chapter 5.) The child's interactions with others tend to be mediated more and more by symbols such as words; they tend to

BEHAVIORAL LEARNING THEORIES AND SOCIALIZATION

An eight-month-old baby is feeding herself. She munches happily on a piece of cheese and gnaws on a ripe banana. Her mother shows her approval by smiling and talking to the baby. Suddenly, the child throws a handful of scrambled eggs on the floor. She laughs heartily. Her mother, taken with her baby's delight, laughs too. The little girl reaches for another fistful of eggs and throws them at her mother—who frowns and says firmly, "No." Eventually, if the mother perseveres, commending her child for not throwing food and showing disapproval when she does, the child will learn not to throw her food.

Learning theorists believe that much behavior is learned through this kind of *reinforcement*—the process by which the tendency toward desired behavior is strengthened by becoming associated with rewards (such as the mother's smile) and the tendency toward the behavior *not* desired is made less strong by becoming associated with punishments (such as the mother's frown and disapproving comments). Learning theorists stress the importance of early learning, since people tend to remember what happens *first* in a chain of events (this is called the *primacy effect*). In their view, if parents want to instill certain behaviors in their children, they should try to provide early, positive experiences in the desired areas. B. F. Skinner, the foremost American behaviorist, has also

found that using an intermittent reinforcement schedule (that is, rewarding behavior only occasionally) yields better results than giving rewards for each desired behavior (Skinner, 1971). Thus parents should reward desired behavior, but not each time it occurs. This is particularly true for the learning of morals and ethics. Moral development is most advanced in children whose parents *rarely* punish them, but reserve the right to do so (Hoffman and Saltzstein, 1967).

A second form of learning that behaviorists believe to be important is *modeling*, or *imitation*. Children act the way they see (or have seen) another person act in a similar situation. For example, one of the classic studies of the role of imitation in socialization (Sears, Maccoby, and Levin, 1957) found that parents' nonaggressive responses to their children's aggressive behavior tended to diminish aggressive behavior among children, whereas parents' aggressive responses (such as spanking) increased children's aggressive behavior. Punishing aggression can itself be an act of aggression and thus provide a model for aggression. Because parents are much more powerful than their children, their aggression against their offspring suppresses the children's aggression in the short run, but also shows the children that aggressive behavior "works."

be guided more and more by understandings shared with others, which are conveyed through symbols and which reflect the world view of the culture in which the child happens to live. Through symbols, the child becomes a truly social self.

Though the verbal period is actually a long and complex continuum, Mead divided it into two stages. In the first, the *play stage*, the child actually begins playing roles (mother, mail carrier, grocery clerk, and so on). More important, the child begins to act out roles in reciprocal or interlocking sets. For example, a little girl may pretend to be an adult mailing a letter. Then she becomes the letter carrier, taking the letter from herself and delivering it to the addressee. Then she becomes the addressee, opening her mailbox and expressing delight over receiving this fine letter from herself. Such rudimentary reflexive play, in which activities are directed back toward the self, is *taking the role of the other*. To Mead, it is crucial to the development of the self, since it prepares children to assume reciprocal roles and gives them practice in seeing themselves as objects in the eyes of others. Goffman (1961, 1967) ingeniously

analyzes this interaction process, though his concern is with a later stage of the life cycle (adolescence and adulthood).

In the next stage, which Mead called the *organized game stage*, the child progresses from the practicing of successions of roles to actual participation in a network of several roles. The child now develops an understanding of the relationship among all the roles and sees himself or herself as a part of that relationship. To illustrate this mental operation, Mead used the metaphor of a baseball game, in which every player must constantly keep in mind not only his or her own role but also those of all the other players and how they work together. For example, if there is a runner on first base and one out, the player at second base must be ready, in case of a ground ball to shortstop, to receive a throw from the shortstop and then to relay the throw to first base for a possible double play.

Mead's metaphor of this stage as an organized game is doubly apt in that children at this stage do spend significant amounts of time participating in just such activities. This is the central means by which they learn

This child, acting out her perception of the role of mother, is exhibiting the behavior that characterizes Mead's *play stage*. In this stage, children learn about various roles through imitation. (© James R. Holland/Stock, Boston)

and stable social self, made up of the standards of the community. The incorporation of this *generalized other* helps to ensure social control. By assimilating the standards of the community (its norms and values), the individual voluntarily behaves in accordance with them.

The hypotheses of Cooley and Mead have received considerable support from research (Rosenberg, 1979). Of particular interest are the studies of Miyamoto and Dornbusch (1956), Moore (1964), and Quarantelli and Cooper (1966), in all of which subjects were asked first to rate themselves on certain personal characteristics and then to rate themselves as they thought spouses, people in a specific group, and "most people" would rate them. The findings, in general, are that people's self-images are extremely close to what they *perceive* are the images of themselves held by other people, and particularly by "most people," a category that would be comparable to Mead's "generalized other."

The "I" and the "me"

A cursory glance at Mead's theory of the development of the social self might lead one to believe that he saw human beings as nothing more than robots programmed with social norms—a view that would fail to account for the phenomenon of social change. Nothing could have been further from Mead's mind. Elsewhere in his writings, he put forth a theory that could account for change and for the combination of individualism and conformity in human beings. He postulated that the self is actually made up of two reciprocally influential forces. One is the *"me,"* made up of internalized social roles and eventually of the generalized other, through the process described above. This "me" stands for stability and social control. Together with the "me" stands the *"I,"* the inner and relatively unfathomable aspect of the self—spontaneous, creative, and critical. Because the "I," according to Mead, is "given"—not, like the "me," formed by the society—the "I" is capable of talking back to the society (Pfuetze, 1961, p. 98) and of deviating from its norms. Mead did not delve into whether the "I" was of divine or genetic origin. Instead, he simply offered this concept as a way of accounting for the obvious interaction, in society as well as in the individual, between the forces of stability and conformity and those of change and creativity.

a new fact of social life: that they are one part of an organized social structure, which exists outside themselves. This understanding helps them, in turn, to organize their inner selves.

Following this basic development—learning to take the viewpoint of specific others in a role system—the child begins to perceive and internalize a more generalized influence, the *rules* that govern behavior within these role systems. Thus the child acquires an organized

SUCCESSFUL SOCIALIZATION: VIEWS OF THE SELF

The Freudian core personality

According to Freud, the major developmental crisis of childhood passes with successful resolution of the Oedipus conflict; the child's personality is by then rather firmly established. What Freud assumed is that underneath the behavior of each individual there is a unified "core" which stays virtually the same throughout life. The people with whom the individual interacts sense that he or she conforms to their expectations in a consistent way. The individual is likely to feel that he or she has an inner being that somehow endures—a being that encompasses memories, perceptions, values, and desires. This core, which the individual senses internally as *self* and others sense as *personality*, is often referred to as an *identity*.

Personality is sometimes described in terms of specific, relatively invariant *traits*. One diagnostic tool based on this Freudian assumption of fixed identity is a widely used psychological test, the Minnesota Multiphasic Personality Inventory (MMPI). A subject is asked to answer "true" or "false" to hundreds of self-descriptive statements (for example, "I usually feel nervous before going to a party," "I have never cheated on an examination," "A lot of people are out to get me"). The responses are interpreted in the form of a personality profile in which the subject is rated according to a number of personal characteristics. This testing procedure reflects a longstanding and dearly held assumption of Western culture: that identity is stable and behavior guided by relatively unchanging personality traits.

The situational self

Many sociologists take a different view. They believe that an individual's behavior, far from being dictated by internal traits, is largely determined by the particular role being enacted at the moment, the context in which it is being enacted, and the way the person has been taught to enact the role (for example, see Goffman, 1969). Mead posited a fixed sequence of stages in the development of the social self. But unlike Freud, he introduced a relatively high degree of indeterminacy and open-endedness; he did not predict any resolution or termination point of development at or after the final developmental stage of childhood. In fact, since the social setting is presumably in a process of continuous change—not only during childhood but also afterward—it is possible to infer that Mead believed the "generalized other" (as internalized in the self) would change continuously as well. In other words, both *personality*—the individual as perceived by others—and the *self*—the individual as perceived by himself or herself—are socially defined and can change to a large extent with the situation. And this flexibility is not inherently pathological (Gergen, 1971).

To present the issue in sharp focus, Orville G. Brim, Jr., suggested a consideration of the situational self as follows:

The personality consists entirely of the learned repertoire of roles. . . . There is nothing else. There is no "core" personality underneath the behavior and feelings: There is no "central" monolithic self which lies beneath its various external manifestations.

But, one says, what then of the self? The answer is that the "self" is a composite of many selves, each of them consisting of a set of self-perceptions which are specific to one or another major role, specific to the expectations of one or another significant reference group. (1960, p. 141)

Status/role rather than self

Brim's hypothesis that the "self" varies with the situation is supported by a number of sociological research studies. For example, Kuhn and McPartland (1954) found that when subjects were asked to make twenty statements in reply to the question, "Who are you?" their first responses were stated as statuses: "I am an insurance adjuster," "I am a woman," "I am a Protestant" (see Figure 6.2). Thus, the key elements of self seem to be statuses rather than traits. Yarrow, Campbell, and Burton (1968) asked a number of mothers to rate their nursery-school children on levels of dependency and aggression; they then asked the children's teachers to do the same. When the two sets of scores for any one child were compared, the agreement between mother's and teacher's scores of the child's traits were extremely low, whereas the agreement between different teachers' ratings of the same child was somewhat higher. In sum, it appears that a child's level of dependency or aggression is less a stable trait, carried over from home to school, than an adjustment to the role requirements of either "son/daughter" or "pupil."

If the adjustment to varying roles explains the dif-

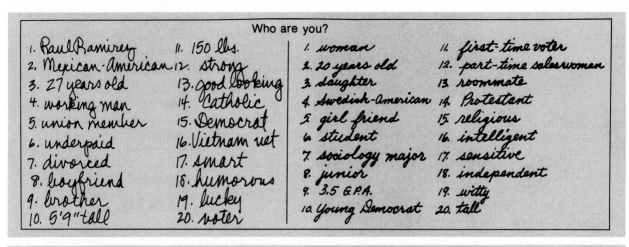

Who are you?

1. Paul Ramirez	11. 150 lbs.	1. woman	11. first-time voter
2. Mexican-American	12. strong	2. 20 years old	12. part-time saleswoman
3. 27 years old	13. good looking	3. daughter	13. roommate
4. working man	14. Catholic	4. Swedish-American	14. Protestant
5. union member	15. Democrat	5. girl friend	15. religious
6. underpaid	16. Vietnam vet	6. student	16. intelligent
7. divorced	17. smart	7. sociology major	17. sensitive
8. boyfriend	18. humorous	8. junior	18. independent
9. brother	19. lucky	9. 3.5 G.P.A.	19. witty
10. 5'9" tall	20. voter	10. young Democrat	20. tall

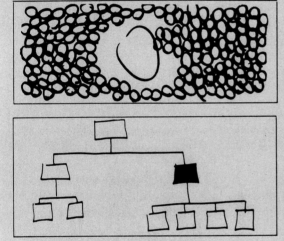

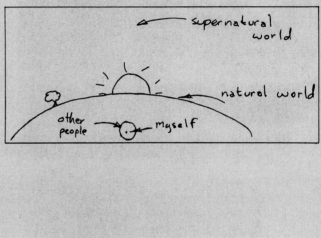

FIGURE 6.2

Top: Two sample Twenty Statements Tests (TST). Can you detect any patterns? How are your own replies similar to or different from these hypothetical answers? *Bottom:* Drawings, like verbal responses on the TST, can be used to express a person's self-identity.

ferences between the ratings of parent and teacher, what might account for the fact that different teachers' ratings of the same pupil were not identical? This disparity suggests that behavior is specific not only to the role being enacted, but also to the person with whom one is dealing at the particular moment of role enactment (Brim, 1960, pp. 132–133). A role is not a script but part of a reciprocal relation—role set (Merton, 1957) or role sector (Gross, Mason, and McEachern, 1958)—so the enactors of the other roles affect one's "performance."

If behavior is governed by situations rather than enduring personality traits, then socialization should ideally prepare the individual to perform adequately in a wide range of different roles (child, student, friend, sister, girlfriend, wife, worker, parent) and with different role partners. A truly successful socialization will, paradoxically, produce a person who is "inconsistent"—flexible enough to meet the varying demands of different roles and role partners. Failure of the socialization process will produce a person who is too "consistent"—a man who does not know how to behave differently with his children and his poker buddies, or a woman who does not know how to switch from her professional role as psychiatrist to her domestic role as wife.

Difficulty in adapting to a new role may stem from a variety of factors (Brim, 1960, pp. 143–147)—accidental or deliberate, located in the individual or in those around him or her—that cause the person to be unaware or uncertain of what is expected in a particular situation. Appropriate role models may not have been available; there may be lack of motivation for a specific role (for example, the bored and irritable woman who has quit her job to stay home with her children only because her husband pressured her to do so); failure may stem from lack of ability (as in the case of a student of moderate ability enrolled in an extremely high-level, academically demanding university).

It is, of course, impossible to prove that we behave in a given way because of our "traits" or because of the situation in which we find ourselves. In fact, both points of view—psychoanalytic and sociological—offer valuable insights. However, sociologists generally believe that society and the relevant social context are more potent determiners of behavior than are the enduring traits that emerge from a universal genetic-maturational process. Both perspectives would agree that the family is the crucial influence on the developing individual. But it is not the only important shaping agent: we must consider as well the impact of the school, the peer group, and the media.

Agents of socialization in childhood

The growing child comes into contact with an increasing number of institutions. Each of them, by teaching the child new statuses and roles, places its own stamp on the child's self; the child, in turn, impresses his or her stamp on them, though to a much more limited extent.

In this section we will discuss the effects of four important *agents of socialization* in American society: family, peer group, school, and the mass media, especially television. In societies with no formal educational system or mass media, other agents serve important roles; in our own society, too, other institutions, such as day-care centers and religious organizations, affect children's socialization. But the four selected for discussion here are the most pervasive and hence the most influential in modern industrialized societies.

PRIMARY-GROUP AGENTS

A primary group, as we saw in Chapter 4, is a small, face-to-face group in which the individual is deeply involved and with which he or she strongly identifies. The child's first primary group is, of course, the family; the second is the peer group.

The family

Unlike other agents, the family deliberately aims at socializing the child; and, being small and dependent, the child is profoundly affected. Also important is the fact that the family's socialization efforts are intertwined with the gratifications the family provides for the child—the satisfaction of physical and emotional needs. The child cannot buy half the package. In the process of receiving nurture, love, and companionship from parents, the child also unwittingly incorporates their norms, values, attitudes—often even their most trivial habits. A young woman may be aware that her political attitudes were inculcated by her parents, but she may be surprised to find herself using with her own child the same baby talk her mother used with her—and even more surprised to hear her child using this same baby talk with a puppy.

One of the fundamental (though involuntary) ways in which the family socializes the child is simply by "placing" the child in the community. "From the moment of his birth, before he has had the opportunity to take any actions of his own, the child is located in society—as middle class or working class, child of a teacher or truck driver, Christian or Jew, member of a dominant or a subordinate ethnic group, member of a family respected or scorned by neighbors" (Elkin and Handel, 1978, p. 22). These designations based on family membership will contribute considerably to the molding of the self.

Another important influence exerted by the family derives from opportunities for practice in group functioning. Through the highly charged *power* and *affective* (emotional) dynamics among family members (see Chapter 17), the child receives the first and most potent lessons in the mechanics of role interaction—com-

The family is the most powerful agent of child-hood socialization. Both parents profoundly affect the child's self-image, values, role behavior, and view of the world. (Hella Hammid/Photo Researchers, Inc.)

last few decades, sociological research (for example, Orlansky, 1949; Lindesmith and Strauss, 1950; Sewell, 1952–1953; Zigler and Child, 1969; Danziger, 1971) has called into question the psychoanalytic assumption that parents determine the child's personality through the specific way in which they feed, wean, and toilet train, among other things. However, there is still little question that the parents' general attitude toward the child is a primary component of his or her self-image and that their attitude toward the world beyond the child is a primary component of his or her image of reality.

Traditionally, the mother has provided the child's first experience of deep intimacy, an introduction to moral standards (what is "naughty" and what is "nice"), and, through her acceptance or rejection, the basis of the child's self-image—whether *he* or *she* is

petition and cooperation, intimacy and distance, relaxation and tension. Of course, not all families teach the same lessons in the same ways. Different social classes and ethnic groups tend to have different child-rearing styles, which produce markedly different individuals. Melvin Kohn (1969) has found that the parent-child relationships characteristic of a particular social class lead to certain behavioral styles that are functional for particular occupations of adults in that class.

Finally, family socialization has a tremendous impact on the child's developing self-image. Within the

naughty or nice. In our society the father's role in the socialization of the young child has received less attention (Nash, 1973). Certainly, however, the traditional father does contribute to socialization by working to loosen the child's dependence on the mother and to broaden his or her experience by drawing attention to both the attractions and restrictions of the society at large (Parsons, 1964; Benson, 1968). This strict role division is now breaking down to some degree, and present trends indicate that in the future fathers are likely to have more intimate relationships with their young children (Hamilton, 1977).

A child's siblings are also instrumental in the socialization process (Brim, 1958; Sutton-Smith and Rosenberg, 1970). There is some evidence that the size of the sibling group affects the way parents deal with the child. James Bossard and Eleanor Boll (1966), for example, found that in large families, household tasks were assigned in a regimented fashion, while in small families, "the children were often spared all household chores in the interests of concentrating on their education, outside activities, and social life" (pp. 39–40). Children in small families also tended to rely on their parents for security, whereas those in large families tended to turn to one another for protection and companionship.

In sum, the members of a family have an overwhelming influence on the child's self-concept and social development. Harry Stack Sullivan is believed to have introduced the term *significant others* to denote those whose treatment of a child is particularly instrumental in molding the self-concept. Of all the "significant others" a child eventually acquires, family members are by far the most significant.

The peer group

Powerful as the family is, its influence is to some degree lessened when the child is old enough to enter a circle of friends. This *peer group* differs from the family in that, by definition, its members are of approximately the same age and social status. Furthermore, unlike the family, the peer group makes no deliberate attempt to socialize the child. It is too busy with its own concerns—playing, deciding who is acceptable and who isn't, hanging around, and the like. Nevertheless, the latent (unintended) socializing functions of the peer group are quite important.

Peer-group interaction influences aggressive behavior in childhood. If aggressive behavior is reinforced in a child's peer-group, he or she is likely to repeat it. (Bill MacDonald/IBOL)

By loosening ties to the family, the peer group may prevent the child from being engulfed in the power-based socialization imposed by adults. In a peer group the child has the earliest experiences in negotiating relatively free and egalitarian social relationships. On the street corner and in the playground, the child for the first time has the opportunity both to choose those with whom to interact and to influence the structure of social hierarchy. Furthermore, experiments can be made with different statuses, roles, and behaviors without fear of any punishment as grave as loss of parental love (Goslin, 1965, p. 67). Being leader, follower, rebel, or goody-goody can be tried out to see how these social positions suit the individual child. Much of this experimentation takes place within organized games, which, as we have seen in our discussion of Mead, have the additional socializing value of teaching the child to internalize the peer group's role networks and the rules that govern them.

SECONDARY-GROUP AGENTS

The school

Upon entering school the child encounters yet another new world, with its own socialization program. Whether or not this program conforms to the parents' values, it differs markedly from the intimate and individually oriented curriculum within the home. Launched into school, the child is to some degree launched into society—for better or for worse.

Since education as a social institution will be covered in greater detail in Chapter 18, here only its most obvious socialization functions will be pointed out. First, the school provides a large peer group with which the child is forced to interact for a long period of time each day, and which offers opportunities to practice the relatively open-ended interactions that are the peer group's specialty.

Second, the school enlarges the child's constellation of significant others by adding not only peers but also teachers. Like the parent, the teacher has authority over the child, has something to teach, and, it is hoped, cares about him or her. Hence, like the parent, the teacher may become an extremely powerful role model. Third, the school is responsible for transmitting to the child the content of the dominant culture: its history, its language, its fund of knowledge, and its norms.

Finally, the school is generally the child's first experience with the more formal mechanisms of institutional control. To use a distinction first made by Talcott Parsons (1951), the child tends to be judged by family and peer group according to *particularistic* criteria, such as love, loyalty, and friendship, which depend on the relationship between the child and family or friends. In the institutions in which we participate as older children and adults, however, the criteria against which we are measured are often *universalistic*—general standards of beauty, competence, affability, and other qualities that tend to be more objective. It is

within the classroom that the child is first systematically subjected to universalistic judgments as a preparation for entering the society at large.

Likewise, in the classroom children are taught a number of skills for participating in the more unyielding institutions of the adult world—waiting one's turn, jockeying for attention, competing and dealing with competition, showing up on time, and following instructions. The school, after all, is the first formal organization the child enters (Goslin, 1965, p. 71). And though it is much more flexible than the organizations of adult life, the school definitely aims to teach the child how to navigate in a world of stricter rules, where there is only one way to spell a word, where "up" staircases are only for going up, and where Mother and Father are not there to cushion the blows.

The mass media

The media exert considerable influence on the socialization process, particularly by providing role models, teaching "correct" attitudes and behavior, and widen-

KINDERGARTEN AS BOOT CAMP

One of the primary goals of kindergarten is to teach children the role of student. Most kindergarten teachers enter their classrooms with idealistic programs for instilling in children a sense of pleasant group interaction and with formulas for making school seem like fun. Yet often this aspect of a child's socialization turns into a perpetual series of drills, which provide very little opportunity for self-assertiveness, expressiveness, or creativity—as Harry Gracey points out in his article "Learning the Student Role: Kindergarten as Academic Boot Camp" (1967). Children leave kindergarten knowing how to perform rituals that have no intrinsic meaning to them, how to follow orders unquestioningly, and how to go through routines, all at the whim of a teacher-leader-authority figure. For many children, the kindergarten experience falls far short of fun.

Consider this condensed example from Gracey's article, which describes a kindergarten class conducted by an experienced and widely respected teacher:

The room is light, brightly colored and filled with things adults feel five- and six-year-olds will find interesting and pleasing.

At 12:25 Edith [the teacher] opens the outside door and admits the waiting children. They hang their sweaters on hooks outside the door and then go to the center of the room and arrange themselves in a semicircle on the floor, facing the teacher's chair which she has placed in the center of the floor. . . . The children seem to know just how much of each kind of interaction is permitted—they may greet in a soft voice someone who sits next to them, for example, but may not shout greetings to a friend who sits across the circle, so they confine themselves to waving and remain well within understood limits.

At 12:35 two children arrive. Edith asks them why they are late and then sends them to join the circle on the floor. The other children vie with each other to tell the newcomers what happened to Mark [an absent child]. When this leads to a general disorder Edith asks, "Who has serious time?" The children become quiet and a girl raises her hand. Edith nods and the child gets a Bible and hands it to Edith. She reads the Twenty-third Psalm while the children sit quietly. Edith helps the child in charge begin reciting the Lord's Prayer, the other children follow along for the first unit of sounds, and then trail off as Edith finishes for them. Everyone stands and faces the American flag hung to the right of the door. Edith leads the pledge to the flag, with the children again following the familiar sounds as far as they remember them. . . .

At 1:30 Edith has the children line up in the center of the room; she says, "Table one, line up in front of me," and children ask, "What are we going to do?" Then she moves a few steps to the side and says, "Table two over here, line up next to table one," and more children ask, "What for?" She does this for table three and table four and each time the children ask, "Why, what are we going to do?" When the children are lined up in four lines of five each, spaced so that they are not touching one another, Edith puts on a new record and leads the class in calisthenics, to the accompaniment of the record. The children just jump around every which way in their places instead of doing the exercises, and by the time the record is finished, Edith, the only one following it, seems exhausted. She is apparently adopting the President's new "Physical Fitness" program in her classroom. . . .

Edith says, "Children, down on your blankets." All the class is lying on blankets now. Edith refuses to answer the various questions individual children put to her because, she tells them, "it's rest time now." Instead she talks very softly about what they will do tomorrow. They are going to work with clay, she says. The children lie quietly and listen. (pp. 291–295)

As Gracey points out, a rigid social structure has been forced on the children. The schoolroom has been furnished and designed by adults; activities have been planned, and specific times allotted for each, by adults; and the teacher has set up a reward system of communication, under which a child's questions will be acknowledged only when they are properly posed and do not seem too "childish." Once children master the mandated routines and drills of each kindergarten day, they are free to explore themselves and one another in small, informal friendship groups; but this activity can take place only during the brief "gaps" or "holes" in the daily schedule—and within the constraints of school rules.

Pursuing his parallel with boot camp, Gracey notes that only the children who thoroughly identify with the rules and routines and completely adapt to them are considered good students, or potential little "generals." Those who follow the rules but do not totally identify with them are regarded as adequate students, or potential little "corporals." Those who reject the system are thought to be bad students, or little "privates." (These are often the children considered "rebels" or "disruptive influences," the ones for whom special guidance is sought.)

Thus, Gracey concludes, even kindergarten is a training ground where children are prepared not only for further routinized education, but also for other highly controlled and regulated social settings. Though Gracey illuminates the kindergarten situation by using a military metaphor, that of boot camp, he is also suggesting that such educational routinization primes children for assimilation into a bureaucratic industrial society.

ing the horizon of the growing child. The medium that perhaps exerts the most influence and certainly arouses the most concern is television—and with good reason:

In the decade of the 1950s, television came to dominate the nonsleep, nonschool time of the North American child. One-sixth of all the child's waking hours, from the age of three on, is now typically given over to the magic picture tube. During the first sixteen years of life, the typical child now spends, in total, at least as much time with television as in school. Television is probably the greatest source of common experience in the lives of children, and, along with the home and the school, it has come to play a major part in socializing the child. (Schramm, Lyle, and Parker, 1961, p. 12)

According to many critics, the socializing influence of children's most constant companion, television, is a thoroughly corrupting one. These critics charge that television teaches stereotypic thinking, instills unrealistic expectations of luxury (two-car garages, appliance-filled kitchens) and prestige ("When I grow up, I will be just like Fonzie"), detracts from reading time, provides an endless succession of models for cruel and violent behavior, and generally wastes children's time.

Other observers have pointed out that television can have beneficial effects. It can broaden the child's outlook by introducing roles that may not be available in the immediate environment (Sebald, 1968, pp. 173–174). It can provide memorable, though vicarious, experiences of a broad range of activities and ideas. And carefully designed shows such as *Mister Rogers* and *Sesame Street* can considerably enhance the child's self-concept and intellectual skills.

Furthermore, not all the charges against television have been supported by research. British and American studies (Himmelweit, Oppenheim, and Vince, 1958; Schramm, Lyle, and Parker, 1961) agree that television has little effect on school performance. On the question

In our society, the average sixteen-year-old has spent at least as much time watching television as she has in school. Yet the effect of all this viewing on the individual's socialization is unclear. (Jean-Claude Lejeune/Stock, Boston)

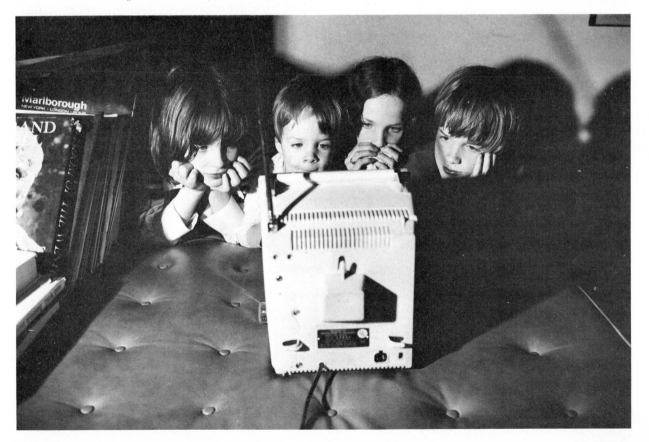

These photographs exemplify the role of reinforcement in imitative learning. This young boy has just seen a film in which a model was praised for exhibiting aggressive behavior toward a Bobo doll. When left alone in a room with a similar doll, the boy imitates with obvious vigor the complex set of behaviors he has just seen. According to Albert Bandura, the boy is behaving as if he himself had earlier experienced the reinforcement of praise.

of whether it cuts down on the reading of books, the evidence is contradictory (Maccoby, 1961). However, it does seem clear that television has displaced movies, radio, and comic books—other forms of "easy" entertainment—in the lives of preadolescents.

As to whether television promotes violence, there are two schools of thought. One holds to the "catharsis" hypothesis: by allowing viewers to participate vicariously in acts of violence and thereby giving some release to their aggressive drives, television actually reduces aggressive behavior (Feshbach, 1955). The other school holds to the modeling hypothesis. This latter theory has been borne out in a number of experiments, including one by Bandura, Ross, and Ross (1961), where a group of preschool children imitated the aggressive behavior of adults they had seen in a movie. Thus it appears that what parents complain of is to some degree true: children *are* eager to emulate the violent activities of their television heroes (Maccoby, 1964, p. 336). However, as Maccoby points out, the aggressive tendencies aroused by television shows are still subject to suppression by parental sanctions.

In regard to the question of why parents feel they must grapple with such an influence instead of solving the problem by turning off the television, there is as yet no answer. Apparently many parents feel they cannot control their children's television viewing; other parents, less concerned, enjoy watching the current shoot-'em-up shows right along with their children (Lyle, 1972).

The puzzle of gender-role socialization

In our discussion of the interactional patterns by which roles are taught and of the socializing agents that teach these roles, we have mentioned certain specific content areas of socialization. Intimacy, morality, achievement striving, competition and cooperation—such are the "lessons" that we learn, either well or poorly. Yet considering the number of socializing processes and agents involved in the teaching of each of these lessons, it is not surprising that it is not at all clear exactly *what* is learned, or how, or from whom. Let us examine, as an example, one specific (and highly controversial) content area of socialization: gender roles. (The terms *sex role* and *gender role* are sometimes used interchangeably. In this text, however, we will use *sex role* to refer to sexual or reproductive behavior. We will use *gender role* to refer to all the other behaviors, not specifically reproductive, that are considered to be appropriate in a particular society for members of each sex.)

Gender-role socialization, although it has been the subject of much investigation and, in recent years, much bitter criticism, is a process about which very little is known. As we are all aware, notions about what is masculine behavior and what is feminine behavior are among the most deep-rooted and persistent in our culture. "Feminine" is thought to mean passive, dependent, emotional, self-sacrificing, and nurturant—as well as (paradoxically) somewhat frivolous and narcissistic. "Masculine" is thought to mean strong, self-reliant, competitive, rational, and unemotional. Children who deviate too far from these stereotypes as the years pass do so at considerable social risk. For a girl to be called a "tomboy" during childhood is not so bad, but if she doesn't conform to the feminine stereotype by adolescence, family members may begin to worry and neighbors to speculate. For boys the rules are stricter. To be considered anything less than masculine, even in childhood, is the greatest insult one can suffer. As Jean Grambs and Walter Waetjen put it, "The most powerful word in the English language is 'sissy'" (1975, p. 115). A slight overstatement, perhaps, but many a boy has had to fight his way out of this category or else slink into semipermanent retirement from equal standing in his peer group.

Current scientific opinion suggests that although there are clear, biologically determined physical differences between males and females, it is unlikely that biological sex dictates complex social and intellectual differences as well. Yet such differences between the sexes apparently do exist. Girls seem to have greater verbal ability; boys excel in visual-spatial ability, at least

Scientific research suggests that gender roles are learned not innate. Boys are often taught that extreme masculinity is the basis for personal success. (© Leonard Freed/ Magnum)

by puberty; boys' mathematical skills increase faster than girls'; and males are more aggressive (Maccoby and Jacklin, 1974). If we assume that these differences are, at least in large part, the result of environmental influences, two important questions remain: What, exactly, are those environmental influences? and How do they operate?

CULTURAL VARIABLES

The most general influences on gender-role socialization are those connected with the culture as a whole: norms and values. The stereotypes outlined above are mosaics of cultural norms and values. And these gender-defining norms and values permeate our language, our literature, our religions, our customs, and our manners, telling us at every turn how boys and girls should behave. And they begin in infancy (Burns, 1976).

Cultural norms and values are not, however, totally uniform. As we have seen, subcultures differ in the values that they place on different things. Lower-class families, for example, are likely to press hardest for their children to conform to stereotypes. Their children are the quickest to learn which toys are for boys and which for girls. Lower-class girls, in particular, seem to be subject to powerful pressure. Not only are they thought to be "unfeminine" if they do not conform, but they may also be seen as threats to their male relatives (Rabban, 1950). Gender roles are also subject to racial differences, sometimes contradicting class differences. According to Joyce Ladner (1971), black girls feel less pressure to play a passive, feminine role. Their mothers often work and are likely to have higher aspirations for their daughters than for their sons (Kandel, 1971).

Norms and values change, not only from subculture to subculture but also from year to year. Recent changes in gender-role expectations are evident in the media. *Glamour* and *Mademoiselle*, two magazines that have specialized in coaching young women in how to catch young (and preferably solvent) men, were by 1980 in competition with magazines like *Working Woman* and *Savvy*, which cater to career women.

Nevertheless, jokes, television programs, advertisements, and textbooks are still rife with stereotypes (Tuchman et al., 1978). In children's books the main character is still usually Johnny, not Jane; and Johnny's teacher is still a woman, his doctor still a man. Advertisers still choose women to sing the praises of dishwashers, men to utter tough-minded judgments on steel-belted tires. Men still go to the "men's room," women to the "*ladies*' room." In Chapter 13 we will discuss these stereotypes in greater detail.

SPECIFIC AGENTS OF GENDER-ROLE SOCIALIZATION

As we pointed out earlier, the most important agents from whom the child learns the norms and values of society are people—the child's "significant others," including family, peer group, and teachers. Consequently, it is important to know who these significant others are, how many of them are present in the child's experience, how they relate to one another, and how they relate to the child. Yet even with this information, we still do not know exactly what parts the different significant others play in the child's gender-role learning.

Take, for example, the influence of the peer group. On the one hand, studies (for example, Hoffman, 1972) indicate that girls are socialized to be more "affiliative" than boys—to depend more on others and to need their approval more. This would suggest that the peer group is more important in female than in male gender-role learning. Yet on the other hand, as Grambs and Waetjen (1975) point out, there are many more male gangs and male sports teams than female gangs and teams. These authors argue that boys, through their involvement in larger and more numerous peer groups, learn "effective ways of competing within the group as well as against other groups" (p. 106); they also develop a wide range of affiliations—a circumstance that allows them to try out assertive and independent behavior without risking the loss of all their friends. The girl, in contrast, is encouraged to rely more on a small group—her immediate family and a few close confidantes—whose disapproval she cannot safely risk by excursions into independence.

Or take the question of same-sex versus cross-sex others in gender-role socialization. On the one hand, the sociological assumption would be that having *cross-sex others* available makes the individual's own gender-role learning easier. Like clay becoming concave when pressed against a convex surface, male learns to be male by interacting with female, and vice versa. On the other hand, if one accepts the social-learning assumption that modeling is a crucial part of the process, then interaction with *same-sex others* would seem to be more important. There is some evidence that modeling is an important factor, if not the only factor, in gender-role learning. Brim (1958) found that children with opposite-sex siblings are more likely to exhibit opposite-sex behavior than children with same-sex siblings, and Hartley (1959) found that if a mother works, or has worked, her daughter is more likely to plan to work when she grows up.

To confuse the issue even further, consider the debate over how children respond to the "clarity" (that is, the closeness to stereotype) of roles as enacted by parents. Some writers (for example, Parsons in Parsons and Bales, 1955) argue that children learn gender roles more easily when their parents' gender roles are clearly differentiated—when the father works, drives the car, and pays the bills, while the mother cooks, cleans, and goes to PTA meetings. Philip Slater (1961), however, finds that stereotyped behavior on the part of adult role models may make it *more* difficult for the child to develop an appropriate gender identification.

THE ACTUAL EFFECTS OF GENDER-ROLE SOCIALIZATION

However gender-role socialization actually operates, it is not always as polarizing as cultural stereotypes would suggest. Of all the differences that are said to exist between male and female, very few have been conclusively validated by research. We do not really know, for example, whether girls are more timid and submissive or whether boys are more dominant and competitive. Furthermore, those purported differences that have been investigated have turned out, as often as not, to be nonexistent. Consider, for example, the following findings:

1. Girls are no more "social" than boys.

2. Girls are no more suggestible than boys.

3. Girls do not lack self-esteem.

4. Boys are no better than girls at tasks that require higher-level cognitive processing and the inhibition of previously learned responses.

5. Boys are no more analytic than girls.

6. Girls do not lack achievement motivation.

7. Girls are not more auditory, boys are not more visual. (Maccoby and Jacklin, 1974)

In sum, there is more sameness between the sexes than we suppose. Perhaps even more important, there is at least as much behavioral variation within each sex as there is between the sexes (Maccoby and Jacklin, 1974). And in view of what we have just seen regarding the number of variables involved in gender-role learning and the number of possible ways in which they can operate, this fact is not surprising. Each child's lesson in gender is a unique blend of different influences—culture and subculture, class and race, parents and peers. The result, predictably, is that each child emerges as his or her own version of male or female—a version more unique than typical.

Childhood socialization: costs and benefits

Looking back over our discussion of childhood socialization, we can see two separate processes at work. The first is the sequence of stages by which the individual becomes a social being: the acquisition of language, the emergence of a self that exists in relationship to significant others, the development of the ability to take the role of the other. Freud saw this process as a battle; the child and society were, in his words, "natural enemies." Socialization was the way the society overcame the child. Yet from the sociologist's perspective, the process is seen as essentially benign: self and society are counterparts.

However, most sociologists understand that the socialization process—by which the society and particular groups work to inculcate in the child their own specific norms and values—is at times less than benign. Tremendous pressures are brought to bear, and sometimes they conflict. Different socializing agents may disagree as to what constitutes proper socialization. For example, the school may hold that all children should salute the flag, or that teenagers should be taught the mechanics of human reproduction, or that black children's speech should be converted to "standard English." Parents, with their own subcultural views, may violently disagree. In such cases, the child often gets bruised on both sides. Faced with conflicting expectations, he or she may or may not be able to decide which socializing agent to disappoint and therefore often disappoints both—and himself or herself into the bargain.

Even without inconsistencies, socialization is not always a rewarding experience, as statistics on child abuse and high school dropouts make clear. Society's gifts can at times look undesirable. Becoming socialized means learning to accept the society's authority structure—mirrored for some, for example, in impersonal, competitive educational "factories." And for children in some social categories (for example, females, blacks,

the working class), it often means accepting a distorted self-image. The latter consequence of socialization—the inequalities it supports and preserves—has been sketched above and will be discussed in detail in Chapter 13. Here we have focused on the socialization process itself—the mechanisms by which it takes place, and the social functions it performs. Basic socialization, as we have seen, takes place in childhood. But it does not stop there. As we will now see, we continue to learn new statuses and roles throughout life.

The socialization continuum: socialization throughout life

The socialization process continues long after childhood for the simple reason that after graduating from grammar school or junior high school, the average person still has sixty or seventy years to live—a near lifetime of new social demands that may be very different from those for which responses were learned in childhood. And if an individual's childhood socialization has not been totally successful, some basic training may be necessary. If, for example, a teenage girl never developed an adequate sense of responsibility as a schoolchild, she may have to undergo some rather jarring socialization, via her boss and her colleagues, on her first job. Second, the social skills developed during childhood need to be adjusted and refined. Childhood socialization gives a certain form to the self, which must then frequently be reinforced and sometimes re-formed to adjust to new demands.

These are the minor adjustments; major ones are necessary as well. Growing up and being an adult mean having to play a large number of new roles. The adolescent is offered a reasonably wide range of new statuses, and the adult an almost limitless set of possibilities. Some of these statuses (juror, PTA member, voter, homeowner, weekend conservationist) involve relatively superficial learning. Others, such as spouse or parent, require major adjustments in social skills, attitudes, and perceptions. Furthermore, once socialized into one job or one marriage, an individual may move on to another job or another marriage, requiring further learning. All in all, this adds up to a substantial socialization

curriculum—one that occupies most adults until the day they die.

SOCIALIZATION IN AGE-GRADED STATUSES AND ROLES

In every society there is an official or unofficial timetable of age-graded statuses and roles. In our early years we learn the statuses of child, student, friend. As adolescents, we learn those of teenager, perhaps worker, perhaps soldier, possibly even sexual partner. As adults we must go on to learn such statuses as worker, mature sexual partner, spouse, parent, grandparent, old person—to say nothing of the general status of adult. *Age-graded statuses and roles* are probably the ones we learn in the most truly "developmental" manner. Growing up and growing older mean inevitable mental and physical changes with which the society *must* cope through cultural mechanisms. It is partly for this reason that in many societies, age-graded statuses and roles are among the most highly institutionalized and thus most eased by public recognition and ceremonies—for example, the birthday party, the confirmation, the bar mitzvah, and the graduation ceremony.

The process of taking on age-graded statuses and roles is smoothed in many cases by maturational readiness. It may also be eased by *anticipatory socialization*, whereby we hear about, read about, play-act, and look forward to future statuses. Certain age-graded se-

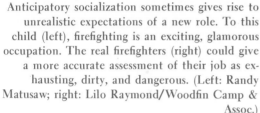

Anticipatory socialization sometimes gives rise to unrealistic expectations of a new role. To this child (left), firefighting is an exciting, glamorous occupation. The real firefighters (right) could give a more accurate assessment of their job as exhausting, dirty, and dangerous. (Left: Randy Matusaw; right: Lilo Raymond/Woodfin Camp & Assoc.)

quences within highly formalized institutional environments, such as the American medical school and hospital, are relatively smooth in that they involve a process of synthesis in learning. For example, the sequence from medical student to intern to resident to attending physician and private practitioner involves relatively little discontinuity: there is little need to "throw out" prior socialization, since most of the new statuses can simply be built on the old ones.

Nevertheless, learning age-graded statuses and roles is seldom easy. Many of the sequences are highly discontinuous: widow-after-spouse, retiree-after-worker, and even adult-after-adolescent involve not only the acquisition of new skills but also the relinquishment of deeply ingrained old skills. Nor is learning age-graded statuses and roles always totally voluntary; most people seem to go through the various stages with a combination of acceptance and reluctance. There is also a "proper time" for most statuses: one reason the seventy-two-year-old father and the fourteen-year-old mother both face some social stigma is because their behavior violates our sense of the "proper time" for parenthood.

Anticipatory socialization can often make actual role learning somewhat painful, since what we anticipate is seldom what we get. It has been found, for ex-

ample, that students entering college "tend to expect the moon and usually find something more mundane" (Stanfiel and Watts, 1970, p. 134). Furthermore, their ideals for their own performance are often equally unrealized and unrealizable (Goodman and Feldman, 1975). The same might certainly be said of those entering marriage or the job market.

The fact that the roles themselves are changing at an unprecedented rate as our society develops new technological and cultural patterns means anticipatory socialization is sometimes almost useless. While children are being taught how to act in the adult world, that world is being altered. Furthermore, as the complexity of adult roles increases, socializing agents become less able to train us for them (Brim, 1966). Consequently, many of us stumble into adulthood baffled by a world for which we were not prepared.

For all these reasons, training for role enactment is incomplete unless it includes "on-the-job" experience; one must assume a status and experience the expectations involved in order to learn it. And as many newlyweds, new parents, and new retirees will testify, the development of skills to meet these new role expectations can be a slow and painful process. This is particularly true of adolescence, which we will discuss below.

ADOLESCENT SOCIALIZATION

As we saw above, both the peer group and the school tug at the strings that tie the child to the family. Year after year, as the child is nudged closer and closer to full participation in the society, the frame of reference is expanded. At the end of this process is adolescence—

and a rather cruel paradox. On the one hand, school, parents, and society are making last-ditch attempts to exact conformity to adult standards of behavior; on the other hand, these very forces are busy denying adult privileges (Goodman and Feldman, 1975). Full of ideas, energy, and sexual interest, the adolescent is not yet allowed to use these resources in adult ways but rather is still being *trained* to use them properly in the future.

The adolescent—neither a child nor an adult—experiences *role discontinuity*. Several decades ago Ruth Benedict (1938) identified three major role transitions the adolescent is called upon to make: from a nonresponsible to a responsible role; from a submissive to a dominant role; and from a role of inhibited sexuality to a role of legitimate sexual activity within the context of marriage. Since then, what society accepts as the legitimate sphere of sexual activity has widened somewhat, but in most respects Benedict's observations still apply. These role transitions require a transformation in the adolescent's sense of self—a task that involves, in addition, the unification of identity inside and outside the peer group and the acceptance of a newly adult body, despite its deviations from advertised ideals.

To make the task of growing up even more difficult, the adolescent must also come to terms with the discontinuities that exist in the society (Elder, 1968, p. 26). But at a time of pronounced idealism and urgent need of admirable adult role models, the adolescent is most likely to spot discrepancies and weaknesses. Finally, the adolescent is required to form a life plan (Elder, 1968, p. 25), or at least some tentative notion of adult goals.

These are formidable challenges, and in most cases the family is not likely to be a refuge. For as the adolescent is undergoing a role change, the parents are undergoing one too—from parents of a dependent and tractable child to parents of an often critical and testy proto-adult, straining for independence. This role discontinuity in both generations is fertile ground for the growth of family strife.

The adolescent subculture

In the adolescent subculture, which seems to offer a haven from the problems caused by role discontinuity, the teenager can find a defined status, a clear set of values and folkways, a sense of stability (bolstered by the emphasis on conformity and group activities), and a feeling of independence from adults. The special clothes and language adopted by adolescents are not trivial idiosyncracies. As Hans Sebald (1968, Chapter 9) points out, they reinforce the sense of group solidarity, signal independence from the adult world, and create a separate society in which the adolescent can linger until socialization into adulthood—through work, marriage, and financial independence—can no longer be delayed.

The importance of the peer group can be overstated, however. Adolescents are actually more responsive to parents on some issues and to peers on others (Goodman, 1969). Moreover, social dependence may well be a product of the anxieties created by not being sure of exactly where one stands. Several investigators (for example, Ralph Turner, 1964; Goodman et al., n.d., p. 89; and Lyell, 1973) suggest that conformity in the peer group is not a result of adolescent rebellion against the adult world, but rather a way of formalizing relationships and protecting insecure adolescents from one another.

The adolescent experience

Adolescents are acutely aware that eventually they will be "moving on." How well the challenges of the future are met and accepted depends in part upon feelings of personal competence and self-esteem. The better the individual feels about his or her capacities, the easier it is to select goals, make decisions and commitments, and enter new relationships (Elder, 1968, p. 26). These decisions, in turn, are shaped by what is open to the adolescent and what goals the society considers to be socially acceptable. The more integrated one's inner feelings and the social environment, the smoother the transition (Elder, 1975).

ADULT SOCIALIZATION

Personal change in adult life can, in rare instances, take place in a sociological vacuum—that is, outside of groups. George Bernard Shaw, for example, literally converted himself into a writer by leaving his job, his family, and his country to go off and write by himself for a period of eight years (Strauss, 1969, p. 128). But most adult development, like that of childhood and adolescence, takes place through interaction with others.

Adult socialization does have some important differences from childhood socialization, however. For one thing, the child has much more to learn in a shorter period of time. In the span of a few years, every child must learn acceptable toilet habits, master spoken language, and absorb thousands of unwritten cultural rules governing everything from eating with a knife and fork to taking turns on the playground. Even the adult who moves to another part of the world and faces a new language and new customs is unlikely to learn much that is completely new (Chinese, like English, has rules of grammar; chopsticks are not so very different from knives and forks). In addition, adult socialization has a more practical slant: adults are more likely to "develop" by learning new skills. Much of the socialization of children, on the other hand, is concerned with values: concentrated efforts are made by parents and teachers to instill the principles of right and wrong. By adulthood, presumably, our basic values are formed, and we move on to develop or adapt the skills we need to cope with our lives as adults.

Agents and contexts

For the adult, as for the child, the family remains the nucleus of primary-group socialization: we learn to be wives, for example, by having husbands, and vice versa. But now formal organizations become increasingly powerful socializing agents. The college, the corporation, the factory provide a constant succession of learning situations in which we adjust and refine our capacity to deal successfully with various kinds of interactions. And while an organization's formal socializing mechanisms are at work, the individual is also a part of various primary groups whose influences contribute to socialization—even within what Goffman (1962) has called "total institutions." First of all, there is the peer group, which exists in and between most institutional settings. We learn to pass courses or do our jobs not only through the guidance of teachers or management, but also through informal training in the subculture of other students or workers, who teach us shortcuts, practical tips, and ways of getting around regulations.

In addition, many elements in our environment socialize us to adapt to that environment. The cities or suburbs we live in socialize us, as do the television programs we watch, the magazines we read, and the films we see. As norms change and as more people enact new roles and roles once considered of low status, such as

divorced person or single parent, the media increasingly provide us with ideas and models for our own socialization. Aside from television, perhaps the most interesting recent entrant into the field of adult socialization is psychotherapy. Each year, a great many people who find they are having difficulty coping with their lives seek the aid of psychiatrists, psychologists, marriage counselors, and other therapists. The ultimate goal of all psychotherapy, whatever the particular technique, is the construction of a more adequate and satisfied self. Once viewed only as a way to cure the sick, psychological treatment has in recent years come to be seen also as an aid to personal growth and fulfillment.

New roles and new meanings

Anselm Strauss (1969) has pointed out that the psychological view of human development generally assumes either a fixed series of "states" or a fixed self—or both. In the first view, human development is seen as a sort of race, with milestones placed at regular intervals along the way and with the goal of maturity at the end. In the second view, the individual is like an egg: scrambled, soft-boiled, or hard-boiled by the vicissitudes of life, but still an egg. "Neither metaphor," Strauss concludes, "captures the open-ended, tentative, exploratory, hypothetical, problematical, devious, changeable, and only partly-unified character of human courses of action" (p. 91).

In the sociological view of human development, "stages" are not fixed and inevitable, as in the race metaphor; nor is the substance of the self unalterable, as in the egg metaphor. Rather, the adult's inner world and progress through life are determined in large part by a vast range of arbitrary and accidental variables: race, class, nationality, generation, age, and so on—along with the race, class, nationality, generation, and age of his or her significant others. Genetic endowment plays its part; whether a person is handsome or plain, brilliant or plodding, will play a part in determining the channels through which he or she can move. But to a large degree, mere circumstance—the fact that one is born the daughter of a mechanic or a professor, that one is elected president of the student body and develops a taste for leadership or loses the election and forgets that one had ever been interested—and the things that happen *to* us create the roles that we will fill. And by enacting this or that role, we develop new ways of classifying, perceiving, and valuing. Pornography, for in-

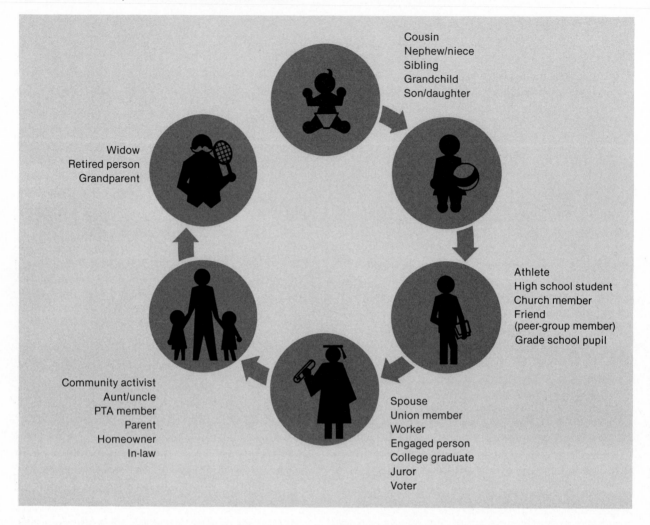

stance, is likely to offend a man once he becomes a father (Reiss, 1967). Another example is Howard S. Becker's (1953) classic study of marijuana smokers, in which he shows that it is only through using the drug—that is, enacting the role of marijuana smoker—that one learns, gradually, to value marijuana. In other words, the roles that we fill transform our structure of meanings, and these revised meanings transform the self. As Strauss puts it, a status tends "to become a way of being as well as a way of acting" (1969, p. 124).

Modes of change

How does the individual assume the new roles that come to constitute the self? According to Becker, personal change in adult life is the consequence of *situa-tional adjustment*, the adaptation of the self to fit the demands of a social situation. Moving from situation to situation, the individual learns what is required for success in each of them. If the individual can supply what is required and is motivated to do so, then, Becker points out, that person "turns himself into the kind of person the situation demands" (1964, p. 44). An interesting example of this mechanism is Wheeler's (1961) finding that prisoners tend to become increasingly "prisonized" (that is, motivated by deviant rather than by law-abiding goals) the longer they are incarcerated, but that as they near the time of their release, the process reverses and they become more law-abiding.

This does not mean, however, that the individual is merely a chameleon, changing the self with each new situation. A second mechanism, that of *commitment,*

FIGURE 6.3
Passage from one age-graded role to another is influenced not just by the biological clock but also by the social clock—the sense of appropriate timing internalized from social norms and expectations.

works to offset the mechanism of situational adjustment (Becker, 1964). Commitment, the renouncing of short-term gains for the sake of a long-term goal, allows the individual to make only a limited number of situational adjustments and thus to maintain a degree of continuity in self and personality. Furthermore, the acquisition of commitments lends stability to the society as well as to the self, since these commitments are overwhelmingly to roles and relationships that form the basis of society itself.

The social clock

All these agents socialize us into a number of age-graded norms, roles, and statuses: we go to college or not and choose a career; we marry, have children, divorce, remarry; we buy a home and become part of a neighborhood or community; we choose hobbies or sports or other pursuits to fill our leisure time. We also gather experience: from our interaction with family members and coworkers, we master our own personal techniques for getting what we want and for getting along. We also build up a store of memories that we blend and use to adapt in new and similar situations.

During our adult years we do all this according to a time sequence, or what Bernice Neugarten (1968) calls the *social clock*, the sense of appropriate timing that we internalize from the norms and expectations of our society. The social clock is what tells us to push harder to do something before a certain date, or to wait a while; it is what told this individual, for example, that it was time to make a career change:

I moved at age forty-five from a large corporation to a law firm. I got out at the last possible moment, because after forty-five it is too difficult to find the job you want. If you haven't made it by then, you had better make it fast, or you are stuck. (Neugarten, 1967, in Kimmel, 1974, p. 68)

It is also what tells us when to marry, when to stop wearing a bikini, when to quit a job and travel the world for a year, when to feel free to let children be responsible for themselves. This internal clock reflects the expectations of the society; it also reflects our changing perceptions of ourselves.

The self's clock

As we grow older and our roles and status change, people come to perceive us differently. Our self-perception changes as well. In fact, our new view of ourselves comes about largely because others' reactions to us change. A young woman, for example, may go through law school and pass the bar. She then finds that friends and relatives, as well as clients, regard her as an authority. The young lawyer then begins to revise her "me" to include a new perception of herself as a professional person who is expected by others to behave in a certain manner.

Sometimes these changes in self-perception come about because of sudden moments of self-consciousness—the first time someone offers a man or a woman a seat on a bus may cause that individual to realize that how he or she appears to others has undergone a change. But usually changes in one's perception of oneself happen more slowly, as a result of experience and the building up of a store of memories. A middle-aged adult can remember a variety of "me's"—student, spouse, young professional, neighbor, community activist, parent, and so on—and at the same time know himself or herself as a current "me" encompassing all the past ones. The adult uses these memories and experiences to meet current situations effectively—choosing the best "me" to get the best result in a given interaction or situation.

We all know that people change as the years go by, but that in some ways they remain the same. The psychological view is that the core personality formed in childhood endures throughout life; the sociological view is that memory, the building up of response habits, and the similarity of the situations in which we find or place ourselves produce the consistency of attitude or behavior that we see as our self and others see as our personality or identity (Kimmel, 1974). In our society, that self or personality becomes the individual's main resource for the years after retirement from the occupational role.

The way an individual perceives herself at a particular age is affected by the social clock, the sense of appropriate behavior that is strongly influenced by societal norms and expectations. Our society expects little if anything of value from the aged and therefore many elderly people feel they are unable to be of use to society. (© Joel Gordon 1979)

THE LATER YEARS

Because our society is only now beginning to cope with a major demographic change—a significant proportion of older people living longer than ever before—the older person currently experiences not a change in role or status upon retirement from the work force, but the loss of both. Unlike every other age-graded status in our society, that of old person involves little expectation of any kind of socially valued activity.

We put away the things of childhood specifically in order to take up the things of adulthood—the socially valued statuses of worker, parent, spouse, homeowner, and so on. The transition from middle to old age, however, offers discontinuity without reward. The individual is quietly nudged out of the statuses of worker, parent, lover, and eventually that of spouse as well: as of 1978, 7.9 million women and 1.3 million men aged 65 or over were widowed (Census Bureau, 1979, p. 42). But our society offers little to replace these lost statuses. Unlike other cultures, in which age is venerated and the status of wise person or leader is reserved for those who have lived long, we have only the status of grandparent, and even that is a part-time one with little social recognition.

As a consequence, adequate anticipatory socialization for aging and the later years has been lacking. Individuals perceive—and experience—this period as one of continuing loss: of occupational role, status, spouse, friends, independence, physical health. But the increase in their numbers as well as the need for individuals to plan for many years of life after retirement has begun to bring about change. Leisure activities, avocations, and hobbies have become signs of the healthy person; someone with no interests other than the job is now seen as a "workaholic" who will probably not be able to survive retirement. Communities for older people are a subject of debate, but one view of these "Sun Cities" is that they provide an opportunity for people to overcome their social losses and to develop new norms and expectations for themselves (Rosow, 1967, 1973, cited in Bengston and Manuel, 1973).

Yet another positive counterpoint to the negative view of old age is the increase in personal freedom that retirement or the end of a long but unhappy marriage can bring (Sheehey, 1979). The person in mid-career is not free: the demands on time and energies are heavy, and many are obligations that cannot be avoided. A fifty-year-old divorced woman with two children has to push ahead at her job even if she hates it; the executive with two ex-wives and heavy alimony payments cannot just go fishing when he feels like it. But the retired or widowed person no longer has heavy responsibilities to others: he or she has the kind of personal freedom to experiment not experienced since adolescence (Bengston and Manuel, 1973, p. 50). Organizations of the elderly, such as the American Association of Retired Persons and the Gray Panthers, and the Senior Citizens groups in many communities, also testify to changing perceptions and the beginning of socialization to a definite role and status.

WHEN SOCIALIZATION FAILS: RESOCIALIZATION

If childhood socialization has been unsuccessful in certain specific areas, developmental socialization in adolescence and adulthood can supply the missing values or skills, while leaving intact the parts of the self that fit the social pattern. But in some cases the individual's entire structure of values and behavior patterns may be pronounced inadequate or deviant—either by others or by the person himself or herself. As a result, the individ-

ual may undergo *resocialization,* the most extreme form of adult socialization, in which the previously constructed self is largely uprooted and replaced by a new one. Resocialization is the aim, for example, of rehabilitation programs in prisons and mental institutions; it may also take place when an individual undergoes "conversion" to a religious sect or an extremist political group.

Thorough resocialization is painful; it is an experience that most individuals—if given a choice—try to avoid. Many resocialization programs succeed primarily through coercion. Yet some processes—such as psychoanalysis—are voluntary. Ultimately, in any type of resocialization process, whether voluntary or not, the person being resocialized *must* accede on some level in order for the program to work. As mentioned earlier, the "other" is internalized as part of the self in any socialization process, and if a person is to be resocialized, there must come a time when the individual begins to side with those who are resocializing him or her. This turning point is a familiar feature of accounts of brainwashing. It is also described in the climax of George Orwell's novel *1984,* when the hero, who has been trying to resist the control of the totalitarian state, gives in and realizes that he loves "Big Brother."

Enlistment in the armed forces is one method of voluntary resocialization, the process by which the previously constructed self is largely uprooted and replaced by a new one. (© Tony Korody/Sygma)

BRAINWASHING: THE ULTIMATE RESOCIALIZATION

The most extreme form of resocialization is brainwashing—the systematic, complete alteration of a person's identity, values, beliefs, and behavior against that person's will. Most of what we know about brainwashing comes from the research done by Edgar Schein (1971) and Robert J. Lifton (1969). Here we shall consider Lifton's work with American soldiers who had been captured and imprisoned by the Chinese Communists during the Korean War in the 1950s. The captors had set out to destroy the identity of each prisoner and to build him a new one: "The reactionary spy who entered the prison must perish, and . . . in his place must arise a new man, resurrected in the Communist mold" (Lifton, 1969, p. 325).

In their attempt to destroy a prisoner's identity, the Communists relied on interrogation and physical torture, coupled with the removal of all support for the individual's existing identity, values, and attitudes. The experience of one of the released prisoners interviewed by Lifton, a physician named Dr. Vincent, illustrates the basic approach used by the Communists. While interrogating and torturing Dr. Vincent, they repeatedly told him that "he was not really a doctor, that all of what he considered himself to be was merely a cloak under which he hid what he really was" (Lifton, 1969, p. 325). Gradually, Dr. Vincent began to lose his sense of who he was and "where he stood in relationship to his fellows" (p. 326).

While the prisoner's identity was being assaulted in this way, his sense of affiliation with the other American POWs was being destroyed by a number of isolating techniques. The Chinese separated the enlisted men from their officers, thus demolishing the supportive leadership structure of the group. They forced the POWs to accuse one another of ideological "crimes" and showed them "confessions" written by their fellow soldiers. They banned all reading matter and radio broadcasts except for the propaganda which they themselves provided."[The resulting] emotional isolation prevented prisoners from validating any beliefs, attitudes, and values through meaningful interaction with others at a time when these were under heavy attack" (Severy, Brigham, and Schlenker, 1976, p. 316).

Once a prisoner lost the psychological support of his group affiliation, he experienced a profound identity loss. Then his captors gradually constructed his new Communist identity by providing him with a group, made up of Chinese Communists and "reformed" prisoners. One prisoner described the experience this way:

Then an official came to see me and he spoke to me in a very friendly voice: "The government doesn't want to kill you. It wants to reform you. We don't want to punish you at all, we just want to re-educate you." . . . It was my first glimmer of hope. I felt finally there might be a way out. I wasn't feeling so hopelessly alone any more. The official had actually shown some human quality. (Lifton, 1969, p. 331)

With the threat of personal annihilation gone, prisoners could "glimpse . . . the Promised Land of renewed identity and acceptance" (Lifton, 1969, p. 331). The need to achieve a new personal identity and a sense of belonging was so strong that prisoners eventually became willing participants in their own "reform."

Socialization, the individual, and social change

By emphasizing the many ways in which socializing agents work on the individual to exact compliance with social norms and assumption of preestablished roles, we invite the following question. In the face of all this conforming, how do we account for differences among individuals and for social change? As we saw earlier, George Herbert Mead answered this question by positing a creative and idiosyncratic "I" as a counterpoint to the more socially responsive "me." But there is another answer: we all conform in different ways and to different things.

In the first place, the social system is extremely complex. A variety of different institutions—family, school, peers, the media, formal organizations—vie for the individual's attention and loyalty. Not only may each of these institutions have different socialization aims (if they have such aims at all), but each individual occupies a unique spot in every one of his or her groups. While three siblings may have been socialized by the same family, for example, the first-born is likely to have been the object of higher aspirations and stricter discipline than the second or third; hence socialization will have been different (Sutton-Smith and Rosenberg, 1970). Furthermore, there is the obvious fact that the content of all socialization processes is not equally beneficial for each individual. A child who has been socialized for five years in a ghetto may be unwilling, or simply unable, to assimilate the middle-class norms valued by the school. In sum, because the society is highly complex, the results of socialization are highly variable.

A second important fact is that social norms are not made of iron. Nor are they uncontested. In any complex society there is bound to be conflict between different institutions, subcultures, age groups, ethnic groups, and socioeconomic classes, resulting in equally inevitable norm conflict. Maneuvering among the various norms, each individual makes a unique resolution. And through this process of individual norm synthesis, social change takes place (Goodman, 1969).

Finally, norms, values, and habits are not simply passed *down:* they are also passed over and up. Regard-less of our age or socioeconomic status, we all socialize one another. The white middle classes have transmitted many of their values to upwardly mobile blacks. Black-power groups have passed along their concern with racial pride to white ethnics. The young have managed to socialize many of the middle-aged into marijuana use and disco dancing.

Thus, what socialization provides the individual, in terms of a social structure, is a collection of loose pieces and movable parts grouped around a few stable pillars. Within limits, each person creates his or her own version of the social context, according to his or her needs, environment, and stage in the life cycle. And as many people come to reject or to prize certain parts of that structure, the society itself changes.

Summary

Socialization is the process through which human beings learn to be human. Through socialization, society teaches children the values and rules of a particular culture—although exactly what is taught depends on a family's socioeconomic status, religious affiliation, and ethnic identity. The process of socialization ensures the continuation of society as a whole—a mechanism known as *social reproduction.*

As children are socialized, they adopt as their own the norms and values of the larger society—a process called *internalization,* which ensures social control. Socialization also acts to develop the individual *self,* for each person's sense of self develops through social interaction.

There are several perspectives on the dynamic process by which socialization takes place in childhood. In the psychoanalytic view, first articulated by Sigmund Freud, socialization is a constant struggle between the "civilizing" demands of society and the strong sexual and aggressive drives of the child. In this conflict, which takes place in the early years of the child, *traits* of personality are formed that endure throughout life. Erik Erikson's neo-Freudian theory focuses on the *self* or *ego* as a mediator between the individual and society and suggests that personality development continues throughout life. Jean Piaget has identified distinct stages of cognitive development (sensorimotor, preoperational, concrete operational, and formal operational) in children and has pointed out that socialization must be related to the child's cognitive level. George Herbert Mead has put forward a sociological view of socialization, which stresses that the self is primarily a product of social interaction, changing through life as the social situation changes. In this view, a crucial step in the development of the self is *taking the role of the other,* in which children learn to see themselves through the eyes of others. Among all these competing views, controversy continues about the relative importance of fixed traits of personality as opposed to changing social situations.

The most important agent of socialization in childhood is the family, which deliberately aims at socializing the child. Less purposeful (but also very important) agents of socialization are the peer group, the school, and the media, which can act to reinforce the family's teaching or undermine it. The exact details of the process by which children are socialized to specific roles remain a puzzle. For example, every child learns the behavior considered appropriate in his or her society for the members of each sex through *gender-role socialization;* yet because of the variety of influences involved in the learning process and the number of ways in which they can operate, each child emerges as a unique version of "male" or "female."

Socialization continues into adolescence and adulthood as each person begins to cope with the varied statuses of adulthood: worker, spouse, sexual partner, parent. The adolescent years are often difficult, since for a time the individual is being trained for adulthood while yet remaining in some ways a child—a situation that has been called *role discontinuity.* The formidable challenge of adolescence is adjusting one's sense of self: learning to take on the identity of "adult."

In adulthood, too, socialization continues, although it is usually a narrower process than in childhood, confined to the learning of new skills rather than broad cultural values. Formal organizations such as the college, corporation, and factory become powerful socializing agents, although the family is still primary, as it was in childhood. The circumstances of the individual—race, class, nationality, and so on—determine in large part the roles that will be followed in adult life. Adults adjust to new roles by a combination of *situational adjustment,* or adaptation, and *commitment,* or devotion to long-term goals. Socialization in adulthood is guided by a sense of proper timing called the *social clock*, which tells when it is appropriate to marry, have children, change careers, and retire; finally it tells that the individual has become "old."

In their later years, many people face a difficult transition as they leave behind the socially valued statuses of worker and parent. As they retire and see their children leave home, they may feel abandoned by the larger society; this feeling may be intensified by the loss of a spouse and, therefore, the status of husband or wife. It has been suggested that "retirement" communities can help solve this problem by providing new activities and social networks for older people, thus compensating for some of the social losses.

Resocialization, the most extreme form of adult socialization, may be necessary for those people whose early socialization has been pronounced inadequate or deviant by themselves or others. Resocialization is the aim of rehabilitation programs for prisoners and mental patients; it may also take place when an individual undergoes "conversion" to a religious sect or political group.

Despite the conformity exacted by agents of socialization, individualism and social change are still possible because socialization is unique to the individual and not always completely effective; because social norms change; and because values are not merely handed down, but transmitted in such a way that all act to socialize one another.

Glossary

AGE-GRADED ROLE The set of behaviors expected of an individual at a specific phase of the life cycle.

AGENT OF SOCIALIZATION A group or institution, such as the family, the peer group, the school, or the mass media, that contributes to the teaching of basic social roles, values, attitudes, and motivations.

ANTICIPATORY SOCIALIZATION The process by which an individual learns about and rehearses the behaviors and values of a particular role or group as a preliminary to possible assumption of the role or membership in the group.

COMMITMENT Becker's term for the renouncing of short-term gains for the sake of achieving a long-term goal.

GENDER ROLE Expected patterns of social behavior associated with masculinity or femininity.

GENERALIZED OTHER Mead's term for the depersonalized set of social norms derived from others' attitudes and expectations as perceived and internalized by a child in role playing and other kinds of interaction.

"I" Mead's term for the spontaneous, creative, and unique element of the self; the element that is capable of criticizing and opposing social norms.

IDENTITY Those relatively consistent and continuous aspects of an individual's social placement, roles, and self-conceptions that constitute answers to the question, "Who am I?"

INTERNALIZATION The incorporation of social norms into the self or personality to such an extent that violation of these norms produces a sense of guilt.

LOOKING-GLASS SELF Cooley's term for the way an individual sees himself or herself in the eyes of others.

"ME" Mead's term for the stable, conforming element of the self, which is produced by the internalization of social norms.

MODAL PERSONALITY The kind of personality considered ideal, "normal," and to some extent average in a particular society.

PEER GROUP A primary (intimate) group or social category made up of people who are very similar in age, social class, or other factors.

PERSONALITY An individual's patterns of behavior, attitudes, values, and beliefs, which other people view as consistent and characteristic of that individual.

RESOCIALIZATION The drastic process of restructuring one's identity and acquiring new social values, norms, and roles.

ROLE DISCONTINUITY The problem that arises when the roles an individual plays do not fit well together, particularly when these roles occur in sequence and no bridge to the change in role prescriptions is provided.

SELF An individual's patterns of behavior, attitudes, values, and beliefs, which the individual views as consistent and characteristic of himself or herself.

SIGNIFICANT OTHERS Those individuals, especially the members of the child's family, who have the greatest influence on the development of his or her self-concept.

SITUATIONAL ADJUSTMENT Becker's term for the adaptation of the self to meet the demands of a social situation.

SOCIALIZATION The process through which persons learn and internalize the culture and the social roles of their society and come to perform the roles expected of them.

SOCIAL REPRODUCTION The perpetuation of a society's cultural patterns, norms, roles, and institutions through the socialization of its children.

TRAIT Any specific, relatively unvarying characteristic of an individual or group that can be observed and measured.

Recommended readings

Brim, Orville G., Jr., and Stanton Wheeler. *Socialization After Childhood: Two Essays*. New York: Wiley, 1966. Brief but excellent statements on the socialization of youth and adults. Brim provides a general theoretical discussion of pertinent issues; Wheeler ties his presentation to the context of "formally organized socialization settings."

Clausen, John (ed.). *Socialization and Society*. Boston: Little, Brown, 1968. The results of a conference of the Committee on Socialization and Social Structure of the prestigious Social Science Research Council, this superb and useful volume contains the papers developed from the conference by some of the most important psychologists and sociologists concerned with the topic of socialization.

Coleman, James S., *et al. Youth: Transition to Adulthood*. Chicago: University of Chicago Press, 1974. This is the report of the Panel on Youth of the President's Science Advisory Committee. This book puts the problem of youth's transition to adulthood into an historical perspective, highlights some of today's major issues, and makes some recommendations for dealing with these issues.

Danziger, Kurt. *Socialization*. Middlesex, England: Penguin, 1971. An interesting brief book by a British psychologist who treats socialization from a perspective that could be endorsed by both social learning theorists and symbolic interactionists.

Denzin, Norman K. *Childhood Socialization*. San Francisco: Jossey-Bass, 1977. A systematic analysis of childhood socialization from a symbolic interactionist perspective. Denzin focuses on the importance of language and the child's active participation in the formation of identity and social behavior.

Dragastin, Sigmund E., and Glen H. Elder, Jr. (eds.) *Adolescence in the Life Cycle: Psychological Change and Social Context*. Washington, D.C.: Hemisphere Publishing, 1975. This volume contains the papers delivered by both psychologists and sociologists at a conference sponsored by the National Institute of Child Health and Human Development. The authors view adolescence as a socially significant phase in the life cycle and examine its relationship to childhood and adulthood.

Elder, Glen H., Jr. *Adolescent Socialization and Personality Development*. Chicago: Rand McNally, 1968. An excellent short analysis of important sociological and psychological issues in the socialization of adolescents. Though technical and somewhat difficult, this book is well worth the effort it requires.

Elkin, Frederick, and Gerald Handel. *The Child in Society: The Process of Socialization*. 3rd ed. New York: Random House, 1978. A well-written, easy to understand introduction to the sociology of socialization.

Goffman, Erving. *Asylums*. Chicago: Aldine, 1962. An absolutely fascinating analysis of the impact of a "total institution" on the individual.

Goslin, David A. (ed.) *Handbook of Socialization Theory and Research*. Chicago: Rand McNally, 1969. A fine collection of articles written especially for this volume on the different theoretical approaches to socialization, as well as its content, context, and stages. A difficult but rewarding book.

Rosenberg, Morris R. *Conceiving the Self*. New York: Basic Books, 1979. The most recent work by a systematic student of the self-concept. Rosenberg carefully explores the nature of the self-concept, its social determinants, and its development. Data from several surveys are brought to bear on and to clarify relevant conceptual and theoretical issues.

Strauss, Anselm. *Mirrors and Masks: The Search for Identity*. San Francisco: The Sociology Press, 1969. A major theoretical analysis of identity transformation.

Zigler, Edward, and Irvin L. Child. "Socialization," in Gardner Lindzey and Elliot Aronson (eds.), *The Handbook of Social Psychology*. 2nd ed. Reading, Mass.: Addison-Wesley, 1968, Vol. 3, pp. 450–589. An excellent but complex overview and bibliography of socialization, using selected personality traits as an organizing principle.

Tropical childhood: cultural transmission and learning in a Puerto Rican village

DAVID LANDY

In the early 1950s a team of social scientists set out to study Puerto Rican culture. David Landy took part in the field study of family patterns and child rearing in the rural community of Valle Caña. Some of his observations of family life there are excerpted below.

. . . ADULT VIEW OF THE CHILD

The infant and small child [are] seen as a kind of doll, an enjoyable, pleasure-provoking plaything. Babies are affectionately regarded more for their entertainment value for parents than because the latter enjoy amusing them. Commonly voiced by the mothers in our sample were such attitudes as the following:

I would lie down on the bed and play with her, making noises for her, caressing her. I would give her a little rattle to entertain herself with. I would dance her the way you do with dolls. . . .

The infant and small child are regarded as *sin capacidad,* which means not merely "without capacity" but lacking the ability to think for [themselves]. One result is that the child is seldom taught anything deliberately, is never, until maturity, considered really capable of acting independently. . . . So a dependency relationship is often maintained and encouraged long after the child maturationally could behave with some degree of independence. . . .

In line with this view, a child is considered *inocente* and is likened to the angels. . . .

However there is a counter-belief, . . . that the male is born with *malicias,* while the girl is born defenseless and corruptible. It represents a basic split in the outlook on child-world relationships and may help explain some otherwise seemingly contradictory behavior patterns and attitudes. Among other things, it aids us in understanding the frequent caprice and whimsy with which the child is treated by the parent on the one hand, and the often violent restrictiveness and punishment on the other. . . .

INFANT CARETAKING AGENTS

As in most cultures, Vallecañese mothers are the chief caretaking agents. . . . Their duties and responsibilities increase with the child's age, while the father comes to play a minor role in day-to-day care. Where the mother, because of illness or temporary employment, cannot fulfill her caretaking responsibilities, usually this is done by a third surrogate. . . .

MATERNAL NURTURANCE TOWARD THE INFANT

. . . Many of these children were unwanted . . . but this does not imply that rejection at conception carried over into the postnatal period. Much apparent neglect may be due to ignorance of what constitutes an objectively dangerous situation (disease, injury, etc.) for the child, the pressing burden of household chores, and economic poverty itself, which may create a generally hopeless outlook.

These mothers are fairly warm toward their infants, though not excessively so. . . . In general they seem to enjoy moderately the duties of infant care and think babies are more fun than older children, but a sizable portion have little liking for these duties and prefer larger children. . . .

MODESTY AND SEX TRAINING

Differential practices and policies toward male and female children are manifested prenatally and shortly after birth become greatly emphasized. While all children receive modesty training fairly early, strictest emphasis is on training the girl properly to conceal her body. . . .

A girl is almost never seen without a dress and loin covering, even during infancy, while boys go about nude or with just a short shirt, genitals exposed, until five or six years normally.

. . . There is a general nervousness of tone in regard to maternal statements on boys which accounts for the variance between what they say they do and what observation indicates they actually do. A large portion of their concern is based on "what other people will think." People, they feel, will think they are bad parents because they permit their children to be immodest. People will think their children are bad. People will think they are worse off than they actually are if they cannot afford even a simple garment for their children. It may get the child into "trouble" with the opposite sex, causing shame and embarrassment. . . .

SEX EDUCATION

. . . The gist of parental responses to children's "facts of life" questions is that they would consider them a terrible affront and a sign that they had lost the child's respect or an indication that they had probably picked up bad ideas from other children. A few fathers but no mothers said they would talk about sex to the boys when older (14-21 years). . . .

While parents occasionally may joke about sexual affairs in front of children, in "serious" discussions about sex, children are always excluded, especially girls. . . . The case of Felipa is illuminating. Her seven-year-old daughter, she says,

> . . . does not know anything about [sex]. These kinds of things have not crossed her mind. Not even Luisa [age eleven] or Lucia [age twenty, also her daughter] have talked to me about these things. If Lucia knows, she found out on the outside. . . .
> Many mothers might tell their children about births and such but I don't. If she asked me where children are born and how, I would give her a slap in the mouth and tell her, "Children do not ask that. . . ."

AGGRESSION CONTROL

Adult Vallecañeses . . . prohibit and punish aggression in their children not only because fighting itself is "bad" but because parents are afraid they will "get into trouble." They have often seen aggressive persons, especially males, end up seriously wounded or in jail. . . . Not only offense-wise, but even in self-defense, they seldom encourage their children to fight back. More generally, parental rules are for the child to come home at once when attacked by another child, complain to them, and have the parents, usually the fathers, settle it at the higher level. . . .

. . . In intrasibling battles, the general procedure is to call once or twice to "break it up." If they persist, the parent punishes all the siblings, not usually bothering to find out which was at fault because of the blanket taboo. The assumption is that it takes two parties to make a conflict. . . .

NEATNESS AND CLEANLINESS

Vallecañese mothers, in spite of primitive living conditions, manage to keep their offspring clean to a surprising degree when poverty, inaccessibility of water, expense of soap (a luxury seldom purchased), and lack of clothes are considered. Keeping one's person clean and clothes neat is taught to many children at a relatively early age. As might be expected, standards are somewhat higher for girls than for boys. . . .

OBEDIENCE

. . . The good child in Valle Caña is first of all the obedient child, and parents are generally insistent and vehement about it. . . .

While mothers are more . . . strict about obedience than fathers . . . , fairly high standards are expected and enforced by both parents. Both are generally more strict with boys than with girls. . . . Because he is given more freedom of movement and action, the boy will find more areas in which to challenge parental authority and therefore is subject to more rigorous obedience demands than the girl. . . . Furthermore, in the everlasting test of his *machismo* the boy will feel constrained to prove himself against authority. This of course runs into direct conflict with the cultural and familial values that demand a "good, obedient, respectful" boy. The essence of maleness is inherent aggressiveness. The boy is born, so to speak, with all the urges of the man, which must be curbed. The girl is conceived of as a submissive, defenseless, delicate creature, who, while respect and obedience are demanded, must not be subjected to the same rigorous treatment as the boy. . . .

THREATS OF DANGERS
FROM THE ENVIRONMENT

Parents use threats of environmental dangers much more often than most other modes of warning and nonphysical punishment, and more often with their sons than with their daughters. . . . The following threats are most often mentioned:

The policeman will catch you (jail you, take you away, etc.).

A madman will come and put you in a sack.

An outlaw (or spastic) will throw you in a sack.

A dog (frog, lizard, *ardilla* [wild squirrel]) will bite (devour) you.

CHAPTER SEVEN
DEVIANCE AND SOCIAL CONTROL

Wearing a crew cut when long hair is in fashion, appearing at a formal party in jeans and a T-shirt, kicking a dog, marrying someone twenty years younger or older, cheating on an examination or an income-tax form—all of these are forms of deviance, as are robbing a gas station and murdering someone. *Deviance* is any violation of social expectations—any failure to do or to be what the values of the society or group in question define as "right." Thus the term *deviance* covers a broad spectrum of behavior, ranging from the most trivial to the most serious, and including acts that many of us have performed at one time or another. A person can be considered deviant without doing anything at all—an illegitimate child is often treated as a deviant. So are those whose physical appearance markedly violates social expectations—the obese, the handicapped, even the very homely.

Individuals are encouraged to conform to social expectations—that is, *not* to commit deviant acts—by a variety of *social controls* (see Chapter 4). Some of these are applied internally, as a result of socialization: most of us learn not only what is expected of us but also how the people around us are likely to respond if we fail to conform. (Socialization was discussed in Chapter 6.) Other controls are applied externally, through *social sanctions*. These are likely to be positive as long as we conform: an appreciative pat on the back or a prize for good work. But if we do not conform, any sanctions are likely to be negative, ranging from the raised eyebrow to the death sentence.

The harshness of the sanction depends, in part, on the perceived seriousness of the violation. Fortunately for most of us, many deviant acts are not perceived as very serious and therefore are not severely punished. A person who drinks too much at a party and behaves foolishly may receive a snub or a sarcastic remark, but that is all. Somewhat more serious are actions that violate the formal rules of organizations or groups. Cheating in school, disrupting a church service, elbowing another player in a basketball game, reporting to management what went on in a closed union meeting—these behaviors, if discovered, can usually be counted on to invoke strong and swift reactions. Graver than these acts of noncriminal deviance are those forms known as crimes: acts forbidden by law because they violate norms that are widely held and highly prized by significant numbers of members of the society.

The nature of deviance

THE VARIETY OF DEFINITIONS

A small number of acts—murder, rape, incest, treason, and theft involving in-group members—have been condemned as criminal deviance by almost all cultures at almost all points in their history. But beyond this core of acts that are generally considered evil in themselves, the definition of deviance tends to vary widely from culture to culture and from decade to decade. In our society, it is acceptable for banks to lend money at interest; American bankers are by no means ashamed of their profession. In the People's Republic of China, however, lending money at interest is considered a crime against the people. One hundred years ago, most Americans viewed divorce as a disgrace; even as recently as the 1950s and early 1960s, the stigma of being divorced stood in the way of the presidential aspirations of both Adlai Stevenson and Nelson Rockefeller. Today, divorce is part of everyday American experience.

SOURCES OF THE DEFINITIONS

Granted that the definition of deviance is relative to time and place, who decides—at a given time, in a given society—what is or is not deviant? An early sociologist, William Graham Sumner (1840–1910), argued that formal social controls are the product of consensus among the great majority of the society's members; the law, for example, defines as illegal what most people find deviant (Sumner, 1959). This explanation is supported by opinion polls showing that most Americans do agree with what the legal code describes and defines as serious deviance. But lack of consensus is also not difficult to find. In our own society, many labels are bitterly contested by dissenting groups. For example, social drinking is presently considered acceptable by *most* middle-class Americans, but there is much more disagreement over the smoking of marijuana. Many people believe that the less serious forms of criminal deviance—misdemeanors such as traffic violations and "status offenses" such as drug addiction—are deviant only because the law defines them as such (Dinitz,

Definitions of deviance tend to vary from culture to culture. (a) Men who kiss each other as a form of greeting would be considered deviant in the United States but not in many Latin American and European countries. (b) In nomadic societies, people are expected to carry all their belongings with them, but Americans who do so—this "bag lady," for instance—are seen as deviant. (Henri Cartier-Bresson/Magnum; © Shelly Rusten 1978)

(a)

(b)

Dykes, and Clarke, 1975, p. 13). Similarly, there is controversy over so-called *victimless crimes* (for example, prostitution, pornography, gambling)—behaviors that, while legally prohibited, do not involve an injured, unwilling, or complaining victim in the usual sense (Schur, 1965; Dinitz, Dykes, and Clarke, 1975, p. 13).

Such disagreements have led a number of conflict theorists to conclude that it is not the society in general, but rather specific groups—the most powerful—who define deviance (Becker, 1963; Quinney, 1970). This view is given further weight by the often-noted lack of congruence between a crime and its punishment. A lower-class person who steals a radio may be labeled a thief and go to jail; a President who obstructs justice is called an "unindicted co-conspirator" and resigns with a large government pension. Although the sellers of legal drugs—the alcohol, tobacco, and pharmaceutical industries—are responsible for many more deaths each year than are sellers of illegal drugs, they are not generally viewed as deviant, much less penalized (Goode, 1975). Consider the ironies involved in the definitions of who is "sick" and who is "guilty." An alcoholic is considered "sick." A heroin addict may be considered "sick" too, but may in addition be thought of as a "criminal," though the addiction is no more dangerous to his or her health than is the alcoholic's. (Narcotics have a different legal status than alcohol, and different groups reap profits from the sale of the two substances.)

Of course, not all matters regarding the definition of deviance can be reduced to questions of economic power. Take, for example, the issue of homosexuality, a type of deviance whose definition is currently much debated. Is homosexuality a "crime" (as laws in some areas still imply), a "sickness," or merely one of several possible "normal" patterns? Clearly, each of these definitions is shaped less by economic factors than by cul-

Prostitution is one of a number of activities that some people consider *victimless crimes*. While regarded as deviant by the majority and prohibited by law, such behavior does not usually involve an injured or unwilling victim in the usual sense. (© Jim Anderson 1978/Woodfin Camp & Assoc.)

tural themes, including Judeo-Christian sexual puritanism, Freudian psychoanalytic doctrine, and the current ethos of increased sexual permissiveness. Noneconomic factors are by far the most important in this particular case. Even in types of deviance that are more obviously connected with economics, cultural and historical factors may still play an important role.

Approaches to deviance

It is not possible for any individual to conform to every social expectation at every point in life; a certain amount of deviance is a part of any social system. The statue of the school's founder gets painted purple one night; New York subways get decorated with graffiti; a town's most upright citizen runs away with his secre-

tary; a salesman gives a politician a large "gift" for help in getting a government contract. This is especially true in complex social systems. Because many different agents socialize each individual in complex societies, and because individuals play multiple and sometimes conflicting roles, each person is always under some degree of role strain. (We discussed these issues in more detail in Chapter 4.)

Given the fact that some deviance is inevitable, however, certain crucial questions remain. Why does person A commit a relatively "serious" deviant act and not person B? What determines whether A's relatively "serious" transgression will be recognized and acknowledged as such by others? Finally, what are the consequences of this process of acknowledgment? These are some of the questions to be considered here. Biological and psychological theories, which will be examined first, offer different perspectives that may complement rather than contradict the sociological theories.

BIOLOGICAL AND PSYCHOLOGICAL THEORIES

The earliest theory, and the most long-lived one, was that the deviant was possessed by the Devil. In the nineteenth century, explanations involving the supernatural gave way to "scientific," particularly biological, ones. Cesare Lombroso, a pioneer Italian criminologist, argued that criminal deviance was the result of inherited biological abnormalities, which also manifested themselves in facial features such as protruding jaw and large ears, by which the "born" criminal could be recognized (Mannheim, 1965).

Some researchers claim that violent criminal behavior in males may be the result of an extra male chromosome that makes the individual an XYY type rather than the normal male XY. This theory received a good deal of publicity after it was reported that Richard Speck, who murdered eight nurses in Chicago one night in 1966, was an XYY type. And it has been shown that the XYY abnormality is four times more common in male criminals than in males in general (*U.S. Public Health Survey*, 1970). But the percentages in both cases are so tiny that it is impossible to establish a significant relationship between chromosomes and crime.

Such theories have found little scientific acceptance. However, the evidence is stronger for the biological origins of certain forms of noncriminal deviance. Some researchers believe that alcoholism and other forms of drug addiction are *physiological* needs. Similarly, some forms of mental illness are attributed to biological factors. Senile psychoses, for example, are known to be connected with specific kinds of brain pathology, and one cause of schizophrenia has tentatively been identified as genetically produced biochemical or physiological abnormalities (Rosenthal, 1970).

Psychological theories attempt to explain deviant behavior as originating in childhood disturbances. Psychodynamic theorists have proposed that parental rejection in childhood may prevent the individual from developing an adequate *superego*, the psychological mechanism that promotes law-abiding behavior and helps to discourage people from violating norms and harming others.

Behaviorally oriented social scientists argue that deviant behavior is the result of inappropriate learning. A child may be socialized into deviant norms, or be the victim of "consequence-less" learning: because of arbitrary discipline—constant indulgence, constant abuse, or simply punishment and reward at the parents' whim—the child never learns to associate rewards and punishments with any specific patterns of behavior, either deviant or conforming (Burgess and Akers, 1966).

SOME SOCIOLOGICAL APPROACHES

Biological and psychological theories focus on the individual's own resources or behavior. Yet deviance is socially defined: it occurs within a social context. Hence it is reasonable to assume that the social context itself may contribute to the development of deviance. This is the assumption on which sociological theories of individual deviance are based.

The *control theory* focuses on the breakdown of factors that can work to promote conforming and law-abiding behavior. Two other theories, *differential association* and *labeling*, focus on the ways in which deviance and a deviant identity are learned, either from peers or from society. Finally, the *macro theories* of deviance, in contrast to differential association and labeling, which focus on face-to-face interactions, try to explain not so much why a particular person commits a deviant act as why deviance is more common among certain categories of people and during certain historical periods. These approaches, as will be seen, are not necessarily opposed; they simply focus on different aspects of the same problem.

Take, for example, the phenomenon of graffiti, which in New York City's subways has reached epidemic proportions. One reason for the virtual explosion of graffiti has been the greatly diminished authority of the police and a chaotic and ineffectual judicial system, as well as a more general breakdown in the consensus on the rules of proper social behavior in an urban setting (control theory). From another perspective, many of those who deface public property have been socialized in a "criminal" or "deprived" setting (differential association) and already labeled delinquent by the soci-ety. From the macro viewpoint, the frustration, rage, and envy revealed by the destructiveness of these graffiti can be linked to the failure of the Great Society programs of the 1960s to fulfill their promises to the poor, as well as to the lack of opportunity for these youths in a city that no longer needs a pool of unskilled labor but provides every kind of comfort and entertainment for the skilled and the wealthy.

Individual theories of deviance

CONTROL THEORY

The central proposition of control theorists is that deviance occurs when internal or external controls are weakened or broken. For Walter Reckless and his colleagues (1956, 1967), the fact that many people are deviant in society means that neither internal nor external controls in the environment are strong enough. The young person who continues to conform to traditional standards even in lower-class, high-delinquency urban areas is thought to do so as a result of having been socialized into a "good" self-concept that serves as insulation from the influences of the environment. It is argued that those who lack this "good" self-concept are likely to engage in deviant behavior.

Travis Hirschi (1969), in a large study of adolescents in California, focused on the controls that are maintained through specific bonds. He found that the more strongly adolescents are attached to parents, conventional adults, and peers, the more they are involved in school and other conventional activities, and the more they are committed to conventional beliefs, the less likely they are to be delinquent. The weaker these ties, the more likely they are to engage in delinquent activities. The Charles Mansons and the Jim Joneses construct whole social worlds of their own; to them, many of the conventional norms and values of the society in which they live are both pointless and meaningless.

Since the 1950s, there has been a succession of deviant groups among British youth—Teddy boys, mods and rockers, skinheads, and today's "punks." Control theorists maintain that this type of widespread deviance occurs when internal and external controls in the environment are weak. (Sygma Photos)

DIFFERENTIAL ASSOCIATION THEORY

As formulated by Edwin H. Sutherland, this idea is that all individuals undergo a similar process in their socialization: what is learned depends on who is doing the socializing. Through symbolic interaction with the primary group and others, a person learns the definitions (meanings given to behaviors), attitudes, and techniques that make him or her willing or unwilling to violate social norms. Whether or not he or she will commit deviant acts may depend on the balance of favorable and unfavorable definitions and the extent of exposure to each—in other words, on how much time is spent with models of deviant or "antisocial" behaviors, and how influential they are (Sutherland, 1947; Sutherland and Cressey, 1974). A pickpocket, for example, is usually part of a subculture in which this skill is highly valued and carefully passed on: young people generally serve apprenticeships with experienced professionals who teach them pride in their "craft" as well as the technique itself.

Every individual, then, acts according to a learned code, whether of deviant or nondeviant behavior. Sutherland's theory was formulated to deal specifically with criminal behavior, but it has been applied to many other forms of deviance as well.

LABELING THEORY

A perspective that uses certain basic symbolic-interactionist assumptions, labeling theory became a major approach to the study of deviance in the early 1960s (Becker, 1963). In this viewpoint, no act or behavior is intrinsically deviant; rather, deviance tends to be defined and dealt with according to the interests of powerful groups in the society. The actions taken to label people as deviant (and to control those so defined) may constitute a self-fulfilling prophecy. Individuals being processed by the criminal justice system (or other institutions, such as mental hospitals) may be cut off from alternatives and pushed into groups and roles that commit them to a deviant way of life. The minor offender may become a serious delinquent after experiences in reform school. Rejection of homosexuals by heterosexual society may push them further into exclusive association with other homosexuals and strengthen a self-image as a homosexual. Persons once hospitalized for mental illness may come to consider themselves "crazy" because people act as if they were.

Some support for labeling theory has been provided by observers who have looked at the agencies of social control created to deal with persons labeled deviant. In most cases, these observers have found a positive correlation between the size of a community's social-control apparatus and the number of deviants it processes. In other words, the more prison cells (and police, judges, and prison guards) a community has, the more criminals it finds to fill them. As Kai T. Erikson (1966, p. 25) notes, "The community develops its definition of deviance so that it encompasses a range of behavior roughly equivalent to the available space in its control apparatus." From this standpoint, it is inevitable that some members of the community will be labeled deviant.

Labeling interactions

Three types of interactions associated with labeling are stereotyping, retrospective interpretation, and negotiation.* *Stereotyping*—using a few cues in behavior to construct a general picture of another person—has long been used to describe ethnic and racial characteristics. (The stereotyping of racial and ethnic groups will be discussed in Chapter 12.) But stereotypes have been found to exist for many kinds of deviance as well. We are all familiar with the behaviors used in films and on the stage to portray mental illness and homosexuality. A study of the blind (Scott, 1969) has shown that similar stereotypes exist for the physically handicapped. The blind, for example, are defined and treated as helpless, with the result that many fail to learn to be as independent as they could be because they have conformed to the stereotype. In the case of criminal deviance, stereotyped beliefs that form the basis for processes and policies of social control can have the same self-fulfilling effect on those defined as criminals.

Retrospective interpretation is the process by which a person's whole life and character are suddenly revised because of a deviant act. The identity of someone arrested for setting fire to a building is changed overnight from "ordinary citizen" to "arsonist." News media then construct biographies of the person in which only those facts that fit the deviant act are included or given significance. The case history or case record is another example, since it generally includes only the acts and behaviors that show why the prisoner or mental patient should be regarded as deviant and that justify the judgment of those who have so labeled him or her (Goffman, 1961).

Negotiation is the term used to describe such processes as plea-bargaining in adult criminal cases and the interactions between officials and young people in the juvenile justice system. Whether a young person is considered delinquent or merely a child in difficulty depends very much on bargaining between the individual and the probation officer (Cicourel, 1968). A similar process of negotiation, though far more subtle, takes place during an initial psychiatric examination. The doctor "hears" only certain information, and the client follows the doctor's cues until the two agree on a mutu-

* This discussion is based on Schur, 1971.

ally acceptable interpretation of why the person has come to the doctor and what the aim of the treatment will be.

Labeling: an assessment

In the 1970s the usefulness of the labeling approach began to be questioned on the grounds that it is much too relativistic and tends to portray society as an evil force that victimizes the deviant. Currently, there is disagreement about the extent to which deviant behavior is uniformly distributed throughout the various social classes.

Wellford (1975) argues that labeling theory has not proved to be correct in the area of crime: "The assumption that labels are differentially distributed, and that differential labeling affects behavior, is not supported by the existing criminological research" (1975, p. 343). Perhaps most basic of all, he points out that not all social psychologists agree that changes in self-concept will inevitably cause changes in behavior. Despite these objections, however, Wellford concedes that labeling theory can have value "as a component of a more comprehensive theory" (1975, p. 343). And Herbert Blumer (1969) holds that labeling theory does not have to be considered a full-blown theory of deviance; it can be useful simply as a sensitizing concept.

Macro theories of deviance

Most macro approaches share the basic assumptions that the various groups, categories, values, and institutions in a society are interrelated as parts of one social system and that what happens in one part of the system inevitably affects other parts. Thus, the major goal of these approaches is to link deviance with certain specific interrelationships among large-scale structural elements in the society. Some macro theorists have attempted to pinpoint strains that might affect the rate of deviance in specific classes, racial groups, ethnic groups, and other social categories. We will examine some of these theories below.

DURKHEIM AND ANOMIE

One of the earliest and most famous macrosociological approaches to deviance is that of Emile Durkheim. He took the functionalist view that a basic purpose of any society is to encourage conformity—and thus to ensure its own smooth, integrated operation—by instilling a commitment to certain essential norms in its members. When for some reason the various parts of the social system lose their integration (that is, cease to mesh smoothly), people may fall into a state of normlessness or confusion—what Durkheim called *anomie*—which may cause rates of deviance to increase.

Durkheim believed that *anomie* and high rates of deviance were particularly widespread during times of rapid change, when values, technology, and social structure were shifting at different rates. In his classic 1897 study of suicide rates in Europe, for example, he was able to demonstrate that rates of suicide went up during periods of economic change. The rates increased not only in times of economic depression, but also in times of unusual prosperity—both periods in which work is not rewarded on the traditionally expected and accepted scale. It was not necessarily economic deprivation that led to deviant behavior, therefore, but people's lack of commitment to stable norms during periods of change (Durkheim, 1951).

MERTON: THE QUESTION OF MEANS AND ENDS

Robert Merton began with the Durkheimian assumption that lack of integration among the structures in a society can result in societal *strain*, which can lead to deviant behavior. Merton focused on the strain that results when goals which are culturally valid *for everyone* (such as the American goal of "making good") are not accompanied by structurally available means *for everyone* to attain them (such as well-paid jobs with prospects of advancement).

TABLE 7.1

MERTON'S MODEL OF INDIVIDUAL ADAPTATION
TO CULTURAL GOALS (+ = CONFORMITY;
− = NONCONFORMITY, OR DEVIANCE)

MODE OF ADAPTATION	CULTURALLY APPROVED GOALS	CULTURALLY APPROVED MEANS
1. Innovation	+	−
2. Ritualism	−	+
3. Retreatism	−	−
4. Rebellion	±	±
5. Conformity	+	+

SOURCE: Adapted from Merton, 1967, p. 140.

Individual adaptation

Merton argued that individuals who lack access to culturally approved means of goal attainment deal with the resulting strain by adapting in various ways. He divided these individuals' modes of adaptation into four categories (see Table 7.1): *innovators*, who seek culturally validated goals by deviant means—for example, professional criminals; *ritualists*, who adhere strictly to norms (that is, to approved means) at the expense of goals—for example, bureaucrats who are more concerned with filling out forms correctly than with personal advancement or achieving the purpose of their organization; *retreatists*, who give up both on goals and on normatively approved ways of behaving—for example, some drug addicts and, perhaps, some of the mentally ill; and *rebels*, who create new norms and goals—for example, political radicals and some of those who seek new lifestyles. (Merton placed individuals who adhere to both the approved goals and the approved means into a fifth category, *conformists*.)

Merton's approach has applicability on various societal levels. In particular, however, the discrepancy between means and ends is likely to be especially acute among lower-status persons. They may hold to the wider culture's ideal of success but lack culturally accepted means to achieve it; subcultures that permit innovative ways of attaining goals may then develop (Merton, 1967).

The delinquent subculture

Delinquency, a type of deviance that many studies suggest is more frequent among the lower classes, has been the focus of a number of studies using Merton's perspective. Albert Cohen (1955) sees the delinquent subculture as a reverse image of the middle-class cultures from which delinquents are excluded. A delinquent subculture may provide criteria of status and achievement that the lower-class adolescent can satisfy, giving a sense of success to the individual who is unprepared to meet the middle-class standards imposed by the school and society. It is thus both imitative of and antagonistic to middle-class society.

Richard Cloward and Lloyd Ohlin (1961) agree that delinquent subcultures arise in response to lack of legitimate opportunities to achieve success and higher status, but they hold that the particular forms they take reflect differences in the availability of illegitimate opportunities in the neighborhood. In the most "disorganized" areas, where even successful criminal models are few, the delinquent subculture is likely to be focused

A delinquent subculture may offer a means of achieving status and success to those lower-class adolescents who are unprepared to meet the middle-class standards imposed by schools and society at large. (J. P. Laffont/Sygma)

on nonutilitarian gang fighting. In other neighborhoods, a more utilitarian theft subculture evolves. Those who fail in both the gang fighting and theft subcultures may resort to a retreatist subculture revolving around drugs.

MARXIST VIEWS ON CRIME AND SOCIAL CLASS

Capitalism is the economic system in Western societies such as our own, characterized by private or corporate (rather than state or cooperative) ownership of the means of production, distribution, and exchange of wealth. Marxist writers believe that because opportunities for ownership are unequally distributed among the social classes in a capitalist system, conflict between the "haves" and the "have-nots" is inevitable. In particular, they argue that the profit motive and the inequalities built into capitalism offer especially strong inducements to crime, including crimes committed by high-status individuals as well as by low-status individuals.

First of all, they maintain, the capitalist system (with its major goal of profit) encourages crime on the corporate level:

Corporations exist to protect and augment the capital of their owners. If it becomes difficult to perform that function one way, corporate officials will quite inevitably try to do it another. When Westinghouse and General Electric conspired to fix prices, for instance, they were resorting to one of many possible devices for limiting the potential threat of competition to their price structures.... (Gordon, 1971, p. 59)

Second, it is argued that the capitalist system encourages crime among workers. Restricted opportunities, working conditions Marxists see as dehumanizing, and an economy based on the need for continuous consumption can be conducive to crime. Blue-collar workers may turn to crime because they are financially pressed, and also because they are bored and frustrated by routine jobs (see Chapters 9 and 18). White-collar workers, too, may commit crimes; although they may have internalized some of the norms of the organization they work for (see Chapter 9), they nevertheless see themselves as exploited by employers. The only difference is the type of crime to which the white-collar workers turn: they are more likely to attempt illegal ways of getting money within the organizational environment. For example, embezzlement is a white-collar crime resorted to by those of relatively high status in positions of responsibility.

Third, Marxist theorists maintain that the capitalist system encourages crime on the lower-class level. Since what is seen as an adequate level of individual financial security is not assured in capitalist societies, lower-class people may commit crimes in order to survive. They may be faced with a choice between low-paid, demeaning jobs with a high risk of layoff and illegal activities—such as drug dealing and numbers running—that can be profitable and may even carry high status within the subculture.

The incidence and distribution of deviance

NONCRIMINAL DEVIANCE

The extent of *noncriminal deviance*, deviance not involving violation of the criminal law, is difficult to measure, primarily because those who practice it seldom come in contact with formal agencies of social control (police departments, hospitals, welfare agencies). Thus, those included in the records of such agencies are but a portion of the broader population of deviants. Much of the information that *is* available takes the form of records kept on crimes committed in connection with noncriminal acts relating to misuse of alcohol

and drugs and to mental illness. Alcoholism, for example, is not a crime, but driving while intoxicated is; similarly, it is not a crime to be a drug addict, but it is illegal to buy, sell, or possess certain addictive substances such as heroin.

Alcoholism

An *alcoholic* may be defined as a person who is addicted to alcohol—compelled to drink alcohol continuously or periodically in order to experience its physio-

TEENAGE DRUNKENNESS

Teenage drinking: to some Americans, these two words stand for a problem of growing, if not already epidemic proportions, a sorry state of affairs that hints at disasters ranging from increasing traffic fatalities and moral misconduct to the coming of crises that promise to affect society as a whole. To others, of course, teenage drunkenness is viewed as natural and inevitable, a reflection of the energy and healthy curiosity of youth and, in short, nothing much to worry about.

Is adolescent drinking a significant problem? Is it deviant behavior? Raw statistics can be used to support all sides of the argument but provide no definitive answers. According to a number of recent surveys, one out of every four seventh graders gets drunk one or more times a year; among all high school students, 23 percent report getting drunk four or more times a year, and 5 percent get drunk at least once a week; and as many as half of all college students get drunk on the average of once a month.

The issue is not teenage drinking, but drinking to the point of intoxication. Although a number of explanations have been advanced to explain the phenomenon—including peer pressure, emotional problems, boredom, and the ease with which intoxicating beverages can be obtained—none of them has been verified. In fact, says Peter Finn, author of a recent study of teenage drunkenness, there is so little agreement in our society as to either the cause or the severity of the situation that no less than six distinct schools of thought on the question can be identified.

Teenagers who get drunk on other than an experimental basis are problem drinkers or alcoholics, according to one view. But Finn challenges this conclusion, pointing out that there is a considerable difference between problem drinking and alcoholism—unlike alcoholics, problem drinkers can control their drinking and are not physically addicted to alcohol—and it's unlikely that large numbers of teenagers are alcoholics. It's more reasonable to assume that teenage drinkers are problem drinkers, Finn suggests, but a satisfactory definition of what frequency or circumstances constitute a "problem" remains to be found.

Suppose instead, as another interpretation does, that youthful intoxication is a warning of future problem drinking or alcoholism. Finn notes that there is some evidence to document this view. Some studies indicate that many adult males who abuse alcohol also drank heavily in their youth, and began drinking at an earlier age than adult males who do not later become problem drinkers. However, other studies dispute these findings, so the cause-and-effect relationship between youthful and adult alcohol abuse that is implicit in the so-called "warning theory" is quite difficult to prove. Besides, says Finn, there is a potential danger in this theory in that "labeling" a youngster as a problem drinker may become a self-fulfilling prophecy by reinforcing a negative self-image.

Perhaps, then, the important question to answer is simply *why* youngsters get drunk. If, as this approach assumes, there are "healthy" and "pathological" reasons for teenage drunkenness, an exploration of motives will indicate whether there is any need for concern. The problem with this perspective, Finn argues, is that it can be quite difficult to determine what is an honest answer and what is a "healthy" motive. And, he adds, the fact remains that getting drunk, even for the best of reasons, can still cause harm. The Italians, for instance, have long been cited for their responsible use of alcohol and for their sanctions against drunkenness, and yet they have the highest rate of cirrhosis (a drinking-related liver disease) in the world because although they drink alcohol moderately, they also tend to drink it continuously. Still, says Finn, insofar as it promotes a dialogue with youngsters about their reasons for drinking, the "motivation" theory makes a lot of sense.

Two other perspectives attempt to explain teenage drinking in societal terms. The first, characterized by the tolerant attitude that "boys will be boys," views the phenomenon as a benign reflection of traditional cultural norms and socialization processes. The other holds that teenage intoxication is a threatening indicator of troubled

logical and psychological effects and to avoid the discomforts caused by its absence. A *problem drinker* is one who drinks alcohol to such an extent that an alcohol-related disability (such as health, behavioral, or mental problems) is manifested (Noble, 1978, p. 9).

A recent government study estimated that about 7 percent of the population of the United States over the age of eighteen, or 9.3 to 10 million people, are problem drinkers, or alcoholics (Noble, 1978, pp. 9–10). Alcoholics pose serious health, economic, and legal problems for American society.

Alcoholism, alcoholic psychoses, and cirrhosis of the liver were identified as the cause of the deaths of 18,492 people in 1974 (Keller and Gurioli, 1976, pp. 14–15). Cirrhosis of the liver, which is almost always alcohol-related, is the sixth leading cause of death in the United States (Noble, 1978, p. 10).

The economic costs of alcoholism are difficult to measure, but the government study cited above (Noble, 1978, p. 17) estimated that alcohol misuse and alcoholism cost the United States $42.75 billion in 1975. This total includes, among other costs, more than

times and of wide social changes, a response to new or emergent social norms. With respect to the first of these arguments, Finn notes that it ignores the negative physical and emotional consequences of drunkenness, and, worse, that it rests on the unjustified assumption that drunkenness is normative teenage behavior. The second viewpoint, that teenage intoxication is a social barometer, is based, Finn observes, on increases in this type of behavior that were noted in the 1950s and 60s but that have since leveled off. Certainly such factors as postwar affluence, the spread of advertising, and even women's liberation have contributed to increases in teenage drinking during recent decades. But, as Finn argues, a theory explaining increases in the condition does not address the question of its effects, nor does it provide any way of knowing whether a youngster is reacting to shifting social norms or to some other unrelated cause.

Finally, there is the view that teenage drunkenness is simply an expression of light-hearted youthful boisterousness. Finn commends this view to the extent that it squares with evidence showing that teenage drinking does not necessarily lead straight to adult alcohol abuse. However, in some instances, teenage drinking does reflect problems, and may lead to others—a fact that the "youthful exuberance" perspective ignores.

Thus, even though some of these perspectives are complementary and illuminating, none of them, alone or in combination, answer the crucial pragmatic question of when one should be concerned by teenage drunkenness. The only sensible approach, Finn concludes, is to consider each case individually, to carefully examine the context in which the drunkenness takes place, and to suspend judgment until all the relevant questions have been answered.

Concerning the original question—Is teenage drunkenness a form of deviance?—there is no easy answer. As the enactment and relatively speedy repeal of Prohibition earlier in this century suggest, there is a tradition of ambivalence toward alcohol consumption in the United States, and that ambivalence persists to this day.

$19 billion in lost production of goods and services on the part of alcoholics; almost $13 billion for hospitalization and treatment of alcoholics; and $5 billion for alcohol-related motor vehicle accidents.

Crimes associated with drinking have placed a severe strain on the legal system as well. In 1977, 1,209,000 arrests were made for public drunkenness and 1,104,000 for driving while intoxicated (Census Bureau, 1978, p. 187).

There is little reason to hope that the incidence of alcoholism will diminish in the near future. Though

More than 3 million American teenagers are problem drinkers. Whether teenage drunkenness signals adult alcoholism and other social problems is a debated question. (Jim McHugh/Sygma)

many people may still think of adolescents as interested primarily in drugs, the proportion of young people who drink is high: more than 70 percent of teenagers report having had at least one drink, and 45 percent say they have been drunk at least once in their lives (Noble, 1978, p. 23). About 3.3 million young people (19 percent) aged fourteen to seventeen are problem drinkers (Noble, p. 10). When applied to teenagers, the term "problem drinker" means one who has been drunk at least six times in the past year or has experienced certain consequences (such as getting into trouble with school authorities or police and driving while under the influence of alcohol) two or more times in the past year (Noble, 1978, p. 23). Whether teenage drunkenness is a warning signal of adult alcoholism and serious social problems is a question currently being debated (see box).

An examination of problem drinkers reveals some patterning by social group. About 10 percent of adult males and 3 percent of adult females are problem drinkers (Noble, 1978, p. 10). A substantial proportion of the elderly (age sixty-five or over) are problem drinkers, though both drinking and problem drinking are less prevalent among the elderly than among younger age groups (pp. 28–29). Little concrete information is available about alcohol abuse among racial minorities in the United States. It is known, however, that American Indians report the highest frequency of alcohol-related problems, that Hispanic Americans have a higher proportion of problem drinkers than the general population, and that black Americans, on the average, drink somewhat less than whites (pp. 29–32). Research into the incidence and distribution of alcoholism continues, but at present it seems safe to say that none of these variables—sex, age, or race—confers immunity from the personal and social ravages of alcoholism.

Addiction to other drugs

Like alcoholism, drug addiction is a form of deviance that can have serious social consequences. According to the National Institute of Drug Abuse (NIDA), there were an estimated 522,000 to 559,000 heroin addicts in the United States in 1974 (reported in the *New York Post*, June 15, 1977, p. 2). Although drug abuse may be increasing in suburbs and small towns, narcotics addicts are concentrated in large cities. The NIDA study shows that San Francisco has the highest rate of heroin addiction—916 addicts per 100,000 population. New York City has the largest number of heroin addicts, 69,000, but ranks eighth in the per capita rate. According to one estimate, about one addict in nine is under twenty-one years of age; only about one in six is female; about half are black (Census Bureau, 1976, p. 91).

Marijuana use is increasing, particularly among the young. In 1971, only 14 percent of those between twelve and seventeen had ever tried marijuana, and only 6 percent were current users; by 1977, the figures were 28 percent and 16 percent. Among young adults (eighteen to twenty-five) the number of current users increased from 17 to 28 percent, and those who had tried the drug increased from 39 to 60 percent (Census Bureau, 1978, p. 123). Like alcohol, marijuana is used more heavily in urban and metropolitan areas. Its use is also greater in the Northeast and West than in other areas of the country (see Table 7.2).

As was noted above, the buying, selling, and possession of certain drugs—narcotics, marijuana, and other "controlled substances" (cocaine, amphetamines, barbiturates, hallucinogens, and the like)—are illegal. Consequently, drug abuse places a heavy burden on police

TABLE 7.2

MARIJUANA USE, BY CHARACTERISTICS AND RESIDENCE OF USER: 1974 AND 1977

CHARACTERISTIC	PERCENT EVER USED		PERCENT CURRENT USER		CHARACTERISTIC	PERCENT EVER USED		PERCENT CURRENT USER	
	1974	1977	1974	1977		1974	1977	1974	1977
YOUTHS, (12-17 YR.)	23	28	12	16	ADULTS (18 YR. AND OVER)	19	25	7	8
Male	24	33	12	19	Male	24	30	9	11
Female	21	23	11	13	Female	14	19	5	6
White	24	29	12	17	White	18	24	7	8
Black and other	17	26	9	12	Black and other	27	27	8	8
12-13 years	6	8	2	4	18-25 years	53	60	26	28
14-15 years	22	29	12	15	26-34 years	30	44	8	12
16-17 years	39	47	20	29	35 years and over	4	7	(z)	1
Northeast	26	35	14	21	Northeast	22	29	7	11
North Central	21	29	11	19	North Central	17	24	7	8
South	17	19	6	7	South	13	17	5	4
West	30	36	19	22	West	29	32	11	11
Large metro. areas	27	37	14	22	Large metro. areas	24	30	9	11
Nonmetro. areas	18	18	10	10	Nonmetro. areas	12	16	4	4

z = Less than 5 percent.

SOURCE: *Statistical Abstracts*, 1978.

forces and courts. In 1977 alone, 569,000 persons were arrested on narcotics charges (Census Bureau, 1978, p. 187). A total of 9,593 were charged in U.S. District Courts for violation of the Drug Abuse Prevention and Control Act. Of these, 2,137 were convicted on marijuana charges; 4,426 on narcotics charges; and 1,011 on controlled-substances (prescription drugs) charges (Census Bureau, 1978, p. 195).

Mental illness

Probably the most difficult form of noncriminal deviance to measure is mental illness. If only those people who are "under treatment" for diagnosed mental illness are counted, the best estimates indicate that less than 1 percent of the population is being cared for in public and private hospitals and clinics (Dunham, 1965). Yet if Karl Menninger's definition of mental health as "the adjustment of human beings to the world and to each other with a maximum of effectiveness and happiness" (Menninger, 1946, p. 1) is taken as the criterion, almost no one would be considered well. One study of city dwellers from the general population (excluding those in institutions) judged as many as 23 percent to be mentally impaired—suffering from marked, severe, and incapacitating symptoms of emotional disturbance (Srole et al., 1962).

Overall rates of hospitalization for mental illness tend to increase with age; and there is evidence that these rates are higher for whites, for men, and for the poor (Hollingshead and Redlich, 1958). Figures for 1975 show a total of 202,971 resident patients in mental hospitals, with 559,058 admissions during that year. Outpatient services cared for over 1.5 million people, and general hospitals had over 500,000 psychiatric admissions.

CRIMINAL DEVIANCE

Types of crime

In considering the incidence and distribution of criminal deviance, it is important first to distinguish among different *types* of crime. *Index crimes*, so called because they are used as the index of the extent, fluctuation, and distribution of serious crime by the Federal Bureau of Investigation in its annual *Uniform Crime Reports*

TABLE 7.3

INDEX CRIMES REPORTED IN THE UNITED STATES, 1978

TYPE OF CRIME	NUMBER	RATE PER 100,000 INHABITANTS
All Major Crimes	11,141,300	5,109.3
Major Violent Crimes		
Murder (and non-negligent manslaughter)	19,560	9.0
Forcible rape	67,130	30.8
Aggravated assault	558,100	255.9
Robbery	417,040	191.3
TOTAL	1,061,830	486.9
Major Property Crimes		
Burglary	3,104,500	1,423.7
Larceny	5,983,400	2,743.9
Motor-vehicle theft	991,600	454.7
TOTAL	10,079,500	4,622.4

SOURCE: FBI *Uniform Crime Reports*, 1979, p. 35.

for the United States, include willful homicide, forcible rape, aggravated assault, robbery, burglary, larceny (any theft, except motor-vehicle theft, that does not involve force, violence, or fraud), and motor-vehicle theft (see Table 7.3). *White-collar crime* includes, on the individual level, crimes such as tax evasion, embezzlement, fraud, forgery, counterfeiting, and bribery; on the corporate level, crimes such as price-gouging, deceptive advertising, price-fixing, illegal monopolistic practices, and consumer fraud; and on the government level, crimes such as illegal search and seizure, unauthorized wiretapping, illegal campaign contributions, political assassination, denial of due process, and questionable procedures such as entrapment (setting up a situation in which a government agent encourages a person to commit a crime that he or she is not predisposed to commit).

Index crimes

What is the incidence and distribution of index crimes among the various classes, racial groups, and other categories of people in American society? Some tentative answers are suggested by the data in the *Uniform Crime Reports* (FBI, 1979), which sketch a profile of

TABLE 7.4

ARRESTS OF YOUTH, 1978

	PERCENTAGE OF ARRESTS		
AGE	ALL ARRESTS	VIOLENT CRIMES	PROPERTY CRIMES
Under 15	7.4	5.8	17.9
Under 18	23.3	21.4	45.5
Under 21	40.0	38.8	63.2
Under 25	56.6	57.5	76.2

SOURCE: *FBI Uniform Crime Reports*, 1979, p. 196.

the "typical" offender by sex, age, region, race, and class.

By Sex. Most crime is committed by males. The arrests of males for index crimes outnumbered those of females by 4 to 1 in 1978 (though unofficial—that is, nongovernmental—studies show the ratio of male to female offenders for self-reported crime to be closer to 2 or 3 to 1). However, there are indications that female crime patterns (or their processing) are changing. In 1978, female arrests for index crimes were up 4.4 percent over the preceding year, in contrast to a 2 percent increase in male arrests.

By Age. Index crime is predominantly an activity of the young (see Table 7.4). An astonishing 76 percent of those arrested for major property crimes (burglary, larceny, and auto theft) and 57 percent of those arrested for violent crimes (murder, forcible rape, robbery, and aggravated assault) are under twenty-five years of age (FBI, 1979). Delinquency and crimes by young adults clearly absorb much of the time of law-enforcement officials. Does this mean that most criminals are under

TABLE 7.5

MAJOR CRIME RATES (NUMBER OF MAJOR CRIMES PER 100,000 POPULATION) AND COMMUNITY SIZE, 1978

COMMUNITY SIZE	TOTAL RATE OF MAJOR CRIMES	RATE OF MAJOR VIOLENT CRIMES	RATE OF MAJOR PROPERTY CRIMES
Metropolitan Areas	5,870.2	583.9	5,286.3
Other Cities	4,363.9	285.4	4,078.6
Rural	1,997.9	174.8	1,823.1
Total U.S.	5,109.3	486.9	4,622.4

SOURCE: *FBI Uniform Crime Reports*, 1979, p. 36.

twenty-five? A look at the age structure of the general population gives a different perspective. About 43 percent of Americans are under twenty-five, so the number of arrests is not quite so far out of proportion for that age group as it first appears to be.

By Community and Region. In general, there is less chance of victimization in the country than in the city; urban areas have a crime rate three times higher than that of rural areas (see Table 7.5). But the situation is changing. According to the 1979 *Uniform Crime Reports*, small and medium-sized cities and suburban towns are not as safe as they used to be. Crime rates in these areas are rising faster than anywhere else, although they still do not approach those of the large cities. The region with the highest overall crime rate, and a significantly higher rate of property crime, is the West. The North Central states have the lowest overall crime rate, though the Northeast has the lowest larceny rate of all regions.

By Race and Class. Considerable controversy exists over the extent to which the *Uniform Crime Reports* profiles of the "typical" offender by race and social class are corroborated by unofficial studies done by sociologists, such as *self-report studies.* According to the 1979 *Uniform Crime Reports*, those with minimum education, low income, and lower-class occupations are arrested in numbers far out of proportion to their numbers in the population; and blacks, who compose about 12 percent of the general population, account for 46.2 percent of the arrests for violent crimes and 30.7 percent of the arrests for property crimes. Yet a number of sociological studies have found no significant correlation between the total number of self-reported crimes and social class (Nye et al., 1958; Akers, 1964; Voss, 1966; Hirschi, 1969). And in many self-report studies, whites admit to committing criminal acts to about the same extent that blacks do. One recent study, however, describes such discrepancies between self-report and official studies as "illusory" (Hindelang, Hirschi, and Weis, 1979).

Which view is correct? This question has not yet been definitively answered, but it is a crucial one: the FBI figures are based on numbers of arrests, so any discrepancy with non-government studies raises doubts about whether the law-enforcement process treats people of different races and classes equally. We will discuss this issue in more detail later in this chapter.

White-collar crime

As we are beginning to realize, in the United States today white-collar crimes are of considerable magnitude. According to one estimate (Gordon, 1971), the losses that can be attributed to embezzlement, fraud, and unreported commercial theft are five times as large as those attributable to crimes against property—larceny, burglary, and so on. Former Attorney General Ramsey Clark states:

One corporate price-fixing conspiracy criminally converted more money each year it continued than all of the hundreds of thousands of burglaries, larcenies, or thefts in the entire nation during those same years. Reported bank embezzlements cost ten times more than bank robberies each year. (Quoted in Gordon, 1971, p. 54)

Nevertheless, it is difficult to establish a reliable picture of the incidence of white-collar crimes. Data are not readily available, especially at the corporate and government level, but the *Uniform Crime Reports* (1979) does include a few figures on white-collar crime at the individual level. In 1978, for example, 262,500 persons were arrested for fraud; 64 percent of them were white, 63 percent were men. In the same year, 77,200 people were arrested for forgery or counterfeiting—66 percent of them white, 70 percent male.

White-collar crimes are more prevalent among the middle and upper classes, whose members are more likely to have ready access to the funds, knowledge, facilities, and positions in business and government that such crimes require.

Are index crimes increasing—and, if so, why?

Crime, especially violent crime, has always been a visible part of American society. Opinion polls show, however, that in recent years it has become a major public and private concern. Some people actually change their lifestyles because of fear of crime—never going out after dark, for example, or never carrying much cash. The crime rate is said to be skyrocketing, and the grim

stories reported in the news seem to confirm this conclusion.

Not all sociologists take these statistics as reflections of actual fact, however. A look at the historical record shows that rates of homicide and assault were much higher in the nineteenth and early twentieth centuries than they are now; in general, our streets are probably

FIGURE 7.1

The percentage change in the overall crime rate and in the rate of index crimes compared to the population increase in the United States from 1960 to 1975. (The crime rate is expressed in number of offenses committed per 100,000 population.) (Adapted from Census Bureau, 1976, p. 5)

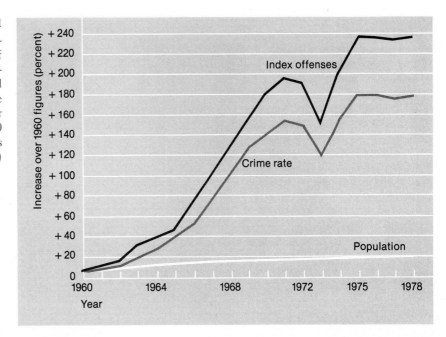

safer today than they were a hundred years ago (Bell, 1962). The figures on crimes against property must also be interpreted with caution. Some sociologists note that demographic changes, such as an increase in the percentage of the population living in urban areas and shifts in the age structure of the population, account for much of the increase. The National Commission on the Causes and Prevention of Violence (1969, Vol. 11, p. 60) estimated that increases in urbanization and in the relative size of the crime-prone younger age groups accounted for 30 percent of the increase in crime between 1950 and 1965. Thus, when other variables are removed, the upward trend in index crimes is not quite as steep as it first appears to be.

Social class and the criminal justice system

Why is it that minimal sanctions such as fines are often the punishment for criminal acts the members of more powerful groups are most likely to commit, while imprisonment, lifelong suspension of voting rights, a permanent "record," and other strong measures are used to punish criminal acts most likely to be committed by the less powerful? Why are some deviant acts called "civil offenses" and others "crimes"? What is our system of legal controls—police, courts, prisons—designed to do? And does it do this?

FIGURE 7.2

The criminal justice system processes millions of reported criminal offenses every year. The system is organized according to the type of offense, the seriousness of the offense, and the jurisdiction of the courts.

DISCRETION IN THE CRIMINAL JUSTICE SYSTEM

If everyone who violated legal norms were reported, discovered, arrested, charged, given a jury trial, and imprisoned if found guilty, the criminal justice system itself would collapse. Even now, with only a fraction of the possible load being handled, the system is overburdened. Of all those arrested for major criminal offenses, less than 20 percent are actually imprisoned. (The percentage is much higher, however, for very serious, relatively infrequent crimes, such as murder.)

Who decides which crimes will not be thoroughly investigated and which criminals will be allowed to avoid imprisonment? Is justice applied in an evenhanded manner, or are certain groups treated more

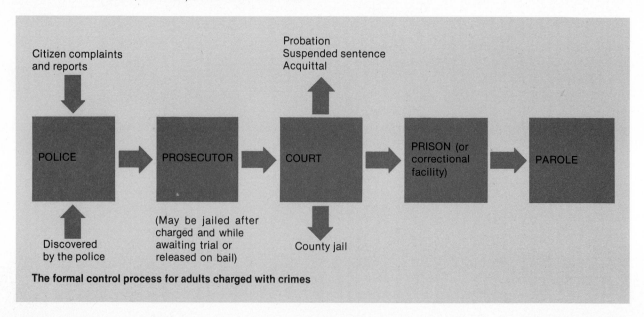

The formal control process for adults charged with crimes

harshly than others? The formal system for processing adults and juveniles charged with violating the law is shown in Figure 7.2. Each step in this system is subject to a profusion of laws and regulations that describe the rights of defendants and the powers and obligations of authorities. In addition, parallel to the formal system is an informal system of discretionary power. The police officer on the beat must often decide whether to ignore, warn, or arrest violators of the law. The prosecuting attorney may, at his or her discretion, dismiss charges, accept a guilty plea to a lesser charge, or formally prosecute the accused. The judge, even after a jury trial, uses discretion in choosing whether to suspend the sentence or incarcerate the convicted person. And the parole board has tremendous discretionary power over how long a person serving an indeterminate sentence will remain in prison.

Such discretionary power keeps the system operating; without it the bureaucracy would be unable to function. But it can also be an invitation to abuse. As was mentioned earlier in this chapter, the FBI crime profile shows a disproportionate number of arrested criminals to be young, male, black city dwellers. Part of the reason for this may be that police are likely to pay disproportionate attention to people with these characteristics, not that the latter are so much more involved in crime and delinquency than other people.

Many police officers have negative attitudes and feelings about black people; at the same time, some young blacks view the police as illegitimate, an "occupation army." However, when behavior rather than attitudes is considered, the focus shifts. A number of studies report that black and white suspects have received similar treatment by police, the prosecuting attorney, and the courts (Terry, 1967; Rosen, 1973). The crucial point is that low-income people, *regardless of race*, are often at a disadvantage in the criminal justice system because of such factors as their inability to post bail or to hire an experienced criminal lawyer. The preponderance of black suspects, convicted offenders, and prisoners may be more a function of their class position than of their race.

HOW EFFECTIVE IS THE CRIMINAL JUSTICE SYSTEM?

In the light of one of its major objectives, if the U.S. prison system "worked," all convicts would end their careers of crime and emerge as law-abiding citizens. This is, in fact, what seems to happen to many juvenile and adult offenders: the majority of minors labeled as juvenile delinquents go on to noncriminal adult lives; one-third of the adults who serve time stay out of prison thereafter; and 43 percent of those who receive probation or suspended sentences—the most common types of punishment—are never arrested again (FBI, 1976, p. 46).

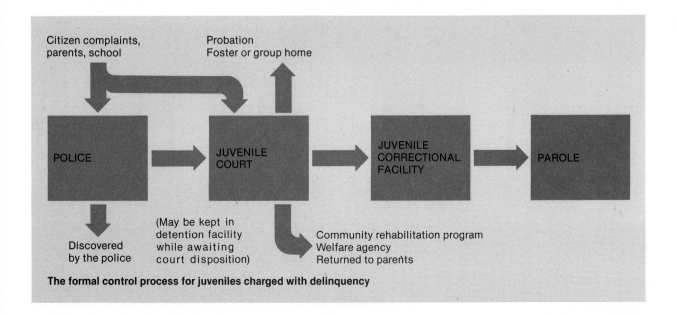

The formal control process for juveniles charged with delinquency

Low-income people, regardless of race, are often at a disadvantage in the criminal justice system: they are less able to post bail or afford a good criminal lawyer, and more likely to be found guilty and given longer sentences. (© Leif Skoogfors 1979/Woodfin Camp & Assoc.)

But rearrest is still common. Even for most people arrested and then released by acquittal or dismissed charges, a majority—67 percent—are rearrested within four years (FBI, 1976, p. 45). This and other figures on the *recidivism*, or rearrest, rate are often used as a measure of the effectiveness of the law-enforcement system as a whole and of specific rehabilitation programs. It should be noted that there are difficulties in using this yardstick. First, it is difficult to know whether convicts who are *not* rearrested have ceased committing serious violations or have simply gotten better at avoiding de-

tection. Also, it is difficult to tell to what degree recidivism is caused by a failure of the prison system and to what degree it is caused by other factors, such as the labeling process. The person with a criminal history is a much less attractive candidate for employment and a much easier target for police.

Bearing in mind these caveats, if we *do* use recidivism figures to measure the effectiveness of formal social controls, we get a bleak picture. A sizable number of the 67 percent of those rearrested within four years were charged with a more serious crime than the one for which they had previously been convicted (FBI, 1979). The recidivism rate was highest for property crimes—81 percent for burglary and 75 percent for auto theft, for example (but only 28 percent for embezzlement). However, it was also high for violent crimes such as murder (65 percent), rape (73 percent), and assault (70 percent).

Such figures have led some observers (for example, Gordon, 1971) to conclude that the system of criminal justice in the United States is actually "exacerbating the criminality it seeks selectively to control" (p. 54). Whether this is true—and *why* it should be true—are

of course unanswered questions. Marxist writers ascribe high recidivism, and the high rate of arrest and imprisonment among the lower class in general, to close connections between government and private industry. They argue that the criminal justice system, by cycling large numbers of blacks (and poor whites) through the sequence of crime, imprisonment, parole, and recidivism, serves to keep under control thousands of people whom industry cannot fully employ except in times of peak economic prosperity, and who would otherwise be likely to rebel against the capitalist system (Quinney, 1977).

The social functions of deviance

On the surface, deviance often seems a threat to the social order. Yet, as a number of sociologists (for example, Coser, 1962) have pointed out, it may sometimes also be functional for the society. In the first place, deviance may serve as an avenue for introducing change and thus for keeping the society vital and flexible. A few decades ago, for example, birth control was seen by most people as a deviant practice; those advocating it were sometimes imprisoned. Today, it is widely used and infrequently questioned.

Deviance may also clarify and reaffirm a society's rules. A rule is most evident when it is broken and the sanctioning process is set in motion; those who witness the deviant's punishment are reminded of the rules and of what can happen to those who break them. This experience may encourage outward conformity in those not deeply committed to certain norms, and it may reward conformity in those who are committed. Deviance may even increase cohesion among members of a group: the collective action of singling out and condemning the rule-breaker may unite the group, reaffirming its members' shared values and their shared identity as rule-observers (Durkheim, 1954).

Kai T. Erikson has provided support for this view in his book *The Wayward Puritans* (1966). The early Puritan settlers of Massachusetts experienced considerable pressure to establish moral boundaries for their new community. Because they were seeking to define the religious values by which they would live in the New World, they felt most threatened by deviance that took

an antireligious, satanic form—and, lo and behold, they began to find witches in their midst. The years of hysterical accusation, trial, and execution that followed served as a crucible for testing and affirming the moral solidarity of the community.

Paradoxically, deviants may be concerned with the same values as conformists: "there are people in any society who appear to 'choose' a deviant style exactly *because* it offends an important value of the group" (Erikson, 1966, p. 20). Thus the witches of Massachusetts—many falsely accused of deviant acts, some not—actually helped to uphold the community's values by seeming to reject them. As Erikson noted,

If deviation and conformity are so alike, it is not surprising that deviant behavior should seem to appear in a community at exactly those points where it is most feared. Men who fear witches soon find themselves surrounded by them; men who become jealous of private property soon encounter eager thieves. . . . In the process of defining the nature of deviation, the [Puritan] settlers were also defining the boundaries of their new universe. . . . (1966, pp. 22–23)

If we look at modern criminal deviance from this functional standpoint, Merton's view is that crime is and will continue to be a function of social conditions. As he points out (1967), crime patterns reflect other patterns—such as the American emphasis on achievement, materialism, and winning—which may be in conflict with norms concerning honesty, integrity, and respect for other people's rights. From another perspective, we might note that crime itself changes. As

Gresham Sykes (1971) has pointed out, we are now seeing an upsurge of new kinds of crime. In addition to index and white-collar crime, we see crimes committed by the relatively affluent and well-educated as a form of sport or recreation (auto theft, shoplifting), as a form of political activity (terrorism, bombings, sit-ins, destruction of records), as a symbol of rejection of the political and social order (trashing, vandalism), and as a result of the removal of ethical or normative imperatives (drug abuse, certain types of sexual behavior).

In each of these instances, not only has crime changed, but cultural themes and institutions as well. There have been changes in attitudes toward business, in perceptions of "acceptable" political behavior, in feelings about the human body, and so on.

Noncriminal forms of deviance also change, as societal definitions of what is "acceptable" and "not acceptable" are altered. It was not so long ago, after all, that women who smoked or wore lipstick were considered deviant. Today's heretics may be tomorrow's saints—or, in more mundane terms, today's eccentrics may be tomorrow's average individuals. But deviance itself is unlikely to go away. For although it may threaten a social order, it may also help a society to change and thus to survive by adjusting to new contingencies.

Summary

Deviance is any violation of social expectations, any failure to conform to social norms. Society attempts to impose conformity on its members by establishing internal and external controls. Some acts, such as murder, rape, and incest, are seen as deviant by nearly all cultures. The definition of deviance, however, is generally relative to culture and time. One sociological theory states that the definition of deviance is determined by social consensus in the interest of societal survival; another holds that powerful groups establish it.

Numerous biological, psychological, and microsociological theories have been advanced to explain the origins of both criminal and noncriminal deviance. Three major microsociological approaches are *control theory*, *differential association*, and *labeling theory*, which is associated with *stereotyping*, *retrospective interpretation*, and *negotiation*.

Macrosociological theories of deviance attempt to explain the deviant behavior of groups and social categories in terms of structural strain. In Durkheim's view, the strain of rapid change may force some people into *anomie*, a state of normlessness that can give rise to deviance. Robert Merton pointed out that the strain between acceptable goals and structurally available means may force some people to search for new, deviant routes to success. In the Marxist view, the capitalist system encourages crime among corporations, workers, and members of the lower class. Marxist theorists maintain that the fact that a higher percentage of lower-class offenders are punished, and more severely, than white-collar criminals supports the theory that powerful groups impose definitions of deviance.

Alcoholism, drug addiction, and mental illness are examples of what sociologists call noncriminal deviance. Criminal deviance involves not only "index crimes," such as murder and assault, but also *white-collar crimes*, such as tax evasion and embezzlement.

The criminal justice system exercises wide discretion in responding to deviance. Rates of *recidivism* remain relatively high regardless of the type of intervention that is applied.

Glossary

ANOMIE Durkheim's term for a state of confusion and normlessness produced in an individual when, as a result of rapid change, social standards become unclear.

DEVIANCE Behavior that violates social norms and expectations.

LABELING A process of social control whereby a person is designated as deviant, with the result that the deviant status may come to dominate his or her self-image.

NEGOTIATION An aspect of labeling that involves bargaining between a person and an agent of social control over whether and to what extent the person should be considered deviant.

RECIDIVISM The rearrest of an individual previously convicted of a crime.

RETROSPECTIVE INTERPRETATION An aspect of labeling that involves the sudden revision of others' perception of a person's entire life and character after he or she is thought to have committed a deviant act.

STEREOTYPING An aspect of labeling that involves the categorization of a member or members of a group on the basis of general beliefs and feelings rather than on the basis of direct knowledge of the person.

WHITE-COLLAR CRIME Criminal deviance that is typical of the middle and upper classes, such as tax evasion and embezzlement.

Recommended readings

Becker, Howard S. *The Outsiders: Studies in the Sociology of Deviance.* New York: Free Press, 1963. An interesting and easy-to-read statement of the labeling approach to deviance.

Cohen, Albert. *Deviance and Social Control.* Englewood Cliffs, N.J.: Prentice-Hall, 1966. A short essay summarizing major efforts to understand deviance.

Goffman, Erving. *Asylums.* Chicago: Aldine, 1961. A provocative analysis of "total institutions," such as mental hospitals and prisons, that are concerned with processing deviants.

Gove, Walter R. (ed.). *The Labelling of Deviance.* Beverly Hills, Calif.: Sage Publications, 1980. An empirically-based collection of articles examining and questioning the labeling perspective.

Inciardi, James A. (ed.). *Radical Criminology: The Coming Crisis.* Beverly Hills, Calif.: Sage Publications, 1980. These articles from a variety of points of view offer a good introduction to the emerging perspective of radical criminology.

Merton, Robert K., and R. Nisbet. *Contemporary Social Problems.* 4th ed. New York: Harcourt Brace Jovanovich, 1976. A wide-ranging collection of readings with articles on topics such as drug use, alcoholism, sexual behavior, and mental disorders.

Quinney, Richard. *Class, State, and Crime: On the Theory and Practice of Criminal Justice.* New York: David McKay, 1977. A critical perspective on the American criminal justice system, stressing its interdependence with the economic system.

Rubington, Earl (ed.). *Deviance: The Interactionist Perspective.* 3rd ed. New York: Macmillan, 1978. A useful collection of readings exploring the ways in which deviance is a product of social interaction.

Sutherland, Edwin H., and Donald R. Cressey. *Criminology.* 10th ed. New York: Harper & Row, 1978. A comprehensive criminology textbook that considers the causes and processes of crime and delinquency.

Sex and temperament

MARGARET MEAD

According to the American anthropologist Margaret Mead, deviancy is culturally defined; in other words, behavior that is considered maladjusted in one society may be totally acceptable in another. In her classic study, Sex and Temperament in Three Primitive Societies, *she examines the sharply different cultural norms for male and female behavior in three New Guinea tribes, one of which, the Mundugumor, is described here.*

We have seen how the Mundugumor ideal of character is identical for the two sexes; how both men and women are expected to be violent, competitive, aggressively sexed, jealous and ready to see and avenge insult, delighting in display, in action, in fighting. . . . If the violent, strongly sexed man or woman is driven to neurotic conflict with his or her society, does the opposite condition obtain in Mundugumor? What happens to the mild man who would like to shelter his sons as well as his daughters, and the woman who would like to cuddle her baby in her arms? . . .

They are the ones in whose purposes no brother will co-operate. These become the men who make the continuance of Mundugumor society possible. They can live near other men without continually quarrelling with them or seducing their wives and daughters. They have no ambitions of their own and are content to play a humble part in the fight, to stand back of their aggressive brothers in an intra-hamlet scrap, an inter-hamlet fight, or on a head-hunting raid. They form the constellations about the leaders, living as younger brothers, as sons-in-law, as brothers-in-law, co-operating in house-building, in feast preparations, in raids. Although the Mundugumor ideal is that every man should be a lion, fighting proudly for his share and surrounded by several equally violent lionesses, in actual practice there are a fair number of sheep in the society, men to whom pride, violence, and competitiveness do not appeal. Because of these men a certain number of the rules are kept, and so are passed on to the next generation; some families of sisters are equally divided among brothers, the dead are mourned for, children are fed. When the proud polygynist quarrels with the son whose sister he is about to use in exchange for a wife for himself, the son can take refuge with one of these milder men. The atmosphere of struggle and conflict would become unbearable and actually impossible to maintain if it were not for them, for each man would have only an army of one to put in the field. Instead of complicating

the social life by taking up positions that are confusing and unintelligible, as do the misfits among the Arapesh, they actually make possible the violent competitive life that is really so uncongenial to them.

And are such men misfits? If by misfit we mean the individual who makes trouble for his society, they are not. But if we include under the term "misfit" all those who find no congenial outlet for their special talents, who never find throughout life a rôle that is suited to them, then they may be called misfits. Where the ideal of the society is a virgin wife, they must be content with widows, with fought-over women, with women whom other men do not want. Where success is measured in terms of number of wives, number of heads taken, and large displays made, they can only point to one wife, often no heads at all, and certainly no large feasts. They are loyal in a society that counts loyalty to be a stupid disregard of the real facts about the essential enmity which exists between all males; they are parental in a society that is explicit about the lack of reward in parenthood.

Beyond the meek acceptance of this minor, undistinguished rôle, there are two courses open to them, daydreaming, or the circumvention of the social emphases. The first is the more common. A mild man will keep his sons by him, and talk to them of the days when people kept the rules, when people married correctly and there was none of this irregularity which causes people to "stand up and stare" at each other, when fathers cherished their sons, and sons were careful to observe all the little rituals that preserve their fathers' lives, even forbearing to walk in the path that their fathers had recently trodden. . . . And this day-dreaming is probably a real drawback to the society. It prevents young people from adjusting realistically to the actual conditions and formulating new rules that would deal with them adequately. It keeps the attention of the more law-abiding paralyzed with a sterile yearning towards the past, and it gives everyone a sense of guilt. If this former imputed Elysium were ignored, a man might find his erstwhile sister classified as an uncle's wife without tingling with shame and anger. The old residence rules, the old marriage exchanges, being gone for ever, new ones might be worked out. All this the day-dreaming maladjust prevents; too weak, too ineffectual, too unplaced to have very much influence in shaping his present society, he serves to confuse the issues. . . .

The other type of maladjusted man is much rarer, and there was only one conspicuous example in the tribe when we were there. This was Ombléan, who was our most gifted informant. He was a slender, delicately made, vivid young man, by temperament committed to none of the Mundugumor ends. He was gentle, co-operative, responsive, easily enlisted in the causes of others. His household was always filled with people for whose care he had no genuine responsibility. . . . None of these people who imposed upon him respected him particularly; he was too slight and too good-natured to beat them with crocodile-skulls or throw fire-sticks at them. As a result, he did a great deal of work himself, growing yams and working sago and hunting to feed his household, where the women often refused to fish. He was indefatigable, resourceful, and too energetic and intelligent to take refuge in day-dreaming. Instead he studied his society, learned every rule and every loop-hole through which intelligence could outmatch brute strength. . . . His own alienation from all the current motivations had sharpened his already superior intelligence to a point very seldom found within a homogeneous culture. But he was cynical where he would, in another context, have been enthusiastic. He had to spend his splendid intellectual gifts in circumventing a society in which he was spiritually not at home. . . .

And who were the maladjusted women in Mundugumor? Kwenda was a good example. Kwenda was plump and soft, where the ideal Mundugumor woman is tall, lithe, and slender. Kwenda loved children. She had refused to throw away her first child, a boy, in spite of her husband Mbunda's request that she do so. While she was suckling the child he had eloped with another woman. Instead of stiffening her back in anger, she had followed him and his new wife. Outraged, he had thrown her out and left her in his maternal village of Biwat, and himself gone off to work for the white man. In Biwat, Kwenda had borne twins; they died. She returned to Kenakatem, and went to live with Yeshimba, a father's brother. Then Gisambut, the reserved sister of Ombléan, bore twin girls, and Kwenda, with no one to help her earn a living, adopted one and soon was able to feed it entirely from her ample breasts. The little twin flourished, grew as tall as the sister who was suckled by her own mother, but on the face of Kwenda's twin there was always a dimpling smile, on the face of the child suckled by her own mother, a harsh set frown. Kwenda's twin was more often about the village, and I was accustomed to greeting it and receiving a happy smile. . . . Not only would she work willingly all day for her six-year-old son and the little twin, but she worked also for others. Anyone who wanted

a coconut-palm climbed had only to coax Kwenda, and disregarding her plumpness and her heavy breasts, which made climbing more difficult for her than for other women, she would be up it, smiling the while. Not only did she suckle the little twin, but often she took on other women's infants for the day. Her husband returned to the village and took a young, sharp-faced wife, for whom he adopted a child so that she would not have to inconvenience him by bearing one. They went every day into the bush to work sago. He hated the sound of Kwenda's name, and declared he would never take her back. . . . Kwenda, young, warm, and vigorous, would remain a grass widow; no strong man would take her for a wife, no weak one would try because Mbunda, not wanting her himself, would nevertheless demand a high price for her. So in Mundugumor the easy-going, responsive, warmly parental woman, like the easy-going, responsive, warmly parental man, is at a social discount.

On the other hand there are other aberrant personalities who are so violent that even Mundugumor standards have no place for them. A man of this sort becomes too continuously embroiled with his fellows, until he may be finally killed treacherously during an attack on another tribe, or possibly a member of his own tribe may kill him and accept the meagre penalty—a prohibition on wearing head-hunting honours. Or he may flee into the swamps and perish there. A woman of equal violence, who continually tries to attach new lovers and is insatiable in her demands, may in the end be handed over to another community to be communally raped. But the fate of these violent persons is consistent with the Mundugumor ideal, which looks forward to a violent death for women as well as for men. . . .

In such a setting, it will be seen that the occasional individual whose greater violence and bad luck resulted in death was not regarded as having had a poor life of it. It was the Ombléans, the Kwendas, who were the real maladjusted persons, whose gifts were spent in a hopeless effort to stem the stream of an uncongenial tradition, where both men and women were expected to be proud, harsh, and violent, and where the tenderer sentiments were felt to be as inappropriate in one sex as in the other.

Primary components of social organization

CHAPTER EIGHT
THE NATURE AND VARIETY OF GROUPS

One Sunday morning in June, a stream of family automobiles unloaded a horde of little boys and their baggage for a two-week stay at Camp Roaring River. The boys were from many different places, and nearly all of them were strangers to one another. In the course of the day they were assigned to lodges, each housing fifteen boys under the supervision of an adult counselor. Residents of each lodge were given a collective name—the Bears, the Wolves, the Cobras. Each group had its own schedule of activities and formed its own sports teams for competition with the other lodges.

Within hours of being thrown together, the boys began to create "social structures." Some boys in each lodge established their popularity; others were considered less popular; and one or two in each lodge were judged unpopular. Within several days the boys in each lodge had forged strong bonds and accepted responsibility for the needs of their group. They were proud to be Bears, Wolves, or Cobras. At the same time, they began to form negative stereotypes about the boys in other lodges—"Bears are cheats," "Wolves are sissies," "Cobras are punks." Furthermore, it became apparent that no lodge group was simply a gathering of fifteen boys. Within each group cliques and coalitions developed, some of which reflected the boys' memberships in various groups outside the camp. Black and white boys tended to form separate cliques, as did Protestant and Catholic boys. Sometimes these factions led to internal conflicts, but these usually subsided the moment the group faced an external challenge from another lodge.

The study of groups

In this account of goings-on at a boys' camp (fictitious, but based on a study of actual summer-camp groups by Muzafer and Carolyn Sherif [1953]), we can see several essential features of the social group. While we discussed some of these features in Chapter 4, we will review them briefly before we investigate the nature and variety of groups in more detail.

In everyday speech, we sometimes use the word "group" to describe a crowd of people waiting to cross a street, or passengers on an airplane, or persons in a theater, and so on. To sociologists, though, such random gatherings are not "groups" but *aggregates* or *collectivities.* Even when, in everyday speech, we use the word "group" more narrowly to denote people who share certain characteristics—factory workers, for instance, or college students—we are talking about what sociologists call *categories* of people.

In sociological parlance, a *group* is a collection of people characterized first of all by a recurrent pattern of interaction; for example, meetings or gatherings tend to take place more or less regularly, and are not random. Within the context of this interaction, the group is structured around recognized positions that are asso-

ciated with recognized roles. In addition to the norms specific to each role, there are also recognized norms that guide all members of the group in their behavior ("We don't talk politics in *this* club"). Another formal characteristic of a group in the sociological sense is that it is oriented toward more or less specific goals—which can range from having fun to trading stamps to starting revolutions—that satisfy certain of its members' needs, whether generated through or outside the group. The sharing of a goal is a critical element in the focusing of a group's activities. Finally, the experience of recurrent interaction, shared goals, and satisfaction of needs is likely to give rise to a feeling of group identity, solidarity, and interdependence. In other words, members of a group feel themselves to be part of a collective whole, and from this feeling comes the sense of sharing a common fate that separates those who belong to the group from those who don't.

This description of group characteristics (Shaw,

Sociologists distinguish between aggregates, categories, and groups. (Upper left) An *aggregate* is a random assortment of people, such as these passengers in an airport waiting room, who happen to be in a given place at a given time. (Lower left) People who share certain basic characteristics—Islamic women, for example—form a *category*. (Below) A *group* is a collection of people—such as these cheerleaders—who interact regularly, hold recognized positions, play recognized roles, and work toward more or less specific goals. (Jeff Albertson/ Stock, Boston; Christine Spengler/Sygma; J. Berndt/Stock, Boston)

1976) is not intended to suggest a particular order of importance; sociologists disagree about what, if anything, is the single most fundamental characteristic of a group. However, all the factors just discussed are known to affect group functioning deeply, as we shall discover in this chapter.

As we have seen in previous chapters, groups are essential not only for our survival but even for the possibility of being what we consider fully human. People spend most of their everyday lives in groups—at work, at school, at play, at home. In these groups we are socialized and learn to enact roles. Indeed, most roles have meaning only within the context of groups. One can enact the role of leader only if one has a group of followers; likewise, one can play the role of mother only in the context of the family. In short, groups are the medium of experience through which we become social creatures, and they serve as the arena for most of our social behavior. Hence, as an elementary unit of social life, groups merit sociological study for their own sake.

In addition, groups are important to sociology because they are microcosms of larger social systems. As Theodore Mills put it, "They present, in miniature, societal features, such as division of labor, a code of ethics, a government, media of exchange, prestige rankings, ideologies, myths, and religious practices" (1967, p. 3). Indeed, in studying groups, sociologists can study such critical and basic phenomena as norms, customs, and culture itself. Thus, for some sociologists, the study of groups is the foundation of all sociological study.

Types of groups

A *group*, in the broadest sense, is any collection of persons who identify with one another and who engage in recurrent interactions structured by recognized statuses, roles, and norms in their pursuit of common goals. Within this general definition fit various types of groups, which were mentioned briefly in Chapter 4: the small group, the formal organization, the community, and even (on the most abstract level) the society itself. In this chapter we will deal with basic sociological concepts that apply to group interaction on any level. Our focus, however, will be on groups that are relatively small.

PRIMARY AND SECONDARY GROUPS

The term *primary group* was introduced in this century by the American sociologist Charles Horton Cooley to describe groups characterized by a high degree of intimacy. In his classic definition (1902), Cooley held that such groups "are primary in several senses, but chiefly in that they are fundamental in forming the social nature and ideals of the individual." As Cooley put it, when people find it natural to describe a group as "we," they are probably describing a primary group.

Cooley stressed the role of face-to-face interaction in defining and maintaining primary groups. Although it is true that face-to-face interaction among members is a common characteristic of primary groups, it is neither a necessary feature nor one that suffices to distinguish primary from secondary groups: as Kingsley Davis pointed out, some relationships, although they involve indirect contacts, may still be very intimate (as among members of a family that is geographically dispersed), and some, although they involve face-to-face contacts, may still be very impersonal (as between prostitutes and their customers). What is characteristic of the relationships among primary group members is at least some degree of emotional content or of especially close feelings (Davis, 1949). Davis also suggested that there are two other conditions characteristic of primary groups: small size and durability, both of which permit extensive and intimate contact only rarely possible in large or temporary aggregations. Thus, the archetypal primary group is the family. Other examples are street gangs, children's play groups, and even some types of social clubs. It is obvious that such groups have considerable impact on our lives. They are the primary locus of our socialization, the scene of our "private lives," and a major source of our identities.

Though primary groups are basic to our experience, much of our lives are lived in groups *not* characterized by close bonds of intimacy. Groups within which relationships tend toward the impersonal are called *secondary groups*. Only a very limited part of a person's loyal-

People who work together on a day-to-day basis exemplify a secondary group. Membership in such a group tends to be based on usefulness to oneself, rather than on intimacy with others. (© George W. Gardner/Stock, Boston)

ties and feelings are invested in his or her secondary groups. Rather, secondary-group relationships tend to be based more on usefulness—in short, on calculation, stereotyping, and instrumentality. We tend to take part in such groups because of what they *do* for us, not for what they *mean* to us. Typical examples are work groups that never meet outside the office or shop, civic organizations, and college classes.

Sometimes, for brief periods, secondary groups—or even simple aggregates of strangers—can be transformed into primary groups, particularly if they are isolated together or subjected to stress as a group. For example, during a strike, a work group may become a primary group. During the blackouts in New York City in 1965 and 1977, many secondary groups of apartment dwellers, and even aggregates of people who were stalled in elevators, briefly resembled primary groups. But unless the conditions that enforced intimacy continue, these groups can seldom retain their primary features, and so they drift back into the category of secondary groups, or aggregates.

It is important to recognize that primariness and secondariness are matters of degree and emphasis. All groups have some degree of intimacy—and all have some degree of impersonality: even spouses do not tell each other everything, nor do they discard all forms of etiquette. Thus, it is generally more accurate to assess the primary or secondary quality of a group in relative rather than absolute terms.

REFERENCE GROUPS

The concept of the *reference group* has become extremely important in sociological analysis (Merton, 1957), although some confusion surrounds the term itself. Strictly speaking, not all reference groups are groups in the sociological sense, so they are sometimes alternatively known as *reference others*. But the important point is that reference groups (or reference others) consist of people we turn to, literally or symbolically, when we are faced with a choice between attitudes or courses of action. Reference groups provide us with values, standards of behavior, and even in some cases a particular self-image (Shibutani, 1955). Individuals use *normative reference groups* (for example, their preferred daily newspaper) to set standards for their own actions; they model themselves on the standards and performance of their *comparative reference groups* (for example, a fledgling violinist might emulate Jascha Heifetz, or a Little Leaguer adopt Carl Yastrzemski's batting stance); and they adjust their behavior according to the evaluations that their *audience reference groups* make of them (for example, a professor might respond to feedback from the formal professor/student evaluations now common in many colleges and universities) (Kemper, 1968). Some groups, such as the family of a young child, may perform all three of these reference functions.

An individual's reference groups may be chosen from among his or her primary or secondary groups, but membership groups and reference groups do not necessarily coincide. Indeed, a person may have as a reference group a group or set of persons who are totally unaware of his or her existence. Lindesmith, Strauss, and Denzin (1975) divide people's reference groups into three categories: "(1) the groups in which they hold official membership; (2) others to which they aspire or to which they hope to belong in the future; and (3) others which they reject and definitely do not wish to belong to" (p. 476). Thus a fourteen-year-old girl may orient her behavior in reference to a rock group that does not even know her name, although she tirelessly copies their manner of dressing and singing. Furthermore, any reference group can serve in a positive or negative capacity. For example, the rock group functions for the girl as a *positive reference group*. Conversely, if she comes from a wealthy background of which she is not especially proud, her family (a primary group) may function for her as a *negative reference group*. That is, their norms and values—as well as their favorite foods, books, clothing styles, and so forth—may serve as a composite model of much that she does *not* want to be. Accordingly, she may judge herself by how well she succeeds in differing from that group.

A person's reference groups can be quite important in determining his or her other actions. In a study of college professors, for example, Alvin Gouldner (1957) found that while some faculty members were attentive to their relationships with local colleagues, others seemed to care little for the approval of their fellow faculty members, attending instead to their reputations among scholars in their field around the world. Gouldner used the terms *locals* and *cosmopolitans* to distinguish between these two types of professors; he found that certain aspects of their behavior could be more easily understood once their reference groups were identified. For example, locals are much more likely to be involved in campus governance; cosmopolitans in their disciplines' professional organizations.

Of course, reference groups never wholly determine a person's behavior. However, the concept is helpful to the sociologist in that hidden loyalties or aversions to reference groups often account for nuances of behavior not easily explained simply on the basis of the individual's primary and secondary group memberships.

How groups are formed

We find ourselves in certain groups, such as the family or the clan, simply by being born into them. Likewise, by enrolling in a college class or taking a certain job, we often find ourselves part of a new secondary group, made up of our classmates or co-workers. Many other groups, however, are formed quite deliberately with a specific goal or goals in mind; for example, couples marry and form families in order to establish stable affectional ties, rear children, and gain economic security. Some groups are formed deliberately with a *diffuse* goal or goals in mind; for example, people may form a social club for the general purpose of having fun. Indeed, *goal achievement* is the most obvious and probably the most common basis of group formation. But how do we choose the people with whom we will ally ourselves, even for a highly specific purpose? Recent research has pointed to two powerful determinants: proximity and similarity.

PROXIMITY

Groups, by definition, require considerable interaction among members. Hence it seems obvious that groups would tend to form among persons who happen to be near one another. However, obvious as the point may be, the extent to which sheer physical closeness shapes our social lives can be surprising.

Perhaps the most extensive and still useful examination of the effects of physical proximity on the formation of friendship groups was carried out by Leon Festinger, Stanley Schachter, and Kurt Back (1950), who

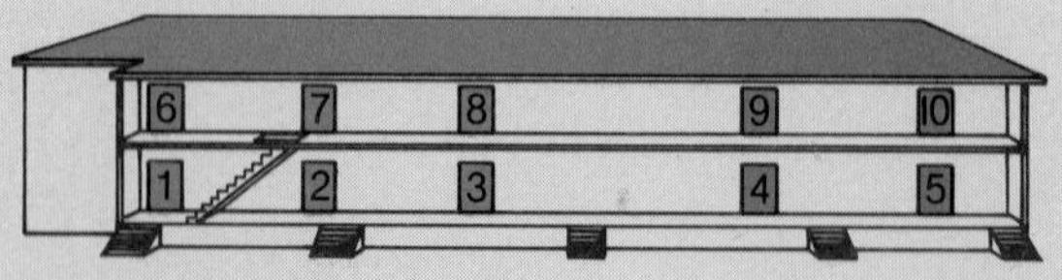

SOCIOMETRIC CHOICE AND PHYSICAL DISTANCE			
Units of Distance	Number of Choices Given	Possible Number of Choices	Percentage Choosing
1	112	8 × 34	41.2
2	46	6 × 34	22.5
3	22	4 × 34	16.2
4	7	2 × 34	10.3

FIGURE 8.1

Top: A housing unit similar to those in the student-housing complex where Festinger, Schachter, and Back investigated the effects of proximity on friendship formation. Bottom: Data from their study, showing that the fewer the units of distance that separated the subjects from other residents, the more likely the subjects were to choose those residents as friends.

studied the development of social interaction in housing units for married students at the Massachusetts Institute of Technology (MIT) just after World War II. Each resident was asked to list his or her best friends in the housing complex. As can be seen from the partial results shown in Figure 8.1, physical proximity, even within very narrow limits, is crucial to the formation of friendships. The MIT students were more likely to list as their close friends the people who lived next door than the people who lived two doors away. The latter, in turn, were more likely to be listed than those who lived three or four doors away. Friendships between couples living in different buildings in the complex followed the same pattern: the closer the building, the greater the likelihood that one of its residents would be listed as a close friend. In conducting their research, Festinger, Schachter, and Back discovered only one pattern that did not at first reflect this proximity principle: certain subjects tended to be listed as close friends somewhat more frequently than would be expected on

the basis of chance alone. The explanation had to do with the fact that these popular people lived in apartments closest to the foot of the stairs, where the garbage can was located. So in taking out their garbage, the residents of the building were brought into daily proximity with the people in these apartments, passing their door and perhaps exchanging a few words. Apparently, the probability that a friendship would develop increased as a result.

In short, then, the closer people live to one another, the more likely they are to form friendships. That distance should make some difference in friendship is of course no surprise; we all know, for example, that when a close friend moves to a town some distance away, the friendship tends to diminish. What is surprising is the fact—corroborated by many other researchers since the MIT study (for example, Ahlstrom and Havighurst, 1971; Schneider, 1976, pp. 469–470)—that someone's living ten feet away as opposed to thirty feet away also makes a substantial difference.

SIMILARITY

Proximity is not the only factor that brings people together into groups. Obviously, we tend to prefer people who resemble us—those who share our interests, values, beliefs, and ideals (Byrne, 1961; Byrne, Ervin, and Lambert, 1970). When people have free choice in forming or joining groups, they gravitate toward those who are similar to themselves in educational achievement, age, class, ethnic background, religion, and politics (e.g., Ahlstrom and Havighurst, 1971). (As we shall see in Chapter 14, the same holds true in the selection of marriage partners.) Furthermore, the more people interact under conditions of equality, the more they come to share values and interests and to like one another.

A very comprehensive study of similarity as a determinant of group formation was conducted by Newcomb in 1950. He followed students at the University of Michigan for an entire academic year, starting on the day they all moved into a cooperative housing unit. Newcomb's research showed that the ties formed between various members of groups resulted largely from the initial similarities and shared interests and values of the individuals involved. Griffith and Veitch (1974) later confirmed Newcomb's findings in a study of people living together for ten days in a fallout shelter. In sum, groups tend to form among people who are already similar, and group membership tends to make people even more similar than they were before. Group members share an initial identity based on certain qualities and interests; these are further reinforced by the common activities of the group.

So far we have briefly discussed various types of groups and two major principles underlying group formation. But once a group is formed, how does it actually operate? The remainder of the chapter will be devoted to this question. We begin with the matter of group norms.

Group norms

A fundamental aspect of group functioning has to do with *group norms*, the guidelines by which groups govern the actions and perceptions of their members. Since groups are so varied, the range of group norms is almost endless. Some of the most familiar types are reflected in common attitudes ("We believe in fair play in our family"), positive in-group identifications ("I'm proud to be a member of this company"), catchwords, and nicknames.

How do group norms come into being, and how great is their power over individual members? In considering these matters, we need to be aware of the fact that most small groups are actually subgroups, or parts of larger social entities; relevant norms are likely to be imposed on them by these larger units, in addition to the norms that emerge from their own activities. For example, a subcommittee of a legislature will develop its own norms, but it is also given a specific mandate and procedures that are based on the norms and goals of the legislature as a whole.

THE FORMATION OF GROUP NORMS

A classic study of norm formation in groups is Muzafer Sherif's 1936 experiment with group responses to a phenomenon called the autokinetic effect: if a person views a single point of light in a setting that is otherwise completely dark, the light will appear to move, though in fact it remains completely stationary. In the first stage of his experiment, Sherif exposed individuals, one at a time, to the autokinetic effect and asked them, on successive trials, to judge the distance that the light had moved—a difficult task, since the subjects, unable to

see anything else in the room, had no point of comparison. Sherif found that each subject soon developed his or her own subjective standard, or norm, against which to measure the extent of movement. However, in the second stage of the experiment, when these subjects were given the same test in small groups, their subjective standards gradually converged into a single group standard; each member, listening to the responses of the others, adjusted his or her own standard bit by bit until an unspoken consensus was reached. In groups whose members had not previously been tested on an individual basis, the convergence of standards occurred even more rapidly. And, most important, individual judgments made after the group experience matched the earlier group standard much more closely than did the individual's initial judgments.

Sherif's finding—later confirmed by other researchers in other types of perceptual tests—led him to conclude that group norms evolve through a gradual process of reciprocal influence among members: "Each compares his judgments with the others, consciously or unconsciously seeking interpersonal support in establishing secure boundaries and reference points where none existed before" (Sherif, 1966, p. xii). This explanation, now generally accepted by sociologists specializing in the study of groups, is easily corroborated by history. For example, contemporary accounts of the early pioneer settlements in the Midwest show that the settlers, faced with the task of developing rules with regard to property lines, town boundaries, election of officials, punishment of wrongdoers, and other essential matters, went through a process of suggestion, disagreement, trial, error, further suggestion, and further disagreement, until they eventually arrived at a workable consensus (Sherif and Sherif, 1969).

Groups reward conformity to their norms with companionship, esteem, and a sense of belonging. (© Lawrence Frank 1980)

CONFORMITY TO GROUP NORMS

As we have seen (and shall discuss further), group norms have substantial power over the behavior of members. Indeed, it may safely be said that small groups are considerably less tolerant than most societies when it comes to the question of members' exercising their free will. Likewise, individuals are generally more attentive to the norms of their various groups than to the norms of the society at large, for it is the group that doles out the majority of the individual's most valued rewards—physical sustenance, comfort, companionship, esteem, and the sense of belonging. As a result, conformity, though it has received a bad name in recent years, is something that each of us practices daily.

A now-famous study of conformity to group pressure was designed and conducted more than twenty-five years ago by the social psychologist Solomon Asch

(1952). The following is what you would have experienced if you had been a subject in one of Asch's experiments.

You and seven other students report to a classroom for an experiment on visual judgment. The experimenter says that you will be asked to judge the length of lines in a series of comparisons. He displays two large white cards like the ones shown in Figure 8.2. On one

FIGURE 8.2

Right: The two cards shown to a subject during one trial in the Asch experiment on conformity and resistance to group pressure. Opposite page: Asch's (1952) descriptions of an "independent" subject and a "yielder" in his experiment.

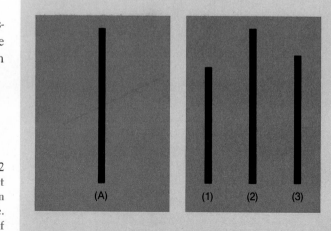

(A)   (1)   (2)   (3)

card is a single vertical line; on the other card are three vertical lines of different lengths. You are to choose the line that is the same length as the line on the first card. You can see that one of the three is equal to the standard, while the other two differ from it substantially. The experiment opens uneventfully. The subjects give their answers in the order in which they are seated in the room; you happen to be seventh, with one person coming after you. On the first comparison everyone chooses the same matching line. The second set of cards is displayed, and once again the group is unanimous. The discriminations seem very easy, and you settle in for what you expect will be a rather boring experiment.

On the third trial, however, something strange happens. You are quite certain that line 3 is the one that matches the standard, but the first person in the group announces confidently that line 1 is the correct match. The second person agrees. So do the third, fourth, fifth, and sixth subjects. Now it is your turn. What you thought was going to be an uncomplicated task has turned into a disturbing problem. You are faced with two totally contradictory pieces of information: your own eyes tell you that one answer is clearly correct, but the unanimous and confident judgments of the six preceding subjects tell you that another answer is correct. What do you do? Do you stick to your initial judg-

ment, or do you go along with the others?

Your dilemma persists through eighteen trials. On twelve of the trials, the other group members unanimously give an answer that differs from what you clearly perceive to be correct. It is only at the end of the experimental session that you learn you have been duped: the seven other subjects were confederates of the experimenter, who had instructed them to respond as they did.

How do most people react to this situation? A large proportion go along with the others and give wrong answers. Of fifty subjects in the Asch experiment, almost one-third conformed to the inaccurate answers of the confederates at least half the time. Later research by Middlebrook (1974, p. 533) raises the possibility that the tendency to conform might be even stronger than Asch's findings originally suggested. What accounts for this conformity? In interviews with Asch after the experiment, very few of the "yielders" reported that they *perceived* the majority's choice as correct. Most yielders said that they believed their own perceptions to be correct but that they yielded to group pressure so as not to appear different from or inferior to the others. Apparently, these subjects felt that if they did not go along with the group, they would be revealing some basic weakness in themselves that they preferred to hide.

INDEPENDENT

After a few trials he appeared puzzled, hesitant. He announced all disagreeing answers in the form of "Three, sir; two, sir." At Trial 4 he answered immediately after the first member of the group, shook his head, blinked, and whispered to his neighbor, "Can't help it, that's one." His later answers came in a whispered voice, accompanied by a deprecating smile. At one point he grinned embarrassedly and whispered explosively to his neighbor: "I always disagree—darn it!" Immediately after the experiment the majority engaged this subject in a brief discussion. When they pressed him to say whether the entire group was wrong and he alone right, he turned upon them defiantly, exclaiming: "You're *probably* right, but you may be wrong!" During the experimenter's later questioning, this subject's constant refrain was: "I called them as I saw them, sir."

YIELDER

This subject went along with the majority in eleven out of twelve trials. He appeared nervous and somewhat confused, but he did not attempt to evade discussion at the close of the experiment. He opened the discussion with the statement: "If I'd been first I probably would have responded differently." This was his way of saying that he had adopted the majority estimates. The primary factor in his case was loss of confidence. He perceived the majority as a decided group, acting without hesitation: "If they had been doubtful I probably would have changed, but they answered with such confidence." When the real purpose of the experiment was explained, the subject volunteered: "I suspected about the middle—but tried to push it out of my mind." It is of interest that his suspicions did not restore his confidence or diminish the power of the majority.

In sum, the opinion of the group is so highly valued that many people will conform to it even when they realize that it is completely in error. Furthermore, it should be noted that Asch's groups were actually aggregates rather than groups—the subjects had not been acquainted with each other prior to the experiment. This is an important point, because the members of an actual group could almost by definition be expected to conform far more readily to the judgment of other members. Moreover, in everyday life, groups tend to focus on matters that are far more ambiguous—such as attitudes about people or events—than such experimental situations devised by social psychologists, which reduces the likelihood that one member of a group would perceive another as being dead wrong in an opinion. But even if it can be clearly shown that group membership implies a high level of conformity, another question remains to be answered, namely, what is it about groups that makes people conform in the first place?

THE DETERMINANTS OF CONFORMITY

Human beings are generally conforming creatures. Nevertheless, some individuals conform more fully than others, and some groups are able to exact more conformity than others. What individual characteristics are particularly conducive to conformity? Several studies (e.g., Marlowe and Gergen, 1968) have found that people with low self-esteem are more likely to yield to group pressure than those with high self-esteem. The latter, obviously, can afford to risk group disapproval. However, it has also been observed that the higher a person's status within a group, the more likely that person is to adhere to group norms (Sherif and Sherif, 1964; Homans, 1950). Thus there is experimental support for the notion that promotions tend to create "company men"—or, at least, that "company men" get promoted.

More crucial to sociologists are the determinants of conformity that relate to characteristics of the group itself. Researchers have isolated a number of group characteristics that encourage faithfulness to the collective norms. One factor that correlates highly with conformity is *group cohesiveness*—the degree to which the members stick together, through friendship with other members and through identification with the group as a whole. For example, in the MIT study cited earlier (Festinger, Schachter, and Back, 1950), it was found that the higher the proportion of friendships within a housing unit, the smaller the proportion of residents who deviated from group standards. More recently, a study by Roger Brown and H. Garland (1971) suggests that a factor in such conformity may be the wish to avoid embarrassment resulting from nonconformity with others with whom one will continue to interact. Another important determinant of conformity within a group is the degree of interdependence among members. When members must rely on one another for their well-being, they are more likely to impose controls on behavior. For example, F. J. Roethlisberger and William J. Dickson (1939), in a classic study of a group of telephone wiremen at the Western Electric Company's Hawthorne Plant in Chicago, found that despite company incentive programs to encourage greater productivity, the men had settled on a clear and unambitious norm as to what constituted a day's work: wiring about 6,000 terminals. To do less was disapproved of as "chiseling." But to do more was very seriously condemned, since the men felt that such zeal could lead the company to raise the work requirements for the entire group or to lay off some of the workers. Hence, those who insisted on working at a pace faster than the group norm were given derisive nicknames ("Slave," "Lightning," "Cyclone," "Speed King," "Rate-buster"), openly criticized, and even semiplayfully punched on the arm ("binged") by the other workers. Hardworking independents were simply not good for the group. (For a discussion of other findings of this study, see Chapter 9.)

All in all, it may be said that conformity to group norms will be taken most seriously by members when they stand to lose something important—be it money or friendship or the achievement of a prized goal—through nonconformity, either by themselves or by others. And since a good deal of what is important to all of us is derived from group interaction, complete autonomy is virtually unknown to human beings. As *social* creatures, we depend on benefits bestowed on us by other individuals and by social groups, and in return for receiving these benefits from others we forfeit some of our freedom for their sake.

Group structure

A group is not an assemblage of homogeneous parts performing identical functions, like a school of minnows swimming in the same direction. On the contrary, every group, when examined closely, reveals an intricate system of highly differentiated statuses and roles, in which different members have different rankings, different amounts of power, and different functions to perform.

ROLES

Roles—a subject discussed in detail in Chapter 4—can best be understood within the context of groups, since it is the group that imposes on each individual many if not most of the behavioral expectations that constitute his or her role. (Furthermore, it is the group—initially the family—that provides the reciprocal interactions that teach us our roles in the first place.) The group may be seen as a system of interlocking roles, learned in sets of two or more, with each member molding his or her behavior to dovetail with the behavior of the other members whose roles are linked with his or her own. In a traditional family, for example, the father's role may include earning the money, disciplining the children, and making major family decisions, such as whether or not to buy a new car or move to a different neighborhood. The mother, in return, may be expected to provide physical and emotional nurturance (cooking, cleaning, cuddling, bandaging skinned knees, encouraging her husband in his work). The children may be expected to love and obey their parents. Thus each member both gives and receives, according to a tacit contract.

Roles, as we have seen, are normative; that is, they are expectations with a degree of social and moral force behind them. Also, members of a group such as the family may play more than one role. Consequently, people can sometimes experience conflict between their different roles, and they can also experience *role inadequacy*—an inability or lack of desire to keep on playing a role. To illustrate, suppose that a mother decides to give up full-time nurturing in favor of law school, or that she simply becomes depressed and ceases to do housework. Other members of the group may react with considerable bitterness because, after all, someone has violated a norm: in this case, the mother is not doing what others think she *should* be doing. Such bitterness is not unjustified, since role failure on the part of any one member is likely to disturb the functioning of the entire mechanism. The group will not return to the prior level of functioning until the "errant" member resumes his or her role or until the other reciprocal roles are readjusted and reapportioned.

If the occupant of a specific role is removed from the group or is incapacitated, his or her role may simply be taken over by another member. This process, called *role appropriation*, is made possible by the fact, mentioned above, that many roles are reciprocal and are thus learned in pairs. We learn the child role by responding to the cues of a person who is enacting the parent role. Consequently, when a mother dies, for example, an older child can often assume a reasonable facsimile of the mother role, having learned it through playing the child role over some period of time.

STATUS STRUCTURE

Just as group members have different roles, so these roles invariably have different rankings. Groups are never made up of equals; inevitably, as George Orwell wryly observes in *Animal Farm*, "some are more equal than others." The pattern of rank in a group is known as its *status structure*. (As we indicated in Chapter 4, the term *status* is usually used by sociologists simply to denote location in a social structure of any sort; but in this particular context, it implies an evaluation of the individual by other group members that results in the individual's being placed on a step in a hierarchy, or ladder of ranks.)

In groups that are relatively highly structured, the social *positions* may be ranked; for example, the positions of chairperson, secretary-treasurer, and committee

STREET CORNER SOCIETY

The workings of gangs have always interested sociologists, but William Whyte approached the subject in an unusual way—from inside. During the 1930s Whyte joined a corner gang in "Cornerville," his pseudonym for a poor, Italian neighborhood in Boston, and *Street Corner Society* (1965) is the product of his observations.

Cornerville had two "classes" of young men: college boys and corner boys. Although Whyte mixed with both groups, they didn't communicate easily with each other. Cornerville also had a settlement house. Its social workers encouraged the college boys' aspirations—but they were glad not to have to deal with the "roughnecks." Instead of working with the social organization as it was, they preferred to deal with those who didn't fit into it:

[The settlement house] accepts those who already are maladjusted in terms of the local society, it rewards them for breaking away from the ties of Cornerville, and it encourages them to better their social and economic positions. To a certain extent, this is a conscious policy. The social workers want to deal with "the better element." (Whyte, 1965, p. 104)

Better or no, the corner boys, specifically the Norton Street Gang, had as complex a social structure as any. Although their organization was informal, the Nortons revealed the power structure and lines of communication and expectation that characterized all groups. Corner boys were actually more cohesive than college boys:

Both the college boy and the corner boy want to get ahead. The difference between them is that the college boy either does not tie himself to a group of close friends or else is willing to sacrifice his friendship with those who do not advance as fast as he does. The corner boy is tied to his group by a network of reciprocal obligations from which he is either unwilling or unable to break away. (Whyte, 1965, p. 107)

What were these reciprocal obligations, and how did they affect the Nortons' lives? Gang members overtly recognized only one norm: members should help each other and not hurt each other. As in other informal groups, the sanctions that mutually bound members operated invisibly—they became palpable only when things went wrong. The group had an unacknowledged status structure, for example, with a leader, Doc, a few high-status friends, and low-status followers. Status only became an issue, however, when a follower needed putting "in his place," and then, ironically, it was most likely other *followers* who were uncomfortable with the threat to the group's equilibrium and who worked, albeit unconsciously, to reestablish the traditional gradations. Take bowling, for instance (bowling was a primary social activity of the Norton Street Gang). When a lower-status member bowled well, he received a much different reaction than a higher-status member, from whom good scores were expected and whose bad scores were seen as bad luck or a temporary lapse:

When a follower threatened to better his position, . . . the boys shouted at him that he was lucky, that he was "bowling over his head." The effort was made to persuade him that he should not be bowling as well as he was, that a good performance was abnormal for him. This type of verbal attack was very important in keeping the members "in their places." It was used particularly by the followers so that, in effect, they were trying to keep one another down. (Wilson, 1978, p. 10)

Thus do followers "make" leaders—literally maintaining their positions for them.

As leader, however, Doc had the highest and most numerous expectations projected on him. He was supposed to relate the group to others outside it, to make good decisions and move the group toward satisfying ac-

members are ranked, with chairperson at the top of the hierarchy. In many small groups, however, it is likely that the individuals themselves, rather than their positions, will be ranked. The ranking of individuals in a group appears to involve three factors (Crosbie, 1975). First are external characteristics of the member based on the social categories he or she belongs in—for example, gender, race, and occupation—many of which are themselves ranked in the larger society as a whole. Second are the other members' first impressions of the individual in question, often affected by his or her physical attractiveness. Third is the individual's performance

of his or her role within the group. Exactly how these three factors affect the group's evaluation of the individual and the status he or she eventually ends up with is a matter of some debate. In a well-known experiment by Fred Strodtbeck, Rita M. James, and Charles Hawkins (1957), it was found that in the early stages of group interaction, the first two factors were most influential, but that as group members came to know one another better, these initial criteria gradually gave way to the individual's role performance as the major basis for status evaluation.

In the Strodtbeck, James, and Hawkins study, the

tivities, and to be generous. He fulfilled his role well; it's a terrible thing to be left behind by the boys, he believed. "If the boys are going to a show, and this man can't go because he is batted out [broke], I say to myself, 'Why should he be deprived of that luxury?' And I give him the money . . . . And I never talk about it" (Whyte, 1965, p. 106).

As Whyte sees it, this attitude toward money was what distinguished those who got ahead in Cornerville from those who remained on the corner; a college education was only part of the larger pattern:

The college boys fit in with an economy of savings and investment. The corner boys fit in with a spending economy. The college boy must save his money in order to finance his education and launch his business or professional career. He therefore cultivates the middle-class virtue of thrift. In order to participate in group activities, the corner boy must share his money with others. If he has money and his friend does not, he is expected to do the spending for both of them. It is possible to be thrifty and still be a corner boy, but it is not possible to be thrifty and yet hold a high position in the corner gang. As a rule, the corner boy does not consciously spend money for the purpose of acquiring influence over his fellows. He fits into the pattern of action of his group, and his behavior has the effect of increasing his influence. (Whyte, 1965, p. 106)

Both Doc's leadership and the group's equilibrium as a whole were destroyed by the Depression. Unemployed, no one could act as he was expected to act.

Whyte's book has become a sociological classic. In answer to questions such as, Who gets ahead in America? Do ties to a neighborhood and community help or hinder? Whose values and ideals do social workers properly represent? *Street Corner Society* holds some disturbing insights.

researchers set up mock juries, which listened to a prerecorded trial, deliberated, and reached a verdict. In the early stage of the deliberations, members of high-status occupations were more likely to be chosen as foremen or forewomen, and their opinions were more readily acceded to by the group. However, the group's respect for external characteristics based on social category evidently diminished with time. Toward the end of the proceedings, when the jurors were asked which types of occupational positions they would like to see represented on a jury judging them or a member of their family, the jurors' choices had less to do with conven-

tional notions of occupational position than with the occupational positions of those who had contributed most to the mock deliberations. In other words, the jurors had come to esteem each other as individuals, and this new esteem motivated them to revise —upward—their esteem for one another's occupations.

Certain later studies, however, have come to the opposite conclusion. Joseph Berger and his co-workers (1972), for example, found that a new member's "diffuse" external status characteristics, such as sex, age, occupation, education, and regional origin, tended to affect other group members' expectations for the newcomer's behavior, and thus affected his or her ultimate status within the group. We should mention that two characteristics of these studies warrant that caution be used in applying their results. First, the particular experimental design limits the actual interaction between participants, though this interaction is crucial in maintaining or changing the effect of external status characteristics on people's judgments of others. Second, in these experiments, the objective feedback or evaluation one might expect in everyday life is absent.

At any rate, status rankings are assigned. Once they are assigned, they have a clear influence on interactions among members. Those with low status tend to show deferential behavior—waiting for cues from others, raising their hands before speaking, assenting to others' opinions, and carrying out others' directives. Conversely, high status gives rise to confident, "take-charge" behaviors, such as expressing opinions, disagreeing openly with others, taking action, and giving orders (Crosbie, 1975, p. 184). Hence the status structure has an immense impact on the actions of the group, since these are generally decided upon by the higher-status members. And because the actions and perceptions of higher-status members are more likely to be perceived as correct (Sherif, White, and Harvey, 1955), the group's faith in the superiority of these members is reinforced, with the result that the status structure becomes self-perpetuating.

POWER AND LEADERSHIP

Power in a group is usually divided among several members; the more complex the group, the more complex the power structure (Collins and Raven, 1969, p. 160). Power may derive from many sources—from information as to how goals are to be achieved, from the ability to punish and reward, from expertise, from identification of persons with one another, or from the individual's affiliation with another group that functions as a positive reference group for the members of the group in question (French and Raven, 1959; Raven, 1965; Collins and Raven, 1969). In addition, various members of the group may hold differing degrees of authority, or legitimate power. An individual's authority is, in essence, based upon the consent of those who are to be influenced. The precise degree of authority that an individual may acquire derives from the recognition by others of that individual's superiority with respect to the group's values, norms, and goals. Thus, the holder of the most legitimate power is the one by whom the other members are most willing to be influenced. It is this ability to elicit voluntary compliance with one's decisions (an ability usually combined with other sources of power) that distinguishes the group leader.

Actually, leadership, like power, may be divided among two or more members. The more complex the group and its tasks, the more leadership tends to be apportioned and specialized. However, even in very simple laboratory groups, two distinctive leadership functions can be observed: *instrumental leadership*, which involves directing the group toward the achievement of its goals, and *expressive leadership*, which consists of maintaining harmony and solidarity among group members. (These two leadership functions parallel the traditional father and mother roles in the family, which is not surprising because, as we will see in Chapter 14, the family is itself a small group. Of course, other role systems are possible within the family, but this small-group process is one of the forces that support the traditional arrangement.) It is possible for a single person to perform both leadership roles, but laboratory findings indicate that this is both difficult and rare in "successful" groups. Although leaders usually begin by playing both roles (being well liked helps them dominate task-directed activities, at least initially), they seldom hold both for very long. For example, in more than half the groups taking part in a series of small-group experiments (Slater, 1955), the same group member was ranked first on both "liking" (expressive leadership) and "ideas" (instrumental leadership) after the first session. After the second session, however, only 12 percent of the groups ranked the same individual first on both instrumental and expressive leadership. The

proportion dropped to 8 percent by the fourth session. One caveat is in order here: these groups were composed of status equals; among status unequals, varying concentrations of power and authority are possible, and even common.

WHO LEADS?

The question of what personality traits distinguish people chosen to be leaders has fascinated many people for a long time. In the 1930s and 1940s this question stimulated a good deal of sociological and social-psychological research, the findings of which are summarized by Paul Crosbie:

Among some of the traits identified in this research were that leaders tend to be taller (Caldwell and Wellman, 1926), bigger and healthier (Bellingrather, 1930), neater (Partridge, 1934), more intelligent and self-confident (Gibb, 1947), better adjusted (Holtzman, 1952), more extroverted and dominant (Goodenough, 1930; Hunter and Jordan, 1939), and more empathetic (Chowdhry and Newcomb, 1952) than nonleaders. (1975, p. 222)

However, these studies and later ones eventually yielded conflicting results, which casts doubt on the notion that there are consistent personality traits that distinguish leaders from followers. Furthermore, it became clear that the qualities of the leader often had more to do with the precise requirements of the particular leadership role in question than with any abstract ideal of "the leader" (Hollander and Julian, 1970). Thus, while acknowledging that there are certain traits that characterize many leaders (for example, intelligence, extroversion, empathy, emotional stability, self-confidence, and a taste for dominance [Gibb, 1947]), sociologists and social psychologists in recent years have given more attention to leadership behaviors, which can be measured with relative precision, than to leadership traits.

First, the behavioral characteristic that appears to be most distinctive in emerging leaders is a high quantity of participation in the group. Leaders-to-be talk more, make more suggestions, and offer more opinions; in short, they seem to be in the role of leader already. Second, the usefulness of the individual's participation—the extent to which it facilitates the group's achievement of its goals—affects his or her chances of being chosen as leader, though quality of participation, surprisingly, has less impact than quantity (Jaffe and Lucas, 1969). Third, it appears that conformity to

Sociologists have identified four characteristics that set group leaders apart from other members—high quantity of participation, usefulness of participation, conformity to group norms, and a high status ranking within the group. (Peter Vandermark/Stock, Boston)

the differentiation of *in-groups* from *out-groups*. They also point out that when group boundaries form, these delineations are reflected in attitudes of self-justification and self-righteousness about the in-group and varying degrees of friendliness or hostility toward outgroups. We saw these hostile attitudes in the negative stereotypes each lodge at the summer camp developed about the other lodges.

Most of the traditional studies of group boundaries have been based on sociometric techniques such as recording and analyzing people's attitudes and perceptions. Here subjects are asked to list those others who "have the best ideas" or "promote group solidarity" or are requested to state "those they like best" and so on. From these judgments, a sociometric diagram (see Figure 8.3) of positive ties, negative ties, and absence of ties can be created and examined. However, more sophisticated approaches to the study of group boundaries have recently been formulated on the basis of the mathematical and analytical precepts of information theory (e.g., Phillips and Conviser, 1972). Apart from

group norms is to some degree a prerequisite for leadership (Hollander, 1960), perhaps as a token of the individual's loyalty to the group. Finally, it should come as no surprise that the qualities that determine status ranking—namely, first impression, external status characteristics, and general performance—also determine leadership. It should be kept in mind that all these behavioral characteristics are relational—they must be assessed in the context of a particular situation involving a specific group of people. Fiedler (1964; 1967; 1971) has continually stressed this interactional model of leadership.

THE GROUP BOUNDARY

The formation of a group's internal structure is likely to be accompanied by the formation of a group boundary, a shared sense that there is a difference between group members (who think of themselves as "we") and other individuals or groups outside the boundary (who are thought of as "they"). Muzafer and Carolyn Sherif (1953), the social psychologists who carried out the summer-camp study mentioned at the beginning of this chapter, describe this process of boundary formation as

FIGURE 8.3

A sociogram showing the pattern of mutual and unreciprocated friendship choices within a six-person group. Persons A, C, and D are the most popular and influential, having been chosen by three of the other members. Persons A, B, C, and D form a subgroup, or clique. Persons B and C are a dyad, as are persons A and D. Person F is almost an isolate.

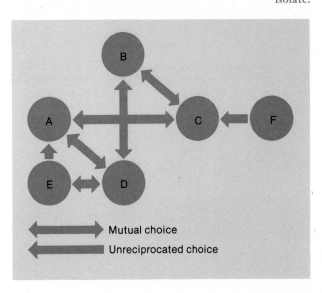

whatever specific findings may eventually emerge from such new directions in the study of groups, it is interesting to note that information theory has also been applied to the study of both very large organizations and computer systems. Thus, in-group/out-group delineation may prove to be a phenomenon of very wide significance. We will return to the concept in later chapters, particularly in Unit Five.

Group processes and interactions

As we have seen, a primary characteristic of groups is a sustained pattern of interaction. Members of groups *act upon* one another—they talk to one another, influence one another, disagree with one another, form subgroups with and against one another, and cling to one another. Essentially, these processes constitute the life of the group.

George C. Homans (1950) pointed out that the group is really involved in two processes at once. On the one hand, it has to survive within its physical, technical, or social environment; thus, some of the behavior of individual members and some of their interactions will be directed toward solving problems that lie outside the group's boundary. On the other hand, the group has to maintain its own inner structure. This is not easy, for externally oriented behaviors may eventually affect activities and interactions *within* the group. Following this line of thought, Robert F. Bales (1950) suggested ways in which adapting to the outer environment may threaten solidarity within the group. For example, to perform an external task, a group may have to set up a more complex division of labor, or it may have to distribute authority, status, and material resources more unequally—thus bringing about changes in group structure that may tend to make the group itself disintegrate.

In sum, group interaction always reflects an uneasy balance; it is subject to pressures both from the external task and from the need to maintain its inner structure and meet the interpersonal needs of its members. In examining group interaction in terms of this balance, we shall focus on three central patterns: communication, conflict, and cohesiveness. We shall also see how these three patterns are affected by the group's size.

COMMUNICATION

Communication within groups is neither randomly nor equally distributed among members. Rather, it is patterned by the structural properties just discussed—roles, status, power, and leadership. Indeed, careful observation of who addresses whom in a group can yield a reasonably clear picture of its status structure. Bales has

TABLE 8.1

ACTS TOWARD OTHERS IN A SMALL GROUP

	TARGET OF ACT						TOTAL INDIVIDUAL-DIRECTED ACTS	GROUP-DIRECTED ACTS	TOTAL OF ACTS INITIATED
INITIATOR OF ACT	A	B	C	D	E	F			
Person A		1,238	961	545	445	317	3,506	5,661	9,167
Person B	1,748		443	310	175	102	2,278	1,211	3,989
Person C	1,371	415		305	125	69	2,285	742	3,027
Person D	952	310	282		83	49	1,676	676	2,352
Person E	662	224	144	83		28	1,141	443	1,585
Person F	470	126	114	65	44		819	373	1,192
Total of Acts Received	5,203	2,313	1,944	1,308	872	565	12,208	9,106	21,311

SOURCE: Adapted from Bales et al., 1951, p. 463.

conducted many studies of communication within small groups. Table 8.1 shows the distribution of all interactions in eighteen sessions of six-person groups in a study by Bales and his associates (1951). These findings show that when group members are ranked according to the total number of interactions they initiate, this ranking is similar to rankings based on: (1) the number of interactions they receive; (2) the number of interactions they address to other specific persons; and (3) the number of interactions they address to the group as a whole. It is easy to see that person A is the leader of the group and that person F is an extremely marginal member—few people talk to him, and he does not talk much to anyone (Bales et al., 1951). Such patterns of interaction are even easier to see when they are presented schematically in a *sociogram* like the one shown in Figure 8.6.

Communication within a group, particularly a stable group (Crosbie, 1975, pp. 261–262), tends to be directed from equal to equal and from higher-ranking persons to lower-ranking persons. Henry W. Rieken and George C. Homans (1954) found that this pattern was influenced by the nature of the group activity. Communication is primarily between high- and low-ranking members in task situations and between equals in social or leisure situations. Similarly, there is more communication with instrumental leaders during task situations and more communication with expressive leaders during social situations.

CONFLICT

The reciprocal influence that constitutes group interaction is, of course, not always harmonious. It is a rare group that is not subject to some degree of conflict. Such conflict may be so severe as to dissolve the group, or—at the opposite extreme—it may be very beneficial, forcing the group to make realistic adjustments in roles, status rankings, and norms. Drawing on mathematical and game-theory models, Letha and John Scanzoni (1976, pp. 348–356) categorized such conflict into three sets of antitheses; although they applied this schema specifically to the family, it is equally applicable to other small groups.

1. *Zero-sum versus mixed-motive conflict:* In *zero-sum conflict*, the combatants are both going for all or nothing; whoever does not win will lose completely. Imag-

ine, for example, an activist group in which two members are engaged in a bitter contest for leadership. Each loudly proclaims his or her own goals for the group—goals opposite to those of the other would-be leader—and each demands the ouster of the other. In this case, the loser, discredited and disgraced, will have to leave the group. In *mixed-motive conflict*, however, neither combatant wants to see the other lose everything, since their relationship and the harmony of the group would suffer too greatly thereby. Hence, each is willing to compromise.

2. *Personality-based versus situational conflict: Personality-based conflict*, as the name indicates, has to do with the clash of incompatible temperaments. Such, for example, would appear to be the problem in a family disrupted by conflict between a dependent, affection-seeking husband and a coldly efficient wife who believes that "the Lord helps those who help themselves." However, in many cases a conflict that appears to be personality-based is actually masking a *situational conflict*—that is, a dispute over some specific reward. For example, it might turn out that the couple in question have had a troubled sex life since the beginning of their marriage and that the husband is now impotent. If this particular situational problem can be solved through sexual counseling, then it is likely that the "personality" conflict will resolve itself—the husband, his confidence restored, becoming less weak and the wife, her source of resentment removed, becoming less cold.

3. *Nonbasic versus basic conflict:* In *nonbasic conflict*, the combatants quarrel, within the rules of the game, over some specific object; in *basic conflict*, the rules of the game are the specific object of the quarrel. Let us take the case of a seven-member English department in a small college. If the faculty members disagree about the sequence of course requirements for English majors, then this is a nonbasic conflict. All members agree that required courses are justified; the only question is whether, say, the modern British novel should precede or follow Romantic poetry. However, if the conflict centers on whether requirements should actually be imposed, with some members arguing that they constitute necessary guidance and others contending that students should be free to choose their own courses, then this is a basic conflict. The rules of the game—that is, what role the department will play in directing the students' education—are in dispute.

Mixed-motive, situational, and nonbasic conflicts are easier to resolve, since less is in dispute. Resolving zero-sum, personality-based, and basic conflicts generally requires massive adjustment on the part of one or all disputants, though in the case of the last two, this adjustment, if it is reciprocal, may still benefit the group.

Up to this point, conflict has been depicted as detrimental to the group's functioning. Lewis A. Coser (1956; 1967), among others, has shown that conflict has positive consequences as well. For example, social conflict can help to clarify group boundaries and group goals, and can promote reintegration through normative regulation of conflict. Normative regulation refers to establishing rules within which conflict is played out (for example, the Marquis of Queensberry rules for boxing contests). To determine whether potential conflict can promote the reintegration of groups, Phillip Bonacich (1972) designed an experiment in which the members of a group of five people stood to gain the most by not cooperating with each other, but also risked losing the most by not cooperating. Since collective action would produce at least some gain for everyone, Bonacich hypothesized that as the temptation to act individually increased, so would the group members' attempts to define noncooperation as negative, immoral, and unethical. In fact, this is just what happened: not only did the members of the experimental groups firmly establish cooperative action as their norm, but they also became increasingly friendly toward one another as they successfully resisted evergreater temptations to place individual interests over the interests of the group as a whole. Thus it seems that conflict in and of itself cannot be viewed as either positive or negative; whether it is positive or negative is determined by the way the group deals with the conflict, and ultimately by the effects of the conflict on the group's activities.

COHESIVENESS

The *cohesiveness* of groups—defined as the degree to which members wish to remain in the group (Cartwright, 1968, p. 91)—has been the subject of considerable research (e.g., Tedeschi, Schlenker, and Bonoma, 1973; Marshall and Heslin, 1975; Terborg, Castore, and De Ninno, 1976). Cohesiveness may be measured in a number of ways. Members may be polled on how much they desire to remain in the group, how intensely they identify with the group, or how they evaluate the group. Another common technique for assessing group cohesiveness is the sociometric method, originally devised by Jacob Moreno (1953) and his associates (e.g., Jennings, 1950). Group members are asked to name their best friends, and the extent to which they choose other group members rather than persons outside the group is used as an index of cohesiveness.

What are the consequences of group cohesiveness? One consequence is that the group itself becomes a more solid entity; membership remains more stable and members are more likely to conform to group norms (Cartwright, 1968; Thibaut and Kelley, 1959). As for members, their performance on tasks, morale, and degree of satisfaction with the group are all improved (Collins and Raven, 1969). Furthermore, a cohesive group gives its members a sense of personal security—a fact that appears to be related to the interesting finding that, contrary to the accepted wisdom, groups tend to take greater risks than individuals (Stoner, 1961; Teger and Pruitt, 1967; Cartwright, 1971). This phenomenon, called the "risky shift," may operate for better or for worse. It is unlikely that any single member of a lynch mob would lynch a man alone; likewise, it is improbable that any one of the original thirteen colonies would have issued its own Declaration of Independence. Apparently, the fact that responsibility for possible failure is spread over the entire group encourages individual members to take chances that they would never take if they had to endure blame alone (Wallach and Kogan, 1965). Although there is some evidence that the "risky shift" phenomenon may depend on the nature of the situation (Middlebrook, 1974, pp. 526–528), a highly cohesive group, no matter how small (for example, a dedicated terrorist group), is a power to be reckoned with.

THE EFFECTS OF GROUP SIZE

In this discussion of group processes and interactions, it is important to raise the question of the effect of group size on communication, conflict, and cohesiveness. We must ask, for example, whether it is logical (or useful) to compare a political power play in a small family with one that takes place among a small group of nations. Georg Simmel (1950) showed that such a comparison could be made. He compared the strategy of a mother-in-law confronting a newly married couple with the ways in which Rome, after subjugating Greece, dealt with Athens and Sparta. "Divide and conquer" was the interaction pattern on which Simmel focused; the point of his comparison was that the *number* of members in a small group makes a great difference in group interaction, whether the group is made up of individuals or countries. If a group is a *dyad* (a two-member group), the members are totally dependent on each other; both must bear responsibility. But if the group becomes a *triad* (a three-member group), one member can shift responsibility to the group. Thus, one member can divide and conquer, play mediator, or profit from a disagreement between the other two. And as the group grows from three or four to ten, fifty, or a hundred, interaction patterns continue to change. Interestingly, the total number of possible relationships in a group increases from one in a two-person group to twenty-five in a four-person group to 966 in a seven-person group.

The larger the group, the more the leadership dominates communications, the more the group tolerates direction by the leadership, and the more formalized the group's procedures become (Bales and Borgatta, 1955). In very small groups, interaction can take place informally, and leadership can be loosely exercised. But beyond a certain size—apparently about five to seven members—domination by the leadership increases rapidly. Michel (1915) has called this the "iron law of oligarchy" (see Chapters 9 and 18). The reason for this domination is obvious. The larger the group, the greater the possibility of chaos; if everyone in a large group tries to talk at once, no one will hear anything at all, and consequently nothing will get done. Hence the need for formalized interactions. This principle clearly holds true for societies. Participatory democracy as practiced in New England town meetings is possible only as long as everyone can fit into the town hall. Mass societies, on the other hand, must resort to more formal and impersonal representative government simply because they are so large, unless they choose to decentralize and devolve authority onto smaller units.

Group cohesiveness is also affected by size (Marshall and Heslin, 1975). Studies of work groups, for example, have consistently shown that as the size of the group increases, job satisfaction decreases. Concomitantly, absenteeism and turnover rates rise, and labor-management disputes become more frequent with increased size (Porter and Lawler, 1965). For most task groups, productivity increases with the size of the group up to a point, beyond which it reaches a plateau and then begins to decline (Steiner, 1972).

Group size, of course, has a great deal to do with the

The number of members in a group greatly affects group interaction. Top: In a *dyad* (two-member group), the members are totally dependent on each other; if one person leaves the group, it will cease to exist. Bottom: In a *triad* (three-member group), interrelationships are more complex; one member can mediate disputes or benefit from a disagreement between the others, for example. (Burk Uzzle/Magnum; © Lawrence Frank 1976)

quality and frequency of interaction among members. The smaller the group, the more opportunity members have for informal interaction; and the sense of intimacy and belonging that results from such interaction often constitutes the social "glue" that binds members together, making the group cohesive. Though cohesiveness decreases as the size of the group increases, conformity has been found to increase with group size (Gerard, Wilhelmy, and Conolley, 1968).

Thus, size can have an important effect on the interaction patterns of a group—on communication, conflict, cohesiveness, and conformity. It can also affect structural patterns, such as the division and interrelationships of roles. We will explore all these factors in more detail in Chapter 9, where we turn to the study of a special kind of group—the relatively large, relatively intricate group known as the formal organization.

Summary

In sociology, the term *group* refers to a collection of people with certain specific characteristics: a recurrent pattern of interaction structured by recognized roles and by group norms, orientation toward a shared goal or goals, and a feeling of solidarity, identity, and interdependence among members. The study of groups is important to sociologists because groups are the means of socialization and the context of much social behavior, and because groups are microcosms of society as a whole.

The most fundamental type of group is the *primary group*, especially the family. Intimate and durable, the primary group has a major influence on each member's identity and social behavior. *Secondary groups* are marked by less emotional and more instrumental significance for their members. An individual's *reference groups* may or may not be the same as his or her *membership groups*, whether primary or secondary. A person looks to a *normative reference group* for an answer to the question "What is the right or appropriate thing for me to do?"; to a *comparative reference group* for an answer to "How can I do it?"; and to an *audience reference group* to answer "How do they think I'm doing?" Sometimes, as in the case of a young child, a single group such as the family may serve all these functions. Reference groups can be either positive (promoting identity and conformity) or negative (promoting dissimilarity) in orientation and behavior.

Groups are formed on the basis of a shared desire to achieve a particular goal or goals. *Proximity* and *similarity* of potential members are the basic determinants of group formation. *Group norms* are established through a gradual process of reciprocal influence among members. Conformity to group norms is encouraged by social rewards, such as friendship. Group characteristics that determine conformity are the cohesiveness of the group and the degree of interdependence among members.

Every group has a social structure, which is determined by the various roles the group imposes on its members. Because these roles interlock, *role appropriation* can take place if a member leaves the group or stops playing his or her role. Every group also has a *status structure*, or a pattern of ranking its members. A person who contributes substantially in quantity or quality to group processes is often defined as a leader, responsible for maintaining the group's solidarity (*expressive leadership*) or for guiding the group toward its goals (*instrumental leadership*).

Group interaction has three basic aspects. The pattern of *communication* often reflects a group's status structure. *Conflict* may involve two or more persons or subgroups and give rise to either the restructuring of roles and norms or the dissolution of the group. *Cohesiveness* is the degree to which members wish to remain in the group. All three factors are influenced by the size of the group.

Glossary

AUDIENCE REFERENCE GROUP A reference group that the individual uses to evaluate his or her behavior.

COMPARATIVE REFERENCE GROUP A reference group that serves as a model for the standards and behavior of the individual.

EXPRESSIVE LEADERSHIP Responsibility for maintaining a group's solidarity and harmony by one of its members.

GROUP Any collection of individuals who identify with one another and who engage in recurrent interactions structured by recognized statuses, roles, and norms in their pursuit of common goals.

GROUP NORM One of the guidelines by which groups govern the behavior and perceptions of their members, formed by a gradual process of reciprocal influence among members.

INSTRUMENTAL LEADERSHIP Responsibility for guiding a group toward the achievement of its goals by one of its members.

NEGATIVE REFERENCE GROUP A reference group that serves an individual as a guide to the self-image, behavior, attitudes, and values that he or she does *not* want to acquire.

NORMATIVE REFERENCE GROUP A reference group that enables the individual to set standards for his or her behavior.

POSITIVE REFERENCE GROUP A reference group upon which the individual models his or her self-image, behavior, attitudes, and values.

PRIMARY GROUP A group characterized by small size, a high degree of emotional intimacy, and (usually) physical proximity.

REFERENCE GROUP A group that serves an individual as a guide in the development of his or her self-image, behavior, attitudes, and values.

ROLE APPROPRIATION The taking over of a role by a group member when the role is vacated by another member.

SECONDARY GROUP A group characterized by relations that are more impersonal than those of a primary group and by the instrumental significance rather than the emotional significance it has for its members.

STATUS STRUCTURE The pattern of rank among individuals in a group, based on each member's external characteristics, as reflected in the social categories into which he or she fits, the group's first impression of the member, and the member's performance of his or her role within the group.

Recommended readings

Cartwright, Dorwin, and Alvin Zander (eds.). *Group Dynamics: Research and Theory.* 3rd ed. New York: Harper & Row, 1968. A classic collection of readings (updated for the second time) of the psychological and social forces affecting groups. Technical reading, requiring considerable—though worthwhile—effort.

Crosbie, Paul. *Interaction in Small Groups.* New York: Macmillan, 1975. A nicely written analysis of small groups and of the existing relevant professional literature.

Hare, A. Paul. *Handbook of Small Group Research.* New York: Free Press, 1962. Although somewhat dated, this book is an extremely valuable, rather complex effort to systematize contemporary theory and research on the small group.

Lindzey, Gardner, and Elliot Aronson (eds.). *Handbook of Social Psychology.* 2nd ed. Vol. 4: *Group Psychology and Phenomena of Interaction.* Reading, Mass.: Addison-Wesley, 1968. See especially Chapters 1, 2, and 3. A detailed, analytic, and bibliographic treatment of group productivity, group structure, and leadership. Quite technical and difficult, but an invaluable reference source.

McGrath, Joseph E., and Irwin Altman. *Small Group Research: A Synthesis and Critique of the Field.* New York: Holt, Rinehart and Winston, 1966. Like Hare's book (above), this volume attempts to bring some order to a field of study that is quite diverse and uncoordinated. Most of the book is given over to cataloging and referencing variables deemed important to the study of small groups, as well as providing detailed annotations of the most significant entries in the bibliography of 2,699 publications.

Ofshe, Richard (ed.). *Interpersonal Behavior in Small Groups.* Englewood Cliffs, N.J.: Prentice-Hall, 1973. An excellent selection of some classic as well as contemporary articles relevant to the study of small groups.

Olmstead, Michael, and A. Paul Hare. *The Small Group.* 2nd ed. New York: Random House, 1978. A simple, brief, theoretical introduction to the sociology of small groups.

Shaw, Marvin E. *Group Dynamics: The Psychology of Small Group Behavior.* 2nd ed. New York: McGraw-Hill, 1976. A well-written, advanced book that explores a number of facets of the small group within a framework of social interaction.

Shepherd, Clovis R. *Small Groups: Some Sociological Perspectives.* San Francisco: Chandler, 1964. A brief, readable presentation of some sociological views of the small group; somewhat more research-oriented than Olmstead's book (above).

CHAPTER NINE
FORMAL ORGANIZATIONS

The times we live in have been given many labels—"the Space Age," "the Industrial Age," "the Atomic Age," "the Age of Anxiety." A plausible addition to this list could be "the Age of Organizations." Twentieth-century life is pervaded by large organizations. It is impossible to get a driver's license, a passport, a credit card, a checking account, a marriage certificate, or a college education without dealing with an organization; it is impossible even to make a telephone call without the help of an organization. When it takes a letter two weeks to travel two miles, an organization is responsible for the delay; when an astronaut walks on the moon, that, too, is the achievement of an organization.

Organizations have emerged time and time again throughout history. Some of the earliest agrarian societies had enormous organizations. Ebla, a recently discovered urban civilization that flourished in northern Syria forty-four centuries ago, had government-run textile and metal-processing industries that were monitored and coordinated by as many as 11,000 administrators and civil servants. The Roman Empire was run with the aid of a huge hierarchical organization. (We discuss organizational hierarchies further on in this chapter.) And 400 years ago, when the agrarian, politically decentralized society of Europe in the Middle Ages began to be transformed into modern society, one of the first large-scale social changes was the development of governmental organizations to administer the newly forming centralized states. In sum, organizations have been an important phenomenon in all structurally differentiated societies; they are as central to such societies as an alphabet or the wheel.

Organizations are of interest not only in their historical context but also in connection with sociological concerns today. Because the organization is a powerful tool for the attainment of group goals, it has been analyzed by sociologists who aim to improve it; and because the organization often has tremendous power over people and resources, it has been studied by sociologists who aim to limit its control. Both approaches, furthermore, have had an additional aim. They have attempted to find out how norms and values learned *within* organizations are carried over into the *nonorganizational* areas of people's lives—and, conversely, how nonorganizational social patterns affect the organization.

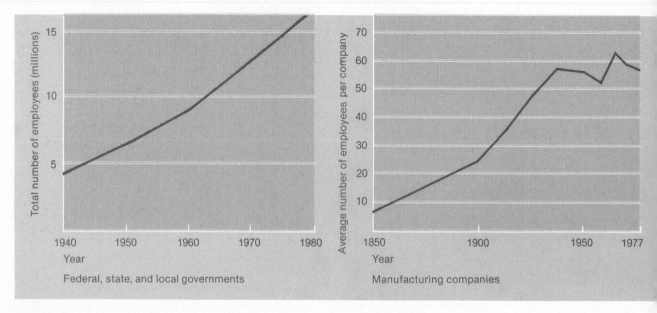

FIGURE 9.1

These charts indicate the growth of the organization in modern American society. (Azumi, 1972, p. 96; Census Bureau, 1976; U.S. Bureau of Labor Statistics, 1980; Department of Commerce, 1980; *Yearbook of American and Canadian Churches*, 1977)

What is an organization?

An *organization*, as we mentioned in Chapter 4, is a type of group. As such, it has a structured interaction pattern, and the people in it share a sense of common membership. But the organization is special in that it is *a group set up on purpose to pursue specific goals* (Blau and Scott, 1962). Industrial corporations, health-care institutions, political clubs—these, and all other organizations, originate with particular goals in view.

The goals of organizations are often much larger in scale than those of other groups. For example, the goal of preparing a meal in a restaurant provides a sharp contrast with the same goal in a small family. When a meal is prepared in a family, it usually involves only one menu with two or three courses and one serving time, and it is prepared for just a few people. In contrast, a restaurant (which is, of course, a type of organization) serves dozens of people at each meal, usually offers a varied menu, keeps many different foods on hand, and serves each patron a short time after he or she arrives. Typically, the goals of organizations are ambitious in terms of time, expense, labor, materials, and product. Many organizations (though not all) also involve large numbers of people.

PLANNING AND RATIONALITY IN THE ORGANIZATION

Not everything that happens in an organization is done on purpose; nor are organizations the only type of group in which conscious planning takes place. But deliberate *planning* is one of the organization's salient features. The people who first set up the organization must create a scheme that deals with questions such as: What are the necessary tasks? Who is to do what tasks? Who is to supervise? How will activities fit together? How will members communicate with one another? Furthermore, these decisions have to be "replanned" throughout the organization's existence—not just once, but many times.

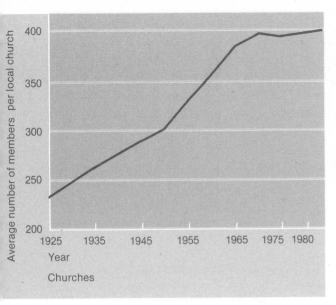

Churches

enon under consideration. No existing social phenomenon (in this case, the organization) will have all the features of the ideal type, nor will the features of an existing social phenomenon be as marked as those of the ideal type. But by focusing on the *ideal-typical organization*, we can gain a clearer understanding of the concept of organizations—small and large, relatively simple and relatively complex. We can then compare this model with organizations that actually do exist and explore the consequences of the differences between the model and reality.

DIVISION OF LABOR

First and most important, the necessary tasks in the ideal-typical organization are divided among many people. Once again we can see this by comparing an organization, such as a restaurant, with a small group, such as the family. In the family, preparing a meal is a project that is small enough to be carried out by one person, who can do all the tasks involved—planning the menu, doing the shopping, cooking, serving, and washing up.

Ideally, the people who make the decisions try to make them as logically and reasonably as possible. Or, as sociologists would say, they try to make them with a high degree of *rationality*—that is, with an emphasis on cause and effect, or means and ends. If the desired "effect" or "end" is to sell hamburgers, then the planners will have to set up activities such as the ordering and reception of deliveries from beef suppliers, the training of short-order cooks, and the acquisition of property on which to put up the hamburger stands. But they will not have to set up mechanisms for hiring gourmet chefs; in fact, to do so would not be consistent with logic or rationality. Rational planning means that all the organization's activities have to be set up with an eye to the key goals; activities that do not further these goals either are not considered or are rejected.

Needless to say, organizations rarely live up to the standard of total rationality. (Most of us can think of organizations that do not.) But organizations do have certain structural characteristics that make them particularly well suited for rational goal attainment. As we look at these characteristics, we will make use of a special kind of conceptual model known as an *ideal type*, which, as we noted in Chapter 1, was introduced by Max Weber. The ideal type is a model that combines—and, for the purposes of study, may even exaggerate—the most typical features of the social phenom-

Division of labor—the assignment of clearly delineated tasks to specific members of an organization—is one of the basic foundations of our health-care system. (© Lawrence Frank 1979)

In any reasonably sized restaurant, each of these tasks is assigned to a different person: shopping and planning the menu to the manager, cooking to the chef, serving to the waiter or waitress, cleaning up to the dishwasher, and so on. Each person performs only one type of task, but she or he performs it many times. This *division of labor* contributes to rational goal attainment by getting things done faster, in greater volume, with more skill, and with fewer wasted motions. Without it, patrons in a large restaurant might not be served efficiently—or even be served at all.

ACTIVITY SEQUENCES AND HIERARCHY

Roles in the ideal-typical organization are planned in such a way that they fit together in a *sequence*, which eliminates duplicated and extraneous activities. The classic example is the assembly line, but there are others: in the university, the student is "processed" by a sequence of workers including the admissions director, the faculty adviser, the professor, and the dean; in the publishing industry, a book order may be processed by a sequence of workers including the field representative (who makes the initial sale), the accounting clerk (who logs in the order), the warehouse clerk (who packs and ships the books), and the marketing manager (who handles complaints and adjustments). No matter what

FIGURE 9.2

The hierarchy of control as seen in the formal structure of a large organization—in this case, a public school system. The teachers and other members of the line staff—those who actually deliver the services of the organization—report to the principals. The principals and the other officials whose function it is to supervise and coördinate the work of the line staff report to a smaller, administrative group, the assistant superintendents. The assistant superintendents, in turn, are supervised by the superintendent of schools, who reports to the smallest group in the hierarchy, the board of education, which establishes policy for the entire school system. (Adapted from an unpublished paper by Richard S. Zeglen in Caplow, 1964)

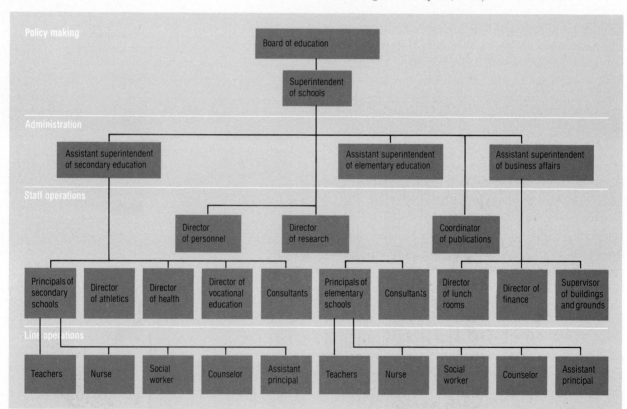

product is being developed or what basic activity is going on, all tasks (and thus all roles) will be arranged in sequences of this sort. Each role links with the next—either spatially or chronologically, or both. Furthermore, in addition to being related in these linear, chain-like sequences, roles are often related in a pyramidal *hierarchy* of control. There is one person, or a small group of people, whose job it is to control and be responsible for everything that happens in the organization. This person or small group is at the top of the pyramid. Reporting to the top level is a slightly larger second rank of people; reporting to them is a larger third rank; and so on. Through the control hierarchy, any activity at the bottom (or on any other level) can be overseen by a chain of supervisors connected all the way to the top.

FORMALIZATION AND DURABILITY

As most of us know, organizations often seem to have a life of their own that extends beyond, or somehow transcends, the particular people in them. Encounters with anonymous, robotlike bureaucracies (as in recorded messages on the telephone or computer-written letters addressed to you personally) are a familiar feature of modern life; and organizations such as government agencies seem to carry on regardless of who is in charge, who joins, who leaves, or what any one person dealing with them may want—almost like the survival-crazy computer HAL in the film *2001*. What lies at the bottom of this amusing and sometimes frightening phenomenon? Surprisingly, it is a factor that has to do with rational planning, one that seems innocuous in and of itself: the organization's dependence on formalized rules.

Rules exist in an organization because, as we have seen, the organization has a complex division of labor and an intricate structure of roles. An organization is a finely spun network that is unlikely to operate well unless clearly defined, precise, stable expectations are connected with each activity. The rules must also be *formalized*, or established so that they are known to all and are relatively permanent—impossible to forget easily, to change at a whim, or to reinterpret to suit members' own private purposes. Putting the rules in writing

helps to formalize them; so does defining them as "official," or having them handed down by the people who make the plans for the organization.

It is only one step from relatively durable rules to a relatively durable social structure. Even if a member of the organization leaves, the rules for his or her job or position remain; someone else can be trained according to the rules to take his or her place. Thus even if there is a high turnover in personnel, the organization can "live on"—one important reason that a huge organization seems to have a mind of its own. (We will discuss other reasons later in this chapter.)

BUREAUCRACY

In addition to rules, organizations need regular record keeping and monitoring. These functions are carried out by a section of the organizational structure known as the *bureaucracy*. Bureaucracy is not, as many people

Bureaucracy developed long before the advent of modern industrial societies. This ancient Egyptian statue, carved around 2400 B.C., shows a scribe, a high-ranking official in the pharaoh's court. (Alinari/Scala)

automatically think, a synonym for delay, meaningless rules, and, in the words of Charles Dickens, "How Not to Do It." A bureaucracy is the part of a formal organization that is responsible for planning, coordinating, and supervising work. It is essentially the administrative machinery of formal organizations.

The negative connotation of bureaucracy is not entirely unjustified. Bureaucracy is often regarded as an enemy of the individual, as in Joseph Heller's novel *Catch-22*, or as a way of achieving the opposite of what is intended. "Those who know do not decide; those who decide do not know," is how a French politician characterized bureaucracy in his country (Peyrefitte, 1976). And at times, bureaucracy seems like a great uncontrollable red-tape dispenser, spewing forth thousands of meaningless forms that no one will ever look at.

Despite these drawbacks, however, bureaucratic management is essential to an organization's functioning. Consider, for example, the administration of the Social Security program, a government service we now take for granted; without extensive records, files, and cross-checks, this essential human service would not be possible.

RATIONAL-LEGAL SYSTEMS: WEBER'S APPROACH TO ORGANIZATIONS

One of the first and most important systematic investigators of organizations was Max Weber, the theorist whose use of ideal types as conceptual models we mentioned above. Weber's pioneering studies in the social context of behavior helped to lay the groundwork for the entire field of sociology. Essentially, Weber did for the study of organizations what Sigmund Freud did for the study of the human psyche. Just as Freud described the components of psychological behavior and tried to identify some of the social and historical forces that influence it, so Weber offered a comprehensive analysis of the internal functioning of organizations and attempted a critique of the historical, legal, and economic factors that favored the development of the organization as a social structure. Weber's view of the organization, like Freud's description of the psyche, remains the classic model and one that is rooted in the functionalist perspective.

BUREAUCRACY: WEBER'S ANALYSIS

During the second half of the nineteenth century, Germany was transformed under the "Iron Chancellor," Otto von Bismarck (1815–1898), from a divided confederation of thirty-nine states into a unified nation that came to dominate European diplomacy. Throughout this period, as the Industrial Revolution ran its course in Europe, economic specialization and commerce advanced rapidly in Germany. Productivity soared, and work settings became increasingly complex as the role of machines in the manufacturing process grew.

It was against this background that Weber embarked on his ground-breaking investigation of highly bureaucratized organizations. Initially his goal was to identify the social patterns—of whatever sort—that made Germany's new productivity possible. As he set about this task, he found himself focusing on complex

Max Weber (1864–1920) conducted a landmark study of bureaucratized organizations and developed a list of specific features that make a bureaucracy successful and productive. (The Granger Collection)

organizations, such as the civil service of the German King Frederick William I (a bureaucracy of outstanding efficiency). Eventually, he developed a list of the specific features that he believed to be responsible for the unusual productivity of these bureaucracies (1947):

1. The organization is guided by a set of explicit and specific purposes from which a system of rules and regulations is derived that governs the behavior of officials (e.g., a charter or articles of incorporation).

2. There is a distribution of activity among offices so that each incumbent has a specified sphere of competence (e.g., job descriptions and organizational charts).

3. The offices are arranged in a hierarchical pattern so that each official exercises authority over those subordinate to him or her and is subject to the authority of his or her superiors, but only in his or her capacity as an officeholder and within the limits established by organizational rules. (The chain of command applies to office activities only.)

4. Officials are personally free, bound to their offices only by a contractual relationship that involves services in return for compensation, normally a salary. Officials do not own their offices, nor are they allowed to appropriate to themselves the means of administration. (This applies to employees only, not to owners or the self-employed.)

5. Candidates for positions are selected on the basis of technical competence, and they are promoted on the basis of seniority, performance, or both. Officials are appointed rather than elected (e.g., the civil service).

6. Officials must carry out their functions in a disciplined and impersonal manner. (There is no favoritism or personal bias.)

7. The organization maintains detailed written records, the contents of which are often treated as "official secrets" (e.g., "the files").

8. The individual's commitment to his or her office is his or her primary work commitment. (The individual will not hold a competing second job.)

THE SOCIAL BENEFITS OF RATIONAL-LEGAL PATTERNS

Taken as a whole, the features of Weber's ideal-typical organization constituted a complex of norms and values that he termed *rational-legal*—a name that he chose to describe the structure of authority in societies in which power is grounded in a "system" of rules and regulations, rather than in a single powerful individual, such as a big-city boss. (See Chapter 17 for a discussion of this facet of Weber's analysis.) Weber believed these rational-legal practices could improve bureaucratic functioning if they were observed more rigorously by actual organizations. They could, for example, help curb the common practice of *nepotism* (filling job positions with one's relatives). They could also cut down on what is sometimes referred to today as "feathering one's nest" (Perrow, 1979, pp. 6–23), whereby an official of an organization uses the organization's resources for his or her own private purposes. In Weber's ideal-typical bureaucracy this problem does not arise, because there is complete separation between the organization's property and the official's personal property.

Weber also believed that rational-legal practices could benefit workers and society as a whole. First of all, rational-legal practices offered certain types of protection. Written rules covering tasks and salaries protected the worker from arbitrary treatment by his or her superiors. While such rules were in force, the worker could not be deprived of preestablished rewards—for example, his or her pay could not suddenly be docked one Friday—or be forced to carry out extra, previously unspecified tasks, such as washing the boss's car. The separation of organizational property from personal property protected the society outside the organization; though the organization might have control over tremendous amounts of money, raw materials, and other resources, no organizational leader could (in principle) subvert these resources for personal ends. The people in charge of gold bullion at the mint could not put any of it in their own safe-deposit boxes. Second, Weber believed that rational-legal patterns could help to decrease inequalities of power, property, and prestige among people in the larger society (see Chapter 10). Competency-based hiring could have the effect of achieving some "leveling" of social classes: people who had talent and ability but came from humble backgrounds could rise in the general social hierarchy by being placed in well-rewarded job slots within organizations. Who they were would not matter so much as what they could do.

Were Weber's analyses of organizational structure and activity used in practice? Did managers and others with control over organizations attempt to improve them along the lines Weber's work had suggested?

Abuses such as nepotism have by no means disappeared, and the continued necessity of affirmative action programs for women and members of minority groups suggests that competency-based hiring is still not universal. But Weberian ideas have influenced organizational planning a good deal. The organization charts for which modern businesses are famous reflect the Weberian emphasis on formalized rules. Tests given to job applicants and educational requirements connected with jobs reflect the Weberian emphasis on expertise. Moreover, the norms and values of the formal organization have been carried over into other areas of social life as well. Most Americans have, as part of their value system, a tendency to favor a systematic, rational approach to planning their activities and their lives. Most people in our society have a deep loyalty to the law; and most Americans believe (at least in theory) that all citizens should be given an equal chance at "life, liberty, and the pursuit of happiness," regardless of sex, religion, race, or class. The new bureaucratic social environment has been an important factor (though not, of course, the only one) in the development of these aspects of the modern world view.

SOME LIMITATIONS OF WEBER'S APPROACH

Ironically, Weber's analysis of the interplay between bureaucratic organizations and culture was in some ways more accurate than his analysis of the organizations themselves. Viewed simply as a tool for management planning, the Weberian approach, while it is correct in some of its outlines, does have limitations. It is often referred to as a "machine model," since "the organization, though consisting of people, is viewed . . . as a machine, and . . . just as we build a mechanical device with a given set of specifications for accomplishing a task, so we construct an organization according to a blueprint to achieve a given purpose" (Katz and Kahn, 1966, p. 71). The trouble with a machine model, as we shall see, is that it does not—and perhaps cannot—take into account the difficulties of running an organization made up of human beings.

Likewise, the Weberian scheme, as used by organizational theorists, is a *closed-systems* model. This means that the organization is sealed off from the things around it; in the Weberian view, the object of planning is simply to establish predictable relationships and to maximize internal rationality. The trouble with a closed-systems model is that it does not encompass the full reality of the organization's context. A completely closed system cannot exist—or exist for very long—in actuality, because outside pressures will always arise to alter, if not thwart, the best and most rational of plans.

An unfortunate result of bureaucracy may be *goal displacement*, in which officials are so involved in the rules of the organization that they lose sight of its true purpose. In order to combat goal displacement, many bureaucrats in China are required to work in factories and on communal farms for a short time each year. Here, Chen Yung-Kuei, vice chairman of the Shansi Provincial Revolutionary Committee and secretary of the party branch of the Tachai Brigade, works with commune members to build terraced fields as part of a national campaign to develop flood-control and irrigation facilities. (Wide World Photos)

To overcome these problems, some researchers have proposed *open-systems* models, which stress the impact of the external environment (social and natural) on the internal structure and performance of an organization. For example, the growing scarcity and increasing cost of oil, a phenomenon at once geological, social, economic, and political, has certainly had its effects on the organizations we know as automobile companies. We could hardly get a clear picture of the functions of the Chrysler Corporation in the past few years without considering the impact of fuel-efficiency standards and the response of the company in its attempts to meet them, including the reorganization of the company's management and the eventual layoff of thousands of workers. On the other hand, an open-systems model by itself sheds little light on the internal workings of the organization. Further, by stressing the role of environmental variables, the open-systems approach introduces a good deal of uncertainty into the analysis of organizations. This is inevitable, since we can never know what natural or social factors will suddenly arise. Most theorists, therefore, combine the two models: the organization is seen as striving for rationality internally while trying at the same time to meet the demands of a changing environment (Zey-Ferrell, 1979).

Thus, although Weber's analysis is illuminating, it is in some ways too simple. Officeholders are not "replaceable parts"; they are people. Planning is not always totally rational; it sometimes involves "politics," mistakes, miscalculations, and guesswork. Even though the organization may originally have been set up by one powerful person or group, it may long since have taken on a life of its own, diverging from its original goals and pursuing new ones. An unfortunate result in some cases may be what has been called *goal displacement*, in which the end, or aim, of the organization is subverted by increasing attention to its rules—a familiar "red-tape" problem. For example, a person applying for welfare assistance might be so intimidated by the form-filling required by the welfare office that he or she would give up and drop out of the enrollment process before receiving benefits. In this case, following the rules of the organization has in effect become more important than its original purpose—aiding the needy. Clearly, organizations are sometimes less than "rational systems" when their original goals are considered.

Natural-systems approaches

The subfield of sociology that includes organizations is almost as complex as the organizations themselves, and there is little agreement as to how theories should be classified. Nevertheless, it is possible to identify a group of theories whose focus is not on the Weberian (or formal and rational) aspects of organizations, but on human and nonrational aspects. These theories have been called *natural-systems approaches*. One of the earliest of these approaches came out of a school of industrial management known as the *human relations school*.

THE HUMAN RELATIONS SCHOOL

During the 1920s, researchers at the Hawthorne plant of the Western Electric Company, a subsidiary of AT&T, had a mystery on their hands. Seeking ways to increase productivity, an industrial psychologist from Harvard University, F. J. Roethlisberger, and a member of Western Electric's management, W. J. Dickson, had conducted experiments dealing with the effect of environmental conditions, such as lighting, on the output of workers (see Chapter 8). The researchers observed two groups of workers at the Hawthorne plant near Chicago, where electrical equipment was made for the Bell System. The researchers increased the intensity of lighting in one group's work area, and carefully observed its effect. Productivity went up. The other group, which was used as a control in the experiment, continued to work under normal conditions. Their productivity also went up. Lighting for the first group was lowered. Productivity continued to increase—for both groups. Over and over, Roethlisberger, Dickson, and Elton Mayo, who had been called in from the Harvard Business School, ran their experiments, varying the type of group used and the kind of work done. But, inexplicably, output for both the experimental and the control groups continued to increase.

The solution to the riddle is what became known as

the "Hawthorne effect." The reason that both groups increased their productivity, the researchers eventually deduced, had nothing to do with lighting levels. The key fact was that the groups had been put in separate rooms, away from the rest of the work force. These groups felt special. They felt that management had taken an interest in them. As a result, their work improved.

The Hawthorne effect and other findings from the experiments conducted at the plant between 1927 and 1932 led to the development of the human relations model of organizations. Mayo (1933) is considered its founder; other influential members include Rensis Likert and Douglas McGregor.

The worker seen as a person

As its name implies, the human relations model differs from the Weberian model in that it describes workers' motivation as a response to personal factors and interpersonal relationships within the organization, rather than to abstract rules, strict discipline, and economic exigencies. Feelings and attitudes, the desire for emotional security and creative satisfaction, curiosity, and the need for a sense of personal worth all affect the worker's performance (and must therefore be integrated into organizational planning). Though not identical with it, in many ways this approach is conceptually consistent with symbolic interactionism, since both place emphasis on the importance of the individual's "definition of the situation" in determining his or her behavior.

Management's task, according to the human relations scheme, is to be employee-oriented rather than work-oriented (Stogdill and Coons, 1957) and to concentrate on fostering worker satisfaction (from which efficient work naturally follows) rather than on enforcing abstract, rigid rules. A basic tenet of this approach is that high worker morale and strong leadership combine to bring about increased productivity. Morale is determined by many factors, but it is seen as emanating primarily from the conditions that exist in the organization member's work group. Managers should attempt, therefore, to create supportive, satisfying group situations by planning work in a way that allows for cooperation rather than competition and by utilizing devices such as rest periods and coffee breaks, which reduce fatigue and allow for relaxed interaction between workers.

The informal structure

Unlike the Weberian model, the human relations scheme recognizes the importance of informal organizational structures that exist parallel to the formal one. A classic example of informal structure is the one, mentioned in Chapter 8, that existed among men working in the bank-wiring room of the Western Electric Company's Hawthorne plant. This structure functioned according to rules that differed from (and sometimes contradicted) those of the formal organization. Whereas the goal of the formal structure was to maximize output of correctly wired electrical apparatus, the goal of the informal structure was to restrict output to a consistent level—high enough so that the workers would not be disciplined by the company and low enough so that all could keep up and could keep their jobs. This behavior was not rational in the light of the company's goals, but it was undoubtedly rational as far as the workers' interests were concerned.

Despite the fact that it recognizes the existence and importance of this informal organizational structure, the human relations perspective is still based primarily on the interests of management—namely management's interest in improving productivity; in this respect it differs from the practice of symbolic interactionists, who are more likely to view things through the eyes of the less powerful, such as the worker (for an example in a different context, see Becker, 1967). Recently, alternative perspectives have been introduced that attempt to address the concerns of workers as well as those of management.

THE ORGANIC MODEL

A second non-Weberian model rests upon the concept of the organization as a "natural whole" (Gouldner, 1959), an "organic" entity. Each organization has a "life history" or a "natural history," just as does an animal or plant. This natural history reflects the changes the organization makes during its lifetime in response to both internal processes and external influences. Not all these changes are planned; many are adaptations that occur as a result of a natural system's tendency toward *homeostasis*—the tendency to survive and maintain equilibrium. Note the similarity of this model to the basic functionalist perspective, which was presented in Chapter 3.

These computer tapes enable an organization to record, store, and retrieve vast amounts of information in a very short time. The development of modern data processing has had a dramatic impact on the organization of most big businesses. (© Lawrence Frank 1976)

As Alvin Gouldner has commented (1959), the organization can become an end in itself. Consider the case of the Women's Christian Temperance Union (WCTU), an organization that dedicated itself to the abolition of drinking during the first few decades of the 1900s. Joseph Gusfield's study (1955) of the WCTU points out that after the repeal of Prohibition, when abstention from alcohol ceased to be a widely held social ideal, the WCTU was left without a goal. But the organization remained viable, though less consequential, by shifting its energies to an attack on the immorality of middle-class values and lifestyles.

To survive, then, an organization, like a living organism, must adapt to its environment. As the environment changes, the structure and even the goals of the organization must change. What are some of the external or *environmental* influences that affect an organization? This question has stimulated an enormous amount of research in recent years. Technology, legal, political, and economic conditions, population density and other demographic factors, social and cultural values—all these aspects of the environment influence the organization. For example, consider the impact of just one technological development—modern data processing—on the organization of most businesses. Our modern systems of banking and credit, the telephone system, and all the organizations that serve airline travel, to name a few examples, might almost be said to be organized "around" the use of the modern computer.

Broad social movements may also affect organizations. For example, the influence of feminism has been felt by most organizations in the United States, especially in the areas of hiring and promotion. Furthermore, *other* organizations influence organizations: the oil companies influence automobile companies, for example, and both are influenced by the federal government. Organizations may conflict, or they may compete for resources. And, as is particularly evident in our society today, they may cooperate (or coexist symbiotically) in complex, interlocking patterns. One key feature of the way this arrangement develops is that after a period of competing, the organizations come to deal with one another through *exchange*: rather than attempting to take away part of a large firm's market, a smaller firm may attempt to provide it with the services it needs. And another pattern that can emerge, as a few organizations come to dominate a field, is the formation of cartels and oligopolies. Once they become dominant, these few organizations can begin to perceive the buyers or sellers with whom they have relationships of exchange as competitors: "The consequent power struggle between buyers and sellers puts the members of

THE RECORDING INDUSTRY: CONSOLIDATION IN A CHANGING ENVIRONMENT

It is an axiom of the open-systems model that an organization is affected by its environment, both social and natural. But is the reverse true? Do organizations create their environments as much as they respond to them? In *Complex Organizations* (1979), Charles Perrow suggests that they do—even displacing their costs of operation onto the environment. Tracing the history of the recording industry, he makes a case for revitalizing organizational theory by taking a more savvy look at the wide variety of often contradictory purposes for which organizations exist—including the creation, selection, and definition of the environment. In the case of the recording industry or any other cultural supplier, that environment is us: our tastes are shaped and our selection preestablished.

The history of the recording industry falls into three periods. Between 1920 and 1955, the industry was oligopolistic: four firms dominated the field. Domination was achieved by vertical integration:

The firms owned the artists through long-term contracts, and hired producers who gathered the ancillary talent, produced the record, and packaged the result. They also owned the manufacturing facilities and controlled the distribution system. . . . The majors also controlled the distribution of the films that featured popular songs, further

rationalizing the system. As a result, the four largest firms accounted for 78 percent of the sales of single records from 1948 to 1955; the eight largest for 96 percent. (Perrow, 1979, pp. 206–207)

Oligopoly suited the needs of the industry well; in fact, Perrow points out, most of American industry reflects production concentrated in a few firms as well as vertical integration, routine production, and innovation only in marginal aspects such as packaging or novelty.

Ironically, the changes that brought an end to this comfortable period for the major recording companies came from within the majors themselves:

Long-playing records made production very cheap.
The advent of television caused a drop in advertising income from radio stations, causing the majors to abandon radio and transfer network programing to TV, making radio stations autonomous and within the reach of local entrepreneurs.
The development of the inexpensive transistor radio increased both set production and the number of AM stations by one third.

With the boom in stations and listeners came a new idea: the audience was no longer seen as a mass audience, but as a number of discrete groups with different tastes.

each group under pressure to unite by establishing agreements and trade associations. In this manner former competitors have once again been transformed into partners . . ." (Blau and Scott, 1962, p. 220). (We will consider these patterns in more detail in Chapter 18.)

THE CONFLICT/MARXIST APPROACH

In contrast to the previous approaches, which stress the way elements of organizations work together toward common goals, some theorists have proposed that the key to an understanding of organizations is not cooperation, but conflict. In this view, an organization is a collection of competing groups, each with a special interest (usually its own welfare or enrichment). The classic analysis of this kind is, of course, Karl Marx's theory of the inevitable clash of interest between workers and capitalists: one class can profit only at the expense of another. Similarly, an organization is made up of a number of groups which may be more interested in some special goal of their own than the overall goal of

the organization. Consider a modern hospital, for example. The staff physicians may be most concerned with having up-to-date facilities and the very latest complex machines for diagnosis and treatment. Nurses, on the other hand, may want the nursing staff enlarged, so that they can do a better job of caring for patients on an individual basis. The service employees—janitors, laundry aides, and kitchen workers—want higher hourly wages. And the hospital management, released by Medicare, Medicaid, and increasing insurance coverage from the constraints of reducing costs, may want to focus on ways to make the hospital grow, enhance its image in the public eye, and gain prestige within the medical community. In such an organization—and it is typical of many in modern society—conflict is likely, if not unavoidable.

Some Marxist analysts have gone one step further with this argument and pointed out that networks of such common interests exist, linking together these "layers" within different organizations. For example, researchers have observed that close ties at the executive level exist between many banks, insurance companies, and private corporations in the United States

Where did all these new tastes come from? "Presumably, they were there all the time, but latent; they had never had the chance to develop because the recording and broadcast segments of the industry were controlled by the majors and devoted to the standard fare" (Perrow, 1979, pp. 207–208). During this period, the four firms' concentration ratio went down from 78 to 44 percent.

In response to the uncertainties of the wide-open years between 1956 and 1960, the industry decentralized and contracted out for services. Of the industry's three functions—producing the master disc or tape, manufacturing the records, and promoting and selling them—producing the record (that is, bringing together the performers, songwriters, recording technicians, etc.) was most affected by the turbulence of the environment. Producers emerged as the most powerful members of the recording process, but if a producer did not have a succession of hits, his latitude could still be easily reduced. Significantly, the costs of the turbulence were not borne by the record companies, but rather pushed onto the producing phase: producers on short contracts, aspiring artists, and those that rent out studios, supply backup musicians, wait for stamping contracts, etc. "Everyone is betting on the big thing, so there are always bettors willing to absorb the costs of turbulence" (Perrow, 1979, p. 211).

But the organization seeks to control its environment, not to be controlled by it, Perrow insists, and after 1960 consolidation again prevailed. From 1962 to 1973 the four-firm ratio went from 25 to 51 percent; the eight-firm ratio from 46 to 81 percent, almost back to pre-1955 levels. The majors began to assert "increasing control over the creative process," through the creation and promotion of new groups, long-range contracts, and reduced autonomy for producers. The majors have also been consolidating their hold on the distribution phase by buying chains of retail stores.

What does such an analysis of an industry in a changing environment "prove"? Among Perrow's conclusions:

New technological developments do not determine cultural outcomes—but the way that they are used by powerful firms can.

"The most salient environment for the majors is other majors; despite competition between them, they collectively evolve strategies to eliminate or absorb threatening minors."

"The public is poorly served in the process. If we have to hope for the accidental conjunction of three major technological changes (LP records, TV, and transistor radios) to have a diversity of tastes served, we are in deep trouble as a public." (Perrow, 1979, p. 213)

(Zeitlin, 1974; Mariolis, 1975). Similarly, some government regulatory agencies have ties to the industry they exist to regulate: personnel at the highest level move from business to government and back again. All these linkages exist to serve the common interests of the elite group, Marxist analysts would argue. At the same time,

it should be pointed out, similar common interest ties exist among labor unions, which frequently support one another when strikes are called, refusing to cross picket lines even when they may have few grievances against their own employers. Thus, networks of interest link individuals across organizations.

The organization at work: whose tool?

Up to this point, our emphasis has been on organizations as whole entities—their characteristics, operation, and place in society. We have discussed them both as social systems, analogous to natural organisms, and as tools for achieving group goals.

At this point, it will be helpful to take a closer look at the "organization as tool." The question here, of course, is "Whose tool?" In other words, we need to study organizational power. First we will discuss how power is distributed in the organization. Then we will investigate why people within the organization or dependent on it comply with organizational power. Last

we will study the ways in which people defend themselves against that power.

POWER AND ALIENATION

As Weber observed, the top of an organization is rarely bureaucratized—that is, there are few rules that the people at the very top are constrained to obey, and there are almost no mechanisms that keep these people from using organizational resources in any way they see fit (though there are, as we have seen, mechanisms that

SELF-MANAGEMENT: THE HUMANIZATION OF AMERICAN INDUSTRY

Millions of Americans punch a time clock five or six days a week every week, then take their places on an assembly line. There they perform the same task over and over and over until their shift ends. True to Max Weber's model, these people's jobs are at the bottom of a hierarchy in which the managers at the top make the decisions that affect those at the bottom.

In many such factories, workers complain of boredom and alienation. One automotive worker told a reporter: "The only gratification you get is a paycheck once a week, and that's too long to go without any kind of gratification from the job" (Kremen, 1973). Weber believed that written rules governing tasks and salaries would protect workers from arbitrary control by superiors, but performing the same tasks every day for years results in more predictability than many people care to live with. Absentee rates run as high as 25 percent per day in some automobile plants, and shoddy workmanship has become a problem in all industries.

In an attempt to boost workers' morale as well as their productivity, factory owners in a number of industries have adopted self-management programs, in which the people who work in a factory make decisions about how it should be run. The self-management concept is flexible, with the exact nature of workers' participation varying from program to program. In the Gaines Pet Food Plant in Topeka, Kansas, for example, all personnel are members of autonomous work teams. Decision making is decentralized, and distinctions between management and workers are minimal. Pay raises are based "not on longevity, bargaining power, or advancement . . . up a hierarchical ladder, but on the basis of number of skills learned. Every employee is encouraged to learn every task in the plant" (Brower, 1975, p. 71). Since everyone rotates through all of the jobs, no one group gets "stuck" with the dullest work. Workers have responded to this new system with tremendous enthusiasm. Absenteeism averages only 1 percent in the Gaines Pet Food plant, and productivity is about 30 percent higher than in comparable plants (Salpukas, 1973).

Self-management is also being tried by the Eaton Corporation in Kearney, Nebraska. Before a new engine valve plant was opened in 1971, corporate planners examined their past personnel policies. "Most," they concluded, "were based on mistrust of employees and on a class system" (Brower, 1975, p. 75). In the new plant, the planners put all employees on the same salary scale and abolished time clocks and other "dehumanizing" procedures and regulations. All plant operators are now responsible for their own quality control and are encouraged to take part in decision making. The results of this self-management program, too, appear to have been excellent. Productivity is reported as 38 percent higher than at traditionally run plants, and absenteeism is under 1 percent. Workers have even been known to come to work when they were ill, complaining that they got bored at home.

Despite their drawbacks—the disputes that may arise when there are "too many chiefs," for example—these self-management programs have generally satisfied plant owners as well as plant workers, since low absenteeism and high productivity mean increased profits. Democratic plant management yields other benefits as well. In traditionally run factories where supervisors earn more than regular workers, preserving personal power can become more important than working for the good of the organization. If supervisors and workers are paid according to the same scale, however, the goals of the organization and the goals of the individual are more likely to coincide. However, as in all democracies, sometimes the views of the leaders (for example, boards of directors, executive officers) are neither accepted nor implemented by the workers. This worker resistance reduces the ability of management to direct a company's practices in what it believes to be the most efficient and economically rewarding fashion, thus making self-management less attractive to owners and managers. Moreover, old habits of management change very slowly, if at all. Assuredly, there are other factors operating as well, but it is important to note that few companies have even experimented with, much less adopted, serious self-management techniques.

deter them from appropriating organizational *property* for their personal use). In his famous "iron law of oligarchy," Robert Michels (1915) states that over a period of time, the leaders of an organization will devote an increasing amount of effort to preserving and perpetuating their power—possibly without realizing they are doing so. And not surprisingly, some (though not all) empirical studies suggest that the higher one's occupational level, the greater one's satisfaction is likely to be (Blauner, 1964; see also Chapter 18).

A corollary is that as one descends the hierarchy of workers in an organization, rewards decrease and the condition that Karl Marx (1964) called *alienation* becomes increasingly common. Marx used the term to refer to the separation of the worker from the means of production: not only did the worker not own his or her own tools but, more important, he or she worked for someone else. Thus all control over the conditions of work was taken from the individual, and he or she was put into the hands—and subjected to the will—of

Workers at the bottom of the organizational hierarchy are likely to suffer from the condition that Karl Marx called *alienation*. They are most distant from the process and the satisfaction of achieving organizational goals, and often view their jobs as meaningless. However, according to the Weberian system, subordinates comply because they believe in the validity of the organization's structure and rules, and they view the organization's power as legitimate. (© James R. Holland/Stock, Boston)

those in control of the organization. In modern parlance, *alienation* refers to the inability of the individual to control the conditions of his or her own life. At the bottom of the hierarchy, one is the most distant from the process and the satisfaction of achieving organizational goals, one is subordinated to a high degree (Etzioni, 1961), and, for some people, work tends to become meaningless. The term "alienation" is usually applied to workers in a business or commercial organization. But it must be understood and remembered that many organizations—such as hospitals, prisons, colleges, and social welfare agencies—have clients, beneficiaries, or dependents who are outside the organizational hierarchy, and such people may also be subject to organizational power (as when a mental patient is put under restraint or in isolation); they too are alienated, in a broad sense, from control over their lives.

COMPLIANCE

Faced with the realities of power and alienation in the organization, how do we explain the fact that workers and clients continue to *comply* with, or obey, organizational leaders' wishes to the extent that they do? Let us

look at how each of the major theories we have studied explains this phenomenon.

Compliance in the Weberian system

Enormous power, as we have seen, is concentrated in the hierarchy of the Weberian system. But according to the Weberian ideal-typical model, subordinates do not obey because they are coerced; they obey because they believe in the validity of the organization's structure and rules. Paradoxically, it is the very impersonality of the organization that makes its power *legitimate*, or acceptable to the workers. The workers can be confident that they are being dealt with not according to some powerful individual's arbitrary whim, but according to formalized written rules. They also know that the rules concern the job slot, not its occupant; thus, they know they are treated no better and no worse than anyone else would be treated in their position. In sum, the Weberian view holds that the acceptability of the impersonal rational-legal power structure, plus economic incentives, form the bases of workers' compliance. This may be an idealized picture. But still, there is a ring of truth in the idea that people in modern society will accept the directives of a rational-legal power structure; an example is the widespread support for the law—most drivers will stop for a red light, even at 4 A.M. with no other persons or cars visible.

Compliance in the human relations model

As we have seen, the Weberian model locates the basis of compliance in organizational structure and impersonal rules; neither of these is necessarily created by those who comply. In the human relations model, compliance is seen as the inevitable outgrowth of a management strategy that plays up the participation of all workers in organization activities. The keystone of that system is the "linking pin" concept: that is, a supervisor relates to his or her subordinates as a group, fosters a supportive atmosphere, and links the group with other parts of the organization through his or her membership in groups on higher levels of the hierarchy, thus forming an interconnecting "organizational family" (Likert, 1967). In essence, the supervisor helps to meet the human needs of the workers at the same time that the organization provides them with adequate pay, safe and sanitary working conditions, and so on.

Compliance in the Marxist model

The Marxist model assumes that organizations are power phenomena—that the central element holding organizations together is power, exercised by those at the top upon those at the bottom of the hierarchy (Clegg, 1979). The exercise of power is not always obvious in today's organizations, however—industries rarely use force or threats against workers openly, at least where labor organizations have obtained some power for workers. According to the Marxist view, analyzing the organization without taking into account the power relations of its components is fruitless. From this perspective, the Weberian and human relations models neglect what lies beneath the "rational" or "human" facade of the organization. Though workers or other subordinates may be "persuaded" to obey, the power of the organization to compel them to obey is always present, even if invisible. The exercise of power in most organizations today is subtle, yet, the Marxists would argue, it is no less important to an understanding of the organization because it is often hidden.

Additional factors in compliance: selection, socialization, and coercion

In addition to the sources of control suggested by the Weberian and human relations models, we should add that organizations have control over members' behavior

FIGURE 9.3

Dull, repetitive work, like that depicted at right, has resulted in alienation among workers. Why do the great majority of these workers comply with the organization's wishes? The most important reasons are summarized in the list at left.

Why workers comply

Workers' perception of impersonal organization's power as legitimate (Weberian model)

Workers' sense of themselves as part of "organizational family" (Human Relations model)

Organization's capacity to preselect and socialize compliant workers

Organization's capacity to coerce workers (Marxist model)

Many factors can encourage normative compliance. According to the human relations model, for example, activities such as this company-sponsored baseball team will foster worker participation in the organization and improve satisfaction and productivity. (© Peter Southwick/Stock, Boston)

by virtue of being able to preselect them and also by being able to socialize them. In Chapter 6 we mentioned some of the differences between socializing agencies that can choose their recruits—such as medical schools—and those, such as prisons, that have to take whomever they get. Businesses are socializing agencies, as are labor unions, government agencies, political organizations, and all other organizations. A business firm can exert control over workers' behavior by being sure to hire workers who already share the values of being punctual, meeting production quotas, and cooperating with fellow workers; it can also help a worker internalize its values fairly painlessly via on-the-job supervision, company clubs, social and athletic activities, and rewards for long service.

In sum, there are many factors that can encourage *normative compliance*—that is, compliance based on the worker's sharing the norms and values of the organization. The Weberian model assumes that the worker shares the values of fairness and economic rationality; the human relations model assumes that workers will aim for high output if treated as responsible, creative people. But there is a darker side to the picture, too. The Marxist model stresses that not all compliance is normative; some is *coercive*, induced by the threatened or actual use of economic or physical force. An industry can fire an employee or limit his or her salary. And,

ironically, certain "service" organizations, such as the military or the penal system, can curtail a client's freedom or even end his or her life.

DEFENSES AGAINST ORGANIZATIONAL POWER

As individuals or as groups, people who are subject to organizational power can resist control in various ways. For one thing, employees can strike. Between 1960 and 1977, the number of annual strikes in the United States rose from 3,333 to 5,506 (Census Bureau, 1979, p. 429); wages and fringe benefits were usually at issue, but working conditions and job security have become increasingly common strike issues. Another form of noncompliance is informal resistance, such as the kind we described among workers at the Hawthorne plant earlier in this chapter and in Chapter 8.

More and more often, formal modes of resistance to organizational power are being used. Demonstrations,

Labor unions are classic examples of organized resistance. Here, union members picket in support of striking hospital workers. (© Lawrence Frank 1976)

boycotts, and sit-ins, especially when they attract media attention, are increasingly part of the organizational landscape. Individual and class-action lawsuits, as well as proxy battles, also add to the armory of weapons that can counter organizational power.

Ties and loyalties that individuals maintain with organizations or associations other than the ones they work for may also serve to reduce the impact of organizational control. A labor union is a classic example of such organized resistance. And one of the most widely noted limits on organizational power is *professionalism:* scientists, engineers, university professors—most people, in fact, who have gone through extensive training in a professional field—are likely to feel capable of rejecting bureaucratic rules in favor of their own internalized or professionally prescribed standards of conduct.

The organization: ally or enemy of society?

Now that we have seen how the organization can control people within it—and how these people can resist that control—it is time to consider a parallel point: the ways in which the organization can control the society around it—or be controlled by it. A hundred years ago our present-day fears of the giant, self-perpetuating, self-extending, resource-devouring organization might have been laughed at. The large majority of individuals were still employed in agriculture and crafts, and the great majority of resources were still controlled by the hereditary aristocracy. But today organizations control much of the wealth of our society, and most people are employed in them or involved in them in some way. Furthermore, not all organizations can be controlled even by the society's highest *authority,* or accepted power—its government. One has only to think of the giant multinational corporations to see that this is true. (We will discuss multinational corporations in Chapter 18.)

Who wins in the power struggle between the organization and society? It hardly needs to be said that there is no clear general answer yet—and there may never be one. There are organizations that have adapted to and become identified with the values of a community or a society. Thus people say, "They can't do away with *The New York Times*—it's an institution." Universities, branches of the United States military, newspapers, venerable local businesses, professional football, the League of Women Voters—all are said to be stable systems in which meaningful social

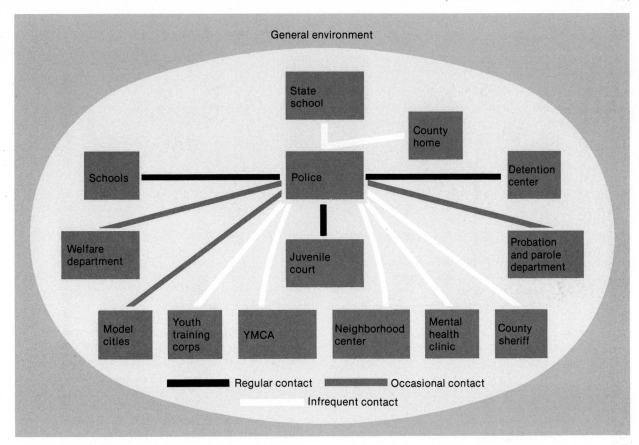

General environment

State school

County home

Schools — Police — Detention center

Welfare department

Juvenile court

Probation and parole department

Model cities | Youth training corps | YMCA | Neighborhood center | Mental health clinic | County sheriff

■ Regular contact   ■ Occasional contact

Infrequent contact

FIGURE 9.4

Interaction takes place not only among the members of an organization but also between the organization and other organizations and between the organization and its general environment. This schematic diagram shows the frequency of interaction between one organization—a city police department—and its environment and other organizations with which it comes in contact in dealing with problem youth. (Hall, 1972, p. 313)

values are enshrined. Of course, an organization's adaptation to local pressures may be of questionable value to the society as a whole. The Crown Zellerbach Corporation, for example, was responsive and adaptive to the community values of Bogalusa, Louisiana, but the values were those of the dominant local white minority rather than those of the society as a whole. Consequently, the federal government had to take legal action to force the company to accommodate overall social values by racially integrating its facilities (Rony, 1966).

Not all organizations mold their activities to the needs and values of the social system around them. In fact, Charles Perrow (1979) suggests that the biggest failure of organizational theory is the failure to see the opposite side of the picture—the many instances in which, rather than the organization's adapting to society, society itself is forced to adapt to organizations. Large formal organizations, surrounded by others that share their basic values, have demonstrated the ability to manipulate even turbulent environments to suit

their own purposes. They do so by lobbying in Congress, by spending millions of dollars on advertising, or even by financing the overthrow of unfriendly governments—as International Telephone and Telegraph (ITT) did in Chile.

The challenge that faces our "Age of Organizations" is to find ways to direct organizations into activities that are as beneficial to society as to the organizations themselves. In most cases, this will probably mean reforming or streamlining the organizations that now exist. Bureaucracy is still, as Weber originally believed, a means of administration that is applicable to a great number of goals. Nevertheless, it is subject to ills—red tape, goal displacement, poor internal communication, inadequate attention to human interpersonal needs, and neglect of those at the bottom of the hierarchy. In the 1970s, collective organizations sprang up across the country—free clinics, "alternative" newspapers, and food cooperatives—in an attempt to replace old hierarchical structures with organizations without hierarchy (Rothschild-Whitt, 1979). These organizations, with their emphasis on equality and democracy, seek to spread power among their members and to minimize rules and the division of labor that leads to stratification. A more "human" enterprise is the goal—surely a noble one. Whether collective organizations will be important in our social life in the future, however, remains to be seen.

Summary

An *organization* is a relatively permanent group that is established for the purpose of pursuing specific goals and is structured by formalized, explicitly defined rules and a hierarchical arrangement of roles. Ideally, a formal organization's activity is rationally planned. Two features of formal organizations are *division of labor* and *bureaucracy*, which is responsible for planning, coordinating, and supervising work.

Max Weber was one of the first to examine formal organizations systematically. He developed an *ideal type*, or exaggerated picture, of the organization. In Weber's *rational-legal model*, the bureaucratic organization emphasizes rationality and rules. Natural-systems approaches, like the *human relations model*, contend that worker satisfaction, rather than strict rules, increases productivity and that the informal structure within every organization is an important factor. The *organic model* deals with organizations as "natural wholes" in which *homeostasis* depends on adaptation to both internal processes and external environment. The *conflict/Marxist model* sees organizations as collections of elements with conflicting interests.

Power is concentrated at the top in an organization. At the bottom of the hierarchy, as rewards decrease, *alienation*—separation from control over one's circumstances—becomes more common. Nevertheless, most people demonstrate *compliance* with the wishes of the organization's leaders. Theories explaining compliance include: Weber's view that workers recognize the impersonal organization as *legitimate* and have economic incentives to comply; the human relations concept of the supervisor as a "linking pin" between his or her subordinates and supervisors, helping to meet the workers' human needs; and the operation of such factors as the selection and socialization of organization members. All these factors can encourage *normative compliance*. However, some compliance—as Marxist analysts would agree—is based on *coercion*. Strikes, labor unions, and professionalism illustrate that the power of organizations does not go unchallenged. Nevertheless, today organizations may challenge even the *authority* of the government.

Glossary

ALIENATION Marx's term for the separation of the worker from the means of production; also refers to the separation of the worker from control over the conditions of his or her life.

AUTHORITY Power derived from a socially accepted, institutionally defined role.

BUREAUCRACY A trained and specialized administrative staff responsible for devising, overseeing, and coordinating the activities of other participants in an organization.

COERCION Exercise of authority based on the threatened or actual use of economic or physical force.

DIVISION OF LABOR The situation in which groups or individuals are charged with carrying out different specific tasks in pursuit of a goal.

HOMEOSTASIS The tendency of a system to maintain internal stability by adapting to situations or stimuli that disturb its normal function.

IDEAL TYPE Weber's term for a contrived, exaggerated mental construct developed from scientific observation and used in comparative analysis of two or more social phenomena.

NORMATIVE COMPLIANCE Compliance with authority based on persuasion and reference to a shared set of values.

ORGANIZATION A group that is relatively complex (meaning that its members perform a number of different functions) and relatively permanent. It is consciously designed to carry out specific tasks and is characterized by planning, division of labor, hierarchical roles, and formalized rules.

RATIONAL-LEGAL SYSTEM Weber's term for his view of the bureaucratic organization as characterized by reliance on members' expertise and based on an impersonal, fair, and predictable set of formalized rules.

Recommended readings

Aldrich, Howard E. *Organizations and Environments.* Englewood Cliffs, N.J.: Prentice-Hall, 1979. An excellent book that focuses on organizations *and* the societal context in which they function. The central theme of the book is organizational change, and Aldrich pursues this idea with adequate attention to historical, economic, political, and demographic factors.

Champion, Dean J. *The Sociology of Organizations.* New York: McGraw-Hill, 1975. A simply written overview of the conceptual models used in the study of organizations, as well as a meticulous detailing of the many typologies of organizations.

Clegg, Stewart. *The Theory of Power and Organization.* Boston: Routledge and Kegan Paul, 1979. A thoughtful, historically grounded Marxist analysis of power and its relation to organizations. A difficult book, well worth the effort required to master this approach.

Etzioni, Amitai. *A Comparative Analysis of Complex Organizations: On Power, Involvement and Their Correlates.* New York: Free Press, 1961. A classic book that approaches the comparative study of complex organizations via an analysis of power relations. This book focuses on the types and consequences of compliance.

Haas, J. Eugene, and Thomas E. Drabeck. *Complex Organizations: A Sociological Perspective.* New York: Macmillan, 1973. After briefly reviewing eight major perspectives in organizational theory, the authors elaborate their own view of organizations as dynamic systems (the "stress-strain" perspective), a framework they use to organize the current research on organizations.

Katz, Daniel, and Robert L. Kahn. *The Social Psychology of Organizations.* 2nd ed. New York: Wiley, 1978. A useful view of the social psychology of organizational life. In this revised edition, the authors elaborate on their "open-systems" approach and provide a worthwhile summary of the findings and conceptual approaches in the field.

March, James G. (ed.). *Handbook of Organizations.* Chicago: Rand McNally, 1965. A massive (1,211 pages), technical, and comprehensive reference source on most aspects of formal organizations. The various chapters are written by recognized specialists, who review and integrate the relevant empirical and theoretical literature.

Perrow, Charles. *Complex Organizations: A Critical Essay.* 2nd ed. Glenview, Ill.: Scott, Foresman, 1979. This sparkling paperback is exactly what its subtitle says: a critical essay on the various models of organizational structure and processes. The style is pungent yet professional, and the book may profitably be read by students at all levels.

Structures and processes of inequality

CHAPTER TEN
STRATIFICATION AND SOCIETY

"I care not how affluent some may be provided that none be miserable in consequence of it," the American revolutionist Tom Paine once wrote. Many people in our society would agree: it is all right for some people to have more than others, as long as the society provides adequate shelter, food, clothing, and other basic necessities to all. Of course, not all Americans feel this way. A considerable number hold that the misery of others is not their—or the society's—concern. They believe that rewards are there for anyone who works hard, and they mistakenly believe that everyone has an equal chance. In their view, failure to rise in the system is the result of a lack of talent and drive; poverty is one's own fault.

Could Tom Paine's ideal be attained in our society, or does unlimited affluence for some mean inevitable misery for others? The question is a crucial one, for an individual's level of affluence means more than the degree to which everyday needs are met. It means the individual's *life chances*—for education, for a pleasant living environment, for interesting and rewarding work, even for better health and a longer life span.

Sociologists refer to the patterns of structured inequality that exist in any particular society as its system of social stratification. Note that the term *stratification* refers to the existence of inequality not only among individuals but also among whole categories of people. These categories are distinguished from one another on the basis of the property they own and the power and prestige (social honor) they have. They can be visualized as *strata* or *layers* of people, like the strata of rock that make up the crust of the earth, arranged in a ladder or *hierarchy*, with the richest, most powerful, and most prestigious categories at the top, and the poorest, least powerful, and least honored at the bottom.

Stratification can be a source of disharmony and conflict in a society. Large gaps in property, power, and prestige between strata mean great differences in modes of life, interests, and even cultures of those strata. As Karl Marx (1867), one of the most important writers on this subject, pointed out, economic conditions in particular may be such that it is not possible for one stratum to enjoy material well-being without others being deprived. What he called *economic contradictions* may then develop. If the system as a whole prospers but only some segments within it are prosperous, the effect may be to put the various strata in opposition to one another. Extreme economic contradictions may be conducive to sudden changes in the social structure through revolution.

Questions about the justification for or the possibility of eliminating inequality thus require us to focus on the sources of conflict among social categories. To understand efforts to bring about change in this area we must know something about the history of human societies and human attempts to master the environment. We will try to explore these questions in this chapter. One approach to understanding stratification and individual inequality is to examine and compare societies with different types of technology. Using an analysis that was carried out by Gerhard Lenski (1966), we will see how five different societies' stratification systems are in part shaped by their technological patterns. (Other theories of social change will be explored in Chapter 22.)

THE SIGNIFICANCE OF LABOR ROLES

One of the central ideas we will use is a basic one proposed by Marx and others: position in the stratification system depends, at least in part, on complex relationships among the person's occupation or labor role, what he or she owns or produces, and the amount of power he or she has. Exactly what these relationships are depends on the stratification system of the particular society. Furthermore, since individuals are grouped into social categories on the basis of their positions in the system of division of labor, some key questions arise about power and occupational roles on the category level. How does a category of people come to monopolize a specific occupation? How does it gain control over the goods produced by another category of people? How is an entire category forced to restrict itself to a low-status, low-reward occupation? And how do these relationships change as the society's occupational structure—which is, in turn, determined to an important extent by its technology—changes? In the space available here we cannot examine all the possible answers to these questions, but we can suggest where some of the essential connections lie.

THREE DIMENSIONS OF STRATIFICATION

Another significant concept is that stratification and inequality are not unidimensional. Modern theorists have conceptualized three dimensions of stratifica-

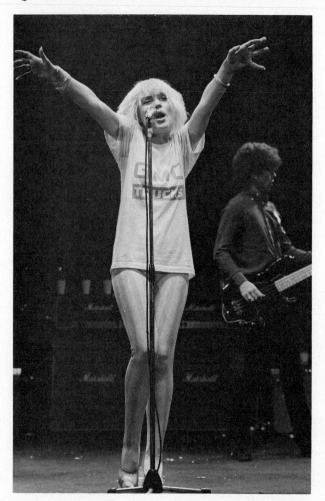

Like many celebrities, Debbie Harry, lead singer for the group Blondie, has property and prestige, but not power. Rating high on one stratification scale does not guarantee a high rating on either of the others. (R. Ellis/Sygma)

tion—material resources (property), power, *and* prestige—based in part upon the insights of Max Weber.

Property

When sociologists use the term *property*, they refer to a set of fundamental rights over things, rather than the things themselves. "Air rights," "mineral rights," or a copyright on a piece of music or work of literature are property as surely as money, jewelry, buildings, and land. The concept of property—of rights over and possession of material assets—is fundamental to human social organization.

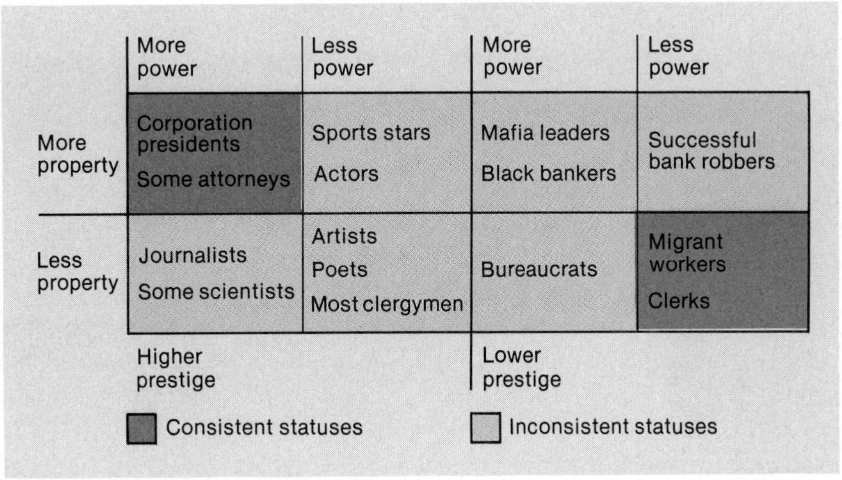

FIGURE 10.1

Because the three major sources of social status—property, power, and prestige—can be independent, high rank on one factor does not guarantee high rank on the others. A person who ranks high on one aspect of status but low on others shows *status inconsistency.* This chart compares certain types of status-inconsistent people with certain types of status-consistent people—individuals who rank equally on all three dimensions of status.

	More power	Less power	More power	Less power
More property	Corporation presidents / Some attorneys	Sports stars / Actors	Mafia leaders / Black bankers	Successful bank robbers
Less property	Journalists / Some scientists	Artists / Poets / Most clergymen	Bureaucrats	Migrant workers / Clerks
	Higher prestige		Lower prestige	

■ Consistent statuses   ■ Inconsistent statuses

The concept of property can take varying forms, however, depending on the resources and customs of the particular society. It varies not only in terms of the items that are considered "property" or "wealth"—shells and beads, wives, land, money, or trademarks—but also in terms of the individuals who can hold property rights. Not all societies, for example, regard land as something that can be individually owned at all.

Power

People differ not only in how much property they have but also in how much power they are able to exercise. Power, however, cannot be quantified and compared as easily as income can; it is a much more elusive phenomenon. As Weber defined the term, power is "the chance of a man or of a number of men to realize their own will in a communal action even against the resistance of others who are participating in the action" (1958, p. 180). Power is more than simply force. As we noted in Chapter 9, when power is exercised as part of an institutionalized role, such as the role of police officer or Chief Justice of the Supreme Court, it includes the dimension of *authority.* (When such power is seen by others as justified, it is termed *legitimate* power.) Power can also include *influence,* the "pull" that comes from personal qualities, unofficial connections, and the like. Thus, power takes many forms, ranging from the capacity of a few men to incinerate the world by starting a nuclear war to the ability of a group to take action, the casting of a vote, and the firing of a worker. (The dimensions of power will be discussed in more detail in Chapter 17.)

Prestige

The individual's desire to gain self-respect and the esteem of others is an important force in human affairs, from the child's search for parental approval to the adult's manipulation of image so as to appear in the best light. In our society prestige, or what Weber called "status honor"—the esteem in which a person or group is held by others—is distributed unequally. Prestige often has something to do with the institutional roles people play and with how much power and property they have. For example, wealth and power are often seen not simply as directly usable resources—as chances to buy a house or send a child to college—but as symbols of success, as "outer signs of inner talents and virtues" (Sykes, 1971, p. 155).

But prestige is seldom reducible to power and property only, and sometimes it is not connected with them at all. In some societies, great prestige may accrue to a person simply for having lived to a great age; in others, such personal traits as beauty, courage, strength, and intelligence may cause a person who possesses little property or power to be held in great esteem.

These comments about property, power, and prestige are, of course, broad generalizations. As we shall see in the following section, the nature of these three dimensions of stratification varies widely in different societies. In order to gain a better understanding of our own society's system of social stratification, we must learn something about the meaning and determinants of property, power, and prestige in other societies. In doing so, we become aware of how variable these aspects of stratification are.

Stratification in five types of human societies

Five principal types of societies have been identified by sociologists. The societies are roughly classified according to the kind of work members generally do, as well as by the resources and technology at their disposal (Goldschmidt, 1959; Lenski, 1966). Of the five—hunting and gathering, simple horticultural, advanced horticultural, agrarian, and industrial—some are more common today than others. The industrial society in particular has become widespread in this century, but all the other types still exist.

As we analyze the stratification pattern of each type of society, one of the major questions we will be asking is: To what extent is the position of each individual in this type of society based on *ascriptive criteria*—that is, on characteristics over which the individual has no control, such as age, sex, family of origin, religious background, or race—and to what extent on *achieved* characteristics—that is, characteristics over which the individual does have some degree of control, such as a learned skill like a craft or a degree in accounting? Can an individual rise in the stratification system through his or her own efforts, or must he or she remain in one stratum for life? As we shall see, no stratification system is based entirely on ascribed characteristics, and none is based entirely on achieved characteristics. The balance between the two varies from society to society and depends in part on technological patterns. (Some functionalists have argued that modern industrial societies are eliminating ascription because such criteria are not functional in complex settings.)

HUNTING AND GATHERING SOCIETIES

As recently as 10,000 years ago, anthropologists believe, all human societies depended for their survival on hunting game and gathering wild edibles. While this basic form of social organization has been supplanted by more complex forms in many parts of the world, societies of hunters and gatherers still exist. The best-known examples are the aborigines of Australia, the Kalahari Bushmen and Ituri Pygmies of Africa, and the Tasaday of the Philippines. People in these societies depend directly on unprocessed natural materials for food, clothing, and shelter. Their technology is limited to the most basic tools, including scrapers made of stone, digging sticks, bows and arrows, simple traps, and rudimentary fishing equipment. They have few means of preserving food or of altering their environment in any significant way. They are therefore nomadic rather than sedentary, for as soon as local resources have been exhausted, they must move or starve.

Perhaps because their existence is so precarious, hunting and gathering societies are usually quite small; they average around fifty members and rarely exceed two hundred. Of the five types of societies to be discussed, these show the least inequality among individuals. The egalitarianism and the small size of hunting and gathering societies are understandable in the light of the limited resources they command.

First of all, property inequalities are lacking in hunting and gathering societies simply because such societies produce almost no *economic surplus*—goods and services beyond what members of the society immediately need—and thus there is very little property for anyone to possess. Inequalities of power are limited for some of the same reasons. It is not easy for one man to coerce another, since all normal adult men in such a society are more or less equally trained and equipped for hunting and fighting; nor can one person control others via bribes, since resources for buying the support of others simply do not exist. Furthermore, possibly because the force or material goods that would be needed to back them up are limited, formal leadership *roles* do not tend to emerge. That is, there is little tendency for powerful roles—"chief," "planner," "second-in-command," and so on—to become an accepted part of the way the group operates, enduring through time despite changes in the specific individuals who fill them.

If people have power in these societies, it is because of their personal qualities, such as skill or intelligence, and not because they occupy recognized leadership roles. (To put this another way, they owe their power to influence, rather than to the authority that would be conferred by accepted leadership roles.) Power thus is

Hunting and gathering societies are usually the most egalitarian because their limited resources don't allow for accumulation of wealth or a division of surplus. However, members who are successful hunters or who have many offspring are often considered prestigious. Sex and age also bring prestige: older persons often have higher rank, and men usually have higher rank than women. (Dr. J. F. E. Bloss/Anthro-Photo)

not formalized but derives from mutual consent; when leaders go against the majority or fail in their tasks, they are often replaced or ignored (Radcliffe-Brown, 1948).

Prestige differences, by contrast, can be reasonably large in hunting and gathering societies. As Lenski (1966) points out, prestige, unlike power and property, is not in short supply in these societies, and inequality in this dimension does not affect the group's ability to survive. Some prestige differences are based on personal accomplishments in specific areas, such as success in hunting, magical healing powers, the ability to find

food or water when others fail, and bearing many children. (It is at this point that *slight* individual property and power distinctions emerge; those who are better at finding food may obtain some power by distributing the food.) The *status* (position in the prestige hierarchy) attained in this way is a form of *achieved status*: it stems from individual qualities.

But status in the prestige hierarchy is also attained in these societies via certain specific *ascribed* characteristics, over which the individual has no control—in this case, age and sex. Older persons often have higher rank than younger ones, and men usually have higher rank than women.

Until recently it was assumed that the dominance of males came from their superior physical strength, but new research has suggested that males' superior prestige may also stem from a complex set of circumstances based on female child-rearing responsibilities. A pregnant woman or nursing mother simply is not free to leave the settlement for long periods of time. Men are more likely to be free to go on hunts away from the encampment; as a result, they are more likely to control basic resources—in this case, meat—needed by all members of the society, particularly since they can carry out large-scale exchanges of meat away from the home (Friedl, 1975).

Male-female prestige differences tend to be smaller in those hunting and gathering societies in which men and women contribute to subsistence more equally. Nevertheless, there is a tendency to emphasize role differences, with their accompanying prestige connotations, even when they are not great in reality. In all hunting and gathering peoples, for example, men claim that hunting is a male activity exclusively—even though women may actually contribute a significant percentage of the group's protein by hunting small nondomesticated animals such as rats, frogs, insects, and young birds (Morren, 1974).

In sum, hunting and gathering societies show some inequality among *individuals*, but it is limited by the constraints on resource supplies. They also show inequalities among *categories* of people, but only among age and sex categories. The forms of stratification found in these societies are very different from those found in societies with other types of technology. The age or sex category may affect an individual's type of work and type of self-concept or self-identification. But an individual is not likely to join with the other members of the category in a struggle for resources against other categories, nor even to think of such a struggle.

What norms and values support these patterns in hunting and gathering societies? First of all, almost all property is owned collectively, with the exception of the tools or ornaments individuals make for themselves. When a hunt is successful, the meat is shared among the hunter's relatives and friends. Among groups such as the !Kung Bushmen of Africa, considerable attention is devoted to repaying the past generosities of others. Bargaining and direct exchange are considered undignified, so artifacts used in daily life are continually exchanged as gifts—with the expectation of receiving a gift of approximately equal value in the future (Lee, 1969, 1972).

SIMPLE HORTICULTURAL SOCIETIES

For approximately 10,000 years human societies have been technologically capable of raising food. The least advanced of these, known as *simple horticultural societies*, rely on small gardens for most of their produce. Among horticultural peoples, cultivation consists of the periodic clearing of new land to replace gardens that have become infertile and must be abandoned.

The major gardening implements of the simple horticultural society are hoes and digging sticks; people in these societies do not fashion tools out of metal. Nevertheless, simple horticultural societies are capable of producing an economic surplus, and they can support larger populations than can hunting and gathering societies. Lenski (1966) estimates their average size at about two hundred, and instances of much larger groups are not unknown (a single Iroquois society, for example, might have had a population of 16,000 members [Murdock, 1934]). Furthermore, simple horticultural societies may consist of as many as ten separate communities, each with its own base of support, whereas links between the more mobile and hardpressed hunting and gathering communities are tenuous at best (Lenski, 1966).

Hunting and gathering societies have little basis for individual inequality in terms of possession of property. Simple horticultural societies, however, show property inequality to a relatively high degree. Since these societies are relatively sedentary, it becomes both possible

and feasible to accumulate property. (Depending on how rapidly their gardens deplete the fertility of the soil, settlements may remain in the same place for ten or twelve years.) As territory becomes important, boundaries appear; one community may covet the property of another and even raid the other community to get it. New values concerning property emerge: decoration, quality of workmanship, and nonutilitarian use become important. Possession becomes an end in itself; people can now afford luxuries.

In these societies, property is the major avenue to prestige. A person's prestige is usually linked to material assets—cowrie shells, gardens, houses. In some simple horticultural societies, wives are regarded as property; they are an important source of wealth because they do much of the gathering. Moreover, women are in limited supply; in many horticultural societies it is customary for married men to have several wives apiece, which cuts down the number of women available for marriage; there is also a high rate of mortality during childbirth. Consequently, a man's prestige increases with the number of his wives.

Prestige may also be obtained through property exchange. As Lenski points out, surplus property in these societies has only limited usefulness to its owner; it is typically not income-producing, as would be *capital goods* (land, machinery, or investments), which are used in the production of other goods (1966, p. 134). People can use only so many plumes, shell ornaments, vegetables, and pigs. When they acquire more than they can reasonably use, they frequently give the surplus to those who cannot repay, thus demonstrating their superior merit. (Wives, who are usually regarded as capital goods, are never given away.) The result of such giftgiving is to reduce somewhat the existing inequalities of property and to increase the inequalities of prestige.

As we have seen, inequality is greater in simple horticultural societies than in hunting and gathering societies because the former have the technological capacity to produce more. But it is also greater for another reason: simple horticultural societies have a more complex division of labor. They can support people who perform specialized tasks—making tools, for instance, or weapons or plans for agricultural activities or ceremonial objects—which are not immediately productive of food. Any specialized-labor role puts the person filling it in the position of having to subsist on what others produce, either by coercing the food producers to give

Although simple horticultural societies—like this Indian village—rely on small gardens for most produce and simple tools like hoes and digging sticks, they are capable of producing an economic surplus. (Bernard Pierre Wolff/Magnum)

up their surplus or depending on their willingness to do so. Because of this, a more complex pattern of power relationships develops.

Leadership roles, those that involve planning and coordinating the activities of the whole community, are essentially specialized-labor roles like any others: they involve providing services needed by the community, and for which the community will offer material rewards. But though a leader may actually *need* only a certain amount of power in order to carry out the coordination of activities, there is a tendency for leadership roles to accumulate more power around them than may be strictly necessary. Chiefs, for example, often have access to surplus property, which they can use to buy the support of more followers, who can in turn help them obtain more property, and so on. Thus the leaders can back up their authority with force, continually increasing the power associated with their role.

As the hierarchy of leadership roles becomes more firmly established over the years, the labor function associated with roles toward the top of the hierarchy may become relatively secondary. People in these powerful positions may contribute services, but at a highly unequal rate of exchange with the food producers; they may be said to be simply *exploiting* the labor of the food producers.

Simple horticultural societies show a fair amount of inequality among individuals. They also show a degree of inequality among categories of people—not only age and sex categories, but also those based on family background. Family background is important because the accumulation of property raises the possibility of its being passed on from one generation to the next within the family or clan; it is also important because the social structure includes powerful roles that continue to exist regardless of "personnel changes" and that can be passed down through families just as property can. Within this system an individual may be able to attain status through achievement, but ascriptive criteria are important determinants of position in the stratification system.

ADVANCED HORTICULTURAL SOCIETIES

Advanced horticultural societies are a great deal larger, richer, and more specialized than simple horticultural societies, and their stratification systems show much more inequality. The basis for the increase in organizational complexity is a web of technological changes. Most important is the mastery of metalworking for tool production. The metal plow, for instance, greatly increases crop yields, allowing farmers to work the soil more finely and deeply than with the digging stick. Advanced horticultural societies also irrigate and ferti-

Advanced horticultural society: Increased productivity yields economic surplus, which means that the time and the resources exist for building monuments such as this Mayan temple in Guatemala. (Courtesy, The American Museum of Natural History)

lize the land; because a wide variety of plants are cultivated, crops can be rotated. As a result, individual farmers are vastly more productive.

This increase in productivity makes possible larger populations and greater population density. Lenski (1966) has estimated that advanced horticultural societies can support as many as one hundred persons per square mile. The Inca population of Peru and the Maya of Mexico numbered in the millions (Steward and Faron, 1959; von Hagen, 1961). The increase in productivity also makes possible the development of relatively large cities, settlements that obtain food supplies from areas outside the settlement itself. At the peak of the Mayan empire, Mayapan, the capital, had a population estimated at 12,000 (von Hagen, 1961).

The increase in the amount and ease of production has many consequences in regard to stratification. First of all, it makes possible the transmission of considerable wealth from generation to generation. In hunting and gathering and simple horticultural societies, wealth cannot be inherited on a large scale because so much of whatever surplus exists is in perishable form. In an ad-

vanced horticultural society, however, assets are more tangible. Since settlements can be much more permanent, land can be considered property, as can cattle and even forms of money. A son or daughter of modest talents can hold on to assets gathered by the parents. If each succeeding generation adds to the holdings, ever greater accumulations of wealth are possible. The result is the emergence of a formal notion of property rights, the development of hereditary strata, and the growth of marked inequalities of property, power, and prestige.

Also important, increased productivity makes possible the development of elaborate government structures and of much larger territorial units, such as states (which we will discuss in Chapter 17) and empires. Government develops a number of levels, from rulers and ministers at the top down to village headmen. Full-time officials appear, as well as full-time soldiers. Unlike simple horticultural societies, advanced horticultural societies have the resources necessary for large-scale warfare, and they are productive enough to make one another's people and holdings appear to be valuable prizes.

Thus, power differentials are marked in advanced horticultural societies. It is in these societies, for example, that organized slavery appears. With increased productivity and social complexity, it becomes feasible to own human beings in order to appropriate the fruits of their labor; slaves produce enough to support not only themselves and their owners but also the standing army that helps to maintain the system.

One can become a slave by being captured in a war, but one can also inherit one's position as a slave. In fact, positions at all levels of the dominance hierarchy tend to be almost exclusively inherited in advanced horticultural societies. (This is also true of agrarian societies, which we will discuss next.) Stratification tends to approximate a *caste* system: that is, the various social strata tend to be mutually exclusive units (castes) between which it is not possible for any individual to move. Not only is each individual's caste position fixed

	HUNTERS & GATHERERS	SIMPLE HORTICULTURE	ADVANCED HORTICULTURE	AGRARIAN	INDUSTRIAL
TECHNOLOGY	Primitive stone tools	Basic tools Slash & burn cultivation	Metal work tools Crop rotation Irrigation and fertilization	Elaborate metal tools Simple machines Development of wheel, plow, and non-human energy sources	Complex machinery Varied and rapidly changing technology
SETTLEMENT	Nomadic bands; temporary location	Semi-autonomous villages or small confederations Transitory: move every few years	Semi-autonomous villages and cities in larger "states" Permanent	Larger, permanent empires with changing political boundaries Urban centers with ethnic diversity and occupational specialization	Larger urban areas Urban/rural split
ORGANIZATION/ FORM OF GOV'T	Limited and informal political roles/ limited authority	Formal leadership roles based in kinship system Limited planning and coordination	Complex multi-level "states" governed by hereditary nobility	Autocratic monarchies ruled by chief landowners	Multi-level bureaucratic states Birth of citizenship
ECONOMIC SURPLUS	Nonexistent	Limited; non-income producing; used for barter	Stable; larger surplus; minimally capital-producing	Larger surplus concentrated in landowners	Great and mostly concentrated yet partially distributed
BASIS OF STRATIFICATION	Property: nonexistent Power: achieved—personal qualities, skill, intelligence, magic Prestige: ascribed and achieved—personal accomplishments, age, and sex	Property: ascribed—small garden plots Prestige: ascribed—material goods (e.g., cowrie shells, garden houses), property exchange, age, and sex	Property: ascribed—inherited wealth Power: ascribed—property ownership Prestige: ascribed—caste membership, property ownership, age, and sex	Property: ascribed—inherited wealth Power: ascribed—property ownership, military might, and tax levy Prestige: ascribed—property ownership, social and economic position (including age, sex, and race)	Property: ascribed and achieved—inherited and acquired capital Power: ascribed and achieved—control over means of production Prestige: ascribed and achieved—wealth, talent, and acquired knowledge, social position (including age, sex, and race)

FIGURE 10.2
This table shows the relationship of five different societies' technologies, settlement patterns, political structures, and forms of economic surplus to their bases of stratification.

by birth, but the distribution of resources among the various castes is fairly fixed as well; established traditions determine the amount of property, power, and prestige available to each caste.

AGRARIAN SOCIETIES

In ancient Greece, Italy, Mesopotamia, and China—among other places—there emerged *agrarian* societies, with relatively elaborate technologies based on improvements in metalworking, the development of the wheel, and the construction of simple machines. Once again, productivity took a leap forward, making possible the support of larger populations and leading to a series of important societal developments.

For one thing, the wealth of these societies encouraged militarism on a hitherto unknown scale. Warfare was highly profitable. Sulla, a ruler of Rome in the first century B.C., is said to have realized 480 million sesterces from his military campaigns—enough to support nearly half a million Roman families for a year. Relatively few farmers were needed to feed an entire army, and the new technology made possible the development of huge transportation and communication networks; thus it was possible to maintain large permanent armies and to deploy them over wide geographical areas. These armies were necessary to defend Rome's borders from neighboring societies as well as to put down the many violent internal power struggles that shook the empire.

Agrarian societies are governed by autocratic monarchs—*because* of the militarism of such societies, in Lenski's view: powerful, unified leadership is a necessity in time of war. Constant warfare also creates a highly developed warrior caste and centralized military power, thus accentuating the division between castes in terms of power and access to accumulated wealth. No distinction is made between the militaristic ruler's personal finances and the national treasury; the annual incomes of the members of the royal family often run into the equivalent of hundreds of millions of dollars. In the nineteenth century, for example, the Russian czars literally owned the 27.5 million serfs who worked their lands. Power differentials are huge. At the ruler's whim, large numbers of people can be enslaved or exterminated; thousands can starve while a few dine on larks' tongues. Commoners may literally be required to grovel in the dust when the king and his retinue pass by; to

Agrarian society: This illumination from a fourteenth-century Italian breviary shows horses, a basic source of energy in this society, being used in the fields. (The Granger Collection)

speak to someone of higher rank before being spoken to may mean severe punishment. Most aspects of life—from work to clothing to speech, food, manners, and entertainment—are ordered so as to reflect the inequalities in the society and to reinforce their legitimacy.

Of all the types of societies discussed here, agrarian societies favor ascriptive stratification patterns most heavily. It is possible for some bold and talented commoners to rise and for members of the hereditary nobility to lose their positions because of incompetence, but these occurrences are rare. Likewise, surplus wealth is highly concentrated in these societies. The castes at the top of the social hierarchy, which possess almost all the property, power, and prestige, rarely exceed 1 or 2 percent of the population.

Agrarian societies are more complex in their structure than horticultural societies. Because they can support larger populations in broad geographical areas and because of their militarism and the frequent changes in their political boundaries, their populations include a variety of ethnic, racial, and religious groups. Sometimes differences between conquerors and conquered disappear in one or two generations; sometimes, however, they persist over the centuries and result in a caste stratification system, as happened in India.

Again, economic activities in agrarian societies are more complex due to technological advances, and there is a greater division of labor. The Paris tax rolls of 1313, for instance, list 157 different crafts—and they do not include such occupations as priest, soldier, farmer, or member of the nobility (Clough and Cloe, 1941). Furthermore, agrarian societies have two social categories that do not appear in hunting and gathering or horticultural societies: the first is the category of *merchants*—now required as a result of the new complexities of production and trade—and the second is the category Lenski calls the "expendables" and Karl Marx called the *lumpenproletariat*—people, such as beggars and thieves, who lack a steady, legitimate source of support. Lenski estimates that 10 to 15 percent of the population of Shakespeare's London were "expendables" (1966, p. 283).

Cities in agrarian societies, with increased production, transport, and need for markets, began to assume some of the character and dimensions they have today. The populations of Rome, Athens, Baghdad, and Hangchow were reckoned in the hundreds of thousands. Thus, to the new complexity of social roles was added an urban social environment on a larger scale. Most of the people continued to live in rural areas, but the new size, density, and heterogeneity of urban environments began to bring changes in norms and values that would ultimately be felt throughout agrarian societies. (These patterns will be discussed in more detail in Chapter 20.)

Inequalities in agrarian societies do not manifest themselves solely as abuse of the weaker by the stronger. Each stratum of such a society has, in addition to its rights, certain distinct responsibilities. In medieval Europe, for example, the feudal nobility was responsible not only for the smooth working of the kingdom but also for the general welfare of those who worked their estates. It was the duty—not just the right—of the noble to participate in public affairs and to serve on courts. In return, subjects were obligated to contribute a certain portion of their annual production, in the form of taxes, toward the maintenance of the noble and his court.

WESTERN INDUSTRIALIZED SOCIETIES

Modern American society, like the societies of Western Europe in general, is profoundly different from the other types we have considered. Western industrialized societies display many of the inequalities that characterize agrarian societies. People still begin life with unequal opportunities for economic and occupational success; huge fortunes, along with the power and prestige that accompany them, are still inherited, and the poor still struggle to keep themselves afloat from day to day; for women and for racial and ethnic minorities, opportunities are still limited by the prevalence of ascriptive status criteria.

But the rigidity that marks the stratification systems of agrarian societies is not evident to the same degree. Life chances are not so completely preordained at birth. It is quite possible to inherit wealth or status, but it is also possible to obtain them through one's own efforts. Caste, in other words, has tended to be supplanted in Western industrialized societies by *class*. The term *class* has a number of meanings, which we will explore in Chapter 11. Here, our focus is on the key fact that in a class system, the various strata are relatively more open; it is possible for individuals and groups to move from one level of the hierarchy to another. Associated with this is the fact that individuals are legally free to choose their own occupations and can compete for any job they wish. (Whether or not an individual is actually hired for a job, of course, is another question.)

This is not to say that conflict among social categories does not exist in Western industrialized societies. But the stratification systems of such societies are complex, and the discrepancies between rich and poor are, relatively speaking, not as extreme as in agricultural societies. We will see this more clearly as we examine how some of these societies developed.

The roots of industrial stratification patterns

Western industrialized societies have existed for about two centuries. In their earliest stages, they retained many features of agrarian societies: aristocrats continued to rule, and impoverished workers continued to produce the economic surplus, merely changing their work site from farm to factory. As in agrarian societies,

The display of advanced technology is one striking characteristic distinguishing modern industrial societies from all other types. (© Phelps/Rapho/Photo Researchers)

an individual's position was determined to a relatively great extent by birth. But when large numbers of lower-class people migrated to the cities, traditional rural patterns of life weakened. In the cities, people were exposed to all the currents of change—economic, social, and political—brought about by the Industrial Revolution.

As early as the Middle Ages, the cities of Europe had been islands of relative freedom from the absolute rule of the hereditary nobility. Centers of commerce and industry, the cities used their economic power to buy a certain amount of autonomy. Merchants accumulated noninherited profits in money, the new and most readily convertible medium of exchange; and a second segment of the urban population—the expanding government bureaucracy—had access to and began to accumulate power. Thus was formed a new stratum of people with relatively ample resources—the *bourgeoisie* (literally, "city-dwellers").

Through their dominance of economic institutions and bureaucratic power, the new urban bourgeoisie challenged the social and political dominance of the hereditary nobility—and eventually won. Merchant and banker princes, like the Medici in Florence and the doges of Venice, assumed positions of power that had previously been controlled by the land-based aristocracy. Monarchs who managed to keep their thrones, like the kings of France, Portugal, and Spain, had to make substantial concessions to the merchant classes.

By the eighteenth century, the power of the bourgeoisie, along with their control over scarce resources, equaled or surpassed that of the nobility. One result was the stimulation of technological advance, financed by the reinvestment of mercantile profits. Because the technological innovations of the Industrial Revolution rapidly multiplied the capacity to process raw materials, they created pressure for increased agricultural productivity to generate those raw materials. But once agriculture had been revolutionized by technology, fewer farmers were needed. Many were forced off the land and came to the cities, where they formed an enormous labor pool from which the new urban industrialists could draw. These peasants-turned-workers were now controlled by the industrialists, rather than by the hereditary landed nobility. Wealth, prestige, and power rested on new and broader foundations. Wealth could consist not only of land, cattle, or houses but also of money and control of new means of production. Prestige could accrue through knowledge and talent.

Most important, individuals now had greater freedom to rise within the system of stratification. Agrarian societies' system of distributing rewards solely on the basis of ascriptive criteria had become inefficient. The complexity of work in industrialized societies greatly increased the demand for individual competence and talent, and even people from lower classes, if they fulfilled the requirements, could in some cases be hired for well-paid, powerful, high-status jobs. Property could be acquired and accumulated by individual effort within one person's lifetime.

These workers, assembling a turbine for a ship's engine, are highly skilled personnel who could not be easily replaced. Increased specialization has created skill monopolies which enable people in subordinate positions to bargain for a larger share of social assets. (© Leonard Speier 1979)

Meanwhile, power, as well as property, was becoming more broadly distributed among the population as a whole. The increase in opportunity opened politics to new groups, and eighteenth-century Enlightenment ideas of rationalism, universal rights, personal liberty, and equality of opportunity reached all strata. A new concept of citizenship emerged, based on a set of fundamental rights—political, economic, and social—to which all were entitled (Marshall, 1964). What group membership had provided in agrarian societies was now provided by citizenship—that is, by membership in the state. (We will discuss these issues in more detail in Chapter 17.)

The consequences of industrial stratification patterns

In what are called the advanced industrial societies of today, the division of labor has become so complex that except for a relatively small number of artisans and craft workers, few people participate in and know all stages of a manufacturing process from raw material to finished product. Those at the highest levels of an organization or of the society no longer understand the work performed by many below them, while some workers have become so specialized that they are no longer interchangeable. The result, in Western industrialized societies, has been skill monopolies for many in subordinate positions, such as plumbers and electricians (Galbraith, 1967; Drucker, 1969). This powerful bargaining position has been used to extract a larger share of social assets.

Furthermore, there has been a growth in the professional and technical segments of the work force, including the sector of public employees who work for government bureaucracies. All these, in Western industrial societies, have been factors in the expansion of the middle classes—people whose prestige, property, and power tend to be independent of the ownership of the means of production.

Greater individual social mobility has been associated with changes in the distribution of scarce resources. It is, for example, more difficult to pass along inherited wealth than it once was. Also, because the total amount of wealth has increased, the absolute living conditions of those at the lowest levels have improved without necessarily diminishing the absolute wealth of those above them. Mass production has made more goods available to more people. There has even been some change in the distribution of capital goods and of the means of production, although ownership of these is still disproportionately concentrated in the hands of a minority of people.

Stratification in Western industrialized societies, in short, is less extreme and less rigid than it is in agrarian societies, and the more equal distribution of resources in Western industrial societies may be a factor in muting the violent class conflict predicted by Karl Marx. Some observers have suggested that such violent conflict, if and when it does take place, will occur not on the national but on the international level; that the "Third World" nations, which are in the process of becoming industrialized, will rise up against the Western industrialized countries in a struggle for the resources that these countries control.

A WORLD SYSTEM
OF STRATIFICATION

Thus far we have focused on individual societies independent of other societies. An alternative approach gaining importance in sociology is to look at the world system of social stratification, where developments in powerful societies have had consequences far exceeding their domestic impact. The emergence of capitalism in the West, for example, has had a major impact on countries and societies all over the world. We will explore the topic further in Chapter 18, but here it will be useful to look at the argument developed by Wallerstein in his *The Modern World System* (1974).

In Wallerstein's view, throughout history individual states have been part of a hierarchically organized system. There has been the world empire, a relatively large territory containing different cultural groups and administered by a single political center, to which capital and tribute flow in return for political stability (the Roman Empire, the Persian Empire, old China, and so on). Since the sixteenth century, another kind of system, the capitalist world economy, has linked separate political units by means of trade. A small number of *core* areas have diversified economies in which the export goods produced by the *semiperiphery* and *periphery* areas are processed. In such a system, a geographical division of labor results in the core areas receiving most of the surplus, which does not have to be redistributed to maintain order throughout the system. Thus the periphery (the countries of the Third World) and the semiperiphery (countries such as Brazil and Korea, which are partly developed and partly industrialized) must remain in subordinate positions in order for the

STRATIFICATION IN THE SOVIET UNION

Is it true that to perform difficult jobs, people have to be motivated by special rewards—as the American functionalists have claimed? Is self-interest the only inducement that will make people go through the long and arduous training many jobs require? Not necessarily, according to Karl Marx. Marx believed it was possible to restructure society in such a way that all citizens would be willing to contribute their time, energy, and special abilities without extra remuneration; they would do so, he believed, if they worked on a cooperative rather than a competitive basis.

What Marx proposed, in essence, was a system that would separate the distribution of resources and the occupational structure from each other. All citizens would receive sufficient material resources for survival and a relatively comfortable life, regardless of what job they did. "From each according to his abilities, to each according to his needs"—thus ran Marx's basic formulation. Like our own American ideology, Marx's ideal envisioned equality of opportunity for all. But it went even further: instead of picturing an open system of stratification (which is what our system is supposed to be), it pictured a society without any stratification at all—a classless society.

How was stratification to be eliminated? Two steps had to be taken, in Marx's view, to achieve this goal. First of all, power and property inequalities had to be erased. In Western societies such as England and the United States, a small category of individuals owned all the wealth-producing property (factories, farms, businesses,

and so on), while a much larger segment—the *proletariat*—worked for the first category as wage-earners, so that the society was polarized into two unequal classes. This polarization could be eliminated, Marx argued, first by taking the means of production away from the private owners and turning them over to the workers themselves, and second by minimizing the boring and fatiguing menial tasks that no one in the society was likely to want to do. In any society with a complex division of labor, Marx saw, some people would inevitably rise to technical, administrative, and professional positions through their superior intellectual qualifications, while others remained tied to menial jobs. But, Marx argued, if technology became sufficiently advanced, the society would have such an abundance of wealth that no members would be forced to spend all their time on drudgery. A cooperative society of the type Marx envisioned could regulate the general production:

. . . and this makes it possible for me to do one thing today and another tomorrow, to hunt in the morning, fish in the afternoon, rear cattle in the evening, criticize after dinner, just as I have a mind. (Marx and Engels, 1947)

It was these two steps which Nikolai Lenin and other early Soviet leaders in the Bolshevik party attempted to follow when they undertook, after the Russian Revolution of 1917, to establish a new socialist Soviet state. And they were able to carry out Marx's ideas to some extent. Factories, farms, and businesses were indeed taken over and in principle given to the people—as represented by the

core areas to be advanced, industrialized economies. Wallerstein's theory has implications not only for stratification *among* nations but also for stratification *within* them. One immediate consequence of a world system is that the poor and working classes of the core areas are better off than their counterparts in peripheral nations. In other words, it is not just the well-to-do living in the core areas who profit from this economic system.

Wallerstein's complex theory has not been put to systematic testing, but it does offer interesting and provocative insights into the world as we know it today, and into how and why inequality, and stratification pervade the modern world. It has provided new directions for sociological research to explore.

Is inequality inevitable?

As we said earlier, all known human societies have shown some degree of inequality. Because inequality seems to be universal, some theorists have suggested that it is inevitable. They maintain that not only has there never been an unstratified society, there can never be one. Others, distressed by what they see as the negative effects of inequality, have argued that unstratified societies could develop if individualism could be replaced with a cooperative ethic and power distributed differently.

This, in fact, was the position of Marx and Lenin, whose views form the basis of the system of social organization known as *communism*—a system in which there is little private property, all major property being held by the community or the state. Certain countries, such as the Soviet Union, have attempted to attain the

---

Communist party—and considerable technological advancement was achieved. Yet, despite Marx's predictions, it has not proven possible to eliminate stratification in the U. S. S. R. *Property* inequalities are less pronounced than in the United States. Strictly speaking, there is no private property, though high-ranking officials may have "perquisites" such as government-owned automobiles and country houses that come with their jobs. But *power* inequalities still exist and even show signs of increasing. How all this came about is an interesting story in itself, and it sheds light on some of our own stratification patterns.

INDUSTRIALIZATION AND THE RESTRUCTURING OF SOVIET SOCIETY

At the time of the Revolution, the need for rapid industrial development was deeply felt. Compared with the countries of Western Europe, Russia was technologically backward, with an economy based largely on agriculture. The building of a perfect socialist state required transformation of the Soviet economy. Moreover, the realistic fear of imminent foreign invasion made it crucial that the new regime industrialize rapidly.

Ironically, in order to pursue the goal of full equality, the Soviet leadership was forced to depart from the very ideal toward which it was striving. Industrial development required the presence of highly trained individuals and po-

sitions of authority. At first Lenin attempted to employ members of the "intelligentsia" and highly skilled workers at wages comparable to those paid to manual workers, assuming that the satisfaction of contributing to the development of the Soviet state would be reward enough. This arrangement, however, proved unworkable. Only by rewarding the intelligentsia with proportionately greater wages and privileges was the Soviet leadership able to motivate them to obtain advanced training or to work at full capacity. So, with industrialization and equality as their goals, the Communists were fostering an occupational hierarchy based on differential salary levels that closely resembled those of Western countries (Goertzel, 1976, p. 88).

Even after making these compromises, the Soviet leaders feared that the goal they sought might still elude them. By the 1920s the Bolshevik party had established a firm political hold on the country, but in many ways its control was no different from that of the czarist government that had preceded it. Russia's millions of peasants still lived pretty much as they had lived for centuries—embracing ancient religious and folk beliefs, working their ancestral plots of farmland, and governing themselves by traditional methods. They had little stake in the new regime. In addition, party leaders feared that the growth of agriculture and industry was leading to the development of a new affluent middle class that would eventually restore private ownership and a return to previous economic patterns. Clearly, steps had to be taken to prevent

(continued)

communistic goal. (As it turns out, the Soviet Union has not been able to eliminate stratification, which has simply taken a different form in that society, as we explain in the accompanying box.) Inequality has persisted in Western societies as well, despite the changes industrialization has wrought.

The two principal sociological positions on this question are those of the functionalists and the conflict theorists, which were discussed in detail in Chapter 3. Let us look at these approaches as they relate to the subject of this chapter.

FUNCTIONALIST VERSUS CONFLICT APPROACHES

Kingsley Davis (1942, 1949, 1955), who took the lead in formulating the functionalist approach to stratification, published the first general statement of the theory with Wilbert E. Moore in 1945. Essentially, their argument was as follows: Societies are complex organizations made up of a great many roles, each of which must be filled by the best-qualified person. If all positions were equally pleasant or important and required equal training and talent, it would not matter who filled what job. But this is not the case: some jobs require specialized skills or abilities, some are more pleasant than others, some are functionally more important. In order to ensure that the best-trained people fill the most important jobs, the society develops a system of unequal rewards that reflects the scarcity of qualified candidates for a given position.

Although the functionalist theory of stratification has the virtues of great simplicity and close congruence with the fact that all societies have been stratified, there is a great deal about social inequalities that it cannot explain.

Conflict theorists, in contrast, hold that societies are more stratified than they need to be. Their explanation of "overstratification" stems from the proposition that people will seek to maximize their self-interest. Therefore, given any degree of inequality to begin with, those

---

the socialist revolution from bogging down before it could surpass its modest early success (Dowse and Hughes, 1972, p. 157).

The solution was a vigorous program of collectivization and reeducation. Private agricultural land was consolidated and turned into large collective farms. Many peasants were stripped of their land and forced into towns and cities, where they were recruited as cheap labor for the nation's developing industries. Government policy also kept living standards low so that capital could be channeled into industrial growth. At the same time, the government sought to end the ideological indifference of ordinary citizens and transform them into loyal and committed members of the socialist state. The educational system was reorganized according to socialist principles. Youth groups such as the Young Pioneers socialized Russian children in Marxist-Leninist philosophy. A universal military draft was instituted, and the armed forces became an additional means of bringing political awareness and class consciousness to the populace (Dowse and Hughes, 1972, pp. 157–158).

The methods used to bring about this large-scale transformation—a transformation that met resistance—included coercion on a scale unknown to most previous societies. Under Joseph Stalin (secretary general of the Communist party from 1922 to 1953 and Soviet premier from 1941 to 1953), a highly disciplined and efficient secret police, using strategies of surprise and torture, unrelentingly quashed all signs of "counterrevolutionary" activity. They consigned dissident individuals to forced-labor camps for "reeducation" through physical deprivation and brainwashing. The effect of the Soviet terrorist program was to create a pervasive feeling of insecurity among the people, a mood of fear that would discourage any organized resistance and would inhibit people's ordinary social ties (Moore, 1954). No one was immune from suspicion—although one could perhaps prove one's loyalty by denouncing neighbors, even friends or relatives, as enemies of the state. Even members of the secret police were repeatedly denounced and purged. After Stalin's death in 1953, the Soviet government's dependence on terrorism as a means of internal discipline decreased, but remnants of terrorism, in a milder and less pervasive form, continue even today.

THE NEW SOVIET CITIZEN AND THE NEW ELITE

Through terrorism, collectivization, and ideological indoctrination programs, the Communists appeared to have produced a "new Soviet person": an obedient citizen, dedicated to hard work and loyal to the leaders of the Communist party (Dowse and Hughes, 1972, p. 160). There were still enormous power differentials in the society—the more so because of the extreme centralization of power in the hands of the state, which leaders had contended was a necessary step in the development of the new society. But this power was now held by a different category of people. The purging and aging of the older leaders of the Revolution had made way for an elite of younger "technocrats" (technical specialists) and adminis-

with advantages will use them to gain even greater advantage.

Conversely, people only give up as much as they must. Power to enforce one's will rather than the social importance of one's job is seen as a key to rewards. Worse yet, those with advantages will cynically defend their position, arguing that it is for the greater good of all, and thus try to pacify the exploited. It is in this sense that conflict theorists call functionalist theories bourgeois and argue that functionalism attempts to hide the self-interest of the ruling classes behind the rhetoric about how inequalities serve the society as a whole.

LENSKI'S SYNTHESIS: ONE PARTIAL ANSWER

Various sociologists have tackled the problem of synthesizing the functionalist and conflict approaches to stratification. One interesting synthesis has been suggested by Gerhard Lenski (1966), who noted a degree

of inevitability in stratification—but also a degree of variability of indeterminacy. Lenski argued that all societies will tend to be somewhat stratified simply because individuals are unequally endowed with skills, intelligence, and other personal attributes; because customs and traditions persist; because humans have a tendency to take the most personally rewarding action; and because there is, inevitably, imperfection in the functioning of any social system. He noted, however, that not all human societies are "equally unequal"—as we have seen in this chapter. Technology can lead, via high productivity, to high degrees of inequality, as in agarian societies. Yet when the division of labor becomes extremely complex (as in industrial societies), a greater proportion of people have skill monopolies which they can use to limit the extent to which they are exploited.

Lenski also noted certain other variable factors that might affect stratification systems. Stratification is likely to be more extreme in societies faced with many external threats; it may also be more marked in societies whose ideologies favor free will (our own is one of

---

trators, who attained their positions by earning high-level educational credentials. Nevertheless there was still a stratification ladder to be climbed; education increasingly became the way to climb it.

Paradoxically, however, what might seem to be the most egalitarian of systems, promising advancement solely through individual merit as reflected in educational attainment, is actually one with inherent class antagonisms: the emphasis on success by educational attainment, instead of increasing feelings of social solidarity, tends to exacerbate status differences between workers in farms and factories and the intelligentsia. (Young people, Soviet writers complain, are unwilling to take jobs involving manual labor—a symptom of this status gap.) There is tremendous competition for jobs in the government bureaucracy. Because they lack private resources to fall back on, members of the administrative and technical elite are always apprehensive about losing their positions of leadership and will go to great lengths to retain them. (In Western societies, by contrast, members of the elite may be able to derive power and security from jobs in the private sector even if they are voted out of office or lose appointed positions in the public sphere.)

Further ill feeling is generated by the elite's use of their power to get their children accepted into universities. Although Soviet spokesmen assert that the educational system of the U.S.S.R. allows far greater opportunity for children of workers and peasants than do the systems of Western countries, adequate data for comparison are not available. Members of the elite tend to be extremely protective of their own positions, and they are

equally anxious for their children to obtain the advanced training that will qualify them for positions of power.

IDEALS VERSUS REALITY IN THE SOVIET SYSTEM

To date, as we have seen, the U.S.S.R. has been unable to reach its goal of a totally egalitarian, classless society. The persistence of stratification in Soviet society has been a cause of some concern to Soviet leaders, since it threatens the very principles of the socialist system. If a small minority of highly educated people control all the wealth-producing property, if they profit from their privileged position, and if they can pass on their control to their children—then, it may be argued, their relationship to that property is really a form of ownership. Property, in other words, may serve the interests of a restricted group of people even if it is not privately owned.

How do Soviet theorists rationalize continued inequality in the U.S.S.R.? Currently, they seem to have retreated from Marx's original vision. Most would claim that stratification is necessary because without it, leadership would disappear and industrial development would cease—an argument that, interestingly enough, runs parallel to that of the American functionalists. And indeed, Russia's economic situation has improved tremendously since the Communists came to power. But clearly, though the Soviet Union may be on its way to attaining many other goals, it is not becoming the unstratified utopia that Marx and Lenin envisioned.

these); and it may be affected by the personal idiosyncracies of the leaders.

Lenski's theory suggests that to understand how and why societies are stratified as they are—and how much they can be changed—we must examine a wide range of factors. It will not suffice simply to examine the needs of the system for scarce talent (the functionalist approach) or to point to the narrow self-interests of ruling classes (part of a conflict approach). Rather, we must try to understand a whole host of factors, from the impact of technology, economic development, and the environment to the effects of religion, politics, population changes, and leadership. We must be familiar with historical trends and events; with the constraints within which societies attempt to survive; with, in fact, anything that bears on how humans organize themselves into groups.

Summary

Every known human society has been characterized by some degree of *stratification*, or inequality among the individuals and groups that make up the society. Social scientists have sought to explain why there is a hierarchy of social rewards. In the view of Karl Marx and others, an individual's position in the hierarchy depends largely on economic position as determined by ownership of the means of production. Drawing on Max Weber's work, sociologists have argued that stratification and inequality involve three major dimensions: *property, power,* and *prestige*.

On the basis of their members' labor roles and of their resources and technology, societies have been classified into five general types: hunting and gathering, simple horticultural, advanced horticultural, agrarian, and industrial. The hunting and gathering type of society has the least inequality among individuals. Simple horticultural societies are characterized by greater property inequality. It is in advanced horticultural and agrarian societies that we find stratification systems based primarily on *ascribed status* of members, known as *caste systems*. In industrialized societies, stratification is based primarily on *achieved status* of individuals and is referred to as a *class system*.

Functionalist theorists believe that at least some degree of stratification and inequality is inevitable by virtue of the division of labor that is an inherent feature of complex societies. Conflict theorists maintain that societies are more stratified than they need to be, because of the central role of power in protecting privilege. Gerhard Lenski has attempted to synthesize these two positions, arguing that stratification is to some extent both inevitable and variable, and that both dimensions are influenced by a wide variety of factors.

Glossary

ACHIEVED STATUS Social position based on characteristics over which the individual has some degree of control, such as acquired skill.

ASCRIBED STATUS Social position based on characteristics over which the individual has no prior control, such as age, sex, family of origin, religious background, and race.

AUTHORITY Power derived from a legitimate, institutionally defined role.

BOURGEOISIE Members of the middle class, including shopkeepers and merchants.

CAPITAL GOODS Machines, tools, and other resources that are used in the production of other goods (as opposed to consumer goods, which are ready for consumption and are not used in any further production).

CASTE SYSTEM A rigid system of social stratification typical of advanced horticultural and agrarian societies. It is based primarily on ascribed characteristics of individuals, and it is not possible for an individual to move from one caste to another.

CLASS SYSTEM A system of social stratification typical of industrialized societies. It is based primarily on achieved characteristics of individuals, and it is possible for individuals to move from one level of the stratification hierarchy to another.

ECONOMIC SURPLUS Goods and services produced in excess of what is needed.

INFLUENCE Power derived from personal qualities or unofficial connections, rather than from authority.

POWER The ability of one individual or group to have its will obeyed by another.

PRESTIGE The esteem in which a person or group is held by others.

PROPERTY Rights over and possession of socially desirable objects.

STATUS Position in the prestige hierarchy of a group or society.

Recommended readings

Bendix, Reinhard, and Seymour Martin Lipset (eds.). *Class, Status, and Power.* New York: Free Press, 1966. An anthology of classic essays in social stratification, including both theoretical and empirical readings on class structure, status and power relations, differential class behavior, mobility, and comparative social structures.

Bottomore, T. B. *Classes in Modern Society.* New York: Pantheon, 1966. An analysis of the gradual shift from inequality toward more egalitarian states, studying the nature of modern social class, social hierarchy, and the possibility of an egalitarian industrial society.

Drucker, Peter F. *The Age of Discontinuity.* New York: Harper & Row, 1969. Western technological change and its effects on pluralism, the poor, success, schooling, and political and economic policy.

Duberman, Lucile. *Social Inequality: Class and Caste in America.* Philadelphia: Lippincott, 1976. A valuable introduction to basic concepts in the study of social stratification, addressed to undergraduates. The book presents key theoretical positions and empirical findings, focusing on social caste in the stratification system of the United States.

Eisenstadt, S. N. *Social Differentiation and Stratification.* Glenview, Ill.: Scott Foresman, 1971. The author combines social stratification and functional analysis in an examination of the process of modernization as it molds modern class systems.

Galbraith, John Kenneth. *The New Industrial State.* Boston: Houghton Mifflin, 1967. An economic approach to the relations of class and industrial and political power.

Giddens, Anthony. *The Class Structure of the Advanced Societies.* New York: Barnes & Noble, 1973. A study of class in capitalist and socialist societies, expanding on Marxist analysis and ending with a discussion of the future of class societies.

Lenski, Gerhard. *Power and Privilege: A Theory of Social Stratification.* New York: McGraw-Hill, 1966. A theoretical approach to class and to systems of distributing scarce resources.

Marx, Karl, and Friedrich Engels. *The Communist Manifesto* (1848). Chicago: Regnery, 1960. Marx and Engels' polemical presentation of an important theory of class relationships: "The history of all hitherto existing society is the history of class struggles."

Caste in India

J. H. HUTTON

In India, elaborate taboos and rituals concerning food and drink both reflect and perpetuate the caste system. According to some observers, the taboo on marriage between certain castes, for example, is the inevitable outcome of the taboo on food and drink, rather than the cause of it. This selection gives some idea of the connection between caste and customs of eating and drinking in India.

. . . Now the taboo on food and water as between caste and caste is subject to many gradations and variations. It is often stated that the test of a 'clean caste,' that is to say, a caste of respectable and non-polluting status, lies in whether or not a Brahman can accept drinking water at its hands. Here, of course, as in the case of marital restrictions, there is room for much variation between one locality and another, and any generalization that can be made must be made subject to local variations of custom which may now and then be very striking.[1] . . . In northern India a Brahman will take water poured into his *lota* (drinking vessel) by men of several Sudra castes regarded as clean, e.g., Barhai (a carpenter caste, claiming an origin from the god Viswakarman, the Architect of the Universe), Nai (the barber caste, the services of which are important in much Hindu ritual), Bharbunja (grain-parchers), Halwai (confectioners), Kahar (fishermen, well-sinkers, and growers of water-nuts). The southern Brahman is more particular, and in any case the water distributors at railway stations are always Brahmans, so that anyone can accept water poured out by them. . . .

Restrictions in regard to eating are generally speaking more severe than those which govern drinking, but do not depend, as in that case, on who supplies the food but rather on who cooks it. The cooking is very important, and a stranger's shadow, or even the glance of a man of low caste,[2] falling on the cooking pot may necessitate throwing away the contents. Members of the same exogamous unit can, of course, share each other's food. So, too, as a rule can members of different exogamous groups who can intermarry, for a man must be able to eat food

cooked by his own household. Blunt[3] maintains that this commensality is a result of intermarriage, and that until such intermarriage had taken place the two groups could not eat each other's food. The other way round, however, is perhaps the more likely, if one comes before the other at all, and intermarriage takes place because there is no taboo on interdining. A Kahar employed by a superior caste—Brahman, Rajput, Kayastha, etc.—may eat their leavings so long as he himself is not married; after marriage he may not do so. Some castes will not take food from their own daughters once these daughters are married, even to men of their own caste.[4] . . .

Food cooked with water as described is known as *kachchā*, and the restrictions associated with it are much more severe than those associated with food known as *pakkā*, which is cooked with *ghī*—it is said that *ghī*, being a product of the cow, sanctifies the food cooked with it, just as the sanctity of the Ganges does the water drawn from her, making it safe against transmitting pollution from one caste to another. Consequently, it is possible for a Brahman even to buy sweetmeats from a Halwai and eat them without any need for preliminary bathing or purification. . . .

Another important point to be noticed is that the severity of the food taboo has no relation to the social position of the caste. Blunt[5] has worked out a classification of castes into five groups as follows:

(i) Those who will eat *kachcha* food cooked only by a member of their own endogamous group or by their personal *guru* (spiritual guide), and *pakka* food cooked only by the same or a Halwai or Kahar; to which he should, I think, have added food cooked (*pakka*, of course) by a Bharbunja.

(ii) Those who will eat similar food similarly cooked by the above castes and also by Brahmans.

(iii) Those who will eat similar food similarly cooked by all the above and by Rajputs.

(iv) Those who will eat similar food similarly cooked by all the above castes and by lower castes of rank which they regard as at least equal to their own.

(v) Those who will eat food cooked by almost anyone.

Under these five heads he deals with seventy-six different castes of the United Provinces, but they do not fall into uniform groups, for some which fall into group one as regards *kachcha* food fall into another in regard to *pakka* food about which they are not so strict, whereas

---

[1] In Bengal a Brahman, or any man of good caste, was forbidden to drink water from the hands of any woman who had no tattoo spot, though this taboo was breaking down in 1883. *Vide* Wise, op. cit., p. 123.

[2] Thurston, *Omens and Superstitions*, p. 109.

[3] *Caste System*, p. 89.

[4] Russell, op. cit., I, p. 179.

[5] *Caste System*, pp. 90 sqq.

there are others who are as strict about *pakka* food as they are about *kachcha*, or even stricter in comparison with other castes. . . . A Kurmi, for instance, in west Bengal, will not take food cooked by any Brahman except his own *guru*, and his wife will not take the food her husband's *guru* cooks. A Kurmi again will take water from a Santal and smoke from the same *huqqa*, but cannot take the food he cooks, though the Santal can take the Kurmi's.[6] . . .

Before leaving the subject of food it should be mentioned that there are restrictions on the material of which eating and drinking vessels are made—earthenware, for instance, is tabooed by all higher castes, the reason usually given being that it cannot be made really clean—as well as on the use of certain animals for food. The only castes that will eat beef are untouchables like the Chamar (leather-worker) or some of the scavenging castes like the Dōm. . . . Certain vegetables are also tabooed in some castes.

Since pollution may be incurred by contact through food or drink it is not surprising that it should be carried by mere bodily contact. . . . It [is] incumbent on a Hindu of caste to bathe and wash his clothes before eating or before undertaking any act requiring ceremonial purity. Similar purification is strictly speaking necessary as a result of contact with certain low castes whose traditional occupation, whether actually followed or not, or whose mode of life places them outside the pale of Hindu society. Such castes are those commonly spoken of as outcastes or untouchables. Thus Chamars (they work in cowhide), Dhobis (they wash dirty, particularly menstruously defiled, clothes), Dōms (they remove corpses), sweeper castes, and many others who are impure because they eat beef or the flesh of the domestic pig, all pollute a Brahman by contact. Castes lower than a Brahman are generally speaking less easily defiled, but the principle is the same, and contact with castes or outcastes of this category used to entail early steps to remove the pollution. . . .

[6] Risley, *Tribes and Castes*, I, p. 536.

CHAPTER ELEVEN
CLASS AND SOCIAL MOBILITY IN THE UNITED STATES

Class systems, as we used the term in Chapter 10, are generally associated with the development of industrial capitalism. The word "class" itself did not take on its modern meaning until the Industrial Revolution, having first come into use in England late in the eighteenth century (Williams, 1966). Relative to systems of caste, class systems tend to be characterized by legal equality, a free and mobile labor force, and the opening, in principle at least, of all careers to all individuals with the ability to perform them. Egalitarianism tends to be an attribute of many class systems—in certain respects. Hereditary privilege is spurned, but only because it is hereditary, not because it is privilege. As Anatole France remarked, "The law, in its majestic equality, forbids the rich as well as the poor to sleep under bridges, to beg in the streets, and to steal bread." Even though individuals have the freedom to find their "rightful" place in the hierarchy, gross inequalities of position remain.

How *class* should be defined is, as we shall see, a matter of debate among sociologists. Class, it is usually agreed, refers in some way to economic groups, but writers disagree about precisely what a class is, how crucial the concept of class is to an understanding of modern society, and how many classes can be distinguished in a particular society.

Although the existence of class is a fact of life in all Western societies, Americans like to think that their society allows people a chance to improve their lot through hard work. Ironically, this belief in the possibility of *upward mobility*, or movement to a higher social stratum, coexists with a widespread acceptance of social inequality. Most Americans, it seems, tend to believe that an individual's class position is largely a matter of personal responsibility. The lower-class individual, according to this point of view, simply lacks the willingness and self-discipline necessary to rise to a higher position. In America this perspective contributes to an absence of class consciousness, or identification with one's own class.

In this chapter, we will examine class in America—what it is, why it exists, and what it means to those who occupy the various social strata. Then we shall examine the question of social mobility and consider how extensive it has actually been in our society.

Two views of class: Marx and Weber

Every contemporary discussion of class owes a debt to Karl Marx (1818–1883). Marx did not coin the term "class," but his theories of class struggle, class formation, and class consciousness have dominated, directly or indirectly, practically every subsequent discussion of the subject. Ironically, Marx never precisely defined *class*; his culminating work, *Capital*, breaks off just at the point at which he was going to address this issue. In fact, Marx used *class* in several different ways. He used it in a general sense, just as we used it in Chapter 10 when we contrasted class societies with those based on caste: class societies are those in which some individual *social mobility*, or movement between strata, is possible, and a class is simply a stratum in such a society. But Marx also used *class* in a more restricted sense, to denote a group of people who "can appropriate the labour of another owing to the different places they occupy in a definite system of social economy" (quoted in Ossowski, 1963, p. 26). A class, in this sense, is a group of people who have in common a particular relationship to the means of production (factories, machinery, raw materials).

Marx argued that classes came into being only when there was a potential for an economic surplus. They were based on an exploitative system of labor whereby one group, because it controlled the means of production, appropriated the wealth created by another. The struggle that takes place between these groups was seen to be the motive force of history; or, as Marx and Friedrich Engels put it in the *Communist Manifesto* in 1848, "all history is the history of class struggle." For Marx, then, class was not so much a descriptive category as a concept necessary to an understanding of historical transformation.

As we indicated in Chapter 10, two great new classes emerged out of the Industrial Revolution in Western societies: those who owned the means of production (the bourgeoisie) and those who were forced to sell their labor (the proletariat). Western industrialized societies operated then (as they do today) under the economic system that is termed *capitalism* (discussed in more detail in Chapter 18). The wealth produced by manufacturing enterprises under this system is owned by private entrepreneurs, who are under no obligation—legal or moral—to redistribute it among the people who work in their factories, beyond paying whatever wages may be necessary to induce these workers to stay on. If workers have no other options for employment, these wages may be very low—just enough to keep the workers alive. Marx argued that the owners of wealth are most likely to reinvest it in raw materials, machines, or more labor for the purpose of producing more profits for themselves.

Marx believed that as industrial capitalism developed, antagonism between classes would be simplified and sharpened. "Society as a whole," he and Engels wrote in the *Communist Manifesto*, "is more and more splitting into great hostile camps, into two great classes directly facing each other—bourgeoisie and proletariat." Marx believed that out of the common situation in which they found themselves, workers (the proletariat) would develop *class consciousness*, a sense of common interests in the struggle against their oppressors, and would unite to overthrow them. This would usher in a new society, truly egalitarian and classless.

Marx's predicted revolutions have not, of course, taken place in the industrial societies of the West. The communist revolutions that have occurred have generally been in countries with little industrial development—Russia, China, Cuba, Vietnam, Korea—although there are active Communist movements in several Western European countries. Why revolutions have not occurred in Western Europe and in the United States has been the subject of much debate. A key factor, as we pointed out in Chapter 10, has been the expansion of the middle class, which serves as a kind of buffer between the classes above and below it in a society's hierarchy. A related factor has been the failure of class consciousness to develop in the way Marx thought it would; we will discuss some explanations of this later in the chapter.

The views of Max Weber are often counterposed to those of Marx, but in many respects the two thinkers held similar ideas. Class, Weber said, "refers to any group of people that is found in the same class situation" (1958). And class situation has to do with *life chances*—the chances that members of a society have to provide themselves with material goods, living conditions, and various life experiences. These life chances are determined by the amount and kind of power the individual has to dispose of goods or skills so as to receive an income within the society's economic order.

But groups can be formed on bases other than the economic one, Weber said. He distinguished three aspects of stratification that correspond to the distinctions we made in Chapter 10 among distributions of property, power, and prestige. While *classes* (in Weber's sense) were formed on the basis of property, *status groups* were formed on the basis of prestige, and *parties* were formed on the basis of political power. But these three aspects of stratification could be somewhat independent of one another, Weber argued, just as status group, party, and what he called class were not always composed of the same people.

Marx and Weber laid the foundation for most later efforts to understand class. What Marx meant by *class* was not simply income or occupation, but relationship to the means of production, which he saw as a major determinant of power and status. Weber, using *class* in a more restricted sense, helps us see the additional com-plexities of stratification and the possibilities that class formations, in the strictly economic sense, are not always the most critical ones in a society. On the practical level, sociologists recognize the importance of both Marx's and Weber's ways of looking at class: in traditional sociological language, the most common measure of class has been a composite one, which combines income, education, and occupational prestige into an index of *socioeconomic status* (SES).

In this chapter we will take both the Marxist and the Weberian approaches to the phenomenon of class in America. Following Marx's line of thought, we will try to determine how wide the economic gaps between American classes are, what causes these gaps, and what factors influence conflict among the various classes. Following Weber's perspective, we will try to identify some of the interrelationships between economic inequality and the other dimensions of stratification. And—also following Weber—we will try to see how people's class situation relates to their living conditions and life experiences. This investigation, a large task, is one that we will carry through several later chapters, particularly Chapters 17 and 18.

Objective aspects of class

In popular usage in our society, people often refer to an upper, a middle, and a lower class. Accepting these categories for the moment, we can ask how extreme the differences are among these groups. To what extent do property inequalities lead to power differences, and how do these power differences in turn help to maintain inequality? These are some of the issues we will discuss in this section. Later in this chapter we will look at the relationships among property, power, and individual life chances.

INEQUALITIES OF PROPERTY

Income inequality

Inequality of annual income has been a pervasive and enduring aspect of American society. And it is more extensive than many people realize. In the United States in 1978, for example, the richest 5 percent of the population received 17.3 percent of aggregate income, while the poorest fifth received only 3.8 percent; the richest one-fifth of the population received a disproportionate 45.2 percent of aggregate income; the entire bottom four-fifths received the remaining 54.7 percent (Table 11.1). In dollar terms for 1977, the top 18.1 percent of households received incomes of $25,000 and over; the majority of families earned less than $16,000, with 16.5 percent receiving less than $5,000. And these are conservative figures. They do not reflect the hidden forms of income that go disproportionately to those in the upper income brackets—for example, capital gains and fringe benefits such as medical insurance, paid vacations, pension plans, stock options, and the use of expense accounts.

Much of the country's income, in sum, goes to the small number of people at the top of the income pyramid. How many people are at the bottom of the pyra-

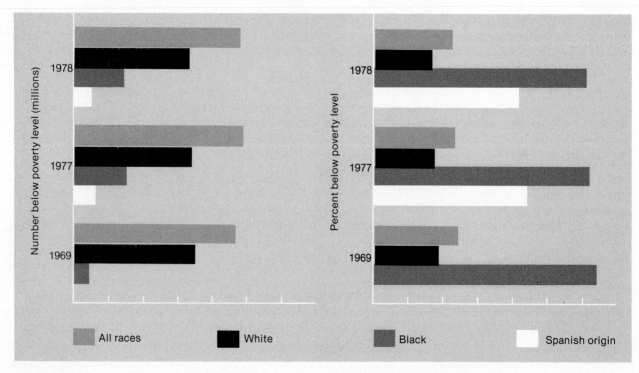

FIGURE 11.1

Persons below the poverty level, by race and Spanish origin. (Census Bureau, *Population Profile of the United States: 1979*, p. 40)

mid, at the poverty level? Of course, the extent of poverty depends on the definition of poverty. According to the calculation of subsistence (the minimum income needed to survive) devised by the Social Security Administration (SSA), an annual income of $6,700 for a nonfarm family of four marked the boundary of poverty in 1979. The incomes of 25 *million* Americans, or about 12 *percent* of the population, fell below that line. This is a reduction from the 22 percent whose incomes fell below the comparable poverty line in 1959. The SSA definition is not the only measure of poverty. Using a different set of criteria, the Bureau of Labor Statistics (BLS), in 1979, calculated that the subsistence income for an urban family of four was $12,585 before taxes.

"Transfer payments" to the bottom fifth of the population—that is, Social Security benefits, welfare payments, and the like—have grown considerably in recent years. Yet although these payments reduce the percentage of the population below the poverty level, they have little impact on the overall distribution of income. Some transfer payments—social security and subsidies for education, for example—may in the aggregate actually benefit the middle and upper classes more

than the poor. One analyst has concluded that "increases in government transfer payments [to the poor are needed simply] to prevent a gradual *erosion* of their income shares" (Pechman, 1969, p. 22; emphasis added).

A number of factors are involved in the great inequalities in personal income in our society. One is the tax system. It is sometimes argued that the federal income tax operates as a kind of institutionalized Robin Hood that takes from the rich to give to the poor. But this comparison stretches the point. The federal tax system has consistently resulted in a slight increase in the relative percentages of income that the lower fifths receive, but in general it has not been an effective tool of income redistribution. When state and local taxes are included, the tax collector begins to look more like King John than Robin Hood (Figure 11.2).

More important, however, is the fact that the people in the top income brackets get their income from different sources than the rest of the population.

TABLE 11.1

PERCENT DISTRIBUTION OF AGGREGATE INCOME TO FAMILIES AND UNRELATED INDIVIDUALS, 1947–1978

	PERCENT DISTRIBUTION OF AGGREGATE INCOME					
	LOWEST FIFTH	SECOND FIFTH	MIDDLE FIFTH	FOURTH FIFTH	HIGHEST FIFTH	TOP 5 PERCENT
1978	3.8	9.7	16.4	24.8	45.2	17.3
1977	3.8	9.7	16.5	24.9	45.2	17.3
1976	3.8	9.9	16.7	24.9	44.7	17.1
1975	3.9	9.9	16.7	24.9	44.5	17.0
1974	3.8	10.1	16.9	24.8	44.4	16.8
1973	3.8	10.0	16.9	24.8	44.5	17.0
1972	3.7	10.0	16.9	24.7	44.8	17.4
1971	3.7	10.2	17.1	24.7	44.3	17.0
1970	3.6	10.3	17.2	24.7	44.1	16.9
1969	3.7	10.5	17.4	24.7	43.7	16.8
1968	3.8	10.7	17.4	24.7	43.5	16.8
1967	3.6	10.6	17.5	24.8	43.4	16.5
1965	3.6	10.6	17.5	24.8	43.6	16.6
1963	3.4	10.4	17.5	24.8	43.9	16.9
1961	3.1	10.2	17.2	24.6	44.9	17.7
1959	3.2	10.6	17.7	24.7	43.9	17.1
1957	3.4	10.9	18.0	24.7	42.9	16.5
1955	3.3	10.6	17.6	24.6	43.9	17.5
1953	3.2	10.8	17.6	24.5	43.8	17.3
1951	3.5	11.2	17.6	24.1	43.6	17.5
1949	3.2	10.5	17.2	24.2	44.9	17.9
1947	3.5	10.6	16.8	23.6	45.5	18.7

SOURCE: Census Bureau, *Money Income of Families and Persons in the United States: 1978*, June 1980, p. 62.

Whereas the vast majority receive their money almost exclusively from wages and salaries, a large proportion of the income going to the top 5 percent of taxpayers comes from business and "capitalist income" sources (dividends and capital gains from investments in corporations). And this leads us to our next point: the income differences among the various groups are a direct consequence of the differences in the extent and kinds of *wealth* that they hold.

Wealth inequality

While income is what people receive over a certain period of time, *wealth* is what they have already accrued, the total monetary value of the property they hold, from a few dollars in the bank to the family car to corporate stock. By any measure, the extent of wealth inequality in the United States makes the unequal distribution of income appear paltry by comparison. A 1979 survey found that 6 percent of American adults possessed 75 percent of the nation's personal wealth (Time Inc., 1979).

Not only is wealth highly concentrated among relatively few people, but there are also important differences in the types of wealth held by different groups. Cars, homes, and small personal savings are held by a substantial proportion of the population, but this is not the case for corporate stock and other investments,

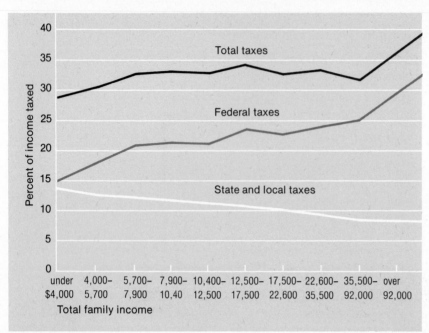

FIGURE 11.2

Total taxes as a percentage of total family income, 1968. (Musgrave and Musgrave, 1975, p. 392)

FIGURE 11.3

Some of the assets of an average affluent adult household, with an annual income in 1978–1979 of $40,000 or more, are shown in this figure. The findings were obtained in a 1979 survey of 7,500 adults by Monroe Mendelsohn Research by Survey Sampling, Inc.

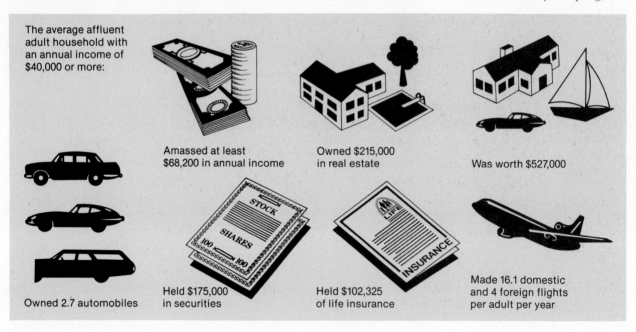

The average affluent adult household with an annual income of $40,000 or more:

Amassed at least $68,200 in annual income

Owned $215,000 in real estate

Was worth $527,000

Owned 2.7 automobiles

Held $175,000 in securities

Held $102,325 of life insurance

Made 16.1 domestic and 4 foreign flights per adult per year

which are by and large controlled by an extremely small minority. In 1972, the top 1 percent of the population held about 58 percent of the corporate stock and monetary bonds (Census Bureau, 1980). Thus the fairly widespread idea that America is a land of "people's capitalism" where almost everyone has "a piece of the action" is misleading. As one group of critics has pointed out, the fact that over 30 million people own corporate stock does not mean that this form of wealth is evenly distributed. "Many people do own a little stock, but the vast bulk of corporate stock is owned by a very few people" (Ackerman et al., 1974, p. 211).

Property differentials and life chances

Inequalities of income and wealth bear directly on what Weber called a person's life chances. In a competitive society such as ours, where almost everything has a

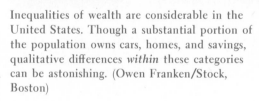

Inequalities of wealth are considerable in the United States. Though a substantial portion of the population owns cars, homes, and savings, qualitative differences *within* these categories can be astonishing. (Owen Franken/Stock, Boston)

Poverty perpetuates itself in a vicious cycle, diminishing the life chances of each generation. (James R. Holland/Stock, Boston)

price, having little money severely restricts freedom and opportunity. What people bring to market greatly affects their access to education and medical care, their self-sufficiency and freedom from taking orders, even their very chances of survival. Furthermore, disadvantage in one area is seldom an isolated factor: it affects the whole life of the individual. People too poor to escape an inner-city ghetto, for example, are thereby a captive population and are prey to crime, to salespeople selling shoddy goods and installment credit deals at high prices, and to higher rents and food prices than those living outside the ghetto—all of which serve to perpetuate their poverty.

INFANT MORTALITY AND LIFE EXPECTANCY. Life chances, quite literally, vary with income and occupation. There is a higher rate of infant mortality and a lower life expectancy among poor people. In the nineteenth century, the differences were enormous. Around 1830, for example, the life expectancy at birth for children of manufacturers, merchants, and directors was about twenty-eight years, while for families of factory workers it was only eighteen years, for families of day laborers, about nine years, and for families of spinners, weavers, and locksmiths, it was only about two years (Antonovsky, 1972). These gaps have narrowed considerably since then, as standards of living and working conditions have improved, medical science has advanced, and levels of nutrition, sanitation, and housing have been raised. But even today white males born in the highest strata of society have a life expectancy seven years longer than those born in the lowest strata (Duberman, 1976).

An analysis by Gortmaker (1979) found that white babies born in poverty ran a risk of neonatal death almost 50 percent greater than nonpoor babies. And 1975 figures show mortality rates for nonwhite mothers to be three times as high as for white mothers, and almost twice as high for nonwhite babies under one year old as for white babies (Census Bureau, 1978). Easily identifiable environmental conditions such as malnutrition, poor sanitation, and inadequate health care are major factors contributing to these differences in mortality rates (Krauss, 1976).

PHYSICAL HEALTH AND SAFETY. People in lower occupational ranks and income strata tend to be exposed to more hazardous living and working conditions and are more likely to become ill. Industrial accidents are an important factor in these differences. In 1970 alone, for instance, an estimated 10 to 20 million workers were injured on the job, while an additional 100,000 died from known occupational diseases (Levinson, 1974, p. 77). Between 1961 and 1970 three times as many Americans died in industrial accidents as were killed in the Vietnam War (Sexton and Sexton, 1971).

Moreover, the Vietnam War itself, like the Korean War before it, took a disproportionate toll of low-income groups. Student deferments favored those wealthy enough to be in college (Krauss, 1976).

The health care that people receive also varies with income. In 1970 only slightly more than one-third of those with family incomes of less than $3,000 had medical insurance, while over 90 percent of those with family incomes in excess of $10,000 did (Krauss, 1976). Although poorer people are often more in need of health services, they tend to go to a doctor only when an accident or illness is incapacitating, while middle-class people are more likely to go for treatment of a much wider range of symptoms (Rainwater, 1974). Differential health care is one reason the poor stay away. Those without medical insurance or its equivalent often receive inferior treatment, usually in overcrowded and understaffed public clinics.

WHO NEEDS POVERTY?

Some 25 million Americans are poor today, despite many government social welfare programs and widespread agreement that poverty is a bad thing. Why does poverty persist? Herbert J. Gans (1971) has looked at this question from the functionalist perspective. He argues that poverty continues to exist because it fulfills certain positive functions for the nonpoor.

Some of the positive functions Gans cites are economic. For instance, poverty provides a labor pool of individuals who cannot afford to refuse the dirty, degrading, dangerous, and menial jobs that no one else wants. And because they work for low wages, Gans observes, the poor often "subsidize" the activities of more affluent classes. The cheap labor of domestics, for instance, frees the affluent for professional, civic, or cultural pursuits. Poverty also creates jobs: without as many poor, there would be less need for public health and social workers, civil servants, penologists, criminologists, and journalists. Poor people also prolong the economic usefulness of a wide variety of goods that no one else wants, from day-old bread to deteriorating cars. And, Gans observes, the poor finance upward mobility: many individuals, especially

MENTAL HEALTH. People who rank differently on scales of income, occupation, and education also tend to have different chances of being mentally healthy, according to three classic studies done by Faris and Dunham (1939), Hollingshead and Redlich (1958), and Leo Srole and his colleagues (1962). These studies showed that the incidence of psychosis—schizophrenia in particular—is higher among low-income people, while neurosis occurs more often among the middle class. What actual relationship may exist between social position and mental health is not clear, partly because researchers do not agree on what "mental health" is. But in any case, people in higher strata are more likely than their lower-stratum counterparts to be treated by doctors in private hospitals and to get psychotherapy, while lower-stratum people are more likely to be treated in state hospitals and are more likely to be given drugs or electric shock treatments (Hollingshead and Redlich, 1958). Rushing and Ortega (1975) found that differences in quality of medical care and in access to preventive care, as well as higher exposure to infectious diseases, contributed to a higher level of brain and schizophrenic disorders among lower-status individuals.

immigrants, begin their climb up the social hierarchy by selling goods and services in slum areas.

Poverty is also socially useful. The poor can be accused of being morally deviant, lazy, dishonest, and spendthrift, in order to legitimize such conventional norms as hard work, thrift, and monogamy. Because the poor are believed to be sexually promiscuous and uninhibited consumers of alcohol and drugs, Gans notes, they offer more affluent groups vicarious participation in the supposed hedonistic side of poverty. Other social uses of poverty include direct contributions in the form of music, artifacts, and even legends or culture heroes, such as the hobo and cowboy, and less direct "benefits" such as helping "to keep the aristocracy busy" with their settlement houses and charity balls.

Poverty also fulfills some political functions, Gans suggests. Poor people, being powerless, bear many of the hardships associated with social change and growth. In the last century, it was the poor who toiled to build cities, and today, as those cities build urban renewal projects for the middle class and expressways for the convenience of suburban commuters, it is typically the poor who are dis-

placed. Furthermore, since the poor generally are not active participants in politics, the political system is free to ignore them and devote its energies to other groups, Gans argues. And he suggests that poverty's stereotype of moral deviance also helps to stabilize the political status quo, because as long as the poor can be depicted as inferior and unwilling to work, there will be little pressure to change America's "survival-of-the-fittest" economic system, nor will there be any incentive for the removal of poverty.

But to say that poverty survives in part because it is useful to society is not to say that poverty should exist. Poverty has more dysfunctions than positive functions, Gans points out. What is true, though, is that even though many of the uses of poverty could be replaced, it would be costly to do so. As Gans puts it, "many of the functional alternatives to poverty would be quite dysfunctional for the affluent members of society." Thus, poverty is likely to persist, Gans concludes, until either it becomes dysfunctional for the affluent or powerful, or the powerless themselves can obtain enough power to change society.

In addition, according to a recent study (Kessler and Cleary, 1980), lower-class people are more emotionally responsive to the stresses they experience—they are more likely to develop symptoms of distress when exposed to stressful events than are middle- and upper-class people.

Given the poorer life chances, more routine jobs, and more difficult lives of low-income people, it is not surprising that they are less likely than wealthier people to report to researchers that they are happy.

FERTILITY AND DIVORCE RATES. People with low incomes tend to have more children, on the average, than those with high incomes. People in lower economic strata are also more likely to get divorced (Krauss, 1976). (These topics will be discussed further in Chapters 14 and 19.)

How life chances are related

Melvin Tumin (among others) has pointed out that many elements of a person's life chances vary not only

with income and wealth but also with education, occupation, and other factors:

One life chance can determine another, and vice versa. If being born into a wealthy family affects significantly the chance of acquiring an advanced education, this advanced education itself largely determines an individual's occupational level. In turn, this occupational level helps determine how much wealth an individual is likely to amass, in addition to that which he may inherit. Both wealth and education will probably be highly relevant in determining the level of health an individual will maintain, and this level of health, in turn, will be relevant in determining how long the individual will be able to continue earning his living. As one can see from this hypothetical example, life chances are mutually determining of each other, even though some may be more basic and occur earlier than others. (Tumin, 1967, pp. 56–57)

Thus, not only are income and wealth related, but they further affect educational attainment, health, and life expectancy. To put it more broadly, Tumin is talking about how one's level of income and wealth tends to determine one's life chances for getting *more* income and wealth—thus, one's chances of moving into a higher stratum.

INEQUALITIES OF POWER

The ownership of wealth not only brings high income to the owner, it also confers power. First of all, the owners of capital have power in the workplace itself; although the workers are not entirely without power— they often have organized strength in labor unions and other occupational associations—the balance of power tends to favor owners and the managers who work for them, from the board of directors down to the assembly-line supervisors. Perhaps even more important, the owners and controllers of corporations tend to have power in other institutional spheres as well, since it is they who hold sway over so much of the nation's resources.

The relation between economic power and political power

Essentially, the economic system and the political system are interdependent; economic decisions are not simply technical matters, but political choices. Thus, it is important to study the class system from a *political economy* perspective: that is, to see the ways in which economic and political power interpenetrate.

Those with economic resources—that is, those who have been successful in their dealings within the economy—have money, organization, and the capacity to develop contacts with political decision makers. In fact, at times they are the political decision makers. The end result is for those with money to consolidate power, or, at the very least, disproportionately influence those who actually hold power. Because they have power and influence, economic elites can assure that a disproportionate number of political decisions will benefit them. In contrast, those without resources have little power and, hence, little ability to influence political decisions in their favor. (Turner and Starnes, 1976, p. 62)

The decisions that corporate power holders make affect millions, from what kinds of cars will be sold to what the price of steel will be to whether a state or region will see some measure of prosperity or swollen unemployment lines. It is no accident, then, that federal, state, and local officials attempt to reach some sort of accommodation with the corporations and the wealthy people who control them. Nor is it an accident that the controllers of corporations try to influence officials to promote policies that will benefit their interests. The influence the wealthy have had on public policy is clearly evident. As we noted, the "progressive" income tax turns out not to be so progressive after all. Corporate taxes, in addition, can often be passed on to the consumer in the form of higher prices, while the government often hesitates to raise taxes on business for fear of discouraging new investment.

The government tends to help perpetuate the position of the rich in other ways as well, through such measures as price supports, import and export policies that keep domestic prices high, oil-depletion allowances, protection for overseas investment, and government contracts for the defense industry prompted by the powerful military lobby. According to some analysts, government welfare policies perpetuate inequality too. Some of these policies may force people at the bottom to take *any* jobs, thereby allowing employers to continue paying poverty-level wages to a guaranteed supply of cheap labor. These and other government policies have led one study to conclude that in many respects the government is run primarily as a "wealthfare" system (Turner and Starnes, 1976).

The concentration of corporate power and the power of major stockholders

Like the distribution of wealth as a whole, corporate power is highly concentrated. There are tens of thousands of businesses in the United States, but a few hundred corporate giants run the show. The top 500 corporations, for example, hold three-fourths of all industrial assets, employ one-third of all workers and two-thirds of all industrial workers, and account for half the total sales of the United States economy. General Motors alone has greater output than most countries. The fifty largest commercial banks, meanwhile, control half the country's total commercial deposits (Katznelson and Kesselman, 1975).

Effective ownership of and control over these vast industrial enterprises and banks, along with the major insurance companies, law firms, and retail chains, are vested in a tiny percentage of the population, as was noted. Of course, no one person owns any of these corporations outright or has personal power in quite the same way that Andrew Carnegie, J. P. Morgan, or John D. Rockefeller did. But holding a controlling interest in today's corporations need not even entail owning a majority of the stock. Because most stockholders are unorganized and cast their votes by proxy rather than in person, an estimated 5 percent (Lundberg, 1968) to 10 percent of stock (Katznelson and Kesselman, 1975) is often all that is needed for effective control of a corporation. Although some modern scholars have argued that control of large corporations is passing from owners to a new group of bureaucratic managers, the weight of the evidence indicates that ownership and control are still closely linked (Useem, 1980).

Subjective aspects of class

So far, we have talked about class mostly as an objective phenomenon, as a distribution of material resources that begets (and is suppported by) power and that is measurably correlated with objective differences in mortality rates and other aspects of life chances. But the subjective aspects of class are important too. People in the same objective position (for example, factory workers with the same amount of education and income) may behave differently depending on how they perceive their social positions. One factory worker may own stock, believe that his children will become professionals, think of himself as middle class, vote Republican, and be vehemently antiunion, while another, identifying himself as working class, may be active in his union, a staunch Democrat, or even a supporter of a socialist third-party candidate. Without some notion of the way people *perceive* their own position and that of others, we would remain blind to this difference and would neglect to ask why these two men might look at their positions so differently.

In this section, we will look at two subjective factors involved with the phenomenon of class. First, we will look at *prestige*—a factor that is often related to an individual's class standing but that cannot always be equated with power nor reduced to dollars and cents, depending instead on the intangible variable of how other people see the social categories to which we belong. Next, we will consider *class consciousness*: how strongly Americans are aware of group inequalities, their own personal standing in the class structure, and the interests they have in common with their fellow class members. Each class, Marx argued, is held together by bonds among members, creating a class not only "in itself" but potentially "for itself." This last point is particularly important because of its implications for class conflict. The more that classes exist "for themselves" and have an awareness of their class interests, the more likely they are to take concerted action to better their standing in the social system.

INEQUALITIES OF PRESTIGE

It has often been noted that ours is a society in which awareness of status, both in community and in occupation, and anxiety about one's place are particularly high. Alexis de Tocqueville, the famous French social observer of the mid-nineteenth century, noted that with the advent of "equal opportunity" in the United States, rankings were no longer a matter of course; they had to be struggled for and actively defended because they were perpetually being called into question by those striving upward from below, while at the same time the individual almost always had a higher status to strive for.

By definition, as we saw in Chapter 10, *prestige* involves how others see us. It "involves at least two persons: one to *claim* it and another to *honor* the claim" (Mills, 1967, p. 310). American sociologists have tried to measure prestige by asking people to rank each other in two main spheres—occupationally and within the community.

Community standing

Some classic studies have centered on how people classify one another in small communities. One influential community study was done by W. Lloyd Warner and his associates (1960) in Newburyport, Massachusetts (thinly disguised by Warner as "Yankee City"). Warner originally expected to find that people would rank one another by wealth, but he soon discovered that their evaluations were more elaborate. How people were ranked depended on where they lived, what clubs they belonged to, what social circles they traveled in, and what church they attended. From his research, Warner was able to create a typology of social standing that he said matched the way community residents themselves had evaluated one another. He called the broad groups into which residents fell "classes," by which he meant social prestige rankings. (His use of the term "class" was different from the other uses we have encountered.)

Warner distinguished six classes in Yankee City, which he called upper-upper, lower-upper, upper-middle, lower-middle, upper-lower, and lower-lower. The upper-upper class was made up of families that had inherited wealth, had been in the town for at least several generations, and were represented in the elite professions. They set the tone for the community. Below them was the lower-upper class, composed of families that had made their fortunes in the present generation and looked up to the old-line families socially. Both segments of the upper class belonged to elite social clubs and were generally members of the Episcopalian and Unitarian churches. Below them was the upper-middle class: people of less wealth who owned stores or occupied less prestigious professions. These were the people "who get things done and provide the active front in civic affairs" in this community (Warner et al., 1960).

Between these top three classes, which constituted only 13 percent of the population of Yankee City, and the bottom three classes, Warner found a considerable social distance. The lower-middle class—about 25 percent of the population—was made up of white-collar workers, tradesmen, and some skilled workers. Less than half of the children of this class were in college preparatory courses (as opposed to almost all the children in the upper classes). The next class "down," the upper-lower class, was made up primarily of semiskilled and unskilled workers and constituted about 34 percent of the population. Last were the lower-lower-class people, making up about 25 percent of the population: they were the poorest, and they were considered by those higher up to be lazy and shiftless, lacking in ambition, and "living like animals" (Warner et al., 1960).

One criticism that has been leveled against Warner's approach—and the use of the "reputational" method in general (that is, the method of asking people to rank their neighbors)—is that because today most Americans live in or near large cities rather than in smaller communities such as Yankee City, the findings

have limited applicability. In urban areas, it has been suggested, people evaluate each other's statuses more superficially, so that "symbols—such as modes of dress, manners, cars, and conversational styles—replace family background and reputation as evaluations become less intimate and less enduring" (Abrahamson, Mizruchi, and Hornung, 1976, p. 166). Another criticism of the Warner method is that these community studies contain an ambiguity about whose typology is actually being used, the respondent's or the interviewer's. In any case, Warner went an important step further. Was there, he asked, any way to predict *how* people would evaluate each other's social standing? He eventually developed an "Index of Status Characteristics" comprising occupation, source of income, house type, and dwelling area. By knowing these characteristics, he found that he could quite accurately predict a person's social standing—in fact, that he could come very close by knowing a person's occupation alone (Warner et al., 1960).

Occupational prestige

The esteem in which a person's occupation is held can be at least as important as the income it brings. To a large extent, occupational prestige determines how a person is treated, from being deferred to as a senator, scientist, or professor to being ignored as "just a worker" or "just a housewife." A detailed scale of occupational prestige is the National Opinion Research Council (NORC) scale, in which a random sample of the population was asked to give "their personal opinion of the general standing" of ninety occupations, grading each one on a scale from "excellent" to "poor." Some of the results of the initial study done in 1947 and a restudy with similar results done in 1963 are shown in Table 11.2 (Hodge, Siegel, and Rossi, 1964).

Various explanations have been suggested for the continuity of such rankings. Income and educational level have been found to be the best predictors of rank (Reiss et al., 1961), but, as we have noted, high prestige is not simply a matter of wealth or sheer power (although prestige itself can be a form of power). Thus doctors rank ahead of state governors, who have much more power, while a board member of a large corporation ranks below many government officials and professionals who undoubtedly make far less money—suggesting that notions of ability, personal power, and an aura of expertise are involved in the shaping of the prestige hierarchy.

According to one interpretation of occupational prestige rankings, people's awe of certain occupations comes from their perception that these roles bring great power or economic reward. Thus, the consensus that some occupations are especially prestigious tends to reflect the facts of power in a society: people "give honor to the privileged" (Vanfossen, 1979). This close correspondence between prestige and privilege has been found in almost all societies (Treiman, 1977): occupations that require the most formal education and provide the largest economic rewards are likely to be found among the most prestigious in a society.

TABLE 11.2

OCCUPATIONAL PRESTIGE RATINGS, 1963 AND 1947

OCCUPATION	1963 SCORE	1947 SCORE	OCCUPATION	1963 SCORE	1947 SCORE
U.S. Supreme Court Justice	94	96	Newspaper columnist	73	74
Physician	93	93	Policeman	72	67
Nuclear physicist	92	86	Reporter on a daily newspaper	71	71
Scientist	92	89	Bookkeeper	70	68
State governor	91	93	Tenant farmer—one who owns livestock and machinery and manages the farm	69	68
Cabinet member in the Federal Government	90	92	Insurance agent	69	68
College professor	90	89	Carpenter	68	65
Chemist	89	86	Manager of a small store in a city	67	69
Lawyer	89	86	Mail carrier	66	66
Diplomat in U.S. Foreign Service	89	92	Railroad conductor	66	67
Dentist	88	86	Traveling salesman for a wholesale concern	66	68
Architect	88	86	Plumber	65	63
Psychologist	87	85	Automobile repairman	64	63
Minister	87	87	Barber	63	59
Member of the board of directors of a large corporation	87	86	Machine operator in a factory	63	60
Mayor of a large city	87	90	Garage mechanic	62	62
Priest	86	86	Truck driver	59	54
Civil engineer	86	84	Fisherman who owns his own boat	58	58
Banker	85	88	Clerk in a store	56	58
Sociologist	83	82	Restaurant cook	55	54
Accountant for a large business	81	81	Singer in a nightclub	54	52
Public school teacher	81	78	Filling station attendant	51	52
Building contractor	80	79	Dockworker	50	47
Artist who paints pictures that are exhibited in galleries	78	83	Coal miner	50	49
Musician in a symphony orchestra	78	81	Restaurant waiter	49	48
Author of novels	78	80	Taxi driver	49	49
Economist	78	79	Janitor	48	44
Railroad engineer	76	76	Bartender	48	44
Electrician	76	73	Soda fountain clerk	44	45
Trained machinist	75	73	Sharecropper—one who owns no livestock or equipment and does not manage farm	42	40
Farm owner and operator	74	76	Garbage collector	39	35
Undertaker	74	72	Street sweeper	36	34
Welfare worker for a city government	74	73	Shoe shiner	34	33
			Average	71	70

Table continues, next page

COMPARATIVE PRESTIGE RATINGS FOR SELECTED OCCUPATIONS IN GOVERNMENT, SCIENCE, AND CONSTRUCTION

95	U.S. Supreme Court Justice Government scientist	Nuclear physicist	
90	Cabinet member U.S. congressman U.S. Foreign Service diplomat	Chemist	Architect
85		Biologist Psychologist Sociologist	Civil engineer
80		Economist	Building contractor
75			Electrician
70			
65			Plumber

SOURCE: Hodge, Siegel, and Rossi, 1964.

Occupational prestige is visible in all aspects of our lives. Compare the workers'
lunchtime environment at left with the corporate dining room at right.
(Bernard-Pierre Wolff/Magnum; Stephen J. Potter/Stock, Boston)

CLASS CONSCIOUSNESS

There is an important *objective* relationship between an individual's class position, in the Marxist sense, and his or her income—a stronger relationship, perhaps, than that between occupational *prestige* and income. For example, in a 1977 study that divided the people in a sample into "capitalists," "managers," and "workers," Erik Olin Wright and Luca Perone found that there was a much stronger connection between each individual's income and position in this tripartite Marxian sense than between his or her income and the prestige that attached to his or her job. But does one's objective status necessarily correlate with one's subjective class consciousness?

Most Americans are quite aware of group inequalities and of their personal position in the class structure, at least as far as attaching a label to that position is concerned. A famous study of how people label themselves by class was carried out by Richard Centers (1949) in the late 1940s. When people were asked to rank themselves as upper, middle, or lower class, the vast majority said they were middle class. But when Centers added "working class" to the possible choices, half the sample chose this response (which shows how critical the particular questions that researchers ask can be to their results). Centers went on to explore how well people's labels for themselves and their political opinions correlated with their position as measured by objective criteria. He concluded that people usually ranked themselves "correctly" and that there was strong evidence of class awareness.

Another study done a few years later found that even when respondents were asked open-ended questions, about three-quarters labeled themselves "correctly" (Kahl, 1959). Additional studies (for example, Bott, 1954) have also shown that perception of class interest tends to correlate with objective class position, but that it conforms even more closely to the labels people attach to themselves.

But although most Americans seem to be aware of class differences, they are less likely to have a strong sense of common class interests. There is some evidence that the wealthy have developed, at least to a certain extent, not only an awareness of their position but also more cohesiveness (Baltzell, 1964; Domhoff, 1967, 1978). But there is less evidence of class consciousness, of the type Marx envisioned, among workers. A study of working- and middle-class people by Gurin, Miller, and Gurin (1980) found that although working-class consciousness exists, it is substantially weakened by an acceptance of the legitimacy of poverty. The working-class people surveyed tended to agree—with the middle-class people—that poverty as well as class disparities based on race and sex "derived legitimately from personal deficiencies of individuals in an otherwise fair, meritocratic system" (p. 45). Although labor unions are to some extent an expression of class interests, there is no workers' political party in the United States (as in European countries, for example), and unions may actually inhibit class antagonisms by their reformist orientation (Perlman, 1923).

Factors that inhibit class consciousness

Numerous writers have attempted to explain the fact that class antagonisms have been relatively muted in the United States. Let us consider some of the factors that have tended to limit the development of class consciousness in our society.

IDEOLOGY. The tendency of Americans to exhibit a low level of class consciousness has roots in American history and ideology. Unlike Europe, the United States never had a landed aristocracy or a feudal system in which class lines were strictly drawn over many generations. Instead, the nation was founded in an era that sought to deny class distinctions ("all men are created equal"). The basic tenets of American ideology, especially individualism and equal opportunity, undermine

In the United States, poverty tends to legitimate itself: working-class people often come to believe that their poverty (as well as sexual and racial discrimination) is related to personal deficiencies—and that the system itself is fair and rewards merit. (Rick Smolan)

class identification. Since class consciousness requires that people identify with their own class, it is unlikely to be a pervasive feeling in a society that emphasizes the possibility and desirability of rising to a higher class. American workers have little incentive to think of themselves as working class if they can win wages high enough to support a middle-class lifestyle. Indeed, if the working-class family can send its children to college (and out of the working class), it will be conforming to a part of the American dream.

THE DEVELOPMENT OF THE MIDDLE CLASS. One reason that the proletariat and the bourgeoisie have not been highly polarized in the United States is that the class structure has not been simplified into just two classes—workers and owners. Instead, there has been the growth of a middle class. Some qualifications should be mentioned here. It is true, first of all, that what is often termed "middle class" today Marx might have considered "working class" by an objective standard. Second, there *has* been a dramatic decline in the occupational categories that Marx thought of as "middle class"—self-employed merchants, artisans, and small farmers. And third, as we have already seen, there is now a tremendous concentration of the means of production in the hands of a very small segment of the population. Despite these qualifications, the middle class is still very evident in this country. (Recent findings indicate that it is becoming increasingly politicized and self-interested [see box].) Marx underestimated the size to which the state and its attendant bureaucracies would grow, and he also underestimated the growth of the professional and technical segments of the work force. The increase in number of public employees in particular suggests that a definition of class must go beyond simple ownership of the means of production.

SOCIAL MOBILITY. The relatively high degree of mobility in our society, which we will discuss in more detail below, has been another factor tending to mute class struggle. As we have seen, class consciousness is built on awareness of permanent membership in a social category. For it to develop in the United States, individuals would have to identify themselves as *permanent* members of a class that shared common interests, and whose unequal social position was determined by the system. But in the United States people tend to focus on where they as individuals "fit" in the class sys-

tem, rather than on the inequalities of class themselves. Class, then, becomes a strictly personal issue (Sennett and Cobb, 1972).

Some sociologists, in fact, argue that in order to account for this phenomenon of mobility, the concept of classes should be replaced by that of "levels" (Nisbet and Perrin, 1977). The level—of which there are several in our society, with the middle one the most important—is a looser category than that of class, and rests not only on wealth or income but also on a set of norms and values relating to such matters as organization of the family, child-rearing practices, and general lifestyle. What distinguishes a level from a class most markedly is that level consciousness makes one aware of one's *differences* from others in the same level, rather than one's similarities, and creates the desire to step up and out of one's level and get to "the top."

STATUS STRIVING. Many differences in American lifestyles bear some relationship to social class. The differences may be blurred by the common phenomenon of status striving, in which people attempt to live the lifestyles of classes above them, or at least to obtain some of the symbols of these lifestyles. The influence of the mass media, the general rise in affluence, and a mass-production, mass-marketing economy have resulted in many consumption patterns that cross class lines. Once again, identification with a higher class is incompatible with identification with one's own.

THE TWO-PARTY POLITICAL SYSTEM. Instead of a multi-party system capable of representing a broad spectrum of political and economic interests, the United States has a winner-take-all, two-party system based on geographical representation. Those chosen by the two parties as candidates balance, to some extent, conflicting class and special-interest group concerns; the compromises involved in such a system tend to limit the extent to which working-class interests can surface. More to the point, the two parties are broad coalitions—at present, we have no workers' party per se.

INCOME OVERLAP AND DIVERSITY. Wide differences in income status *within* the working class have inhibited workers from perceiving that they may have common class interests and might benefit from a class-oriented ideology. Today, white- and blue-collar salaries overlap to a considerable extent. Some small capitalists,

THE MIDDLE CLASS IN THE EIGHTIES: SQUEEZED OR MISPERCEIVED?

The middle class may have a hard time in the eighties. Of course all classes suffer from recession and inflation, but the reciprocal effects of these two trends are causing the middle class a kind of identity crisis, forcing it to re-examine its values and repudiate its standard operating procedure. Traditionally progressive and socially aware, altruistic and optimistic, the middle class is growing self-interested and insular, according to some observers. It is as if the American Dream were finally failing its firmest partisans. Of course the idea of an American Dream—that hard work will eventually ensure a good life—has always had critics, but the reasons for rejecting it have changed: "The middle-class formula for success, along with so much else, is being called into question—not, as it was in the 1960s, for moral and political reasons, but because it may not work" (William Severini Kowinski, "The Squeeze on the Middle Class," *The New York Times Magazine*, July 13, 1980, p. 28).

Insecurity is one of the main factors precipitating the change. Inflation, or a decline in buying power, is disorienting for the middle class. If money loses its value economically, it loses its value morally as well, which leaves many middle-class people feeling shaken: what is the point of playing by the rules if the rewards aren't going to follow?

In addition to the increasing insecurity that is pervading its outlook, the middle-class character itself may have altered in the past decade, decreasing its ability to weather an economic squeeze. Traditionally, middle-class values were grounded in the idea of sacrifice and deferred gratification. Children were encouraged to stay in school, and college educations were saved for. Higher education has always been *the* approved route for upward mobility among the middle class, and that hasn't changed. But expectations about personal sacrifice have: people's beliefs about what they should be expected to do altered during the seventies, or "Me Decade." In a word, the quick prosperity of the last two generations may have altered the middle-class character to the extent that equal weight is now given to instant gratification *and* still greater subsequent rewards.

The economic squeeze feels sharper, then, because the middle class has added new priorities to its old ones. As one result, becoming accustomed to living on credit means that many people no longer have the savings that would formerly pay for major expenses. For another, most parents no longer assume that they must sacrifice something in order to send their children to college, preferring instead that the children assume more of the cost through loans and demanding more outside aid. The 1978 Middle Income Student Assistance Act, which provides grants for middle-class students, testifies to the ability of the middle class to make tuition a salient issue in Congress.

Demographically, according to pollster Pat Caddell,

the American electorate is becoming increasingly middle class. Until recently, however, it did not unite as a constituency to elect officials and effect legislation favorable to its own interests. The middle class used to be altruistic, and when, in the sixties, it was prosperous, it willingly underwrote social welfare programs such as those of the Great Society. The effects of inflation seem to have brought such altruism to an end, however, and middle-class people no longer appear to be willing to pay high taxes for services that go disproportionately to those less fortunate than themselves. The growing middle-class electorate now intends to emphasize its own needs.

Ironically, the straw that broke the camel's back may have been a misperception. Although the middle class feels that inflation and higher education costs affect it differentially, economists demur. According to Joseph Minarik of the Brookings Institute, who has studied the situation in detail, "On almost every account, the average middle-class family is in a very good position in regard to inflation. They are the winners in inflation, in relation to both those above and below." The poor, he observes, have lost ground because welfare payments and other forms of aid have not kept up with inflation, and the rich because the bulk of their investments has generally done badly. Because salaries have climbed, however, the middle class has held its ground—especially if a mortgage is involved, since the price of homes has increased faster than prices in general through the worst of inflation.

Another area in which the middle-class perception of differential hardship isn't borne out by the facts is tuition: middle-class people often feel that the rich can afford tuition and the poor are given a free ride, yet the middle class has actually done better than either in keeping up with rising tuition. "College costs have indeed risen over the last decade or two, but not, according to the Congressional Budget Office, as fast as the incomes of middle-class families with college-age children. . . . Between 1967 and 1976, the percentage of income both lower- and upper-middle-class families spent on education actually declined" (Kowinski, 1980, p. 29).

Nevertheless, though the middle class may not have lost ground, and though middle-class students reach college, graduate, and go on to earn graduate degrees far more often than lower-income students, many middle-class families are staggering under the extra burden of their children's educational expenses, and it is becoming clear that traditional middle-class expectations will not be met as easily in the future. Inflation is robbing many of the secure retirement they worked for, and the recession is making their children unable to become established in secure livelihoods, which prolongs their financial dependence. Middle-class anxieties are not likely to disappear very soon, and, because the middle class is powerful, they will have political consequences for the nation.

**The man who lives on the left owns a sports car.
The man who lives on the right fixes them.**

If the guy who fixes your sports car seems to be living beyond your means, maybe we have a solution.

It's called the Karmann Ghia.

And it was built for people who want to answer the call of the open road without making a lot of expensive pit stops along the way.

That's why we started with the guts of a Volkswagen. The same advances that went into the Beetle to make it so monotonously reliable, went into the Karmann Ghia.

Next, we turned things over to the Ghia Studios of Turin, Italy. (And you know how the Italians are when it comes

to great bodies.)

Then the Karmann Coach Works translated the Ghia design into a reality.

At that point we had a beautiful sports car that was as economical and trouble free as a Volkswagen.

So we stopped right there.

The Volkswagen Karmann Ghia

Though humorous, this advertisement reflects a social reality: a considerable number of blue-collar workers do earn as much as—and in some cases more than—white-collar workers. This income overlap between occupational levels, along with the wide range of incomes within the working class itself, is one reason a high degree of class consciousness has not developed in the United States. (Courtesy, Volkswagen of America)

such as owners of small businesses, earn much less than salaried or unionized employees. These income overlaps can help to obscure economic and class distinctions; the terms "workers" and "owners" are no longer automatically synonymous with "poor" and "rich."

ETHNIC AND RACIAL DIVERSITY. The ethnic and racial diversity and wide range of multiple group affiliations that characterize industrial societies cut across class lines, and also work against purely class considerations as a basis for political decisions. In looking at the American labor movement after the Civil War, Marx's colleague Engels noted that because manual workers were split into many different nationality groups and spoke different languages, it would be impossible to forge class solidarity by uniting groups as diverse as the Irish

Molly Maguires of eastern Pennsylvania, the black miners of southeastern Ohio, the German radicals of Chicago, and the Italian anarchists of New York and Boston. The language barriers have now largely disappeared, but a degree of mutual suspicion and economic competition remains among many of the various ethnic and racial groups within the working class. White owners have sometimes used impoverished black and Hispanic workers to break strikes called by white-dominated unions. In turn, many white workers have resented the minorities and have often tried to exclude them from union membership.

Trends in class consciousness

Are class consciousness and class antagonisms likely to increase in our society? It may prove that the economic strain of the 1970s and 80s—rising inflation, economic recession, unemployment, cutbacks in public services, and so on—has eroded many people's faith in the "American dream." To the extent that it becomes more and more difficult for working- and middle-class families to get credit, buy a home, and send their children to college, it may be expected that their desire for "bettering themselves" will be frustrated. This may lead to resentment of the more privileged and to increasing class consciousness.

Although the "working class" now includes a number of those whose jobs are actually white-collar positions—secretaries, typists, clerks, and the like (Vannerman, 1977)—it is unlikely, to judge from the American past, that the United States will see the rise of a self-conscious working class as envisioned by Marx. When people in our society do become more aware of the society's inequalities, they tend to translate this awareness into various forms of political action aimed not at overturning the system, but merely at changing some of its aspects. Americans are less likely to demand the overthrow of the privileged classes than a chance to rise into them.

STATUS ATTAINMENT
AND SOCIAL MOBILITY

Historically, American society has seemed more open to change than have European societies. In the relatively static, rigidly stratified, and tradition-bound agrarian societies that existed in Europe before the Industrial Revolution, one's position in the stratification system was inherited, and so was one's occupation. The son of a village blacksmith became a blacksmith (usually in the same village); the king's son ascended the throne on his father's death. From decade to decade, and sometimes from century to century, there was very little change in the labor roles that were traditionally associated with the various strata. What little *social mobility* (movement from stratum to stratum) did exist tended to be *downward mobility*: the number of high-ranking positions remained relatively constant, and the upper strata bore more children than were needed for simple replacement, so some children from high-stratum families were forced to either experience a degree of downward mobility or leave (Lenski, 1966). Historically, some of the impulse toward wars of conquest and the expansion of empire came from younger sons who had no access to their fathers' wealth and position. Often, their only option was to seek fortune elsewhere,

at the expense of other societies and often of their own.

During and after the Industrial Revolution, by contrast, *upward mobility* began to predominate. Industrialization greatly expanded the number of higher-status, better-paid skilled positions, and at the same time reduced the proportion of jobs in the agrarian sector. As industrialization advanced, the proportions of agrarian workers, blue-collar workers, and white-collar workers changed markedly. Reporting on the effects of this change on the United States, for example, Peter M. Blau and Otis Duncan (1967) note that in 1900 Ameri-

When waves of Italian immigrants arrived in New York City at the turn of the century, they generally had to take the most menial jobs because they lacked special skills and fluency in English. As a result, the Irish immigrants, who had previously been at the bottom of the social ladder, in effect moved up one step. (International Museum of Photography at George Eastman House)

can farm workers outnumbered professional and technical workers by almost ten to one. Today, professionals and technicians outnumber farmers by nearly five to one (see Chapter 18).

Two other factors that were conducive to upward mobility in the industrialized countries of Europe and in the United States were class differences in fertility rates and population shifts. Industrialized societies generally show class differentials in fertility rates that are different from those seen in agrarian societies. In industrialized societies, the upper strata bear *fewer* children than do the lower strata (see Chapter 19). As societies become industrialized, people from the upper strata cannot fill the increasing number of high-level jobs. Individuals from the lower strata then move up to meet the demand. Population shifts—immigration of unskilled labor from other countries and migration of unskilled labor from rural to urban areas—also can force movement up the social ladder. Immigrants often come without special skills; some do not speak the language of the host country. They are forced to take the menial jobs that others are unwilling to do. At the turn of the century, for example, most of the laborers building New York City's subway system were recent Italian immigrants. The Irish, who had come a half-century earlier, were pushed up a notch; they became police officers and fire fighters, clerks and owners of small businesses.

Both these sets of factors affecting upward mobility—the expansion of the occupational structure and the demographic changes—operated in European countries as they industrialized as well as in the United States. Yet the impression remains widespread that mobility has been more marked in the United States than in Europe. Later in this chapter we will consider certain studies that have addressed the question of whether this is indeed true. But first, let us consider studies that have sought to measure the extent of mobility in the United States.

Mobility patterns in the United States

What do we mean when we talk about mobility patterns? Mobility can be studied with respect to change on any dimension of the stratification system: a gain (or loss) in income or wealth or both, a gain (or loss) in power, or a gain (or loss) in prestige. But mobility has most often been measured in terms of occupational change, because in American society—and in other industrialized societies—occupation is usually an accurate indicator of such other determinants of position as property, power, and prestige. Thus a factory worker who becomes plant manager is an example of someone who is *upwardly mobile*, and a supervisor of a sales force who is demoted to salesperson is an example of someone who is *downwardly mobile*. (A car mechanic who becomes a truck mechanic illustrates another kind of movement, *horizontal mobility*.) In studying mobility, sociologists look at both *intragenerational* and *intergenerational* mobility. The first term refers to changes in position within one person's lifetime; the second has to do with changes in position from one generation to the next. The factory worker's promotion, for example, shows *intragenerational* upward mobility. The son of a lawyer who becomes a blue-collar worker exemplifies *inter*generational downward mobility (see Figure 11.4).

The American belief in unlimited opportunities for mobility, as we have mentioned, is widespread. However, some people also believe that the rise of American capitalism has created a permanent class of poor people and that changes in this century, such as the closing of the frontier, the halting of mass immigration, the decline of medium-sized and small business, and the continuing need for unskilled and semiskilled labor, have made the society less open and the social structure more rigid than it once was. Which view is more accurate? If we look for "either/or" explanations, we find from an examination of the research that the answers are both confusing and contradictory. But if we take the various patterns as complementary, as forming part of a complex whole, we begin to see how stratification and mobility interact to form a system that exhibits elements of both rigidity and fluidity. (Note that the studies discussed below generally do not include data on women, though the numbers of working women have always been sizable and are steadily increasing. Later in the chapter we will look at such data as are available on women's mobility.)

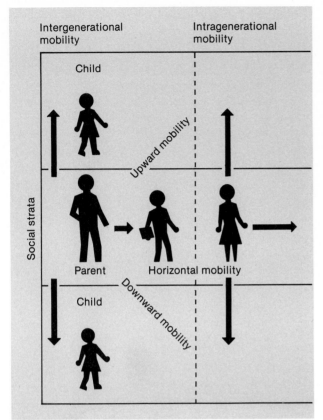

FIGURE 11.4

A schematic representation of social mobility. An individual's social position may be higher than, lower than, or the same as his or her parents' (intergenerational mobility, at left). An individual's social position may also change within his or her own lifetime, either upward, downward, or horizontally (intragenerational mobility, at right).

minority—about 3 percent—came from the lowest classes (Keller, 1953; Lipset and Bendix, 1959; Bendix and Howton, 1959). It seems, then, that opportunities for the kind of upward mobility that involves jumping many steps up in one lifetime have always been, and still are, quite limited.

In a study of the nineteenth-century working-class mobility patterns, Stephan Thernstrom (1966) found that unskilled and semiskilled laborers, such as farmers and factory workers, did move up, but only a step or two. He also found that it usually took several generations for a family to make significant progress. Thus in the nineteenth century, upward mobility was not uncommon, but it was limited.

Studies of mobility in the twentieth century show a continuation of these patterns. Blau and Duncan (1967), for example, who surveyed the educational and occupational background of 20,000 males and their fathers, found that both intra- and intergenerational upward mobility were common, but limited. Intergenerational mobility in particular was not extensive; it tended to occur *within* the three broad occupational brackets—white-collar, blue-collar, and farm—rather than *between* brackets (Table 11.3). Robert Perucci (1961), in his studies of intergenerational mobility

PAST AND PRESENT PATTERNS OF MOBILITY

Considerable research suggests that mobility patterns in the United States have been relatively consistent ever since the American Revolution. A number of historical studies of business executives have found that an overwhelming majority of the nineteenth-century business elite were the sons of business leaders, and only a

TABLE 11.3

OCCUPATIONS OF MEN WORKING IN 1962 (25–64 YEARS OLD) AND OF THEIR FATHERS

FATHER'S OCCUPATION WHEN SON WAS 16	SON'S OCCUPATION IN MARCH 1962		
	WHITE-COLLAR	BLUE-COLLAR	FARM
White-Collar	71.0%	27.6%	1.5%
Blue-Collar	36.9%	61.5%	1.6%
Farm	23.2%	55.2%	21.6%
Total	40.9%	51.4%	7.7%

SOURCE: Adapted from Blau and Duncan, 1967, p. 496.

among engineers, showed that sons of high-status fathers held the majority of high-status positions, and sons of low-status fathers held the majority of low-status positions. More recent studies (Hauser, 1975; Lipset, 1976) have confirmed these findings.

Other studies, however, show a slightly different picture. Mabel Newcomer (1964) found high-status occupations becoming increasingly accessible to people from the lower strata. In 1900, 45.6 percent of corporate executives came from the upper classes, but by 1950 the proportion had dropped to 36.1 percent, and by 1964 to 10.5 percent. At the same time, corporate executives from the working classes increased from 12.1 percent in 1950 to 23.3 percent in 1964. One interpretation of these findings might be that children of the working class now have greater access to higher education; thus, lower-stratum individuals may now have increased opportunities to move upward to those jobs that require relatively high degrees of education and skill. It is also important to note that the proportion of such jobs is increasing; in their study of occupational mobility from 1962 to 1970, Robert M. Hauser and David L. Featherman (1973) found that the pattern among the male work force had shifted away from self-employment, unskilled labor, and farm work toward occupations as salaried professionals, managers, craftsmen, and supervisors.

IS THE UNITED STATES MORE MOBILE THAN OTHER INDUSTRIALIZED SOCIETIES?

Two somewhat contradictory patterns seem to characterize mobility in American society: it is relatively difficult to move from the lower strata into the highest ones, yet it is quite possible to move upward within any broad occupational bracket. How much we can rise or fall seems to depend on where we start from. Although the "land of opportunity" myth has some basis in truth, opportunity is not unlimited. In this connection, let us look at the results of comparative studies among industrialized nations.

Lipset and Bendix began their 1959 comparative study of the United States, Sweden, Great Britain, Switzerland, and the Netherlands with the assumption that there was in fact greater overall mobility in the United States. What they found, however, was that

mobility rates were similar in all the countries studied, although there were distinct variations from country to country (Figure 11.5). More recent comparative studies indicate that the United States is the country in which people from low-status, manual-labor families have the greatest chance of moving into elite occupations, even if most will not make a significant change. Yet America is also the country in which the sons of the elite are most likely to retain their positions. In a comparison of four industrialized nations (Great Britain, Japan, the Netherlands, and the United States), Thomas G. Fox and S. M. Miller (1965) found that the sons of American elite and middle-class people were most likely to inherit their fathers' positions.

Thus, it seems that in the United States, the nonelite may be *more* mobile and the elite *less* mobile than in other countries. Although lower-class Ameri-

FIGURE 11.5

This chart shows upward, downward, and total intergenerational mobility in six societies. Note that, for example, total intergenerational mobility for the United States and Switzerland is about the same, but the two societies differ considerably in the percentages of people who are upwardly and downwardly mobile. (Adapted from Lipset and Bendix, 1959)

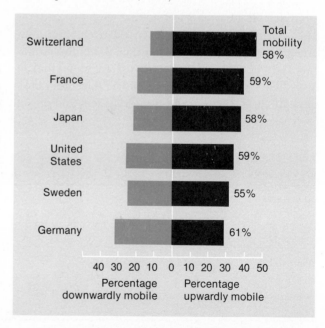

cans continue to have considerable opportunity, class origins as a restrictive factor still count heavily in the upper reaches of society. Now perhaps we can begin to see why the United States might appear to be the land of opportunity to an unskilled white immigrant from southern Europe but less so to an educated minority-group member; why a laborer can rise relatively easily to foreman or skilled machinist, but is not likely to become president of the company. The greater opportunities on the lower rungs of the social ladder may support the myth that in the United States anyone who tries hard enough can gain wealth and renown.

Sources of mobility

Thus far we have looked at broad patterns of mobility in the American past and present and at relative mobility in the United States and other industrialized societies. Now we turn to factors that influence mobility chances for each *individual*.

FACTORS IN INDIVIDUAL MOBILITY

Occupation

Paradoxically, occupation itself can make a difference in an individual's chance for future advancement. Occupations involve people in specific social milieus and affect a person's life chances in direct ways. Aside from the effects of occupationally related accidents and diseases noted earlier, work plays a critical role in determining where one lives, the hours one keeps, one's potential for fulfillment, stability of employment, and access to information and opportunities for advancement. To take just one example: a blue-collar worker's chances of being unemployed are almost twice as great as a white-collar worker's (Census Bureau, 1977). As is true of other situations we have considered, a favorable position in terms of one's life chances improves one's chances in other areas. Thus, those in top echelons are particularly well placed to advance their own interests.

Education

Social scientists generally agree that education is the most important key to upward mobility in an industrial society, although by no means the only one. In a study done in 1962, Blau and Duncan (1967) found a direct correlation between educational achievement and chances for upward mobility: the proportion of men experiencing some upward movement went from a low of 12 percent among those reporting no education to a high of 76 percent for those who had gone beyond college. Virtually the same results were found in a follow-up study (Featherman and Hauser, 1977, 1978). Since in recent years the proportion of children of the American working class attending college has grown to nearly one-third, the number of individuals who are likely to be upwardly mobile is increasing.

High educational achievement generally matters most in obtaining the first, entry-level job. But getting to that first job—which is often a matter of one's educational credentials—is the problem, for educational opportunities themselves are tied to class origins. For example, one large study found that an upper-class student's chances for education or training beyond high school are 2.5 times greater than those of a lower-class student; chances for attending college are four to one; for graduating, six to one; and for attaining a postgraduate degree, nine to one (Sewell, 1971).

There can be no doubt that a college degree matters: those who complete college earn substantially more than those with only a high school diploma. According to a study of American men by Christopher Jencks (1979), a high school graduate has a 15 to 25 percent earning advantage over a nongraduate, and a college graduate's advantage jumps to 49 percent. Moreover, the kind of college attended also makes a difference. Jencks found that those who graduate from such "selective" colleges as Harvard and Yale earn 28 percent more than those who graduate from "nonselective" schools.

Ironically, however, in some respects education is another kind of advantage that can be passed down through families. Although no one inherits a college degree, parents' wealth, the milieu in which children

TABLE 11.4

COLLEGE EXPERIENCE OF PERSONS 16–24, BY FATHER'S EDUCATION AND FAMILY INCOME

FATHER'S EDUCATION	FAMILY INCOME	PERCENTAGE OF YOUTHS WHO HAVE ATTENDED COLLEGE
Attended college	Less than $5,000	52.3%
	$10,000 or more	88.6
Graduated from high school	Less than $5,000	41.5
	$10,000 or more	50.0
Did not graduate from high school	Less than $5,000	12.6
	$10,000 or more	40.8

SOURCE: Krauss, 1976, p. 135.

grow up, and the people with whom they associate are conducive to keeping children in the stratum of their parents. Table 11.4 demonstrates the interrelationships among fathers' education, family income, and children's college attendance.

Race

Education cannot always fully compensate for the other social factors—such as race—that may limit a per-

son's chances for upward mobility. Blau and Duncan (1967) found that the higher a black person's educational level, the greater the difference between his or her occupational level and that of whites with comparable education. Part of this difference may be traceable not only to discrimination but also to differences in the quality of education received (see Chapter 15). Blau and Duncan point out that even though a black person and a white person may have completed the same number of years of schooling, the chances are that the black person has actually received less and poorer education.

Over the last decade, however, younger, better-educated blacks have made substantial gains in upward mobility. Federal legislation such as the Civil Rights Act of 1964 combined with increasingly positive self-images have enabled blacks to achieve higher occupational levels than ever before. Featherman and Hauser (1973) found that the effect of race fell from a 30 percent to a 19 percent "deficit" between 1962 and 1973 (although their study included only employed black

The past two decades have seen substantial gains in upward mobility among younger, better-educated blacks in the United States. (Tyrone Hall/Stock, Boston)

men). They also found that black mean earnings rose from 47 percent to 65 percent of white mean earnings.

Hispanic Americans have not fared so well. Mexican-Americans and Puerto Ricans may also face the barrier of a different language. In 1975, only 38 percent of Americans of Hispanic origin had four years or more of high school education, compared with 65 percent among the dominant (white) group. Not surprisingly, they also lag behind the rest of the population holding relatively high-paying jobs. Only about 7 percent of Hispanic Americans—as compared to 15 percent of the total labor force—hold jobs classified as "professional" (Census Bureau, 1976). (For further discussion of the obstacles faced by racial and ethnic minorities see Chapter 12.)

Sex

Women have consistently encountered barriers to upward mobility, regardless of their educational achievement. Traditionally they have filled a disproportion-

ately large number of the more tedious, low-paid, low-status jobs. For example, in 1940, women made up 52.6 percent of American clerical workers and 27.9 percent of sales workers. By 1978, these numbers had climbed to 79.6 percent and 44.8 percent, respectively. The data that are beginning to appear on women's mobility patterns strongly suggest that women face some of the same obstacles as do minority groups when they enter professional-level jobs (Epstein 1970). If they enter traditionally male occupations, they may not be accepted by colleagues or clients. Advancement often depends on being part of an informal, "old-boy" social network of peers and patrons; women may have trouble becoming either mentors or protégées in that predominantly male network.

Although women have recently made advances into prestigious areas of employment previously closed to them, their salaries may still be substantially lower than those of male colleagues in similar jobs. (Jean-Claude Lejeune/Stock, Boston)

Because the subject has not been thoroughly explored, there is considerable controversy over the exact nature and degree of mobility among American women. One study, by Peter DeJong and his colleagues, found patterns of intergenerational mobility among women to be essentially identical to those of men. That study reported great similarities between women and men in occupational inheritance, degree of mobility, and progression by short stages rather than long jumps (DeJong et al., 1971). Elizabeth M. Havens and Judy Corder Tully (1972), however, have severely criticized this research, especially on methodological grounds. They claim that the conclusions do not necessarily follow from the data, and that DeJong and his colleagues ignore discrepancies in occupational distribution and income differentials between the sexes. They also point out that the study uses job categories suitable for a male-dominated occupational structure, categories that are inappropriate for women.

A neglected but highly important factor in women's mobility is mother's occupation (in addition to, and perhaps even more than, father's occupation). A recent study by Rosenfeld (1978), for example, found that whether the mother had an occupation outside the home and which type of occupation she had strongly influenced her daughter's occupational position.

The traditional avenue to upward mobility for women has been marriage. Andrea Tyree and Judith Treas (1974) contrasted women's occupational mobility with their marital mobility (defined as the change in status that results when a woman moves from her father's occupational category to her husband's). Marital mobility for women is an important reality: a woman may be mobile either through her own occupational rise or through that of the husband or father, whereas a man's mobility depends much more on his own job achievements. Not surprisingly, Tyree and Treas found that female marital mobility patterns were reasonably close to those of male occupational mobility, and that female occupational mobility was *lower* than female marital mobility. Of course, a woman may have both occupational *and* marital mobility: a 1976 study by Linda Burzotta Nilson, for example, found that when people in a community assess a woman's social standing, they are likely to take into roughly equal account both her husband's occupational attainments and her own.

Finally, it is interesting to note that although women have recently made some advances into prestigious occupations, they have neither the income nor the authority in the workplace of men in the same fields (Acker, 1980). Thus a woman who becomes an architect, lawyer, or university professor may be somewhat more "mobile" on paper than she is in reality: her salary may be substantially below that of men in her field.

Demographic factors

A major set of influences on individual mobility—demographic variables—may affect access to education and the shape of our hopes. Families with fewer children, for example, are on the average better able to provide those children with a wide range of opportunities. Blau and Duncan (1967) found that men from families with fewer than four siblings attained higher educational levels and substantially higher occupational status than those from families with five or more. Families of low socioeconomic status tend to be larger than those of higher status; children of such families suffer a double disadvantage, in that the family's resources are limited and they must be distributed among more people. Order of birth can also determine how great a share of total family resources a child receives; according to Blau and Duncan, on the average the oldest and youngest children get the largest portions. The lower success of children from broken homes may also relate to family resources. Limited resources may mean that some single parents have less to give their children.

Other influences

A number of other minor factors exert some influence on individual social mobility. Physical beauty probably plays a part, especially in a woman's chances for marital mobility. Height may influence a man's occupational success; compared to other males, corporation executives are disproportionately tall, and corporate personnel officers seem to prefer tall men for management training programs (Deck, 1971; Feldman, 1971). Sheer luck may also affect mobility (Wohl, 1953): in the classic Horatio Alger tale of rags-to-riches, success depends more on luck than on hard work.

The consequences of mobility

Most Americans think of upward mobility as an unqualified good. Mobility means success—usually, greater financial rewards, more prestige, and increased power. But not all its consequences are positive. Widespread and sudden mobility may create severe strain in transitional societies, where considerable pressure for movement among the lowest classes is combined with a lack of flexibility in the system. If a society trains and educates more people than it really needs to fill the available high-status positions, frustration and unmet expectations may generate pressures for radical change (Germani, 1964).

few agreed-upon, permanent signs of high (or low) status, a constant tension may be generated among the mobile. Because occupation is one such established sign, one result of the scramble for status in such a society may be an unwillingness on the part of many young people to enter manual occupations, even though the material rewards of these occupations are sometimes equal to or greater than those of many higher-status, nonmanual occupations. Conversely, the struggle for higher status may lead to a counterreaction: some young people "drop out," refusing to enter the "rat race" at all.

ADVERSE PSYCHOLOGICAL EFFECTS

High rates of mobility may also have negative effects on individuals, especially in success-oriented societies like our own. Concern over mobility and the changes it brings may result in anxiety, adjustment problems, and tension (Blau, 1956; Lipset and Bendix, 1959; Tumin, 1967). The person who moves up must constantly cope with new people and new surroundings, new values and customs. The person who moves down may experience similar upheavals, in addition to the loss of prestige.

STATUS STRIVING

In a country like Great Britain, which, though industrialized, retains many of the values supporting a traditional hereditary stratification system, distinctive behavior patterns typical of each stratum are fixed and almost universally accepted; people can therefore display them without concern. In the United States, where the idea of class differences conflicts with such basic values as democracy and equality, those who claim higher status may have a difficult time convincing others of their position, and they may consequently feel they must constantly assert that claim in a variety of ways (dress, manner, vocabulary, material possessions) or lose their right to it. In other words, where there are

CHANGES IN ATTITUDES AND VALUES

It is not surprising that newcomers in a stratum tend to internalize the norms and values that are characteristic of it. For example, some (though not all) studies have found that the children of manual workers who rise above their fathers' occupational status tend to give up their former political orientation and adopt the politics (generally more conservative on economic issues) of the class they join (Lopreato and Hazelrigg, 1972). One explanation for this tendency has been offered by Joseph Lopreato (1967), who suggests that those who attain occupational success feel such gratitude toward the system that they may oversubscribe to the prevailing middle-class values.

Some research suggests that many of the downwardly mobile may become more radical in their politics, but only to a point somewhere between the politics of the middle class and the nonmobile working class (Lipset and Bendix, 1959). Melvin Seeman (1977), in an examination of some of the consequences of mobility in France and the United States, concludes that there is great similarity between the two countries in the overall commitment to upward striving. More interestingly, he finds that the effects of mobility—in terms of such factors as political attitudes, feelings of powerlessness, or social isolation—are much more limited than has been believed. Such differences as do exist imply that, in France, downward mobility causes more problems, while moving upward is generally less unsettling than it is in the United States.

In Chapters 10 and 11, a major theme has been the relationship among technology, the occupational structure it has created, and stratification patterns in the United States. As we have seen, many aspects of our stratification system can be understood more clearly if we see them in the technological context; but not all aspects of stratification can be reduced to a simple, objective equation involving power and resources. Stratification also involves personal, subjective meanings, which can be powerful forces in themselves. There are differences in the way the members of the various strata behave, differences in the way they are socialized, differences in the way they feel about themselves, and differences in the cultural myths concerning them. We will see this point even more plainly when we look at certain types of stratification: racial and ethnic stratification in Chapter 12 and stratification by sex and age in Chapter 13.

Summary

Karl Marx viewed class struggle as the basic force behind historical change. He believed that exploitation by the ruling class would generate *class consciousness* among the proletariat, or working class, which in turn would lead to revolution. Thus, in Marx's theory a *class* is a group of people who have in common a particular relationship to the means of production. To Max Weber, groups of people found themselves in various economic "class situations" that largely determined members' *life chances*. In addition to "classes" formed on the basis of property or economic power, Weber observed, groups could be stratified on the basis of prestige (status groups) and political power (parties).

The objective aspects of class have to do with inequalities of property and power. The major dimensions of property inequality are inequalities of *income* and of *wealth*; both types of inequality remain extensive in the United States. They exert a profound influence on such life-chance factors as infant mortality, life expectancy, physical health and safety, mental health, and divorce rates. Besides being related to income and wealth, life chances are related to one another and to such factors as education and occupation. Power is also related to income and wealth, and such economic power is intimately connected with political power in our society. Economic power tends to be concentrated in relatively few corporations, and those corporations are controlled by relatively few people.

The subjective aspects of class include *prestige* and *class consciousness*. Two areas in which inequalities of prestige come into play are community standing and occupation. For various ideological, social, and political reasons, Americans do not show the degree of class consciousness that tends to characterize European societies.

Although class differences in the United States are far-reaching, Americans like to think of their society as allowing for a high degree of social mobility, or movement from one stratum to another. Mobility is most clearly seen in occupational changes. Most studies have found that both intragenerational and intergenerational mobility are relatively common, but limited. Most mobility involves slight movement upward or downward, rather than movement from the lowest occupational stratum to the highest.

The major factors in individual social mobility are occupation and education, both of which are influenced by family origin. Other factors in mobility are race, sex, demographic variables (such as family size and birth order), and individual physical characteristics.

Upward mobility means more property, power, and prestige. But it can also have negative consequences.

Glossary

CLASS Defined by Marx as a group of people who have in common a particular relationship to the means of production; classes come into being when the potential for economic surplus exists. Marx saw two major classes in capitalist society: those who own the means of production and those who sell their labor.

CLASS CONSCIOUSNESS The awareness shared by members of a class that they have certain interests in common and, often, a set of political beliefs and orientations toward action arising from this awareness.

HORIZONTAL MOBILITY Changes in social position that do not appreciably alter a person's status.

INCOME The amount of money or monetary equivalents earned or received over a certain period of time.

INTERGENERATIONAL MOBILITY Changes in social position within one person's lifetime.

INTRAGENERATIONAL MOBILITY Changes in social position from one generation to the next.

LIFE CHANCES Defined by Weber as the opportunities a member of a society has to obtain material goods, living conditions, and various life experiences.

OCCUPATIONAL PRESTIGE The esteem in which an occupation is held.

SOCIAL MOBILITY The movement of people from one social position to another.

SOCIOECONOMIC STATUS (SES) A commonly used sociological measure of class, usually based on income, education, and occupational prestige.

WEALTH The monetary value of accrued property.

Recommended readings

Abramson, Mark, Ephraim H. Mizruchi, and Carlton A. Hornung. *Stratification and Mobility*. New York: Macmillan, 1976. A synthesis of sociological theories of stratification and mobility with the realities of everyday life. The book's emphasis is on social mobility both in American and in cross-national perspective.

Baltzell, E. Digby. *Puritan Boston and Quaker Philadelphia: Two Protestant Ethics and the Spirit of Class Authority and Leadership*. New York: Free Press, 1980. An inquiry into the nature of class differences in two major American cities.

Blau, Peter M., and Otis Dudley Duncan. *The American Occupational Structure*. New York: Wiley, 1967. The classic empirical work linking careers to status, ascribed and achieved, and showing how mobility actually works and how a stratification system is created.

Krauss, Irving. *Stratification, Class and Conflict*. New York: Free Press, 1976. A useful text that shows how stratification and class are elemental to human group life.

Lipset, Seymour Martin, and Reinhard Bendix. *Social Mobility in Industrial Society*. Berkeley: University of California Press, 1959. In an analysis of the existing literature on mobility's causes, consequences, and dimensions, the authors propose that social mobility is a continuing part of the process of industrialization.

Mills, C. Wright. *The Power Elite*. New York: Oxford University Press, 1957. A classic work arguing that a single elite rules social, political, and economic spheres via a tight "old-boy" network that works smoothly and unseen.

Thompson, E. P. *The Making of the English Working Class*. New York: Vintage, 1963. An historical perspective on class, showing how a class becomes a class through ideology, leadership, and class culture.

Vanfossen, Beth E. *The Structure of Social Inequality*. Boston: Little, Brown, 1979. A readable text summarizing the basic materials on stratification and mobility.

Veblen, Thorstein. *The Theory of the Leisure Class* (1899). New York: Doubleday Mentor, 1953. A classic, often satirical, analysis of economic consumption as both cause and effect of class differences.

CHAPTER TWELVE
RACE AND ETHNICITY

Almost everywhere we look, conflict and competition among different races and ethnic groups can be seen. In the Middle East, Muslims, Christians, and Jews are caught in a struggle that has global ramifications. Iran has had a religious revolution; Afghanistan, a secular one. In Africa, rival tribes vie for power in newly created states, while the white supremacist government in South Africa attempts to stem black liberation movements. In Europe, resentment builds between migrant workers from the Mediterranean countries and workers native to the more industrialized countries of the north. In Canada, the French-speaking people of Quebec struggle to preserve their cultural heritage in the midst of a dominant English-speaking society. And in our own country, racial and ethnic issues have been front-page news for over twenty-five years—among them school integration, bussing, open housing, the growth of black, Mexican-American, Puerto Rican, and Indian protest movements, and the resurgence of "white ethnic" organizations among Italians, Irish, Poles, and Slavs.

What lies behind these antagonisms? Is there more competition and conflict between various races and ethnic groups today than before? What factors bear on the outcomes of these struggles? These are some of the questions we want to explore in this chapter. They have a special urgency in relation to the American experience, because ours is a nation of immigrants. And these questions affect our lives directly, because membership in an ethnic or racial group remains an important source of individual identity. To begin our investigation, we need to look at what races and ethnic groups are, how they have come to be, and what roles they play in contemporary society.

Races, ethnic groups, and minorities: an overview

To sociologists, the term *race* means something different than it does to physical anthropologists or geneticists. To the latter, a race is a group of people who possess similar, genetically transmitted physical characteristics. Scientists do not agree on how many races there are or where the lines should be drawn between them. In fact, some scientists have even abandoned the

WHAT IS RACE?

In the nineteenth century, Darwin's theory of the origin of species (1859) had a powerful impact on many areas of human thought. Enthusiastic social scientists tried to extend Darwin's ideas to the analysis of human societies. One of the inferences drawn by many people from Darwin's work was that the human species could be divided up into clear-cut groups, called "races," and that these races were so different, biologically, as almost to constitute different species, like lions, tigers, and leopards. Moreover, the differences between races were thought to include substantial differences in behavior and ability. Since the nineteenth century was also an age of imperialism, with European powers competing for domination of large parts of Asia, Africa, and Latin America, such ideas about race were politically very convenient. They could be used to help justify the subjugation of "inferior" or "primitive" peoples by the "more advanced races"—that is, white Europeans and Americans.

Similar ideas about race are still held by many people today, but they are not supported by modern genetics. To a geneticist, a race is simply a semi-isolated breeding population: a group of people who tend to mate with others of their own group much more often than with outsiders. Eventually, such inbreeding causes members of the group to resemble each other more and more closely because they come to share more and more of the same genes. But there is no single gene that produces the differences in appearance that we often think of as "racial." Many different genes are responsible for such characteristics, and not all of them vary together. For example, we often associate dark skin with kinky hair and broad noses. People in southern India, however, have dark skin but straight hair and relatively narrow noses. Genetic researchers (for example, Cavalli-Sforza and Edwards, 1963) sometimes use similarities in blood groups to study the differences in gene frequencies among different populations, and so locate the geographical boundaries of different races. But this method still does not produce the simple, self-con-

tained categories popularly associated with the idea of race. The geneticist Theodosius Dobzhansky (1962) has identified thirty-four "races." Moreover, these "could have been combined into fewer races, or any of them could have been subdivided further," depending on the particular criteria used (Mazur and Robertson, 1972, p. 69). The boundaries of the human races, therefore, are really rather arbitrary. Many biologists argue that human beings are so similar that race is really a social rather than a biological category. As one writer has remarked, "Given the amount of genetic intergradation and overlap among human populations, what people have perceived as 'races' . . . or as 'people of different blood' are largely cultural constructs" (Kirk et al., 1975, p. 731).

The tendency toward isolation and inbreeding that separates human groups, and may lead to the emergence of the small genetic differences that are sometimes called racial, has two origins. One is geographical. It seems likely that past geographical isolation helped to produce some of the more noticeable physical differences among groups, such as skin color. Much more important, however—especially in today's world, with geographical barriers largely abolished by rapid transportation—are the social isolating mechanisms. These may be highly subjective, with no biological basis, but they are very powerful. People tend to perceive those who look physically different from themselves as somehow different in more profound ways as well—different in feelings, behavior, and morals. Frequently, this perception is accompanied by negative value judgments: members of other groups are regarded as "lazy" or "stupid" or "cruel." These ideas naturally tend to deter interbreeding, and thus maintain whatever genetic differences do exist. Moreover, as we shall see in Chapter 15, many societies give members of different races widely different access to money, power, status, and liberty. Thus, in the words of one recent writer, "the important thing about race is what human beings have made of it" (Kirk et al., 1975, p. 731).

concept of biological race as a meaningless, if not harmful, way of dividing humanity.

Sociologists are interested not so much in the physical differences that may actually exist between people as in the differences that people *believe* to exist and, most important, the meaning that people assign to these perceived differences. Sociologists are concerned about how people view race because they want to understand human interaction. As one cardinal principle of modern sociology has it: "Human beings interact not so much in terms of what they actually are but in terms of the conceptions that they form of themselves and one another" (Shibutani and Kwan, 1965, p. 38).

Therefore, in this chapter we talk about race as a social category—a means by which people classify one another in everyday life—not as the biological classification some scientists use in discussing genetic transmission.

In the sociological sense, then, a *race* is "a human group that defines itself and/or is defined by other groups as different . . . by virtue of innate and immutable physical characteristics. . . . It is a group that is *socially* defined but on the basis of *physical* criteria" (van den Berghe, 1967, p. 9). The term *group* is used here in a slightly different way than is usual in sociology. Ordinarily, the term refers to an aggregate of people who

The bonds that unite an ethnic group may be built on common territorial origins, religion, or language or dialect. The French Canadians are united by all three factors, and many Québecois—political leader René Levesque, for example—are working to maintain their heritage in the midst of a dominant English-speaking society. (Sygma Photo)

interact with one another in a structured pattern. Strictly speaking, a racial or ethnic group is really a social *category*: individual members of the group do not necessarily interact with one another, and they may or may not be aware of one another's existence. On the broader level, however, a racial or ethnic group does resemble other groups in having a boundary perceived by people both inside and outside the group.

The concept of the *ethnic group* is distinct from, though related to, the concept of race. Like race, ethnicity involves descent. But whereas race refers to a group defined on the basis of its physical characteristics, ethnicity implies a group defined primarily on the basis of its cultural characteristics. An ethnic group is a "people"; it "consists of those who conceive of themselves as being alike by virtue of their common ancestry, real or fictitious, and who are so regarded by others" (Shibutani and Kwan, 1965, p. 47).

The consciousness of common ancestry in an ethnic group may be built around any of a number of group attributes, reflecting the circumstances under which such groups are formed and struggle to survive. It may be based on common territorial origins (for example, Germans, Poles, British), on religion (for example, Lebanese Christians), on language or dialect (for example,

the Basques of southern France and northern Spain), or on a combination of these factors (for example, French Canadians, who have common territorial origins, language, and religion).

THE GENESIS OF MULTIETHNIC SOCIETIES

Before the state developed, each society was essentially a single ethnic group, as anthropologists Charles Wagley and Marvin Harris (1958) point out. Primitive social organization is based not on territory but on kinship. It has no way of incorporating groups of individuals "who are not related by descent or by marriage, who follow different customs, who stress distinctive values, and who, in sum, are an alien people" (pp. 11–12).

But when the institution of the state developed—that is, when the political organization of society changed from one based on kinship to one based on control over a geographical area and all the people in it—*multiethnic societies* became possible. The state provided a political structure that had a monopoly of coercive power over all the people in its territory, regardless of their kinship affiliations; it was able to "bind masses of culturally and physically heterogeneous 'strangers' into a single social entity" (Wagley and Harris, 1958, pp. 11–12).

It is possible for the boundaries of a state to match those of a single ethnic group, but historically this has seldom been the case. Today, most states are multiethnic. In fact, a survey showed that of the 132 states extant in 1971, fewer than one in ten was ethnically homogeneous; in fifty-three states (40.2 percent of the total), the population was divided into more than five major groups. In some cases the number of ethnic groups within the state ran into the hundreds (Connor, 1972). And although some ethnic groups may be in the process of merging with others in their area, new ones are constantly being formed, since national boundaries are constantly shifting. In this century alone, for example, world wars have transformed the control of whole continents, while cartographers have been kept busy by events such as the partition of Korea, the creation of Pakistan, Bangladesh, and Israel, and the emergence of new nations in Africa. In addition, new ethnic configurations are constantly arising due to movements of peoples in search of work, better living conditions, or political refuge.

ETHNIC STRATIFICATION AND MINORITIES

Ethnic stratification tends to occur with the belief that certain groups possess qualities that make members inferior or superior to members of other groups. With respect to economic stratification, these beliefs often play a special role. They provide a convenient means of denying whole segments of a population equal access to social resources—and a justification for doing so; they also facilitate and justify denial of full participation in the society's political, social, and cultural life.

Groups subordinated in ethnic stratification systems are known as *minorities*. The term is often misleading because sociologists use *minority* to refer to a group's relative lack of power in society, not its numbers. For example, blacks in the United States are a minority both demographically and sociologically; blacks in South Africa are a minority because of their subjugation by whites—even though they make up more than two-thirds of South Africa's population. To describe the group that is dominant in an area where one or more minorities exist, sociologists use the term *majority*. Thus the tiny British colonial administration that ruled India for many years is called a majority by sociologists, while the millions of Indians under its control are referred to as a minority.

Patterns of racial and ethnic relations

Clearly, almost every state in the world is faced with ethnic issues, and in every area of the globe minority confronts majority. Of course, this is not to say that antagonism is the only result, or even a necessary result, of intergroup contact. The meeting of different ethnic and racial groups can be the source of great cultural richness and of social change (see Chapter 22). When ideas and techniques are shared, a new surge in creativity often follows, as people discover new ways of seeing things. It is, after all, no accident that great cities with their ethnic mix have been noted for their cosmopolitan atmospheres, for they serve as unique meeting grounds for people of diverse cultures. Nevertheless, when the interpenetration of cultures produces a dominant group and subordinate groups, antagonism is common.

The intergroup relations that result fall into several patterns. At one pole lie the most brutal patterns, those of *genocide* and *expulsion*: the dominant group simply exterminates the minority or removes it from the society. History gives ample testimony that both courses have been followed. The Turks killed thousands of Armenians in 1915; Hitler's Nazis organized the massacre of 6 million Jews; former president of Uganda Idi Amin deported 27,000 Indians, many of them second- and third-generation Ugandans. Extreme patterns of *exclusion* from the territory and institutions of the dominant group may also be present—for example, in the system of *apartheid*, or legal segregation, in South Africa.

Toward the other pole are patterns of racial and ethnic relationships in which the dominant group does not attempt to eliminate or rigidly exclude the minority. The dominant group may attempt to partly incorporate the minority into its social order, while keeping it in a subordinate position. Sometimes this is done by encouraging or forcing it to take on the dominant group's cultural characteristics (such as dress, language or dialect, music, foods, myths, manners, and world view) and sometimes by allowing it to keep its own culture. Allowing various cultures to coexist is called *cultural pluralism* (Gordon, 1961). *Structural pluralism*, allowing "separate but equal" facilities, is another pattern: in the United States, for example, there are parallel "black" and "white" Baptist churches. Minorities may also be allowed to participate in a common political system while being kept socially subordinate: blacks in the United States have had equality before the law since 1865.

In the course of time, a minority group may come to participate more fully in the dominant group's institutions, and the cultures of the two may become increasingly similar. The two groups may fuse as one un-

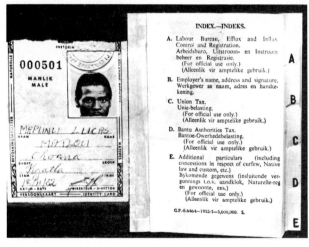

Expulsion and exclusion are extreme results of antagonistic racial and ethnic relations. (Above) In the early 1970s, Idi Amin of Uganda deported 27,000 Indians, many of whom were second- or third-generation Ugandans. (Left) In South Africa, the system of *apartheid*, or legal segregation, requires blacks to carry an identity card at all times and excludes them from white territories and institutions. (W. Campbell/Sygma; Wide World Photos)

differentiated ethnic group. (This has largely happened in the United States, for example, among groups from northern Europe.) But this fusion, or *assimilation* (see Chapter 4), is not necessarily inevitable. The minority group may resist assimilation, desiring to maintain its autonomy. For many generations, ethnicity can continue to be an important emotional anchor and source of positive identification and cultural direction, supple-

menting age, sex, class, nationality, and other sources of identification in the individual's self-concept.

Racial and ethnic relations in the United States

The United States has seven major ethnic groups that are not directly of European origin. In addition to more than 26 million blacks (12 percent of the population in 1981), there are at least six other non-European groups of more than 400,000 individuals each. Intergroup patterns in the United States have ranged all the way from extermination (of Native Americans, or Indians) to widespread intermarriage (between the white Protestant descendants of the early English and Scottish settlers and the descendants of other northern European immigrants such as the Germans and Scandinavians). American views of appropriate intergroup relations have never been very clear. They have included the "melting-pot" goal, the idea that the different cultures would "melt" into a new combination, and various forms of pluralism, some more equitable than others. The "separate but equal" doctrine of the late nineteenth century is an example of the idea of pluralism. In the late 1800s and in the early part of this century, it was common policy to enforce a high degree of cultural assimilation, as can be seen in the following remarks of an American educator from that time:

Our task is to break up these groups or settlements, to assimilate and amalgamate these people as a part of our American race, and to implant in their children, so far as can be done, the Anglo-Saxon conception of righteousness, law and order, and popular government, and to awaken in them a reverence for our democratic institutions and for those things in our national life which we as a people hold to be of abiding worth. (Ellwood P. Cuberly, 1909)

Some writers have called this the "transmuting-pot" approach. Instead of aiming to "melt" all ethnic groups together on an egalitarian basis, it aimed to "transmute" the behavior of the minority groups into patterns more acceptable to the white Anglo-Saxon Protestants (Yetman and Steele, 1975). The underlying assumption in such cases, whether explicit or not, was that "deviant" cultural traditions were inferior and that

people would surrender them willingly to embrace the culture of the majority.

Since that time many observers have come to question the desirability, or even the possibility, of total assimilation in the United States—as we shall see in the sections that follow. Intergroup relations have varied considerably, depending on the groups in question. The assimilation of white immigrants from Protestant, northern European countries, who arrived singly and voluntarily at a time when their labor was needed, was one thing; that of the Native Americans, the Indians, quite another. The Indians had their own culture and social structure and were on their own territory; it was this territory the white settlers wanted, not the Indians' labor. And this situation, in turn, proved different from that which occurred when whites interacted with blacks. Not only were the blacks torn from their native lands; their traditional culture and social structure were largely destroyed, and centuries of slavery in the New World led to suspicion and hostility in much black-white interaction.

In this chapter, we will concentrate on the history of intergroup relations in the United States and on the current opportunities and life experiences of the various minorities. As we do so, we will focus on the ways in which intergroup relations have been shaped by the needs and values of both majority and minority. As we will see, minority responses to domination have changed in the recent past, with results that have been felt in many areas of our society.

Ethnic stratification in America

COLONIALISM AND SLAVERY

A central historical factor in the formation of today's multiethnic states—our own especially—is European colonialism. During the height of Europe's overseas expansion—from the sixteenth to the eighteenth century—ships set sail from Europe's ports bound for destinations from the West Indies to Africa, Asia, or Australia in search of gold, raw materials, and increased trade. Where there were important trade routes, where the prospects of finding gold or raw materials looked favorable, or simply where a competing state might otherwise

stake a claim, colonists often established settlements that became permanent. By the nineteenth century, these empires extended throughout the world.

European colonizers invariably disrupted the societies of the lands they invaded, transforming the local subsistence economies into systems of exploitation designed to benefit themselves and the mother countries. Two broad patterns of colonial control emerged (van den Berghe, 1967). In places like Mexico, where settled, hierarchically organized agricultural societies already existed, the Europeans simply replaced the ruling group or superimposed their own rulers on it and subjected the native population to some kind of forced labor. In places like Brazil and the American colonies, where the native populations were more nomadic, smaller, less rigidly stratified, and unaccustomed to agricultural labor, the colonists found no ready-made social structure to dominate and soon discovered that the local populations made poor slaves. "The general outcome was virtual genocide of the natives" and "encapsulation of their scattered remnants in human game reserves" (van den Berghe, 1967, p. 125). Instead of using native laborers, the colonists imported laborers from other places.

At first, such laborers were brought to colonial America as indentured servants—white servants from Europe and black ones from Africa. But as the demand for labor grew, it became necessary to provide European laborers added enticements in the form of legislation designed to make the conditions of indenture more profitable. This legislation, by setting up protections for white indentured servants, had the effect of supporting and codifying *less* favorable conditions for black laborers, and ultimately of defining their servitude as a lifelong condition. Their non-European culture and their highly visible "differentness" made black laborers seem alien to their ethnocentric masters; furthermore, unlike the indentured servants from Europe, they were not backed by powerful governments that might take action if they were mistreated (Noel, 1968). The pattern of subjugation that resulted was to last for centuries.

The black slaves in the United States lived under a *caste* system, in which status is ascribed and intermarriage forbidden. Although slavery was officially banned in 1865—shortly before this photograph of newly freed blacks was taken—the caste system persisted for many years afterward, as segregation and limited opportunities restricted blacks' chances for social mobility. (Courtesy, The New-York Historical Society, New York)

BLACK-WHITE RELATIONS: FROM THE CIVIL WAR TO TODAY

The stratification system in which blacks in the United States were enmeshed under slavery was basically one of *caste* (see Chapter 11). In a caste system, status is ascribed and intermarriage prohibited. Caste lines usually correspond to a rigid division of labor, and movement into strata occupied by the dominant group is forbidden. Only certain occupations are open to the subordinate group, and the differences between castes in standards of living and access to such social benefits as education and health care are enormous.

The caste system was "officially" dissolved in 1865, when slavery was legally abolished by the Thirteenth Amendment to the Constitution, but it survived for many years thereafter. Many of the jobs that were made available to freed blacks were concentrated in agriculture. Segregation of schools lessened blacks' chances of moving up the job ladder through education; voting restrictions blocked their routes to political power. During World War I, job openings in new industries encouraged migration to northern cities; this demographic shift was further spurred by a second industrial boom during World War II and by the mechanization of agriculture in the South. Blacks arriving in the North were generally shut out of unions by the other groups with whom they were now directly competing. Thus they were underrepresented in the expanding industrial job hierarchy.

The castelike lines between whites and nonwhites have only recently begun to blur. Intermarriage, for example, is still rare; race is still a fairly good predictor of life chances. Despite all the changes of the postwar period—general prosperity and affluence, the civil-rights movement, and the war on poverty—real change in the status of blacks has only recently become marked in some areas, and it has been neither steady nor rapid.

Blacks have achieved some gains in political power. Voter registration drives in the 1960s have shown results in terms of an increase in the number of elected black officials at various government levels. In 1979 the number of black representatives in Congress and in the state legislatures was 315, compared to 182 in 1970; 2,647 blacks held such city and county offices as mayor, council member, and commissioner in 1979, compared to 715 in 1970 (Census Bureau, 1979). Black participation in local, particularly urban, politics has also increased.

Nevertheless, in education, income, occupational level, housing, and general living conditions, the record is decidedly more mixed. Although between 1950 and 1980 the percentage of blacks in professional and white-collar occupations more than tripled, so that one-third of blacks are now in such positions, slightly more than half of all whites are in these occupations. Blacks continue to predominate in manual, unskilled, and service jobs that offer low pay and little chance for advancement. Blacks are similarly disadvantaged in terms of unemployment. The unemployment rate for whites was slightly more than 5 percent in the fall of 1979; the rate for nonwhites was much higher, close to

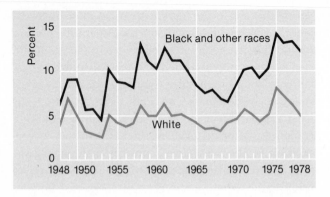

FIGURE 12.1

Unemployment rates in the United States, 1948 to 1978. (Census Bureau, 1979, pp. 59 and 185)

11 percent. And the rate for nonwhite teenagers (ages sixteen to nineteen) was over 35 percent, three times that of their white counterparts (U.S. Department of Labor, 1979).

In 1977, 74.4 percent of blacks between the ages of twenty-five and twenty-nine had finished high school (compared to 22.2 percent in 1950 and 37.7 percent in 1960), and 12.6 percent had gone on to receive college or graduate degrees. But better education has not brought rises in income comparable to those of whites (Census Bureau, 1979, p. 142). The median income of male black college graduates is about the same as that of white high school graduates; a black full-time worker earned $162 a week in 1976, while his or her white counterpart earned $202 (U.S. Department of Labor, 1977a, p. 2). Though median income for black families rose from $6,962 in 1967 to $9,563 in 1977, it was still only about 57 percent of the median income of white families (U.S. Department of Commerce, 1979, pp. 189, 201). In 1978, 30.6 percent of blacks lived below the poverty line, compared to 8.7 percent of whites. In addition, a much higher proportion of black families are headed by a woman—39 percent, compared to 11 percent of white families (U.S. Department of Commerce, 1979, p. 157). (We discuss the "earnings gap" between men and women in Chapter 16.) Job opportunities are limited as well: blacks face difficulties in commuting to well-paying jobs, now that many industries have moved out of the central cities. Though some black families joined whites in fleeing to the suburbs, there is still a great deal of residential segregation. One

TABLE 12.1

WHERE BLACKS WORK, BY TYPE OF JOB

	1958	1978
Professional and technical	4.1%	11.7%
Managers, administrators	2.4%	4.8%
Sales	1.2%	2.8%
Clerical	6.1%	16.9%
Skilled trades	5.9%	8.8%
Operatives, including vehicles	20.1%	20.5%
Laborers (nonfarm)	14.7%	7.9%
Household workers	15.3%	3.6%
Other service jobs	17.7%	20.5%
Farm managers	3.7%	0.5%
Farm laborers	8.8%	2.0%

SOURCE: U.S. News & World Report, May 14, 1979, p. 50

indication of this pattern is the fact that in 1978, 55 percent of blacks and only 24 percent of whites lived in central cities (U.S. Department of Commerce, 1979, p. 171; see Chapter 20).

In considering all these data, it is important to remember that blacks' low economic status is connected not only with ethnicity, but also with other factors. People who work in agriculture and people living in the South earn less than the national average—as do younger people, people who are less well educated, and people in rural areas. And there happen to be disproportionately high numbers of blacks in all these categories. These nonethnic variables, though they do not by any means account for *all* the discrepancies between blacks' income and that of whites, do contribute to the magnitude of the differences. The other point to remember is that black gains, though erratic, are solid: in the North and West, young black couples earn about the same incomes as young white couples; women, whether black or white, earn roughly equal pay. There is a young, affluent black middle class. So whether blacks are poor or affluent also depends on age, sex, education, occupation, and region: the picture is a complicated one.

OTHER ETHNIC GROUPS

The first great wave of immigration to the United States was made up of European colonizers and the slaves they imported; the second was the enormous influx during the nineteenth and early twentieth centuries of people, again primarily from Europe but also from China and Japan, responding to the surge in American industrial development and contributing to it in turn. The rate of immigration rose and fell with the severity of conditions in Europe and Asia and with the receptiveness of American society. This population expansion occurred mainly between 1870 and 1920, although by 1850 enough Irish had been driven from their homeland by the great famine of 1846–1850 to account for more than one-quarter of New York's population (Glazer and Moynihan, 1963). Along with the Irish, the Germans, British, and Scandinavians were the first to come in large numbers, followed by peoples from eastern and southern Europe—Slavs, Jews, and Italians. Between 1899 and 1910 alone, 2.3 million Italians entered the United States.

The European immigrants

The European immigrants entered an ethnic stratification system that approximated the *class* type, whereby individual mobility is possible, and the emphasis is on achievement rather than ascribed status. To begin with, these immigrants had a degree of choice that had not been given to the blacks who came before. Though often driven by famine or exclusion from their own societies, or enticed by false promises, these immigrants were nevertheless not brought in chains. Furthermore, the established population was receptive to some degree, depending on economic conditions. In times of depression, though they were resented by native workers as competitors, these immigrants were welcomed by capitalists, who saw them as a source of cheap labor. (Capitalists also used the immigrants to undercut the bargaining power of native skilled workers; factory owners similarly took advantage of new technology to replace skilled labor with machines.) Also important was the fact that most European immigrants were not physically different from the dominant group. They were also able to fight successfully for education. (We will discuss the expansion of education in the United States in Chapter 15.)

Mobility for these groups was relatively high. Many white immigrants eventually left the slums and the menial jobs they took when they arrived. They moved to better housing within the city and then, after World War II, into the expanding suburbs. Today, an average of about 57 percent of "white ethnic" persons graduate from high school, as against a national average of 62.5 percent (Census Bureau, 1976, pp. 34, 124). Median family income is only slightly below that for all white Americans—$12,217 for German-Americans and $12,520 for Italian-Americans in 1972, for example, compared to a median income for the total white population of $13,088 (Census Bureau, 1976, pp. 34, 412).

The rapidity of the white ethnics' rise can perhaps be seen most dramatically in the change in the proportion of those in the lowest tenth of the income scale between 1910 and 1970. In 1910, when only 10 percent of native whites were in this category, between 20 and 40 percent of southern and eastern European immigrants were considered poor. By 1970, the proportion of native whites below the poverty line was still 10 percent, but only 5 to 9 percent of southern and eastern European immigrants were in this group (Lebergott,

An interesting side effect of the black civil rights movement has been the increased sense of identity and pride among members of white ethnic groups. (Richard Kalvar/Magnum)

1976, p. 47, Table 2). These figures contrast sharply with comparable figures for blacks: in 1910, 40 percent of blacks were in the bottom 10 percent of income; in 1970, 35 percent were.

The other major ethnic groups in America—Native Americans, Hispanics, Chinese, and Japanese—do not exactly fit into either the black caste pattern or the white class pattern. Each has had a different experience.

Native Americans

The only racial or ethnic group mentioned by name in the Constitution, Native Americans have been profoundly affected by shifts in governmental policies reflected in laws and treaties. (It is somewhat misleading to refer to Indians as a racial or ethnic group in the sense in which we have been using those terms, because they are the aboriginal people of this continent—the truly native Americans.) They were hounded off their lands and then nearly exterminated in the Indian wars of the late nineteenth century, and are at the bottom of the socioeconomic scale today. In 1970, about half of the 793,000 Native Americans were on reservations and still under the trusteeship of the federal Bureau of Indian Affairs. By 1977, there were about 1 million Native Americans (U.S. Department of HEW, November 1979). Native Americans are poorer than blacks (median per capita income in 1975 was $2,453) and have

one of the highest unemployment rates of all ethnic groups (12.5 percent for males in 1976). Yet, overall, Native Americans are not less educated than other minority groups: in 1976, 70 percent of males and 55 percent of females between twenty and twenty-four had finished high school (U.S. Commission on Civil Rights, 1978).

On the reservations, land and housing tend to be poor, and residents generally have no option but to patronize stores owned mostly by outsiders. The incidence of tuberculosis is four times as high among Native Americans as among the rest of the population. The infant mortality rate was 23.8 per 1,000 in 1971, compared to a national rate of 19.2. Alcoholism and suicide are critical problems, particularly among the young. Though some efforts have recently been made to initiate economic self-help programs, most Native Americans still do not have adequate access to jobs or opportunities for economic mobility.

Hispanics

Spanish-speaking immigrants from Central and Latin America have come to the United States from different backgrounds and at different times. Many have been hampered by lack of ability to speak English. Many, too, have had physical characteristics that differentiated them from the majority. Most twentieth-century Hispanic immigrants, with the exception of the skilled

Native Americans are at the bottom of the socio-economic ladder in the United States today. They are beset by poverty, high unemployment, disease, and alcoholism. (© Lawrence Frank 1977)

and professional Cubans who came in the 1950s and 1960s, have come as unskilled, uneducated cheap labor. In 1978 there were 7.2 million people of Mexican descent in the United States (U.S. Bureau of the Census, June 1979). Many are descendants of Mexicans who lived in territory annexed by the United States in the nineteenth century (and some trace their ancestry to early Spanish settlers). Others emigrated more recently from Mexico, primarily to look for work.

Mexican-Americans live mainly in the West and Southwest, many either in rural poverty as migrant farm laborers or in urban *barrios* ("districts"). In 1977, median income among them was $11,742, and occupational levels were all much lower than for non-Hispanic white Americans. Only 34.3 percent of those over twenty-five—but 59.9 percent of those twenty to twenty-four—had finished high school. Figures for 1978

Hispanic Americans are one of the poorer ethnic minorities, and the language barrier has kept them apart from the mainstream. Many are concentrated in urban *barrios*, where their language and culture prevail. (Susan Shapiro)

showed that 21.4 percent of Mexican-Americans lived below the poverty line, and 9.6 percent were unemployed (U.S. Bureau of the Census, June 1979).

The same is true for the Puerto Ricans who migrated to the cities of the Northeast, especially New York, after World War II. Not only do differences of language, skills, and culture separate them from the mainstream, but because of the intermarriage among blacks, native Indians, and the Spanish, many Puerto Ricans are considered nonwhite and thus suffer the effects of racial prejudice as well (see page 279). Many of the 1.7 million Puerto Ricans in the continental United States have access to only the most menial jobs and, as with urban blacks, unemployment rates are very high: 11.7 percent. As of 1978, 47.7 percent of those twenty to twenty-four (and 36 percent of those over twenty-five) had finished high school. Median income is lower than that of blacks ($7,972 in 1977), and 39 percent of Puerto Ricans live below the poverty line (U.S. Bureau of the Census, June 1979).

Chinese and Japanese

Both Chinese and Japanese immigrants suffered discrimination, but the experiences of the two groups have been markedly different. Most of today's 435,000 Chinese-Americans are the descendants of those who came to the United States during the late nineteenth century to work the mines and build the railroads. As a group, the Chinese were at first welcomed as cheap labor and then subjected to violence and exclusion when economic conditions changed. They were long confined to certain low-status occupations, such as running laundries, and they tended to remain in tightly knit urban ghettos. Language remains an obstacle for some, and median income is low ($5,223 in 1970). According to a special census report, 57.8 percent of Chinese-Americans complete high school, and 37 percent go beyond high school.

The 591,000 Japanese-Americans in the United States, clustered on the West Coast and in Hawaii, also came originally as cheap labor for the farms and plantations of California and Hawaii, but many accumulated capital, bought farms of their own, and set up small

During World War II, when the United States was fighting Japan, the entire West Coast Japanese community was driven into internment camps such as this one at Manzanar, California. Today, however, a high percentage of Japanese Americans are well educated and hold good jobs. (UPI)

businesses. Their mobility may have been aided by the fact that, like the dominant culture, their values stressed hard work and education. During World War II, the entire West Coast Japanese community of 110,000 was forced into internment camps and deprived of liberty and possessions in one of the most blatant episodes of discrimination in American history. Today, many Japanese-Americans are well educated (69 percent graduate from high school) and hold good jobs (median income was $12,772 in 1970). In certain areas where they are highly concentrated (such as Hawaii), they are also a powerful political force.

Maintaining inequality

Once a racially and ethnically stratified social order in the United States had emerged, what sustained it? And what sustains it now? There are no easy answers to these questions, yet a number of general factors can be noted. First, various attitude and behavior patterns on the part of the dominant group—among them physical repression, social distance, prejudice, and discrimination—sustain this stratification. Second, minority responses to these patterns may help to sustain or lead to changes in the system.

DOMINANT-GROUP BEHAVIOR AND ATTITUDES

Physical repression

One highly visible way of keeping a minority group in its place is through the use of terror. This can take the form of relatively spontaneous acts by an individual or group; it can be organized and carried out by the state; or it can occur in the "twilight zone" of covert official encouragement but overt disclaimer.

White-black relations in the United States offer a living arsenal of the various forms physical repression can take. Recent violence against blacks engaged in school bussing struggles in Boston and Louisville and the beatings and murders of civil-rights workers in the South in the early 1960s are examples of white resistance to the demand for social change. The most prominent example of physical repression was lynching. During the 1890s, when this activity was at its height, more than 1,000 black men were lynched in the South, helping to create a climate of fear that aided whites in maintaining social control.

Social distance

In addition to the threat or actual use of physical violence, systems of ethnic stratification may depend on the maintenance of some form of separation of majority and minority.

The form this "social distance" takes depends on the type of stratification system involved. In what Pierre van den Berghe (1967) has called a "paternalistic" system of race relations (which corresponds to the racial caste system discussed above), majority and minority can intermingle physically because there is never a question of their relative statuses. The groups live as if in different social universes. Detailed rituals of etiquette, a common feature of paternalistic systems, help maintain this social distance in the midst of physical proximity. The master calls the slaves he has bought by their first names; they call him "Sir."

In what van den Berghe calls a "competitive" system (that is, one of class), where the caste barriers have broken down and social distance has decreased, the situation is quite different. The relative positions of the two groups are not always clear. The threat of assimilation looms, and the dominant group often tries to ward it off via physical segregation, avoidance of close personal relationships, or the creation of separate social institutions, such as churches and schools. Table 12.1 presents a schematic outline of the features of both types of race relations.

These ideas offer us a clue to why legalized segregation, or "Jim Crow," developed in the South when it did. The South's segregated institutions, far from being a creation of slavery, were not established until about the turn of the century (also the peak period of lynchings), when a series of state laws effectively disenfranchised blacks and segregated everything from schools to

TABLE 12.2

FEATURES OF THE PATERNALISTIC AND THE COMPETITIVE TYPES OF RACE RELATIONS

	PATERNALISTIC (CASTE)	COMPETITIVE (CLASS)
GENERAL STRUCTURAL FEATURES		
1. Economy	Nonmanufacturing, agricultural, pastoral, handicraft; mercantile capitalism; plantation economy	Typically manufacturing, but not necessarily so; large-scale industrial capitalism
2. Division of labor	Simple ("primitive") or intermediate (as in preindustrial large-scale societies). Division of labor along racial lines. Wide income gap between racial groups.	Complex (manufacturing) according to "rational" *universalistic criteria*; narrow gap in wages; no longer strictly racial
3. Mobility	Little mobility either vertical or horizontal (slaves, servants, or serfs "attached" in space)	*Much mobility* both vertical and horizontal (required by industrial economy)
4. Social stratification	Caste system with horizontal color bar; aristocracy versus servile caste with wide gap in living standards (as indexed by income, education, death and birth rates); homogeneous upper caste	Caste system but with tendency for color bar to "tilt" to vertical position; complex stratification into classes within castes; narrower gaps between castes and greater range within castes
5. Numerical ratio	Dominant group a small minority	Dominant group a majority
6. Value conflict	Integrated value system; no ideological conflict	Conflict at least in Western "Christian," "democratic," "liberal" type of society
SPECIFIC FEATURES		
1. Race relations	Accommodation; everyone in "his place" and "knows it"; paternalism: benevolent despotism	Antagonism; suspicion, hatred; competitiveness (real or imaginary)
2. Roles and statuses	Sharply defined roles and statuses based on ascription, particularism, diffuseness, collectivity orientation, affectivity; unequal status unthreatened	*Ill-defined* and based on achievement, universalism, specificity, self-orientation, affective neutrality; unequal status threatened
3. Etiquette	Elaborate and definite	Simple and indefinite
4. Forms of aggression	Generally from lower caste: slave rebellions; nationalistic, revivalistic, or messianistic movements; not directly racial	Both from upper and lower caste: more frequent and directly racial: riots, lynchings, pogroms; passive resistance, sabotage, organized mass protests
5. Miscegenation	Condoned and frequent between upper-caste males and lower-caste females; institutionalized concubinage	Severely condemned and infrequent
6. Segregation	Little of it; status gap allows close but unequal contact	Much of it; narrowing of status gap makes for increase of spatial gap
7. Psychological syndrome	Internalized subservient status: no personality "need" for prejudice; no "high F"*; "pseudo-tolerance"	"Need" for prejudice; "high F"*; linked with sexuality, sadism, frustration; scapegoating
8. Stereotypes of lower caste	Childish, immature, uninhibited, lazy, impulsive, fun-loving, good-humored; inferior but lovable	Aggressive, uppity, insolent, oversexed, dirty; inferior, despicable, and dangerous
9. Intensity of prejudice	Fairly constant	Variable and sensitive to provocative situations
"SOCIAL CONTROL" FEATURES		
1. Form of government	Aristocratic, oligarchic, autocratic; either centralized or "feudal"; colonial	Restricted or pseudo-democratic
2. Legal system	Lower caste has definite legal status; law on side of racial status quo	Lower caste has no definite legal status; resort to extra-legal sanctions (e.g., lynchings)

* This refers to the "F-Scale," an index of authoritarian personality traits devised by Adorno *et al.* (1950).

SOURCE: Adapted from van den Berghe, 1967, pp. 31–33.

public toilets and waiting rooms. Under the paternalistic caste system, such segregation was needless as well as impractical. But as Southern society began to become industrialized and to shift toward a competitive class system, the social position of whites became less secure.

White Southerners therefore attempted to create in physical space what they were losing in social distance.

When the final vestiges of the Jim Crow laws were struck down in the courts in the 1950s and early 1960s, *de jure* (legally approved) segregation ended. Nevertheless, *de facto* segregation (segregation that is not approved by law but still exists in reality) continues, in the North as well as in the South. Residential segregation has increased with the disproportionate white exodus to the suburbs. And physical distance maintains social distance, for residential segregation also means school and job and recreational segregation. The result has been more separation between blacks and whites (see Chapter 20). In fact, some observers argue that we are moving toward "the permanent establishment of two societies: one predominantly white and located in the suburbs, in smaller cities, and in outlying areas, and one largely Negro located in central cities" (Kerner Report, 1968, p. 398).

But despite the prevalence of certain kinds of segregation, as with other measures of stratification, reality is far more complex than this idea of two separate societies. As Chapter 11 shows, residential (and hence job and school) segregation has a class as well as an ethnic or racial aspect; middle- and upper-class blacks are also moving to the suburbs, leaving lower-class blacks in city ghettos. Perhaps what is being most accentuated are the divisions between the privileged and the disadvantaged sectors of the black community (we discuss these changes in more detail later in the chapter).

Prejudice

Another major way in which ethnic inequalities may be perpetuated (and symbolized) is through *prejudice*. Prejudice involves an attitude of prejudgment toward a group, a generalization about the members of that group. We all generalize about people and categorize them, but prejudice involves generalizations that are not likely to change in the face of new evidence. In one specific category of prejudice, *racial* prejudice, the attributes of the group in question are thought to stem from biological inheritance. (We should note here that racial prejudice is only one component of the system of beliefs and actions known as *racism*; one manifestation of racism is the practice of discrimination, a topic we discuss below.)

Prejudice has a belief component—blacks are thought to be lazy and violent, Jews to be pushy and clannish, and so on—and an emotional component, consisting of the way the prejudiced person feels about the group in question (see box). The belief component of prejudice is often called a *stereotype*—which, as we saw in Chapter 7, is a categorization of a group based on general feelings or beliefs about a supposed characteristic of its members. In the shift in American society from a paternalistic system to a competitive one, stereotypes also changed: "Stereotypes of the subordinate group changed from the humble, happy-go-lucky, 'good' Negro or 'Native' who 'knew his place' to the cheeky, uppity, insolent, treacherous, sly, violent 'new Negro' or 'detribalized scum' who threatens the status quo" (van den Berghe, 1967, p. 128).

Discrimination

Prejudice is often confused with *discrimination*, but there is an important difference between the two. Prejudice refers to beliefs or attitudes; discrimination refers to behavior and social roles. Discrimination involves differential, negative behavior toward a member of a minority group solely because the person belongs to that particular group (excluding Jews from a country club, for example, or hiring blacks as dishwashers and busboys but not waiters or managers, or excluding Catholics from prestigious private schools). Although prejudiced people often practice discrimination, there is no one-to-one link between prejudice and discrimination. In other words, people can be prejudiced without being discriminatory or discriminatory without being prejudiced (Merton, 1940). For example, an executive who knew himself to be prejudiced might nevertheless avoid discrimination in his company because he knows it to be illegal and bad for business.

In many instances, habitual discrimination may be systematic and institutionalized and not dependent for its maintenance on individual prejudice. Actions may have discriminatory consequences even if they are not intended to produce them, and actions in one area may support inequality in another. A focus on *institutional discrimination and institutionalized racism* means we must consider the dominant group's total set of practices toward a minority and the direct and indirect ways in which inequality is perpetuated.

For example, many obvious instances of institutional racism stem from inequality of income: blacks find themselves closed out from many geographical areas and spheres of activity because of low income, not because of "color" per se. Families with very low incomes, for example, must often live in public housing and send their children to nearby public schools—both of which may be virtually segregated. Urban renewal programs, ostensibly aimed at improving the quality of city life for all residents, have often intensified these patterns of segregation. Owners of businesses in predominantly black neighborhoods may be unable to get insurance or bank loans. The insurance companies and banks would claim that their actions are not based on race but on the fact that ghetto properties are bad risks. Such policies do not require that the insurance agents or bankers themselves be prejudiced; in fact, they might even be sympathetic to minority problems. However, banks and businesses in our society concern themselves above all else with making a profit. This seemingly neutral goal results in discrimination as surely as does prejudice.

The functions and costs of racism

A racially and ethnically stratified society can also be maintained and sustained because it benefits certain groups. Some businesses, for example, may profit from discrimination. Prejudice can divide workers and keep them from forming effective unions, with the result that wages stay low. Moreover, an ethnically divided work force can exert little political power. Keeping a large pool of cheap labor (unemployed blacks and minorities) is easier when those in power do not need to deal with a united labor force demanding full employment.

Racism also provides scapegoats for social problems and justifications for the status quo. In the South, slavery was justified as being divinely ordained, and it was argued that blacks were slaves because they were inferior people. Today, equivalent arguments can be used to explain inequality and to keep minorities from equal job opportunities.

On the international level, racism can fuel antagonism toward other peoples in time of war; it can also be used to justify imperialism, the affluence of a few nations at the expense of the poverty of many (Sherman and Wood, 1979, pp. 114–118). Although racism has its "functions," however, it certainly has its costs as well. Besides taking an obvious toll in human suffering, racism wastes the abilities of the excluded group and compromises the moral values of the society as a whole.

Dominant-group ideology

Prejudice and discrimination, then, are powerful weapons in the perpetuation of ethnic stratification. Often, they are particular manifestations of the dominant group's ideology. The dominant group must believe that it has the *right* to rule, and may succeed (at least partly) in convincing many members of the subordinate group that existing inequalities are only natural and just. Prejudice provides the needed rationale; by convincing themselves and others that the subordinate group is indeed inferior, individual *members* of the dominant group conclude that they therefore have a right to the privileges they enjoy. In a paternalistic system, blacks were portrayed as carefree children; thus it would appear only natural for the "adult" whites to take them in hand—and enslave them. In class systems, the right to rule is based more often on the supposed inferior culture, capacity, or will of the minority—for example, the belief that blacks are mentally inferior or that Mexicans are lazy.

The dominant group's ideology inevitably affects the minorities at which it is aimed. Even if members of minority groups know intellectually that the images projected of them are not true, they are still likely to experience emotional wounds—inner doubts, feelings of rejection, loss of human dignity. And the socialization process may to some extent actually succeed in inducing many minority individuals to accept the dominant group's ideology and the legitimacy of its rule. The actual distribution of income, status, and power is usually consistent with beliefs about which groups are subordinate and which are dominant and with arguments concerning God's will or the dominant group's moral superiority, which the inequalities of situation then appear to "prove." The dominant-group culture, to which the minority is constantly exposed, may further support the majority's position in various direct and subtle ways—through textbooks, advertising, the arts, jokes, and language.

MINORITY-GROUP RESPONSES

These, then, are some of the mechanisms by which the dominant group's power is exerted. Faced with them, minority-group members may, in certain instances, respond in ways that (paradoxically) help to maintain their own subjugation: for example, self-deprecating humor, scapegoating of other minorities, and aggression against in-group members may serve to displace hostility away from the dominant group. Some minority-group members may adopt a posture of resignation; others may use drugs and religion as escapes.

Needless to say, however, not all minority responses fit this category. In the past seventy-five years, and particularly in the past thirty years, there has been an increasing tendency toward minority-group responses that are more active and more clearly oriented toward bringing about changes in the system. We will discuss some of these changes in the section that follows.

Recent changes in the system

The orientation of a minority group toward the dominant group is partially related to the way the dominant group receives it. As it becomes clear to a minority group seeking assimilation that large segments of the dominant group are likely to continue to reject it, the minority may shift toward more pluralistic or even separatist aims. This pessimism about the likelihood of increased acceptance has been one of several factors underlying recent changes in the position and orientation of the various ethnic groups in the United States, as we will see below.

CHANGES IN BLACK-WHITE RELATIONS

Historically, black people have been divided in their orientation toward the dominant society. Some black leaders, such as Roy Wilkins of the NAACP, have aimed at integration through legal change; some, such as Marcus Garvey in the 1920s and Elijah Muhammad in the 1950s and 1960s, have advocated separatism. At one time, integration seemed to be the most desirable and easily attainable goal. With the coming of President Franklin D. Roosevelt's New Deal policies of large-scale government intervention in the economy and other spheres, blacks gained new recognition and opportunities.

After World War II, when African and Asian nations newly freed from colonial control began to send their diplomatic representatives to the United States, black leaders found that the U.S. government—embarrassed by discriminatory treatment of these diplomats in this country—was more receptive to change than it had been in the past. Blacks sponsored a series of legal

battles that culminated in the Supreme Court's 1954 *Brown v. Board of Education* decision ending school segregation. At last many Jim Crow practices were forbidden by law. When they did not disappear in practice, Southern blacks, in alliance with some whites, turned to nonviolent protest. This protest brought more legal victories (the Civil Rights Acts of 1964 and 1965 and the Voting Rights Act of 1965).

The civil-rights and black-power movements broadened their emphasis from integration to a new concern with community building and economic advancement. The vast majority of blacks continued to desire equal treatment and equal participation in American life. A smaller but significant group began to question whether they wanted to remain part of traditional society at all. The increased media coverage of racial problems and the rise of outspoken leaders such as Malcolm X also stirred black awareness and the pride of many blacks in being a *separate* people. There was some breaking down of the barriers between the black middle class and the black lower class, caused not only by the new ethnic pride but also by disappointment in the limited gains brought about by the civil-rights movement.

Thus, the movement toward assimilation lost some of its followers; groups that were separatist and often hostile to the traditional, dominant American society received increased attention. When the ghetto riots of 1964 to 1968 broke out, a number of blacks perceived them as a *legitimate* expression of mass dissatisfaction. Significantly, this dissatisfaction was with the economic system as a whole, rather than with more symbolic issues such as seating on busses and at lunch counters.

In the decade since the riots, other issues have received attention. Wilson (1978) argues that the growth of a black middle class after 1960 has made class a more significant factor in maintaining stratification than race. Inner-city blacks are continuing the battle for equal opportunity, but the battles are conducted over social and political issues, not race. Wilson's critics (Marston and Morse, 1978; Marrett, 1980; Pettigrew, 1980) argue that racism continues to be highly significant and that the position of the black middle class is by no means secure. As evidence, they cite the ongoing battle over affirmative action programs and the effect of economic recession and cutbacks in government bureaucracies, where large numbers of blacks have found employment and advancement. These critics suggest that the significance of race is changing, but not declining.

But Wilson (1980) maintains that in terms of economic opportunity, middle- and upper-class blacks simply have many more options than they did a generation ago; it is the black underclass that has fewer. This growing gap within the black community can result in a "divide and rule" phenomenon, weakening the overall power of blacks, just as labor's power is weakened by black-white divisions. It also points up even more sharply the plight of young lower-class blacks trapped in city ghettos: for them, the chances for improvement grow dimmer and dimmer as education and social (class) skills come to mean more and more in the job market.

Reynolds Farley (1977), however, finds that for blacks as a whole, the gains of the 1960s were not lost in the recession of the 1970s, and gains in some areas (for example, occupational level) continue to be made. Nevertheless, the black underclass—the unemployed and the underemployed—continues to be economically subordinate. Yet at this point, militant separatist movements and mass action seem to be in abeyance. Among the factors responsible for lessening social-movement activity since the 1960s may have been clear legal and other victories; accommodative gestures by the dominant group (in the form of manpower training and other urban programs); the co-optation of protest leaders and an increased stake in the system for middle-class blacks; a sense of hopelessness about change; and direct repression (as in the suppression of the Black Panthers). However, the riot in Miami in May 1980, in which eighteen people were killed, was a powerful illustration of the frustration and anger that still exist among

blacks. In that case, a series of police abuses ignited long-smoldering discontent over joblessness and economic hardship. As long as such conditions affect the black community disproportionately, outbursts of rage such as that seen in Miami can be expected.

CHANGES IN OTHER GROUPS

In addition to effecting a certain degree of direct legal and attitudinal change, the civil-rights and black-power movements had indirect effects on other ethnic movements and groups. They tended to spark a renewed interest in ethnicity; during the 1960s, Native Americans, Mexican-Americans, Puerto Ricans, and others mounted their own protests, parallel in some ways to those of the blacks.

Native Americans, for example, used violence at Wounded Knee in 1973, and in Washington, D.C., in 1972, and civil disobedience at Alcatraz in 1969 to draw attention to their plight. They have also attempted in recent years to use the system to regain control of valuable land or resources by suing in the courts. In northern California, Klamath Indians sued for the right to fish a river commercially and won. A number of tribes have sued for the return of lands in Massachusetts, Rhode Island, western New York, and Maine. (The Maine claim encompasses about one-fourth of the state, much of it valuable timberland.) The gains made by some blacks also intensified feelings of competition among several groups.

ETHNIC RELATIONS

The late 1970s saw increasing evidence of tension among certain ethnic groups, especially those at the bottom of the economic hierarchy. The admission to the United States of hundreds of thousands of Cuban refugees was thought to have been a contributing factor to the riot in the black ghetto of Miami in 1980. To many blacks, the presence of the Cubans represented a threat to their own economic well-being. Not only would the Cubans be competing directly with blacks for increasingly scarce jobs but, as refugees, they were eligible for a variety of kinds of aid not available to blacks.

THE NEWEST IMMIGRANTS

Eugenio Gonzalez, a 34-year-old computer programmer, spoke to a reporter in Florida recently: "I refused to join any of the party organizations, so I worked as a laborer for under $50 a month in a coffee factory. When you apply for a better job you must have proof of revolutionary activities. When they fired me as a computer expert, I got so desperate I bought a rubber inner tube, and I was going to float across to Florida . . . (*Time*, May 19, 1980, p. 18).

Gonzalez didn't have to use his inner tube. Instead, he joined thousands of Cubans fleeing their island on crowded boats in a chaotic flotilla to Key West, Florida. The mass evacuation began suddenly in May, 1980, when Fidel Castro granted Cubans the right to leave their country. Since the years just following the Cuban Revolution, when 750,000 Cubans emigrated to the U.S., few others have managed to leave. So, with Castro's unexpected policy change, thousands more were eager to join relatives in this country, or, like Gonzalez, simply sought personal freedom. In just one day in May, 4,500 Cubans arrived in Key West.

Most of the refugees were young men with working-class backgrounds. Three-fourths said they had relatives in the U.S. And while they sought to escape from political oppression, many seemed equally troubled by the lack of "jobs, food and clothing."

The American reaction to this new wave of Hispanic immigrants was mixed. To soften what had seemed to be a hostile reception, President Carter declared: "Ours is a country of refugees seeking freedom from Communist domination. . . ." But by early July, when the number of Cuban boat people arriving at Key West had grown to 114,000, Representative Sam Hall, Jr., asked, "How long is this country going to be the recipient of people from all over the earth? When is this going to end?" In south Florida, where the influx of new arrivals would have the greatest impact, one town circulated a petition to send the Cubans away.

The strongest reaction, both in favor of and against the refugees, took place in Miami. In the city's Little Havana, where 500,000 Cubans already live, money, food, and clothing were collected for the new arrivals. But in Miami proper, others feared competition for jobs, housing, and social services. Dade County officials forecast a strain on schools, and have already asked the federal government for $20 million in aid.

For years now, long before the dramatic escape of thousands of Cubans to this country, south Florida has been handling another group of immigrants—the Haitians. Over 17,000 Haitians are known to live in Miami, and immigration officials estimate that an equal number may be there illegally. Unlike the Cubans, the Haitians are not considered refugees fleeing from political oppression. They are, instead, escaping from the worst poverty in the Western Hemisphere. As such, they do not qualify under U.S. immigration law as legitimate refugees, and the Justice Department is working to send most of them back. Living in the poorest section of Miami, the Haitians receive $10 million worth of social services each year. Nevertheless, many are going hungry, and city officials have asked Washington for help.

Even though the Haitians have been in Miami longer than the newly arriving Cubans, they remain at the bottom of the economic and social ladder. "In a city where whites look down on Cubans, where Cubans look down on blacks, and where blacks from the Bahamas and other Caribbean countries have their own system of castes, the Haitians are at the bottom of everybody's lists" (*The New York Times*, May 14, 1980, p. 10).

The dominant population rejects the Haitians for many of the same reasons that other Americans, one hundred years ago, despised the newcomers from southern and eastern Europe: fear of economic competition; the language barrier—Haitians speak neither English nor Spanish in this bilingual city; fear of diseases brought by the new group; dislike of the immigrants' social habits. Finally, one source of the resentment toward them may simply be that they are black. With the continuing immigration of these groups from the Western Hemisphere, as well as of Vietnamese, Cambodians, and Chinese, the United States is again cast in the role of a refuge for immigrants. The newest waves of immigration remind us that our social order is in constant flux.

Similar tensions between blacks and Hispanics had been growing for years in areas such as New York and Los Angeles, where a large Hispanic community competed directly with blacks for jobs and social services. To blacks, the increasing visibility of Hispanics and their needs has served to divert attention from the continuing plight of black Americans. It has been frustrating for some to see large sums of money allocated for programs—such as bilingual education—aimed at helping the Hispanic population when budget cutbacks are eliminating other social services. This competition for a slice of a shrinking economic pie has not only affected blacks and Hispanics, however; in Denver, for example, there have been a number of clashes between Hispanics and Vietnamese refugees in conflicts over jobs and increasingly scarce public housing.

Black and Hispanic leaders concerned about conflicts between their communities have pointed out that both groups would ultimately benefit from cooperation. A coalition between blacks and Hispanics would represent a voting bloc of about 50 million people. However, cultural differences and economic competition have so far kept the groups apart. As the Hispanic population continues to grow—and Hispanics will soon be the largest minority group in America—further conflicts can be anticipated.

ETHNIC STRATIFICATION
IN THE FUTURE

Robert Park, an influential observer of American ethnic patterns, theorized that relations between the immigrant groups and white Anglo-Saxon Americans evolved through a sequence of stages, from *contact* to *competition* to *accommodation* to *assimilation* (see Chapter 4). Park believed that this sequence would ultimately be experienced by all minority groups (1949). But though it tends to fit the experience of whites from northern Europe, there is some question of how well it fits the experience of even other European immigrant groups. Gordon (1964) notes that most immigrant groups were assimilated at the secondary-group level (political and economic institutions), but that there has been little assimilation at the primary-group level (intermarriage, personal friendship, recreation, and religion). Richard Alba, in a study of descendants of nineteenth- and twentieth-century Catholic immigrants, has found "extensive and increasing social assimilation" (1976, p. 1045), especially in the case of descendants of English, Irish, German, Italian, and Polish Catholics. (He found less assimilation of Hispanic and French Canadian Catholics.) But he cautions that "the increasing social assimilation of the groups in these data does not mean that they are blending into an ethnically homogeneous mass" (1976, p. 1045).

Blacks: a special case?

If the history of some European immigrant groups diverges from Park's prediction, blacks have not yet come

even close to it. The question is, will they do so in the future? In part, the answer depends on whether one takes a short-range or a long-range perspective. Some observers who believe that the assimilation model is applicable to blacks argue that blacks do not yet fit the pattern because they are such late arrivals to urban life, large numbers of them having migrated to the cities only in the past half-century (Glazer, 1968).

In support of this position, some have suggested that cultural factors—a lack of "value congruence" between blacks and the dominant group—play an important role. But this type of argument can be misused: it can involve a tendency to "blame the victim" (Ryan, 1976)—or the victim's culture—for inequalities, rather than looking at factors in the social situation in which the minority finds itself. Another view agrees that there are similarities between the experiences of blacks and those of other urban immigrants, but notes that there has been a crucial change in the conditions faced by urban immigrants. Today, poor immigrants to the cities find themselves amid general affluence; they encounter a more developed and formalized society whose capacity for assimilation has in some ways declined. One important change, for example, is the erosion of local urban power bases, as control over many aspects of city affairs increasingly shifts to the state and federal levels.

But other observers believe that talk of a common American ethnic experience can be deceptive or even irrelevant. True, blacks have some things in common with other ethnic groups; but they also differ from them in crucial ways. They are set apart by the experience of slavery. And they are set apart by their color, which seems to arouse greater antipathies—at least among Americans—than do language and other differences. None of the European ethnic groups has faced a comparable degree of oppression, nor have any been denied opportunity to the same extent as blacks.

Some of these observers have suggested that in many ways blacks and other American "people of color" have more in common with colonized peoples of the Third World than they do with white European immigrants; therefore, they suggest, it is the colonial model, not that of assimilation, that best fits the black experience. Robert Blauner, for example, focuses on the fact that unlike the European immigrants, the people of color had no choice in their initial contact with the dominant group or in the outcome of that contact.

This, to Blauner, is a significant factor in the failure of black-white integration. As he points out, "choice is a necessary condition for commitment to any group, from social club to national society" (1972, p. 341). Moreover, blacks, again like "colonized" people, were denied access to the free labor market, which existed mostly in urban, industrial settings. Finally, unlike the European immigrants, blacks and other people of color were systematically deprived of aspects of their culture by the dominant group. Not only were black families broken up, but the dominant group also outlawed everything from drums in the slave states to most Native American tribal religious ceremonies.

In emphasizing the colonial parallels, Blauner points out, we sharpen the focus on factors that create unique barriers to the assimilation of more than a token number of individuals. Implicit in the model of "internal colonialism" is the thesis that whites have a vested interest in keeping blacks in a subordinate position. This vested interest may be connected with the fact that we have what some economists term a *dual economy*. Employers in core industries like steel, autos, and chemicals want a reliable corps of workers and are willing to pay for it; there is no longer a need for a pool of unemployed but available workers in these industries. But there is a need for workers to fill low-paying jobs in "secondary" industries, like the garment, hotel, and restaurant industries. Blacks and other minorities may therefore be maintained in a subordinate position because they fill an important economic need (Piore, 1970). (The dual-economy concept will be discussed further in Chapter 18.)

Beyond the assimilation model

So it may not be appropriate to use the assimilation model in predictions concerning future black-white relations—not only because of blacks' unique past, but also because of unique economic factors in their experi-

ence. In fact, some sociologists even debate whether it is racism itself or, instead, economic interests (particularly large corporate interests) that are at the root of the continuing subordination of blacks. Sidney Willhelm, for example (1970), argues that legal discrimination has ended precisely because it is no longer needed; urban blacks have been bypassed by technological change, and discrimination is now built into the economic system.

More generally, we might inquire whether the assimilation model is totally appropriate in the case of *any* current ethnic group. As Greeley (1974) points out, even our governmental institutions have been set up with pluralism, rather than unity, in mind. In areas with large Hispanic populations, for example, voting instructions and other public documents are usually given in Spanish as well as English. Ethnic differentiation provided immigrants with certain advantages: the ethnic group became a special market, an auxiliary "social mobility pyramid" that the individual could ascend, a link with the parent culture, and an avenue to political power. And as Greeley suggests, it seems quite likely that ethnic differentiation still offers many of these advantages, even to second- and third-generation descendants of immigrants.

In sum, it may be more appropriate to view ethnic groups as elements of society that, rather than being on the way to disappearance, are likely to remain and perhaps even grow more salient. These groups are constantly in the process of change. In the long run, the American ethnic groups as we know them today may change tremendously: Jews, for example, may practically disappear (current population statistics indicate that the Jewish population is not reproducing itself); a single Native American group may emerge as tribal distinctions disappear; and there may be a Spanish-speaking or Latin group into which the various Spanish-speaking groups now in existence may merge. But some forms of ethnic distinctiveness are likely to remain.

Summary

In nearly every nation, people are enmeshed in two forms of social organization: one based on ethnicity and one based on territory. Thus, most societies are *multiethnic*, not homogeneous. Beliefs about the innate qualities of a *race* or an *ethnic group* affect economic stratification and can be used to justify denying certain segments of a population equal access to social resources and full participation in the society's political, social, and cultural life. Racial and ethnic relations range from *genocide* and *apartheid* to *accommodation* and *assimilation*.

Originally, both blacks and whites were brought to this country as indentured servants. The position of blacks evolved into that of slaves in a *caste* stratification system. Today, despite some political gains, blacks are still unequal to the white majority in education, income, occupational level, housing, and general living conditions.

The biggest influx of immigrants into the United States occurred between 1870 and 1920. White European immigrants entered an ethnic stratification system of the *class* type, where mobility was relatively high. Native Americans today are at the bottom of the socioeconomic scale. Hispanic-, Chinese-, and Japanese-Americans have also felt racial discrimination and still do today to varying degrees.

Sustaining the racially and ethnically stratified social order are the attitude and behavior patterns of the dominant group, among them *physical repression, social distance,* *prejudice,* and *discrimination.* Beyond individual attitudes are the systematic devices of institutional discrimination and institutionalized racism, and the benefits these policies bring to the dominant group. Minority responses vary from seeking assimilation to movements for separatism.

Robert Park has envisioned a four-step process of relations between minority groups and white Anglo-Saxon Americans: contact, competition, accommodation, and assimilation. However, complete assimilation of blacks into white American society has not yet occurred. Park's model fits earlier immigrants from northern Europe better than those from southern Europe or nonwhites. The situation of nonwhites in the United States is in some ways parallel to that of the colonized peoples of the Third World, although there are important differences as well.

Glossary

ACCOMMODATION A reciprocal process by which distinct racial or ethnic groups mutually adjust their discordant attitudes and behaviors.

ASSIMILATION The process through which one group, either voluntarily or under compulsion, adopts the styles of life, attitudes, and behaviors of a politically or culturally dominant group, leading eventually to the former's disappearance as an independent, identifiable unit.

DISCRIMINATION Behavior toward a person based only on that person's group membership, rather than his or her individual behavioral characteristics.

ETHNIC GROUP An aggregate of people that defines itself and is defined by others as distinct primarily because of cultural characteristics.

GENOCIDE Systematic extermination of an ethnic or racial group.

MAJORITY In sociology, the term used to designate the relatively dominant aggregate of people in a society, independent of the size of the aggregate.

MINORITY In sociology, the term used to designate the relatively subordinate aggregate of people in a society, independent of the size of the aggregate.

MULTIETHNIC SOCIETY A form of social organization that is based on territory rather than kinship and encompasses more than one ethnic group.

PLURALISM The social situation in which a variety of ethnic groups and subcultures maintain a degree of autonomy and develop their own social structures and cultural traditions within a single complex society.

PREJUDICE An attitude of prejudgment toward members of a particular group.

RACE An aggregate of people that defines itself and is defined by others as distinct because of innate and immutable physical characteristics.

RACISM A system of beliefs and behaviors based on the idea that a subordinate group's race makes it inherently inferior.

Recommended readings

Feagin, Joe R. *Racial and Ethnic Relations.* Englewood Cliffs, N.J.: Prentice-Hall, 1978. A useful introduction to the historical experience and sociological background of eight American racial and ethnic groups.

Glazer, Nathan, and Daniel Patrick Moynihan. *Beyond the Melting Pot: The Negroes, Puerto Ricans, Jews, Italians, and Irish of New York City.* Cambridge, Mass.: MIT Press, 1963. Contrasts the experiences of various racial and ethnic groups in New York City and emphasizes the continuing importance of ethnicity.

Gordon, Milton M. *Assimilation in American Life.* New York: Oxford University Press, 1964. An inquiry into the assimilation process of American ethnic groups.

Shibutani, Tamotsu, and Kian M. Kwan. *Ethnic Stratification: A Comparative Approach.* New York: Macmillan, 1965. A book rich in comparative examples focusing on how systems of ethnic stratification arise, are sustained, and break down.

Simpson, George E., and J. Milton Yinger. *Racial and Cultural Minorities: An Analysis of Prejudice and Discrimination.* 4th ed. New York: Harper & Row, 1972. A comprehensive textbook emphasizing the study of prejudice and discrimination.

van den Berghe, Pierre I. *Race and Racism: A Comparative Perspective.* New York: Wiley, 1967. Contrasts patterns of race relations in industrial and nonindustrial settings.

Vander Zanden, James W. *American Minority Relations.* 3rd ed. New York: Ronald, 1972. A concise treatment of factors involved in race relations.

Williams, Robin W., Jr. *Mutual Accommodation: Ethnic Conflict and Cooperation.* Minneapolis: University of Min-nesota Press, 1977. An analysis of the changing position of blacks in recent decades, and a theoretical discussion of intergroup cooperation and conflict, by a major figure in the study of race and ethnic relations.

Wilson, William J. *Power, Racism, and Privilege.* New York: Macmillan, 1973. A historical and sociological analysis of black-white relations, with a contrast between the United States and South Africa.

Yetman, Norman R., and C. Hoy Steele. *Majority and Minority: The Dynamics of Racial-Ethnic Relations.* 2nd ed. Boston: Allyn and Bacon, 1975. A useful anthology dealing with majority-minority interactions.

Magubane's South Africa

PETER MAGUBANE

Peter Magubane, a black South African photojournalist, has documented the tumultuous racial scene in his own country. In this moving account, we see the incredible difficulties he must surmount in order to take his pictures of the black people's experience under apartheid.

. . . In June 1969 I drove to Pretoria to take clothes and fruit to Mrs. Nomzamo Winnie Mandela, the wife of imprisoned African National Congress leader Nelson Mandela. At that time she was in detention too. I arrived at the women's section of the Pretoria Prison and asked to speak to a black woman warder to whom I had spoken earlier on the phone. I could feel that there was something wrong. I could feel that I was surrounded. But then I asked myself, why would I be surrounded? I handed over the clothes and fruit to the black warder and was walking back to my car when four policemen grabbed me and threw me to the ground, and throttled me, and then loaded me into a car that was parked next to mine and took me to the Compol Building, where the Security Police have their headquarters. I later found out that they had thought I was plotting to get Mrs. Nomzamo Winnie Mandela out of prison. The entire prison was surrounded.

That day was the start of my interrogation. I was made to stand on three bricks for five straight days and nights without a wink of sleep, and to drink black coffee through the night. At two-hour intervals the two officers interrogating me would be relieved by others. Only when I needed to go to the toilet would they let me off the brick platform; when I needed to urinate they would merely hand me a tin to make use of.

After five days my feet were swollen and I started to urinate blood. They called Major Theunis Johannes Swanepoel (nicknamed "The Redman"), who gave me tablets to ease the pain and told them to take me to a cell. In the cell I was held in solitary confinement. They gave me five dirty blankets, two mats, an empty bucket to shit in, a mug, a bucket of water, and a spoon. I complained to the warder about the dirty blankets. It was not a five-star hotel, he told me. If I wanted clean blankets I should go to a five-star hotel.

I had been detained, along with many others, under the Suppression of Communism Act of 1950. . . .

In September 1970, when we were finally acquitted, the government was not done with us yet. Within two weeks orders came that we were banned for five years.

A banning order is signed by the Minister of Justice and means this: a banned person is not allowed to talk to more than one person at once, to attend any gathering,

to enter any educational premises or any building containing a printing press, to enter another township without a permit, to talk with another banned person, or to live in the magistracy of Johannesburg without a permit. Being banned meant that my job as a newspaper photographer was finished, it meant the end of my profession. My pictures couldn't be captioned with my name, and of course I couldn't take a picture of more than one person at a time.

A banning order leaves you naked. Unless you make up your mind to fight it with all your might, you will become a lunatic. At any time of the night police may come to your house and ransack it, keeping your whole family awake, going through each and every piece of paper in the house. You no longer have privacy. You cannot even talk to your wife while the police are there. Should a neighbor come by to offer help, he is threatened with arrest. Your employer will be interrogated, your fellow workers questioned, informers are planted around you. You are no longer a human being, people run away from you, it is as if you have leprosy. Your relatives, your friends are afraid to come near you, afraid even to greet you. I had married again in 1962 but was divorced three years later, and now in the absence of my children I spent lonely days and nights in my five-room house in Diepkloof (a part of Soweto). There was no one to talk to, even my sweethearts ran away like rats. I was not bothered, though; I was already used to isolation, from prison.

During this period I lost all my friends and have since fallen out with some of my relatives. For two years I kept my head by buying carpets, clothes, and furniture and selling them in Diepkloof. But people came to buy and sometimes promised to pay me the next day, then never came back. As a result I lost a lot of money in that project. I was not much of a merchant. Finally I got a job as a debt collector. . . .

Soon the action started again. I covered the demonstrations outside the new Johannesburg Supreme Court during the National African Youth Organization political trials; people were chased by police with attack dogs and I got good pictures. Clive Emdin and I covered the bus boycott in Newcastle. But it was in June 1976 that the really big story began. It isn't over yet. Maybe it will never be over.

I mentioned how back in the 1950's most demonstrations were run by serious adult political leaders and how most of the participants were adult too. By the 1970's nearly all the adult black politicians had been detained or jailed and their parties outlawed. This may explain why the riots that broke out in Soweto in June involved mostly children. The South African government, with its police and troops and its version of law, had succeeded in shattering organized black opposition. Now, almost without any control or organization, black high school students were acting out their anger.

I remember that the *Star* newspaper had a placard on the 15th of June 1976 saying that demonstrations were planned for the next day by Soweto pupils. Soweto is the main black area outside Johannesburg; more than two million blacks live there. The next morning I headed into Soweto to see what was going on and was quickly swept up. I photographed such things as policemen firing at students carrying signs protesting the fact that they had to learn Afrikaans in school, students burning cars, police shooting tear gas into crowds of students, all sorts of scattered violence. This went on for several days. . . .

The Soweto riots broke out again in August and I went out again to cover them. I saw, and photographed, people being assaulted by the police for taking part in "stay-away" days (refusing to go to work in a kind of general strike). On one occasion while I was taking pictures, a white policeman attacked me and smashed my nose; I had to spend five days in Baragwanath Hospital.

I suppose that the worst thing I saw was Zulu men from the hostels who armed themselves with knobkerries, assegais, and shields and went right through the township systematically breaking down doors and windows and assaulting people. These were men from tribal areas far away, living as single men in the hostels in Soweto. They resented being told what to do by the students. It was easy for the police to encourage them to fight other blacks, and this is exactly what happened. I saw it myself. When I went to a police station to report what the Zulus were doing the police asked me what I expected them to do. "Why doesn't black power fight back?" they said. And later that day when I went into another police station and found it full of blood and packed with women and children who had been injured by the Zulus, I was told by an officer in charge that black power must taste its own medicine.

On following days I tried to cover the actions of the Zulus in Soweto and saw how when the residents attempted to fight back, the police would attack them with tear-gas bombs. Several times the police warned me to get out of the area. I knew that trouble for me was on the way. At last on August 26 I was detained again; they had enough of my nuisance. I was locked up under Section 10 of the Internal Security Act, without charges, in Modder Bee Prison in Johannesburg. I was not in solitary, but again my life was shattered, my freedom taken away from me, and my cameras put to rest. . . .

I do not know what will happen next to me. I will go on working in South Africa, taking the best pictures that I can. I hope they will not all be pictures of violence.

Yet as long as there is no dialogue between the government of South Africa and the black man, there will be no turning point from violence. As long as the government is not prepared to recognize the black man as a citizen and give him his full rights in the country of his birth, I can see no change except for the worse. The black man does not want to drive the white man into the ocean. White and black should share the fruits of the country equally and together. . . .

CHAPTER THIRTEEN

SEX AND AGE STRATIFICATION

Sex and age are the most universal criteria for social stratification. In every known society, the sexes and the age categories have (or have had) different roles and positions in the social hierarchy. In this chapter we will explore some of the causes of stratification by gender and by age in societies similar to those from which our own evolved; some of the effects these past patterns have had on our society; and some of the ways in which patterns have been changed by industrialization. We will also look at the circumstances in which people in particular sex and age categories have become conscious of themselves as having distinct and separate interests.

Stratification by gender and by age has only recently attracted serious, systematic attention from sociologists, and much is still unknown. Renewed interest in this area has been kindled by the political activities of women, the young, and the elderly, and by dramatic changes in the condition of people of these three categories. These developments, in turn, have provoked debates about what the roles of men and women should be at work and in the family, and about whether the young and the old should be better integrated into the mainstream of society.

Are sex and age stratification similar to class and race stratification? Many sociologists, feminists, and others have pointed out strong parallels. One similarity is that a person's sex, age, and race are all *ascribed* (assigned) rather than *achieved* statuses (see Chapter 10). In addition, women and the elderly share several characteristics with racial minorities. One is high visibility. Blacks, for example, stand out because of their skin color; women because of their unique physiological features; and old people because of their white hair, wrinkles, or other signs of age. Furthermore, all three groups have been objects of discrimination rationalized by the majority. It was thought, for example, that blacks were "happy in their place" and that "a woman's place is in the home." Such myths served to justify barring these groups from supervisory positions, political importance, and social and professional integration (Hacker, 1951).

In spite of these striking resemblances, there are important differences that set sex and age stratification apart from racial discrimination. Of the utmost significance is the fact that role differentiation and ranking by age and sex are intricately woven into the fabric of the family in a way that is not true of class or race. In the family, affection, authority, resentment, and reverence are so intertwined as to complicate all our beliefs and feelings about age and sex. Moreover, although there is massive evidence of inequality between men and women and between age groups, these disparities are not always matters of simple oppression. Women, for instance, are "the only exploited group that has been placed on a pedestal by its oppressor" (Gray, 1976); young people in our society "are simultaneously the most indulged and oppressed part of the population" (Coleman et al., 1974). We need, then, to take a fresh look at these forms of stratification.

Gender-role differentiation and sex stratification

To study the relationships between men and women in sociological terms, we need to look first at their different roles. As we saw in Chapter 6, most of us are taught from birth to see certain roles as befitting men, others as befitting women. Those thus differentiated include not only *sex roles*—the "natural" roles taken in sexual reproduction—but also *gender roles*—nonreproductive behaviors considered suitable and sometimes obligatory for each sex in a society. Gender roles cover a wide variety of behaviors, from appropriate occupations to intricate distinctions in style and manner (Gagnon, 1977). In past years, particularly in the past one hundred years, men in the middle class of our society have been expected to work for money in the outside "real" world, while women have been expected to stay home tending the children and keeping house. Men have been expected to be active, to exemplify aggression, reason, and self-control, while women have been expected to be passive, submissive, irrational, and emotional. Although belief in these norms has been undermined in recent years, particularly by the resurgence of the women's movement, notions about what is masculine behavior and what is feminine are deeply rooted and persistent in our culture.

GENDER ROLES IN CROSS-CULTURAL PERSPECTIVE

The evidence anthropologists have gathered about other societies reveals a striking fact: our traditional beliefs about "suitable" masculine and feminine roles are not universally shared. This point was illustrated by George P. Murdock's extensive survey (1937) of the sexual division of labor as seen across cultures (see Table 13.1), which, although carried out almost two generations ago, appears still valid. In Murdock's findings there is a broad pattern that fits, to some degree, our modern Western conceptions of gender roles: in the vast majority of societies the tasks involved in hunting and the collection of most raw materials are done by men, while those connected with "domestic" life—food collection and preparation, child care, and clothing manufacture—are ordinarily done by women. Yet within this pattern there is great diversity. In some societies agriculture, trade, pottery making, or house building is the province of men; in others, these tasks are done exclusively by women. In fact, of the tasks Murdock surveyed, there are very few that a man does in one culture that a woman doesn't do in another. It can therefore be concluded that "it is not the nature of the task, but rather the cultural assignment of the task to one sex or the other that determines who will undertake it" (Grambs and Waetjen, 1975, p. 14; italics deleted).

A similar conclusion can be reached regarding the behavioral traits considered masculine or feminine, which vary tremendously from culture to culture: "If those temperamental attitudes which we have traditionally regarded as feminine—such as passivity, responsiveness, and a willingness to cherish children—can so easily be set up as the masculine pattern in one tribe, and, in another, be outlawed for the majority of women as for the majority of men," Margaret Mead argued in a classic study, "we no longer have any basis for regarding aspects of such behavior as sex-linked" (1935, pp. 279–280).

Since both the work roles and the behavioral expectations assigned to the sexes vary greatly from one society to the next, we might also expect to see great variability in the sexes' relative standing. But here we encounter a puzzle: no matter what tasks are assigned to men and to women in a culture, the work considered economically or politically more valuable is that done

TABLE 13.1

COMPARATIVE DATA ON THE DIVISION OF LABOR BY SEX

ACTIVITY	NUMBER OF SOCIETIES IN WHICH:				
	MEN ALWAYS DO IT	MEN USUALLY DO IT	EITHER SEX MAY DO IT	WOMEN USUALLY DO IT	WOMEN ALWAYS DO IT
Metal working	78	0	0	0	0
Weapon making	121	1	0	0	0
Pursuit of sea mammals	34	1	0	0	0
Hunting	166	13	0	0	0
Manufacture of musical instruments	45	2	0	0	1
Boat building	91	4	4	0	1
Mining and quarrying	35	1	1	0	1
Work in wood and bark	113	9	5	1	1
Work in stone	68	3	2	0	2
Trapping or catching of small animals	128	13	4	1	2
Lumbering	104	4	3	1	6
Work in bone, horn, and shell	67	4	3	0	3
Fishing	98	34	19	3	4
Manufacture of ceremonial objects	37	1	13	0	1
Herding	38	8	4	0	5
House building	86	32	25	3	14
Clearing of land for agriculture	73	22	17	5	13
Net making	44	6	4	2	11
Trade	51	28	20	8	7
Dairy operations	17	4	3	1	13
Manufacture of ornaments	24	3	40	6	18
Agriculture: soil preparation and planting	31	23	33	20	37
Manufacture of leather products	29	3	9	3	32
Body mutilations, for example, tattooing	16	14	44	22	20
Erection and dismantling of shelter	14	2	5	6	22
Hide preparation	31	2	4	4	49
Tending of fowls and small animals	21	4	8	1	39
Agriculture: crop tending and harvesting	10	15	35	39	44
Gathering of shellfish	9	4	8	7	25
Manufacture of nontextile fabrics	14	0	9	2	32
Fire making and tending	18	6	25	22	62
Burden bearing	12	6	35	20	57
Preparation of drinks and narcotics	20	1	13	8	57
Manufacture of thread and cordage	23	2	11	10	73
Basket making	25	3	10	6	82
Mat making	16	2	6	4	61
Weaving	19	2	2	6	67
Gathering of fruits, berries, and nuts	12	3	15	13	63
Fuel gathering	22	1	10	19	89
Pottery making	13	2	6	8	77
Preservation of meat and fish	8	2	10	14	74
Manufacture and repair of clothing	12	3	8	9	95
Gathering of herbs, roots, and seeds	8	1	11	7	74
Cooking	5	1	9	28	158
Water carrying	7	0	5	7	119
Grain grinding	2	4	5	13	114

SOURCE: Adapted from Murdock, 1937.

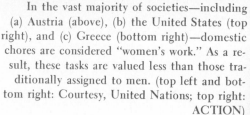

In the vast majority of societies—including (a) Austria (above), (b) the United States (top right), and (c) Greece (bottom right)—domestic chores are considered "women's work." As a result, these tasks are valued less than those traditionally assigned to men. (top left and bottom right: Courtesy, United Nations; top right: ACTION)

by men. It appears that in every society men have gained the power of the legendary King Midas; they are able to transmute whatever they touch into the social gold of authority, while whatever women do is base metal by comparison.

The universality of this difference in status is matched by the fact that, according to Gough (1977), every known society has been, to one degree or another, *patriarchal*—ruled by men. Although many cultures feature myths to the contrary, Gough points out that there is no evidence that any society has actually been *matriarchal*—ruled by women. "This does not mean," he cautions, "that women and men have never had relations that were dignified and creative for both sexes, appropriate to the knowledge, skills, and technology of their times. Nor does it mean that the sexes cannot be equal in the future, or that sexual division of labor cannot be abolished" (1971, p. 761). But still, women so far have been everywhere the subordinate gender—or, in Simone de Beauvoir's words, "the second sex" (1953).

THE ORIGINS OF GENDER-ROLE SEGREGATION AND INEQUALITY

Various attempts, none of them complete or satisfactory, have been made to explain the sexual division of labor and the unequal valuations of men's and women's contributions. While most of these explanations are based partly on physiological differences between the sexes, biology alone cannot account entirely for gender roles or their valuation. The wide variety in the content of the sexual division of labor indicates that this is not a simple case of biological determinism. (For a more detailed exploration of this issue, see the box "The Sexes: Biology and Behavior.")

THE SEXES: BIOLOGY AND BEHAVIOR

When Sigmund Freud made his often-quoted observation that "anatomy is destiny," he was merely giving pointed form to a very old idea. For centuries, most people had taken it for granted that God, or "nature," had provided men and women with profoundly different temperaments and behavioral tendencies to go with the physical differences in their reproductive anatomy. Some nineteenth-century thinkers, for example, asserted that women represented a lower evolutionary stage than men; others claimed that women's metabolisms were more plantlike than men's. Quite typical was the opinion of one social scientist that "neither political nor technological change could alter the temperamental tendency for males to be active and aggressive and females to be quiescent and passive" (Geddes, cited in Conway, 1973, p. 144).

Nowadays, however, it is not uncommon to hear the diametrically opposite position being vehemently argued: namely, that women differ from men in personality and behavior *only* as a result of their upbringing and social conditioning. The old stereotypes—that women are more emotional, passive, nurturant, while men are more rational, aggressive, independent—have been dismissed by many writers as either false or, if true, the product of social rather than biological forces, of feminine socialization rather than female genes. Today most social scientists tend to agree that social factors do indeed play the decisive part in shaping gender roles. (This subject is explored in Chapter 6.)

Nevertheless, it seems possible that genetic factors may also play *some* part—though the exact extent of their influence is unclear—in predisposing men and women to different patterns of behavior. As with so many other aspects of the debate between heredity and environment, clear evidence on this question is hard to come by. Most of the significant research in this area has focused on one particular set of genetically determined influences: the influences of the sex hormones, a group of hormones whose concentration is different in the two sexes. Hormones are chemical messengers that are secreted into the bloodstream by a variety of glands and that help to regulate many aspects of our physiological functioning. It is reasonably well established that *estrogens*, the hormones that help to regulate female reproductive processes such as the menstrual cycle, can affect the individual's moods, emotions, and behavior in certain instances. Some women—though by no means all—find that they are unusually irritable and prone to depression around the onset of their menstrual period, when the level of estrogens in the blood is lowest; and psychologists have found that at this point in the menstrual cycle, women's feelings of anxiety seem to be relatively high and their self-esteem low, while two weeks later—around the time of ovulation, when estrogen levels are elevated—positive feelings are much stronger and anxiety less evident.

Less well established are the effects on behavior of the male hormones, or *androgens*. Ever since ancient times, it has been known that castration (removal of the testes, the chief source of androgens) will make many animals more docile. Human beings seem to be affected in much the same way. This has led many people to assume that androgens are associated with aggressiveness or competitiveness—an association reflected in the slang use of the word *balls* to mean courage, audacity, or toughness. Yet this assumption has also been questioned; one writer has recently asserted that "There is growing evidence for rejecting the view that androgen is the 'aggressive' hormone, responsible for sex differences in combativeness" (Rossi, 1977). Other research has suggested that hormone levels may be as much a *result* of certain sorts of behavior or social situations as a cause. In male monkeys, for example, it has been found that reduction in status within the group seems to lower levels of testosterone (the chief male hormone), while exposure to females, whom the male monkeys can dominate, causes a rise in testosterone production (Rose et al., 1968, 1969, 1971, 1972; Mazur, 1976).

Thus, the relationship between sex hormones and day-to-day behavior is still far from clear. But what about the influence of sex hormones on longer-lasting behavior patterns? One approach to this question is that of biologists John Money and Anke A. Ehrhardt (1972), who have investigated many cases of a special type of physiological "accident": the situation that occurs when a genetically female individual develops under the influence of male hormones. Some weeks after conception, the primitive sex glands of every normal fetus begin to develop into either testes or ovaries, depending on whether its genetic program is male or female. Beyond this point, the completion of sexual development is controlled largely by hormones—specifically, the androgens, which are secreted by the testes in the male and by the adrenal glands (in small quantities) in both sexes. Under the influence of the large quantities of androgens present in its bloodstream the male fetus develops the male sexual anatomy. The female fetus, having only small quantities of androgens, matures physically as a female. Occasionally, however, a female fetus may receive unusally large quantities of androgens from a malformed adrenal gland; a fetus of this type, though genetically female and usually possessing female internal reproductive organs (such as the uterus), will at birth tend to resemble a male in its external sexual anatomy.

It was a group of individuals of this type whom Money and Ehrhardt followed in their study. Of the group, all had been brought up by their parents as girls; plastic surgery had been employed to "correct" their physical appearance. Money and Ehrhardt were curious as to whether the heavy doses of male sex hormones had somehow programmed their subjects' nervous systems for behavior patterns not typical of ordinary girls. They found that most of the girls studied did seem quite "boyish" in their styles of play, choice of activities and games, preferences in clothing, and attitudes toward marriage and babies (generally negative or indifferent). Among the older girls, interest in the opposite sex was distinctly late in developing, and sexual fantasies were unusually rare.

Yet when Money and Ehrhardt studied a group of older women who had similar medical histories, they found that the biological influence on behavior had ultimately been far from decisive in the lives of these individuals. Despite having exhibited similarly boyish behavior and lack of interest in marriage and children in their youth, not one of the group studied felt that she had been raised in the "wrong" gender. More than half, indeed, had eventually married, and several had borne children and cared for them successfully. Money and Ehrhardt, along with others who have studied their work, concluded that sex hormones probably do affect the brain and thus influence, to some extent, the behavior patterns that an individual will tend to acquire: "fetal exposure to hormones may lay down propensities for male, as opposed to female, behavior after birth" (Rossi, 1977). Yet it is equally obvious that environmental factors can often override biological ones in psychosocial development.

We are still far from understanding fully the complex interaction between these two forces in shaping male and female identity. Passions on the subject continue to run high. In a recent essay, the sociologist Alice S. Rossi (1977) has noted that feminists have often felt compelled to adopt the position that there are no intrinsic behavioral differences between the sexes on political grounds—as a way of proclaiming the equality of men and women. She points out, however, that "different" does not necessarily mean "inferior"; even if men and women differ, women can still demand equal rights and equal respect. Rossi then goes on to discuss some of the evidence, drawn from recent research in anthropology, sociobiology, and endocrinology—such as that discussed above—that points toward at least the possibility of sex-related behavioral orientations. The fact that Rossi—herself a noted feminist as well as a social scientist—is willing to consider this possibility dispassionately and objectively, suggests that we may soon be ready to put both the myths of the nineteenth century and the sexual politics of recent years behind us and to examine the issues unswayed by either prejudice or ideology.

Functionalist explanations

Sociological explanations associated with the functionalist school tell us something about the origins of the division of labor between the sexes, but they are almost totally silent on the inequality that has developed in association with it. They suggest that every society is continually faced with two tasks—executing its purpose and keeping itself together. Because women must nurse and care for infants, they argue, efficiency dictates that men take on the "instrumental" roles of providing the means of subsistence and security and women take on the "expressive" roles of providing group cohesion and caring for children at all stages of their growth (Zelditch, in Parsons and Bales, 1955).

A close analysis of Murdock's survey findings, however, shows that women in many societies play a crucial "instrumental" role outside the home. While the functionalists assume that men are the family breadwinners, in the more than 800 societies examined women contribute an average of 44 percent of the family's subsistence (Aronoff and Crano, 1975). And a more recent paper (Crano and Aronoff, 1978) reports that fathers are increasingly sharing "expressive" tasks with their spouses; their participation in child care during infancy and early childhood has become especially notable.

Findings such as these suggest that other theoretical approaches might be useful as supplements or correctives to the functionalist view.

Conflict theories

Conflict theories of sex stratification trace differences in role content not to functional adaptations of the species as a whole but to differences in "class" interest between the two sexes. Some have suggested that the fear of rape was a causative factor in the subjugation of women to men (Brownmiller, 1975, p. 16). Another "conflict" theory, classic in this area, is that of Friedrich Engels, who argued that the subjection of women coincided with the emergence of a social surplus and the development of the state. Wanting to pass on property to their own offspring, men forced monogamy on women as the only way to be sure of their paternity. Kathleen Gough (1971, 1977), looking at Engels' ideas in the light of modern anthropological knowledge, also locates the systematic subordination of women in the development of the agriculturally based large states; but she traces its *early* beginnings, along with the sexual division of labor, to the dawn of hunting among hominids, when nursing women were not able to accompany the men far from home.

In Greece, the social structure permits men to do very little work. According to conflict theories, once such a pattern of sex stratification is established, it is in the interest of the dominant group—men—to maintain it.
(Susan Shapiro)

Some of these ideas are very suggestive, but much about the origins of gender-role segregation and the subordination of women remains pure speculation. Gender-role segregation *may* originally have had adaptive functions related to the survival needs of hunting and gathering societies. There were, perhaps, no *inevitable* connections between this role segregation and the inequality that went with it, but as technologies became increasingly elaborate and more wealth was produced, role differences between men and women meant differences in their access to property, power, and prestige. (For a survey of sex stratification in hunting and gathering, horticultural, and agrarian societies, see Chapter 10.)

Whatever the original cause of sex stratification in a society, once the pattern is established it is in the inter-est of the dominant group (men) to maintain it. Accordingly, it is reinforced and supported by a variety of powerful social-psychological and social-control mechanisms. These mechanisms, in certain respects parallel to those that help to sustain the stratification of ethnic and racial groups, include sanctions, stereotypes, and myths that help both dominant and subordinate individuals to perceive their positions as legitimate; they also include socialization patterns that transmit gender roles from one generation to the next (see box).

Sex stratification is, then, a phenomenon whose particular form is in part related to a society's technological patterns, but which is also reflected in and supported by language, art, and institutional norms passed down from generation to generation as part of the culture. It has been observed that different elements of the culture change at different rates. Ogburn (1927) termed this *cultural lag*. Generally, cultural patterns such as words, stories, and stereotypes change more slowly than technology; this point should be borne in mind when we look at sex stratification in any one era. In our own era there is particularly marked tension between traditional norms and values and the new roles offered to the sexes by technological change. Bottle

HOW SEX STRATIFICATION IS SUSTAINED

Like racial and ethnic inequalities, sex stratification, once begun, is perpetuated by powerful forces. These include: the transmission of gender roles from one generation to the next through socialization; a mythology that legitimates the respective positions of dominant and subordinate alike in an unequal system; sex stereotyping; and a set of "ultimate" sanctions.

SOCIALIZATION

In Chapter 6 we saw how gender roles are inculcated in children. Much of what people see around them appears to confirm that men are naturally dominant. At home it is usually the man who makes the important decisions. At work it is usually the man who commands, the woman who assists and obeys—doctor and nurse, business executive and secretary, dentist and technician. And everyday patterns of behavior accustom both men and women to their respective places. Men usually initiate encounters with women—dates, sex, marriage—while the rituals of the man paying for dates, opening doors, and walking on the outside have come to signify that the woman is in need of protection and support (Henley and Freeman, 1975).

Gender-role segregation and inequality tend to be self-confirming in another way. Differences in socialization encourage differences in behavior. People observe these differences, infer that they are physiologically based, and

then argue that physiology dictates that the status quo in gender roles be maintained. "This is the perspective subscribed to by most behavioral scientists, clinical psychologists, and psychoanalysts," one sociologist claims, "despite the fact that the women they have studied and analyzed are the products of a society that systematically *produces* such sex differences through childrearing and schooling practices. There is no way of allocating observed sex differences to innate physiology or to socio-cultural conditioning" (Rossi, 1976, p. 84).

MYTHS

An important way in which sex stratification is perpetuated is through myths. Their function is to demonstrate that women are by nature fit for inferior roles.

One central theme that is common in many societies' myths about men and women is the association of men with culture, women with fertility and nature. Men are the bearers of culture, women the bearers of children. Napoleon only put it most crudely when he said, "Women are nothing but machines for producing children" (quoted in Deckard, 1975, p. 3).

Women, as wives, mothers, witches, midwives, nuns, or whores, are defined almost exclusively in terms of their sexual functions. A witch, in European tradition, is a woman who sleeps with the devil; and a nun is a woman who marries her god. Again, purity and pollution are

feeding, birth control, automation, and labor-saving domestic devices, among other technological advances, have radically altered earlier conceptions of appropriate gender roles.

SEX STRATIFICATION AND THE INDUSTRIAL REVOLUTION

Prior to the Industrial Revolution, women had lower status than men but played an important and integrated part in the production system. Women's labor was needed, and men depended on women as much as women depended on men. For one thing, the home was often a locus of production. For another, housework, considered by many people today as the epitome of unskilled and mindless drudgery, required far more skill and had higher status in the preindustrial world. To take just one example, a great variety of skills was needed to transform the wool on a sheep's back into a shirt; today that shirt would either be purchased from a

department store or perhaps handmade as a hobby. In the family, a woman was valued not so much for what she shared with her husband as for her separate but necessary roles and for her contribution to the production of the family's subsistence.

With the coming of the Industrial Revolution, however, the status of certain work roles was diminished.* It is often noted that major casualties of the Industrial Revolution were the craftworkers, who could not compete with the cheaper, standardized factory production performed by semiskilled labor. But women, too, were casualties of the Industrial Revolution. Although preindustrial life had not been idyllic, and women did reap some of the benefits of technological change, the advent of industrialism stripped them of important economic roles by shifting a large part of domestic production to industrial settings (Abbott, 1909).

---

* Much of the rest of this section is based on the work of Joan Huber (1976).

ideas that apply primarily to women, who must either deny their physical bodies or circumscribe their dangerous sexuality. (Rosaldo, 1974, p. 31)

But there is a paradox here, because if women are unreasonable creatures, they nevertheless have the power to corrupt reasonable men. Eve is Everywoman in this conception. Morally weak because unable to resist temptation, she succumbs to the wiles of the serpent. But she possesses the power to seduce Adam. As sex incarnate, as tempestuous nature, as unreason, women have the power to destroy the culture men have built and therefore must be kept in a subservient position.

A second important theme in the myths about women emphasizes women's status as secondary to and derivative of men's. One aspect of this is that women are meant to serve their husbands. "Women's entire education," the French Enlightenment philosopher Jean-Jacques Rousseau announced, "should be planned in relation to men. To please men, to be useful to them, to win their love and respect . . . these are women's duties in all ages" (quoted in O'Faolain and Martines, 1973, p. 247). Another aspect emphasizes that women exist only in and through men. While men derive their status from the world, women derive theirs from the men to whom they are attached— "He for God only, she for God in him," as the English poet John Milton put it. Saint Augustine elaborated this idea when he argued that man alone or husband and wife together were "the image of God," but woman alone was not.

STEREOTYPING

A related way in which the gender-role system is perpetuated is by projecting stereotypes about each sex. Stereotyping, as we saw in Chapter 7, involves the casting of a diverse group of people into a single mental mold on the basis of some characteristic some members of the group may share. As society has moved increasingly toward embracing the idea of awarding social position on the basis of ability, stereotypes about the incompetence of women have become the most prominent. The famous "woman driver" is one example, while others play variations on this statement about women that appeared in an 1848 medical text: "She has a head almost too small for intellect but just big enough for love" (quoted in Ehrenreich and English, 1973).

What stereotyping ignores is that, regarding many aspects of behavior, variations within each sex are greater than variations between the sexes. "Still," says one social scientist of her colleagues, "in reporting research findings we tend to concentrate on the 10-point difference between, say, the average black child and the average white child, overlooking the 50-point spread between the highest and the lowest child among blacks and among whites. And so, analogously, do we look at distributions of sex differences. . . . Despite all the evidence of great intrasex differences . . . we still speak—and think—as though 'women' were a homogeneous population" (Bernard, in Kaplan and Bean, 1976, p. 17). In any case, discrimination

What were some of the factors that prevented women from taking on industrial roles to the same degree and for the same rewards as men? Most crucial, perhaps, were pregnancy and child-care responsibilities. Though the birth rate had already begun to drop (a phenomenon characteristic of industrialization, discussed in Chapter 19), women still had what we would consider large families, which kept them at home at least part of the time. Then, too, alarmed by the falling birth rate, governments were unwilling to support programs encouraging women to work in factories, which might make it seem desirable to avoid childbearing. In addition, working-class women were in demand as nurses for middle-class children; the norms of the time dictated that middle-class women merely bear the children and adorn the home (Stern, 1944, p. 444), but that they not do any work.

When women did work, their wages were lower than men's in jobs open to both sexes as well as in sex-segregated jobs such as teaching, nursing, and clerical work. Those who had to work to supplement their

husbands' meager earnings were vulnerable to exploitation by employers, who could use women's labor to undercut the bargaining power of men (Fuller, 1944). In addition, laws were enacted that limited the work settings and hours of women. Middle-class humanitarians viewed women as needing protection from the fatigue, dirt, and danger of early industrial jobs; working-class men viewed women as competitors. Thus, for a number of reasons, women were prevented from putting in the long hours of steady work needed to achieve seniority. In addition, they were excluded from labor unions (Chafe, 1972) and from opportunities for training and education (Abbott, 1909; Clark, 1919; Holcombe, 1973).

While these and other factors combined to edge women out of full and equal participation in the industrial labor force, they did gain a toehold in light industry and clerical work. Over the past hundred years, the expansion of white-collar jobs, combined with the continuing drop in the birth rate (see Chapters 11 and 19), has brought more and more women into the work force.

against women on the basis of intersex differences, Bernard argues, would be analogous to denying all men driver's licenses because men are more likely than women to be color-blind.

SANCTIONS

"Everything which is usual appears natural," John Stuart Mill wrote in 1869 in his treatise on the subjection of women. "The subjection of women to men being a universal custom, any departure from it quite naturally appears unnatural" (quoted in Deckard, 1975, p. 9). Perhaps the most common sanction against people who stray from their gender roles is to label them unnatural to their sex. Thus, women who deviate from the "feminine" norm are stigmatized as "bitches" or "dykes."

More serious sanctions abound. It is men, after all, who control the instruments of force and the machinery of state. And at the personal level, the greater physical strength of many men makes domestic tyranny possible, as the not uncommon cases of wife-beating attest.

Women have, in addition, been barred from many roles in past and present societies by taboo or written law, which both codify stratification and legitimize the punishment of deviations from it. Historically, Western legal systems have systematically discriminated against women. In England and, to a lesser extent, the United States, the informing principle of women's legal position has been English common law. Upon marriage, women underwent "civil death." In the words of Sir William Blackstone, the great eighteenth-century English jurist,

"By marriage, the husband and wife are one person in law; that is, the very being or legal existence of the woman is suspended during the marriage, or at least is incorporated and consolidated" (1872).

The men who made the laws apparently agreed with Rousseau's dictum that "Women have, or ought to have, but little liberty" (quoted in Swerdloff, 1975, p. 11), for women were placed under virtual house arrest. In many areas, they could not own property, make contracts on their own, and, upon marriage, ceded their rights to their own earnings and their children to their husbands. Although particulars have often varied from state to state, throughout the nineteenth century and extending well into our own time there have been laws barring women from sitting on juries, laws imposing stiff penalties for female adultery but little or none for male, and laws providing greater punishment for women than for men who committed the same crime. In addition, there were paternalistic laws meant for women's "own good," such as protective labor legislation; and there have been laws that were indirectly discriminatory in that they affected women more than men, such as those prohibiting contraception and abortions.

In view of the fact that all these powerful forces have been at work to perpetuate it, it is not surprising that sex stratification has been so pervasive and enduring. What is surprising is the strength and rapid spread in recent years of the determination of many women—and some men—to overcome these forces and to destroy the inequities of stratification by sex.

Whereas in 1890 women constituted only 17 percent of the work force, and only 18 percent of women worked, in 1978 women made up 41 percent of the labor force and 49.1 percent of all women were either working or looking for a job. At first, the large majority of working women were young and single, planning to work for only a few years to save money for their marriages. They thus held all the "right" ideas and were no threat to the established system. During and after World War II, however, married women began to enter the work force in appreciable numbers. Recently, a complex set of demographic factors resulting in fewer young unmarried women workers has contributed to a trend in which more and more married women with children have gone to work outside the home (Oppenheimer, 1973); by 1978, 41.6 percent of married women who worked had children under 6 (Census Bureau, 1979, p. 359). As Joan Huber puts it, "The (middle-class)

working woman is no longer a deviant, obliged to explain why she works" (1976, p. 381), and the working-class working woman is no longer an object of pity.

WOMEN IN THE MODERN INDUSTRIAL ECONOMY

Women are still on an unequal footing in the industrial economy, and their life chances are different from those of men. A variety of indexes can be used to demonstrate this pattern—mental health, "human capital" (which measures occupational attainment for any given educational level), mobility, and others. Here we look at three basic indexes: occupational distribution, earnings, and education.

Occupational distribution

First of all, though women now make up a larger percentage of the work force than ever before, their distribution by occupation is not the same as men's. They do not, for example, have an equal share of professional jobs. The percentage of women among professionals and technological workers, having increased early in the century, has actually been declining since the 1940s and is now about the same as it was in 1900 (Udry, 1974). The disparities between men and women are especially great in the most prestigious professions—medicine (except nursing), law, government, and so on (see Table 13.2).

The jobs women *have* filled have been concentrated in a few areas, which have come to be thought of as "female" occupations—nursing, social work, library science, elementary-school teaching, retail sales, clerical jobs (about three-quarters of the workers in this category are women), domestic service (where women make up close to 100 percent), and miscellaneous service jobs (waitress, hairdresser, and the like). In fact, almost half the women who entered the labor force between 1950 and 1960 ended up in jobs that were already 70 percent or more female.

Earnings

The gap between earnings of men and women is large and has generally been growing wider in recent years. In 1950, women's median wage was only 65 percent of men's. By 1970, it had shrunk to 59 percent; it crept up to only 60 percent in 1975 and was back down to 58 percent in 1977 (see Table 13.3). Married women in the labor force earn an average of only about half as much as their husbands (Treiman and Terrell, 1975, p. 198).

TABLE 13.2

PERCENTAGES OF MALES IN PRESTIGIOUS PROFESSIONS

PROFESSION	1940	1950	1960	1970	1979
Architects	97.7	96.0	97.7	96.5	94.0
Authors	63.9	61.2	74.4	70.7	N.A.
College presidents and faculty	73.5	76.8	78.1	71.6	N.A.
Lawyers and judges	97.6	96.7	96.2	95.2	87.6
Physicians and surgeons	95.4	93.8	93.0	90.8	89.3
Social and welfare workers	35.7	30.8	37.2	37.3	35.7
Teachers	24.3	25.4	28.3	29.8	29.2
Librarians	10.5	10.9	14.3	18.1	19.1
Photographers	86.3	82.7	88.0	86.2	78.5

N.A. = Not available.

SOURCE: Census data as cited in Udry, 1974, p. 31. Data for 1979 from Labor Department, 1980.

During World War II, married women began to enter the work force in significant numbers. Here, women in California assemble nose cones for fighter planes.

TABLE 13.3

WOMEN'S MEDIAN WAGE AS PERCENT OF MEN'S

YEAR	PERCENT
1950	65
1955	64
1956	63
1957	64
1958	63
1959	61
1960	61
1961	59
1962	60
1963	60
1964	60
1965	60
1966	58
1967	58
1968	58
1969	61
1970	59
1975	60
1977	58
1978	60

SOURCES: Labor Department, 1970, p. 1. Figures for 1975, 1977, and 1978 from Census Bureau, 1978.

The factors usually seen as "reasons" for these differences—higher quitting rate, greater absenteeism, less education—account for very little of the disparity. One factor that *is* significant is the occupational distribution of the sexes. As we have seen, most working women hold low-prestige jobs, and these occupations simply do not pay as well as those that men are more likely to pursue. Nevertheless one study of men and women workers has shown that even when the extent of education, occupational status, work experience, and proportion of year worked were held constant, women still earned only 62 percent of men's income (Suter and Miller, 1973)—a pattern these authors attribute to simple sex discrimination in wage rates. However, it is easier to claim discrimination than to prove it: one recent study of the reward system for scientists concludes that "the functionally irrelevant statuses of sex and religion are *not* influential in determining several forms of recognition in the stratification system of American sciences" (Cole and Cole, 1976, p. 82; italics added).

Education

In education, women and men have been equal in the median number of school years completed for over three decades (Udry, 1974), but women have regularly received a considerably smaller percentage of the advanced degrees awarded (see Table 13.4). It is true that

TABLE 13.4

PERCENTAGE OF ACADEMIC DEGREES EARNED BY WOMEN, 1890–1978

YEAR	B.A.	M.A.	PH.D.
1890	17%	19%	1%
1900	19	19	6
1910	23	26	10
1920	34	30	15
1930	40	40	15
1940	41	38	13
1950	24	29	10
1960	35	35	11
1970	42	40	13
1973	42	41.5	17.8
1978	47.1	48.3	26.4

SOURCES: Labor Department, 1969, and Blitz, 1974, p. 38. Figures for 1973 are from Census Bureau, 1976, p. 146, and figures for 1978 are from National Center for Education Statistics, 1980.

the proportion of women getting such degrees rose significantly during the 1950s and 1960s, but this only restored them to the same relative position they had held forty years before. And the proportion of Ph.D.s going to women was only slightly smaller in 1920 (15 percent) than in 1973 (17.8 percent), though it has risen to 25.4 percent in 1978.

Though the figure is rising, it is clear that women still experience difficulty in attaining professional status. Women's educational and occupational choices are a two-edged sword: "Barriers to occupational attainment are found within educational institutions, and discouragement from educational goals is often based upon assessments of occupational barriers" (Lipman-Blumen and Tickamyer, 1975, p. 307).

CHANGES IN THE SEX STRATIFICATION SYSTEM

Revival of the women's movement

Given the inequities between men and women in such basic areas as earnings and jobs, it is not surprising that many women have for many years experienced a sense of common interests and common aims analogous to "class consciousness." Organized political action on the part of women, aimed at reforming education, industrial working conditions, and discriminatory laws, dates back to the period after the Civil War. But after the ratification in 1920 of the Nineteenth Amendment, which gave women the right to vote, feminism as a mass-based social movement disappeared. It was not until the mid-1960s that enough changes had taken place in women's perception of their situation for a mass-based women's movement to take hold once again.

Joan Huber (1976) has traced mass participation in the women's movement to the increasing numbers of married women, especially young women with children, who were drawn into the labor force in the 1940s and after. During the 1950s—the years of the postwar "baby boom" (a demographic phenomenon to be discussed in Chapter 19)—child care and family life were glorified in books and the mass media. But women were attaining higher educational levels. By the 1960s many more middle-class women were conscious of being dissatisfied with housework and baby tending as a full-time occupation. The time was ripe for rebellion among "middle-of-the-roaders" and progressives alike; the mood of this period is captured in Betty Friedan's book *The Feminine Mystique* (1963). In 1966, Friedan helped to found the National Organization for Woman (NOW), which today has a large middle-class membership. It aims at instituting paid maternity leave and publicly supported child care, and at ending sex discrimination in employment and education; its methods of promoting change (especially through legislation) are primarily "within the system." Other, more radical groups have organized rape clinics, shelters for battered women, child-care centers, women's centers, self-defense classes, and legal counseling services (Freeman, 1975). "Anti-establishment" methods such as collective action are employed by these more radical groups, and targets for change include women's own world views and sense of self (hence the spread of "consciousness-raising groups").

Achievements of the women's movement

The greatest success of the women's movement has been the substantial shift toward greater equality in legal status. Legislation passed in the last two decades guarantees women equal pay for equal work and makes sex-based discrimination illegal. Nevertheless, the Equal Rights Amendment—a major piece of legislation that reads quite simply, "Equality of rights under the law shall not be denied or abridged by the United States or by any State on account of sex"—has yet to be passed. There are also other areas in which the women's movement has to date not had total success. An unresolved problem in industrial society is the continuing need for supportive services in the home. If a man works all day outside the home, he has less time to take on domestic duties; these responsibilities then continue to be allocated largely to women even when they too hold outside jobs. A study by Robert Tsuchigane and Norton Dodge (1974) indicates that *if* women shared domestic responsibilities with men, and *if* they were not the objects of differential socialization, their pay, occupational distributions, and rates of labor-force participation would be the same as men's. But so far only a few men have taken on an equal share of housework (Coser and Rokoff, 1971; Hedges and Barnett, 1972), and the proportion of children being cared for in group facilities is still small (Labor Department, 1975, p. 33).

The greatest success of the women's movement has been the trend toward equality in legal status between men and women. However, the Equal Rights Amendment, whose terms appear on the banner held by these demonstrators, has not yet been ratified. (© Lawrence Frank 1979)

Prospects for the future

Whether change in the occupational structure will be favorable to women in the near future is not certain. Many of the "female" occupations tend to be located in the smaller and more competitive industries of the American economy, which cannot raise wages without the risk of going under. In contrast, the large, more unionized, and predominantly male corporations, because of their near-monopoly position, are able to pass on wage increases to the consumer (Deckard, 1975). Blau (1976) predicts that in the present stagnant labor market, the "earnings gap" between men and women is not likely to close.

FEMINISTS IN SPAIN: GETTING ANGRY

In Madrid, eleven women were on trial for the serious crime of having had abortions. To protest this trial, 300 women locked themselves into the main courthouse. Outside, men brandishing clubs and hurling insults gathered their strength and then attacked, forcing the women to flee. This tale of passion and persecution might almost be mistaken for an episode in some medieval chronicle, but in fact it appeared in a *New York Times* report on feminism in Spain.

In many ways, Spanish women are still living in the middle ages, and change, when it occurs, is hard-won, indeed. For example, in the trial mentioned above, it took an open letter signed by 1,300 prominent Spanish women, all of whom announced that they, too, had had abortions, to get the case dismissed. And at that, the presiding judge based his decision on a technicality, so that the law against abortion remained on the books.

In Spain's larger cities, women behave and dress like their counterparts elsewhere in Western Europe; increasingly, they ignore taboos against premarital sex; they belong to women's organizations, attend feminist seminars; frequent feminist bookstores, and patronize bars and other gathering places where men are not welcome. And yet, despite these signs of strength and feminist consciousness, it was only five years ago that the Spanish government altered the rigid and patriarchal civil code that placed women in the category of deaf mutes, the mentally incompetent, and minors.

An opinion poll taken in early 1980 shows that five years after the death of Spain's autocratic ruler Generalissimo Francisco Franco, neither the growth of political democracy nor of the women's movement has had much of an impact upon established ways of thinking. For instance, 63 percent of a cross section of Spanish women said they do not consider themselves the equals of men (versus 27 percent who did), and 37 percent said they did not participate as equals in conversation with men (versus 35 percent who do). Seventy-one percent of the women were "absolutely against" the legalization of abortion—even though some 300,000 abortions are said to be performed in Spain every year, with as many as 10,000 women dying as a result of crude methods used.

In fact, a well-known lawyer in Madrid told the *Times*, Spain's feminists have yet to achieve a major legal victory. "Only two laws have been changed," she said. "Women are no longer being sent to jail for adultery, and contraceptives have been decriminalized." A proposed revision of the paternity code, she added, was dying of ne-

Meanwhile, there are other barriers to equality between the sexes. Much of what happens between the sexes goes on in the home, where legislation doesn't reach; any push toward greater equality can easily result in marital strains (Rossi, 1969). As Alice S. Rossi has also pointed out, women, unlike black people, are not residentially concentrated and therefore cannot exert the same kind of collective pressure blacks can. Furthermore, wide class and race differences in women's attitudes and interests serve to undercut a united movement.

Among men, there have not yet been large-scale changes in attitude in regard to matters that bear on sex inequality. In a study surveying the attitudes of male Ivy League college students toward the careers of their future wives, it was found that 24 percent expected to marry women who did not work outside the home and 48 percent favored their wives working until they had children, then staying home to take care of the children, and perhaps returning to work when the children were older. Only 7 percent of the men said that they would be willing to alter the course of their own careers in order to foster those of their wives (Komarovsky, 1973).

Among women, however, there have been signifi-

cant shifts in attitudes in recent years. In one study, for example, about 50 percent of the women polled between 1958 and 1969 said they would vote for a qualified woman of their own party for president—fewer, incidentally, than men who answered "yes" to the same question. But when the question was asked again in 1972, 69 percent said they would, and the differences between men's and women's responses had disappeared (Feree, 1974). Other studies also show considerable shifts in recent decades, with employed and more educated women tending to express the most egalitarian attitudes. A review of five opinion surveys shows that women are today more likely to believe that men and women should share housework, that women should have equal pay and equal opportunity, that it is not harmful for children if the mother works, and that it is not necessarily more important for a woman to help her husband's career than to have one herself. Interestingly, these attitude changes began to occur *before* the spread of the women's movement, and the subsequent changes are not easily traced to that movement (Mason, Czajka, and Arber, 1976; Thornton and Freedman, 1979).

However, the feminist movement may be having some impact on moves toward sexual equality that are

glect in the parliament, partly due to the reluctance of many men to accept a law that would force them to recognize their illegitimate children, and partly due to the resistance of the powerful Roman Catholic Church.

The church is not the only obstacle to progress for women in Spain. Another strong influence is the deep-rooted tradition of "machismo," or male supremacy. In general, Spanish feminists do not agree whether they should conduct their struggle only in the context of political subordination, or whether they should also direct their energies at all structures of male domination. But for some feminists who belong to the tiny communist movement, there is no doubt. One of their leaders recently pointed out that from a communist perspective, working-class men are among the oppressed groups in society, but from a feminist point of view, these men are also oppressors. "We are enslaved by the powerful, and at the same time we are enslaved by the oppressed," she told a rally of 3,000 feminists. "We must be against capitalism and against men."

Even progressive Spanish men are not yet convinced that anything needs to be done. When one left-wing magazine called El Viejo Topo conducted a round-table discussion on "the crisis of macho," the participants at the conference all concluded that the subject did not exist.

And even in Catalonia and Barcelona, which were never subjected to Napoleonic laws governing family matters, and where married women therefore possess property rights, the conservative influence of machismo continued to make itself felt. One lawyer in Barcelona observes angrily that there are children registered as the offspring of unknown fathers, even when everyone knows exactly who the father is. "I have even had cases of public scandal," she said, "brought by husbands when their wives refused to sleep with them for one night."

Thus, the Times report concludes, the prospects for Spain's feminist movement is one of "gradualism" and "piecemeal victories." Notes one lawyer, "There is a certain disenchantment with politics today, and this has affected the feminist movement. There has been some backsliding." Another lawyer, this one in Barcelona, argues that politics are less important to the movement's success than economics. "So few women work in Spain," she explains. "It's a question of economic pressure." But, she adds, small signs of change can still be seen. "It's difficult to go to a meeting in which someone doesn't talk about the rights of women. At least men are beginning to be a little ashamed of themselves."

now taking place in society. An increasing number of divorcing fathers press for custody of their children, and several major corporations and government offices have introduced more flexible work schedules to assist employees who have special needs and interests, for example. Furthermore, it has been argued (Greiff and Munter, 1979) that today's upper-level corporate management prefers to recruit individuals who balance personal, family, and organizational concerns rather than those who resemble the "organization man."

Predictions concerning the future of sex stratification in the United States are still tentative. In a cross-cultural study, Weiss, Ramirez, and Tracy (1976) have shown that economic and political development increases the participation of women on the lower rungs of the labor force, but the crucial factor in increasing participation at all levels, including the upper rungs, is women's increased entry into colleges and graduate schools: women's penetration of one high-status institutional area seems to have a positive effect on their penetration of another high-status institutional area. But answers to related questions—such as whether the women's movement will have significant long-range effects or whether change, if it comes, will result from other factors—remain unknown. Similarly, more subtle changes in attitudes, values, and role prescriptions for traditionally gender-linked social positions cannot be predicted on the basis of present trends.

Stratification by age

Age stratification, like stratification by gender, is a universal phenomenon. Every society has graded its members by age and on that basis accorded differential treatment and access to social resources. But in contrast to what we have seen of sex stratification, in industrialized societies at least, there has been a distinct shift in the age group that holds dominant status and power. Historically, in almost every society, there has been ambivalence toward old age and youth (Fischer, 1977; Thomas, 1977); but authority, both within and outside the family, has increased with age. Propertied (male) elders of a society were its leaders, and relative age de-

There is a historic ambivalence toward old age. Although we are taught to "respect our elders," old people tend to be pushed to the sidelines of economic, social, and political life. (A. Keler/Sygma)

termined succession. Today, life expectancy has lengthened. People aged forty to sixty are what we think of as the middle-aged; these are the people in power in most arenas of economic, social, and political life. The young are barred from the field and the "old" (people aged sixty and above) are pushed to the sidelines. Age stratification in our society, then, is "curvilinear" (Elder, 1975). The changes in a person's social power and status tend to trace the same trajectory as bodily growth and decline, rising from birth to its height at midlife, then diminishing toward death. To understand this and other elements of age stratification, we need first to examine the two dimensions of this stratification: age strata and age cohorts.

THE TWO DIMENSIONS OF AGE STRATIFICATION

If we were to descend into the earth, it would be like taking an expedition into the past. Discrete strata, or layers formed at progressively earlier periods in geological time would become visible as we went down. Society's age structure is somewhat similar: If you arrange people according to age, you see not only successive stages of individual development and decline but also different slices of history—people formed at different times and, like geological strata, inevitably marked by their era of formation, and influenced even more by successive eras. Knowing someone's age, then, locates that person in two dimensions—in the individual life course and in history. Sociologists call the collections of people who share a common chronological age or stage in the life cycle *age strata*, and the collections of people born at particular historical periods *age cohorts*.

Age strata

Every society divides the life cycle into stages, distinguishing at least among childhood, adulthood, and old age. Each stage is differentiated from the others by a host of intertwining biological and social-psychological factors and by distinct roles and norms. Significant among the latter are age-graded behavioral expectations (see Chapter 6). Children in our society are allowed certain liberties of behavior not approved in adults, but they are expected to obey their elders. Adults have more legal rights than children and are expected to act in a responsible manner and to support themselves and their children. The elderly, who have the same legal status as the middle-aged, are often restricted in employment.

Age grading also affects the allocation of rewards. In the past and in the present, age has affected inheritance, as in the case of the trust that is made over to the inheritor at the age of twenty-one. Age is often used by parents today to grant differential privileges and responsibilities to children. In education, age grading is rigid and pervasive. There are also age-graded systems of seniority with respect to pay and job security in industry, in the military, and in government.

Age cohorts

Some of the differential advantages among age groups may be based not on the fact that they are young, middle-aged, or old, but on their relative numbers and the experiences they have shared. Thus when contrasting different age groups, we need to look at each group as an age *cohort* as well as an age stratum. The age cohort bears on the individual's life chances in two broad ways: through demographic and historical conditions.

DEMOGRAPHIC CONDITIONS. An individual's year of birth is connected to his or her life chances quite literally, in that life expectancy has changed dramatically. Today's college students, for example, can expect to live to a greater age than their grandparents, or even their parents. A person born in 1900 could expect to live only 47 years (Krauss, 1976); a person born in 1940 could expect to live 62.9 years; in 1960, 69.9 years; and in 1977, 73.2 years (Census Bureau, 1979, p. 70).

Also age cohorts vary in size, both absolutely and in relation to other groups. This difference can greatly affect the extent of competition for jobs or for schooling. Changes in the proportions of one's own cohort in relation to other cohorts can make a great difference in the financial burdens the various cohorts must bear; for example, a smaller number of younger working people now must pay higher Social Security taxes to support a larger number of retired elderly people.

HISTORICAL CONDITIONS. Varying historical conditions often mean wide differences in cohorts' world views, and they also bear dramatically on life chances. For example, education has changed since today's older people went to school; many careers now require kinds of education that were not available in earlier years (see Chapter 15). Likewise, the meshing of an individual's life cycle with economic cycles can affect life chances, as in the case of the cohorts that came to adulthood during the Depression.

Too much can be made of the similarities within a cohort. After all, "social change generates differences within as well as between cohorts: historical events do

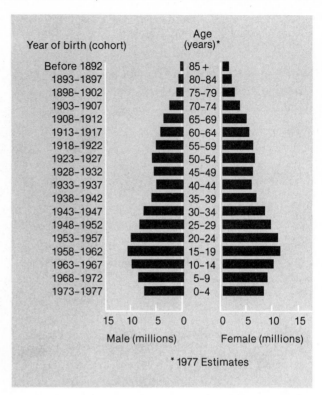

FIGURE 13.1

This figure depicts eighteen different age cohorts in 1977. The bulge in the groups between ages 15 and 34 represents the "baby boom" that followed World War II. (Census Bureau, *Current Population Reports*, Series P–20, No. 303, 1978, Figure 3)

not impinge uniformly on members of a cohort" (Elder, 1975, p. 172). Thus, class is sometimes a much more important basis for similar experience than age group. But still, age cohorts appear to be much more than mere statistical devices—they structure the context within which other influences occur.

THE RELATIVE POSITIONS OF YOUNG AND OLD

Now that we have taken a brief look at age stratification, we will concentrate on the age groups on either side of middle age: the elderly and the young (or adolescents). Both groups are subordinate to the middle-age range, both have grown considerably larger in absolute numbers and as a proportion of the population in recent years (though it is projected that the proportion of youth will decline and the proportion of elderly will increase as the decade progresses), and both have been the focus of recent attention because of political rumblings in their ranks. Yet each group is subordinate in its own way.

The elderly

The elderly are a large and growing segment of the population. In 1900, only 4 percent of the United States population was sixty-five or over, while in 1978, the figure had risen to 20 percent (Krauss, 1976; U.S. Bureau of the Census, 1979). By the year 2000, the United States population aged sixty-five and older is expected to increase by 40 percent (Wynder and Kristein, 1977). (We will discuss the bases for this prediction in Chapter 19.)

How do the elderly compare with other age groups in terms of treatment and life chances? The author of one major study of aging, Simone de Beauvoir (1972), suggests that the special problems of the elderly revolve around three issues: income, illness, and isolation.

INCOME. In our society, where for most people basic livelihood depends on employment earnings, it is no accident that retirement or loss of a job late in life signals a decline in income. Retirement, whether compulsory or voluntary, age discrimination in hiring practices, and general lack of reemployment opportunities have meant that in 1978, only 19.7 percent of men and only 7.8 percent of women over sixty-five were still working (U.S. Bureau of the Census, 1979). Postretirement income in the form of Social Security payments and private pension plans simply does not amount to much. Thus, while the average household income in 1977 was $16,009, for families headed by a person sixty-five or older the figure was 51 percent of that (Census Bureau, 1979, pp. 448, 456). This difference represents a relative worsening of the position of the elderly since 1945 (Spengler, 1966).

HEALTH AND HEALTH CARE. The aged are more susceptible than younger people to chronic disease, especially cancer, heart disease, stroke, and arthritis. They occupy one-third of all acute-care hospital beds and consume one-quarter of the drugs sold (*Newsday*, Octo-

ber 19, 1976). As a result, medical expenses incurred by people over sixty-five are more than three times as high as those of younger people, and, although a significant part of these expenses is met by government programs, the remaining cost must be paid by the elderly at the time when they can least afford it (Botwinick, 1973).

This situation is especially regrettable because it results from our health-care system's focus on treatment rather than prevention. A shift to an emphasis on preventive medicine might not only reduce the medical bills of the elderly but enable them to avoid chronic illness and prolong their good health and productivity (Wynder and Kristein, 1977). And, indeed, both our health-care and Social Security systems will *have* to adapt to handle the needs of the increasing elderly population (Payne and Whittington, 1976).

ISOLATION. A common problem for the aged in our society is social isolation, although it is not a universal plight of the elderly (see Table 13.5). In the United States, the social isolation of old people takes various forms. Surprisingly, only about 5 percent of the population aged sixty-five and over live in nursing homes. Most elderly people live at home, and of these about 7 percent are housebound (*Newsday*, October 19, 1976). "There is a continuing and growing trend, however, of living away from their children" (Botwinick, 1973, p. 2). Nevertheless, most elderly people are integrated into a modified extended family system. A 1975 study (Shanas, 1979) found that of people sixty-five and older with living children, 53 percent had seen a son or daughter "today or yesterday"; 77 percent within the preceding five days. Only 11 percent had not seen one of their children for thirty days or more. The study also found that for old persons without children (21 percent of the total sample), brothers, sisters, and other relatives tended to substitute for a child. Geographically, there are heavy concentrations of the elderly in rural areas and in parts of Florida and Arizona, and retirement communities have sprung up all across the country. The elderly are more concentrated in central cities than are younger people, and 35 percent live in small towns (Botwinick, 1973).

The larger issue, although one harder to approach statistically, is the loneliness and isolation that often follow retirement and separation from activities of the past. There is also the decline in status that comes with

TABLE 13.5

LIVING ARRANGEMENTS OF PEOPLE OVER AGE 65 IN FOUR COUNTRIES (PERCENTAGES)

COMPOSITION	JAPAN		GREAT BRITAIN		U.S.		DENMARK	
	M	F	M	F	M	F	M	F
Couples:								
Alone	16	15	67	68	77	82	80	84
With child	79	79	29	28	18	15	17	14
With relatives	4	5	3	5	3	2	1	—
With nonrelatives	1	1	1	2	2	1	2	2
Total	100	100	100	100	100	100	100	100
Single:								
Alone	10	8	37	45	52	46	58	63
With child	82	84	41	37	38	37	20	21
With relatives	6	6	14	13	11	22	6	7
With nonrelatives	2	2	8	5	8	5	10	9
Total	100	100	100	100	100	100	100	100

SOURCE: Palmore (1975), Table 1. Reprinted with permission. Data from Shanas et al., (1968); Nasu, S. *The Aged and the Development of Nuclear Families.* Metropolitan Institute of Gerontology, Tokyo, 1973.

retirement: "The role of the retired person is no longer to possess one" (Burgess, quoted in Beauvoir, 1972, p. 266). There is the isolation that besets those who simply do not have the money to participate in many social activities or to visit friends and relatives. And there is the loneliness that comes with the death of a marital partner—especially for women, because they tend to marry younger and to live longer than men. In fact, elderly women are in "double jeopardy." Not only do they suffer loss of status and isolation, but they also bear the stigma of physical unattractiveness far more than do their male contemporaries. In our culture, young women are generally admired as the ideals of beauty, and as women age, their self-image is likely to be damaged (Kimmel, 1974). As Simone de Beauvoir wrote in *The Coming of Age* (1972):

I have never come across one single woman, either in life or in books, who has looked upon her old age cheerfully . . . . Neither bloom, gentleness, nor grace are required of [the elderly male], but rather the strength and intelligence of the conquering subject: white hair and wrinkles are not in conflict with this manly ideal.

In consequence, older men who are divorced or widowed are in a better position to find a suitable, if not younger, marriage partner than are elderly widows or divorced women (Kimmel, 1974).

The young

The most important demographic fact about young people today is related to the one major exception to the general decline in fertility in this century. As was mentioned above, during the late 1940s and the 1950s the United States experienced a "baby boom" in which the number of births per married woman rose dramatically for a time and then receded again in the 1960s. The infants of the baby-boom era have become the youth of today. The population segment between the ages of fourteen and twenty-four grew by 52 percent during the 1960s as a result; it also rose significantly as a percentage of the total population. As those born of the boom grow older, the number of young people is expected to decline, first relatively and then in absolute figures (see Figure 13.2).

The young do not share with the elderly the problem of illness, but they do have the two other special problems in common: low income and isolation from the rest of society. And their political power, already discernibly lower than in the 1960s and 70s, is likely to decline even further.

INCOME. Rulers of private industry smelled larger profits in the golden youth of the baby boom, and the

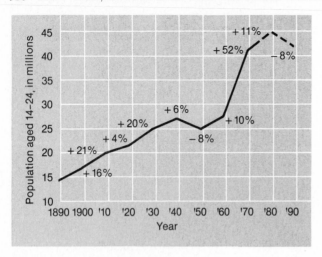

FIGURE 13.2

Changes in the size of population aged fourteen to twenty-four. (Adapted from Coleman et al., 1974, p. 46)

market was quickly glutted with the latest fads in music, clothing, and cosmetics. There was much talk of the new affluence of youth, and there surely were teenagers with a great deal of money. But in retrospect, it appears that the affluence of youth was more a product of their increased numbers and their sharing in their parents' rising income than of their increased individual wealth.

Until at least the age of seventeen, the vast majority of young people are dependent on their parents for financial support. But even after they leave school, young people are comparatively poor. The unemployment rate among young people is much higher than for the rest of the population, and it has increased since 1960. For those who do get jobs, the pay outlook is not good. In 1969, for example, the median wage for men aged sixteen to nineteen was less than $1.75 per hour. And "the median usual weekly earning of 16- to 24-year-old males fell by about 12 percent between 1967 and 1971 relative to the earnings of those aged 25 years and over" (Coleman et al., 1974, p. 75n). The trend has continued, and between 1970 and 1978 the differences have grown sharper (U.S. Bureau of the Census, 1979, p. 420). In 1978, for example, the median weekly earning of 16- to 24-year-old males was $185, whereas that of males 25 years and older was $294.

SEGREGATION. Like the elderly, but perhaps to an even greater extent, young people are physically and socially segregated from the rest of society. Until the age of sixteen the young are kept apart from most adults, and even from youth of different ages, by compulsory school attendance. As a result, their only significant contact with adults is likely to be with parents and teachers. Within school, there is usually a very narrow age range within each grade, so that few children have more than superficial contact with peers over a year older or younger.

THE CULTURAL ORIGINS OF AGE STRATIFICATION

"There is a wicked inclination in most people," the English man of letters Samuel Johnson once remarked, "to suppose an old man decayed in his intellects. If a young man or a middle-aged man, when leaving a company, does not recollect where he has laid his hat, it is nothing; but if the same inattention is discovered in an old man, people will shrug up their shoulders and say, 'His memory is going'" (quoted in Beauvoir, 1972, p. 479). Johnson was making an important point about age prejudice, but the onlookers' comments are not without some basis in fact. In contrast to the unfounded biological rationales of most other forms of stratification, there is a biological basis for some aspects of age stratification: the ability to function consistently and reasonably in social roles does vary significantly with age, at least at the two extremes of the life cycle. Two-year-olds, for instance, no matter how much their parents may feel dominated by them, are forever incapable of ruling society, while most octogenarians can no longer perform physically demanding tasks. But, as with gender roles, the connection between the biological manifestations of age and cultural role norms is quite limited: most roles do not require extremes of experience or physical strength. It is how we choose to define people, not only their actual capacities, that makes for stratification.

Most young people in industrialized societies have the capacity to perform the most complex mental operations by the age of fifteen or sixteen. In fact, some mental functions are actually at their height during adolescence. At the other pole, certain forms of memory do tend to decrease with age, although that does not happen as early or as completely as is commonly thought. General intelligence does *not* decline steadily with age; it drops significantly only right before death (Botwinick, 1973). While resiliency of mind diminishes with age, experience and certain forms of knowledge accumulate.

Age grading by chronological year is almost as arbitrary as discrimination by gender or race. Maturation and aging vary from individual to individual. There may be a degree of incapacity at the extremes, but it does not often correspond to society's boundaries of eighteen and sixty-five. And even when people are not at the height of their powers, there is still the possibility for integration into many roles, both for the young and for the elderly. For both groups, the limits of age are primarily cultural. In fact, a brief look at history reveals that only a little more than a century ago the roles of the young and the elderly were considerably different from those of today.

DECLINE IN THE ROLES OF THE YOUNG AND THE OLD

Industrialization and the changes associated with it spelled doom for the high status of elderly people. Experience, once so valued in the elderly, counts for little in many segments of contemporary industrial society. Today there are no elaborate rituals that need to be handed down by word of mouth, nor are there elderly guardians of special technical knowledge. And experience is of little help in many areas of work—in keeping up with an automobile assembly line, for example, or pushing papers in a bureaucracy.

But industrialization by itself does not explain the real decline in the roles of the elderly compared to the middle-aged. In 1900, well after industrialization was under way in the United States, two out of three men over sixty-five were still in the labor force, while today, as we have noted, only one out of five is. What happened? Early retirement is actively sought by many workers, of course, especially those with the most unsatisfying jobs. But workers' self-interest does not appear to be the overriding factor in this historic shift. The turning point, according to one account, came with the Depression:

The Great Depression drastically reduced the total demand for employable persons. During this period, retirement, through Social Security benefits, became a conventional tool for dealing with our unemployment problem by eliminating

part of the population from the competition for scarce jobs. In recent years, when unemployment has never fallen below 3.5% of the civilian labor force, pension plans have become a primary means for distributing an inadequate amount of work. (*Work in America*, 1973, pp. 66–67)

The decline of the extended family since the advent of industrialization and the increasing tendency of the elderly and their children to live apart mean that the family roles of the elderly have declined as well. And with the elderly no longer part of the household or integral to the workplace, it has become easier to keep them "out of sight, out of mind" (*Work in America*, 1973).

Industrialization also transformed the social roles of young people. One historical survey (Coleman et al., 1974, pp. 9–29) outlined the change as follows: In the home, at work, in many parts of society, what characterized the preindustrial world—and set it off from our own time—was a "promiscuous assemblage of ages." People of widely varying ages lived and worked alongside one another. From the age of seven or eight, boys were expected to help on the farm, and by the age of twelve or fourteen they could often be found living and working on a neighbor's or a relative's farm or serving an apprenticeship. Until they reached twenty-one, boys were expected either to work directly for their families or to send their earnings home. Most young people in preindustrial societies worked at irregular intervals, lived at home intermittently, and attended school when the rhythms of agriculture permitted.

Industrialization and related social developments changed all that. The school-reform movement of the mid-nineteenth century brought increased segregation by age. "The assumption of many school reformers was that the proper 'culture' of childhood demanded a segregation of children from adults in asylumlike institutions called schools" (Coleman et al., 1974, p. 18). And throughout the latter half of the nineteenth century, the haphazard schooling of the past was increasingly replaced by the regimentation and measured movement of age achievement, as society moved from labor based on the farm to labor based on the factory.

By the turn of the century, industrialization and urbanization had stripped young people of their economic roles in the family. And during the period in which young people's roles became less highly valued, schooling increasingly took up the slack. As with the elderly, what industrialization started among young

people, the Depression finished. Humanitarian and educational reformers had been agitating for the passage of child-labor laws for some time, but the Depression gave the critical push. As one member of the National Child Labor Committee put it in 1933: "It is now generally accepted that the exploitation of children, indefensible on humanitarian grounds, has become a genuine economic menace. . . . Children should be in schools and adults should have whatever worthwhile jobs there are" (quoted in Coleman et al., 1974, p. 35). And despite the booming economy of World War II and the 1950s, this philosophy prevailed

Although industrialization and associated changes have reduced the roles that both young and old people play in Western societies, there are still exceptions to the rule. (Left) An adolescent helps out on his family's farm, where his labor is needed. (Below) Henri Matisse produced some of his greatest paintings in the years just before his death in 1954 at the age of eighty-five. (left: Burk Uzzle/Magnum; below: Robert Capa/Magnum)

as more and more young people completed college. During the 1960s, graduate education boomed, keeping many middle-class young people out of the work force far beyond the voting and drinking age. Lower-class youth frequently got neither schooling nor jobs. In the 1980s, because of the weak economy and the spiraling costs of higher education, it is likely that undergraduate and graduate enrollments will decline and that unemployment will rise. Thus, more middle-class youths may find themselves in circumstances similar to those faced by their lower-class contemporaries.

POLITICAL MOVEMENTS AMONG THE YOUNG AND OLD

Some of the elements of age stratification that we have examined—differences between age strata, increased age segregation, and differences in experience of age cohorts, all of which tend to encourage the development of age subcultures—help explain the underpinnings of recent age-based social movements. The youth movement of the late 1960s and early 1970s, for example, coincided with the coming of age of the children of the "baby boom." In the view of some observers, this cohort was not so much rebelling against society's treatment of it as it was expressing new values, formed as a result of experiences that were different from those of previous cohorts and crystallized because the group was isolated from the rest of society (Braungart, 1975).

Political developments among the elderly, however, suggest a more direct consciousness of their treatment as an age group. Recent years have seen the growth of several organizations dedicated to promoting social legislation and increased respect for the elderly. Groups like the Gray Panthers have worked for abolition of mandatory retirement by age, improved nursing-home care, and increased Social Security and health benefits. They are also seeking ways to combat the isolation to which many elderly people are consigned. The growth of the elderly population and the fact that voting rates tend to increase with age have contributed to the political clout of the elderly in recent years.

Both young and old are beset by problems in organizing effectively on their own behalf. For children, the difficulties are obvious; they are able to gain only the rights adults see fit to give them. But eighteen-year-olds now have the vote, and legislators are not anxious to offend this segment, which has often formed the core of

In the United States, child-labor laws were passed in the 1930s to prevent the exploitation of children. Elsewhere—in rural Colombia, for example—children are still expected to work. (J. P. Laffont/Sygma)

political activists in election campaigns, even though the proportion of this age group that votes is smaller than that of other age groups. Nor have the elderly been quiet: they are now a political force, as changes in federal, state, and local legislation have shown. The continuing pressure for medical services and property tax relief is ample evidence that this group is aware of its needs and of how to see that they are met.

THE FUTURE OF AGE STRATIFICATION

In spite of our growing awareness of age stratification, it is unlikely to disappear given present conditions and trends. But there are signs that it may be becoming less rigid, and youth and the elderly may be able to assume greater control over decisions that affect their lives. Such modifications in our age stratification system will help to reduce the institutionalized "agism" that many critics have pointed out in our society and that—like sexism and racism—is a cause of social divisiveness and fragmentation (Butler, 1969).

One thing is quite certain, though: American society is "graying." The "baby boom" generation—babies born between 1947 and 1957—now comprises one-fifth of our population, and it will remain a critical factor to society at each phase of its development. When this group reaches retirement age in about the third decade of the next century, it will still be a dominant force (*Newsweek*, February 28, 1977). The social, economic, and political implications of this trend are enormous, and it is likely that old age, in the near future, may be a very different experience than it is today.

Summary

The two major bases of social stratification are gender and age. Gender-role differentiation and stratification by sex are universal, with "men's work"—whatever form it takes—regarded as more valuable than "women's work." All known societies have been *patriarchal*. Neither the functionalist nor the conflict-theory explanation of the origins of gender-role segregation and inequality between the sexes is entirely satisfactory. It is clear, however, that the lower status of women was accentuated even further with the Industrial Revolution, when much domestic production shifted to factories.

In today's industrial society, women remain unequal to men, as demonstrated by such indexes as occupational distribution, earnings, and education. The women's movement has brought about some significant changes in the sex stratification system, especially a substantial improvement in women's legal status.

Stratification by age is also universal. Each person belongs to an *age stratum*—an aggregate of people of the same chronological age or at the same stage in the life cycle—and an *age cohort*—an aggregate of people born at a particular point in history. The strata of the young and the elderly are faced with problems of lower income and social isolation; the elderly have the additional problem of higher susceptibility to illness.

There is a sound, though limited, biological basis for some aspects of age stratification, but many of its features seen today were brought about arbitrarily by the Industrial Revolution. The elderly lost their high status because their special knowledge and experience were no longer needed; this trend accelerated during the Depression, when older workers were encouraged to retire earlier. The elderly also lost many of their family roles through industrialization. Young people's social roles were also dramatically altered by industrialization. They not only lost their economic importance to the family, but they became segregated from the rest of society by longer and more regular schooling. Political movements among the young and, especially, the elderly are now attempting, with some success, to improve the status of these groups.

Glossary

AGE COHORTS The group of people born at a particular period in history.

AGE STRATA A group of people who share a common age or stage in the life cycle.

GENDER ROLES The nonreproductive behaviors considered suitable and sometimes obligatory for each sex in a society.

MATRIARCHY A society ruled by women.

PATRIARCHY A society ruled by men.

SEX ROLES The roles assumed by men and women in sexual reproduction.

Recommended readings

Atchley, Robert C. *The Social Forces in Later Life: An Introduction to Social Gerontology.* 3rd ed. Belmont, Calif.: Wadsworth, 1980. A multidisciplinary textbook for the field of social gerontology. It provides a useful overview of the important theoretical and methodological concerns in this field.

Elder, Glen H., Jr. *Adolescent Socialization and Personality Development.* Chicago: Rand McNally, 1968. A detailed review and integration of the research literature on adolescence.

Kaplan, Alexander G., and Joan P. Bean (eds.). *Beyond Sex Role Stereotypes: Readings Toward a Psychology for Androgyny.* Boston: Little, Brown, 1976. A useful collection of readings on various aspects of gender roles, including the biological and sexual factors, social and cultural influences, and the consequences of traditional and alternative gender-role socialization.

Maccoby, Eleanor E., and Carol N. Jacklin. *The Psychology of Sex Differences.* Palo Alto, Calif.: Stanford University Press, 1974. An excellent analysis and critique of the vast research literature on sex differences. The authors separate fact from fiction, suppositions from truths.

Panel on Youth, President's Science Advisory Commission. *Youth: Transition to Adulthood.* Chicago: University of Chicago Press, 1974. An action-oriented report on the problems of transition to full adult status in society. This volume considers, among other topics, the economic problems and legal status of youth, age segregation, and the educational environment; it then sketches several directions for change in society's treatment of individuals at this critical stage in their life cycle.

Riley, Matilda White, Ann Foner, and Marilyn Johnson, in association with others. *Aging and Society.* New York: Russell Sage Foundation, 1968 (Vol. 1, *Inventory of Findings*), 1969 (Vol. 2, *Aging and the Professions*), and 1972 (Vol. 3, *A Sociology of Age Stratification*). One of the most ambitious attempts in the field of social gerontology to pull together the recent research literature, put it into a sociological framework, and make it useful to those who work with the aged. Volume 3 is the most relevant to this chapter and most important in initiating a more sociological approach to the field of gerontology.

Sebald, Hans. *Adolescence: A Sociological Perspective.* New York: Appleton-Century-Crofts, 1968. A comprehensive textbook on the sociology of youth. Chapters 1, 3, 5, 6, and 8 are especially relevant.

Stockard, Jean, and Mariam M. Johnson. *Sex Roles: Sex Inequality and Sex Role Development.* Englewood Cliffs, N.J.: Prentice-Hall, 1980. An examination of continuing sexual inequality in the context of sex roles and sex differences, this volume draws on different social science perspectives in the course of analyzing its subject.

Stoll, Clarice Stasz. *Female and Male: Socialization, Social Roles, and Social Structure.* Dubuque, Iowa: William C. Brown, 1974. This textbook for undergraduates examines from a sociological perspective the consequences of being male or being female.

Walum, Laura Richardson. *The Dynamics of Sex and Gender: A Sociological Perspective.* Chicago: Rand McNally, 1977. A thorough sociological review that integrates the research literature on gender and considers its pertinence to everyday life.

Social institutions

CHAPTER FOURTEEN

THE FAMILY

We tend to take family life—and our particular "average" family of man at work and woman at home with children—for granted. We think of what we know as "natural" and "right" as the way things should be. If we look around us, however, only 17 percent of all families in the United States actually conform to this image of the "average" family. And although the family is a fundamental feature of all societies, its forms vary enormously across time and across cultures as well. A survey of 250 societies conducted a generation ago, for example, revealed that the vast majority—80 percent—found nothing unnatural in three people or more belonging to the same marriage.

As different societies evolved, so did different forms of the family. And as societies continue to change, so do their family forms. Indeed, even within the same society, norms surrounding family life may show considerable variation.

In this chapter, then, we will look at the family as a social creation and as a social group. We will first examine basic functions and forms before analyzing the past and present of the American family and attempting to speculate about its future. There is, as we'll see, a wealth of material on the contemporary American family, for this institution and the changes taking place in it have become a major object of concern to sociologists.

Universal functions

As we have seen in Chapter 3, structural-functionalists tend to look for the universal and necessary features of all societies. The family is often cited as just such a universal feature. In fact, one reason for the current concern about the American family is that, in the view of structural-functionalists (among others), the viability of the family as an institution is crucial to the health and survival of the society as a whole.

One of the traditional vital functions of the family, for instance, is to ensure the survival of a population. In addition, the family regulates sex and reproduction, provides for the care and socialization of children, forms a basic economic unit, and maintains a society's stratification system. In recent years, it has also become an important source of fulfillment of needs for intimacy and companionship.

Even as a society evolves from traditional to industrial, the family continues to perform these functions. Thus, in almost every known society, a *family* can be defined functionally as "a social arrangement based on marriage and the marriage contract, including recognition of the rights and duties of parenthood, common residence for husband, wife, and children, and reciprocal economic obligations between husband and wife" (Stephens, 1963, p. 8).

SEX AND REPRODUCTION

Sexual activity is controlled to some extent in all societies, perhaps because the continuous sexual receptivity of the human female would have fostered disruptive competition between men. This, at least, is one theory. Another holds that the female's capacity to bear children is such an abundant resource that men imposed sexual controls in order to guarantee their ability to distinguish their own offspring from those of some other male. In either case, the permanent partnership of marriage solves the problem by setting clearly defined limits on sexual accessibility (Ember and Ember, 1973, p. 323). In turn, the social recognition of parenthood confers on a child the benefits of protection and status; it also minimizes conflicts over the inheritance of property or office.

On an Israeli kibbutz, or agricultural commune, children live in dormitories and are looked after by special caretakers. Here the responsibility for a child's socialization rests not with one family, as in our society, but with the community as a whole. (Louis Goldman/Rapho/Photo Researchers, Inc.)

special caretakers; their socialization is the responsibility of the group and the community, rather than of the nuclear or extended family.

SOCIALIZATION OF CHILDREN

Human children are born helpless and need a longer period of care than the young of any other animal species. They also must be socialized into the complex network of norms, values, and rituals that characterize human culture. The family is ideally suited to perform these functions and also to teach traditional values to those who will eventually assume control of the society, thus maintaining stability.

In many societies, children are not cared for or socialized exclusively by their parents; a large network of aunts, uncles, grandparents, and cousins—the extended family—feeds, changes, and teaches children right from wrong. A less common nonexclusive pattern is that of the Israeli kibbutz, or agricultural commune, where the child is the responsibility of the entire community. Children live in dormitories and are looked after by

ECONOMIC COOPERATION

In preindustrial societies, the labor necessary to feed, clothe, and shelter people was divided by sex, men doing the work that required greater mobility (for example, hunting), and women the tasks that enabled them to stay closer to home to care for children (making clothing, preparing food). In industrial societies, by contrast, technology has made rigid work-role specialization unnecessary. Either sex can buy food at the supermarket or give the baby a bottle. Both husband and wife can have jobs that require travel. Complete sharing of work roles is still relatively uncommon in Western societies, but changes have taken place. There are also continuities, for the kind of cooperation that enables the family to function as an economic unit is still needed. Family members may no longer work together on the farm or in the shop as they once did, but hus-

PLAYING SOCIAL-PSYCHOLOGICAL "PASSWORD"

It seems reasonably safe to assume that people in a close relationship, such as marriage, have high empathy and are usually able to communicate better than people who are less closely related. But how can we find out for certain? How can such intangibles as empathy and communication be measured? An unusual and revealing attempt was made by Professors Norman Goodman and Richard Ofshe in their study of "Empathy, Communication Efficiency, and Marital Status" (1968). Goodman and Ofshe designed an experiment to test communication and empathy among married couples, engaged couples, and strangers. They attempted to show that "the more two people are 'in tune with' one another, the fewer units of information are required to transmit meaning between them" (p. 597).

The professors devised an experiment, utilizing forty-five men and forty-five women (all college students or college graduates), paired in three sets—strangers, married couples, and engaged couples. They all took part in tests, which were akin to the popular word game "Password," in which player A "cues" player B in an attempt to get him or her to say the particular word that player A has in mind.

The experiment was conducted in two phases. In the first phase, which was designed to test communicative ability, each pair of subjects was given a series of twelve words, which were divided into two categories—family-related words and general words. The family-related words were *birth, family, hospital, house, in-laws*, and *marriage*. The general words were *beef, bite, hope, party, sin*, and *symphony*. Taking one word at a time, the subjects were asked to keep giving one-word clues until their partners guessed the particular word. For instance, in the case of two strangers, with one trying to communicate the goal word *family* to the other, the interaction sequence went like this:

PLAYER A'S CUE	PLAYER B'S RESPONSE
1. nuclear	1. warfare
2. group	2. atoms
3. primary	3. electrons
4. father	4. Einstein
5. primary	5. reactor
6. children	6. molecules
7. human	7. matter
8. mother	8. family

In this example the communicators had to rely on the kind of knowledge that is relatively standard and universal, because they were strangers and had not had time to develop a degree of empathy with each other.

Overall, the experimenters found that the results of the tests with family-related words "reveal[ed] that greater [communicative] efficiency is associated with marital status, but for general words, the strangers were found to be more efficient at communication than the engaged

couples, though the difference was not significant" (p. 599). The experimenters argue that the greater communicative efficiency which couples display, in connection with words related to the family, can be attributed to the fact that these individuals have been together for relatively long periods of time; during this time they have developed a mutually conditioned system of communication through which meaning can be more easily transmitted. Communication was most efficient in those areas which were central to the pair's existence as a unit. For example, one wife was trying to get her husband to say the word "in-laws." The exchange was very short:

PLAYER A'S CUE	PLAYER B'S RESPONSE
1. Trouble	1. In-laws

In this case, the wife, displaying a high degree of empathy, was able to draw on her knowledge and recall of her partner's personal attitudes and values in selecting her cue, and her husband was able to provide the correct response very quickly.

In the second phase of the study, which was designed as a test of role-taking ability, the experimenters asked the subjects to differentiate the same twelve goal words by placing them at some point on a ten-step rating scale, from "good" to "bad," "pleasurable" to "painful," and so on. After this process was completed, they were again asked to place the words on a scale, this time giving them the same ratings they thought their *partners* had. For instance, one woman rated the word *birth* as very pleasurable; her partner said he thought she had rated the same word as moderately painful. The number of steps between these two choices (four in this case) was then squared and a score computed (sixteen), which represented the couple's ability to empathize with each other. The process was repeated for all twelve words, and a final score was computed after all words had been scaled.

As expected, the engaged and married couples were much better at taking the roles of their partners than the strangers were. But the interesting result of the study was that wives were *less* adept than engaged women at taking the role of their partners. The experimenters suggested that this surprising finding might be explained by the theory that after marriage, men traditionally become more involved than women in instrumental activities outside the home. This may make it more difficult for wives to empathize with their husbands' roles than it is for engaged women to empathize with their fiancés' roles. Consequently, the role-taking scores of married women in this study were lower.

Undoubtedly a second experiment along these lines—conducted after ten additional years of the changes that women's liberation, men's liberation, and other new trends have wrought in the American institution of marriage—would yield some interesting results.

band and wife increasingly pool salaries and other resources for the support and maintenance of their family.

MAINTENANCE OF THE STRATIFICATION SYSTEM

Closely related to its economic activities is the family's role in preserving and perpetuating a society's stratification system (see Chapter 10). In most societies, a family rich in goods, money, and education passes down to its children both the expectation of these benefits and, eventually, the benefits themselves. More generally, in both rich and poor families, parents pass on to children both life chances and life styles. Through laws and customs, society supports this family-based transfer of goods, status, and opportunity, for it promotes stability, an important goal in all societies. The transfer process also keeps those at the top of the social hierarchy secure in their power. In serving itself, then—by keeping its fortune intact, for instance—the family also serves the social system of which it is a part.

INTIMACY AND COMPANIONSHIP

In the past, traditional families not only worked together to make a livelihood but were one another's friends and companions; social life centered around family and kin. For the most part, today's families no longer spend all day working together; nor are their friendship networks limited to relatives. But because of the trend toward frequent relocation, the immediate family has become more important than ever as a source of emotional support, intimacy and companionship.

In the idealized view of modern family life, husband, wife, and children gather at the end of the day to reveal their inner feelings and share experiences and frustrations in an atmosphere of empathy and affection (see box). While few families manage to measure up to this rosy standard very consistently, even alienation and conflict within a family can provide its members with emotional reinforcement and meaningful, if not always tranquil, contact.

Variations in structure

The family unit that performs these basic functions can take a number of forms. There is no universal family type, per se; a variety of structures have proved efficient at different times and in different situations. Today we can identify two major forms: the nuclear family and the extended family.

Extended families are common in agricultural societies because they provide more hands to do the work that farming requires, and because collective land ownership and use is preferable to repeatedly subdividing the land for use by smaller family units. In contrast, hunting and gathering societies as well as industrial societies require geographical mobility and favor the nuclear structure.

THE NUCLEAR FAMILY

The basic unit of all known family organizations is the *nuclear family*, consisting of a married couple and their immature offspring (Lowie, 1920, pp. 66–67; Murdock,

1949, p. 2; Stephens, 1963, p. 29). In isolation, this unit can fulfill all of the basic family functions outlined above. In some societies, notably our own, the nuclear family sometimes functions with only one parent in the home. In the vast majority of societies, however, the nuclear family truly is only a nucleus, with a number of relatives—including other, interlocking nuclear families—grouped around it.

THE EXTENDED FAMILY

The *extended family* consists of several nuclear families united by parent-child relationships and living together, either in the same house or in a compound. It may include an elderly man and his wife, their sons and the sons' wives, and the children of the sons' marriages—in other words, grandparents, parents, and children. The extended family may also be polygamous, meaning that either the man or the woman, or both of them, has more than one spouse. Whether monoga-

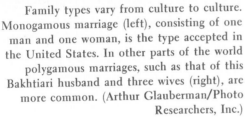

Family types vary from culture to culture. Monogamous marriage (left), consisting of one man and one woman, is the type accepted in the United States. In other parts of the world polygamous marriages, such as that of this Bakhtiari husband and three wives (right), are more common. (Arthur Glauberman/Photo Researchers, Inc.)

mous or polygamous, the extended family form is far more common world-wide than the relatively independent nuclear family normally found in the United States.

Since family form has an enormous influence both on the individual and on society, the advantages and disadvantages of the two patterns have been widely debated. The extended family offers a number of assets: continuity through time, work efficiency made possible by the large number of persons available to assume different responsibilities, assured care for the aged and helpless, greater capacity for group self-protection, and a comforting sense of permanence and stability. The extended family member belongs to a quite substantial unit: a large, permanent, diversified grouping of human beings who are bound together by blood, marriage, and loyalty. But, on the negative side, there is little privacy and great pressure to conform. As a rule, the individual is not encouraged to use his or her initiative or to leave the family setting.

By comparison, the nuclear family, containing only two adults and their young children, may seem to be a rather fragile structure. But this family form also offers certain advantages: social and geographical mobility, privacy, and greater leeway for individual freedom. Furthermore, because they are concentrated in a small group, affectional ties in the nuclear family tend to be more intense than in the extended family, where they are distributed among a larger membership. It is debatable, however, which affectional pattern is more conducive to individual emotional stability and happiness.

AMERICAN FAMILY STRUCTURE

So far in this chapter we have spoken of the nuclear family as "independent"—as operating alone, without the need to solicit help or advice from others. Yet there remains some question as to how independent the American nuclear family actually is. In 1951, the sociologist Talcott Parsons offered his conceptualization of the American family as an "isolated nuclear family," sheared from its traditional roots by industrialization. Social mobility, geographical mobility, emphasis on achieved rather than ascribed (that is, inherited) status—all these offshoots of industrialization, according to Parsons, left the American family more closely connected to its car than to its kin.

Subsequent studies, however, have modified this rather extreme interpretation. Eugene Litwak (1960a, 1960b), for example, has shown that neither social nor geographical mobility has the power to dissolve all ties to kin. Indeed, according to Litwak's study, it was the *least* mobile members of the society, the manual workers and the poor, who were most isolated from their relatives. The typical middle-class family was still tightly enough bound to its kin to merit the label of "modified extended family." Likewise, a study by Marvin Sussman (1963) has shown that middle-class nuclear families, regardless of geographical distance, tend to maintain an active "service network" with their relatives, giving and receiving advice, money, and help with young children.

So despite the popular notion of the American nuclear family as an atom floating in the void, our families are *not* truly isolated. Nevertheless, what has changed is the nature of our kinship ties. With individual ability and industriousness becoming stronger influences on a person's future than family resources, the duties that once bound adults to their parents, siblings, aunts, and uncles have weakened. These obligational ties appear to have been supplanted by emotional ties (Pitts, 1964, p. 90). Kin still help one another, particularly in times of need, but they tend to look to their relationships with one another more for the satisfaction of emotional needs—love, intimacy, a sense of belonging—than of practical and material needs.

Setting up a family: mate selection and marriage

Love, marriage, and sex are three different behavioral systems. While almost all societies recognize the interrelationship of the three, each society has its own way of defining this interrelationship. The conventional wisdom of middle-class America is that ideally the three systems amount to a single whole; to allow any of them to exist without the others (for example, sex without marriage or marriage without love) poses a threat of one kind or another. Many other cultures, however, regard marriage as far too crucial an event to be influenced by considerations of love or sexual preference.

THE CONTROL OF MATE SELECTION

All known societies, without exception, impose some controls on the selection of marriage partners (Belkin and Goodman, 1980, pp. 12–21). One reason for this regulation is that when a man and woman marry, their two kin groups become allied, and the status of these kin groups determines to a large degree that of the children born of the marriage. Thus the stratification system of a society, to say nothing of its political and economic systems, is greatly affected by marriage patterns. If, for example, Americans decided overnight to ignore racial, social, economic, and educational differences and to engage in totally free mate selection—black marrying white, rich marrying poor, semiliterate marrying college graduate—the entire existing social structure would probably change considerably. But although no society allows completely random mating, the control mechanisms differ.

Exogamy and endogamy

The most fundamental principle of mate selection is *exogamy* ("marriage outward"), which requires that a person marry outside a specified group, usually consisting of particular kinds of relatives. The exogamy principle is actually an extension of *incest taboos*, the prohibition of sexual relations between certain family members. How far these taboos extend and the kinds of relatives they apply to will dictate the limitations on marriage choice. Almost invariably, the incest taboo includes members of one's nuclear family. And in all societies it extends to certain other relatives as well (Leslie, 1973), though there is little cross-cultural consistency as to *which* relatives. Indeed, there is no single relative outside the nuclear family, not even grandparents, to whom the incest taboo applies in all known societies.

Complementary to exogamy in the regulation of marriage is *endogamy* ("marriage within"), the principle that requires one to marry *within* one's own group—whether that group be defined as one's tribe, community, social class, religion, or some combination of these. The communities of the world are somewhat more consistent regarding endogamy than exogamy, because group solidarity and entire social structures are founded on endogamy. The majority of societies, for example, disapprove of interracial marriage (Murdock, 1949, p. 265), and most peoples prefer individuals to marry within their own religion, social class, and community, whether this community is one village or an entire nation (Belkin and Goodman, 1980, pp. 182–188).

Arranged marriage

"It's not a man that marries a maid, but field marries field—vineyard marries vineyard—cattle marry cattle." This sentiment, expressed by a German peasant (quoted in Goodsell, 1915, p. 189), is endorsed by most societies in the world. And in order to ensure that their field marries the right field, families in such societies tend to arrange marriages rather than to let their young choose mates at the whim of chance, love, or sexual attraction.

One of the most common means of controlling marriage choice is *child marriage* (Goode, 1959). At an age when he or she is too weak to oppose the family's preference and, in any case, too immature to have a mean-

ingful preference, the child is officially married to another child from an appropriate family. Consummation is postponed until it is biologically feasible. In another type of *arranged marriage*, two families decide to ally themselves through marriage and then simply introduce the couple to each other on their wedding day. In traditional China, where arranged marriages were customary, "the Chinese elders claimed that the old god in the moon bound together the feet of males and females destined for each other, and parents and intermediaries merely acted as instruments to carry out his will" (Scanzoni and Scanzoni, 1976, p. 106).

LOVE AND MARRIAGE

Few societies share our belief that the best marriage is one based on love. This is not to say that other societies reject the notion of love completely. Rather, as William J. Goode has pointed out, cross-cultural attitudes toward love must be seen as a continuum: "At one pole, a strong love attraction is socially viewed as a laughable or tragic aberration; at the other, it is mildly shameful to marry without being in love with one's intended spouse. This is a gradation . . . ranging . . . from low to almost nonexistent institutionalization of love to high institutionalization" (1959, p. 41).

At the low-institutionalization pole we would place China and Japan, although they have recently shown

The belief that marriages should be based on love, or even that love is a precondition for marriage, is not universal. Although this Chinese husband and wife may love each other, they do not subscribe to what William J. Goode calls the "romantic love complex," which abounds in our society. (Paolo Koch/Photo Researchers, Inc.)

some movement toward the center. Urban and village India, as well as many southern European societies, would fall near the middle of the continuum, where love may be viewed as a desirable *result* (not precondition) of betrothal or marriage. Here, the ideal would be *conjugal love*—the love that can develop between spouses on the basis of companionship, mutual understanding, and shared experiences.

At the high-institutionalization pole we would find the United States and, according to Goode, a handful of other societies, including those in northwestern Europe and Polynesia. Goode has termed this firmly institutionalized expectation of love as the prelude to marriage the *romantic love complex* (1959, p. 42): it involves a type of love based on sexual attraction and on idealization of the loved one's personality that is seen as a highly desirable basis for courtship and marriage.

SEX, LOVE, AND MARRIAGE IN THE UNITED STATES

In the American value system, love, marriage, and sex are considered three aspects of a single process. How closely does our behavior conform to these values?

As regards sex and love, it appears that Americans—or at least American youth—remain somewhat romantic. Despite the current preoccupation with sexual freedom and sexual "performance," research indicates that young people are neither promiscuous nor bent exclusively on physical pleasure. Young people, and particularly young women, have become freer in their sexual behavior, though. Traditionally, young men in early adolescence have been far more likely than women in the same age range to have intercourse. But surveys increasingly demonstrate that the gap is narrowing (Baumann and Wilson, 1974; Zelnick and Kantner, 1977). Between 1950 and 1975, for instance, the proportion of women having intercourse by age 16 rose from about 8 percent to 25 percent. Another survey showed that between 1970 and 1975, the proportion of nonvirgins among 17-year-old women rose from one in four to one in three.

When surveys distinguish between women who plan to go to college (or are actually attending) and those who do not, the latter are far more likely to have premarital intercourse. One reason for this is that women who are not college-bound are typically more deeply involved in selecting a mate, which increases the likelihood of sex. At the same time, however, there has been a steady increase in the proportion of young women who are nonvirgins by the time they leave college, which in turn seems to reflect a definite liberalization of attitudes regarding premarital sex. In other words, women are less likely to "hold out" for an engagement ring before having intercourse. This is suggested by a survey in which women reported that sex was as acceptable with someone they were in love with as with someone to whom they were engaged (Kaats and Davis, 1970). Similarly, in a key study conducted by Robert R. Bell and Jay B. Chaskes (1970), the number of college women having intercourse with men they were simply dating or going steady with doubled in the ten years between 1958 and 1968. But the number of premarital coital partners each person has remains small; particularly among the college-educated, there appears to be a definite trend toward viewing sexual intercourse as part of a serious emotional relationship (Turner, 1970, pp. 331–332; Hunt, 1973a, 1973b; Udry, 1974, pp. 122, 128–129; Zelnick and Kantner, 1977). In short, as Morton Hunt concludes from his own study, "the much-touted philosophy of recreational sex is definitely a minority view" (1973b, p. 75).

As for love and marriage, there is no question that in our society love leads to sex more often than it leads to marriage. Yet when we do marry, we tend to marry for love. Or at least we think we do. There is ample evidence that, *objectively* speaking, the fluttery sentiment that impels us down the aisle is actually something other than pure romantic love—an exclusive passion for one person that occurs spontaneously and is free of any drab practical considerations. If such a passion occurred spontaneously, we would expect it to be as common in other cultures as in our own; but it decidedly is not. Rather, because romantic love is so firmly institutionalized in our society—because it is so much in evidence in our fairy tales, television programs, movies, popular literature, and advertisements; because parents tell their children that falling in love and getting married (in that order) are part of "growing up"—it becomes a self-fulfilling prophecy. We hope and expect to fall in love. Therefore, when we meet someone whom we find emotionally, sexually, and socially attractive, we respond by "falling in love."

That social attractiveness—indeed, social sameness—is a component of mate selection in the United States has been established by numerous studies. Like most other societies in the world, we are a *homogamous* people. That is, we are extremely likely to marry our "own kind" (Belkin and Goodman, 1980, pp. 182-188)—people of our own race (Census Bureau, 1970), our own religion (Monahan, 1971), and our own social class (Centers, 1949; Hollingshead, 1950). Furthermore, we stand an excellent chance of marrying someone who lives within walking distance of us (Katz and Hill, 1958; Catton and Smircich, 1964; Kephart, 1977). Whatever Americans may subjectively feel when they marry, their mate choice is, objectively, the result of a careful selection process engineered by the society, the family, the peer group, and the bride and groom themselves.

American family dynamics

Like any other group, the family is a system of roles. To some degree the matter of who will play which role and how he or she will play it is determined by cultural values and norms, but considerable flexibility remains. In a sense, the family drama is a bit like an improvisational play: the actors are assigned to roles and given a rough outline of the script, but they have considerable leeway to improvise according to their needs and desires, and even to change the basic guidelines, with the agreement of the other actors. Still, there are some common patterns in family interactions, as in those of any other group.*

FAMILIAL LOVE

Familial love can be thought of as a sentiment: "a socially defined complex of feeling that indicates a characteristic relationship to a social object and is accompanied by tendencies to behave in the socially appropriate manner" (Turner, 1970, p. 225).

First, the social sentiment of love operates—or at least can operate—to defuse conflict among family members. The halo of romantic love with which Americans tend to surround their marriages sheds a certain warm light over the early period of adjustment, easing tension and smoothing out conflict. Likewise, the tender, more realistic, conjugal love that develops later in the marriage supplies the tolerance and generosity that make it possible for spouses to live together, as they must, without perfect justice.

Second, familial love can serve as a buffer between the judgment of the larger society and the individual who deviates from social norms. Familial love is supposed to include a certain compassion, a predisposition toward forgiveness, so that family members' misdeeds—ranging from a small child's taking a toy from a store to a parent's incipient alcoholism—can be handled with a degree of tenderness and understanding they would not meet in the society at large.

Third, familial love can provide relief from the kind of bargaining that prevails in many other kinds of relationships. This is not to imply that bargaining does not go on in the family; in fact, it is crucial in family role dynamics. But love among family members can prevent interactions from assuming the more rigid equal-exchange quality common to our relationships with employers and often with friends as well. In the family, gifts, favors, or forgiveness can, through the medium of love, be given freely, without the giver thereby "getting the upper hand" or implicitly obligating the receiver to make an equal return.

Thus, whereas other primary groups depend upon other kinds of sentiments—companionship, *esprit de corps*—to bind members together and to ease their interaction, the family relies on the socially prescribed sentiment of love to smooth over quarrels, to temper social regulation with compassion, and to provide some relief from social bargaining.

The common coin or medium of all the transactions and interactions in the family system is communication. It is important not only for the performance of agreed-upon or assigned roles, but also for the carrying out by adults and children alike of yet another extremely significant function: the family is the arena in which identity is formed, developed, and also transformed (Goodman, forthcoming). In short, the family is a rich field of investigation for sociologists with a

* This discussion is based on Turner, 1970, Chapters 9–10.

symbolic-interactionist point of view as well as, increasingly, for those with an interest in conflict theory.

ROLE DISTURBANCES

The husband-wife bond, with which the family begins, is subject to a number of strains. We will consider two aspects of the traditional husband-wife role system that are currently being seriously questioned by many American couples—power and sex.

Power and authority

"The institution we call marriage can't hold two full human beings—it was only designed for one and a half." This opinion, stated by Andrew Hacker (quoted in *Time*, December 28, 1970, p. 35), is shared by a number of feminists, who contend that the power structure typical of marriage in our society is designed to suppress the woman's will and individuality.

Despite such arguments, marriage is still extremely popular. "In 1972 and 1973, there were 10.9 marriages for every thousand Americans. This was the highest rate since 1950 (at 11.1), which was the tail end of the post-World War II marriage boom" (Scanzoni and Scanzoni, 1976, p. 141). The latest figure (1978) is 10.3 marriages for every thousand Americans (Census Bureau, 1979, p. 81). The women's liberation movement, along with the recent increase in the number of working women, has generated considerable social controversy—and considerable bargaining between individual husbands and wives—over the allocation of power.

What are the sources of power in marriage? One

LOVE IN THE FAMILY: A SEARCH FOR ITS ROOTS IN HISTORY

Can you picture yourself sending your newborn baby to live with a wet nurse miles from home or leaving it, unguarded, in front of an open fire? Can you imagine being unsure how many children you have had, or how many have been stillborn? Our modern view of the family makes such things seem inconceivable, yet in European societies before the eighteenth century, this apparent lack of feeling for one's offspring was the norm. That, at least, is the contention of the social historian Edward Shorter.

In his book *The Making of the Modern Family* (1975), Shorter maintains that in traditional European society, parents cared little about the well-being of their infants.

Mothers in villages and small towns across the continent . . . seldom departed from traditional—often hideously hurtful—infant hygiene and child-rearing practices. . . . Nor did these mothers often (some say "never") see their infants as human beings with the same capacities for joy and pain as they themselves. Parents were not, in other words, able to put themselves in their infants' tiny shoes, to imagine the world from their viewpoint, and thus to make it as agreeable and delightful a world as possible. . . . (p. 169)

Relations between husbands and wives were similarly grim, claims Shorter. Marriage was a matter of economic convenience, arranged by a couple's parents. Courtship was carefully supervised, and "before 1800, people seldom has sexual intercourse before it was absolutely certain they would marry" (p. 166). Even after marriage, writes Shorter, "sex served the larger ends of procreation and the continuation of the lineage, rather than being in itself an object of joy and delight" (p. 166).

Then, during the late eighteenth century, all this began to change. There was a rise in legitimate and illegitimate birth rates, a drop in infant mortality rates, and a decreased use of wet nurses after 1750. Men and women started choosing their own mates, and mutual affection—not mutual property—became the goal. Attitudes toward sex changed, and in the decades after 1750 Shorter sees the first "sexual revolution" of modern times. Children too became the objects of love instead of neglect. Mothers began to nurse their infants themselves and became more attentive to their needs.

And so, Shorter maintains, the modern family was born. The question, though, is why? What freed young men and women to choose their own wives and husbands? Why did sex become a source of joy and not just of children? And why did women start caring for their babies with affection and concern? For answers to these questions, Shorter looks to the crucial economic changes that took place in the eighteenth century. With the rise of capitalism, men and women left their communities for jobs in industrialized towns. Young people, no longer dominated by familial and community pressures, could respond to their own needs and feelings. Shorter's thesis is that "contact with the marketplace gave local people a new sense of individual gratification and a corresponding unwillingness to conform to traditional community values of self-abnegation and self-denial" (p. 266). Under such conditions, Shorter claims, premarital sex would become more common, people would marry for love, and this love would carry over to the mother child relationship.

major source is a society's pattern of norms. For example, despite recent trends, our society still expects the husband to be "in charge" or "the head" of the family. This cultural assumption is reflected in our language. "A *man's* home is *his* castle," though the woman is likely to spend many more hours there. The person in charge of a family is the one who "wears the pants," not the skirt. And if the pants-wearer cedes to his wife too much of his culturally ordained authority, he is said to be "henpecked." (We do not speak of "roosterpecked" wives.) Thus the culture, and the language that reflects it, makes it quite clear to young people that the power they will have within marriage will be largely determined by their sex.

There is another important determinant of power in marriage—the control of resources. In a classic study by Robert O. Blood and Donald M. Wolfe (1960), it

Shorter's theory has received much attention, but he has also been criticized for both lack of evidence and faulty analysis. For example, the testimony about the indifference of mothers comes from physicians' reports, and the latter may have been biased in their observations (Lasch, 1975, p. 52). It is certainly possible that infants died not because of maternal neglect, but because of poor sanitation and limited medical knowledge. It is also possible that women avoided becoming emotionally attached to their babies precisely because losing them to disease would then have been unbearable. In sum, the drop in infant mortality rates in the nineteenth century may owe more to improved sanitary facilities and medical care than to heightened maternal feelings.

Shorter also provides little documentation of the loveless premodern marriage and the joylessness of sex. It is one thing to say that there was less premarital sex before 1750, but "it is quite another matter to infer a change in the meanings of the sex" (Gordon, 1973, p. 170). Too, critics have faulted Shorter for assigning a vanguard role in family change to the working classes. On the contrary, they say, it was the commercial classes, with their increased affluence, who could afford to lavish time and money on children (Plumb, 1975, p. 3).

Despite these possible shortcomings, Shorter's work raises intriguing questions, and reminds us that some of our most basic habits, those we take most for granted, may be surprisingly recent phenomena and may also have some unexpected connections to the economic institutions of our times.

was found that a husband's power within the marriage tended to increase in proportion to the amount of "resources"—such as education, salary, and job status—that he had to offer. Likewise, wives who were gainfully employed had more say in important family decisions than wives who stayed at home. The resources that confer power are those which pertain to the marketplace—those which bring in money. The talents and services a housewife has to offer—cooking, cleaning, entertaining, preventing the children from being hit by trucks—do not increase her power, no matter how essential they are to the family's and to society's existence. It seems that one way for a wife to gain more say in family decision making is to earn money (Benson, 1969; Gillespie, 1971, p. 457).

Of course, we all know of families where personality traits outweigh economic prerogatives. Many a husband has more power than his wife even though she earns half the family's income. Conversely, many a wife has more power than her husband even though she earns no money. If a husband is unable to assert himself, or if he simply prefers to leave household decisions to his wife, then she will gain power.

When power is considered legitimate (that is, earned or deserved) by those who are subject to it, then it is called *authority*. The authority holder makes the decisions; those under his or her authority comply; and peace reigns. But when power is exercised without the consent of those subject to it—in short, when it becomes simply *domination* (Scanzoni and Scanzoni, 1976, p. 316)—then conflict is likely to result. This appears to be the case in many troubled marriages, where the wife may feel the husband simply is not entitled to the power he insists on wielding.

This kind of analysis is important for micro-oriented conflict theorists, who are interested in applying their views to groups smaller than society. Power and authority in the family constitute an area of inquiry that has come increasingly to the fore with the growth of the movement for equality between men and women, a point discussed more fully in the previous chapter.

Sex

Another potential source of strain in marriage is the couple's sex life. This is particularly true in our culture where, as noted above, we tend to see sex and love as being intimately related. Thus, trouble in the marriage

Until recently, the respective roles of marriage partners in our society were clear-cut and widely accepted. The quotations from the Bible used to decorate this marriage certificate by the noted lithographer Nathaniel Currier in 1848 support the traditional view of the husband as provider and protector and the wife as "the weaker vessel." (Library of Congress)

is likely to cause trouble in the marriage bed (Turner, 1970, p. 341); conversely, trouble in bed is readily interpreted as trouble in the marriage. Any deficiency of sexual interest or response, for whatever reason, may elicit the complaint, "You don't love me anymore."

Marital sex is currently a subject of intense interest, as is evidenced by the spate of sexual "how-to" books published in the last decade. Much of this interest is focused on two related topics, female orgasm and sexual reciprocity—that is, the ability of husband and wife to communicate to each other their sexual needs and to respond to each other's needs. Such cooperation, thought to be a major determinant of female orgasm (Masters and Johnson, 1970), appears to be lacking in a large number of marriages.

It appears that in lower-class marriages, in particular, men "still hold openly to the *macho* concept of masculinity where the man is insistent on taking his own pleasure without reference to the woman's needs" (Rainwater, 1965). In middle- and upper-class marriages as well, many women complain that their husbands are not "romantic" enough before intercourse (Seaman, 1972). Another source of conflict may simply be a difference in sex drive beween the two partners—though the degree to which this is biologically determined or socially learned is still subject to debate. In addition, differences between men and women in sexual perception and arousal complicate mutual understanding of sex roles in marriage (Belkin and Goodman, 1980, 219–224).

Many sexual conflicts between husbands and wives may stem not from any real difficulties in their marriages, but from inadequate socialization for sexual behavior. According to F. Ivan Nye and Felix M. Berardo (1973, pp. 332–333), the information available to most children and adolescents teaches them primarily that sex is dark, secret, and mysterious; that it is charged with emotional meaning (often guilt, sometimes "ecstasy"). Once dating begins, it is a struggle between the female, who teases but holds back, and the male, who pushes toward the gratification of his own needs. Young people often fail to learn that sex—and marriage itself—can and should be a cooperative venture, an attentive and tender give-and-take between two human beings.

THE PROBLEMS OF PARENTHOOD

The interaction between parent and child, like that between husband and wife, is a system of interlocking roles (Brim, 1957). Here, too, there is an exchange of costs and rewards. Essentially, children are expected to be obedient—that is, tractable to the process of socialization—and in return they are nurtured. Parents are expected to care for the children—to feed them, house them, and socialize them—and in return they expect to be obeyed. Furthermore, as we have seen, both parties are expected to love each other.

The parent-child role system, based on the unalterable fact of the child's dependency, thus appears simple. Yet the truth is that in modern industrial societies, performing the parent role has become increasingly difficult (Belkin and Goodman, 1980, Chapter 10). In the first place, the arrival of the first child puts a tremendous strain on the husband-wife relationship, cutting down on leisure time and sexual spontaneity and shifting the balance from shared duties and activities to role specialization (Udry, 1974, p. 377). As time passes and the number of children increases, the strains multiply. Husband and wife labor separately to spend as efficiently as possible their limited resources of time, money, and energy on the resource-devouring system of the family. It is thus no surprise that reported marital satisfaction tends to decline steadily from the birth of the first child to the time when the children begin to leave home (Rollins and Feldman, 1970). The stress of young children on parents also increases the probability of depression (Pearlin and Johnson, 1977).

And what of parental satisfaction? Can it compensate for the loss of marital satisfaction? At present there are no definitive studies on whether American parents experience child rearing as more pleasure than pain, but some researchers have found increased marital dissatisfaction associated with the child-rearing phase of the family cycle (Burr, 1970; Rollins and Feldman, 1970; Renne, 1976). Indeed, American parents are faced with a rather cruel cultural paradox. On the one hand, the culture is decidedly pro-parenthood. Voluntary childlessness is still viewed as somewhat unnatural, even selfish. Furthermore, it is not enough simply to

Parents in our society are expected to enjoy their children. Yet the truth is that children increase parents' probability of depression (Pearlin and Johnson, 1977) and decrease their overall freedom. (Elizabeth Crews/Stock, Boston)

have children; parents must *enjoy* their children. Parenthood should be fun, our society tells us (Wolfenstein, 1955, pp. 174–179), and if it is not, then perhaps there is something wrong with the parent.

On the other hand, the society does very little to make it possible for parents to fulfill this imperative. Indeed, behind the parental mystique is a rather grim reality—a society in which parents are expected to shoulder the burden of parenthood without the help of any clear child-rearing standards or of such practical aids as adequate day-care facilities. In the extended family there are extra hands to help with washing, feeding, and supervising children. But in the American nuclear family, and particularly in the single-parent family, children fall into what Arlene Skolnick calls a "nurturance gap" (1973, p. 278), where parents struggle alone, totally free and totally responsible. Supermarket aisles do not easily accommodate baby carriages; baby sitters are expensive; and each year brings a new crop of child-rearing manuals, promulgating a revised set of firm dos and don'ts, guaranteed to arouse guilt in the parent who has already committed multiple don'ts. If the parents admit discouragement, this is tantamount to failure. Yet it is difficult to see how parents can fail to feel discouraged when asked to fill so taxing a role.

FAMILY VIOLENCE

Familial love can defuse conflict, but as a system of roles involving power and dependency the structure of the family itself can be a source of conflict, and the family a setting for force and violence. Husband and wife may use force to resolve their power struggles; parents may use force to coerce their children.

One kind of force is, of course, physical violence. Wife beating and child abuse are probably as old as

human society—but they are also, it seems, more common in the dynamics of the modern American family than has been generally understood. In the last decade, the problem of family violence has become an object of concern and of study as its dimensions have become clearer: each year, millions of wives and children in families of all socioeconomic levels seek legal and medical help because of abuse in the home (Steinmetz and Straus, 1974; Gelles, 1973, 1977, 1978).

This would hardly seem to conform to the ideal of American family life—and particularly to the middle-class stereotype. But if we look at the American family as part of the larger society, the picture is a little different. Violence as a solution to conflict situations is part of the American ethos; "spare the rod and spoil the child" was until a few years ago a major guideline for parents; and a husband's right to use physical force against a wife was so taken for granted that, until recently, under the law a wife could not accuse her hus-

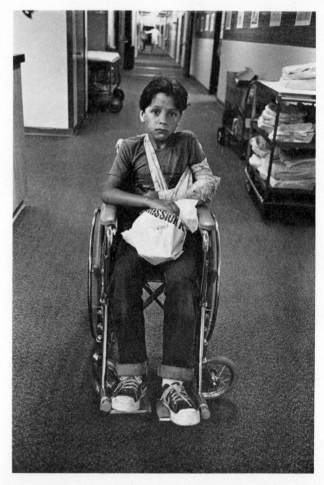

A child abuse victim awaits medical treatment. Many parents who beat their children deny them medical attention for fear that their abuse will come to the attention of authorities. In the last decade, the problem of family violence has become an object of concern and study as the true scale of the problem has become clearer. (Barbara Alper/Stock, Boston)

band of rape. Indeed, in the early 1800s it was considered a husband's prerogative, if not his responsibility, to beat his wife. When one battered spouse threw herself on the mercy of the court, the town magistrate responded by handing down what might well have been considered enlightened justice at the time: no husband should beat his wife with a stick thicker than his own thumb.

Physical punishment of children is almost universal; one survey showed that 93 percent of all parents spank their children.* And Steinmetz and Straus (1974) found that physical punishment or the threat of it was experienced by half the students in their study sample as late as senior year in high school.

Violence, it seems, begets violence; many studies have shown that abused children become abusive parents, that those who see and experience violence in the home as children are more prone to use this solution to conflict throughout their lives. Efforts at solving the problem have so far focused on teaching individuals new ways of behaving and of coping with conflict and frustration. But this approach does not deal with the social and cultural basis of the problem—the general approval of the use of violence that pervades American culture. Doing something about family violence, then, seems to require doing something about our society and not just for or with individual husbands, wives, or parents (Gelles, 1973, 1977, 1978).

The changing American family

As we have seen, the American family is clearly under pressure. The raising of children is becoming an increasingly lonely and trying task. ("It should not escape attention," Richard R. Clayton notes, "that if the median duration of first marriages is seven years, this coincides with the stage in the family life cycle when there are one or more preschool children present in most homes" [1975, p. 497].) And under the influence of the women's movement, many women are beginning to regard child rearing as a burden they are under no obligation to bear, or bear alone.

Changing gender roles have also injected considerable confusion and discord into many husband-wife role systems by bringing into question the traditional pattern of the husband exerting overt dominance and the wife depending on the power of covert influence. Indeed, the very institution of marriage—not just parenthood and gender roles—has now come under increasing attack. The traditional view of the sanctity of the family has been replaced by the wisdom of the 1960s and 1970s, which insists on the ideals of freedom, intensity, and variety. Most of all, the new requirement that a relationship provide maximum emotional fulfillment for both partners has proved a severe test for traditional marriage.

* Rodney Stark and James McEvoy, "Middle Class Violence," *Psychology Today*, 4 (November 1970), 52–65.

FRAGMENTATION

The result of all these strains has been that although many people stay married, many do not. Families are increasingly fragmented by divorce and separation, and many children grow up living with one parent and only occasionally visiting or seeing the other. The high rate of remarriage has created "reconstituted" families (Duberman, 1975), new family and kin relationships for which we do not as yet even have names. And because people may belong to several different familial units in a lifetime, the continuity and stability that were once the hallmark of family life do not exist for a growing number of people in quite the way they once did.

Divorce

In 1975, there were more than one million divorces granted in the United States. This was the first time the number passed the million mark, but the divorce rate has been rising steadily since 1950 and doubled between 1964 and 1975 (Clayton, 1978). Since then, it has continued to break records.

Although the numbers clearly suggest that there are a lot of divorces taking place in our society, the term "divorce rate" can be highly misleading because that rate can be computed in a number of ways. The simplest method is to record the number of divorces in a

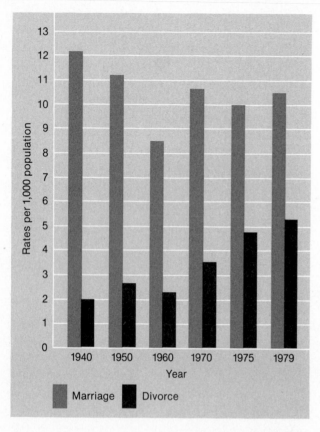

FIGURE 14.1

Rates of marriage and divorce in the United States, 1940-1979. (Adapted from Census Bureau, 1976, p. 68; and National Center for Health Statistics, *Monthly Vital Statistics Report: Births, Marriages, Divorces, Deaths*, March 1980, p. 1)

given year per 1,000 people in the population. In 1977, for instance, there were 1,091,000 divorces in the U.S. (Census Bureau, 1979, p. 84), for a rate of about 5 per every 1,000 Americans. The most dramatic method, and therefore the most appealing to the media, involves calculating the ratio of couples getting married to those getting divorced. In 1976, for instance, 50 couples got divorced for every 100 couples that got married in the United States, which yields a rate of 50 percent. The rate will be lower using a third method that factors in the known divorce rates for both first marriages (38 out of every 100) and second marriages (45 out of every 100), as well as the remarriage rate (about 3 out of every 4 divorced women marry a second time). So of the 38 women whose first marriages end in divorce, 29 will

remarry, and of those 29, 13 will get a second divorce, for a grand total of 51 divorces out of 129 marriages—or 40 percent. Finally, it's possible to compute the number of divorces per 1,000 existing marriages. This method compares the proportion of married couples who decide to stay married to the proportion of married couples who don't, and the result may be the most informative estimate of the extent of significant marital strain in our society.

No matter how the rate is computed, however, the fact is that almost everyone in America today has a relative or friend who is divorced, and most people in their early thirties speak of their generation as "on the second marriage."

One frequently cited explanation for the rising divorce rate is that many states have replaced stringent laws requiring court suits, formal charges, and the like with comparatively more permissive procedures. In a "no-fault" divorce, for example, neither party need offer any explanations nor assume any guilt. Many people have objected to "no-fault" divorce on the grounds that it would drive the divorce rates even higher, but so far—though it's still too soon to tell what the ultimate impact will be—the effect of "no-fault" statutes has been minimal.

The number of children involved in divorce has also increased dramatically—1,095,000 in 1977, with a mean of one child per divorce (Census Bureau, 1979, p. 81). Today American couples are less likely to "stay together for the sake of the children." In 1970 for the first time, more children suffered disruption of the home through divorce than through the death of a parent, which until then had been the leading cause of a child's losing a parent.

Despite the high rate of divorce and the great numbers of families involved, not all families or all marriages are equally susceptible. Divorce is more common, for example, among blacks than among whites, but the lower rates for older middle-class blacks are the same as those for older middle-class whites: for those now over 35, the likelihood of divorce decreases as income and education rise. The great increase has come among those born since 1940. Of those in this group whose first marriages ended in divorce, over 50 percent were divorced in their twenties (Clayton, 1978). There is a greater chance of divorce for the nonreligious than for the religious; for those who marry young rather than in their mid or late twenties; and for the less rather than the more educated—but the differences are becoming smaller. The social pressure to continue an unsatisfactory relationship is simply less for Americans of all races and classes than it once was. And the traditional economic pressures have dwindled in importance, too. This is especially true for married women, whose increasing presence in the labor force has given them an economic independence that makes it far easier now than in the past to leave an unfulfilling marriage.

These changing values, however, do not mean that Americans have abandoned marriage as an institution. They continue to marry in record numbers, and the extremely high remarriage rate for divorced people, who in any age group are more likely to marry than the single or the widowed (Clayton, 1978), seems to support Udry's (1974, p. 405) conclusions that "marriage has become so important a source of emotional satisfaction . . . few people can endure a relationship which does not provide this" and that "divorced persons are rarely soured on marriage as such but only on *that* marriage" (p. 401). Americans, it seems, now practice not simple monogamy but *serial monogamy*, going from spouse to spouse as the years pass.

Single-parent families

Serial monogamy does not mean that one is *always* living with a spouse. There is usually a gap of several years between divorce and remarriage, and during these peri-

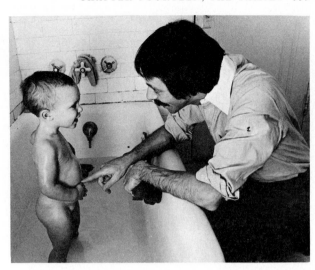

This child, being bathed by his father, is one of the more than one million children of single parents. With the increasing frequency of divorce, nearly 20 percent of all children under the age of eighteen are being raised by one parent. (Mark Antman)

ods—and sometimes permanently—the family may be a single-parent one. This pattern, long common among American blacks, is now found among all races and classes. Census data show that between 1970 and 1978, the proportion of children under 18 living with one parent increased from 12 to almost 20 percent. When the number of families headed by women are separated

FIGURE 14.2

The percentage of children under eighteen living with one parent only increased significantly between 1970 and 1979. (Census Bureau, *Marital Status and Living Arrangements for March 1979*, February 1980, p. 5)

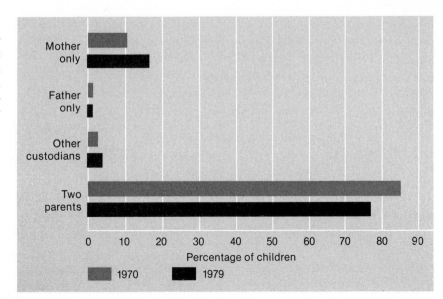

out by race, the increase for white women heads of households was 106 percent and for black women, 149 percent.

What these figures mean is that a great many American families no longer fit the stereotypes still used in most commercial advertising. As we said at the outset of the chapter, only about 17 percent of American families consist of a working husband, a nonworking wife, and children at home. Instead of the smooth-running, sparkling suburban home to which the father returns each night for a delightful family dinner and then an evening of shared intimacy, many children know only a harassed mother trying to do everything and be everywhere at once. The household often does not run smoothly; there is generally not as much money as before, so the living standard is usually not so high; and both the parent and the children may be cut off from the social life of the community, which centers around married couples and their offspring. Still, there appear to be compensations: a recent survey done by a market research firm (*Newsday*, October 23, 1979, Part II, p. 7) shows that most single parents like their new status, although most miss adult companionship and want eventually to remarry.

ALTERNATIVE FAMILY FORMS

Serial monogamy, single-parent families, the rise in "living together" arrangements, the growing number of those who choose to remain single, and the growing number of those who choose to have fewer or no children has led many critics to prophesy the death of the family. Others have focused instead on the idea of a metamorphosis, and on the development of new family forms to meet new needs. In fact, there have been changes; Americans have been experimenting with a variety of arrangements (Libby and Whitehurst, 1977).

Dual-career marriages

In the "ideal" family described earlier in this chapter, the husband works and the wife stays home to keep house and look after the children. In a dual-career marriage, by contrast, *both* the husband and wife pursue separate careers, and do so by choice. Their careers provide them with considerable satisfaction, as well as with a good salary and chances to advance professionally,

but the couple also remains committed to being married and to having a family. Typically, there are seldom more than two children in a dual-career family, which stands to reason considering the formidable demands imposed on the parents by full-time, often more than 9-to-5 jobs.

The dual-career marriage is a relatively new phenomenon; little is known about how many there may be. From the few studies conducted to date in this area, it is possible to construct a sort of general outline or profile of this family form. Normally, dual-career couples marry late, after the woman has completed college and often not until she has finished her graduate or professional training. There is no definite moment at which the husband and wife decide that both will have careers; instead, the situation seems to develop in stages, with the crucial moment, if there is one, coming at the birth of the first child.

Rather than promoting competition between two ambitious and hard-working people, a dual-career marriage seems to favor precisely the opposite, the husband and wife each taking pride and satisfaction in the other's work. In addition, income may be a less critical problem in this type of marriage: as a rule both the man and the woman earn salaries in the five-figure category. Some of the income may be used to hire household help, baby sitters, and the like, reducing to some extent the pressures on both the man and the woman in coping not only with their careers but also with such domestic and time-consuming matters as cleaning the house and feeding the children.

But things do not always work smoothly in dual-career marriages; it seems that both the man and the woman generally have more work than time to do it in. Unlike traditional marriages, however, in which the husband may resist any responsibility for household chores, in a dual-career marriage, husbands and wives report that they share such chores, and that this sharing can be a source of deep satisfaction. At the same time, children are usually pressed into service—to set the table, to wash the dishes, and so on—at the earliest possible moment. This sharing of duties, plus other factors mentioned above, may account for the fact that women in dual-career marriages who work by choice have shown a higher level of "marriage adjustment" than women who work because they have to (Orden and Bradburn, 1968).

Still, a dual-career couple is often forced to make

sacrifices. The wife may in fact be saddled with more responsibility for the home and children than the husband: one report states that working women enjoy considerably less free time than their husbands—who "help out" along with the kids. Also, long-distance moves (to another county or state) often mean that the wife will drop out of the labor force for at least a while, or take a cut in earnings, suggesting that the move was dictated by the husband's career. On the other hand, men seem to move to another county or state less frequently if their wives work, so it may also be true that husbands make sacrifices for their wives' careers. Both the husband and wife, however, seem to stand a statistically better chance of moving within a county or state, probably to a better neighborhood.

Indeed, dual-career couples seem to be more mobile than average. This, plus their heavy workloads, means that their circle of friends will be small. Besides, so little leisure affords limited time for lavish entertaining or socializing. The mobility and hectic schedules may also prevent either member of a dual-career couple from having much contact with parents or relatives, and some strain may develop in these relationships. In short, there are pluses and minuses in this as in all family forms. As more is learned about dual-career marriages, it may become easier to answer a crucial question: how do they compare to traditional marriages? For now, it is simply too soon to tell.

The communal family

Both married couples and single parents have joined together to raise children in common, regard one another as kin, and sometimes extend sexual privileges beyond the marital unit (Skinner, 1948; Stoller, 1970; Schulz, 1972). The idea of communal living is not new; there were a number of short-lived experiments in the United States in the nineteenth century, most of them based on religious ideas. The revival that began in the 1960s has been part of the trend toward greater personal fulfillment and satisfaction and against the perceived alienation of modern American life. Most communes have not survived for long, but the experimentation continues in both rural and urban settings. Particularly for the divorced parent with children, the commune offers help with child care, the companionship of other adults, emotional support, and an easing of the economic burden of raising a family alone.

Group marriage and polygamy

Like communal living, group marriage and polygamy are old forms now being revived in a new context. Group marriage today is generally the joining of already existing pairs in a cooperative living arrangement that allows for sexual variety within a defined structure (Constantine and Constantine, 1977). There is no one pattern for group marriage; each unit makes its own rules for living. At least one strong advocate of sexual freedom (Ellis, 1970), however, has suggested that the inherent difficulties of such an arrangement will limit its popularity.

Open marriage

One of the basic tenets of traditional monogamy is sexual exclusivity. For those who like all the aspects of marriage but this one, the freer attitudes toward sex of recent decades have led to the idea of "open marriage" (O'Neill and O'Neill, 1966; Thamm, 1975), defined by anthropologists Nena and George O'Neill as "a relationship in which the partners are committed to their own and to each other's growth," and that "is flexible enough to allow for change, which is constantly being renegotiated in the light of changing needs, consensus in decision-making, acceptance and encouragement of individual growth, and openness to new possibilities for growth" (1972).

Typically, these "new possibilities for growth" mean that while maintaining a traditional monogamous home and family life, a couple rejects the notion of sexual exclusivity; separately, the husband and wife enjoy variety in sexual partners. In a broader sense, however, the "open marriage" concept refers to more than sexual freedom: it points to a relationship in which the individual fulfillment and personal preferences of each member lie at the core of the marriage, rather than the more traditional values of duty, obligation, and durability (Melville, 1980).

Shared parenting

Until very recently, custody of the children of a divorcing couple was almost automatically given to the mother on the basis of the so-called *tender years doctrine*, which held that children are better off with Mom than with Dad. She was the full-time parent with whom the children lived; the father saw them only at certain prearranged times and for specified periods. The father, in effect, became an outsider to his own family.

In the last five to ten years, divorced fathers wanting to maintain close ties with their children have begun to seek custody themselves or shared custody with the mother. And the courts have recently begun to consider cases in a new light (Belkin and Goodman, 1980, 451–453).

During the 1970s, studies began to indicate that a father could be as good a "mother" to his children as their biological mother. Simultaneously, as part of the expanding social role of women, many mothers were beginning to hold jobs and earn incomes, removing the age-old argument that the father was the children's (and mother's) sole financial support. This gave rise to a new legal doctrine called *joint custody,* based on the idea that both parents are at least theoretically equal in their ability to care for children. The key breakthrough occurred in 1973 when a judge in New York's Family Court threw out the *tender years doctrine* in a custody case on the grounds that it was based on outdated stereotypes of both mothers and fathers.

Thus, today, living arrangements of children of divorced parents show considerable variations. Some children live with their mother half the week and their father the other half; some go back and forth on a weekly or monthly basis. But whatever the schedule, both father and mother remain equally active parents of their children, though they no longer function as a couple.

Living together

Divorced people who want to live with someone but do not want another legal marriage and couples who would like to live together instead of or before taking on the responsibilities of legal marriage have developed another new/old form: "living together" or cohabitation. Once called "common-law marriage," if it lasted long enough, and definitely frowned upon, this style has been adopted now by some middle-class people, both young and old. College students live together, as do young professionals beginning their careers. Older couples who could not afford the reduction in social security benefits that would result from their marriage are also cohabiting in increasing numbers. The law regarding social security benefits was changed in 1979, but whether this will affect cohabitation rates remains to be seen.

Staying single

Although marriage and couple-living are still the overwhelming norm in America, the greater tolerance for different life styles and the easing of the pressure to have children has led still others to decide to stay single. Those who choose this style, whether never married, widowed, or divorced, live most often in urban settings. They may live with someone for a period of time or perhaps share in a communal arrangement, but their basic orientation is not toward couple-living.

The single life style is also more characteristic of certain age groups than others, due to the increasing tendency of young men and women to postpone marriage. In 1960, the median age at first marriage was 22.8 for men and 20.3 for women; by 1977, the figures were 23.0 for men and 21.1 for women (Census Bureau, 1979, p. 81).

Staying single as an alternative to marriage is becoming more widely accepted. Those who do marry are doing so at a later age and thus are remaining single longer. (Amy Meadow)

The future of the American family

In 1927, the psychologist John B. Watson predicted that "by 1977 marriage would no longer exist in the United States" (Clayton, 1978, p. 594). Watson was mistaken, of course, but the forms and functions of the family have certainly changed and will continue to do so.

In terms of form, there are now a number of alternatives, and social scientists predict even more. Trial marriage is one suggested alternative that might help the divorce rate and shield children from the trauma of separation. The best known of these schemes is Margaret Mead's "marriage in two steps" (1966). In this arrangement, a couple would first enter into an easily dissolvable "individual marriage," with the goal of mutual happiness but with the proviso that they have no children. Then, if they eventually wanted to have children and were emotionally and financially prepared to do so, they would move on to the second step, a "parental marriage," which would be much more difficult to enter and to dissolve than "individual marriage," thereby ensuring the well-being of the children.

Another proposal, again an adaption of older customs, would be written marriage contracts setting out the rights and duties of each of the partners, especially with regard to having and raising children (Sager et al., 1971; Edmiston, 1972; Weitzman, 1974; Ramey, 1977). More radical are proposals such as Tyler's (1975) plan to have people marry according to sexual compatibility: young men at the peak of their sexual activity would first marry experienced older women who had previously been married to older men. These men would then leave the first marriage to marry younger women, who would bear the children. By the time parents were ready to switch partners, the children would be nearly grown and able to cope with the change. Casler's (1974) "permissive matrimony" proposals are equally radical: he argues that marriage as we know it has outlived its usefulness and should be replaced by new forms, such as conventional monogamy, modified monogamy (sexually nonexclusive or child-free), nonmonogamous relationships (polygamy, group marriage, communal arrangements), and nonmarital relationships that are free of any legal constraints.

All these proposed alternatives are based on changes in the legal basis of marriage. Although some are already being tried, they have no legal sanction, as is shown by recent court cases over division of property when a "living-together" arrangement ends. What some social scientists predict is that some of these forms of marriage and family will eventually have legal status: a "living-together" arrangement or a trial marriage will be registered just as a monogamous marriage is today, and there will be laws specifying rights to property and the status of children similar to those that now exist for husbands and wives.*

In terms of function, some of the five basic functions of the family may be transferred to other institutions. Society already provides some families with a measure of financial support (through welfare, family assistance, food stamps, Medicaid, Medicare) and to a large degree has assumed various aspects of the socialization function. In the future, these functions may be to a greater or lesser extent taken over by society, as is the case on the Israeli kibbutz (Spiro, 1968).

As tax laws continue to change and affirmative action programs increase, the family will be less able to support the stratification system by passing on parental resources to children or jobs to relatives. The regulation of sexual activity is already changing and will continue to, although reproduction will probably remain the province of married couples.

Intimacy and companionship are likely to become an even more important—and perhaps the central—function of the family. The frequency of marriage, divorce, and remarriage in our society indicates that a large number of people already consider emotional gratification an essential part of marriage, and there is no sign that this trend will be reversed. The ascendancy of intimacy in the hierarchy of family functions may well be aided by the trend toward increased equality and flexibility in the family role structure. Power and authority, it appears, will be more equally distributed in the family of the future: husband and wife will have an equal say in important decisions, and older children will be granted more autonomy and authority.

* Edgar W. Butler, *Traditional Marriage & Emerging Alternatives*, New York: Harper & Row, 1979.

As Belkin and Goodman (1980, pp. 464-468) indicate, all these alternatives and trends in both family form and function point to greater openness, choice, and flexibility. Marriage and the family will continue to exist (Bane, 1978), but there will be a variety of socially and legally sanctioned ways in which men and women may structure their intimate lives and rear children.

Summary

In one form or another, the *family* has existed in every known society throughout recorded history. The basic functions of the family are the regulation of sex and reproduction, care and socialization of children, economic cooperation, intimacy and companionship, and maintenance of the social stratification system.

There are two major types of family structure: the *nuclear family* and the *extended family*. The type of family favored in a society is an outgrowth of that society's values and economy. Thus, hunting and gathering societies and industrial societies favor nuclear families, while agrarian societies favor extended families.

All known societies exercise some control over marriage as a safeguard against dissolution of the existing social structure. Mate selection is governed by the complementary principles of *exogamy* and *endogamy*, and by *homogamy*, the tendency to marry someone of like background and status. *Child marriage* and other forms of *arranged marriage* are often used as a means of regulating marriage choices. Views on the importance of love in marriage vary greatly among the world's societies. In the United States, love, marriage, and sex are considered three aspects of a single process.

The family is a system of roles enacted according to personal needs, cultural requirements, and expectations of family members. Familial love serves to defuse conflict between members, to ease interaction between the family member and society, and to provide relief from the rigid bargaining that often marks other social relationships. The family can also be a source of strain and conflict, and sometimes a setting for violence. Conflicts between husband and wife over power and authority, and dissatisfaction with sex, as well as the difficulties of child rearing in contemporary America, can result in physical abuse and family violence.

Many changes—the women's movement, economic upheavals, the acceptability of divorce, experimentation with new marital forms and arrangements—have put a great deal of pressure on the traditional family and monogamous marriage. But these are still strong and vital institutions: they are likely to change form and function to meet changing needs, but they are by no means about to disappear.

Glossary

CONJUGAL LOVE Love that can develop between spouses on the basis of companionship, mutual understanding, and shared experiences.

ENDOGAMY Marriage within one's own group.

EXOGAMY Marriage outside a specified social group usually consisting of particular kinds of relatives.

EXTENDED FAMILY Several nuclear families united by parent-child relationships and living together.

FAMILY Defined by Stephens as a social arrangement based on marriage and the marriage contract, including recognition of the rights and duties of parenthood, common residence for husband, wife, and children, and reciprocal economic obligations between husband and wife.

GROUP MARRIAGE One form of polygamy involving marriage of two or more men and two or more women in a single union.

HETEROGAMY Marriage between people of different races, religions, and social classes.

HOMOGAMY Marriage between people of the same race, religion, and social class.

INCEST TABOO The prohibition of sexual relations between certain family members.

MONOGAMY Marriage involving one man and one woman at the same time.

NUCLEAR FAMILY The basic unit of family organization, consisting of a married couple and their immature offspring.

POLYANDRY A form of polygamy involving marriage of one woman to two or more men at the same time.

POLYGAMY Marriage involving more than two partners of opposite sexes at the same time.

POLYGYNY A form of polygamy involving marriage of one man to two or more women at the same time.

ROMANTIC LOVE COMPLEX Goode's term for the type of love—based on sexual attraction and on idealization of the loved one's personality—that in some societies is seen as a highly desirable basis for courtship and marriage.

SERIAL MONOGAMY A series of monogamous marriages.

Recommended readings

Belkin, Gary S. and Norman Goodman. *Marriage, Family, and Intimate Relationships*. Chicago: Rand McNally, 1980. An unusual and excellent textbook that blends the knowledge, training, and experience of a counseling psychologist and a sociological social psychologist. The book provides an initial examination of marriage and family patterns across the world and throughout history as backdrop to a description and analysis of the contemporary American context.

Clayton, Richard R. *The Family, Marriage, and Social Change*. 2nd ed. Lexington, Mass.: D. C. Heath, 1978. A well-written textbook on the family that attempts to integrate this subfield with general sociological theory.

Gagnon, John H. and Cathy Greenblat. *Life Designs: Individuals, Marriages, and Families*. Glenview, Ill.: Scott, Foresman, 1978. A fine textbook that adopts a life-cycle approach to the study of the family and critically assesses the relevant research literature, particularly on topics such as gender-role learning, the effects of growing equality between men and women, and alternative models for male-female relationships.

Greenblat, Cathy S., Peter J. Stein, and Norman F. Washburne. *The Marriage Game*. 2nd ed. New York: Random House, 1977. This remarkable book is a combination of selected readings and an instructional game designed to give youthful readers the experience of courtship, marriage, and family life. The "players" become involved in the manifold day-to-day decisions of courtship and marriage and learn the necessity of making certain choices as well as the likely consequences of their decisions.

Libby, Roger W. and Robert N. Whitehurst (eds.). *Marriage and Alternatives: Exploring Intimate Relationships*. Glenview, Ill.: Scott, Foresman, 1977. An interesting collection of articles that center around the restrictive nature of contemporary marriage. The selections provide a serious discussion of alternative modes of intimacy; the editors call for more public debate of these issues.

Skolnick, Arlene. *The Intimate Environment: Exploring Marriage and the Family*. 2nd ed. Boston: Little, Brown, 1978. An unusual textbook that takes as its premise the notion that the family is problematic, rather than an essential "given" in human society. Its orientation is strongly influenced by the view that families should be seen as behavioral *systems*, not merely as collections of individuals.

Turner, Ralph H. *Family Interaction*. New York: Wiley, 1970. An excellent textbook by a widely respected sociologist with broad interests. This book adopts the social-psychological view of the family as a small group, focusing on its internal interaction and its relationship to outside social forces.

Aspects of the family among the Bedouin of Cyrenaica

E. L. PETERS

In any society, the marriage ceremony reveals much about the connections between generations within the family. Among the male-dominated Bedouin of Cyrenaica, marriage means the restructuring of the father-son relationship so that the son begins to have more independence and authority.

When a marriage takes place among the Bedouin of Cyrenaica, a nuptial tent is set up some distance away from that of the groom's father. There is no particular significance about the nuptial tent itself, but it must be pitched at a distance so that the father "will not see it"—although, obviously, in a country of large level plains, it stands out conspicuously. This pretence that the tent remains unseen by the father is pushed to the point of his denying any knowledge of what is afoot. A middle-aged or elderly man with a family adopts a similar attitude to any marriage in which his son participates, as groom or as guest. . . . Prior to the wedding festivities, the father will have participated in negotiations, although even in these he will have remained silent, leaving an affine, as a rule, to arrange the details with the girl's father and his kinsmen. The father feigns aloofness from the start of negotiations until after the wedding celebrations have ended. Before inquiring into this seemingly odd behaviour, a few further details of marriage ceremonies need to be mentioned briefly.

The bride is carried to the nuptial tent on a camel, seated in a cagelike structure placed on the camel's back, this canopy covered over with carpets and at least one long blanket—later to be used to divide her tent into male and female quarters—which constitute part of the goods given to a woman on marriage. On her arrival, while she is still seated in her canopy, the camel is led round the tent seven times by a small boy. She then descends and is hustled into the tent by a number of women who make a show of their attempts to conceal her from view. Inside the tent the bride is enclosed in one corner in a kind of cubicle partitioned off by a length of blanket.

In the meantime, the groom has affected to escape, but is "caught," while running away, by his fellows, who "compel" him to return to the nuptial tent, to the accompaniment of their lewd songs telling of the sexual pleasures awaiting him. Much of this is horseplay, but the young men carry it out brazenly and the groom is re-quired to show reluctance to continue with the ceremonies. His entry into the nuptial tent is marked by an expectant hush that falls over the crowd of men gathered, as they await the result of the virginity test the groom is about to perform, which he does by wrapping part of his toga round one of his fingers to pierce the hymen. Sharp shrieks from the bride give the signal that the test has been undertaken; not a stir moves the crowd until evidence of its success has been publicly displayed, which is given by the groom hoisting the blood-stained portion of the toga through the corner of the tent on a pole, followed by firing three shots from his rifle. Jubilantly, the men gathered fire volley after volley from their rifles just over the nuptial tent, and the seven-day celebrations begin.

A full descriptive account of a marriage, or many of the ritual details woven into it need not be given here. What is included is intended to illustrate certain relationships between father and son, and between one generation and another. . . .

The fiction that nothing has happened, which characterises the father's behavior, does not cease with the termination of the celebrations. Each morning, soon after daybreak and before the camp is astir, the groom must leave his bride and repair to his father's tent to lie at his father's side "as he always had done in the past, as if he had not left him." This conventional ruse is followed, not just for the seven days of wedding festivities, but is continued after the groom has moved back into the camp proper, and pitched his tent alongside his father's, with the ropes of the two tents crossing.

In matters other than sleeping arrangements, this fiction that "nothing has happened" is maintained. Marriage does not mean the immediate creation of a wholly separate domestic unit. Save for the appearance of an additional tent, the ordinary run of daytime activities is scarcely altered. To mention perhaps the most important feature of the relationships between father and son, the groom continues to eat with his father. . . .

The son who continues to eat with his father "as he always had been doing," also continues to accept his authority. Indeed he could do little else at this stage, for he lacks the economic means to cut away. Neither at marriage nor after is there any transfer of wealth from father to son. The new tent recently pitched is no more than a dormitory to which the young couple retire at night. During the daytime the son is still to be seen in his father's tent, and, in the male quarters, things appear to be much the same as before. In the female quarters, the only superficial change is the more frequent appearance among the women of one who, before marriage, often sat among them if she had been a close neighbour or a close cousin previously; or of an additional helper if she had come from afar. On the surface things remain "as they always have been," although in fact, a whole set of changes have been initiated. . . .

After marriage, the Bedouin argue, a son has a tent of his own, a woman over whom he has authority and soon children to make him a father. Marriage causes split, branching. A new family is created, holding the potential of a new lineage. The separation is so painful a matter for the father that he cannot contemplate it, hence his pretence that he has no knowledge of wedding festivities, and his subsequent attitude that nothing has happened. . . .

In what sense can marriage mean split? Bedouin men marry "so that we may beget many sons, to make a big lineage later on." The worst fate that can befall a man as a result of his son's marriage is that he, in later generations, will become the focal point in a series of branching descent lines. The alternative—that his sons remain unmarried—can only mean that his name would disappear through want of successors to carry it on, which is one of the greatest evils which can befall a man, according to Bedouin sentiment: better split than oblivion. If the key to the interpretation of the father's attitude to his son's marriage is not that it causes split, it must lie elsewhere in their relationship. What marriage does is alter the distribution of authority between father and son. In order to pursue this, it is necessary first to clarify the types of authority involved, and then assess them in a post-marital situation. . . .

In the tent his [the father's] authority over his son is so overwhelming as to keep the son in almost complete subordination. The son is referred to as a slave, and in daily life he has to behave as one. He must obey every command, for, were he to rebel, he would find little or no support among his agnates, whatever the extent of the provocation. Retreat from his father is hardly an alternative, since, while his father is alive, he has no animals of his own, and to leave camp would only mean that he would have to move outside his group to seek employment elsewhere as a shepherd. If he did this he would forfeit status, and almost certainly cut himself off from property which would fall to him after his father's death. A man who "denies" his father loses too many privileges for the practice to become widespread. . . .

The question still remains: why is marriage the occasion of such ebullient celebration? The formal authority a father exercises over his son changes little on marriage. Economically the son is still harnessed to the father. The latter still shouts his orders at him, and obedience remains unaltered. Any sign of an independent view on a matter is met with a gruff rebuff. If the marriage turns out to be disagreeable to the father, he has the authority—if not always the power—to break it. Marriage does not mean a change in the general mode of behaviour between the two; the legal relations remain unaltered, albeit modified in practice, as the married son matures in age. But marriage does mean the acquisition of rights and status previously denied a son. Henceforward, he has a domain of his own. This is high drama, indeed, for although every effort is made to give substance to the expressed view that "nothing has happened," for the first time in his life the son has seized publicly, amid the jubilations of his fellows, a status which hitherto was the possession of the father. . . .

CHAPTER FIFTEEN
EDUCATION AND SOCIETY

Institutions of formal education are among the most prominent and all-embracing parts of complex societies, particularly industrialized ones. In the United States, for example, well over 60 million people, or one-quarter of the population, are involved in formal education as students; over 3 million are involved as teachers; and millions more are involved as suppliers of buildings, textbooks, blackboards, and other necessary goods and services. In fact, education is the United States' largest industry. And because of the increasingly high educational requirements of certain jobs, many Americans now spend one-quarter to one-third of their lives going to school.

The growth of formal education that has taken place in the United States and Western Europe in the past hundred years has been part of the larger pattern of *modernization*—the great societal transformation that has included industrialization, the growth of the middle classes, the shift of political allegiances from local groups to the national government, and the spread of bureaucratic or rational-legal values and procedures. (All these matters are discussed in Chapters 9–11, 17, 18, 20, and 22.)

But sociologists differ in their interpretation of the connection between education and other parts of the modern social fabric. Functionalists (whose general theoretical approach was discussed in Chapter 3) believe that our educational system is the way it is because it has taken shape in accordance with the needs of our society. To the functionalists, schools are a crucial part of the total social system, performing the important task of socializing the young and preparing them for particular jobs—and thus for particular niches in the social system. Conflict theorists (also discussed in Chapter 3) agree that schools perform this function—but they would say that they perform it all too well. In their view, the powers in control of the educational system act to keep the social classes in their place, ultimately channeling the children of the poor into menial or less skilled jobs and the children of the prosperous into college and well-paying and more prestigious careers. In this chapter we will consider these perspectives on education, and questions related to them. Our focus will be on the relationship between education and the modern industrial economy and on the way in which these two institutions relate to the stratification system.

A functionalist view of American education

Taking a cross-cultural view of the growth of secondary and higher education in industrial societies, sociologists such as S. N. Eisenstadt (1956), Martin Trow (1961), and Burton Clark (1962) have argued that this growth is the result of the extensive economic and professional specialization that exists in these societies. These writers believe that because the family alone cannot transmit all the technical knowledge such a society accumulates, a need arises for schools in which this knowledge can be transmitted (Solari, 1967).

EDUCATION AND WORK IN THE UNITED STATES

The United States is a country whose mushrooming secondary and higher education facilities appear to confirm this viewpoint. True, the roots of our educational system lie partly in the early Puritan emphasis on being able to read the Bible. But the thrust toward *mass* education did not come until the process of occupational specialization began after the Civil War. Around 1870, economic activity in many parts of the United States began to shift from agriculture to industry. Life changed in the developing industrial towns and cities: increasing specialization multiplied occupations by the thousands, and new professions began to emerge. Successful operation of the new industrial economy required that workers master new skills and techniques only extensive education could provide.

There seem to have been historical connections between the changes in economic and educational institutions. In 1870, there were relatively few middle-class and elite occupations. (Typical ones were law and the ministry.) Correspondingly, there were few secondary and higher education facilities; of the approximately 80,000 students enrolled in secondary schools in 1870, the 16,000 who were to graduate that year made up only about 2 percent of the seventeen-year-olds in the country. After 1870, however, the economy shifted from small industry to huge bureaucratized organizations characterized by centralized decision making, mass production, and mass marketing. Organizational growth demanded new skills for the reception, recording, retrieval, evaluation, and transmission of information; industries needed white-collar employees with better credentials than the bare literacy that elementary schools could provide. Accordingly, during this period there was a phenomenal expansion in the public high school system. By 1910, nearly 15 percent of the fourteen- to seventeen-year-olds (a total of more than 1 million students) were enrolled in secondary schools, 90 percent of them in the more than 10,000 public high schools then in operation. As the 1930s drew to a close, public and private secondary schools enrolled 65 percent of children from fourteen to seventeen. By the end of World War II in 1945, a mass system of secondary education was providing a useful and increasingly voca-

FIGURE 15.1

Enrollment rates in secondary and higher education in the United States from 1870 to 1980 (projected).

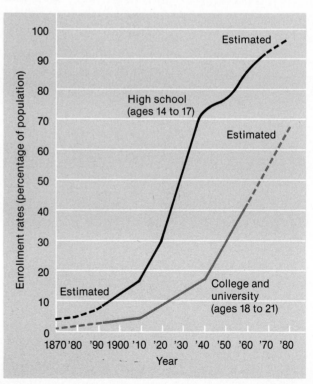

The members of this nineteenth-century high school graduating class probably came from wealthy families, and the men most likely went on to college and then into elite occupations. Most young people from less advantaged families either did not complete high school or got jobs as soon after graduation as they could. (Courtesy Title Insurance and Trust Co., San Diego)

tionally oriented education for more and more white-collar workers.

After World War II, sustained economic prosperity brought further changes in occupations in the United States, matched by further changes in secondary and higher education. Between 1950 and 1975, the number of white-collar workers nearly doubled; between 1950 and 1960, the total labor force increased by only 8 percent, but professional and technical positions grew by 68 percent. In parallel fashion, there was a boom in college enrollment. In 1940 college students represented only 15 percent of the eighteen- to twenty-one-year-old age group. By 1954 that proportion had risen to 30 percent; by 1979 to 32 percent. Since 1930, the rate of college enrollment has increased nearly *eight times* as fast as that of the total population, and since 1910, graduate school enrollment has multiplied more than *forty times* as quickly as the total population.

EDUCATION AND THE CLASS STRUCTURE

The functionalist view is that education grew *in response to* the increasing specialization of the occupational structure, and that education was supported by various groups because it made further industrialization possible. If it is indeed true that the two institutions—education and the economic system—are closely tied, then it might logically be expected that people with higher educational attainment would, in general, attain higher job levels; in other words, education should aid in the upward mobility of individuals. Indeed, as we saw in Chapter 11, such is the case today—at least for white males. In addition, since the number of jobs associated with higher status and rewards was increasing, it might also be predicted that education (the prerequisite for these jobs) would tend to bring higher status and rewards to larger numbers of people. In other words, it might be expected that education would tend to aid in the expansion of the middle and upper classes as categories. As we have seen, this too was the case. Before 1870, when there were relatively few middle-class or elite occupations, most students who were prepared for these occupations through education had middle- or upper-class backgrounds to begin with; thus, little change in the class structure took place through education. But after 1870, an increasing number of young people from less advantaged backgrounds were able to rise, through education, to the middle classes (and a few to the upper classes).

EDUCATION AND THE "AMERICAN DREAM"

In sum, the functionalist view sees education as serving three purposes: facilitating industrialization, acting as a "conveyor belt" for individual social mobility, and tending to broaden the middle classes as a whole. There has been enough truth to this picture for it to have been widely accepted, not only by social scientists but also by large numbers of other American citizens. The growth of education has been partly due to the fact that it has been widely perceived as a route to social mobility. As increasing numbers of young people have gone to high school and college (many of them then going on to relatively well-rewarded jobs), values and expectations favoring higher education have spread, and more groups have claimed education as a right. Thus education has become part of the American up-ward-mobility dream.

But how well does the functionalist view actually fit American reality? Conflict theorists argue that not all the functionalist assumptions are entirely valid. They see education in a different light—as we shall explain in the next section.

Education and stratification: a conflict view

Basically, conflict theorists question whether education really operates in a "hand-in-glove" fashion with other institutions in the society or with groups that are striving to improve their position. One reason for their doubt is that cross-cultural data fail to support the idea that education is the mechanism that has been responsible for the expansion of the middle classes in all industrialized societies. Sometimes, industrialization and its effects on the stratification system have come about *before* the expansion of education, or concurrently with it, rather than afterward. In fact, industrialization occurred in Western Europe and the United States after only 30 to 50 percent of the seven- to fourteen-year-old age group was in school.

In line with this point, Randall Collins (1971) has questioned the closeness of the relationship between education and occupations in America. First, Collins estimates that only 15 percent of the increase in educational requirements imposed on the American labor force during this century can be attributed to a replacement of low-skill by high-skill jobs. Most of the upgrading has taken place *within* job categories: the education required to obtain a particular job has been raised over time. (Figure 15.2 illustrates the increase, within various job categories, in the percentages of workers with four years of high school or more education.) Second,

Collins points out that most skilled manual workers acquire their skills on the job or in union apprentice-ships, rather than in vocational education programs. Occupational attainment in manual positions is virtually independent of vocational education; contrary to what one might expect, graduates of vocational programs are *not* more likely to be employed than high school dropouts (Plunkett, 1960; Duncan, 1964; Davis and McGurn, 1975). And although much has been said in recent years about the need for expanding the traditional vocational-education concept of specific skill training into "career education" that would encompass training and planning for a working lifetime (see, for example, National Academy of Education, 1979), these ideas have by no means been translated into practice (Marland, 1971). Nor is it totally clear how important education is for *nonmanual* occupations. While traditional professions such as medicine and law have legal requirements that prohibit noncertified individuals from practicing, the importance of formal schooling for other nonmanual occupations is more difficult to pinpoint. In 1970 approximately 40 percent of those in occupations labeled "engineer" lacked a bachelor's degree, a fact that indicates that even highly technical skills may be acquired on the job (Engineering Manpower Commission of Engineers Joint Council, 1976).

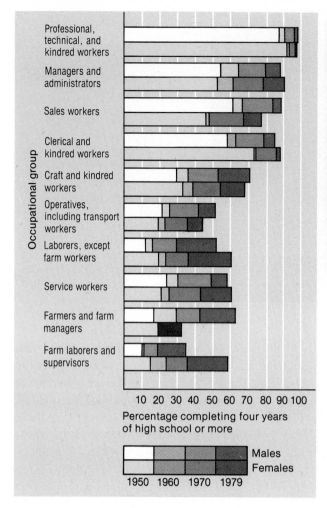

Students in a printing class. Research indicates that graduation from a vocational program is *not* a guarantee of related employment. (© Leonard Speier 1979)

FIGURE 15.2

This graph shows that the percentage of workers who have a high school education or more has increased in all ten of these job categories from 1950 to 1975. For example, whereas only 61 percent of male sales workers had four years of high school or more in 1950, 89 percent did in 1975. This is one manifestation of what Collins (1971) sees as a general increase in the amount of education required to obtain a particular job. (Adapted from Census Bureau, 1975, p. 5; Bureau of Labor Statistics, 1979)

THE CONFLICT MODEL

As a basis for his perspective, Collins uses the idea that society is made up of *status groups*—aggregates of people who share a position in the stratification system and who also interact among themselves, especially to fur-

ther the interests they have in common. (Labor unions and professional associations are examples.) Membership in these groups plays an important role in the development, maintenance, and transformation of the social identity of the members; and position in the stratification system is crucial to the members' lifestyles. In Collins' opinion, most of the conflict over valuable goods in a society is conflict between status groups; and much of the increase in secondary and higher education, and in educational requirements for jobs, results not so much from the need for more formal training as from the desire of status groups to maintain their positions in the occupational hierarchy.

Educational institutions do provide students with skills, but they also provide them with values and patterns of behavior that will identify them with certain status groups and therefore make them eligible for certain positions. Educational requirements for jobs limit applicants for elite positions to members of elite subcultures; for example, high-prestige corporations and law firms consistently recruit from upper-class Ivy League schools, thereby perpetuating the employment of elite "WASPs" in top positions. Likewise, educational institutions provide graduates with credentials. The professional teachers', social workers', and nurses' associations have consistently tried to make educational certification a legal necessity. Such credentials

Conflict theorists believe that educational institutions help to perpetuate the structure of society at large. Thus, students in a select club at a prestigious college can be expected to enter top positions in business and the professions. (Jim Smith)

do not necessarily guarantee that the holders are better trained than those who do not possess them; but they do strengthen certified individuals' leverage in the labor market.

A related idea, which fits in with this model, is that educational requirements can also be used by one group (those in charge of the educational system) to control the behavior of others. Let us look, for example, at the scope and functions of the public secondary school. In this century, the curricula in these schools have expanded to include social and civic responsibility, healthful living, and recreation. One might ask, are these topics intended to enrich the student's life, or to force him or her willy-nilly into the American mold (Cremin, 1964)?

To take another example, Samuel Bowles and Herbert Gintis (1976), in their study of American education as a part of the capitalist economic system, argue that two major reform periods in America—the emergence of the public school system in the mid-nineteenth century and the Progressive movement of the early twentieth century—can be viewed as periods of conflict among status groups in the capitalist system. Entrepreneurs needed to incorporate new groups into the industrial work force; workers, for their part, demanded access to education as an avenue of social mobility. The result was a series of compromises in which the workers got expanded education, but the higher-status groups shaped this education's form and content

to fit the needs of their own enterprises. In the various levels and kinds of schools, students learned the virtues needed for the various places in the economic hierarchy: in elementary and secondary schools they learned working-class characteristics—promptness, neatness, respect, obedience; in colleges they learned the characteristics needed by middle-level workers—dependability, responsibility, ability to work without constant supervision. The few colleges that encouraged independent thinking and initiative trained the leadership group—the elite.

All in all, then, the conflict model emphasizes the way educational institutions operate as a mechanism of occupational placement and of behavioral control for different status groups. There is some evidence that this view of the roles schools play is at least in part an accurate one. For example, employers in large corporations are dubious about how much actual skill is acquired in formal settings, but they still require a college degree for management trainees.

THE RELATIONSHIP OF EDUCATION TO ACHIEVED AND ASCRIBED STATUS

As Collins (1971) and Scimecca (1980) have pointed out, the functionalist theory of education is an application of the more general theory of stratification in industrialized societies developed by Kingsley Davis and Wilbert E. Moore (1945) (see Chapter 10). Davis and Moore suggested that power, property, and prestige are to some degree "necessary": they are rewards the society makes available to especially able individuals in consideration of the long and arduous training they undergo to prepare for important occupational roles (see Table 15.1). Looking at education this way, one can see it as the mechanism that screens and selects candidates for these important occupational roles and then starts them on their way to their new achieved statuses. Education, the broadener of the middle class, is thus also the creator of a *meritocracy*—a new system of stratification in which individuals attain status and rewards on the basis of their talents and achievements, rather than on the basis of ascribed characteristics such as sex, race, or family origin.

Yet, as we saw in Chapters 10 and 11, merit is only one of the many bases on which an individual may occupy a particular position in our stratification system—and merit does not by any means always outweigh ascriptive factors. Family origin, sex, and race or ethnicity still determine one's standing to a significant degree; furthermore, ascriptive criteria affect the quality of education one receives.

Educational achievement, class, and sex

First of all, educational achievement itself depends on social class origins. William Sewell and his associates

(1971) followed the career development of 9,000 randomly selected Wisconsin high school seniors for fourteen years beginning in 1957. Dividing his sample into four socioeconomic-status (SES) groups, Sewell found that those in the highest 25 percent had a 2.5 times greater chance of continuing in some kind of higher education than those in the lowest 25 percent. Individuals in the highest SES groups were four times more likely to attend college, six times more likely to graduate, and nine times more likely to receive graduate or professional training.

Educational achievement was also found to be correlated with sex, especially in higher education. Males were more likely to attain higher education than were females. Again, social origin was an important factor in determining probabilities. In the highest SES group, males were 28 percent more likely than females to complete college, and they were 29 percent more likely to go on to graduate or professional school. In the lowest SES group, sex differences were much more marked: males had an 86 percent better chance than females of graduating from college and a 25 percent better chance of going on to professional or graduate school (Sewell, 1971).

What is behind the relationship between educational achievement on the one hand and class and sex on the other? In Chapter 13 we investigated some of the reasons why women tend to be disadvantaged in education, and we discussed the limited progress that has been made on certain educational levels. Here we

TABLE 15.1

INCOME AS A REWARD FOR EDUCATION: MEDIAN ANNUAL INCOME AND LIFETIME INCOME OF MALES BY EDUCATIONAL ATTAINMENT, 1978

| | ELEMENTARY | | HIGH SCHOOL | | COLLEGE | |
	LESS THAN 8 YEARS	8 YEARS	1–3 YEARS	4 YEARS	1–3 YEARS	4 YEARS
Median Annual Income Age 18 and over	$5,566	$7,478	$8,550	$12,345	$12,487	$17,426
Median Annual Income Age 18 to 24	$3,417	$5,108	$3,323	$6,961	$4,498	$7,752

SOURCE: Adapted from *Current Population Reports*, 1979, p. 212.

Educational achievement correlates with sex: males are more likely to graduate from college than are females. This tendency is especially strong among low-socioeconomic-status groups. (Frank Siteman/ Stock, Boston)

will glance briefly at a factor affecting the poor and the working classes, the increasing "class segregation" of American students at the primary and secondary levels. In particular, the suburbanization of the middle classes has had dire consequences for lower-class students. Between 1950 and 1960, the populations of major metropolitan areas increased by 26.4 percent, but the bulk of that increase, 48.6 percent, took place in suburban areas. From 1960 to 1970, growth in the central cities essentially stopped while the suburbs continued to expand, though more slowly than before. And between 1970 and 1975, the populations of central cities actually declined. This growth of suburban populations has involved the migration of relatively young, well-educated, and wealthy parents of school-age children, so that

the central cities are increasingly composed of rural and small-town migrants of a much lower socioeconomic status. The consequence of this population shift is poorer education for the central-city child. Because school districts are supported by local taxes, the migration of upper-income groups out of the city has meant less tax expenditure on the educationally segregated lower-class student.

In addition, schools in urban slums are staffed for the most part by new teachers who lack tenure and job experience and therefore cannot get work in more attractive school districts. These teachers generally leave the slum schools as soon as possible, and their feeling that they are "doing time" is often reflected in their treatment of students. Teachers in deprived areas seem

Inner-city school districts have been increasingly plagued by problems such as shrinking revenues for education. Many sociologists believe that the quality of education in these areas has been adversely affected as a result. (Jim Smith)

to view their students as inherently inferior and incapable of profiting from normal curricula (Trow, 1966). The same is apparently true for suburban teachers as well (Knight, 1978). These attitudes in turn affect the students' performance: when students are perceived as incapable of learning, they accept this definition of themselves and do not learn (Rosenthal and Jacobson, 1968). Further problems are caused by the fact that many teachers have middle-class attitudes toward education that lower-class youth do not necessarily share—for instance, that staying in high school long enough to graduate is better than dropping out early to accept a low-paying job or to join one's friends on the street corner. One result of this discrepancy is that much of the daily educational routine is more disciplinary and custodial than academic. That is, teachers spend more time keeping classrooms quiet and under control than teaching (Silberman, 1970).

Educational achievement and race

Recent studies indicate that blacks and other minority groups actually constitute a small fraction of those disadvantaged by inequality of education; the majority of such persons are white. The studies show that cumulative inequalities stem from social origins and that social class is therefore a better predictor of educational achievement than is race. The number of blacks and other minorities attending college has increased in recent years. (We discussed this increase in more detail in Chapter 12.) Nevertheless, according to the Coleman Report (1966), racial minorities do score significantly lower on achievement tests than do whites upon entering school, and these differences increase with each grade level. By the twelfth grade, blacks, Puerto Ricans, Native Americans, and Mexican-Americans are on the average three to five grade levels behind whites in reading comprehension and four to six grade levels behind in mathematics.

The reasons for this pattern are not known for certain. One major factor may be the class segregation of urban youth described above; though various ethnic groups are concentrated in urban areas, blacks are perhaps the most highly segregated group—a pattern caused partly by economic forces and partly by discriminatory practices, among other factors (see Chapter 12).

Also involved is the fact that children from poor areas, and from cultural backgrounds other than that of the dominant group, may be behind in the battle from the first day they enter school. Sociological research has documented the fact that motivation and intelligence, like wealth and power, are not distributed randomly throughout the population, but reflect the stratification system itself. At this point, there is no agreement on the extent to which intelligence is genetically determined. But it is widely accepted that regardless of possible genetic influences, intelligence is clearly susceptible to the influence of the environment. Children in disadvantaged environments may lack the stimulation necessary for the development of basic cognitive abili-

Racial minorities—Native Americans, for example—tend to score lower on achievement tests upon entering school than do whites. This gap widens at each grade level. (Nicholas Sapieha/Stock, Boston)

THE CONTROVERSY OVER RACE AND IQ

In our society, race has often been used to categorize people in a way that powerfully influences their access to jobs, education, social status, and even the protection of the law. Not surprisingly, people denied these advantages generally achieve less than people who enjoy them, but those who believe in biological differences in ability between the races point to these differences in achievement to support their belief. This sort of reasoning confuses cause and effect. At present there is little convincing evidence for significant genetic differences between racial groups in talent, or in such socially desirable behavioral traits as cooperativeness, altruism, idealism, or diligence. The variations from individual to individual within any race are far wider than whatever differences—whether genetic or cultural—may exist between the races.

But the question of racial differences in ability refuses to die. In fact, no debate has raged with greater bitterness in recent years than that over inherited racial differences in intelligence—especially between blacks and whites in our society. According to most studies (reviewed in Loehlen, Lindzey, and Spuhler, 1975), the average IQ of blacks in this country is some 15 points lower than that of whites. Controlling for occupation and income may reduce this gap somewhat, but it does not eliminate it. In the late 1960s, at a time when many people were disillusioned with the ambitious social programs of the preceding years, the psychologist Arthur Jensen (1969) suggested that the differences between black and white IQ scores might be due in significant part to genetic differences. Attacked by critics who have argued that the causes of the gap were environmental—the result of poor education, low social status, and the social and psychological effects of centuries of discrimination—Jensen and his followers have contended that IQ has been shown to be a highly heritable trait, affected much more by genetic than by environmental factors.

As we shall see, this claim—a key issue in the debate—is open to serious challenge.

THE NATURE OF IQ AND IQ TESTS

It is important to realize that IQ ("intelligence quotient") is not necessarily the same thing as "intelligence." "Intelligence," as we use the word in everyday language, is a vague and complex concept. It subsumes many different sorts of abilities, some of which are hard to define and quantify: creativity, for example; insight, resourcefulness, and common sense; verbal ability, mathematical ability, and the capacity to grasp many different sorts of logical relationships. The IQ test measures only a few of the elements of what we ordinarily call intelligence.

The function of the IQ test is basically predictive. It is designed to forecast how well an individual will do in a particular environment—namely, the predominantly white, middle-class schools of the United States. Thus the test itself may be unfair to minority children. Its questions measure learned skills as well as innate ability, and draw heavily on material that is much more likely to be familiar to white children from middle-class or upper-class homes. Often they involve attitudes, value judgments, and cultural assumptions that students from poor or minority backgrounds may not share. A recent writer cites an example from one of the most common tests:

"What's the thing for you to do when you have broken something that belongs to someone else?" (The correct answer must include an offer to *pay* for it as well as an apology. "Feel sorry" and "Tell them I did it" are wrong answers.) (Kirk et al., 1975, p. 778)

Moreover, the attitudes of the tester and the student toward each other may influence the results of the test. A large social or ethnic gap between the two can lower scores (Krech *et al.*, 1976). A child who wishes to impress the tester will perform better, other factors being equal, than one who does not; and discrimination lowers incentives to do well. Thus, while the tests may "predict the ability of black children to compete with white children in a white school system" (Harris, 1975, pp. 504–505), they do not necessarily reflect absolute ability.

IS IQ INHERITED?

The data on the heritability of IQ are not completely convincing to most social scientists, for there are great methodological difficulties in testing the heritability of any trait among human beings. To assess the effects of hereditary differences, for example, the best method would be to find people who have grown up in identical environments. But this is almost impossible to do, especially with blacks and whites in this country. Similarly, one of the best ways to evaluate the effects of environmental differences is to find people who possess the same genes. Only identical twins, who develop from a single fertilized egg, have identical genetic programs. Thus the chief evidence of the heritability of IQ has come from studies of identical twins who were raised from birth in separate households. Despite their upbringings in different environments, such pairs of twins, it has been claimed, have generally shown a fairly close correlation in their IQs. This result has been taken by hereditarians to indicate that IQ is determined more by the genes than by the environment. But it has recently been revealed that the most widely cited twin studies—those by the British psychologist Cyril Burt—may be fraudulent, and therefore useless for scientific purposes. Furthermore, it has been objected that many such studies did not adequately allow for the possible influence of environmental factors. A review of several of the original studies reveals that twins were generally placed in homes that were quite similar in social and economic class (Wade, 1976).

IQ AND ENVIRONMENT

Even if IQ is ultimately found to exhibit a significant degree of heritability among individuals, large gains in IQ may still be possible for disadvantaged groups through improved environmental conditions and educational opportunities. As one writer points out, "High or low heritability tells us absolutely nothing about how a given individual might have developed under conditions different from those in which he actually did develop" (Hirsch, 1970, p. 101). To take a physical analogy, height is obviously a highly heritable trait: tall parents tend to have tall children. Yet in countries where the level of nutrition is low, the average height of the population is much less than in well-fed nations such as the United States. Short immigrants to this country are often astonished to see how tall their children and grandchildren, who benefit from improved nutrition, grow. If it is found that IQ is in part inherited, therefore, it will still not be proved that the IQs of blacks, as a group, are lower for hereditary reasons.

THE HISTORICAL PERSPECTIVE

A recent study of the performance on IQ tests of other "outsiders" to American society—the immigrant groups that came to this country during and after World War I—reveals a pattern very similar to that of blacks and other minority groups (Native Americans, Mexican-Americans, and Puerto Ricans) today. Early testers concluded that the Jewish, Polish, Chinese, Italian, and Greek immigrants who came to this country during the first decades of the twentieth century belonged to innately inferior "races." But as these groups were assimilated into American society and improved their social and economic condition, their IQ scores rose. Today the grandchildren of these immigrants have IQs that equal or surpass the national average (Sowell, 1977).

Summing up the IQ controversy, one writer has concluded that "the evidence for inherited differences in intelligence between racial and social classes is a pyramid of hypotheses, resting on assumptions that lack scientific validity and conclusive data" (Kirk et al., 1975, p. 779). One way of determining the exact degrees of genetic and environmental influence on the black IQ gap has been suggested by psychologist Robin Dawes:

The assertion that the discrepancy between the average white and average black IQ in the United States is due in some part to genetic differences is equivalent to the assertion that if there were no differences in the environments of whites and blacks there would still be a difference in their average intelligence. It may not be productive to examine this assertion with correlational studies of samples drawn from United States society as it exists. Perhaps a better method would be to attempt experimental evaluation of how IQ differences would change if in fact the environments of blacks and whites were equivalent. In other words, the best way to settle this controversy might be to eliminate racism. (1972, p. 230)

ties. Minority children may also be deficient in the skills and learning considered important by the dominant group, so that they tend to "test out" low on IQ tests that may be culturally biased.

Inequality in higher education

Research conducted since the great expansion of American higher education, particularly the work of Martin Trow (1962), suggests that this growth has not removed inequality at the college level. Social-class origins still affect not only an individual's chances of going to college in the first place (see Figure 15.3) but also *which* college he or she attends. Private schools, which are

FIGURE 15.3
This graph shows the percentage of black, white, and Hispanic families at various income levels and with one or more members 18 to 24, in which at least one of those members attends college fulltime. (Census Bureau, October 1979, p. 40)

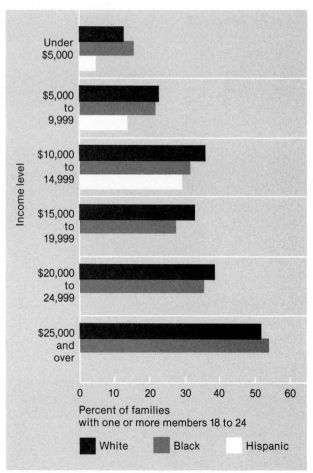

selective and often expensive, draw students from higher social strata than do large public universities, state colleges, and junior colleges. It is the nonselective institutions that have the highest dropout rates (Newman et al., 1971)—a fact that further decreases the statistical likelihood that a student in such an institution will go on to an elite position or to graduate and professional training. Like class, membership in a minority group also affects access to education (Research Triangle Institute, 1976, and Brown and Stint, 1977).

One example of a trend toward stratification in American higher education is provided by the California system, which comprises three independent systems—junior colleges, state colleges, and the University of California. Each system's admissions policies tend to determine the socioeconomic composition of the student body. The junior colleges have an open-door policy; they are required to accept any individual with a high school diploma. The state colleges recruit their students from the top half of high school graduates. The University of California system selects from the top 12 to 13 percent of the high school graduates in the state. Although tuition fees are minimal in all the schools, the fact that the junior and state colleges are nonresidential, while the University of California campuses provide dorms, means that a family's ability to support a student away from home will be a factor in deciding which college that student attends.

Not only does the California system reflect the various social classes in the community, but it also offers different opportunities for students once they enter the system. Clark's important case study (1960) of a junior college indicates that only about one-third of the students go on to a four-year program; the rest are channeled into two-year vocational courses. Clark considers this an important "cooling-out" function of the junior college, one through which the student is helped to redefine his or her aspirations and to settle, with a degree of dignity, for a lesser level of achievement. The result is that the student is more likely to receive, say, an associate degree as a laboratory technician than a bachelor's degree as a medical technologist. Similarly, the four-year degree offered by the state college usually does not lead to graduate study or to the professions. Only the University of California system provides a center for graduate research and professional training; thus, only the university affords the student full opportunity to achieve elite occupational status.

Educational credentialism

The changes in the role of education in American society have produced a paradoxical situation. At one time, education was one of a number of factors leading to upward social mobility. But now—in the view of many critics—it is the *only* avenue to success. Failure in school cuts the student off from crucial opportunities even in nonacademic spheres. As Don Adams notes,

. . . it appears that failure in schools, *no matter what the content of the schooling*, works against the person in the allocation process. If the student decides to become a nuclear physicist, schooling offers the appropriate training. Success in the schools will speed the student toward his goal, while failure in the school will prevent him from reaching that goal. But suppose the student wants to be an insurance salesman or a store manager. Then the relationship between his schooling and job aspiration may not be as direct. Nevertheless, like the student who wants to be a physicist, this student's chances are best if he succeeds in school, and failure in school may prevent him from entering his chosen occupation. (1972, p. 120)

True, schooling helps to make it possible for the student who is educationally successful to attain higher status on the basis of his or her own individual abilities. But to the student who is *not* educationally successful it affixes the label "failure"—a label that he or she may have trouble shaking off.

Contemporary American education

Public debate over the quality of American education was heightened when the Soviet Union launched its first space satellite in 1957. As a nation, we were concerned that another country had been able to outpace us to such a degree in scientific and military achievements, and the bulk of the blame fell on our educational system. Educators, critics contended, had become more concerned with the psychological adjustment of the child than with basic subject competence, especially in mathematics and science.

The furor led to unprecedented government aid to education, primarily at the college level. America finally won the race to the moon, but in the last fifteen years the turmoil over the quality of education has continued to intensify. No area of education has escaped controversy and criticism.

Trow (1966) has pointed out that there are two distinct problem areas at the center of the recent debate: the preparation of students going on to higher education, and the education of the culturally deprived. As Trow has suggested, the criticisms in these areas are based on several different conceptions of the overall nature and purpose of education. First of all, there is the liberal conception that if adequate teachers and facilities are provided, students can learn the skills they need in order to succeed. Motivation to do well or innate intelligence is not the point of the debate; the point is access to better educational opportunities. Then there is the conservative view, which stresses a reduction in the role of schools in the child's development; this view stresses the need for a return to the basic "three Rs," with the family and religious institutions resuming many of the functions that have gradually been adopted by the educational system (for example, sex education, value clarification, and driver education). Last, there is a more radical conception that focuses not only on the expansion of educational facilities but also on the expansion of the school's responsibility for the child's development; it also stresses the importance of diversity in the educational system. This radical perspective, which is heavily influenced by findings concerning the influence of the environment on intelligence and performance, holds that the school should work actively to supplement the opportunities for intellectual growth that are offered by the family. In order to overcome inadequate education, radical educators argue, we must also overcome barriers to learning created by family, teachers, and other parts of the environment. This is sometimes referred to as the "compensatory" approach.

ATTEMPTS TO IMPROVE EDUCATION

Compensatory education

The more radical conception of education has been gaining momentum in recent years. By the middle 1960s, *compensatory education* programs funded by the federal government had begun in many urban school systems. One example was Head Start, a program established by the Office of Economic Opportunity that was aimed at applying compensatory educational methods in the most direct fashion. Preschool training would be used not so much for traditional nursery-school purposes as to make up for deficiencies in family training. For example, there was an emphasis on verbal experiences—children listened to stories read by the teacher, listened to their own voices on tape recorders, and became familiar with the letters of the alphabet.

Marion Stearns' (1971) report on preschool programs under Head Start and the Elementary–Secondary Education Act—programs that reach about a half-million children a year—points out that, measured in terms of improvements in children's test scores and other "objective" measures, the success of these programs has been limited. Stearns indicates that the programs are initially successful in changing intellectual and social behavior, but that the effects of preschool training gradually decrease. By the end of the first grade, children who have not been involved in preschool programs begin to catch up with those who have. By the third grade, there are no significant differences in either intelligence or academic achievement between disadvantaged children who have had preschool compensatory education and those who have not; both groups have fallen behind their grade level. However, the most recent review of the existing literature on early childhood compensatory education programs (Palmer, 1977) concludes that the weight of evidence supports the value of such programs in improving measured IQ and scholastic achievement. Obviously, the value of these programs remains a matter for debate, as do the reasons for what some critics see as a lack of enduring success.

Compensatory education programs have also been criticized on the ground that they co-opt minority children and enforce behavioral assimilation to the dominant culture; in teaching these children the language, arts, and scientific and mathematical concepts of the dominant group, critics maintain, the programs confuse the children—or, worse, make them traitors in their own and in their peers' eyes. (Of course, the difficulty of learning another culture's skills may itself be one of the causes of failure in compensatory education programs.) Yet, as Kenneth Conklin points out, there need be nothing "immoral about teaching or learning the folkways of another group, and there is no need to re-

THE SCHOOL BUSING BATTLE: EDUCATION AS AN ARENA OF RACIAL *AND* CLASS CONFLICT

"My children will never ride a bus" (Stuart, 1976, p. 60). The Louisville parent who shouted these words spoke for thousands of American parents, to whom the big yellow bus that has carried generations of children to and from school has become anathema, a symbol of a government policy to which they are bitterly opposed.

Even though the Supreme Court declared segregation unconstitutional in 1954, opposition to integrated schools is still widespread, and the policy of busing children to achieve racial balance in public schools has been the focus of intense debate. It has been widely assumed that white opposition to desegregation has been based on racial prejudice. Recent research suggests, however, that for many whites, resistance to integrated schools stems from *class* prejudice as well. It is a sociological fact that people "prefer to interact with others of equal or higher social status" (Giles, Gatlin, and Cataldo, 1976, p. 281). And it is also true that blacks tend to be on the low end of the status hierarchy. Thus, the objection to integration may not only be that it brings black and white children together; it may also be that integration brings together children of different social classes.

Sociologists Michael W. Giles, Douglas S. Gatlin, and Everett F. Cataldo (1976, pp. 280–288) were interested in understanding the part that class prejudice played in white anti-integrationist feelings. Other researchers have found that as social status increases, *racial* prejudice *decreases* (Lipset, 1960), but *class* prejudice *increases* (Laumann, 1966; Hollingshead, 1949; Frazier, 1957; Baltzell, 1958). From this Giles and his associates hypothesized that in situations where the social status of the commu-

nity is high, public protests would be found to stem more from class prejudice than from racial prejudice.

To test their hypothesis, the researchers selected seven county school districts in Florida that were in the process of desegregating their schools. The districts they chose provided a variety of sociodemographic characteristics and geographical dispersion throughout the state. All respondents were randomly selected from school records and from census data, and all recorded responses were from white parents whose children attended public schools.

Using data from questionnaires, the researchers divided their sample into 1,500 people who did not protest against desegregation and 340 who did. Next, they measured racial attitudes and class prejudice, assigning a score for each of these variables to every respondent. Annual family income and years of schooling were used to determine respondents' social status. The researchers also took into account the concentration of blacks in the school population, a factor that has been found to influence white opposition to school desegregation (Giles, Gatlin, and Cataldo, 1976). After studying their data, the researchers identified the following five independent variables, or factors likely to have determined who protested:

Income:

1. Less than or equal to $14,999 a year (67% [of the sample population])
2. More than $14,999 a year (33%)

Education:

1. High school diploma or less (75%)
2. Education beyond high school (25%)

nounce one's heritage in the process. . . . The point is that schools can render a valuable service by teaching everyone the folkways of other groups and the skills needed for success" (1974, p. 41). And because the dominant group does set the criteria for success in society, the success of minority group members may depend on knowing its rules. Furthermore, compensatory education can help children of the dominant group gain a better understanding of the subculture of the minority.

Integration of schools

Another target for compensatory efforts is that suggested by the problem of residential segregation, which we have mentioned above. Research by James S. Coleman et al. (1966) and by William Sewell (1971) indicates that as a result of residential segregation, students

of lower-class origins usually end up in schools with others who have not been encouraged by teachers and parents to achieve. The net effect is an environment that discourages performance at every level.

Coleman's research (1966) demonstrates that a child's performance, especially a lower-class child's performance, is greatly benefited when the child attends school with children of stronger educational backgrounds. As long as the school enrollment is 60 percent or more middle class, the smaller group of lower-class students has no detrimental effect on overall performance. A pattern of cultural dominance seems to emerge: middle-class norms prevail, and students and teachers strive to maintain the relatively high standards of performance characteristic of middle-class schools.

Such research findings have greatly influenced court decisions ordering racial integration and bussing. But such programs may in some instances have only a lim-

Percent Black:
1. Those whose children were either attending schools less than 30 percent black in both 1971–72 and 72–73 or more than 30 percent black in both years (81%)
2. Those whose children attended a school less than 30 percent black in 1971–72, but attended a school more than 30 percent black in 1972–73 (19%)

Racial Prejudice:
1. Those below the median score on the summed racial prejudice scale (48%)
2. Those above the median score on the summed racial prejudice scale (52%)

Class Prejudice:
1. Those below the median score on the summed class prejudice scale (53%)
2. Those above the median score on the summed class prejudice scale (47%) (p. 283)

Through statistical analysis, Giles and his associates found that their hypothesis was correct. For respondents low on both education and income, racial—and not class—prejudice was highly related to protest against desegregation. In contrast, "among respondents high on both education and income, racial prejudice is unrelated to protest; but respondents high on class prejudice are more likely to protest than those low on class prejudice" (p. 286). It seems then, that although we like to think of education as "the great equalizer," many parents believe that equal education should be shared only by social equals.

ited effect. For example, although blacks constitute a minority of only 11.5 percent of our society, the large majority live in urban areas where they represent much greater proportions of the population. The sheer logistics of busing enough students to achieve the desired balance is staggering; furthermore, the high resistance of various groups to busing may make it politically difficult, if not impossible, in many places (see box). The results of recent studies of busing's effectiveness are unclear and controversial, and the future of busing remains in doubt (Scimecca, 1980, pp. 178–183).

Improved teacher training

The social background and academic qualification of teachers have become topics for discussion and debate. Teaching is often an avenue out of the working class (National Education Association Research Division,

1977). However, teachers' qualifications are low when compared with other college-educated and professional groups. In the 1950s, extensive studies of national samples by the Educational Testing Service and others (for example, Chauncey, 1952) showed that students who majored in education scored lower on tests of verbal and mathematical competence than did majors in almost all other fields.

Teacher training has been upgraded somewhat by new rules that require teachers to pursue college majors and minors in subject fields other than education. The National Science Foundation has provided opportunities for older teachers to return to school to improve their knowledge and skills in English, science, social science, foreign languages, and mathematics. But the impetus for reform has usually come from outside forces, such as anxious parents, college administrators, and college faculty. Teacher-training institutions generally resist reform. No doubt the traditional low pay and low prestige of schoolteachers contribute to the recruitment of those who are less academically able, and—ironically—this pattern has been reinforced, until recently, by the tremendous growth of higher education: academically able men and women who are interested in teaching have been drawn not to high schools, but to colleges and junior colleges, in hopes of obtaining higher prestige and higher pay.

Improved methods and materials

Efforts to upgrade the quality of education in recent years have produced many innovations in the methodology and technology of education. Perhaps the most widely used—and certainly the most controversial—alternative teaching method is the open classroom, in which students are free to move about the classroom and to pursue individually tailored courses of study at a flexible rate. Technological developments include such sophisticated learning aids as computer-assisted instruction, filmstrips, language laboratories, and courses taught via closed-circuit television or tape cassettes.

DO SCHOOLS MAKE A DIFFERENCE?

One of the many criticisms that has been leveled at the educational system in recent years has gone beyond the traditional appeal that schools be made better. According to some influential research by Christopher Jencks (1972, 1979), schooling is less important in determining a person's ultimate success in society than his or her parents' social standing. In other words, children of the well-off tend to do better than those of the poor regardless of schooling. Although this was hardly news, it *was* news that Jencks, a liberal social critic, was willing to throw cold water on the traditional liberal belief that better education was the key to the advancement of the poor. Improving the schools, Jencks concluded, was not enough; what was needed, if progress was to be more than "glacial," was redistribution of income. This suggestion met with little enthusiasm among those in power. Instead, Jencks' research was widely interpreted as showing that it was pointless to keep pouring public monies into education, since schools "didn't make a difference."

The publication of Jencks' first book stimulated a good deal of research, and it is likely that in the next decade we will begin to see studies that support or contradict his conclusions. Meanwhile, some English researchers have published the results of their extensive study of the effects of secondary schooling (Rutter et al., 1979). Although English schools are different in certain respects from those in the United States, the results of this study may eventually be shown to have some applicability in America. What the study concluded was that although parents' background did have an influence on students' performance in school, so did the quality of the school itself. Certain schools could clearly be identified as good schools, and students in these institutions, regardless of their ability or social background, did better than similar students in other schools. Good schools were not necessarily those with modern facilities, small classes, or stern discipline. Instead, what was important was the "ethos" of the school—what it considered important and expected of its students. Good schools, the researchers concluded, are "schools which set good standards, where the teachers provide good models of behaviour, where they [the students] are praised and given responsibility, where the general conditions are good and where the lessons are well conducted" (Mack, 1979). In addition, it was found that schools in which a significant proportion of the students were of high ability were in general schools in which students of all ability levels did better. This would seem to confirm the findings of Coleman, which, in turn, is likely to set off further debate on the value of bussing to achieve integration. But the findings of Rutter and his associates are clearly hopeful ones for educators: good schools apparently can produce better performance from students of all ability levels.

The future of American education

While controversy over the schools has continued, federal administrators and policy makers at all levels have been struggling with larger political and economic issues that affect education—shrinking urban tax bases, the distribution of federal funds, the problem of jobs for the urban young. All these problems have been exacerbated by the world energy crisis, the lagging economy, population shifts, and the declining proportion of the young in the total population. The issues facing educators and society as a whole now are not only what the goals of education should be but also what priority should be given to education in the allocation of increasingly scarce resources.

Until recently, there has been a widespread belief that improving education is a way of counteracting inequality in the society as a whole. This belief has appealed to both ends of the political spectrum. Liberals have chosen educational institutions as an arena for battles over desegregation and civil rights. As Godfrey Hodgson (1973) points out, the connection in the public mind between education and equality makes the schools an easier social setting to integrate than public accommodations or housing, and desegregation cases brought before federal courts have resulted in more expeditious change than have innumerable local battles. Conservatives, meanwhile, have countenanced education as an avenue of social mobility for the poor because it does not directly attack the economic establishment and because it appeals to the "self-improvement" ethos. Thus, until recently, both sides have been able to unite to support an ever-expanding educational establishment.

Today, however, many of the basic assumptions about education held by both sides are under attack.

To begin with, a lowered birth rate and economic inflation have caused resistance to school taxes in some localities. Findings indicating poor performance on reading tests and a yearly decline in College Entrance Examination Board test scores have raised doubts about whether increased educational expenditures are producing the desired results. Furthermore, complications have arisen in the implementation of educational reform. Drastic measures such as busing are expensive and politically divisive, and they have aroused not only controversy but violence in some cases. Finally, the old relationships between education and the occupational structure seem less strong; our technology changes so rapidly and unpredictably that it is difficult for educational institutions to predict and match its needs, and economic recessions have put many people, even those with high-level educational credentials, out of work.

Population shifts and the economic slowdown would seem to bode ill for higher education in particular. As the number of people in the eighteen-to-twenty-two age bracket continues to decline, and as costs continue to rise, colleges will face increasing competition for students. Already some colleges have launched intensive recruitment drives, and others are drawing up long-range plans for attracting foreign students and members of the adult population who never attended college (such as many adult women), did not complete degrees, or need additional vocational training. Substantial increases in the numbers of older adult students can be expected throughout the coming decades, with greater percentages of women and minorities. (See *The Chronicle of Higher Education*, April 21, 1980.)

It is no longer clear, however, that improving education at any given level can greatly help to offset social inequality. Murray Milner (1972) argues that within a society such as ours, the value of an education actually *decreases* as the average level of education increases. Although persons from the working class who receive a college education do obtain higher status than they would have if they had not attended college, spiraling education has had the net effect of creating "status inflation": educational requirements for jobs may have increased, but individuals who are better educated than their parents are not guaranteed a significantly higher standard of living as a result.

All in all, if people in the society want to ensure a more just distribution of resources, they may have to tackle the problem in more direct ways. And if change in education is desired, other assumptions may have to be framed concerning the ultimate significance of education. Regardless of the complexity of its connection to the stratification system, education has definite and far-reaching effects on the everyday life of the individual, as we have discussed above. Moreover, it clearly affects—and is affected by—activities in other major social institutions, such as the family, the economy, and the political arena. Modern industrial society places substantial weight on the institution of education for

The return of increasing numbers of older adults to college and vocational programs is a current trend in American education. (Jim Smith)

Education serves as a bridge between society's past and its future, perpetuating its traditions and developing new skills. (© R. Lynn Goldberg 1980)

its continuity and future development—to carry on its traditions and knowledge and to develop the skills to meet future needs. Consequently, sociologists have an important stake in understanding the nature of education as a societal institution and the ramifications of its activities throughout the rest of society.

Summary

Education is the largest industry in the United States. With modernization came universal secondary education and a system of mass higher education.

Functionalist theorists regard the growth of education as both a response to and a contributing factor in the economic and professional specialization of industrial societies. In their view, education also serves as an avenue to individual social mobility and an agent for expansion of the middle class.

Conflict theorists believe that the increases in secondary and higher education and in educational requirements for many jobs are the result not of an objective need for more—and more specialized—training, but of conflict between *status groups* trying to maintain their positions in the occupational hierarchy. In the conflict model, educational institutions are mechanisms of occupational placement and behavioral control.

Though mass education has aimed at making our stratification system a *meritocracy* of achieved status, such ascriptive factors as social class, sex, and race are still correlated with educational achievement. Systems of higher education are still marked by admissions policies that result in inequality of opportunity. An increasing tendency toward educational credentialism has made it essential for a student to succeed in school if he or she is to succeed in other areas of life.

Other trends in contemporary education in the United States include various attempts to improve educational quality and opportunity—compensatory preschool education programs, such as Head Start, and efforts to integrate schools and to improve the training of teachers—and struggles among various groups in many areas for control of school systems.

In the near future, individuals and groups concerned with the education system will have to contend with such issues as increasingly scarce resources resulting from inflation and shrinking urban tax bases; the declining birth rate; worsening overall performance on standardized tests; the bussing controversy; and the effectiveness of education in eliminating social inequality.

Glossary

COMPENSATORY EDUCATION An effort to overcome environmental barriers to learning by making up for deficiencies in family training through special programs for disadvantaged students.

MERITOCRACY A system of stratification in which individuals attain status and rewards on the basis of their talents and achievements rather than on the basis of ascribed characteristics such as sex, race, and family origin.

STATUS GROUP An aggregate of people who share a position in the stratification system and who interact among themselves, especially to further their common interests.

Recommended readings

Adams, Don, with Gerald M. Reagan. *Schooling and Social Change in Modern America*. New York: David McKay, 1972. An interesting analysis of the American educational system in the context of its social and economic environment, particularly industrialization and modernization. The authors use their analysis to support their recommendations for educational change.

Berg, Ivar. *Education and Jobs: The Great Training Robbery*. Boston: Beacon, 1971. A fascinating book that tries to demonstrate that the accepted relationship between level of education and level of job performance and salary is much more complicated than economists generally realize. Berg demonstrates that under certain circumstances, increased education may actually be detrimental to individuals in their occupational roles.

Bowles, Samuel, and Herbert Gintis. *Schooling in Capitalist America: Educational Reforms and the Contradictions of Economic Life*. New York: Basic Books, 1976. A neo-Marxist analysis of the function of the educational system in maintaining and legitimizing inequality in American society.

Brookover, Wilber B., and Edsel L. Erickson. *Sociology of Education*. Homewood, Ill.: Dorsey, 1975. A good standard textbook in the sociology of education, with an emphasis on a social-interactionist perspective. The authors analyze the reciprocal influence of education and other social institutions. They also examine the school as a social system and the nature of the learning process within that context.

Coleman, James S., et al. *Equality of Educational Opportunity*. Washington, D.C.: U.S. Government Printing Office, 1966. Coleman, James S., et al. *Supplemental Appendix to the Survey on Equality of Educational Opportunity*. Washington, D.C.: U.S. Government Printing Office, 1966. A massive and highly technical compilation of a series of studies on the education of minority-group members in the United States. It has stimulated heated debate because of its complex methodology and its major conclusion that the attitudes, values, and habits students bring to the schools are more important to student achievement than what the schools provide in the way of facilities, curriculum, and so on.

Corwin, Ronald G. *Education in Crisis: A Sociological Analysis of Schools and Universities in Transition*. New York: Wiley, 1974. This well-written paperback tackles some of the critical issues facing American education (for example, equality of opportunity, increased militancy among teachers, and student activism) in a useful and interesting fashion. Corwin also sets out his strategies for educational reform.

Jencks, Christopher, et al. *Inequality: A Reassessment of the Effect of Family and Schooling in America*. New York: Basic Books, 1972. Though technical in spots, this is an important book, written for the well-informed general reader in an interesting and provocative style. The authors examine the effects of family and schooling on income, thus tying in to but extending Berg's analysis (above) of education and income. Many of the variables in academic achievement that concern Coleman et al. (above) are also discussed. Finally, the book addresses the complex and politically charged issues of the effects on IQ of genetic inheritance and environmental influence.

Scimecca, Joseph A. *Education and Society*. New York: Holt, Rinehart & Winston, 1980. An historically grounded analysis of education in the U.S. From the perspective of conflict theory, Scimecca focuses on power relations in the educational system and assesses both liberal and radical reform strategies.

A country school in Cuba

JOE NICHOLSON, JR.

Education in a communist state is, as Joe Nicholson, Jr., found out during his visit to Cuba, radically different from education in a capitalist country such as ours. For one thing, in rural schools, students and teachers alike are expected to work in the fields in order to increase the country's agricultural production.

. . . The visit to the secondary school selected by Vega seemed a good place to begin a tour of Cuba, however much it might be a showcase. Cubans say they are still constructing socialism and that they will not arrive at true communism until the New Cuban Man has been formed. Naturally the formation of this new man is a top priority: the Revolution has conducted a crash program to train teachers and build new schools, an effort that also springs from the goal of providing children in the furthest interior sections with the same educational opportunity traditionally available only to city dwellers, particularly wealthy city dwellers. For those who grew up before the Revolution's new schools and universities were built, the armed forces and factories provide adult education classes that lead to the universities. . . . As a result, Cubans now boast that UNESCO statistics show that Cuba has the lowest illiteracy rate in Latin America, only 3 percent.

While bringing classes to the factories, the Revolution has also brought work to the schools. Beginning in junior high school and continuing through graduate schools, students study part time and work part time. Just before I arrived in Cuba, Castro had inaugurated forty-five work-study boarding schools for junior high school students, all located in the countryside where the students can do the agricultural work that is still Cuba's basic industry. Half work in the tobacco fields or citrus groves during the morning while the rest attend classes. In the afternoon they reverse positions. At harvest time, the schools shut for several weeks so the students can work in the fields full time.

At the work-study school I visited, the teachers as well as the students were products of Revolutionary training. . . .

Georgina Alvarez, a twenty-four-year-old member of the Young Communist League, was the school principal. . . . Of the school's forty-eight teachers, only four were over twenty-six, and the oldest was thirty. They had grown up largely under the Revolution, learning a lifestyle I soon began to discover. . . .

The dormitory was clean, spacious, breezy. Except for two sick girls who were asleep under their blankets, the thirty-two bunk beds were neatly made up. The building, constructed around open courtyards of gardens, had marble floors and prefabricated concrete walls, freshly painted white and trimmed with red. Large windows allowed fresh country breezes to sweep through the rooms. . . .

Students at the Turcios Lima School cultivated lumber-producing ceiba trees, citrus fruit, pineapples and coffee. They were assisted by professional technicians and agricultural engineers. "Our students work three hours a day and they do more than half the work an average worker does in a day," Georgina boasted. . . .

As with all school activities, teachers work alongside students in the fields. Special facilities have been built near the school for the teachers' children, including a day-care center, nursery school, and a primary school. The school has a university division for student-teachers to attend classes, and, like any work center, chapters of the mass political organizations. . . . Georgina explained that the teachers were too young to be admitted to the Party. However, thirty of the forty-eight teachers were Young Communists. All teachers and students old enough were members of the Committees for the Defense of the Revolution and all the women teachers belonged to the Federation of Cuban Women.

Georgina introduced me to Ismael Castañeda, a twenty-one-year-old teacher of English. . . .

Asked whether a boarding school run on the principles of collectivism provided enough privacy, the students looked puzzled. Ismael said, "We do not understand what you mean." I started to explain my concept of privacy. . . .

"Oh, well, we don't need privacy because all our activities are group activities," Ismael replied.

But suppose, I persisted, a student wanted to be alone for a few minutes, for example to take a walk away from the school? I pointed to the woods and rolling fields that surround the school.

"That isn't permitted during the week," he said. "On Saturday night the students go home to be with their family for a day. Besides, the students don't want to be alone because they're involved in activities. They believe in doing things the normal way here." Both students nodded. "Of course," Ismael added, "when they first come here, they may think about their parents and be homesick for a while."

What role do the parents play at the school?

"We don't fight, school versus home," said Georgina. "We teach the students to love their home and to bring their parents to school. The students clean their own dormitories. But many of the mothers volunteer to help with the cleaning and other work here. At our last biweekly meeting of parents, the fathers were mad because they wanted to participate like their wives. If a student is ill or has a problem, the parents come to the school. With a discipline problem, the first persons we call are the parents." . . .

How is school discipline handled?

"Discipline here is completely natural," replied Georgina. "Our students are very happy and love the school a great deal. But they are young people going through their adolescent change in life. So discipline, of course, is sometimes needed. We have various kinds. When the students come here we go over the rules with them. They can propose changes. But when they agree to the rules, they are expected to live by them. Respect for the teachers is a very fundamental thing here. If a student speaks back badly to a teacher, he is called to my office. We analyze the problem and criticize the student inside my office. If it happens again, we criticize the student in front of all the students and let them decide what to do. They may decide the student's parents should be called. . . .

What happens when a teacher does badly?

Ismael replied: "First we tell him he is doing badly. If he continues to do badly we can change him to another school. If he keeps on doing badly there, he should be transferred to another job which he likes more or works harder at."

Can teachers change jobs if they want?

"If they put me in a school I didn't like," said Ismael, "I would ask to change. It's not too difficult. I've seen teachers change jobs because they were working too far from their homes. The Revolution changed them according to its needs and their needs too."

Are male students—all had closely cropped hair—permitted to let their hair grow long?

"It's not correct for a boy's hair to be long," said Ismael. "So we would cut it. We work in collective groups, and it's important for the students to be the same. Otherwise, we'll have controversies, and that wouldn't be correct. If we permit one student to be different in dress, hair, or behavior, what can we expect from the rest? If they were in New York, they would be molded as very good capitalists. We have to create similarity among the students and form them with a collective philosophy. That is a basic tenet of communism."

The week after the school visit, Marcos and I walked through the campus of the University of Havana, bustling with students matriculating for a new semester. Off the main quadrangle we came upon the familiar Alma Mater statue, the seated woman with a book in one hand and the other hand upraised. "Here we have a statue that we call the Alma Mater," said Marcos, believing the statue to be a Cuban exclusive. Such provincialisms are among the most revealing indications of the isolation in which Cubans live. . . .

I returned to the university alone the next day, hoping to find some students for a rap. But not in Cuba. Cuban students have no time to sit about the campus strumming guitars, tossing Frisbees or haggling in bull sessions. In the quadrangle, they were all rushing off somewhere, including several in army uniforms. The soldier-students carried holstered pistols and wore their uniforms with pride—not swagger—the way American ROTC students did before Vietnam. The only loiterers were a half-dozen children who were playing war games on a life-size army tank, cranking the snub-topped turret a full 360 degrees to sweep the buildings on each side of the quadrangle. . . .

CHAPTER SIXTEEN
RELIGION AND SOCIETY

The study of religion by social scientists enjoyed a golden age from the latter part of the nineteenth century until the first part of the twentieth. All the prominent early figures of social science, including Karl Marx, Emile Durkheim, Max Weber, Sigmund Freud, and William James, paid considerable attention to religious institutions and religious behavior. But near the end of World War I, the study of religion declined. One reason was that the battle between religion and science, so bitter during the disputes over Darwin's theory of evolution, had died down. Religion no longer threatened science. Furthermore, as James H. Leuba's studies (1916) showed, most American scientists and social scientists no longer rigidly adhered to traditional religious beliefs. Social scientists therefore assumed that religion was on the wane. Why study a subject that would soon be unimportant? they reasoned.

But then, in the 1950s, membership in the traditional religions reached a high point—50 percent of Americans were attending church or synagogue weekly (Gallup, 1957). And although that figure began to decline in the 1960s, the past two decades have seen a resurgence of fundamentalism and a growth in sects and cults so great that the mass media has called it a "religious revival." In fact, when we compare the United States with other nations, we find that Americans profess a degree of religious commitment second only to that found in India. A 1976 Gallup poll revealed that 94 percent of adult Americans said they believed in "God or a universal spirit." And whereas only 27 percent of Western Europeans described their religious beliefs as "very important," 56 percent of Americans did. In 1978, surveys showed that 71 percent of Americans believed in life after death, 49 percent felt the Bible should be taken literally, and 82 percent indicated belief in the resurrection of Jesus Christ (table). But as Table 16.1 suggests, the beliefs of the various denominations differ considerably.

In some ways, the strength and durability of religion in the United States may seem surprising. The fact that the people of a highly industrialized country profess a high degree of religious commitment challenges some basic assumptions about both the nature of religion and the nature of industrialization. Religion is often thought of as being concerned with the relationship of human beings to some supernatural entity or plane of reality whose existence cannot be scientifically demonstrated and must therefore be taken on faith. Sociolo-

TABLE 16.1

DENOMINATION AND PROFESSED RELIGIOUS BELIEF

DENOMINATION	PERCENT INDICATING BELIEF IN EXISTENCE OF GOD	PERCENT INDICATING BELIEF IN VIRGIN BIRTH	PERCENT INDICATING BELIEF IN JESUS' WALKING ON WATER	PERCENT INDICATING BELIEF IN JESUS' FUTURE RETURN	PERCENT INDICATING BELIEF IN MIRACLES	PERCENT INDICATING BELIEF IN EXISTENCE OF DEVIL
Congregational	41%	21%	19%	13%	28%	6%
Methodist	60	34	26	21	37	13
Episcopalian	63	39	30	24	41	17
Disciples of Christ	76	62	62	36	62	18
Presbyterian	75	57	51	43	58	31
American Lutheran	73	66	58	54	69	49
American Baptist	78	69	62	57	62	49
Missouri Lutheran	81	92	83	75	89	77
Southern Baptist	99	99	99	94	92	92
Sects	96	96	94	89	92	90
Total Protestant	71%	51%	50%	44%	57%	38%
Roman Catholic	81%	81%	71%	47%	74%	66%

SOURCE: Stark and Glock, 1968.

gists have traditionally assumed that as societies become more industrialized, individuals come to be guided more by rational forms of thought. It has seemed that the explosion of scientific knowledge would leave little room for beliefs that could not be grounded in empirical proof. And yet religious belief in the United States is strong. In order to understand this seeming contradiction, we need to look more closely at the nature of religious experience and at the role religion plays in a society.

What is religion?

Sociologists look at religion not in terms of belief or dogmas, but in terms of those aspects that make it a social phenomenon—important to the community as well as to individuals. The contemporary sociological approach to religion is thus a *functionalist* one, based on the work of Emile Durkheim, whose ideas we have already encountered.

DURKHEIM'S DEFINITION

Durkheim provided the first important step toward a workable definition of the term *religion* in *The Elementary Forms of the Religious Life* (1954), first published in 1915. Durkheim began by arguing that religion is based on a separation of all aspects of reality—thoughts, words, actions, and objects—into two opposed categories, the *sacred* and the *profane*. Sacred things, in Durkheim's analysis, are "set apart and forbidden," whereas profane objects are simply ordinary. An object considered sacred in one society or subculture may not be so in another; what causes something to be considered sacred is what that particular society values. The cow, for example, is a sacred animal in India and a commonplace food-producing beast in most of the rest of the world; circumcision is a sacred rite to many Jews and a simple act of minor surgery to non-Jews.

Working from this basic distinction, Durkheim proposed the following definition of religion:

A religion is a unified system of beliefs and practices relative to sacred things . . . beliefs and practices which unite into a single moral community called a Church, all those who adhere to them. (1954, p. 47)

Emile Durkheim distinguished between the sacred and the profane, but what is sacred to one society or subgroup may not be to another. This monument, which honors an Indian warrior, is a target for vandalism and the end of a road to other groups. (© Lawrence Frank)

Religion as a social phenomenon

As is evident from his definition, Durkheim believed religion to be important because it is something people share. In Durkheim's view, there are three basic elements that operate to unite adherents into a "single moral community": (1) *beliefs*—shared ideas that explain the nature of things the religion defines as sacred; (2) *rituals*—prescribed acts that are sacred, ways in which people can interact to represent to themselves and to one another the important experiences of the religion; and (3) *symbols*—objects, images, or words that represent these beliefs and rituals and that ultimately take on meanings of their own, becoming sacred in their own right.

As an example, we might consider the Catholic and Episcopal ceremony of the Eucharist, or Holy Communion. In this ritual, participants reenact the events of the Last Supper (when Jesus Christ gave bread and wine to the Apostles in token of his imminent sacrifice of his life for humanity) and reaffirm their relationship to their religion and to one another as members of a religious community. This ritual involves a belief concerning the sacred wafer and, sometimes, wine that are taken by participants: at a certain moment in the ritual, these substances are believed to become transubstantiated, or transformed into the actual body and blood of Christ. The wafer and wine symbolize, or represent, Christ and the salvation of humankind; furthermore, they themselves are the objects of awe and reverence.

As this example illustrates, beliefs give meaning to rituals and symbols and, in turn, are reinforced by them. The wafer and wine and the Communion rite itself are meaningless without beliefs concerning transubstantiation, God, and redemption through Christ. Conversely, these beliefs might not remain as strong as they do without the symbolic representation and reenactment the ritual provides. (Beliefs and symbols were discussed in more detail in Chapter 5.)

Participants in Holy Communion reaffirm their relationship to the Catholic Church and to one another as members of a religious community. This ritual and the symbols (wine and wafers) and beliefs (transubstantiation) it involves all reinforce each other. (Rick Smolan)

Religion as the worship of society

Moslems kneeling in prayer may seem quite different from Catholics participating in the Mass. But for sociologists, the differences among the beliefs, rituals, and symbols of the religions of the world are less significant than their similarity of function—that of bringing people together into a religious community.

Durkheim himself argued that this strengthening of group cohesiveness was religion's most important function. He went on to hypothesize that regardless of the beliefs in which worship is clothed, what adherents really worship is their own "moral community." In short, Durkheim concluded that *religion is the worship of society* (in his words, religion is "a system of ideas with which individuals represent to themselves the society of which they are members" [Durkheim, 1954]). He based this conclusion on anthropological accounts of small tribal groups with a high degree of cohesiveness—high agreement on norms and values and close relations among group members. As the anthropological accounts suggested, these groups seem to show the highest expression of group solidarity during religious ceremonies and celebrations.

What Durkheim suspected was that because the society imposes moral pressure on its members, the society itself becomes the object of awe and reverence; people come to think of it as sacred. It is inherent in the very nature of societies, Durkheim wrote, that "outside of us there exists something greater than us, something with which we enter into communication." This "something" is, of course, society itself. Likewise, society gives the sensation of perpetuity; it is not the gods but society itself that is eternal.

MODERN DEFINITIONS

Modern sociologists have changed Durkheim's definition somewhat. According to one definition, religion is an institutionalized system of symbols, beliefs, values, and practices focused on questions of ultimate meaning (Glock and Stark, 1965). The word "institutionalized," which indicates that religion is a relatively permanent property of groups, of course fits in with the definition proposed by Durkheim. But the key phrase "questions of ultimate meaning" suggests an important difference. Questions of ultimate meaning are questions about the purpose, origin, and fate of the world: Why do we exist? What can we expect? and—very important—What happens when we die?

Value orientation

The definition of religion given by modern sociologists is broad enough to encompass not only systems based on belief in the supernatural, but also Marxism and a variety of other doctrines and scientific efforts that address questions of ultimate meaning without supernatural elements. From this definition, even atheistic systems can be seen as "religious." To avoid possible confusion, some sociologists have suggested that the term "value orientation" be used in this broad sense instead of the term "religion."

"Civil religion"

Modern American culture includes a uniquely significant value orientation that deals with ultimate meaning without reference to the supernatural. Robert Bellah (1968) observes that the religious pluralism of the United States is unified by other kinds of values, such as faith in democracy and the rule of law. A deity and common symbols, derived from but not identical to Christianity, are invoked on solemn political occa-

The American flag is one of the major symbols of our civil religion. (Anestis Diakopoulos/ Stock, Boston)

sions. According to Bellah, these elements constitute a "civil religion." This civil religion does not displace or oppose traditional religions; anticlericalism is not part of its heritage. It portrays the United States as a new Israel, a light to the nations, answerable to a God not of personal salvation but of public rectitude. The civil religion has its symbols—the American flag, the bald eagle; its "hymns"—"The Star-Spangled Banner" and "America the Beautiful"; its Holy Writ—the Declaration of Independence and the Constitution; and even its saints—Washington, Jefferson, and Lincoln. This collection of symbols and beliefs unites American society politically by instilling essentially religious attitudes toward the nation. For most Americans, the civil and traditional religions complement and reinforce one another: we call ourselves a nation "under God."

Civil religion can be seen as one example of a general tendency that Durkheim pointed out—every society tends to invest its mores, traditions, history, important offices, and so on with a sacred character that elevates them to "religious" status. But what happens when some of a society's members no longer feel that its customs and traditions are worthy of such status? When Robert Bellah looked at the cultural and political upheaval of the 1960s, and the counterculture groups it spawned, he concluded that the "major meaning of the sixties was purely negative: the erosion of the legitimacy of the American way of life" (Bellah, 1976).

He ventured to project three possible scenarios for the future of society, and thus for the future not only of civil religion but of religion as a whole. In one, the "liberal" scenario, society would continue to be dominated by individualism and the idolization of technical reason. The major religions would have disappeared, and oriental religious groups and the human-potential movement would play only a marginal role. In the second, the "traditional authoritarianism" scenario, which would be triggered by worldwide economic collapse, there would be a single orthodox vision of truth and reality. The third and ideal—but, Bellah admits, improbable—scenario would be the "revolutionary" system, firmly committed to the quest for ultimate reality and founded on a greater concern for harmony with nature and between human beings.

Thomas Robbins (1976) suggests that some of the sects popular among youth represent attempts to create new civil religions to replace the one eroded by political apathy and disenchantment. The Unification Church of Sun Myung Moon, in particular, which has attracted a large following in the United States, provides the experience of intense community solidarity for individuals from a society they find increasingly isolating. Beyond that, it and other sects of its type can provide the kind of recommitment to threatened values—both religious and patriotic—that the old civil religion represented.

Religions and modern society

The relationship between modern societies and the religions that exist within them is a complicated one. Some religions may tend to *legitimate* the social structure; they may support and lend approval to the society's dominant values and uphold the authority of the group that holds power. Other religions may reflect opposition to the status quo and may act to challenge political authority. In some instances, the same religion may take different positions in different societies: in Spain, for example, the Catholic Church was an important supporter of the Franco regime, while in Hungary after World War II it challenged political authority. A religion may also shift from opposition to support in the same society. Islamic religious leaders, for example, played a major role in the 1979 overthrow of the Shah

of Iran. They then sought to reconstruct Iran as an Islamic state run according to religious precepts.

Karl Marx and Max Weber are two social scientists who have attempted to analyze the relationship between religious institutions and the larger society. Others, such as the historian Ernst Troeltsch and the theologian H. Richard Niebuhr, have extended this analysis to the question of how religions arise and change.

THE VIEWS OF KARL MARX

Marx, like Durkheim, viewed religion as a reflection of society—particularly of its economic relations. But Marx disliked what he saw. He concluded that reli-

The Ayatollah Ruhollah Khomeini, an Islamic religious leader, was instrumental in the overthrow of the Shah of Iran in 1979. Khomeini's assumption of power was legitimated by religion, and he and his followers have tried to reconstruct Iran as an Islamic state run according to religious precepts. (UPI)

gion's underlying function is to make sacred the social arrangements under which most people in the society are exploited. In his view, the religious ideas of a society are those of the ruling classes; religion, he said, serves as "the opiate of the people." As long as workers believe that kings have a divine right to rule over them or that worldly success reflects the will of God and the virtue of the wealthy, they will remain victims of exploitation. Among the numerous studies that support this argument is the classic *Millhands and Preachers*, by Liston

Pope (1942), which discusses the way churches in North Carolina supported the interests of the textile mills that were dominant in the state.

Marx also argued that in its earliest stages a religion can serve as a disruptive force in a society. He pointed out that most early revolutionary movements were organized under the banner of religion—that new religious ideologies arose in order to integrate and justify the rise to power of a new class. Observers such as Marx and Friedrich Engels, and later Karl Kautsky (1953), argued that early Christianity, for example, was essentially a proletarian movement. Whether this argument holds for all proletarian movements, especially those of the nineteenth century, is open to debate, as will be seen later in the chapter. What does seem generally valid, however, is the identification of a relationship between religion and the economic structure of a society.

THE VIEWS OF MAX WEBER

Weber, who agreed with much of Marx's analysis, used it as a base to develop a new, functionalist, perspective. He rejected the Marxist premise that religious ideas are basically determined by the economic interests of specific social classes. In his classic essay *The Protestant Ethic and the Spirit of Capitalism* (1930), first published in 1905, Weber argued that both religious and nonreligious values may in some instances be reflections of economic relations, but they may also play an independent role in governing such relations. Instead of shaping religious values to justify economic institutions, societies may over time see their institutions shaped to fit values. The rise of Protestantism, Weber pointed out, preceded the development of capitalism; he argued that capitalism would not have been possible without Protestantism. Whereas the traditional religious values of Catholicism had deterred the development of rational and disciplined economic activity, Protestantism stressed the importance of work as an end in itself and regarded worldly success as evidence of God's favor. Eventually this belief led to the concept of hard work and worldly success not merely as signs of salvation, but as means for earning it. This theological position, according to Weber, motivated the economic zeal and pursuit of wealth that were capitalism's underpinnings. Furthermore, Protestant values encouraged both the pursuit of money and personal frugality; profits were not to be spent on luxuries but were to be plowed back into one's business to earn more money.

Priest and prophet

Like Marx, Weber believed religion could sometimes oppose the status quo. He identified two major types of religious leaders, with two different stances toward economic and political authority. The *priest*, a religious leader whose authority comes from the power of an office, is the official and authorized celebrant of ritual. Because the authority is derived from a religious organization, the priest usually defends it and its support of the status quo. The *prophet*, by contrast, holds authority on the basis of charismatic qualities. (We will discuss the concept of charismatic leadership in Chapter 17.) The prophet is not bound to an official institution and so is more likely to criticize both religious institutions and the general social structure.

There is often conflict between priestly and prophetic functions in the clergy of a religion at a particular time. Jeffrey K. Hadden illustrates this point in his book *The Gathering Storm in the Churches* (1969), in which he surveys the involvement of the Protestant clergy in the civil-rights movement of the 1960s. During this period, many members of the clergy sought to emphasize the prophetic tradition by taking an active role in the civil-rights movement. But most congregations strongly disapproved of such activism, preferring their leaders to remain in the traditional role of priest.

Church-sect theory

Weber pointed out that the contrast between priestly and prophetic orientations extends beyond leadership into the whole organization of religions. He drew a distinction between two types of religious institutions— the church and the sect. This analysis was later extended by the German historian Ernst Troeltsch (1949). *Churches*, highly institutionalized religious organizations, are dominated by the priestly role and are relatively at ease with the cultures that surround them. Their membership constitutes a significant part of the society as a whole, and most members are born into a church rather than converted into it. Worship is public, ritual systematized, theology codified, and divine grace mediated by formal means such as sacraments. *Sects*,

on the other hand, are less highly organized; defining themselves as opposed to the surrounding culture, they are dominated by the prophetic role. Since the sect separates itself from society in general, its members may even be quite hostile toward outsiders and toward society's institutions. Moreover, the sect emphasizes membership through voluntary conversion instead of by birth; it sees itself as a society of the saved.

Changes in religious institutions

H. Richard Niebuhr (1929) applied similar concepts to formulate a theory of religious change. Niebuhr suggested that a sect is inherently unstable. It is founded by people whose religious needs are currently not met by the churches of their society. These disenchanted people break away and start a new faith to give expression to their religious concerns. Sects tend to appeal to the socially disadvantaged and disinherited; they often begin as societies of committed converts embattled against the world. But this posture does not last. Sometimes they are crushed as heresies. Sometimes they merely die out as members get old. But frequently they begin to come more and more to terms with the surrounding society, *eventually becoming churches*. In fact, sometimes they replace the previous churches.

This transition may in some instances take place after the death of a charismatic founder, when new leaders are faced with administering a rapidly growing organization. This process, in which an institution is developed to take the place of the charismatic founder, Weber called "routinization of charisma." Other mechanisms that promote the change from sect to church include the arrival of the second generation, when the sect is no longer composed exclusively of converted members. It begins to have members who did not join out of conviction or dissatisfaction with society. Another factor is that over time some members may improve their economic position. As they cease to be uniformly dispossessed and as the wealthier members begin to play a prominent role in sect affairs, the group becomes less hostile to the outside world. When they begin to require clergy to undergo formal training for the ministry, sects are well on their way to becoming churches.

At this point, the process repeats itself. The sect in transformation begins to lose those qualities that originally attracted alienated and dispossessed members.

RELIGION, RADICALISM, AND RACE

Uncle Tom, finding solace in spirituals, and Rev. Martin Luther King, singing as he was led off to jail, are two aspects of black religion and black militancy. What is the relationship between the two? This question has been debated by historians and also by students of the contemporary drive for racial equality. On the one hand, as Gary T. Marx (1967, p. 64) points out, "Slaves are said to have been first brought to this country on the 'good ship Jesus Christ,'" and "most slaveowners eventually came to view supervised religion as an effective means of social control." But on the other hand,

the effect of religion on race protest throughout American history has by no means been exclusively in one direction. While many Negroes were no doubt seriously singing about chariots in the sky, Negro preachers such as Denmark Vesey and Nat Turner and the religiously inspired abolitionists were actively fighting slavery in their own way. All Negro churches first came into being as protest organizations and later some served as meeting places where protest strategy was planned, or as stations on the underground railroad. (Marx, 1967, p. 65)

Some sociologists argue that the Negro church functioned as a "refuge, an escape from the cruel realities of the here and now" (Essien-Udom, 1962, p. 358). But others say that "if there had been no Negro church, there would have been no civil-rights movement today."

Actually, as Marx's 1967 study revealed, the relationship between militancy and religiosity depends on the nature of the individual's religious commitment. Sect members, predictably, are least militant. (Said one evangelist, "I don't believe in participating in politics. My church don't vote—they just depend on the plans of God" [quoted in Marx, 1967, p. 67].) Likewise, the more religious members of conventional churches (those with the most orthodox beliefs, those who attended church most frequently, those who attached the most subjective importance to religion) were less likely to be militant. But, Marx found, there was no corresponding lack of religious commitment among those individuals who were militant. Although militants were twice as likely as conservatives to be rated "not very religious" or "not at all religious," two-thirds of all militants still ranked as "very" or "somewhat" religious.

What were the crucial factors involved? One factor Marx identified was the particular religious themes that the individual felt were important. One Christian theme, for example, focuses on other-worldly concerns, such as the power of God and the submission of humankind; another focuses on the temporal or the "here and now," emphasizing the importance of righting conditions on earth today. Blacks with a strong commitment to the first theme, Marx found, were more likely to be very religious and less likely to be militant. Some blacks with a commitment to the second theme, on the other hand, were willing to enter the equal-rights struggle: almost 40 percent of the very religious or somewhat religious who had a temporal orientation of this kind were found to be militant. In sum, religiosity and militancy were not found to be mutually contradictory in themselves. What mattered was the particular religious themes the individual espoused.

These then frequently split off to found a new sect. Niebuhr isolated an endless cycle of schism, birth, development, schism, and rebirth. Most Protestant denominations began as sects within the Christian community. Indeed, Christianity itself began as a small sect within the Jewish community.

This theory not only offers powerful insights into the formation and transformation of religious groups but may also provide insights into the development of political and other social movements (see Chapter 21). As with religious sects, such movements frequently begin with very radical positions that reject the institutions of their society. But if they grow and endure, these movements then move toward increasingly moderate positions and eventually become institutions themselves.

RELIGIOUS SECTS AND RADICAL POLITICS

We have drawn a parallel between sects and radical political groups because the two seem to be alternative value orientations. Both focus on questions of ultimate meaning, but from different positions. As Niebuhr pointed out, no important sect movements have occurred among the Western European working classes since the rise of Methodism in the eighteenth century. He suggested that since the beginning of the nineteenth century, working-class dissatisfactions have been channeled mainly into radical politics *instead of* into religion. This trend was also noticed by early socialists. In fact, Leon Trotsky was so aware of the similarity of revolutionary Marxism and sectarianism that in the latter part of the 1890s he successfully recruited the first

In the United States, sects have continued to emerge in considerable numbers. They include (left) Sufis, an Islamic group, (below) Hare Krishnas, and (right) Christian Scientists. (Left: © Jerry Berndt 1980/Stock, Boston; below: © Shelly Rusten 1974; right: John Running/Stock, Boston)

working-class members of his South Russian Workers Union from among adherents of religious sects (Lipset, 1960).

In the United States, meanwhile, the opposite trend has been seen: sects have continued to emerge in considerable numbers. Such bodies as the Nazarenes, the Mormons, the Seventh-Day Adventists, the Chris- tian Scientists, and the Jehovah's Witnesses are only the most prominent of the hundreds of sects in the United States (Landis, 1963). One observer, Seymour Martin Lipset (1960), suggests that continuing forma- tion of sects in the United States is one of the reasons radical politics has failed to develop here to any signifi- cant extent.

Religion in the United States

Religion in the United States does not present a simple picture, chiefly because the population is made up largely of immigrants who brought with them a great number of religious traditions. Although more than a third of the population are not church members or otherwise formally affiliated with a religion, only 8 per- cent of those questioned in a 1978 Gallup Poll reported no religious "preference." In that poll, 60 percent said that they considered themselves Protestant; 27 percent, Catholic; 2 percent, Jewish; and 2 percent, other. (See Tables 16.2 and 16.3 for profiles of church membership and distribution of major religions.) However, the di- versity of groups within each of the major religions greatly complicates this picture. Within Protestantism, there are more than a dozen large denominations and countless small ones. (A denomination is a group of

TABLE 16.2

CHURCH MEMBERSHIP STATISTICS FOR A CROSS-SECTION OF U.S. DENOMINATIONS, 1940–1977

DENOMINATION	1940	1950	1960	1970	1974	1977
American Baptist Churches in the U.S.	1,543,976	1,561,073	1,521,052	1,472,478	1,579,029	1,304,088
American Lutheran Church	1,129,349	1,587,152	2,242,259	2,543,293	2,437,862	2,390,076
Assemblies of God	198,834	318,478	508,602	625,027	751,818	939,312
Christian and Missionary Alliance	22,832	58,347	59,657	112,519	144,254	152,841
Christian Church (Disciples of Christ)	1,658,966	1,767,964	1,801,821	1,424,479	1,312,326	1,256,849
Church of Jesus Christ of Latter-Day Saints	724,401	1,111,314	1,486,887	2,073,146	2,683,573	2,486,261
Church of the Brethren	176,908	186,201	199,947	182,614	179,387	177,534
Church of the Nazarene	165,352	226,684	307,629	383,284	430,128	455,648
Episcopal Church	1,996,434	2,417,464	3,269,325	3,285,826	2,907,293	2,818,830
Jehovah's Witnesses	N.A.	N.A.	250,000	388,920	539,262	554,018
Lutheran Church in America	1,988,277	2,760,442	3,053,243	3,106,844	2,986,970	2,967,168
Lutheran Church–Missouri Synod	1,277,097	1,674,901	2,391,195	2,788,536	2,769,594	2,673,321
Mennonite Church	51,304	56,480	73,125	88,522	92,390	96,609
Presbyterian Church in the U.S.	532,135	678,206	902,849	958,195	896,203	869,693
Reformed Church in America	163,135	183,178	225,927	367,606	354,004	351,438
Reorganized Church of Jesus Christ of Latter-Day Saints	106,554	124,925	155,291	152,670	156,687	186,414
Roman Catholic Church	21,284,455	28,634,878	42,104,900	48,214,729	48,701,835	49,836,176
Salvation Army	238,357	209,341	254,141	326,934	366,471	396,238
Seventh-Day Adventists	176,218	237,168	317,852	420,419	479,799	522,317
Southern Baptist Convention	4,949,174	7,079,889	9,731,591	11,628,032	12,513,378	13,078,239
United Church of Christ	1,708,146	1,977,418	2,241,134	1,960,608	1,841,312	1,785,652
United Methodist Church	8,043,454	9,653,178	10,641,310	10,671,774	10,063,046	9,785,534
United Presbyterian Church in the U.S.	2,158,834	2,532,429	3,259,011	3,087,213	2,723,565	2,561,234

N.A. = Not available.

SOURCE: *Yearbook of American and Canadian Churches*, 1979.

church members, often formed as the result of one individual's teaching, who share a roughly common doctrine. The Lutherans, for example, were originally the followers of Luther; the Presbyterians, of Calvin; the Methodists, of John Wesley.) Despite its appearance of unity to outsiders, Catholicism too is a heterogeneous collection of denominations, mainly of ethnic origin, including Irish Catholics, Polish Catholics, and so on (Greeley, 1972). Catholicism has in addition given rise to a number of splinter groups, of which the Catholic evangelical movement is only one example. Judaism has three branches—reform, conservative, and orthodox; the orthodox branch is further divided into several smaller groups with strong European ties, such as the Hasidim.

Religion in the United States today is thus varied and complex: an individual may belong to a huge established church with millions of members in this country; to an isolated outpost of a religion that is well established in some other part of the world; to a large or small sect; to a tiny cult; or to no formal group at all.

RELIGION, SUBCULTURES, AND SOCIOECONOMIC CLASS

Religious affiliation can be correlated with a number of social, economic, and political factors. Each religion— even, to some extent, each Protestant denomination— can be seen to have a particular profile. A large portion of Episcopalians and Presbyterians, for example, have attended college and earn high incomes. They are also more likely to call themselves Republicans than are other Protestants. On the other hand, Jews also show relatively high socioeconomic status, yet a majority designate themselves as Democrats. A majority of Catholics are Democrats as well, yet as a group they rank below Jews in average income and representation in business and the professions (see Table 16.3).

Religious affiliation, therefore, can often reveal something about people's socioeconomic status and political preference. It cannot tell everything, however; other factors are obviously at work. Race, for example, is far more important than religious affiliation in determining political preference: blacks in our society tend to vote Democratic, even if they earn high incomes and call themselves Protestants. Geography is also important. Large numbers of Baptists, for example, live in small towns and rural areas—places in which there are

fewer opportunities to earn large incomes. In addition, there are subcultural differences. Many Catholics and Jews are second- and third-generation immigrants who have settled in cities, yet the demographic profiles of the two groups are different. The Jewish subculture, with its stress on education, may be one important reason for the difference.

RECENT TRENDS

As was mentioned at the beginning of the chapter, religion has been and continues to be a strong element in life in the United States. Yet if we look at recent trends in church attendance, at the growth of new religious groups, at individual religious experience, and at the revival of fundamentalism, we again see a complicated picture of diversity and change.

Church attendance

If religious strength is measured by church attendance, it is seen that the major denominations experienced significant growth in the 1950s, followed by a decline, stabilization, or substantially slower growth in the 1960s and 1970s (see Figure 16.1). The strength of insti-

FIGURE 16.1

Church attendance in an average week, 1955–1978. Note that after several years of decline, especially among Catholics, church attendance began to stabilize in the mid-1970s. (Adapted from *Public Opinion*, March/May 1979, p. 34.)

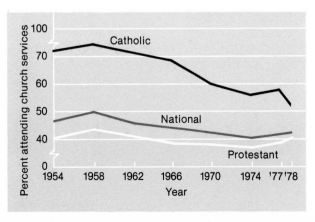

TABLE 16.3

PROFILES OF THE MAJOR RELIGIOUS FAITHS IN THE UNITED STATES, ACCORDING TO A 1977–78 GALLUP POLL

	POPULATION DISTRIBUTION	PROTESTANTS	ROMAN CATHOLICS	JEWS	ALL OTHERS	NO RELIGIOUS PREFERENCE
National	100%	100%	100%	100%	100%	100%
Sex						
Male	48	46	47	48	51	62
Female	52	54	53	52	49	38
Race						
White	88	85	96	98	75	88
Non-White	12	15	4	2	25	12
Education						
College	29	27	28	58	33	47
High School	55	55	58	34	52	43
Grade School	16	18	14	8	15	10
Region						
East	27	20	39	65	21	26
Midwest	27	28	29	5	23	21
South	28	35	18	13	23	19
West	18	17	14	17	33	34
Age						
Total under 30	29	23	31	31	43	55
18–24 years	17	13	19	18	25	31
25–29 years	12	10	12	13	18	24
30–49 years	34	35	36	32	32	26
50 & older	37	42	33	37	25	19
Income						
$20,000 & over	21	19	23	43	21	22
$15,000–$19,999	17	16	20	16	12	12
$10,000–$14,999	23	23	23	21	22	23
$ 7,000–$ 9,999	11	11	10	4	8	11
$ 5,000–$ 6,999	11	11	10	7	10	12
$ 3,000–$ 4,999	9	10	7	5	16	9
Under $3,000	8	10	7	4	11	11
Politics						
Republican	23	27	17	8	18	11
Democrat	46	44	53	56	35	37
Independent	29	27	28	36	39	47
Occupation						
Professional & Business	25	22	26	53	26	30
Clerical & Sales	9	8	10	15	11	9
Manual Workers	42	41	44	11	38	41
Non-Labor Force	19	21	15	18	16	13
Farmers	3	4	2	1	1	1
City size						
1,000,000 & over	19	13	28	52	31	23
500,000–999,999	13	10	15	16	12	20
50,000–499,999	25	25	28	16	25	25
2,500–49,999	16	17	15	5	12	13
Under 2,500, Rural	27	35	14	11	20	19

* Less than one percent.

SOURCE: Gallup Opinion Index, *Religion in America 1977–78*, p. 57.

tutionalized religions thus seems to fluctuate with changes in the larger society. In recent years, the relaxation of sexual mores and cynicism following events in the political sphere (Vietnam and Watergate, for example) may have contributed to the decline in church attendance.

A number of explanations have been offered for the declines particular religious groups have suffered. Judaism may be waning, for example, because it is the religion of a minority who are now becoming relatively assimilated into the American mainstream. Of its three branches, it is the most modernized and "Americanized" branch, the reform, whose congregations are shrinking the fastest. Another example of declining attendance is the recent history of the Roman Catholic Church. In 1964, 71 percent of all Roman Catholics attended Mass in a given week; but a study in 1973 showed a drop to 55 percent. Several explanations have been offered for this rapid and substantial decrease. One researcher, Andrew Greeley (1976), suggests that the decline may have been linked to the papal encyclical on birth control issued in 1968. In 1970, according to one estimate (Westoff and Bumpass, 1973), 65 percent of Catholic couples in the United States were using forms of birth control other than the rhythm method, the only church-approved form of contraception (see Figure 16.2). Immediately after the issuance

of the encyclical, there was a sharp drop in church attendance. Greeley (1976) suggests that many American Catholics, unable to reconcile their own feelings about birth control with those of the Church, withdrew from active participation.

Exactly how social change affects church attendance—and religious institutions—is a matter of debate. The rapid rise in church attendance that began after World War II continued during the 1950s until it reached a high point in 1957, when the Gallup poll reported that 50 percent of Americans claimed to attend church weekly. Some sociologists now believe that part of the postwar religious revival stemmed from the "baby boom," or sharp rise in the birth rate, that began immediately after the war. (The "baby boom" will be discussed in more detail in Chapter 19.) It is known that family church attendance rises when there are younger children in the home and declines when the children are grown (Glock, Ringer, and Babbie, 1967; Nash, 1968). The "baby boom" peaked in the 1950s, and there may be some relationship between the subsequent decline in the birth rate and the steady decline in church attendance between 1957 and 1971.

Not all sociologists, however, accept this explanation for the drop in church attendance. A study by Robert Wuthnow (1976) suggests that the rise of the youth counterculture in the 1960s may also have played

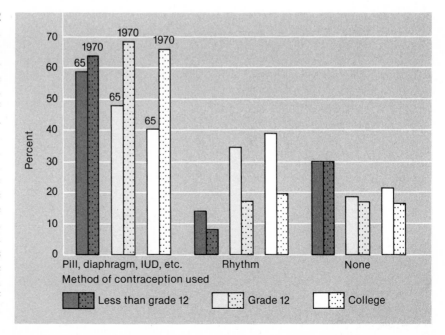

FIGURE 16.2

The extent to which Roman Catholics deviate from official church doctrine on birth control is illustrated by this graph. It shows the percentages of white, married Catholic women with various levels of education who used methods of contraception forbidden by the church, the church-approved rhythm method, and no contraception in 1965 and 1970. Note that the use of such methods as "the Pill," the diaphragm, and the intrauterine device increased at all educational levels in 1970, after the 1968 papal encyclical affirming the church's ban on the use of all contraceptive measures except the rhythm method. (Adapted from Westoff and Bumpass, 1973, p. 42)

a role. Wuthnow points out that the decline in church attendance was particularly marked in the age group between twenty-one and twenty-nine. This was the group most involved in experimenting with drugs, politics, and sex, and the subculture it evolved was at least partly concerned with finding new answers to questions about human existence. Perhaps even more important, most members of established religions were deeply offended by this group's rejection of traditional values and thus were not likely to encourage its members to become more involved with the churches. In sum, Wuthnow argues, while large-scale changes in the society may have important effects on religious institutions, it is also important to consider the more discontinuous changes affecting particular generations. If his theory is correct, we should expect to see fluctuations in church attendance that will, at least in part, reflect the different experiences of the generations that are young now. Thus we might expect to see an increase in church attendance as the youth of a less turbulent time enters the twenty-one to twenty-nine age group. And, indeed

FIGURE 16.3

The percentage of Americans who expressed the belief that religion as a whole is losing its influence on American life, 1957–1976. (Adapted from Gallup Opinion Index, 1977–78, p. 18)

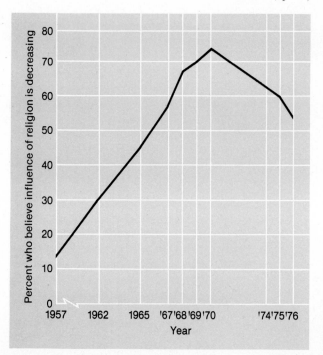

JONESTOWN

On November 18, 1978, in Jonestown, Guyana, more than 900 men, women, and children in a religious sect called the People's Temple gave up their lives at the command of their leader, the Reverend Jim Jones. Few events in recent years have inspired the horror, shock, and bewilderment of that so-called "white night" in the jungle. *The Nation,* an influential political journal, pronounced the event "an aberration—in the sense that disease is an aberration of the healthy body." The *Wall Street Journal* also attempted an explanation, but could do no more than to describe Jonestown as a dark symbol of inexplicable human nature.

But does the self-liquidation of the People's Temple truly defy understanding? Not according to John R. Hall, a sociologist who has studied the behavior and organization of both historical and contemporary sects. In an article entitled "The Apocalypse at Jonestown" (*Society,* Sept./Oct. 1979, pp. 52–61), Hall argues that in many ways, the People's Temple resembles other sects of a similar type, and he suggests that the people of Jonestown considered their final macabre ritual an act of salvation, not of self-destruction.

Founded in 1964 by a former fundamentalist minister from Indiana named Jim Jones, the People's Temple was an offshoot of American revivalist evangelism. Hall places the People's Temple in the category of "other-worldly" sects since it aimed to withdraw from a society it considered totally evil and, in its last days, to live instead in a timeless heaven on earth.

The rejection of "this world" for some other, says Hall, was seen by sect members as a spiritual—and, in this case, physical—journey that required replacing the (evil) values of the dominant society with their (good) opposites. Thus, where American society valued the individual, the other-worldly sect valued the group; where American society valued the nuclear family and dyadic sexual relationships, the People's Temple styled itself one big family and discouraged the dyadic bond. The notion of private property, by the same token, was rejected in favor of communal ownership, and so on. The goal of such reversals, Hall points out, is to escape what is seen as the corrupting influence of society; beyond this, he says, between the sect's version of reality and the society's, there is "no encompassing rational connection" (as

(except for Catholics), the decline seems to have ended in 1971: the figure of 40 percent church attendance seems to have held firm through 1975 and even increased slightly to 41 percent in 1978. Moreover, the percentage of those who think the influence of religion is decreasing has declined after a steady rise in the 1960s and early 1970s (see Figure 16.3).

one might expect to find, for instance, in a political movement). And the result is therefore that

the interchange between the other-worldly sect and the people beyond its boundaries becomes a struggle either between 'infidels' and the 'faithful," from the point of view of the sect, or between rationality and fanaticism from the point of view of outsiders.

As a self-exiled community of 900 souls, the People's Temple was of course more than a mere religious group: like any other community, even a heaven-on-earth must be governed in order to remain cohesive. In this sense, the People's Temple was a civil as well as a religious organization, and the Reverend Jim Jones ruled it with an iron hand, imposing a harsh discipline on his followers. This particular pattern, says Hall, is typical not only of sects of the past, such as the communal groups that established themselves in the United States during the nineteenth century, but also of such modern-day collectivities as the Children of God and the Hare Krishna society. This autocratic style of leadership serves a very specific purpose, Hall notes:

mechanisms of mutual criticism, modification of conventional dyadic sexual mores, and other devices . . . decrease the individual's ties to the outside . . . and increase the individual's commitment to the collectivity as a whole.

Indeed, Hall adds, the very things that critics find "abhorrent in the life of the People's Temple at Jonestown prior to the final 'white night' of murder and suicide are the core nature of other-worldly sects," for they reinforce the members' sense of living outside the boundaries of society. This sense of being different in turn inspires a kind of paranoia. The sect becomes wary and fearful of the society it has abandoned, and sees that society as dangerous, not only because it is larger and more powerful than the sect, but also because it is evil. "The persecution complex," Hall concludes, "is a stock-in-trade of other-worldly sects."

Thus, while various authorities conducted investigations into some of the People's Temple's questionable fund-raising activities, for example, the Reverend Jim Jones used the opportunity to reinforce in his followers their mistrust of the outside world, and in this way to draw them even closer together. Similarly, Jones initiated the notorious "white nights" of trial suicide in Jonestown as an elaborate means of strengthening his followers' loy-

alty. Jones was, in essence, a totalitarian ruler who was able to increase his sect's sense of isolation through his unchallenged and absolute control over information. Hall observes that "Jones manipulated fears among his followers by controlling information and spreading false rumors about news events in the United States."

At the same time, Jones warned his followers that the Apocalypse—the Judgment Day when good would triumph over evil once and for all—was near at hand. And so if life in Jonestown was not the heaven on earth that had been promised, Jones could blame it on the evil forces of social persecution. As pressures grew in the U. S. for a full-scale investigation of the People's Temple, Jones increased the harshness of his regime: he barred outsiders from the commune, and Jonestown came to resemble an armed camp more than a religious community.

Finally, Jones was forced to capitulate, and he allowed a group of reporters and relatives led by Congressman T. K. Ryan to inspect conditions at Jonestown. That visit, however, seems to have convinced Jones that the end was near. Some members of the People's Temple pursued the Ryan party to a nearby landing strip and mowed them down as they were boarding their plane. Jones, meanwhile, ordered the distribution of the "white night" potion of deadly cyanide. Since he had been training the sect's members to drink the elixir unquestioningly, few resisted.

Once again, says Hall, we see a pattern typical of the other-worldly sect: "the demanding regimen of everyday life," he explains, "predisposes people in such groups to respond to the whims of their leaders, whatever fanatic and zealous directions they may take." More to the point, Hall suggests that having been thoroughly indoctrinated in Jones' upside-down logic of good and evil, the people of Jonestown "would rather die together than have the life that was created together subjected to gradual decimation and dishonor at the hands of authorities regarded as illegitimate."

By the dictates of the religious beliefs that they had adopted, then, the members of Jonestown had to accept their "white night" as the final stage of their spiritual journey—to a better life—in other words, as the only possible means left to escape the corruption and evil they saw in American society. To an astonished world, the mass suicide and murder in Jonestown represented a senseless killing spree. But to the majority of those involved, it was likely a road to salvation.

New religious groups

Another way to measure the vitality of religion in the United States is to look at the substantial number of new sects and cults that have arisen in recent years. *Cults*, religious groups or movements concerned mainly with some particular, specialized belief or form of wor-

ship, are no longer confined to a handful of people convinced that the world is about to end. Some of the more ambitious cults have attracted thousands of members, many of whom have left families and jobs behind. Such a cult was the People's Temple of San Francisco (see box), which tried to build a utopian community in the jungle of Guyana and ended up a scene of carnage.

Cults draw many of their members from those under thirty or those who live on the socioeconomic fringes of society; some are quite large and influential. Reverend Sun Myung Moon's Unification Church, one of the largest of such groups, was estimated to have anywhere from 2,000 to 7,000 American followers in 1978, depending on whose figures one used (Bromley and Shupe, 1979). One explanation for the success of such groups is that they offer a promise of identity for the young and the idealistic who are seeking their place in society. A group such as Moon's, with its strict regulations, may also speak to the person who feels adrift.

Another recent development in American religious life has been the conversion by many people to spiritual beliefs and practices that have come from the Eastern traditions of Hinduism and Buddhism, although conversion for most has been more a matter of experimentation, trial, and tentative acceptance than an "instant" event. A wide variety of such groups have appeared on the scene, ranging from the Hare Krishna cult to the Transcendental Meditation movement, which presents itself almost as a self-improvement course (successfully enough to have attracted 6 million followers). Yoga, a more familiar import from the East, has gained an even larger following. The Eastern religions themselves, and Zen Buddhism in particular, have attracted numerous converts.

What all this suggests is that millions of people in the United States are actively seeking some kind of religious experience beyond that offered by traditional congregations.

Fundamentalism

In addition to the appearance of new religious sects and cults, yet another recent trend in the United States has been the revival of fundamentalism, a variety of Christianity that differs from the mainstream religion in its strict interpretation of the Bible as the word of God, and in its belief in the imminent Second Coming of Christ. While the rate of growth of church membership in general has lagged behind the population growth, many fundamentalist groups have grown more rapidly. Between 1952 and 1971, for example, while the population as a whole increased by about 27 percent, membership in the Southern Baptist Convention grew by 45.5 percent and in the Seventh-Day Adventists by 73.8 percent (*Yearbook of American and Canadian Churches*, 1975, p. 264). In a 1976 Gallup poll, 34 percent of Americans reported that they had been "born again" or had a "born again" experience in committing themselves to Christ. This shows a substantial proportion of the population to be committed to a basic fundamentalist tenet.

In recent years, membership in fundamentalist groups has increased rapidly in the United States. About one-third of all Americans now report that they have been "born again." (J. R. Holland/Stock, Boston)

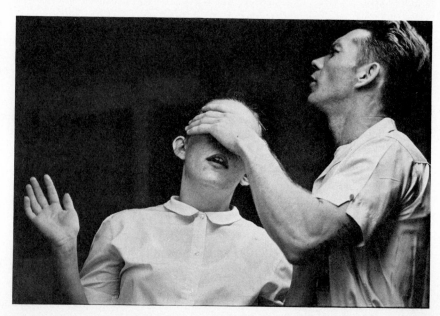

The "electronic church" is one of the most recent and profitable developments in organized religion. (Amy Meadow)

The electronic church

In a society so dominated by its communications networks, it is not surprising that a considerable number of Americans now absorb their religion wholly or in part via radio and television.

The lure of the "electronic" church is not restricted to the marginal members of society, although the poor are more apt to be attracted to radio evangelism than to its sophisticated television counterpart (Martin, 1970). Pastor Gene Scott of Channel 38 in San Francisco ("The Voice of Faith") appeals not only to individuals but to corporations, from whom he asks 10 percent of their profits as a contribution (Mariani, 1979).

The wide-ranging styles of broadcasting reflect the variety of audiences. A typical radio program consists primarily of taped segments from a live "healing and blessing" service, and a closing pitch for money. On television, by contrast, evangelism may take the form of a variety show, mixing testimony with musical acts, reminiscent more of the Ed Sullivan Show than of a religious service.

Like all religious groups, the media churches invariably ask for money—and much radio and television religion is "big business." The Church of God, run by California evangelist Herbert Armstrong, tops the list of well-known organizations with $65 million in donations each year, 80 percent of it from individuals (Mariani, 1979).

Why do people listen and watch rather than attend church in person? For radio listeners—other than those

for whom the medium is just a stopgap until they can get to an actual healing service—the evangelists offer answers to the whole range of human problems, physical, emotional, and financial. For television viewers, the medium seems to have taken over the fervor once generated by established religion but now declining. The special drama of the color and light of television, and the willingness of Americans to take not only their entertainment but their laws and social instruction from the tube, have turned religious experiences for many into inspirational events readily available at the flick of a switch.

The nontraditional "seekers"

Many Americans who belong to no church, sect, or cult have experiences and follow practices that may be considered religious, although they do not take place in a traditional or formal setting. A nationwide survey by the National Opinion Research Center (Greeley, 1975) found that fully 40 percent of all Americans report having had at least one mystical experience. A study by Wuthnow and Glock (1974) of a young, affluent, and presumably trend-setting group found that although only one-third of the sample ever attended church or synagogue, the majority still believed in the supernatural, in the efficacy of prayer, and in the possibility of life after death. Fewer than 25 percent rejected astrology outright. Only 8 percent were fairly sure that extrasensory perception (ESP) does not exist. A majority said that they had at some time felt close to something sacred, and at least 25 percent reported having had an experience that was definitely mystical in nature.

What the evidence suggests, according to these researchers, is an enormous pool of what William R. Catton, Jr. (1957), has called "seekers," people who may have rejected some of the doctrines of traditional religion but who are open to new beliefs. As Wuthnow and Glock observe,

God is not dead, He has simply changed clothes and come down from the clouds into the body. . . . The idea of God, as an abstraction out in space, has less reality for many than ESP, the belief in inward and personal mystery, communion with nature. (1974, p. 131)

WHY A RELIGIOUS RESURGENCE?

As Allan Eister (1972) points out, underlying the growth of religion seems to be a discomfort with traditional values. Eister argues that times of cultural crisis promote the growth of cults outside the mainstream religions. To many observers, the United States has appeared in recent years to be going through such a crisis period. Values that have traditionally been dominant, such as achievement and success, activity and work, morality, efficiency, material comfort, and rationalism, have at this point become sources of controversy. If they have not been rejected outright, they are being reinterpreted by certain small but highly visible groups. Many Americans have begun to distrust science, technology, and efficiency because they have produced such terrifying new possibilities as nuclear annihilation and world-wide pollution. For some people, the pace and scale of modern industrial society, with its emphasis on change, mobility, materialism, and relativism, may generate a deep need for a simpler way of life with fixed answers, strong leaders, and a tightly knit community. These may be some of the reasons many Americans seem to be turning to cults and other groups that purport to offer clear answers.

Paradoxically, the cultural crisis (if there is indeed a crisis) may be one of the causes not only of the growth of new religions but also of the recent resurgence of fundamentalism. Dean Kelley (1972) suggests that the fundamentalist churches succeed *because of* their strictness, rather than in spite of it; their strictness gives members definite answers to some of the bewildering puzzles of existence and provides them with a firm sense of belonging. Reginald W. Bibby and Merlin B. Brinkerhoff (1973), while agreeing with Kelley that the strictness of these churches has encouraged their growth, suggest that his emphasis on their evangelical appeal to potential converts may be misplaced. As these researchers point out, over 70 percent of such churches' "new members" have been reaffiliates—people who were previously members of evangelical churches—and another 20 percent were in fact children of members. In their view, strictness of evangelical doctrine does not so much attract converts as retain members—people who are already familiar with such churches.

In an important 1966 book, *The Secular City*, the theologian Harvey Cox defines the modern age as the age of "no religion at all." And Peter L. Berger, in his influential book *The Sacred Canopy* (1967), argues that in modern society, people live in a world of many religions and many nonreligious "reality-defining agencies," none of which is dominant. He claims that because traditional religious definitions of the world have lost their strength, the context of religion has shifted from the external world into the realm of individual consciousness.

It may be true to some extent, as Berger argues, that religions have changed from faiths that bound believers into a social and moral community to faiths that have become "privatized"—faiths each individual must construct alone because no dominating religious institution exists to do it. Yet a totally privatized religious experience is by no means typical. Even among the nontraditional "seekers," the mystical ideas that predominate—ESP, astrology, and the possibility of another world—are very much socially shared. Clearly, regardless of the complexity and rationalism of their society, Americans still have a strong need to deal with ultimate questions of existence through religious institutions.

Summary

Social scientists once assumed that religious belief would gradually give way to scientific rationalism. However, despite the ascendancy of science and technology in American society, religious beliefs and practices have persisted. There is still considerable interest in religion, although some of it has taken on new forms.

Emile Durkheim defined *religion* as a social phenomenon, uniting adherents into a community by means of beliefs, rituals, and symbols. He argued that religious worship is actually worship of society. A modern definition of religion describes it as an institutionalized system of symbols, beliefs, values, and practices focused on questions of ultimate meaning. *Value orientations*, such as the "civil religion" of the United States, may direct people's attention to ultimate questions without reference to the supernatural.

Karl Marx believed that religion acts to sustain, and make sacred, the existing order. Max Weber, however, argued that religious values may shape, as well as be shaped by, economic relations. Weber defined two types of religious leaders: *the priest* (associated primarily with *churches*) and the *prophet* (associated with *sects*). Sects appeal mainly to the socially disadvantaged, may be politically more radical than churches, and often evolve into churches.

Religious life in the United States presents a complex picture. The three major religions, Protestantism, Catholicism, and Judaism, are further subdivided into groups whose doctrines and practices differ. (This is especially true of Prot-

estantism, which is organized into a number of denominations.) Religious affiliation can be correlated, although imperfectly, with such factors as political preference, income, and social class.

Although declining church attendance through the 1950s, the 1960s, and the 1970s suggested that public interest in religion might be waning, church attendance actually increased slightly at the end of the 1970s. At the same time, several million Americans became involved in religious groups outside the mainstream: cults, meditation, Eastern religions, and Christian fundamentalist groups. A large number of others are content to experience their religion filtered through the mass media.

It has been suggested that the pace and scale of modern industrialized society, with its emphasis on change, mobility, materialism, and relativism, may be encouraging interest in these nontraditional religions. The continuing interest Americans have shown in seeking religious experience suggests that even though the forms of religion may shift, religion itself is among the most enduring of human institutions.

Glossary

CHURCH According to Ernst Troeltsch, a highly institutionalized religious organization dominated by the priestly role and characterized by compatibility with its surrounding culture, membership of a significant part of the society, membership usually by birth, public worship, systematized ritual, codified theology, and formally mediated divine grace.

CULT A religious group or movement that is concerned mainly with a particular, specialized belief or form of worship.

PRIEST A religious leader who derives authority from his or her religious organization.

PROPHET A religious leader who derives authority from his or her own charismatic qualities.

RELIGION An institutionalized system of symbols, beliefs, values, and practices, focused on questions of ultimate meaning.

RITUAL A prescribed religious act.

SECT According to Ernst Troeltsch, a loosely organized religious organization dominated by the prophetic role and characterized by opposition to its surrounding culture, a primarily converted membership, and a self-image as a society of the saved.

SYMBOLS The objects, images, or words representing the beliefs and rituals of a religion that ultimately take on meanings of their own, becoming sacred in their own right.

Recommended readings

Durkheim, Emile. *The Elementary Forms of the Religious Life.* Joseph W. Swain (tr.). Glencoe, Ill.: Free Press, 1954. A classic book that laid much of the groundwork for the development of the sociology of religion. It stresses the implications of religion for the group.

Weber, Max. *The Sociology of Religion.* Ephraim Fischoffs (tr.). Boston: Beacon Press, 1964. A classic work showing the power of historical and cross-cultural analysis and stressing the interdependence of religion and other social institutions.

Wilson, John. *Religion in American Society: The Effective Presence.* Englewood Cliffs, N.J.: Prentice-Hall, 1978. An integrative textbook on American religion in the last two decades.

Wuthnow, Robert. *Experimentation in American Religion: The New Mysticisms and Their Implications for the Churches.* Berkeley, Calif.: University of California Press, 1978. A nice balance of quantitative data and theory focusing on the relationship of American religious experimentation, such as Zen, astrology, and mysticism, to conventional religion.

Yinger, J. Milton. *The Scientific Study of Religion.* New York: Macmillan, 1970. A balanced and readable textbook that can serve as a good introduction to the sociological study of religion.

The faith and the faithful in the Islamic state

BERNARD LEWIS

As indicated in this chapter, there seems to be a revival of religious faith in America. This revival, however, although it may affect private morality and may also influence the stands that people take on certain public issues such as legalizing abortions, is a secular one. For unlike an Islamically ruled country like Iran—where, as described here, church and state are the same thing—in America, according to the Constitution, church and state are to remain strictly separate.

The word Islam has several different meanings. In the traditional sense, as used by Muslims, it connotes the one true divine religion, taught to mankind by a series of prophets, each of whom brought a revealed book. . . . Muhammad was the last and greatest of the prophets; and the book he brought, the Qur'ān, completes and supersedes all previous revelations. . . .

Islam means the religion taught by Muhammad himself, through the Qur'ān and through his own precept and practice. By extension, it is used of the whole complex system of dogma, law and custom, which was elaborated, on the basis of his teachings and of others ascribed to him, during the centuries after his death.

In a still wider sense the word Islam is often used by historians, and especially non-Muslim historians, as the equivalent not of Christianity but of Christendom, and denotes the whole rich civilization which grew up under the aegis of the Muslim empires.

The basic religious precepts of the Qur'ān are already contained in the early chapters, those revealed at Mecca before the migration of the Prophet and his followers to Medina. They teach that there is one God, omnipotent and omniscient, creator of all that exists; that it is the duty of men to submit themselves completely to the will of God; that those who rebel against the prophets sent by God to guide them and who persist in their unbelief are punished both in this world and the next; that after death there is a heaven and a hell where the good are rewarded and the wicked chastised; that at the end of time and the end of the world, there will be a resurrection of bodies and a universal judgment.

The Qur'ān may be supplemented as a source of guidance by *hadīth* ('Sayings'), the technical name for reports concerning the actions and utterances of the Prophet, who is believed by Muslims to have been divinely inspired in all that he did and said. . . .

Qur'ān and *hadīth* form the basis of the *sharī'a*, the Holy Law. This great corpus . . . is one of the major intellectual achievements of Islam, and in many ways the fullest and richest expression of the character and genius of Islamic civilization. . . .

The *sharī'a* covers all aspects of the public and private, communal and personal lives of the Muslims. In some of its provisions, especially those relating to property, marriage, inheritance and other matters of personal status, it is a normative code of law, which men were expected to obey and society to enforce; in others, more especially in its political prescriptions, it is rather a system of ideals towards which men and society were presumed to aspire and strive.

THE RULE OF LAW

The Islamic state as conceived by pious Muslims is a religious polity established under divine law. The source of its sovereignty is God; its sovereign, the caliph, has as his primary task to maintain and spread Islam. Its law is the Holy Law revealed by God and elaborated by the recognized interpreters of the Faith. This law is not limited to matters of belief, ritual and religious practice; it deals also with criminal and constitutional matters, with family and inheritance and with much else that in other societies would be regarded as the concern of the secular, not the religious, authorities. In classical Muslim theory there is no secular authority, and no secular law. 'Church' and state are one and the same, with the caliph as head; the Holy Law, which he exists to uphold, regulates the whole range of human activities. Where the basic tie between subject and sovereign is conceived as a religious one, political and religious attitudes coalesce. Political protest, itself perhaps socially determined, finds religious expression; religious dissent acquires political implications. In such a society, adherence and resistance to the existing order both tend to manifest themselves in religious terms—in attitudes and ideologies which may be characterized in Western parlance as orthodoxy and heresy. Some critics are moderate in their dissent and passive in their opposition; others are more radical in their divergence from accepted beliefs, and more violent in their methods, seeking to overthrow the existing order by means which may be described as revolutionary.

There were many such movements of religious dissent and revolt in Islam. The coming of Islam was itself a revolutionary change, with a new state, a new social order and a new doctrine to replace or transform existing institutions and ideas. In Islam as conceived by the first Muslims, there was to be no church and no priests, no kings and no aristocrats, no castes and no estates, and no privileges other than the natural and rightful superiority of those who accept the new dispensation over those who wilfully reject it.

In fact, however, the revolutionary change was less than complete. Some inequalities inherited from the old order—such as those of women and of slaves—were maintained in the new dispensation. True, these were softened by Islam. A slave was no longer a mere chattel but a human soul with definite legal and moral rights. Woman, though still subject to polygamy and concubinage, was given substantial protection in property and some other matters. By the moral and social standards of the time, neither slavery nor the inferiority of women was in any way objectionable. By recognizing and therefore regulating these institutions, Islam was able to bring some improvement in the situation of both groups. . . .

The tensions and conflicts which shook medieval Islamic society resulted not from those forms of inequality and discrimination which were sanctioned by Islam and regulated by Islamic law, but rather from those which survived in spite of Islam and in violation of its principles. . . .

In principle, the Islamic state was created to serve and spread the Islamic religion. Instead, in the view of many contemporary critics, it served the interests of small groups of ambitious men who ran it by methods that in-creasingly resembled those of the Persian and Roman empires which the Islamic state had superseded. Pious Arabs, joined by resentful non-Arabs, denounced the caliphs as perverters of the true faith and as the creators of a secular tyranny. Others, both Arab and non-Arab, pursuing a variety of grievances and ambitions, joined them in rebelling against this alleged tyranny, and by their actions gave rise to a series of civil wars which convulsed and disrupted the community and the government of Islam. . . .

Out of these struggles there emerged a series of religious groups differing from one another in their doctrines and in the nature of their support, but having as their common purpose to restore the radical dynamism of what they saw as the authentic and original Islam. In early days, when Arab and Muslim meant more or less the same thing, the religious struggle was a civil war between Arabs. Later, as the process of conversion brought increasing numbers of non-Arabs into the Islamic fold, converts, and especially Persians, began to play a growing role. This could be no better proof of the appeal and power of the Islamic message than the fact that all the great opposition movements in the Islamic empire were movements within Islam and not against Islam, having as their purpose not to overthrow the Faith but to purify, restore and enforce it. . . .

CHAPTER SEVENTEEN
POLITICS

In the course of a typical working day, the various divisions of the United States government may be occupied with problems and situations like these: A small town wants funds to build a sewage treatment plant. New York City needs a loan of $1 billion to pay its bills. A large corporation submits a bid for a government contract. A Midwestern agricultural lobby asks for subsidies for farmers whose crops were ruined by drought. A feminist organization demands that a woman be appointed to the Supreme Court, and a civil-rights group calls for a black to be appointed to the Cabinet. A state asks for federal approval of its plans to build an interstate highway, while a conservation group voices its opposition to the highway on the grounds that it would harm the environment. And a lawyer appeals a court decision that would sentence a federal offender to life imprisonment.

These examples illustrate a fundamental aspect of governmental organization. Any government controls the distribution of wealth and other resources within the social system it governs. It also has *some* control—though often specifically limited control—over these groups' and individuals' everyday actions. Because of this, any government is the focal point of *politics*—the struggle among interested groups and individuals for control over decision making.

Political activity goes on in a social system of any size. Large systems—communities and societies—have separate, differentiated governmental organizations (like the Supreme Court) and institutions devoted solely to political activity (like the Democratic party). But political activity is also part of the workings of smaller, less highly differentiated systems. In private corporations and public bureaucracies, workers compete for better jobs and bigger salaries; in academic settings, faculty members jockey for tenure; in clubs, members hold elections and may pull strings behind the scenes to choose officers; in families, parents and children wrangle over rules, decisions, and plans. In almost any social relationship, in fact, people compete for resources and struggle to control one another's behavior. That is, almost any social relationship is political in that it has a dimension of struggle for *power*. We touched on the nature and sources of power in Chapter 9; let us begin our discussion of politics by reviewing briefly what we covered there.

Power and its sources

Power can appear in a number of complex forms, but it has a simple definition. It is the ability of one person to have his or her will obeyed by another, or the ability of one group to have its way regardless of the intentions of others. Power is both the potential for control and this control made manifest.

Let's look at some sources of power. One of the easiest to recognize is *force*. When power is derived from force, it is based on a threat, which may be implicit or explicit: refusal to submit will result in harm. The point hardly needs to be illustrated, but a police officer with a gun is an obvious example of a person who exerts power by force: "Don't move or I'll shoot." Implicit in this form of power is the ability to carry out the threat and actually use force.

It is obvious, of course, that police officers in the United States do not have to wave a pistol every time they give an order. In fact, they rarely do. They are usually heeded anyway. This is because the power of the police is generally not based on force alone. For most members of society, police also have a somewhat less concrete source of power called *authority*. Authority is present when a person carries out a leadership role, or one involving control, that is seen as *legitimate*. Legitimacy means that the propriety or necessity of the authority is recognized and accepted by a relatively large proportion of the members of the social system. The police officer's authority does not derive from personal characteristics (for example, physical strength, size, or possession of a gun), but from the fact that he or she is performing a role involving control that, by and large, is socially accepted and institutionally defined. In this sense, the authority of the President of the United States is no different from that of the police officer: for the vast majority of Americans, both have authority because of the roles or offices they occupy.

A third source of power, *influence*, is somewhat more difficult to define. Whereas authority is usually based on formalized norms, such as laws, influence has a more informal basis. On the individual level, influence can stem from persuasiveness: a member of Congress, for example, may be able to convince his or her colleagues of the importance of a certain bill by skillful

argument. Influence may also come from knowledge: one factor in consumer activist Ralph Nader's success in influencing the automobile industry was his expertise about automobiles. Influence may also come from an individual's control over specific resources, such as money, or over a production facility, such as a large company with many jobs. It may result from inherited status in the nonpolitical sphere: an individual may

Isaac B. Singer accepts the 1979 Nobel Prize for Literature. Influence can be an important source of power, even if it stems from achievements in a nonpolitical sphere. (Andanson/Sygma)

have influence by virtue of being a member of one of the oldest families in a town. Or it may come from the individual's own achievements in the nonpolitical sphere: a Nobel Prize winner may be able to make his or her opinion count among members of a governing body. Influence can be held not only by individuals but also by aggregates of people: for example, the voters in the home district of an elected official can exert influence by virtue of the fact that the official is guided by a desire to be reelected by these voters.

Politics in the community and the society

Politics is of special interest, on the level of the community and the society, to both sociologists and political scientists. But whereas political scientists are generally more interested in the formal institutions that exist in a given community or society, sociologists are generally more interested in the relationships *between* these formal institutions and other social structures, and in the ways formal political institutions reflect broad cultural values and norms (Lipset and Schneider, 1973). Why do people in a society accept its governmental and political institutions? Under what conditions do they cease to accept them, and how do new institutions evolve? What are the lines of cleavage—diversity of interests and values—in a society, and how are they reflected in the society's political patterns? These are some of the major questions sociologists consider.

FUNCTIONALIST APPROACHES

Broadly speaking, sociological theory and investigation in the area of politics can be said to have followed two different lines of thought. The approach taken by functionalists, such as Emile Durkheim, has in essence looked for the basis of a political system's *legitimacy*—that is, the sources of agreement among the members of a society concerning the way the society is governed and the way that political struggle takes place. In other words, functionalists tend to focus on the *authority* dimension of the power structure.

Types of authority

Max Weber, one of the classic writers on the subject, identified three general types of authority in human societies (1922). The first, *traditional authority*, is characteristic of preindustrial societies. According to Weber, authority based on tradition is legitimated on the basis of "belief in the sanctity of immemorial traditions." An example of this attitude is the old saying, "The king is dead—long live the king!" In other words, there has always been a monarch and there will always be one. In the traditional system, obedience is owed to the person of the ruler, such as the feudal lord, and not to abstract rules. The ruler exercises authority not in accordance with formal principles, but on the basis of social customs or free personal decisions.

During periods of transition or crisis, another type of authority, which Weber called *charismatic authority*, tends to arise. Charismatic authority derives from belief in a leader's exceptional abilities, superhuman gifts, or divine characteristics. Obedience is strictly a matter of personal commitment to a specific individual. Charismatic authority is usually short-lived; it lapses almost as soon as the crisis has passed or when the leader dies. If a charismatic leader is to maintain power, it is usually necessary to convert his or her legitimacy to a traditional basis or to the third type of authority, which Weber called *rational-legal authority* (a typical characteristic of formal organizations, as we noted in Chapter 9). Here power is based on enacted laws, and obedience is owed not to an individual but to an impersonal order of norms and regulations. One of the hallmarks of rational-legal authority is that instead of rulers, there are holders of office. The legitimacy of the officeholders rests on the acceptance of the political system by the members of the society. In contrast to the emotional magnetism of charismatic authority and the arbitrariness of traditional power, rational-legal authority is abstract and routinized.

Authority and effectiveness

In simple societies, Durkheim argued, the social order is based on a "collective conscience," or set of shared values. Members have a common *ideology*, or coherent set

The Nigerian King of Akure and his wives (top left). When authority is based on tradition, as is common in preindustrial societies, obedience is owed to the person of the ruler, not to abstract rules. In times of transition or crisis, according to Weber, charismatic authority— belief in a leader's exceptional qualities—may prevail; for example, Mohandas Gandhi (bottom left), the political and religious leader, was instrumental in India's movement for independence from Great Britain. Rational-legal authority is based on impersonal laws and norms; in rational-legal systems, there are officeholders (bottom right), not rulers. (© Marc & Evelyne Bernheim/Woodfin Camp & Assoc.; The Granger Collection; Tim Carlson/Stock, Boston)

of beliefs regarding human existence and the validity or "rightness" of their particular social order. (In such societies, political beliefs are often intertwined with religious ones.) Complex societies lack a "collective conscience," since their complex division of labor and wide range of social roles make the sharing of values and interests among all members problematic. But though a complex society may thus be subject to political conflict, such conflict need not lead to disintegration of the social order. Members may be in conflict but still share

a commitment to political *procedures*. That is, although members may not have common goals, they may all believe in, or at least accept, the ground rules by which political decisions are made. Functionalists, then, study the basis of the common ideology in a simple society; in a complex society, they look for the ways in which the members "agree to disagree."

In addition, functionalist approaches may weigh the balance between the legitimacy of a government and its *effectiveness*—the degree to which people perceive it as actually performing its expected functions. A political system that is low on both these dimensions is likely to be unstable and is more likely to be overturned (Lipset and Schneider, 1973). The American political system, viewed from this perspective, can be said to have enjoyed—at least until recently—a high degree of both legitimacy and effectiveness. But with the war in Vietnam, the Watergate scandal, the failure of much-touted urban programs, the energy and environmental crises, and the state of the economy, our system may have become less stable—a point we will explore in more detail later in this chapter.

Conflict approaches

Karl Marx and other social scientists with a conflict perspective play down the role of agreement on values, ideology, and procedures in the maintenance of a political system. As they point out, even if a government has a low level of both legitimacy and effectiveness, it may still survive by coercion. In general, these observers emphasize the role of external force in a society's political workings. In their view, the form that government and political procedures take in a society is the outcome of struggle among competing groups, not of consensus. The dominance of particular groups ultimately rests on those groups' control over specific economic and political resources, and not on the willingness of most people in the society to abide by the "rules of the game." Institutionalized procedures for nonviolent struggle may exist, but their function is really cosmetic; coercion is the underlying mechanism. Conflict theorists also examine the question of legitimacy, but their concern is more with how political elites attempt to legitimatize their authority over a relatively powerless mass of people. One approach to this problem is to focus on the degree to which dominant groups are able, through their influence over mass media, schools, and other agents of political socialization, to control subordinate groups' perceptions of political reality.

LEGITIMACY, EFFECTIVENESS, AND FORCE

A commonsense assumption might be that democratic political systems are maintained almost wholly by means of legitimacy and effectiveness, and totalitarian systems almost wholly by force. But this would be an overstatement of the case and an oversimplification of something that is in reality very complex. The totalitarian state does not police every individual at every moment, yet it continues to exist. Some proportion of the population grants legitimacy to the government. (We discussed the Soviet Union's stratification system and the ideology that supports it in Chapter 10.) Conversely, consensus in Western democratic political systems is not total, nor is force absent, as is evident from prompt police reaction to noninstitutionalized forms of protest. (Think, for example, of the Ohio National Guard's role at Kent State; see Chapter 21.) In this chapter, we will take a close look at the balance among legitimacy, effectiveness, and force in our own political system. But first, we will survey the way the modern state and the Western industrialized democracies developed.

The modern state

By definition, a *state* is a society's supreme governmental institution, and the one that holds a monopoly over the legitimate use of force. The state is not a recent development. States of varying size, strength, and complexity have existed in many societies throughout history. But in most, power was typically applied to a narrow range of activities, most of which ultimately had to do with increasing the wealth of the ruler or rulers. Moreover, the state shared its power with numerous secondary governmental and political institutions: in pre-modern states, the rulers' power was not absolute. For example, kings had only limited control over their nobles. A ruler had to depend on these nobles for armies, which except in time of war were always under the control of individual nobles rather than directly responsible to the ruler.

In the modern state, however, political power over a wide geographical area is *centralized*, or concentrated, in the hands of the state government. Furthermore, it extends into many areas of social life. The typical modern state is directly involved in such diverse activities as educating and protecting its citizens, regulating commerce and agriculture, and building and maintaining recreation facilities—to name just a few. The roots of the modern state are to be found in the broad historical currents that helped transform European society from an agricultural basis to an industrial one. Among the factors involved were bureaucratization, the growth of capitalism and urban markets, and the spread of new values regarding power and authority.

INCREASING CENTRALIZATION

The process of centralization began in the feudal period with the gradual emergence of urban merchants, who manufactured and sold goods for money, thus making possible the accumulation of a new kind of wealth. The growth of urban markets, and of trade between them, created new routes to power and new political relationships. The new wealth also helped to finance military and colonial expansion, which in turn led to the development of political regimes commanding vast resources. Under feudalism, the state had been like a patchwork quilt consisting of individual, agriculturally self-sufficient units, each under the control of its own lord. Power was extremely decentralized. What emerged to replace this fragmented system was a tightly knit society consisting of increasingly interdependent, trade-linked regions.

This new industrializing economic setting was exceedingly hospitable to a centralized government. Administration of the growing industrial and commercial network was a task that could no longer be carried out by a monarch and a handful of trustworthy ministers. Special bureaucracies were required for the planning and management of so many diverse activities. And because of colonial expansion and the growth of capitalism, the economic system became worldwide in scope, necessitating even more control, planning, and direction. In this world system, those states that developed centralized governments and specialized bureaucracies became dominant (see Wallerstein, 1974; see also Chapters 10 and 18).

The shift to rational-legal authority

One of the earliest government bureaucracies was the English Exchequer, which was set up to oversee tax collecting and financial administration, still among its functions today. Other bureaucracies came into being during periods of colonial expansion, when foreign offices were established to maintain contact with governors and staffs that had been sent to manage the far-flung regions of the empire.

What the rulers did not realize, or perhaps could do nothing about, was the fact that bureaucratic institutions helped bring about a crucial cultural transformation, from values favoring traditional authority to values favoring authority of the rational-legal type. Traditional European rulers and aristocrats had tended to use their power—which was not greatly restrained by rules and regulations—to support the status of the hereditary classes, rather than to advance the well-being of the people as a whole. But with the growth of government bureaucracies, powerful roles such as those of king and ministers began to be seen less as private sources of gain than as public offices in which power was expected to be used for the ultimate benefit of all citizens. As these government bureaucracies penetrated more deeply into Western society to satisfy the need for specialized services, they carried their rational-legal norms with them, socializing both those who became bureaucrats and those governed by bureaucratic organizations and rulers.

The greatest scope of government activity

As bureaucracy grew, so did the scope of the government's activities. In Western Europe, state governments became ever more concerned with supporting the capitalist system and with protecting it from serious disruptions. In the early nineteenth century in France, for example, Napoleon created a new judicial system to administer a legal code that reconciled feudal customs with modern realities. Significantly, it stressed the property rights of the growing industrial and commercial middle class, or *bourgeoisie*. (Capitalism is discussed in Chapters 10, 11, and 18, the bourgeoisie in Chapter 10.)

In most modern Western democracies, the government sooner or later makes at least minimal provision for many of the population's basic needs through unemployment benefits, welfare programs, social security, medical programs, and the like. A small minority in such societies, particularly in the United States, thinks the government goes too far in undertaking these responsibilities, since they constitute an interference in the workings of the free economic market. But for the most part, business has profited from this system of "welfare capitalism." By protecting the majority of workers from extreme poverty or excessive hardship—during or after their working lives—the state has helped maintain a stable labor force. "Welfare capitalism" has also provided workers with enough money to function as the consumers who are needed by a high-production economy. (We will discuss these issues in detail in Chapter 18.)

Government authority gradually entered other areas of social life. One example is offered by the creation of the London police force in 1829 to protect "respectable" citizens against crime and violence. This bureaucratic involvement in society, as Allan Silver

points out, quickly spread beyond crime prevention: "In a broader sense it represented the penetration and continual presence of central political authority throughout daily life" (1967, p. 161). Similarly, educational activities came increasingly under government direction during the 1880s, partly as a result of industry's growing need for educated workers and technicians. Thus, in the course of the nineteenth and twentieth centuries, citizens in Western industrial states became increasingly dependent on the government for specific services. One result has been that the responsibility for allocating various resources has become ever more concentrated, or centralized, at the national level.

CENTRALIZED POWER

The product of the gradual increase and centralization of power in modern states can be thought of as a two-edged sword. Powerful, wide-ranging, and highly bureaucratized governments have the capacity for great benevolence. They can protect the fortunate and at the same time ensure a standard of living that benefits everyone, and they can use their power to try to help solve social problems. But such power also carries with it a potential for abuse in the form of invasion of pri-

As government becomes more centralized, government buildings often come to resemble temples (an interesting aspect of the "civil religion" discussed in Chapter 16). (Erich Hartmann/Magnum)

vacy, manipulation, unequal distribution of privilege—and dictatorship. At the root of the totalitarian regimes of Stalin in Russia, Mussolini in Italy, and Hitler in Germany lay the gradual expansion of state power.

THE DEVELOPMENT OF PLURAL ELITES AND MASS PARTICIPATION

In examining the emergence of plural elites (diverse privileged groups) and mass participation in Western societies, we once again trace a process that began with the breakdown of the feudal system. First, traditional authority came under attack: the urban merchants and manufacturers, resentful of interference by old-guard aristocrats, pushed for laws favoring free competition. Once this process had begun, members of the bourgeoisie began to acquire not only new wealth but also new social and political advantages. They could no longer be excluded from the traditional avenues to power and status, such as the university, legislative bodies, courts of law, and military systems. Political power, so closely

guarded by royal families under the old system, was gradually dispersed. In this way, new economic opportunities made possible the formation of multiple, or plural, elites within a society, in place of a single, monolithic elite.

An indication of this political change was the development of *egalitarian* ideals among the bourgeoisie. The French and American revolutions, two of the most radical movements of the eighteenth century, were fought in the name of free economic competition *and* "liberty and equality." Needless to say, there were gaps between the revolutionary rhetoric and the true goals of the new bourgeois class. But once the new ideas were put forth, they gained acceptance—at least on certain levels—among increasingly wide segments of society.

Meanwhile, and partly as a result of the growth of this new ideology, the political status of the common man (and woman) was changing as well. The lower classes gradually acquired certain political rights—for example, the right to vote. The new elites needed mass support: a pluralistic system was seen to require the participation of all free men, regardless of whether or not they were also property owners. This need for mass

Egalitarianism was an ideal of the French Revolution, which began with the storming of the Bastille, a notorious prison, on July 14, 1789. (The Granger Collection)

support was related to the expansion of economic rights for workers; unions were one result. Finally, in a last step, what Thomas H. Marshall (1963) calls "social rights" were extended to the masses. Government undertook the responsibility for their education and protection.

Not all these political changes came about solely through shifts in the goals of elites. In many cases, they came about because the masses fought for them. Before the development of representative institutions (primarily popularly elected legislatures) and universal suffrage, the masses frequently took collective action, often of a violent nature, to make their desires known. Gradually, as Charles, Louise, and Richard Tilly (1975) point out, collective action shifted its focus from small-scale local disputes or brawls over limited resources (which the Tillys call *competitive action*) to *proactive action*: politically coherent, national mass movements aimed at gaining rights and privileges not previously enjoyed. In other words, a local battle between one powerful factory owner and his workers became just one part of a regional or national battle over broader issues such as the right to work or the quality of life.

Only in recent times have Western societies come to view mob action as relatively illegitimate: in eighteenth-century England, according to Silver, riots and disorders were seen by many people as politically meaningful activity that "provided the unorganized poor with a language by which, in the absence of representative institutions or the ability to participate in them, they might articulately address the propertied classes" (1967, p. 169). But as political and economic relationships became more tightly woven in the United States and England, these societies became less willing to tolerate such disruptive collective action. States instituted formal mechanisms of social control, such as civil-disorder laws and police organizations.

Sociologists often disagree about how best to interpret violent protest. Some of this disagreement involves theoretical discussions about the nature of crowds, the causes and effects of riots, and so on. (We will discuss these issues in greater detail in Chapter 21.)

Elites and masses in the American political system

How meaningful is the access to decision-making power that the masses have gained in Western political systems? Is popular democratic power being weakened? These are much-debated questions. Some theorists argue that in any system, whether it is the United States or the Soviet Union, a small elite will tend to appear, and this elite will become more concerned with perpetuating its power than with serving its constituents' interests. The social theorist Gaetano Mosca (1939) believed that rule by elites was inevitable: throughout history, small elites have governed the masses by virtue of their superior talents and organization.

Vilfredo Pareto (1935), studying what he termed the "circulation of elites" in political systems, predicted that power might shift from one small group to another, but the lives of the masses would remain the same. And Robert Michels (1915) stated as an axiom—known as his "iron law of oligarchy" (rule by the few)—that in an organization of any size, power would tend to fall into the hands of a small group of leaders, simply because as the organization grows those with the most time, energy, and ability will take over (see Chapter 9).

So far, forms of pluralism with mass participation have survived in many Western countries, particularly in the United States. But certain questions concerning pluralism remain, especially regarding the American system. Do the masses really participate in the political process? Does the government give all groups a reasonable chance to have their voices heard? Is the government a neutral arbiter of conflicting interests? How independent is the government from powerful interest groups, such as corporations? What might recent events and situations—such as the civil disorders in Miami, student demonstrations against the draft, the anti-nuclear reactor protests, the war in Vietnam, unemployment, the pollution of the environment, Watergate, and strikes by police and teachers—tell us abut the actual workings of American political institutions? In the following sections we will present the viewpoints of two different groups: those who maintain that political decision making in the United States is dominated by a tightly knit monolithic elite, and those who believe that power in American society is more widely dispersed among the plural elites.

THE MONOLITHIC ELITE THEORY

Marxist and other conflict theorists, who believe that the state functions basically to protect and further the interests of business, have pointed out numerous links between the United States government and the corporate sector of private economic enterprise. On the policy-making level, government and big business regularly exchange personnel; between 1940 and 1967, for instance, of the ninety-one individuals who served as secretaries or undersecretaries of state or defense or as heads of military services, the Central Intelligence Agency, or the Atomic Energy Commission, seventy had previously worked for major corporations or investment houses. Power is seen to have become increasingly concentrated in the hands of the federal government and large corporations (Dye, 1976).

C. Wright Mills has argued that a strong, unified elite exists in the United States, but he rejects the Marxist notion that the elite is simply a steering committee for the capitalist ruling class. In *The Power Elite* (1956), he described a group of approximately 500 Americans who, emerging after World War II, gained control of the country's economic, political, and military institutions. This "power elite" derived its cohesiveness, in Mills' view, from the fact that its members came from the upper class and had similar backgrounds. Having attended the same universities, joined the same clubs, and learned the same set of values along the way, the members of the elite behave according to the same "rules of the game." Members of the elite, in Mills' view, do not agree on every issue, but the values they share make accommodation through bargaining possible most of the time.

Some of Mills' ideas were empirically examined in studies by G. William Domhoff (1967, 1971, 1978), surveying individuals who Domhoff felt could be categorized as belonging to the upper class. Domhoff's criteria included not only millionaire financial status but also high prestige (as reflected by membership in exclusive men's clubs, education in select private schools, and being listed in the *Social Register*). Domhoff's data did not prove that this elite was literally a "governing class," but his findings did show that members of this tiny category—which represents only about 0.5 percent of the total population—hold a high proportion of controlling positions in governmental *and* business organizations, foundations, elite universities, opinion-making associations, and so on. Baltzell's (1979) study of the elites of Quaker Philadelphia and Puritan Boston sheds some new light on the theory of the monolithic elite—or at least on the idea of this elite as monolithic in all ways. The Quaker leaders of Philadelphia were as wealthy and as bright and educated as the Puritan leaders of Boston—yet in one city public service was regarded as something a "gentleman" did not engage in, and in the other it was considered a duty. Thus it is clear that forms of elite involvement can differ—the Boston elite has a long tradition of such public service; the Philadelphia elite does not. Moreover, there even are elites within elites. A study by Michael Useem (1979) found that an "inner group" and an "outer group" could be discerned within the economic elite; members of the inner group were usually directors of several corporations, while outer-group members directed only one. Members of the inner-group elite were more likely to serve as directors of nonprofit organizations and in high positions in government agencies than were the outer-group elite.

The extreme concentration of power described by the monolithic-elite model is perhaps easiest to visualize on the national level, where decisions are far-reaching and many political processes are hidden. (It is, perhaps, even easier to visualize on the international level, as we will point out in Chapter 18.) But some research also points to the existence of monolithic elites on local levels. In a study conducted in Atlanta, Georgia, Floyd Hunter (1953) found a ruling elite, composed of business and financial leaders, that operated behind the scenes to set the policies carried out by elected officials. In their famous study of "Middletown" (Muncie, Indiana), Robert and Helen Lynd (1929, 1937) found an even more concentrated power structure. This elite was dominated by the "X" family, which owned the largest industry, and was composed chiefly of other wealthy local manufacturers. One Middletown man summed up the influence of the powerful "X" family in these words:

If I'm out of work, I go to the X plant; if I need money I go to the X bank, and if they don't like me I don't get it; my children go to the X college; when I get sick I go to the X hospital; I buy a building or a house in the X subdivision; my wife goes downtown to buy X milk; I drink X beer, vote for X political parties, and get help from X charities; my boy goes to the X YMCA and my girl to their YWCA; I listen to the word of God in a X-subsidized church; if I'm a Mason, I go to the X Masonic temple; I read the news from the X morning paper; and if I'm rich enough, I travel via the X airport. (1937, p. 74)

ARE THERE PLURAL ELITES?

Although there is much evidence to support the single-elite hypothesis, there is also a great deal of data suggesting that the American political system is composed of a variety of power centers. In *The Power Structure* (1967), written to refute Mills' theory of the power elite, Arnold Rose argued that rather than having a single nucleus of influence, the American power structure contains multiple power centers that can—and do—conflict with one another. Support for Rose's contention can be found in the geographical and ideological cleavages that exist within many elite groups. In the economic sphere, for example, large corporations and small businesses frequently disagree in their support of candidates for office, as well as over such matters as tariffs, the regulation of credit, and federal welfare policies.

In the two parties that dominate political life in the United States, leaders differ over a broad range of policy issues. Herbert McClosky, Paul J. Hoffman, and Rosemary O'Hara (1960) examined the political attitudes of Democratic and Republican delegates to the 1958 national conventions. Leaders from each party differed significantly on twenty-three out of twenty-four issues the researchers had listed. Democrats tended to favor aiding underprivileged members of the society through social-reform legislation and spending policies. They also backed the enforcement of integration and the use of taxation to redistribute wealth. Republicans, by contrast, were inclined to support a laissez-faire doctrine of personal effort, private incentive, and self-denial as the means of overcoming hardship. After twenty years, these broad distinctions still remain, despite considerable diversity within the parties—especially the Democrats (Kirkpatrick, 1976).

Plural elites can also be seen on the local level in certain areas. One of the most famous studies of these patterns is Robert A. Dahl's (1961) investigation of the decision-making process in New Haven, Connecticut. Dahl found that although the number of people involved in making decisions constituted only a fraction of the community, power was exercised by different elites over different sets of issues. Dahl's findings seemed to indicate that power in New Haven was not transferable from one sphere of influence to another, and that there was the potential for competition and conflict among elites.

Three years before Mills argued that influence in America had become concentrated into a "power elite," David Riesman came to the opposite conclusion in *The Lonely Crowd* (1953). Pointing to patterns such as those seen in metropolitan areas, where federal, state, and local programs often seem to thwart one another, Riesman argued that America had actually become *overly* pluralistic, entangled in multiple tugs of war between elites whose efforts tended to cancel one another out. Where Mills saw increasing domination by a single elite, Riesman saw a weakening of leadership overall.

THE ASSUMPTIONS BEHIND THE SINGLE- AND PLURAL-ELITE THEORIES

The distribution and exercise of power in our system cannot be described in terms of "either/or." Whether one finds a monolithic or a plural elite depends on the particular political unit—community, area, or state and, perhaps, even issue or institution—one is studying. But there is also a deeper question, a question concerning the definition of power itself. Is power a *potential* capacity that may be exercised indirectly, secretly, or even unconsciously? Or is the ability to prevent certain issues from being raised or to shape how they are presented a major attribute of power? Or is power best approached as a *behavioral* phenomenon, attributable only to those who can be seen exercising it? Sociologists who see elites as monolithic tend to deemphasize the public discussion of issues. They look instead at behind-the-scenes power transactions and at the factors that shape which issues surface in the political agenda. Sociologists who see elites as pluralistic give closer attention to the issues that emerge into public consideration, and assign less weight to matters, even important ones, that do not reach the public arena.

Were the "founding fathers" of the United States a pluralistic or a monolithic elite? As the *Federalist Papers* show, these men disagreed on many issues during their constitutional debates, and, in this sense, they could be termed a gathering of plural elites. But when it was presented, the Constitution appeared to have been conceived in a spirit of unanimity, and its originators combined their political resources to give it monolithic backing. (Courtesy, Wadsworth Atheneum, Hartford, Conn.)

Whether one finds conflict or consensus among elites also depends on the issues one looks at. The "Pentagon Papers," a secret Defense Department study of the Vietnam War leaked to the press in 1971, revealed considerable disagreement among elites over *how* the war in Southeast Asia should be waged; there was little disagreement, however, about *whether* the United States should be involved, because there was a long-standing elite consensus that it was necessary to contain the spread of communism.

It is easier to contrast pluralistic and elitist arguments on the theoretical level than to resolve them with empirical evidence. The truth probably lies somewhere between the two. There is not a homogeneous, monolithic elite in the United States, but neither do major societal groups have anything like equal influence on the political process.

NEW ELITES: THE MULTINATIONALS

The growth of extremely powerful multinational corporations in recent years has led sociologists to examine a new "power elite." Since the 1960s, a few corporations—most of them based in the United States—have come to have enormous power over hundreds of millions of people (see Chapter 18). As Richard Braungart has put it:

Multinational corporations in their daily operations have more power or impact on the lives of ordinary citizens than many armies, nation-states, and municipal governments. They are successful in penetrating and influencing the life styles of communities and nations alike. This involves changing family, work, and leisure, and political, educational, and consumer habits of millions of people throughout the world. The primary source of this power is derived from the control over national and international technology, capital, and market place ideology. (1978, p. 120)

The multinational corporations thus form a "super-elite" whose power stretches around the globe. Their ultimate impact on the nations of the world is unknown, but two ominous facts must be considered. First, their growth is continuing, and individual nations are essentially powerless to control or regulate their activities. Second, since their business is often in defense-related technology and strategic supplies (arms, electronics, oil), world instability and conflict—at least up to a point—are in their interest.

The American political system: mass participation and mass support

Mass political participation has been one of the most conspicuous and often-praised features of the American political system. But how much influence do "the people" actually have on the decision-making process? Do they really provide a foundation for the political system, as the classical pluralist model assumes, or are they instead buried helplessly beneath a top-heavy structure—and manipulated at that? There are two key questions here: Who actually participates? And, how likely are the participants to attain their political goals?

WHO PARTICIPATES?

Compared with other industrialized countries, the United States shows a strikingly low turnout of voters in elections. (This is in great contrast to the nineteenth century, when voter participation was more widespread than in other nations.) In the five presidential elections between 1952 and 1968, an average of 61 percent of all eligible citizens voted; but in 1972, only 55.5 percent of the electorate voted, and in 1976 there was a further drop to 53 percent. In off-year elections, when all members of the House of Representatives and many senators and governors run for office, even fewer voters go to the polls—usually less than 50 percent. In the 1974 post-Watergate elections, when American disillusionment with politics was unusually high, only 36.1 percent of voters cast a ballot (Census Bureau, 1976, p. 467).

Ironically, those groups that might most profit from changes in government practices and increases in social services—minorities, ethnic groups, the elderly, and others—tend to participate least on the average. Socioeconomic status is a crucial factor in determining participation (see Figure 17.2). The less education one has, for example, the less likely one is to vote. In 1976, 44 percent of those with eight years of school or less voted, compared to 60 percent of those with a high school education and 73 percent of those with more than high

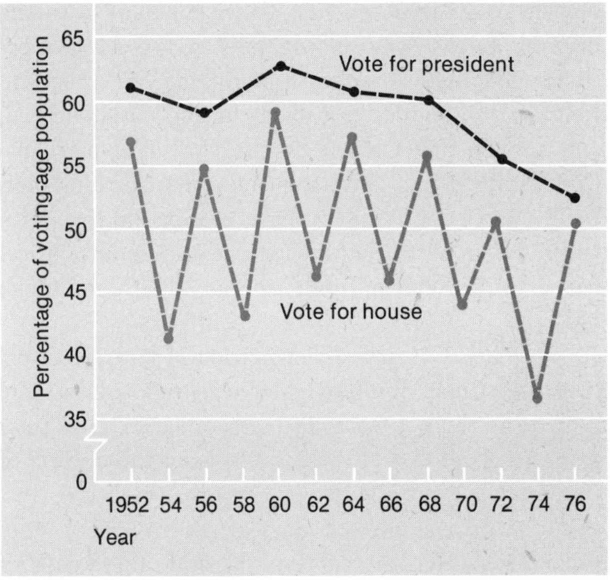

FIGURE 17.1

This graph shows the percentages of eligible citizens who voted in elections for President and members of the House of Representatives from 1952 to 1976. (Census Bureau, 1976, p. 467)

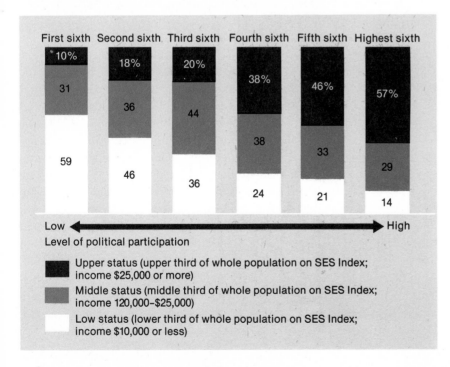

FIGURE 17.2

This chart shows the percentages of individuals at six levels of political participation, from high to low. The majority (59 percent) of those in the one-sixth of the population whose level of political participation was lowest were found to be in the lowest socioeconomic status (SES) group. The majority (57 percent) of those at the highest level of participation were found to be in the highest SES group. (Verba and Nie, 1972, p. 131)

TABLE 17.1

PROFILE OF REGISTERED VOTERS IN
JANUARY–APRIL, 1980

	PERCENT REGISTERED
National	70
SEX	
Male	70
Female	71
RACE	
White	71
Non-white	65
HOUSEHOLD INCOME	
$25,000 & over	78
$20,000–$24,999	76
$15,000–$19,999	71
$10,000–$14,999	67
$ 5,000–$ 9,999	65
Under $5,000	63
EDUCATION	
College	77
High school	67
Grade school	66
OCCUPATION OF CHIEF WAGE EARNER	
Professional & business	77
Clerical & sales	71
Manual workers	62
REGION	
East	71
Midwest	76
South	67
West	67
POLITICS	
Republican	79
Democrat	75
Independent	59

SOURCE: Gallup, 1980, p. 63.

school (Census Bureau, 1978, p. 520). Poor people vote less than rich people; blacks vote less than whites, and Hispanics vote less than blacks. Catholics tend to vote less than Protestants. Age also makes a difference: less than 25 percent of those aged eighteen to twenty-four and less than 56 percent of those aged sixty-five and over voted in the November 1978 elections. Whether or not a person votes can also be affected by occupation: in 1978, 35 percent of blue-collar workers, 39 percent of service workers, and 55 percent of white-collar workers voted (Census Bureau, September 1979).

Aside from voting, there are a number of other kinds of political participation in the United States. They include running for office, being active in campaign work, making financial contributions to candidates, engaging in community action to obtain collective benefits, and making contacts with government officials for special benefits. To what extent do members of nonelite groups take part in these activities? Although American political parties are not subject to tight central control (especially at the national level, and to some degree at the state level as well), participation requires time and often money. As a result, less than 3 percent of adult Americans ever run for office, and only about 15 percent are ever active in political parties and campaign fundraising (Milbrath and Goel, 1977).

Why *don't* most people participate? Until recently, in certain areas, complex voter registration laws were used expressly to discourage disadvantaged groups from going to the polls. There has also been the decline of the unofficial but highly effective urban political "machine," which before the days of government welfare programs handed out money, jobs, and other favors to newly settled urban immigrants in return for their votes.

There are more general barriers as well, many observers believe—barriers created by the political system's failure to address itself to the needs of the nonparticipating groups. Some evidence suggests that nonparticipation levels vary from region to region and from community to community, and are related to the degree to which local elites are monolithic or pluralistic. When competition among leadership factors in a community declines, so too does citizen participation; fewer issues are submitted to voters, and the distribution of power becomes more elitist. Conversely, as a monolithic elite structure begins to lose its control and becomes more pluralistic, political competition within the community increases on both mass and elite levels (Agger, Goldrich, and Swanson, 1964). Political participation, then, seems to be related to the individual's belief that he or she may successfully influence government (Huber and Form, 1973; Wright, 1976).

HOW DIRECTLY IS PARTICIPATION REWARDED?

The way an individual votes obviously does not necessarily result in his or her candidate's doing what the individual wants. Voting for one plank in a candidate's platform means, in effect, supporting the other planks. And there are constraints inherent in the two-party system. In the United States there is a tendency for each of the two major parties to try to be all things to all people, including poor and rich, Southerners and Northerners, farmers and factory workers, and so on. Publicly parties tend to play down partisan and narrow appeals to special interests in an effort to attract both undecided voters—usually about 10 to 15 percent of the electorate—and moderates of the other party. Thus a vote is seldom directly translated into the specific action the voter intends.

Furthermore, even when candidates do take clear positions, they may be misunderstood or misperceived— one can vote for someone who is actually planning something different from what one has in mind. Not only is the average American voter relatively unin-formed about politics, but his or her perception of a candidate's stand on an issue is often affected by the voter's own opinion on it (Berelson, Lazarsfeld, and McPhee, 1954). Finally, as many studies have shown, voters' opinions are often inconsistent (for example, see Key, 1960); they do not tend to be shaped by strong ideological perspectives (Wolfinger et al., 1976, p. 100).

Until recently, party affiliation has been a reasonably good indicator of voting behavior. And ostensibly, party membership reflects some cleavages in interests among classes, races, religions, ethnic groups, and regional groups. The reasons *why* people belong to one political party rather than another include not only membership in specific ethnic and religious groups, but also the individual's class position and parents' party

Compared with other industrialized countries, the United States shows a strikingly low turnout of voters in elections. This could suggest that many Americans are essentially satisfied with the government and its actions—*or that they believe that nothing can be done to change them.* (© Lawrence Frank 1976)

choices during the individual's childhood. Interestingly, party choice is *not* directly correlated with region of birth, urban or rural residence, the social class of one's father—or one's educational level, according to studies by David Knoke (1972, 1976). Education does, however, have an indirect effect on party identification through its effects on occupational status and the individual's subjective class identification.

But if a significant number of Americans do not participate in politics, does that mean our political system lacks broad support?

HOW GREAT IS MASS SUPPORT FOR THE POLITICAL SYSTEM?

Have the frequently low rewards of political participation in the United States caused people to become disillusioned with government? Does the small voter turnout at elections indicate that many people believe political decision makers are unresponsive to their needs? The extent to which Americans are satisfied with the existing political system is the subject of much debate. Although some have argued that many Americans' political apathy is a sign that they essentially approve of the government and its actions, others (Wright, 1976) point out that surveys consistently show that as much as half the population is alienated from political life. According to this interpretation, the failure of many people to vote reflects not agreement with things as they are, but a belief that nothing can be done to change them.

Public opinion, party support, and ideology

For more than four decades, since the "New Deal" reforms made in response to the Great Depression, American political institutions have maintained a relatively stable society and supported a capitalist system agreeable to the middle-class majority. Demands for deep structural change have not been effectively articulated. Now, however, many people's feelings about the political system seem to be changing. According to Gallup polls, between 1966 and 1972, the proportion of the American public that agreed with the statement, "People who run the country don't care what happens to people such as myself" nearly doubled, from 26 percent to 50 percent. In 1964, 20 percent of the population said that the government could not always be trusted to do what was right; by 1972, 40 percent felt that way.

According to a Gallup poll, the proportion of Americans "dissatisfied with the way this nation is being governed" went from 54 percent in 1971 to 66 percent two years later. In another set of surveys, the proportion of citizens who believed that government officials "don't care what people like me think" increased from 36 percent in 1952 to 56 percent in 1973 (Nie, Verba, and Petrocik, 1979). This evidence points to a weakening of support for the dominant ideology, which holds that the government is good, responds to the needs of citizens, and represents the will of the majority.

Partly for these reasons, and partly because of the rise of other institutions (such as television and schools) that compete with the parties as agents of political socialization (*see box*), support for the two major parties is shrinking. Third parties have cut into the moral, if not the numerical, support enjoyed by the Republicans and the Democrats. And more people now call themselves independents than identify with either party (see Figure 17.3). Neither party can count on the automatic support of its traditional backers—Republicans have gained considerable support in the once-Democratic South, and many of the young college graduates and professionals who once would have voted Republican are now Democrats and independents (Braungart, 1978).

The decline of party politics has been accompanied by marked increases in ideological concern. In *The Changing American Voter* (1979), Norman H. Nie, Sidney Verba, and John R. Petrocik document some of these developments. Chief among them are an increased concern for political issues and reliance on them as guides in voting, a more pronounced tendency to vote across party lines or for particular candidates regardless of party, and a significantly greater coherence of individuals' political attitudes than was the case in the 1950s. Another development noted by Nie and his colleagues is the increasing tendency of citizens to perceive wide political concerns, such as world peace and inflation, as directly affecting their lives. These changes, the authors conclude,

add up to an "individuation" of American political life. Membership in a population group no longer predicts politi-

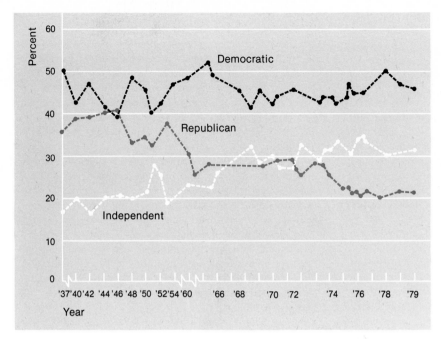

FIGURE 17.3

This graph shows the shifts in political party identification in the United States from 1937 to 1979. Note the steady climb in the percentage of people who identified as Independents. (Adapted from Woll and Binstock, 1979, p. 219)

cal behavior very well; region, class, religion are still associated with party affiliation and the vote, but not as closely as they once were. Nor does party affiliation predict political behavior very well; fewer have such affiliation and fewer of those with affiliation follow it. The individual voter evaluates candidates on the basis of information and impressions conveyed by the mass media, and then votes on that basis. He or she acts as an individual, not as a member of a collectivity. (p. 347)

Political support or "false consciousness"?

Does this pattern mean that Americans want significant changes in the political system? Many observers believe not. They interpret the relative lack of political protest during recent years as a sign of contentment on the part of most Americans. Other observers disagree. Marxists feel that the American people are kept quiet by a "false consciousness" fostered by schools, the mass media, and the government, which prevents people from seeing that the government is acting not for them but for exploitative economic elites. Marxist critics argue that the rich not only exercise most political and economic power in American society, but conceal it in a variety of ways. Millions of working-class Americans face the "choice" between an elite Republican and an elite Democrat at election time; candidates without substantial support from big business are unlikely to get very far. The same Americans learn from schools and the mass media (both controlled by the elite) that their country is a land of liberty and equal opportunity, and their government one "of the people, by the people, and for the people." By disguising the interests of the ruling class as those of all, the dominant ideology is able to legitimize the social system. Since this ideology stresses equality (political, not economic), the failure of a citizen to get a good job or earn a decent wage is interpreted as a personal shortcoming rather than a defect in the structure of the society.

Examples of the way the government may attempt to shape people's thinking through its definitions and perspectives are legion. One occurred in 1972, when President Richard Nixon declared that the urban crisis was over—meaning that order had been restored. In reality, the situation of many black and Hispanic urban groups on some economic and social dimensions had

POLITICAL SOCIALIZATION BY GOVERNMENT AND THE MEDIA

More than 95 percent of the households in America contain a television set. Over 50 million households (out of a total of about 73 million) watch network news programs each night. The daily circulation of newspapers in America is 61 million (as against a population of about 214 million people). And the federal government allots approximately $400 million annually for public information activities. Thus, government and the media are two of the main institutions through which people receive information about politics in the United States. Along with schools, these two agents of political socialization are the most important communicators of the dominant values of our society.

The broadcast media, especially television, have the potential to act as a forum for change and to sharpen people's awareness of critical issues in this country; and they sometimes do. But the media tend mainly to sanction existing ideology (directly or indirectly), and thus to perpetuate it. Television and radio stations may hesitate to criticize prevailing institutions or forms of government, partly because their very existence depends on government licensing. As Ira Katznelson and Mark Kesselman state in their book *The Politics of Power* (1975), "Through government licensing, control over most of the air waves—a community resource as public as air and water—is granted to private business to use for a profit" (p. 371). Thus, station owners may be reluctant to risk losing their source of profit by antagonizing the government that gave it to them. Corporations on whose advertising dollar the broadcast media depend may also limit the extent to which controversial issues are aired. True, television stations did broadcast the brutal unleashing of police dogs on unarmed young black people during civil-rights demonstrations in the 1960s. TV stations also

broadcast the Senate hearings that led to widespread public pressure for the impeachment of President Richard Nixon. But when NBC televised a program entitled *The Migrant*, depicting miserable working conditions at a plant owned by the Coca-Cola Company, NBC found itself without the Coca-Cola account the following year—a loss of advertising that brought home a very important message.

Television and radio news also tends to be handled superficially, in a way that inhibits reflection and public analysis, in the view of Katznelson and Kesselman. Most stations do little investigative reporting, instead relying mainly on official government or police accounts. Information presented in these half-hour news shows is highly condensed; hard news is combined with a rapid-fire assortment of commercials and humorous features—a mixture that tends to lessen the impact of any critical or controversial subjects and leaves little or no time for news analysis and commentary.

Most people would think of television and radio news as foremost in political socialization of the public by the media. But Katznelson and Kesselman suggest that it is advertising, not news, that plays the most important part in this process. Media advertising oversimplifies and stereotypes the world, and tends to suggest to people that the answers to all their problems lie in material goods:

Television advertising suggests that political change is never the answer. Thus, have you no friends? Use our mouthwash or deodorant. Fed up with your job? Sneak a week in the Caribbean. Unable to pay your bills? "Consolidate" your debts with a loan or credit card. The advertising political parties sponsor at election time provides an exact parallel to this approach. Want to solve the country's problems? Vote for our party and everything

actually deteriorated since the late 1960s. Another striking example occurred in 1973, when all federal agencies were ordered to replace the word "poverty" in their official documents with the more neutral term "low income." In the Marxist view, if disadvantaged groups can develop symbols and definitions strong enough to counteract the quieting effect of official "reality," they will no longer be apathetic, but instead strongly motivated toward change.

The political protest of the 1960s

During the 1960s, there was much talk of significant political change. Frequent civil disturbances and unrest challenged the social order and indicated dissatisfac-

tion with traditional methods of applying political pressure: there were ghetto revolts, student strikes, antiwar protests, and demonstrations against segregation. In 1967, over 200 civil disturbances occurred throughout the United States. In April of 1968, following the assassination of Martin Luther King, Jr., about 200 more took place. In that same month, 1 million students boycotted classes during an antiwar moratorium.

Many of these actions were considered politically illegitimate by elites and, by legal standards, some of them were criminal. But violence, when present, should not distract us from the fact that these disturbances can be seen as forms of political protest related to the belief that traditional political activity was unlikely to bring about change. Research conducted in the aftermath of

will be fine. . . . The constant barrage of television advertising can be considered political propaganda that infects American culture with materialism, competitiveness, a manipulative attitude toward one's own body and toward others, and an acceptance of corporate capitalism. (pp. 378–379)

The entertainment content of television is also very important. Most entertainment shows tend to simplify reality and deflect political awareness, thus reinforcing existing norms.

. . . Entertainment programs glamorize and slant reality. Authorities are usually warm, concerned, and sincere people attempting to help the community. Although facing manifold difficulties, they usually manage to come out on top. In the strange world of television, crimes never go unsolved, patients rarely die, and defendants are almost never convicted of crimes they did not commit. As for those at the bottom, they are beset by problems, but none so great that—thanks to the good will of authorities—they cannot be solved within their half hour of allotted television time. The possibility of rebellion is never evoked, except by a radical, a hippy, or a militant black—whose harebrained schemes are proved wrong by the patient efforts of wise, moderate authorities. Even more than in news broadcasts, the message of entertainment programs is that there is no reason for fundamental change, since dominant institutions are responsive to individual grievances—and serious group grievances of class and race do not exist. (pp. 377–378)

Various segments of government may also attempt to shape the political attitudes of the public—particularly by changing people's perceptions of reality, rather than changing the reality itself. Consider this example:

The transcripts of taped conversations in the White House relating to the Watergate break-in reveal that what

dominated discussions was the question, as Mr. Nixon says at one point, "how do you handle that PR-wise?" On March 21, 1973, the President discussed in detail the options available to keep the truth from coming out. He suggested that a White House statement be issued, saying that the initial payments made to the Watergate defendants (which were, in fact, supplied by presidential aides as hush money to buy silence) had come from a Cuban defense committee.

Presidential adviser John Dean III replied, "Well, yeah. We can put it together. That isn't of course quite the way it happened, but—."

"I know, " said Mr. Nixon, "but that's the way it's going to have to happen." (pp. 380–381)

How strong are the effects of mass media and government efforts at political socialization? Katznelson and Kesselman suggest that their power is not absolute, and they point out that recently many people have lost their faith in the dominant ideology. These writers have come to conclude:

A convergence of social, economic, and political problems has weakened the hold of the dominant ideology in recent years. As economic growth has slowed down, American corporate capitalism, which requires constant expansion both to provide benefits for capital and to hold out the promise of social mobility to workers, becomes less able to attract support. Institutional mediators, such as parties and Congress, have lost their hold. Revelations by crusading journalists, public interest lawyers, and critical scholars concerning injustice and the illegal activities of public officials from the President down, have further weakened the dominant ideology. It is becoming clear to increasing numbers of Americans that the procedures of democracy, which the dominant ideology uses to legitimize present arrangements, can also be used by discontented groups to air grievances. (p. 383)

ghetto disorders, for example, shows that most rioters were neither criminals nor vagrants, but instead were broadly representative of their communities (Caplan, 1970; Paige, 1970). Many persons who did not participate in the riots as such nevertheless sympathized with the rioters.

Riots as a means of political expression are rarely translated into political terms by the authorities. Instead, they are treated as ordinary criminal behavior and quickly suppressed. The restoration of order is the first priority for the community. In their review of the literature dealing with violent protest, Robert R. Alford and Roger Friedland (1975, pp. 464 ff) note another response, an effort to co-opt angry citizens into relatively powerless forms of bureaucratic participation

such as the Model Cities program and some community action agencies. In this way, the system may reduce the likelihood of future challenges while presenting the appearance of fostering change.

WHAT LIES AHEAD?

Supporters of a pluralistic approach have pointed out that in comparison with totalitarian societies, the United States shows a remarkable degree of civil liberty. American citizens do have choices, both through elections and through referenda, and they receive some protection from the American system of checks and balances (as seen, for example, when Congress, the courts, and public opinion forced President Nixon out of office). If there are gaps between the pluralistic model and the American reality, these gaps may be gradually reduced as fundamental American values stressing equality and citizenship become more fully institutionalized.

Others, however, take a less benign view of American political patterns, at least recent ones. Walter Dean Burnham (1976) has described the current political situation as an "authority crisis" in which the political system is widely seen as unresponsive to citizens and uncontrolled by leaders. Burnham uses the image of "a geological fault in the earth." As pressures build for a new order, tension is generated along the fault line. Finally, an earthquake occurs, a brief crisis follows, and the rocks settle into a new position.

To the extent that such a crisis is emerging, what might its outcome be? Nie, Verba, and Petrocik (1979) suggest three possibilities: (1) a system that retains party alignments but in which parties play only a modest role in determining how citizens vote; (2) a volatile electorate that is easily swayed by extremist and/or single-issue causes, such as antiabortion and antigun control, reflecting the decline of political parties as stabilizing forces in politics; or (3) a long-hoped-for "responsible" two-party system based on an increased concern of the citizenry over issues, and featuring parties with clearly distinguishable positions.

An alternative version of our political future, one with roots in economic analysis, has been elaborated by James O'Connor in *The Fiscal Crisis of the State* (1973). O'Connor, a Marxist, sees the problems in the American economy as harbingers of a crisis that will eventually be caused by contradictory economic and political forces. Like Marx, O'Connor believes that capitalism contains within it the seeds of its own eventual destruction, but his analysis departs from Marx when he takes into account the changes that have occurred in the world economy in the past century. O'Connor sees capitalism's continued survival as making ever-increasing demands on the state. (High-technology industries, for example, need large numbers of workers with advanced education—which is usually paid for in large part by the state.) In turn, to obtain revenues, the state must help the private sector expand and make high profits (which are in part returned to the state in taxes). The problem is that the two processes feed on each other. The activities of business constantly place more and more demands on the state. Government must educate workers for private industry and provide for their social needs when employers do not. It must subsidize the roads that private industry uses to move its products. It must clean up the pollution and toxic waste produced by industrial activities. Thus, the state's budget is always increasing, its deficit growing ever larger. According to O'Connor, the problem is "central to capitalism and can only be resolved by [capitalism's] transcendence." Non-Marxists, of course, would disagree. The recent efforts of Congress to balance the federal budget (an effort that failed) suggest that decreasing some of the demands for state services will be a priority in the 1980s and beyond.

Summary

Almost any social relationship may be characterized by competition for control of resources and of others' behavior. This struggle as it takes place on the level of the social system—private corporations, public bureaucracies, and, especially, government—is known as *politics*.

Political activity thus has a dimension of *power*—the potential or actual control over the actions of others. The sources of power include *force, authority,* and *influence*.

Sociologists tend to focus on politics on the level of the community and the society. Functionalists concentrate on the power structure's dimension of *authority*. Max Weber identified three types of authority: *traditional, charismatic,* and *rational-legal*. Emile Durkheim noted that simple societies were marked by a "collective conscience"; a complex society, however, though its members may agree on political procedures, is not so unified, since its complexity makes the sharing of values and interests among members problematic. Conflict theorists like Karl Marx concentrate on the role of *force* in a society's politics.

In the modern *state*, power tends to be *centralized* in the government. As a result, government tends to be highly bureaucratized (which has produced a shift toward values that favor rational-legal authority). The scope of governmental activity has widened; and the power of government has increased. In Western industrialized democracies, governmental power is balanced to some extent by a degree of mass participation and by the development of pluralism among elites.

Observers of the political system of the United States disagree about the existence or extent of the balance between masses and elites. Some have argued that an elite does dominate the political decision-making process. Some research suggests that power is increasingly concentrated in the hands of a monolithic elite. Other studies point to the existence of a pluralistic elite, with multiple centers of power struggling for control.

The classic pluralist model assumes that the operation of a variety of interest groups is the foundation of the American political system. But the proportions of citizens who vote and engage in other traditional forms of political activity have been decreasing steadily; and there is no guarantee that those who do participate will be rewarded by seeing their wishes translated into government action. Mass support for the dominant ideology and for the two major political parties has in some ways been decreasing. Though fewer Americans are politically active, more seem to be politically aware. Lack of political participation in the conventional sense is not the same as apathy. Some citizens *are* apathetic, of course, and others may be lulled by "false consciousness"; but many people, especially the poor, do not vote because they believe that their vote does not affect the political process. Political pressure may also be applied in nontraditional ways, such as with disturbances and demonstrations.

Glossary

AUTHORITY Exercise of a leadership role that is perceived by others as legitimate. According to Max Weber, there are three types of authority: traditional, charismatic, and rational-legal.

EGALITARIAN Characterized by belief in the equality of all people.

ELITE A privileged group exercising the major share of authority or control within a larger organization, such as a political system.

IDEOLOGY A relatively coherent set of political and cultural beliefs that are shared by members of a particular group or of a society.

POLITICS The struggle among interested groups and individuals for control over decision-making processes; studied particularly with reference to government.

POWER The ability of one person or group to have its will obeyed by another through the potential or actual application of force, authority, or influence.

STATE A society's supreme governmental institution and the one that tends to monopolize the use of force.

Recommended readings

Braungart, Richard G. *Society and Politics: Readings in Political Sociology.* Englewood Cliffs, N.J.: Prentice-Hall, 1976. A balanced collection of classical and modern materials emphasizing the connections between society and politics.

Dahl, Robert. *Who Governs?* New Haven, Conn.: Yale University Press, 1961. An influential work in the study of community power holding, with a decision-making approach to power studies.

Gamson, William A. *Power and Discontent.* Homewood, Ill.: Dorsey, 1968. A theoretical discussion of power—its forms, definitions, and applications. Gamson examines social-influence and social-control models of power holding.

Katznelson, Ira, and Mark Kesselman. *The Politics of Power: A Critical Introduction to American Government.* New York: Harcourt Brace Jovanovich, 1975. An analysis of the evolution and workings of political institutions and practices in the United States, with emphasis on the relationship between American capitalism and politics. The authors also stress the educational, political, economic, and social inequalities that exist among groups and how those inequalities affect a group's ability to understand and protect its interests.

Lipset, Seymour Martin. *Political Man.* Garden City, N.Y.: Doubleday, 1960. A modern classic in political-sociological analysis. The author seeks the key to stable democracy, and his analysis of empirical work links industrialization and political alliances, political choices and social cleavages.

Mills, C. Wright. *White Collar: The American Middle Classes.* New York: Oxford University Press, 1951. A modern analysis of power, success, and work as they affect the middle-class segment of society.

Orum, Anthony M. *Introduction to Political Sociology: The Social Anatomy of Body Politics.* Englewood Cliffs, N.J.: Prentice-Hall, 1978. A short eloquent text summarizing research in the field.

Szymanski, Albert. *The Capitalist State and the Politics of Class.* Cambridge, Mass.: Winthrop, 1978. An effort to synthesize empirical research on politics, class, and the state within a Marxist framework.

Tocqueville, Alexis de. *Democracy in America.* Phillips Bradley (tr. and ed.). New York: Random House, 1954. A classic in social thought. De Tocqueville's insights into the link between political form and culture in nineteenth-century America are still relevant today. The book is crucial to all modern views of American democracy.

CHAPTER EIGHTEEN

ECONOMICS AND THE WORLD OF WORK

Work is what most adults do for at least half their waking hours, and our success at it determines, to an important extent, what we will be able to do with the hours that remain. For some, work is drudgery, doing what *must* be done in order to do what we *want* to do with the rest of our time. For others, work is much more than a source of livelihood: it is an attempt to create something of value, to practice a craft, to be helpful, to be respected or admired, or to get rich.

Through the centuries, the meaning of work in Western society has changed as much as the types of work performed. For the ancient Greeks—whose word for work, *ponos*, was derived from the word for sorrow—work was a curse, a form of enslavement, an activity that corrupted the soul. Among the Hebrews, work was regarded as a form of atonement. To the early Christians, work was ethically neutral; practical activity was considered to be part of the earthly city (as opposed to the City of God). But from the time of the Protestant Reformation in the sixteenth century, the Christian conception of work changed dramatically. Influenced by Martin Luther's idea of a religious "calling," Christians began to believe in the fulfillment of religious duty by involvement in worldly affairs. Work became even more highly charged with ethical meaning in the Calvinist doctrine of predestination, which came to be interpreted to mean that individuals must prove through worldly activity that they were among the elect, those chosen for salvation.

For most of us, work is no longer a symbol of salvation. But neither is it an ethically neutral activity. Although some have suggested that the "Protestant ethic" of work is fading, it remains a powerful force. Those who can work but do not are targets of derision. We tend to sympathize with those who want to work but cannot find jobs. And we recognize the perils of being out of work in a society where work is not just a source of sustenance but of self-esteem as well. We tend to judge others by the type of work they perform, how well they do it, and what they get paid for it, and we apply similar standards to ourselves. We relegate to second-class status the kinds of work, such as housework, for which no paycheck is received.

This chapter deals with the economic institutions that frame the world of work. In thinking about these economic institutions, we can ask several questions regarding the production and exchange of goods: What goods will be produced? Who will produce them, and how? How are tasks divided among workers, and how are people motivated to work? And, finally, how will goods be distributed and exchanged?

Economists have studied these questions, of course, but they are also of great concern to sociologists. Many social analysts—following Karl Marx—have regarded the economic system as the mainspring of society itself. They see it as more important than other institutions such as the family or the political system. In fact, as we noted in Chapter 1, the science of sociology began in the nineteenth century as an attempt to understand and solve the problems created in Western society by rapid industrialization and the new social and economic arrangements that accompanied it. Therefore, in our examination of the division of labor, the reorganization of the work process, and the motivations for and satisfactions of work, we will be exploring questions that are at the very center of the sociological tradition. But to understand the meaning of work in our society today, it is useful first to review what work has meant in Western society in times past.

Preindustrial society

In the preindustrial society from which our society developed—as in those in many parts of the world today—work activities were closely related to activities and relationships in other social spheres. Work and its fruits were seen not so much as ends in themselves, but as part of the larger web of status relationships and the larger pattern of interdependence among individuals in the community. Individuals usually "inherited" their occupations, learning their skills from their parents.

THE MEDIEVAL PATTERN

In feudal Europe, for example, the worker and the landlord were often committed to certain forms of mutual support and aid. The serf (a peasant bound to the land) took an oath of fidelity to the lord, and the lord in turn owed certain duties to the serf. Journeymen and apprentices learning their trades often lodged with their masters and formed long-term bonds with them. The mutual obligations that bound employers and employees were far more extensive than the wage contracts that were to take their place in Western industrial society.

Medieval society did not favor the types of economic activities that would enable individuals to make a profit at the expense of others. Guilds (associations

A master craftsman passing on the skills of hat making to an apprentice. Masters and apprentices in preindustrial societies were bound together by long-term mutual obligations going far beyond the exchange of wages for labor that characterizes employer–employee relations in Western industrialized societies. (Culver Pictures)

that regulated the practice of specific crafts) strictly limited economic competition, forbade advertising, and even discouraged technical progress—it was considered disloyal to the other members of the guild. The church, too, tried to restrain the profit motive through its doctrine of a "just price" for every service and good.

Nor did the form of exchange support values that were economically rational—that is, values that stressed efficiency and productivity above all other considerations. In the countryside, the economic activities on which most people depended for their livelihood were based on *barter* rather than money: peasants raised their own food and paid their debts "in kind" with foodstuffs and handcrafts. In town, the same pattern prevailed: the remuneration that apprentices received, for example, was food and lodging, rather than money. For most people there was relatively little incentive to produce more goods or services than could be exchanged directly for the goods and services one needed at the moment. All this was to change, however, from the late Middle Ages onward.

THE TRANSITION TO MODERN PATTERNS

On the eve of industrialization in Western Europe, three key trends emerged that were ultimately to transform economic activity and to affect other areas of life as well.

First, employers gradually came to regard labor as a commodity—something to be bought and sold in the marketplace—rather than a human activity closely tied to noneconomic concerns. Second, as the relationship between employer and employee gradually changed, so did the system of exchange. Regional markets, and even highly organized trading bodies, had been common for centuries. By the eighteenth century, most parts of Europe were connected by a true *market economy*—one in which the price of a given product or service, and the quantities in which it was produced, rose and fell with demand. What made this market economy possible was the increasingly widespread use of money, a fluid medium of exchange. What the market economy encouraged in turn were values that favored a separate sphere of economic activity, one that was set apart from the rest of the individual's social life and religious obligations.

The third and final development provided the ideological justification for the new economic order. In contrast with the earlier attitude of the church, which discouraged both the getting of wealth and the enjoyment of it, the Calvinist doctrine of predestination seems to have resulted in a new religious value on worldly activities. The belief developed that the more successful a person was, the more worthy he or she was. And, as we mentioned in Chapter 16, Calvinist doctrine provided much of the impetus for what Max Weber would call "the spirit of capitalism." The sixteenth-century Reformation leader John Calvin approved of diligence in one's business, but not the frivolous enjoyment of the fruits of one's labor. Thrift, he argued, was a virtue. Economic growth and material improvement received ideological justification in his concept of accumulating wealth and putting it to work in investments. While such doctrinal innovation was not the only factor involved in the social and economic upheavals that were to follow, it is striking that industrialization first developed in the Protestant countries where Calvin's influence was strongest.

The industrial system

By the end of the eighteenth century in England, industrial manufacture on a large scale was becoming the most prominent economic activity, and one that reshaped the social order as it redefined the work process. It began as a combination of new energy sources (such as the steam engine) and industrial inventions (such as the spinning jenny, an early yarn-making machine); the result was a dramatic increase in output. As the new machines came into use, it became less sensible for manufacturing to take place in homes or small shops. So production shifted to factories, which became the centers of new social habitats for peasants-turned-industrial-workers. Over the next century, visitors to the new industrial cities in England were horrified by their squalor and expressed a deep-seated fear of the industrial process itself, which had torn work out of the traditional protective context of the guild, the village, and the family just as certainly as it had broken the ancient attachment between human beings and the soil.

Perhaps the most visible effect of the industrial process was that it changed the scale of things. Even the early industrial cities, which included thousands of tenements constructed by factory owners to house workers, were considerably larger than most preindustrial towns. And the increased size of the productive unit—now the factory—was equally significant. Less visible but equally important was the continuing change in the relationships between employers and employees. In the industrial system, the entrepreneur buys both labor and materials, and regards both as commodities to be purchased as cheaply and used as efficiently as possible. New laws granted individuals the freedom to choose their occupation and gave capitalists the freedom to set wages as they pleased.

Capitalism and society: theoretical approaches

For various historical reasons, industrialism in Western Europe (and, a little later, in the United States) developed within a capitalistic system. *Capitalism* is an economic system in which it is primarily private individuals and corporations, rather than cooperative groups or the state, that invest in and own the means of production, distribution, and exchange for the purpose of making a profit. Both industrialism in general, and capitalism specifically, have had complex effects on other aspects of social life. Here we will consider two of the best-known theoretical perspectives on industrial and capitalistic institutions. The first is that of Adam Smith, an apologist for the capitalist system; the second is that of Karl Marx, whose criticisms of the system changed the world.

ADAM SMITH AND THE FREE MARKET SYSTEM

The genius of the free market system, according to Adam Smith (as he explained in *The Wealth of Nations* in 1776) is that it makes a virtue of acquisitiveness. By encouraging each person to maximize profits, said Smith, the "invisible hand" of the free market determines prices, directs resources to their best use, encourages economic innovation, and contributes to the greater wealth of the entire society. What is the role of the government in such a system? In Smith's view, its task should be to remove all restraints on free trade, such as certain taxes and customs barriers.

What would then prevent one firm, or a few, from controlling the market and fixing prices at a high level? Smith's answer was that in a "perfectly competitive" market, no one could gain control of an industry because competing firms would be formed as soon as others discovered they could make a profit by turning out a similar product. Free competition would help to keep prices within most people's reach.

Smith's analysis, as a description of the workings of the economic system and its relations with government and the public, is more useful as a historical perspective than as a picture of these institutions today. Our system now would best be described as a mixed market and command economy. As Richard Flacks puts it, by the twentieth century "an economic system organized around problems of capital accumulation and the need for saving, entrepreneurship and self-reliance—a system of free market and individual competition—has been replaced by an economic system organized around problems of distribution and the need for spending, interdependence, bureaucratic management, planning, and large-scale organization" (1971, p. 21).

Government regulation

Today the "invisible hand" is guided to a large degree by political decision makers. Especially since the Great Depression of the 1930s, the federal government has taken on more responsibility for regulating the economy, increasing spending to stimulate it during periods of recession, and providing some benefits to the poor and those who cannot find employment. Such benefits—unemployment insurance, medicaid, and other social programs—have had the effect not only of helping to maintain a stable labor force upon which industries can draw but also of ensuring a sufficient number of consumers for the products put out by industry.

Oligopoly and the multinational corporations

A parallel development has been the increasing concentration of corporate economic power. While Smith envisioned free enterprise as being beneficial to the society as a whole and in a sense responsive (if not actually answerable) to it, today's capitalistic enterprises generally are not directly responsive to people's needs as they are expressed through the workings of a free market. In part, this has been because of the shift from individual to "group" entrepreneurship. Group entrepreneurship is made possible by the institution of the *corporation*—an enterprise that has no single owner, but instead thousands (and sometimes even hundreds of thousands) of stockholders. (In most corporations, a high proportion of the stock is owned by just a few wealthy people, but the remainder is owned by a large number of "small investors.") Compared with partnership, stock ownership limits the individual's liability, but it also tends to greatly limit the individual's participation in corporate decision making on the day-to-day level. Ownership by stockholders also makes it possible for an enterprise to amass and deploy far greater amounts of wealth than could an individually owned enterprise. It is because the stakes in corporate capitalism are so high and free competition so risky, in the view of economist John Kenneth Galbraith, that our

twentieth-century economic system has moved away from the free market pictured by Adam Smith.

As we mentioned in Chapter 9, competitive relationships among organizations have had a tendency to become tempered by cooperation and interdependence. Both in this country and abroad, many industries are dominated by just a few companies—a situation known as an *oligopoly*. The American domestic automobile industry, for example, is dominated by just three companies. To the extent that they "cooperate" to set prices and affect market conditions, the laws of supply and demand do not operate.

Another development that illustrates how far some modern industries are from the situation described by Smith is the growth of multinational firms. These giant corporations, most of which are based in the United States, are able to reap enormous profits by moving parts of their operations to underdeveloped countries. Workers in Korea or Mexico, for example, can be paid a few cents an hour for work that in the United States would command at least the minimum wage. Moreover, by concentrating production in underdeveloped countries, the multinationals escape antitrust, antipollution, and worker-protection laws in force in the United States. Since these corporations can shift capital and production from one country to another, they are able not only to avoid price competition but also, as Richard J. Barnet notes, "to divert resources from the

Multinational corporations based in the United States reap large profits by transferring parts of their operations to developing countries—for example, this aluminum plant in Surinam. They can pay workers far less than they would at home, and they escape expensive American antipollution and worker-protection measures.

places where they are most needed (poor countries and poor regions of rich countries) to those where they are least needed (rich countries and rich regions)" (1976, p. 11).

The "world capitalist economy"

Barnet's analysis of the multinational firm points to yet another development Smith did not foresee: the growth of a world economic system in which the concentration of power and the division of labor would extend far beyond the border of the individual nation-state, and in which the nation-states would be allotted roles like those given to the various sectors of a national economy. Smith believed the free market economy would be self-regulating; free competition would act to promote a rough equality. Immanuel Wallerstein (1974), who has focused on what he calls the "world capitalist economy," argues just the opposite. In his view, the capitalist economy is a global system of exploitation, in which inequalities are perpetuated through the dominance of what he calls *core areas*— zones of strong states characterized by skilled wage and tenant-based labor systems, industry, and differentiated agriculture.

Core areas draw their supplies from two other zones: (1) the surrounding semiperiphery, where labor is primarily sharecropping and the economic activity primarily agriculture; and (2) the periphery, which is characterized by one-crop agriculture and by slavery or "coerced cash-crop labor." Although technology and industrialization are now spreading throughout the world, Wallerstein believes that the system is likely to continue working in favor of the core areas and against the semiperipheries and peripheries. In other words, there may be an IBM Indonesia, but there is not likely to be an Indonesian IBM.

All in all, our economic institutions today are quite different from those of Smith's "classical" economic analysis. Smith did not give adequate attention to the social and political variables that can interfere with the free market. Yet the cultural themes underlying his "free market"—such as private property, individual enterprise, and competition—have endured.

KARL MARX AND THE CRITIQUE OF CAPITALISM

The first generation of sociologists—which included Saint-Simon, Auguste Comte, Herbert Spencer, and Karl Marx—all lived through at least a part of the great social upheaval that took place in Western Europe between 1750 and 1850. Among writers in that first generation, no one conducted so comprehensive an analysis of the breakdown of feudal society and the rise of in-

According to the theory of a world capitalist economy, the dominance of core areas works to the disadvantage of peripheral areas, where one-crop agriculture or "coerced cash-crop labor" prevail. Here a farmer plows a rice paddy near Djakarta, Indonesia. (Jean-Claude Lejeune/Stock, Boston)

dustrial capitalism as Karl Marx. Certainly no other analysis of that great transformation has been so influential, both intellectually and politically.

Marx's analysis

Marx believed that the most important element to examine in any society is its *mode of production*. In any complex society, he argued, there is an inherent and inescapable conflict between those who own the means of production (in feudal times, the lord who owned the land; in industrial society, the capitalists who control the means of production, such as machines) and those who perform the labor.

Marx contrasted the simple societies of the past, in which the products of labor were divided more or less equally among all members of the group with the situation he felt characterized industrial society, where workers received only their wages while owners got rich by accumulating the surplus value produced by those workers. In effect, said Marx, capitalism repeated some of the circumstances that existed when feudal lords, because they owned the land, could require their serfs to hand over to them most of the crops they produced. But in a sense, industrial laborers were even worse off, because they received very little of the protection that feudal lords offered to serfs. Capitalists were free to force laborers to work long hours for subsistence wages, with little obligation in turn.

Under capitalism, the use of interchangeable parts of mass production (techniques that revolutionized the industrial process) created a situation in which workers themselves were treated as interchangeable parts. Marx argued that under capitalism there was no other "nexus between man and man than naked self-interest, than callous 'cash-payment.'" And, he pointed out, the new factories had changed the meaning of work. Work now corresponded to the rhythms of the machine. There was a new concern for efficiency and rationality, for a careful calculus of gains and losses, for impersonal rules and scientific management. For Marx, the specialization and fragmentation of work were dehumanizing for the laborers, who no longer exerted any control over the work process. (In his terms, work was *alienating*, a concept we discussed briefly in Chapter 9.)

Capitalism, Marx believed, contained the seeds of its own destruction: conditions under this system would lead inevitably to a revolution of the masses. Marx regarded the workers' riots that were taking place in factory towns in the mid-nineteenth century as the first expression of the class consciousness—workers' awareness of their common plight—that would ultimately

In his classic 1936 film *Modern Times*, Charlie Chaplin bitterly satirized the impersonality of the industrial process, which can treat workers as interchangeable parts of a huge machine. (The Granger Collection)

lead to a proletarian revolution. He also foresaw some events that have since taken place, and that had not been envisioned by Adam Smith. Economic necessity and technical progress, Marx predicted, would force the capitalists to replace workers with machines and to reduce the wages of the remaining workers. Economic competition would also force capitalists to combine their enterprises into ever-larger organizations in order to reduce competition.

But he foresaw one pattern that has not so far emerged in the industrialized countries of Western Europe and North America. He predicted that the large numbers of workers required to operate factories would learn from the capitalists and form their own organizations, which would foster class consciousness and hasten the revolution. When that happened, capitalism would be destroyed by a socialist system in which the distinction between owners and workers would be dissolved and eventually everyone would receive rewards commensurate with his or her needs.

Changes since Marx

In Chapter 11, we discussed some of the reasons why class consciousness and class conflict have failed to develop in the United States to a significant degree. High mobility rates, values and loyalties shared among the various classes, income overlap, ethnic and racial diversity, and social control are some of the factors that have tended to prevent classes from coming into violent conflict more frequently.

These forces have been aided by certain factors specific to the economic system and the work-place itself. For one thing, what Marx had no way of knowing was that, at the time he was writing, conditions for factory workers were at their very worst; there was to be improvement over the next half-century. Likewise, government programs would eventually provide some security for the worker. And, in addition, the potential for

revolution was to be diminished by trends in the bureaucratic setting, such as the use of rational-legal procedures, professionalization, and the development of management ideologies like the scientific management approach and the human relations perspective. These filtered into workers' value systems and helped to justify the new industrial order. (We discussed these topics in more detail in Chapter 9.)

American labor unions, too, while they may be a sign of the development of some class consciousness, have also operated to neutralize class struggle by allowing reform to take the place of revolution. As the economic historian Selig Perlman (1923) observed, American workers organized into unions and sought to improve their wages, working conditions, and job security, but generally refused to support a radical critique of the economic order. Perlman was led to reject Marx's assumption that lack of ownership of the means of production would lead workers to revolt. Instead, he argued, workers were concerned primarily with the conditions for marketing their labor; they were motivated primarily by the desire to maximize their personal gain from their labor, which is what labor unions helped them to do. According to Perlman, as unions flourished, they would lead not to greater class consciousness and an organized base for revolution, but to concessions to labor and a reduction in class conflict. To an important extent, this is what happened. American unions have generally lost their reformist zeal; their main role now is to put pressure on industry for higher wages and better working conditions. In the United States today there is

The objectives of the American labor movement have changed; no longer zealously concerned with broad reform of the capitalist system, American unions now concentrate on achieving higher wages and better working conditions. (© Joel Gordon 1980)

very little union interest in bringing about broad changes in the capitalist system, in marked contrast to the role unions play in some European countries.

The potential for revolution may also have been reduced by changes that have taken place in the American occupational structure. Today, employers and employees are not so sharply polarized into two opposing factions. Managers, for example, tend not to own the means of production but are held responsible for the work of others. Some employees, such as farm laborers and domestic workers, still face the kind of unstable work environment envisioned by Marx; others, however, enjoy far better conditions. Yet this does not mean that American workers love their jobs. Dissatisfaction may be expressed subtly and in individual ways, through absenteeism, frequent job changes, wildcat strikes (those not sanctioned by the union), work stoppage, "working according to rule," and sabotage.

The American labor force today

Over the decades, the greater efficiency and productivity that technology allows has wrought a remarkable transformation in the American occupational structure (see Table 18.1). First of all, the percentage of people employed in agricultural production has fallen dramatically. A century and a half ago, in 1820, about 70 percent of the work force consisted of farmers. By 1900, this percentage had fallen to about 37 percent. Currently, because of mechanization, the use of fertilizers and pesticides, and scientific breeding, it takes only 2.7 percent of the labor force to grow food for the entire population.

There has also been considerable change in the non-agricultural sector. Over the past fifty years, a large and relatively stable part of the American labor force—about 35 to 40 percent—has been employed as blue-collar workers in manufacturing, but a dramatic increase has taken place in the number of white-collar workers (a category that includes professional and technical workers, managers and proprietors, and clerical and salespeople). In 1920, only about 25 percent of the labor force performed such work; today, more than 50 percent do. The growth rate in the white-collar area has recently slowed down. However, within the past twenty

TABLE 18.1

PERCENT OF AMERICAN WORKERS IN MAJOR OCCUPATIONAL GROUPS, 1900–1980

	1900	1910	1920	1930	1940	1950	1960	1970	MARCH 1980
Total labor force (in 1,000s)	29,030	37,291	42,206	48,686	51,742	59,648	66,681	78,627	96,264
White-collar workers	17.6%	21.3%	24.9%	29.4%	31.1%	37.5%	43.1%	48.3%	52.5%
Professional and technical workers	4.2	4.7	5.4	6.8	7.4	7.5	11.2	14.2	16.4
Managers, officials, and proprietors	5.8	6.6	6.6	7.4	7.3	10.8	10.5	10.5	11.3
Clerical workers	3.0	5.3	8.0	9.1	9.6	12.8	14.7	17.4	18.6
Sales workers	4.5	4.7	4.9	6.3	6.7	6.4	6.6	6.2	6.3
Blue-collar workers	35.8	38.2	40.2	39.6	39.8	39.1	36.3	35.3	31.7
Craftsmen and foremen	10.5	11.6	13.0	12.8	12.0	12.8	12.8	12.9	12.8
Operatives	12.8	14.6	15.6	15.8	18.4	20.4	18.0	17.7	14.4
Non-farm laborers	12.5	12.0	11.6	11.0	9.4	5.9	5.5	4.7	4.4
Service workers	9.0	9.5	7.8	9.8	11.7	10.9	12.5	12.1	13.4
Private household workers	5.4	5.0	3.3	4.1	4.7	3.1	3.3		1.1
Other service workers	3.6	4.6	4.5	5.7	7.1	7.8	9.2		12.3
Farmworkers	37.5	30.9	27.0	21.2	17.4	12.4	8.1	4.0	2.4

SOURCES: Census Bureau, *Historical Statistics of the United States, Colonial Times to 1957*, p. 74 (for data before 1950); Census Bureau, 1976, p. 372; Bureau of Labor Statistics, 1980, p. 42. Data beginning 1950 not strictly comparable with earlier years due to reclassification of occupations.

years, America has become the first society in which a majority of workers engage in service occupations rather than in the production of food and other goods.

This shift away from manufacturing and toward a service-oriented labor force and economy is part of what sociologist Daniel Bell (1973) sees as an overall change from industrial society (in which the machine is the central force) to a "post-industrial" society (in which the central force is the organization of theoretical knowledge and the production of information). It is also an economy that is more and more bureaucratized, in which labor is more and more segmented and controlled.

Unfortunately, the very division of labor on which modern industry depends has had unhappy results for many laborers. Before the advent of the assembly line, most workers practiced crafts; that is, starting with raw materials, they performed all the steps necessary to produce a finished product. The modern industrial worker, however, usually performs only one step in the production of the finished product. Not only is this kind of work likely to be boring and alienating; it may seem worthless. Unlike the craft worker, the modern worker no longer has the knowledge necessary to produce a thing; that has been appropriated by management, which designs the assembly line. Harry Braverman, in his book *Labor and Monopoly Capital* (1974), has called this process "the degradation of work": specialization has deprived workers of knowledge, skills, and a chance to make decisions or exercise control over their work. The result is that workers become easily replaceable "cogs" in a machine, and their labor a cheapened commodity. This has in turn produced discontent among workers and is spurring both sociologists and corporate managers to consider ways in which job satisfaction can be increased.

SOURCES OF CONFLICT IN THE OCCUPATIONAL SYSTEM

The dual economy

A comparison of the three major types of employers in today's economy—small-capital firms, the government, and large-scale corporations—shows that wages, job security, and the types of labor performed in each sector vary considerably.

The small-capital sector, which includes local factories, small businesses such as real estate firms, and family enterprises, typically depends on low-paid labor rather than advanced technology for its profitability. About one-third of the American labor force works in such settings, where workers have little job security and few employee benefits such as health care or retirement plans. According to one assessment, "because these workers are usually without union protection, have few marketable skills, and are more numerous at any given time than the number of jobs available, they are America's most exploited workers" (Katznelson and Kesselman, 1975, p. 86). They are also less likely to be able to move to another, more secure sector.

Work conditions, job security, and employee benefits are typically better for those who work in the second sector, the government. The percentage of the labor force working for the government—including those directly employed by public agencies as well as those in firms working under government contracts—has grown rapidly in this century and now comprises about one-third of all workers. (It is particularly in the government sector that the white-collar portion of the occupational structure has expanded most.)

Large-scale corporations, even though they employ roughly the same percentage of workers as the first two sectors (about one-third) dominate the American economy because of their size and capital resources. All the largest private business firms are organized as corporations. Corporate employees belong to unions more often than do those who work in smaller firms, their wages are typically better, and employment is relatively more secure.

Thus, in the present American labor force, there appear to be two different labor markets (Piore, 1970). The "primary market" consists of jobs for which workers receive relatively high wages and enjoy good working conditions and considerable job stability. (Heavy industry and large corporations are parts of this "primary market.") Jobs in the "secondary" sector offer none of these advantages. In fact, the productivity of workers in the secondary market tends to bear little relation to the income they receive. These jobs are characterized by low pay, bad working conditions, arbitrary discipline, and few opportunities for advancement. (Jobs in this "secondary market" include jobs on farms, in restaurants and laundries, and in road-work crews.) Discrimination, a lack of educational credentials, and the ab-

Family-owned small businesses like this grocery store have declined in numbers and importance in today's economy. The only way many such enterprises can make a profit is to give their employees low wages and benefits. (Sepp Seitz/Magnum)

sence of valued work habits such as regularity and punctuality all serve to keep many workers in this secondary sector; and public assistance programs may discourage some from seeking steady full-time work (though data from the negative income tax experiments suggest that this is generally not so).

The presence of a dual economy may be regarded as an instance of what Marx predicted—that certain workers would be kept at or near subsistence levels, with little hope for advancement, because it is in the economic interest of some employers that there be a pool of low-paid, unskilled workers who can be recruited as needed. But the dual-economy theory is still controversial, and some economists (Evans, 1973) think it describes the situation in developing countries more accurately than it does a complex postindustrial system like that of the United States, where there are sharp lines of cleavage not only between sectors but within them. Within a sector, "internal labor markets" (Kerr, 1954)

comprise systems of rules and classifications that regulate access to jobs and promotion ladders inside units such as large corporations and craft unions. What this means is that in the United States, not only can a worker be stuck in a less advantageous sector, but he or she can be denied access to better jobs even there (Kalleberg and Sorensen, 1979).

Inequalities at work: age, sex, race

As we observed in Chapter 13, it has become increasingly common for young people to remain in school well into their twenties, and workers in large organizations are usually encouraged to retire at age sixty-five,

An office building janitor. Although the number of women in the work force has risen considerably, most women still work at poorly paid clerical and service jobs. (Owen Franken/Stock, Boston)

regardless of their productivity. This exclusion of the young and the old from the work force has to do with structural considerations. It has been a source of conflict—as has the exclusion of women and of minority group members from well-paid, high-status jobs. There have been some improvements in these areas recently, but much inequality of opportunity remains.

Women and minorities remain overwhelmingly in the lower-status and lower-paid jobs: they are the assembly-line workers, the assistants, the secretaries, the dishwashers, and so on (see box). Although the number of women in the work force has risen considerably, most women still work at poorly paid clerical and service jobs. And even though many thousands of blacks have entered technical and professional jobs in the past few decades, black family income on the average still remains less then two-thirds that of whites. Affirmative action programs so far have enabled relatively few women or minorities to enter jobs that had always been reserved for white males, and these "pioneers" often must cope with the problem of tokenism: they may be treated differently from the other employees in their group or at their level and are subject to special strains and pressures. Women sales trainees, for example, are sometimes subjected to sexual harassment, and, as are black workers, to stereotyping. The tokens, because they are so few in number, often find themselves in

impossible positions. They may be forced to concentrate on their own survival, thus perpetuating tokenism and the broader and continuing discrimination it conceals (Kanter, 1977, pp. 238–242).

In considering such situations, a Marxist analyst would raise questions about the formation of class consciousness and class conflict. In Chapters 12 and 13 we discussed some of the reasons why awareness of inequality has become more evident in recent years.

Unemployment

Official unemployment rates include those who want to work but who have been unsuccessful during the previous four weeks in their efforts to find work. These rates include those who are unemployable because of lack of qualifications, those who cannot find jobs that correspond to their skills, and those who may have work skills but are unable or unwilling to move to where the jobs are. This may seem to be a clearly defined measure of unemployment but, like other social measurements, it is a human construct whose meaning is not a "given"; as such, it is subject to controversy. Many observers feel that the current measure of unemployment underestimates the potential work force. For example, it does not include those who have become so discouraged that they have stopped looking for employment, nor does it

PINK-COLLAR WORKERS: THE INVISIBLE PROLETARIAT

Waitresses. Beauticians. Clerks. As has been the case since the turn of the century, the overwhelming majority of women who work are in occupations disproportionately filled by women. For these women pay is low, compared with that of men with the same or lower educational levels, and the equal-pay-for-equal-work laws are inapplicable, since only women perform their jobs. Their unions are weak or nonexistent. In most ways, in fact, the lot of the average woman worker—not the first-in-the-field, not the career woman, not the token—hasn't changed much since 1900, in spite of the fact that the service area in which they work is the largest growth sector in the American labor market.

In other words, the most dramatic distinctions among American workers exist not between blue- and white-collar workers but between male workers and the noncollege majority of female workers: pink-collar workers—the invisible proletariat. Pink-collar workers do the jobs accorded the lowest status in our society. They earn very low wages and are treated with very little respect, on the whole (humiliating uniforms, restrictions and regulations, insulting remarks, expectations to do ancillary work such as cleaning or serving, and sexual harassment). Although many have small children with whom they would much rather be at home, believing it important to be with a child at a young age, all *must* work—even though married women workers earn so little that their wages form on the average only a quarter of the family income. It's a bewildering and embittering situation, as Louise Kapp Howe discovered in researching her now-famous study *Pink Collar Workers* (1977)—even more puzzling because the women themselves somehow manage *not* to be engulfed by bitterness.

Since seven out of eight women in the labor force do not have college degrees, Howe concentrated on the jobs most typical for noncollege women. She settled on five traditional female occupations: beautician, saleswoman, waitress, clerical worker, and homemaker, the largest of all. What she learned undermined all the upbeat stories about the firsts, the breakthroughs. It undermined the theoretically good news about more women working than ever.

Low wages and sex discrimination are the hallmarks of pink-collar work. For example, the *haute cuisine* restaurants—where wages and tips are highest—hire only waiters. Most food in this country, however, is served by women: of waiters and waitresses in 1975, 91.1 percent were waitresses. The sales field seems well-integrated—on paper: although women are employed in sales roughly in proportion to their numbers in the labor market—around 40 percent—women generally aren't allowed into those areas in a department store where there are commissions

to be made—such as large appliances, furniture, carpets, TVs, men's wear—or if they are, they don't get commissions. Beauticians earn roughly a third less than barbers, for doing more demanding, complicated work.

Economically, the status of women who have been full-time homemakers is even more grim. In oft-cited estimates made by the Chase Manhattan Bank, back in 1972 the twelve services—among them laundress, cook, dishwasher, nurse, seamstress—that a homemaker performs, if paid for on the open market, would cost $13,391.56 a year to duplicate (of course, this figure would vary with size of family and lifestyle). But the ninety-odd hours a week spent at housework are *un*paid, and in our society that means unrespected. Worse still, not only hasn't the homemaker been paid for her work, she also hasn't been paying *into* any system of credit for it—and if she becomes divorced or widowed, she is often surprised to find herself in a harsh and precarious position.

Unlike blue-collar workers, whose unions gain them significant wage and benefit packages, pink-collar workers have never been substantially unionized, for several reasons. For one, many women do not see themselves in their jobs "for good," but rather as a response to economic exigencies "for a while." Many are also under severe time pressures, having to rush home after work to full homemaker responsibilities; they literally do not have time to attend union meetings. Many unions—where they exist—do not address themselves to issues or needs that relate to women, nor do they attempt to ascertain these needs in order to address them in the future. Beauticians who were in the beauticians and barbers' union, for example, left over the issue of pensions: they did not see themselves as beauticians until age sixty-five—unlike the barbers, many of whom also owned their shops.

Union organizers also cite the fact that many pink-collar workers work for extremely large, powerful companies adept at using both carrot and stick to decrease employee interest in unions. The large insurance company for which many of the clerical workers interviewed worked, for example, prided itself on a delicious free lunch for employees and a commitment to "job enrichment"—but the high school graduates hired at the minimum wage soon reached the top level possible in their departments, and the unspoken assumption was that enough would leave so that more young graduates could be hired—at minimum wage. The firm eventually moved from Chicago to the suburbs, where taxes—and wages—were lower. It should be noted that this firm did attempt to tackle discriminatory practices: when women workers complained that the company's pension plan discriminated against them, the firm sat up and took notice—and reduced the men's pensions.

TABLE 18.2

ANNUAL AVERAGES OF UNEMPLOYMENT FOR SELECTED CATEGORIES, 1960-1979

				SELECTED CATEGORIES					
YEAR	TOTAL	MALES, 20 YEARS AND OVER	FEMALES, 20 YEARS AND OVER	BOTH SEXES, 16 TO 19 YEARS	WHITE	BLACK AND OTHER RACES	MARRIED MEN, WIFE PRESENT	MARRIED WOMEN, HUSBAND PRESENT	FEMALE FAMILY HOUSE-HOLDER, NO HUSBAND PRESENT
1960	5.5	4.7	5.1	14.7	4.9	10.2	3.7	(NA)	(NA)
1970	4.9	3.5	4.8	15.2	4.5	8.2	2.6	4.9	5.4
1974	5.6	3.8	5.5	16.0	5.0	9.9	2.7	5.3	7.0
1975	8.5	6.7	8.0	19.9	7.8	13.9	5.1	7.9	10.0
1976	7.7	5.9	7.4	19.0	7.0	13.1	4.2	7.1	10.0
1977	7.0	5.2	7.0	17.7	6.2	13.1	3.6	6.5	9.3
1978	6.0	4.2	6.0	16.3	5.2	11.9	2.8	5.5	8.5
1979	5.8	4.1	5.7	16.1	5.1	11.3	2.7	5.1	8.3

SOURCE: Census Bureau, *Population Profile of the United States: 1979*, p. 35.

reflect the loss of employed skills that occurs when a highly trained person who has lost his or her regular job works part-time as a laborer.

But even if we look only at the official rate of employment, we can see how large a part of the American labor force has recently been out of work, especially since the economic slowdown that began in the early 1970s. The policy objective of the federal government has been to maintain "an acceptable level of unemployment"—generally considered to be 4.5 to 5 percent of the labor force—rather than to achieve full employment. Presumably, an increase in consumer spending sparked by full employment would result in a dramatic, "undesirable" increase in the rate of inflation as demand outpaced supply. At the optimum level of 4.5 to 5 percent, both inflation and unemployment rate are "acceptably" low—to government policy makers, though not, of course, to those who are unemployed. (This reasoning has been called in question in recent years when high rates of both unemployment and inflation have occurred at the same time.) However, the average rate of unemployment in the United States was 5.8 percent in 1979.

Unemployment poses a threat not only to an individual's financial situation but also to his or her self-esteem. Studies of the effects of long-term unemployment on men (Komarovsky, 1940; Wilcock and Franke,

1963) suggest that it is often as devastating—both financially and psychologically—as it was during the Great Depression of the 1930s, despite the cushion of unemployment benefits that is now available. The men studied felt embarrassed and helpless; having already lost their community of co-workers, they gradually withdrew from other friends and social groups. Many of them became hostile and self-incriminating, blaming themselves for a situation over which they actually had little control.

Underemployment

Underemployment is more difficult to measure than unemployment, but essentially it refers both to the fact that many workers are employed irregularly, at low levels of skill and salary, and more generally to the underutilization of people's skills and talents. Many of those who are employed—especially those with only part-time jobs—are unable to support themselves and their families with their low wages. Many others—most of whom are currently working full-time—have skills and talents that are not utilized in the job they hold.

In the 1950s, there was wide discussion of a coming "automation revolution" which forecasters believed would eliminate certain menial or repetitive jobs almost entirely, while increasing the demand for skilled

Unemployment, though on the increase throughout the United States, is particularly devastating in Detroit, as a result of the recession in the auto industry. (Owen Franken/Stock, Boston)

workers. But this "revolution" did not come to pass. So far, at least, it has not been economically feasible nor technically possible for many industries to introduce extensive automation. Nor has it been possible to mechanize menial "jobs of last resort"—such as waiting on table, digging ditches, collecting garbage, and making beds and taking out bedpans in hospitals.

Thus, one of the main questions about the future of the American labor force is not what the results of automation will be, but who will fill the menial jobs that cannot be automated. In the past, these jobs were filled disproportionately by members of racial minorities, women, immigrants, and those only marginally able to obtain and hold any job, such as mentally retarded people and people with personality disorders. But rising expectations, greater egalitarianism, and increased formal education, as well as more generous welfare and unemployment benefits, mean there are fewer and fewer people willing to take such jobs. One writer suggests that the pattern of the future may be that the young people who have not yet graduated from high school or college will perform an increasing number of the menial, "dead end" jobs as an initiation into the world of work (Faltermaver, 1974).

JOB SATISFACTION

Judging from reports in the news media over the past few years, it would appear that dissatisfaction with work is growing. When automobile workers at a Lordstown, Ohio, assembly plant went on a wildcat strike in 1972, for example, it was headline news: Lordstown was supposed to have been a model plant, yet workers were so discontented with the company's work rules that they walked off the job. There have been reports of increasing absenteeism, declining productivity, and an apparent rejection of the work ethic by disaffected young people. We now hear about the "white-collar woes" as well as the "blue-collar blues," suggesting that it is not only factory work that is unsatisfying.

THE MOTIVATION TO WORK

Clearly, most people work because they have to make a living. It is often assumed that without the proddings of necessity, people would stop working entirely. But this assumption is far from true. The motivation to work is strong and prevalent. As Barbara Garson reports, "I have spent the last two years examining the way people cope with routine and monotonous work. I expected to find resentment and I found it . . . . But the most dramatic thing I found was quite the opposite . . . . *People passionately want to work* (1975).

Several years ago, the Department of Health, Education, and Welfare conducted an experiment to predict the impact of one income maintenance program that has been suggested as an alternative to our present welfare system. This program, called the negative income tax, would, in effect, provide a minimum income for the entire population. When members of the low- or non-income families receiving payments found employment, cash payments from the government would be reduced, but by an amount less than the worker's salary, thus providing an incentive for paid employment. An obvious question about the effect of such a negative income tax program is whether its recipients might decide to work less, or not at all. The most striking conclusion from this experiment was that the prospect of a guaranteed minimum income from the government did not substantially undermine the incentive to work, especially among male heads of households. "I'm amazed to observe how strong the urge to work is," one of the experiment's directors remarked. "Despite the fact that many of the people we studied had repeated experiences with discrimination, low wages, poor working conditions, and arbitrary layoffs, the work ethic and the desire for higher incomes are all very strong" (quoted in Melville, 1974, p. 14).

Such findings are consistent with a number of studies that report that most people say, perhaps unreflectively, that they would continue working even if they did not have to. And more and more, people would rather work. Today, half of all housewives plan to get salaried jobs. They want to work not only for the money, but because they feel working women lead more interesting, autonomous lives (Lesem, 1979).

But this does not necessarily mean that people regard work as a highly satisfying experience. Assessing satisfaction turns out to be a very difficult task. Like the answers to questions about marital satisfaction or general contentment about one's life, the answers researchers get can be significantly affected by the way they phrase their questions. For example, one can simply ask people if they are happy with their work. Several studies of this nature are summarized in Kerr and Rosow's *Work in America* (1979), a report issued by a special task force to the Secretary of Health, Education, and Welfare that investigated the problems and prospects of the American worker. Polls conducted over the past several decades have consistently shown that about 75 percent of those questioned feel their work is satisfying when asked the question in this way. Much recent research has shown that all people, regardless of social characteristics, claim to believe in the inherent moral value of hard work (Kerr and Rosow, 1979). Another consistent finding is that as people increase their earn-

ings and their wealth, they do not choose to reduce the amount of time and energy they spend working.

But we get a somewhat different impression from studies that ask a different question: "Would you choose the same type of work if you had your life to live over?" One study of this sort found that while 41 percent of skilled steelworkers said they would choose the same type of work again, only 16 percent of unskilled automobile workers gave the same answer. In general, white-collar workers express considerably more job satisfaction than do blue-collar workers, and the job satisfaction of professionals is considerably higher than that of white-collar workers. For example, 83 percent of lawyers, 89 percent of physicians, and 97 percent of university professors said that they would choose the same profession again (Kerr and Rosow, 1979).

This is consonant with the classic view in sociology (Mills, 1951; Vollmer, 1960, 1965; Blauner, 1966) that suggests that overall job satisfaction is strongly influenced by occupational status and level of autonomy. In his study of white-collar employees (1951), Mills found a direct correspondance between the prestige and skill level of an occupation and feelings of job satisfaction: 86 percent of professional employees, 74 percent of managers, 56 percent of skilled workers, 48 percent of semiskilled workers, and 42 percent of commercial employees were satisfied with their work.

Most recent research, particularly that of Laslett (1971) and Kalleberg (1977), however, does not support these earlier findings. After reviewing the work of Blauner and others, Laslett concluded: "The assertion that there is a positive relationship between occupational level and work satisfaction is . . . not as conclusive as some authors have suggested" (Laslett, 1971, p. 30). She found that the relationship held only *within* blue- and white-collar categories, but not across the whole occupational hierarchy.

Another influence on work satisfaction is job autonomy. Blauner contrasted the working conditions of two types of industrial employees—those on assembly lines and those involved in continuous-process industries, such as petrochemical plants, where much of the work is automated. Assembly-line jobs consist of simple and repetitive tasks, are tightly supervised, and are paced by the production belt. Blauner found that such work produced the greatest amount of dissatisfaction among workers. Perhaps this is why assembly-line workers sometimes sabotage the process; it may be their only means of exerting some personal influence on their work. Workers in continuous-process industries, in contrast, displayed considerably more job satisfaction. They enjoyed greater flexibility in the timing and performance of their jobs and were able to introduce such personal touches as a hotplate in the control room that allowed them to take a "soup break" at the time of their choice (Blauner, 1966).

Yet another factor in work satisfaction and how people evaluate it may be what Curt Tausky and R. Dubin (1965) call "career anchorage"—whether they are looking at where they have come from or where they hope to go. One person, for example, may look back at his or her point of origin and derive satisfaction from the distance covered; another may look ahead, see only how far there is to go, and express dissatisfaction. In their study of middle-level managers, Tausky and Dubin found career anchorage to be a factor in satisfaction. Of those who looked forward, 78 percent said they would be dissatisfied if they did not reach the top, whereas only 44 percent of those who looked back felt this way.

But to study the correlates of work satisfaction as these studies do still does not tell much about what work satisfaction is. In a 1977 study, Arne C. Kalleberg asked a representative sample of 1,500 workers about their perceptions of themselves, their jobs, and other aspects of their lives. The results suggest that six aspects of work can be sources of reward and job satisfaction: (1) intrinsic aspects—whether or not the work is interesting and allows the worker to be creative and self-directing; (2) convenience—the "creature comforts" of a job, such as easy commuting and good hours; (3) financial rewards—pay, fringe benefits, job security; (4) relations with co-workers; (5) career opportunities; and (6) resource adequacy—enough help, good equip-

One way of assessing what motivates people to work is to consider the nature of the rewards they receive. Extrinsic rewards, such as money and prestige, may be important sources of motivation for the commercial artist. Intrinsic rewards—the satisfaction gained from performing the activity itself—may be more important to the Navajo sand painter. (Alan Mercer; Michal Heron)

ment, access to information. Kalleberg's results showed intrinsic satisfaction to be the most important factor, followed by financial reward. Convenience and relations with co-workers were relatively unimportant, as were career opportunities and resource adequacy.

Job satisfaction is not a simple phenomenon but a complex one, involving not only the kind of job but also the kind of person who does it. Efforts to increase job satisfaction, such as improving working conditions or changing management styles, may have the desired effect for some people and under some conditions, but not others. And people themselves do not expect to receive satisfaction, as if it were a paycheck, regularly and always in the same amount. They often make trade-offs among different kinds of satisfactions to achieve what is seen as best for them, given their particular circumstances, background, and resources. Furthermore, the mix of satisfactions may change throughout life as circumstances, needs, and aspirations change.

MANAGING JOB SATISFACTION AND PRODUCTIVITY

That how workers feel about their jobs has become a real problem for employers is evidenced by the current focus in management studies and practice on the use of psychological techniques to make work rewarding (Sennett, 1979). Three important approaches are used: one is based on Maslow's human potential movement and is aimed at making workers happy by increasing the intrinsic rewards of the job; the second uses behavioral techniques to increase productivity by a system of rewards and punishments. The third is based on the idea of cooperative decision making, or consulting workers about how a job can or should be done.

All these techniques are currently being used, but their consequences are open to debate. Productivity has been shown to increase, but generally only for the short term, and sometimes to the point of inefficiency for the company: workers (and managers) may become so involved in doing a job right that they actually slow down; rewards and punishments cost money to administer, and can be expensive enough to offset any increase in productivity. Furthermore, Sennett argues, because the real aim of all these techniques is manipulation, not autonomy, they are likely to exacerbate what some see as a crisis of legitimacy for all our institutions. If workers are now questioning the authority of the boss or the point of caring about a job at all, just as they have questioned the authority of the church, the family, and the government, attempts to persuade them to like their jobs may be viewed as nothing more than manipulation.

Work in the future

Looking back over the past two centuries in the United States and Western Europe, it is no exaggeration to say that our emphasis on productivity and economic growth and the widely shared belief—especially powerful in the United States—that work endows one's life with meaning and purpose have constituted significant aspects of modern industrial society. A strong commitment to the work ethic in the nineteenth century was one of the most important factors in the phenomenal growth of industry and output during the century.

THE NEW LEISURE

Now, however, there seem to be changes. The influence of the Protestant ethic may have declined somewhat. It is possible that an increasing number of people are coming to feel "less committed to the entrepreneurial character and its virtues. Increasingly, self-worth and worth in the eyes of others is organized as much by one's style of life and one's consumption pattern as by one's occupational status as such" (Flacks, 1971).

A century ago, when the average work week was considerably longer than it is today, the gospel of hard work had an unchallenged authority. Today, we identify ourselves by our leisure activities, just as earlier generations identified themselves by their work. A new Porsche with a Playboy Club bumper sticker identifies the driver just as surely as the station wagon next to it with a Disneyland sticker says something about the family that owns it.

Indeed, leisure has become a booming business. Between 1955 and 1974, the amount the American people spent for leisure activities and products in-

As the desire for an enriched lifestyle gains momentum in America, industries that supply our leisure needs are enjoying an economic boom. (© Hazel Hankin 1980)

creased by 550 percent, while the population increased by about 28 percent and the gross national product increased by about 80 percent (Census Bureau, 1976, pp. 10, 218, 393).

STRUCTURAL TRENDS

This change in values may in the future be spurred by current structural trends. For one thing, the work week is now shorter in certain occupational categories. The average work week has been reduced from 70.6 hours in 1850 to 39.4 hours in 1975 (Census Bureau, 1976, p. 380). Fifty years ago, when the Ford Motor Company introduced the five-day work week, it was considered a great breakthrough for laborers. The contract settlement between Ford and the United Auto Workers union in 1976 called for 25 thirty-two-hour, four-day weeks a year, suggesting that a thirty-two-hour work week may be a prospect for many workers.

For another thing, "skill obsolescence" as well as new attitudes toward personal fulfillment may well cause many to leave work for retraining at mid-career,

or to change careers in middle age. For centuries, people could learn a trade or profession when they were young and then spend the rest of their working lives practicing what they had learned in their youth. But as technology changes more and more rapidly, what an individual originally learned may quickly become out of date. It has been estimated, for example, that half of what an engineering student learns today will be out of date within ten years. Consequently, educating oneself for a given career is being regarded more and more as a lifelong pursuit, rather than a one-time affair.

It is also becoming more and more common for people to rethink their careers at middle age and to plan second careers substantially different from the first. A 1974 American Management Association survey found, for example, that almost half of the 3,000 management-level employees studied had either changed or considered changing their occupation during the five years prior to the survey (Institute of Life Insurance, 1974, p. 5).

Interestingly enough, despite high unemployment, possible changes in the work ethic, and the failure of many jobs to tap the abilities cultivated by higher education, many college-educated youths—though still a minority—are "turning on to work," according to a survey by Daniel Yankelovich (1974) of 3,500 young people. The study showed that, in contrast, "the majority who lack a college degree are turning off . . . , searching for outlets outside the job" (p. 41). In conclusion, Yankelovich sees college students as the least alienated group in the society. The students Yankelovich studied place considerable emphasis on self-fulfillment and reject a nose-to-the-grindstone attitude toward work; yet they also express a strong willingness to pursue an education in order to get a good job. A survey of college freshmen in 1980, however, suggests that today's young people are hardly interested in work solely for its own sake: nearly two-thirds of those questioned said that "being very well off financially" was to them a very im-portant goal. The same number of students said that an important reason for attending college was "to be able to make more money." It may be that increasing emphasis on the financial rewards of work—which has been noted among working adults as well as college students—is a compensation for the alienating nature of much work, an alienation that appears to be less tolerable nowadays. A study by Yankelovich (1978) found that many people, failing to find much personal satisfaction in their work, express their discontent by demanding more pay and fringe benefits, as if to make up for what they are missing.

Although Yankelovich found that most people do want to work, he also found that today's workers share a widespread "preoccupation with self." According to Yankelovich, workers of the future are going to be increasingly likely to look for personal fulfillment in their jobs. The "flex-time" work schedules now offered by some corporations—in which employees choose their own working hours—represent one effort to respond to these demands.

Summary

With the coming of industrialization in eighteenth-century Europe, employers began to regard labor as a commodity to be bought and sold; the system of exchange shifted from *barter* to a *market economy*; and the "Protestant ethic" placed a religious value on hard work and thrift. Under the economic system of *capitalism*, industrialization not only redefined the work process but reshaped the social order.

In the view of Adam Smith, the capitalist system should be as free of government restraint as possible. The "invisible hand" of free market forces would ensure that capitalism operated for the best interest of society. In the view of Karl Marx, however, capitalism dehumanized, exploited, and alienated workers; he predicted that class consciousness among workers would ultimately result in a revolution that would replace capitalism with a socialist system.

The occupational structure in the United States today is characterized by a far smaller number of farm workers, a relatively stable number of workers in manufacturing, and a shift among white-collar workers from production areas to service occupations. Sources of strain in the occupational system include a dual economy with "primary" and "secondary" labor markets; inequality of work opportunity on the bases of age, sex, and race; high rates of unemployment; and underemployment of many workers.

Most people are highly motivated to work, but the degree of satisfaction they derive from their work depends on the influence of a number of factors—whether or not the job is interesting and/or convenient, its financial rewards, career opportunities, and the congeniality of co-workers.

Glossary

BARTER A system of trade whereby goods are exchanged for each other.

CAPITALISM An economic system in which private individuals and corporations, primarily, invest in and own the means of production, distribution, and exchange for the purpose of making a profit.

CORPORATION A business enterprise consisting of an association of individuals created by law and having powers and liabilities independent of those of the individual owners of its stock.

MARKET ECONOMY A system in which the price of a given product or service, and the quantities in which it is produced, rise and fall with demand.

OLIGOPOLY A market condition in which a few companies dominate a particular industry.

Recommended readings

Kerr, Clark, and Jerome Rosow (eds.). *Work in America: The Decade Ahead.* New York: Van Nostrand Reinhold, 1979. A collection of articles by leading scholars, critically reflecting on current and future work issues.

Mills, C. Wright. *White Collar.* New York: Oxford, 1951. A provocative, classic analysis of the situation of the white-collar worker.

Polanyi, Karl. *The Great Transformation.* Boston: Beacon Press, 1957. An account of how economic relations changed as the West industrialized.

Rosow, Jerome M. (ed.). *The Worker and the Job: Coping with Change.* Englewood Cliffs, N.J.: Prentice-Hall, 1974. An interdisciplinary anthology that considers change in work and innovations designed to improve work.

Smelser, Neil J. *The Sociology of Economic Life.* 2nd ed. Englewood Cliffs, N.J.: Prentice-Hall, 1976. A short book focusing on the economy as a social system and its interconnectedness with other institutions.

Terkel, Studs. *Working.* New York: Random House, 1974. Americans describe what work means to them.

Weiss, Robert S., Edwin Harwood, and David Riesman. "The World of Work." In Robert K. Merton and Robert A. Nisbet (eds.). *Contemporary Social Problems.* 4th ed. New York: Harcourt Brace Jovanovich, 1976. A useful summary of issues on the sociology of work.

Work in America: Report of a Special Task Force to the Secretary of Health, Education, and Welfare. Cambridge, Mass.: MIT Press, 1973. A report of a federal commission, typical of many issued in the last decade. It analyzes work from many perspectives, some critical, with a concern for policies that the federal government might adopt.

Organizing production in China

WILLIAM HINTON

In 1946–47, the Communists and Nationalists were fighting for control of China. In the territory occupied by the Communists, economic cooperatives were organized in an attempt to overturn the economic foundations of feudal rule and to move the country toward a collective economy.

. . . Mutual-aid groups for labor exchange on the land and the pooling of resources for subsidiary occupations did not simply appear. They were organized and promoted on a vast scale. The whole purpose of the land distribution, as envisioned by the Communist Party, was to remove the fetters that bound production, to release the energy and enthusiasm of the peasants, and to lay the basis for a transition from "individual labor based on an individual economy to collective labor based on a collective economy." Once the question of land ownership was settled the mutual-aid movement—the embryonic form of co-operation in production—was considered to be the key to progress in the rural areas.

Mao spoke many times of the two great "organizings"—organize to overthrow feudalism and organize to increase production. One without the other was futile. Mutual aid, labor exchange, and co-operation in production were impossible on any large scale as long as landlord-tenant relations predominated. Where one man owned all the means of production—the land, the implements and the draft animals—and the other man owned only his own two hands, there were no grounds for getting together. There was no basis for exchange. The rich man simply hired the poor man. . . .

In the Taihang Mountains in 1946 and 1947, mutual aid was not only relatively easy to initiate, it was absolutely necessary if the peasants were to produce at all. There simply were not enough carts, donkeys, oxen, seeders, or even iron hoes to go around. In order to produce, people had to share. Mutual aid was necessary for still another reason. Primitive as the means of production were, no family could afford to have a complete set of the implements and draft animals necessary for production. . . .

Since there were not enough draft animals and implements to go around and since the landholdings were too small to engage efficiently any complete set of equipment, it was essential that people get together, swap and share what they had, and help each other out. Labor exchange, which had existed in China for thousands of years on a

spontaneous but limited basis, suddenly became a great agricultural movement.

Yang Chung-sheng, a landowning Long Bow peasant with a large family to feed, led the best-organized local mutual-aid group. Starting with five families who joined together of their own accord in 1946, it soon grew to include 22 families who owned a total of over 80 acres of land. Among the earlier members were four soldiers' dependents and two families without able-bodied members who had been left out by other groups. But even this dead weight did not dampen enthusiasm. The group produced so well that new families constantly applied for membership. As finally constituted the 22-family constellation mustered 12 able-bodied men, two "half-labor-power" children, and two "half-labor-power" old people for field work. In spite of the fact that they had a very large area to till per man, they were always the first to finish any work, whether planting, plowing, hoeing, or harvesting. This was because they got along well and helped each other out, not only in the fields but also in solving all problems of livelihood. . . .

Aside from the fact that the members of Yang Chung-sheng's team were good friends to begin with, they attributed their success to the fact that they organized well, met often, discussed every problem thoroughly and worked out a good system of keeping records so that the exchange of labor time balanced out in the long run. Yang never tried to tell the group what to do. When they met they talked things over and only when they agreed did they act. They always tilled the land of soldiers' dependents first, asking only their meals in return. Families without manpower paid wages for all work done, but the group did not demand that these wages be paid at once. Those who had no grain could wait until after the harvest to settle up. A committee of four was elected to report on all hours put in and on all exchanges of implements and draft power. One member who could write and figure on the abacus was appointed to tally up the accounts. At the end of every period—that is, planting, hoeing, harvesting, etc.—a balance sheet was drawn up and a settlement made. Everyone paid up what he owed except those who were in difficult circumstances and needed more time. This satisfied all participants and helped to maintain morale at a high level.

The group met briefly every evening to plan the next day's work. When the cocks began to crow before dawn, no time was wasted in consultation. Everyone went straight to the field without having to be called. When the six animals possessed by the group members were not needed in the fields, they were taken by their owners on transport work that was individually planned and executed. In other words, the group did not try to pool all

the activities of its members. They worked together where the advantage was greatest and went their separate ways where that was more suitable. . . .

Mutual-aid type organization was not confined to work on the land or to the labor of male craftsmen. Women also organized mutual-aid groups, most of which concentrated on textile production. Because of the inroads of machine-made textiles in the previous decades, many wives and mothers no longer knew how or had never learned to make cloth from raw cotton in the home. The Women's Association therefore had to start from the beginning with a spinning and weaving class whose students, coming from dozens of families, lived together in the "Foreign House" of General Hsu, and learned by doing. Once the students became proficient they transformed their class into a spinning and weaving group rather than return to their homes for individual production. This was

because the women, young and old, found it much more congenial to work together in a large group than to sit isolated in their homes endlessly spinning or pushing a shuttle. Also, when one worked alone at home, it was easy to fall asleep early in the evening and thus shorten the hours of work. By meeting together, exchanging gossip, studying, and singing, the long evenings passed quickly and productively. Some husbands and fathers soon complained over the absence of their women from home for such extended periods. When complaints could no longer be ignored, the women compromised by working at home during the day and with the group in the "Foreign House" in the evening.

I have no record of the amount or value of the cotton cloth which this one large Long Bow group created, but a similar group of 70 women in another Taihang village won region-wide recognition by producing enough textiles in one season to buy 55 sheep, 35 pigs, two draft animals, and farm implements worth $335 in U. S. currency.

Almost as important as mutual aid in stimulating production was the new tax system introduced on the heels of land reform by the Border Region Government. . . .

The old tax system, when it did not simply take everything that police and troops could find, penalized the conscientious producer by demanding a fixed proportion of the actual crop harvested. The bigger the crop, the bigger the tax. The new tax system reversed this and rewarded the conscientious producer by basing its demands not on the actual crop harvested in the current year, but on the average amount harvested in previous seasons. What was taxed was not the land as such or the crop as such but standard *mou*. A standard *mou* was defined as any amount of land that yielded 10 tou (one *tou* = 0.285 bushels) of millet. To determine how many standard *mou* a man possessed one only had to calculate his annual average yield in *tou* and divide by ten. The tax that he paid was set as a proportion of this standard. Anyone who worked hard, applied new methods and increased his yields, paid no tax on that part of the crop exceeding the fixed standard no matter how large it was, and this was true for a definite number of years. If, for instance, a peasant dug a well, irrigated his fields, and thereby doubled his crops, this made no difference at all to his tax base until three years had passed. Similar provisions rewarded other forms of effort such as reclamation.

All crops grown on virgin land (land uncropped for more than six years) were tax free for three years. Crops grown on reclaimed land (land uncropped for any period up to six years) were tax free for two years.

To guarantee that all families retained enough grain after taxes to survive (a matter with which the old regime had never concerned itself), the yield from one standard *mou*, or 2.85 bushels of millet per capita was entirely exempted from all taxation. These exemption provisions were similar to the $600 exemptions of the United States federal income tax law. However, the Border Region tax regulations went the United States one better in this respect. Oxen and donkeys were granted an exemption equal to 40 percent of a standard *mou*, or 1.14 bushels of millet, while horses and mules were granted 70 percent, or 1.9 bushels, thus guaranteeing a minimum of food for livestock as well as for their masters.

The proportional features of the law also paralleled the United States income tax provisions. Families harvesting an average amount of land per capita paid 25 catties of millet, or approximately 20 percent of the yield on all taxable standard *mou*, but families who held more than the average amount of land and hence harvested more than the average paid a proportionately higher tax.* . . .

Other families, fully convinced of the need to produce, were discouraged by lack of capital. Here mutual aid, by pooling the meager resources of several poor families, solved part of the problem. But credit from the local co-op or the newly organized People's Credit Bank of Lucheng County was also important. . . .

At the same time the dampening influence of middlemen's high profits and speculatory manipulations was mitigated by the creation of a vast network of village-controlled and financed consumer co-operatives. These popular institutions provided staples at low prices and an outlet for rural produce at a fair return.

An expanding market was also greatly aided by the growth of transportation facilities. . . . So did the improvement of roads and highways. Most striking of all was the construction of a narrow gauge railroad which, under the direction of the embryonic Railroad Bureau of the Shansi-Hopei-Honan-Shantung Border Region Government, pushed halfway through the Taihang Mountains from the east. . . .

The government also went heavily into mining, smelting, and munitions manufacture, to mention but a few important areas of public production. . . . Gradually the peasant-style rifle-and-hand-grenade army was being transformed into a modern force that boasted both tanks and artillery.

Twice a year, by government decree, every peasant in the Fifth District was required to bring five catties of ash to the new plant housed in an empty building on Long Bow's eastern rim. For this ash the peasants were paid a standard price. The demand for organic ash soon mushroomed far beyond anything that could be satisfied by the embers of the peasants' cooking fires and stimulated an endless search for waste material. Over the hills and valleys of the district arose wisps of smoke that were visible for miles, as young and old burned the leaves, weeds, roots, and trash that would make it possible to blast Chiang Kai-shek, "The Old Root of Reaction," right out of Nanking.

Whether or not Chiang Kai-shek could ever actually be blasted out of Nanking depended in large measure on the uninterrupted progress of this production movement and the solid basis which it alone could provide for a new politics and a new culture. Yet, as the months passed, many signs indicated that all was not entirely well on the home front. The full potential of the economy was being undercut by several negative trends, all of which arose

---

* These were wartime rates. After 1950, rates were cut to between 12 and 15 percent.

from the same source—the very thoroughness with which the drive of the poor to *fanshen* had smashed down all feudal barriers and then gone on to "level the tops and fill the holes."

One of these trends involved a clear violation of policy. In spite of repeated warnings by the Central Committee, in spite of the clear language of the May 4th Directive, the expropriation proceedings against the gentry had not stopped with feudal property. To the young activists in the villages a landlord was a landlord, a rich peasant was a rich peasant, and an exploiter was an exploiter. They did not recognize any such phenomenon as a dual personality—a landlord capitalist, or a capitalist landlord. When they attacked they took everything—land, housing, stock, tools, buried treasure—and also business ventures. As a consequence, in the whole of Lucheng County, very few enterprises of a private nature survived the 1946 campaigns. Most of them had either been destroyed by a division of their assets or had been taken over by various mutual-aid groups to be run as co-operatives. The over-all effect of such expropriations was to stifle private initiative, a drag on production which the underdeveloped state of the economy could ill afford. While co-operative efforts filled a great need, they could not, on their own, provide all the capital and incentive necessary to an all-around development of production. For this, private enterprise was considered essential.

An even more serious drag on expansion was the growing reluctance of those families who had been attacked as exploiters and those of their more prosperous brethren who feared such an attack, to produce with zest. While the poor who had *fanshened* went at production with unprecedented enthusiasm, those who had helped to make their *fanshen* possible, or feared that they would be called upon to contribute to it later, hung back. The "chive-cutting thought" that had sprouted in the spring of 1946 spread with accelerated speed in the following fall and winter. At a time when the majority were doing their best to create wealth and make themselves as rich as Li Hsun-ta, a substantial minority hesitated.* They did only as much as was necessary to feed their families and guarantee another year's crop. In the meantime they waited to see what the shape of the future might be.

Most serious of all was the political friction which the deepening of the expropriation drive and the broadening of its target produced. The excesses of the movement divided the peasants as surely as its over-all objectives had united them. And it was this tragic division which served as seed-bed for the growth of all kinds of abuses of power and arrogant misbehavior on the part of some leading cadres and militiamen when they began to be confronted with apathy and opposition from unexpected quarters.

* Li Hsun-ta was a famous labor hero of the Yenan region.

Aspects of modern society

CHAPTER NINETEEN
THE POPULATION PROBLEM

Population is in one sense a very simple subject. The study of any human population involves just three main elements: size (that is, how many people there are); distribution (where they are); and composition (who they are—how many women and how many men, how many children under the age of five, how many adults over the age of seventy, and so on). Moreover, there are only three variables that can change a population: the *birth rate;* the *mortality rate,* or *death rate;* and *migration,* the movement of people from one place to another. The relationships among these variables are extremely simple: the difference between births and deaths gives us the *net natural increase* (or *decrease*) of a population, and if we add *net migration* to this, we get the population's total growth or decline in a given period (see Figure 19.1).

Yet these seemingly uncomplicated phenomena can have very complex causes and results, and it is these causes and results that are of primary interest to sociologists. For example, a population's birth rate can be affected by religious beliefs, by people's average age at marriage, and by the population's *sex ratio* (the proportion of males to females)—all of which are cultural factors, or are related to cultural factors. A population's death rate, likewise, is affected by cultural factors such as sanitary practices and medical techniques; and its migration rate is affected by socially determined "push factors," such as unemployment, food shortages, and racial or religious discrimination, and by "pull factors," such as cheap land and the availability of jobs.

Behind population statistics, in sum, are myriad complex social forces that are of central sociological concern. Perhaps of greatest concern to sociologists—as well as many other observers—are the social forces that are shaping the future of world population. Will world population continue to grow at its present rate? For how long? And how will the pattern of growth affect the world we live in?

World population trends

Viewed in historical perspective, the current population explosion is relatively recent. Until about 1750, the world population was no more than 791 million (United Nations, 1973), and was almost stable in size (annual growth was under .1 percent) (Nam, 1968). Almost all human societies had high rates of fertility;

FIGURE 19.1

The formulas on page 441 are used by demographers to arrive at a population's birth rate, death rate, net rate of immigration, net rate of natural increase (or decrease), and net growth rate. Each formula is illustrated with rates for the population of the United States in mid-1978. The graph at near right shows these rates for the United States from 1940 to 1978. (Census Bureau, 1980)

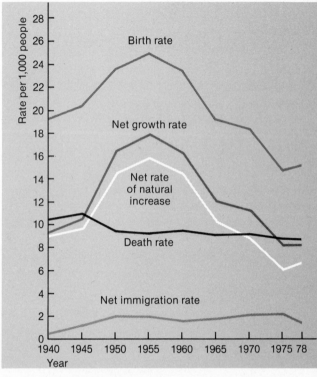

but their mortality rates were almost equally high. Death rates tended to fluctuate widely from year to year, as a result of unpredictable natural disasters such as floods, droughts, and plagues. During the Middle Ages in Europe, death rates soared at various times owing to famines and epidemics; between 1346 and 1350, for example, some 25 million people—one-quarter of the population of Europe—were wiped out by the bubonic plague or "Black Death" (Deaux, 1969; Shrewsbury, 1970). But even in times of prosperity, death rates stayed high enough to keep population growth from shooting upward to any great degree.

After about 1750, however, these patterns began to change. From 1750 to 1900, the growth rate of the world population climbed to about .5 percent per year—a more than fivefold increase in just 150 years. Then, during the twentieth century, with advances in medical knowledge and the introduction of public-health measures in many parts of the globe, the growth rate leaped to 2 percent by 1971 (Matras, 1977). The decade of the 1970s witnessed some slackening of the rate; in 1977, it stood at 1.7 percent (Population Reference Bureau, 1978). Viewed in historical perspective, however, this is still a dramatically high figure; and no one can be certain that it will not rise even further (see Figure 19.2).

World population growth *may* threaten our survival, and it will undoubtedly have political implications, for reasons we will make clear later on. In order to expand our understanding of these problems, sociologists and *demographers* (social scientists who specialize in the measurement and analysis of population changes) are asking many different types of questions about population growth in the various societies of the world. What are the cultural factors behind various societies' norms for reproduction and the family—such as the Indian preference for large families and early marriage and, conversely, the American patterns of marriage after college (or even later) and the "two-child"

FIGURE 19.2

This graph shows worldwide population growth rates from 1750 to 2000. The implications of these growth rates come into sharp focus when they are considered in relation to doubling time—the number of years in which the size of a population will double, a figure that is calculated according to the formula: Doubling Time = 70 ÷ Growth

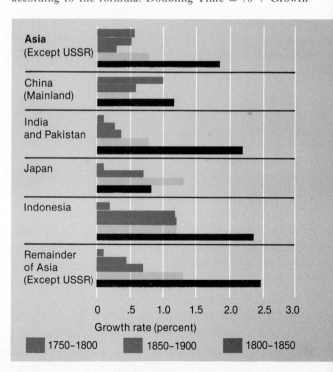

Population growth: basic formulas

Birth rate	$\dfrac{\text{Births in a year (3,932,000)}}{\text{Population at midyear (215,653,000)}} = \text{Crude birth rate (.018)}$
	Crude birth rate (.018) × 1000 = Birth rate (18 per 1,000 people per year)
Death rate	$\dfrac{\text{Deaths in a year (2,093,000)}}{\text{Population at midyear (215,653,000)}} = \text{Crude death rate (.0097)}$
	Crude death rate (.0097) × 1000 = Death rate (9.7 per 1,000 people per year)
Net immigration rate	$\dfrac{\text{Number of immigrants (386,000)}}{\text{Population at midyear (215,653,000)}} = \text{Crude immigration rate (.0018)}$
	Crude immigration rate (.0018) × 1000 = Net immigration rate (1.8 per 1,000 people per year)
Net rate of natural increase (or decrease)	Birth rate (18) − Death rate (9.7) = Net rate of natural increase (8.3 per 1,000 people per year)
Net growth rate	Net rate of natural increase (8.3) + net immigration rate (1.8) = Net growth rate (10.1 per 1,000 people per year)

Rate. At the time of Christ, the world population (estimated to have been no more than about 300 million) was doubling every 1,400 years. From 1750 to 1900, however, the world population increased by .5 percent a year, a rate that doubled the population in that century and a half. Between 1900 and 1950 the rate rose to .8 percent a year, and the doubling time decreased to 88 years. The estimated rate of increase over the second half of this century is an average of 1.8 percent. At that rate, the world's population would double in 39 years. As calculated (Hauser, 1969), an annual world population growth rate of just 2 percent would produce one person for every square foot of land on earth in 650 years. (Durand, 1967)

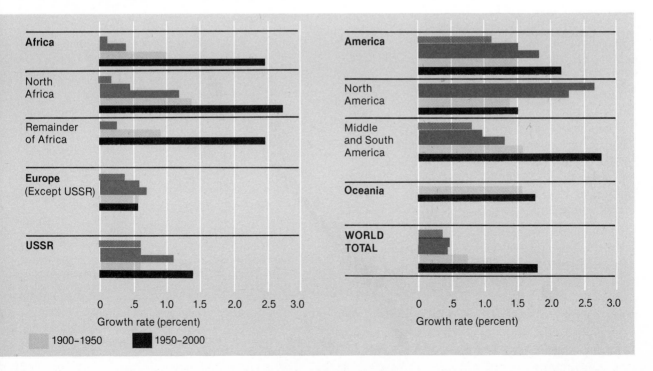

Africa / North Africa / Remainder of Africa / Europe (Except USSR) / USSR

America / North America / Middle and South America / Oceania / WORLD TOTAL

Growth rate (percent)

Growth rate (percent)

■ 1900–1950   ■ 1950–2000

In the mid-fourteenth century, many Londoners fled to the countryside in an attempt to escape the bubonic plague. (The Granger Collection)

family? What does having a large family mean to a Nigerian woman and a Nigerian man, as opposed to an American woman and man? Can people in a country such as Bangladesh be expected to change their attitudes and expectations about reproduction, and if not, why not? Will American attitudes in this area change, and with what consequences? How do world political relationships affect demographic patterns, and what has aid from industrialized nations done to population patterns in less developed areas? Needless to say, the implications of these questions are complex; in this space we can only outline some of the main trends. To begin with, let us look at the Western industrialized nations, and pinpoint some of the cultural factors behind their population patterns.

Population trends in the Western industrialized nations

From about the ninth century B.C. to the seventeenth century A.D., the birth rate in Europe was high—about thirty-five to forty-five births per 1,000 each year—and the death rate was almost equally high. During the seventeenth century, however, Western nations began a process known as the *demographic transition*. The term "demographic transition" is used to describe an historical process in which there is a major change in the pattern of birth and death rates of a society. Although there have been demographic transitions of varying degrees at other times and in other parts of the world, the term is generally used to describe the specific set of population changes that occurred in Western Europe between the mid-seventeenth century and the mid-twentieth century. Briefly, this demographic transition consisted of three stages: first, a high birth rate with a declining death rate; second, a declining birth rate with a still-declining death rate; and third, a relative balance of birth and death rates at a low level.*

Many of the technological and social changes that took place during the seventeenth and eighteenth centuries probably contributed to the gradual decline in mortality rates with which the demographic transition began. During this first phase of the demographic transition, perhaps the single most influential factor was better nutrition; new food crops introduced from the Americas gradually spread throughout Europe, providing cheap and reliable dietary staples for the poor:

* It should be borne in mind that this is a highly simplified and schematic summary of what was in reality a very complex process. Some researchers, for example, have found that in certain countries during the early phase of the demographic transition, when death rates were beginning to decline, there was also an *increase* in birth rates over and above their already high level—a phenomenon also seen in developing countries today (Habbakuk, 1953; Biraben, 1967; Rele, 1967; Davis, 1967). Nevertheless, in its general outlines the concept remains a valid one, at least as applied to the history of populations in Western Europe.

". . . by 1800 the potato had become the principal food of the lower classes throughout northern and central Europe, while in the southern countries and the Mediterranean area maize (Indian corn) . . . displayed an analogous role in vastly enlarging the food supply" (Langer, 1977, p. 4). At the same time, advances in agricultural technology increased food production, and improvements in transportation facilitated wide distribution; people were no longer at the mercy of sudden changes in their immediate natural environment. Improved diets in turn made people more resistant to disease, and the prevalence of severe epidemics gradually declined. The reduction of disease was accelerated by the development, during the nineteenth century, of public-health and sanitation measures. Infanticide, too, is thought to have gradually disappeared (Langer, 1977). Because of all these factors, during the period from about 1650 to 1850, the population more than doubled (Carr-Saunders, 1936): death rates no longer counterbalanced birth rates, and more women lived to childbearing age. These women had enough children to push birth rates even higher.

Some time during the middle to late nineteenth century, the second phase of the demographic transition became evident. Mortality rates continued to decline, but there was now a drop in fertility—so that population growth slowed. As we mentioned in Chapters 10 and 18, industrialization drew people to urban areas during this period, and this change in settlement patterns may have been one reason for the unprecedented drop in the birth rate. Children became more of a liability than an asset. They increased household expenses, and in the new urban environment, fewer of them were able to work to contribute to family incomes. Moreover, adequate housing in the rapidly growing cities was scarce, and large families meant crowded quarters. Thus, for people living in an urban, industrialized setting, small families were much more practical than large ones.

The new pressures of the urban environment, plus the decline in infant mortality that had resulted from improved diet, public health, and sanitation, served as powerful incentives to married couples to control their fertility (Banks and Banks, 1964). For the first time, contraception began to be widely employed. It was first taken up in the 1870s and 1880s by the urban middle classes; many people in this segment of society were literate and well-informed, and were thus most likely to be aware of the advantages and various techniques of contraception. Furthermore, the middle classes were strongly oriented toward economic rationality; they wanted to lead planned and prudent, not accidental, lives and quickly realized that limiting family size could be a big step toward prosperity (Petersen, 1975). After the 1880s, the practice of contraception spread rapidly through all classes of society: it was adopted by the working classes and people in rural areas of Europe and Britain in less than two generations.

As a result of the spread of contraceptive practices, the Western countries—in the third phase of the demographic transition—moved to a low-growth, relatively stable pattern characterized by low rates of both birth and death. There are still fluctuations in the population growth of these societies, but these fluctuations are not due to variations in the rates of *mortality*, as they were during the years before the demographic transition took place. (As we have mentioned above, nutrition and sanitation have improved, and in the twentieth century there have been major advances in medical science.) Instead, fluctuations in growth are due to variations in the rates of *fertility*—caused by shifts in economic conditions, value trends, and changes in lifestyles. We will see this especially clearly as we look specifically at the United States.

Population trends in the United States

TRENDS SINCE THE DEMOGRAPHIC TRANSITION

Population trends in our society have offered some interesting examples of post-transition patterns. The death rate has been relatively steady. Fatal infectious disease has been all but eliminated; for example, the rate of deaths from influenza and pneumonia, which were 202 per 100,000 in 1900, had fallen to about twenty-nine per 100,000 by 1972 (Thomlinson, 1976). The birth rate fell steadily through the first four decades of this century, and leveled off during the Depression of the 1930s at the quite low figure of eighteen births per 1,000 population each year, yielding an annual population growth rate during this period of less than 1 percent. After World War II, there occurred an unexpected rise in the birth rate; couples began having more children more often, which resulted in a "baby boom" that lasted from about 1946 to 1957, with a crude birth rate of between twenty-four and twenty-five per 1,000 per year (see Figure 19.1). Then after 1957 the birth rate suddenly began to fall again; it dropped steadily, to twenty-one per 1,000 in 1964, and then began to decline even more rapidly, dropping by 1978 to 15.3 per 1,000 per year. All told, between 1957 and 1978 the birth rate fell by some 40 percent (Census Bureau, 1979, p. 60).

One factor in the drop in the birth rate has evidently been a change in desired family size. As recently as 1967, the majority of women aged eighteen to twenty-four expected to have three or more children; today, the majority expect to have only two or fewer (see Figure 19.3). These figures point to a decline in the *fertility rate*—the number of births that 1,000 women would have in their lifetimes if, at each year of childbearing age, they experienced the birth rate occurring in the specified year. (Thus, the fertility rate and the birth rate are related, but not identical.) In 1965, for example, the fertility rate was 2,928 births for the lifetimes of 1,000 women, or 2.9 children apiece; in 1977, it was 1,826 or 1.8 apiece (Census Bureau, 1979, p. 61).

Indicators suggest that fertility may continue to drop and attitudes concerning childbearing may continue to be altered. Why are these changes taking place? The answer cannot be known with certainty, but a number of explanations have been offered.

POSSIBLE REASONS FOR THE DECLINE IN THE U.S. BIRTH RATE

Changing lifestyles and values

Part of the drop in the birth rate may be attributed to the influence of the women's movement. Today, with more women becoming involved in careers outside the home, many see childbearing as a matter of choice rather than an inevitable necessity. Many women are realizing that they may legitimately aspire to adult

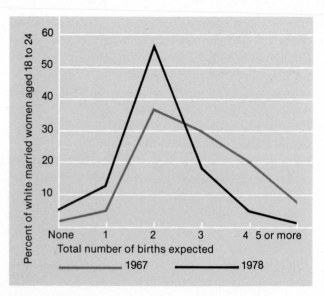

FIGURE 19.3

This graph shows the number of children various percentages of married white women aged eighteen to twenty-four expected to have in 1967 and in 1978. In 1967, 44.5 percent of women in this age bracket expected to have two children or fewer, and 55.5 percent expected to have three or more. In 1978, however, 73.5 percent expected to have two or fewer children, and 26.5 percent expected to have three or more—a significant shift in only eleven years. (Adapted from Census Bureau, 1979, p. 26)

roles other than or in addition to those of wife and mother. The nationwide legalization of abortion by a 1973 Supreme Court decision, to which the women's movement gave substantial impetus, has helped make these options more of a reality. In 1977, according to the Center for Disease Control, 1,079,430 legal abortions were performed in the United States. It has been suggested, too, that the heightened environmental concern of recent years has played its part in changing our reproductive patterns. Organizations that have sprung up recently have helped make people aware that the old pattern of large families threatens eventual disaster through overpopulation and destruction of the environment. These organizations have made a concerted effort to encourage people to limit family size, remain childless, or adopt children (Matras, 1977).

However, neither the women's movement nor the

environmental movement began to have a substantial impact on the national consciousness until after 1970. By then, the birth rate had already been falling sharply for more than a decade. Though these forces may be contributing factors, they were certainly not the initial, or necessarily the ultimate, cause of the decline in fertility.

Economic factors

The low fertility of the 1930s is often explained in economic terms. This was the time of the Great Depression, and it seems plausible that fertility was low because people could not afford to have children. Similarly, many observers (for example, Becker, 1960) account for the high birth rate after World War II by saying that prosperity made large families economically feasible again. But the facts do not fit this interpretation. The birth rate did hit a historic low during the Depression, but it had already been falling sharply throughout the prosperous decade of the 1920s. Although fertility was high in the prosperous 1950s, it declined rapidly in the no less prosperous early 1960s. Moreover, fertility today is below Depression levels, though our current economic problems are hardly comparable to the conditions of the 1930s. In fact, the response of the birth rate to economic conditions has generally been slight. Economics alone does not explain the baby boom or the decline in the birth rate that followed it.

A more subtle, social-psychological explanation has also been advanced, which hinges not so much on objective economic conditions as on *expectations*. According to this theory, young married couples of the 1960s and 1970s became accustomed to the high standard of living in which they were raised during the prosperous postwar years, and decided to limit their family size in order to maintain that standard. Forced by economic inflation to choose between a new home and a second (or third) child, many couples nowadays may be inclined to pick the former. People who grew up during the Depression and World War II, by contrast, having spent their formative years under conditions of scarcity, may have set their sights lower. Since they were not conditioned to expect a high material standard of living, when times improved after the war they did not hesitate to use their new resources to have large families (Becker, 1960). This theory has a certain plausibility,

but just how much of the falling birth rate it actually accounts for is very hard to determine.

Birth control

Perhaps the most commonly cited reason for the decline in fertility in the United States is the recent widespread use of birth control, especially the diaphragm, the birth-control pill, the intrauterine device (IUD), and—less common but still a significant and extremely controversial factor—abortion. At least in part because of the availability of these techniques, contraception for child-spacing purposes in the early years of marriage has become more common and much more effective. Whereas a decade ago, about 40 percent of married women between the ages of twenty and twenty-four used contraception prior to their first pregnancy, today that figure has climbed to nearly 65 percent (Rindfuss and Westoff, 1974).

It is important to note, however, that birth-control methods do not determine whether people will *want* to have a child or not; they merely make it easier not to have one if that is the preference. And even in this role, the importance of birth control may be somewhat overrated. The low fertility of the 1930s, for example, was achieved in the absence of most of today's contraceptive methods. Moreover, in many European countries, where there has not been the rapid diffusion of contraceptive techniques that has occurred in the United States, fertility is as low as it is here. Thus there is no firm proof that a falling birth rate is really a *direct result* of safer and more readily available contraceptives, though clearly the two are related.

It is certainly true that modern methods of contraception have come into widespread use in our society with remarkable rapidity. Evidently, when the motivation for fertility control already exists, people will eagerly adopt any methods or devices that are likely to make contraception cheaper, safer, or more reliable. As we pointed out earlier, the less sophisticated techniques of the late nineteenth century (chiefly the condom and the douche) were taken up with enthusiasm by the middle class—in the United States as well as in Europe—once the economic advantages of contraception became apparent. Incentive, rather than technology, was the key factor.

Interestingly, the widespread motivation to control births is also reflected in a change in the basic nature of contraceptive practices. With the more traditional contraceptive methods, the contraceptive device or method must be used before or during each separate sex act. But today many contraceptive devices, such as the pill and the IUD, are used independently of the sex act, and a separate, additional action is necessary to reverse their effect: that is, a woman must stop taking the pill or have the IUD removed if she wishes to become pregnant. The popularity of these techniques may be both symptom and cause of a subtle but pervasive shift in our attitudes toward birth control. It seems possible that we are well on the way toward accepting contraception as the normal, rather than the exceptional, practice; it is increasingly the case that conception, rather than the avoidance of conception, must be deliberately chosen and actively pursued (Westoff, 1976).

TRENDS IN THE FUTURE

Toward zero population growth

We do not fully understand why the baby boom occurred, and we do not know whether another one will occur. But we do know that, setting aside the issue of migration, if the present low fertility rate persists, the *rate* at which our population is increasing will gradually decline. By the middle of the next century, then, the population of the United States will level off at about 270 million (Census Bureau, 1979, p. 9). The number of births each year will equal the number of deaths, so no further increase will take place. This state of equilibrium, which many see as the essential goal if we are to avoid overtaxing the capacity of our environment to feed and support us, is known as zero population growth, or ZPG.

It would seem logical that the way to achieve ZPG is for parents to have only enough children to replace themselves—that is, two children per family on the average. (To be more exact, the average number of children per couple should be slightly greater—perhaps 2.1 or 2.2—to compensate for those people who do not marry or do not survive long enough to have children.) Many people are surprised to learn that in the United States this has already been achieved. In 1972, the total fertility rate was 2,022 births per 1,000 couples—below the replacement level (which is now 2,110) for the first time in this nation's history—and it has since fallen even lower (to 1,826, as we have seen). Yet in 1979, the number of births was 3.5 million and the number of deaths 1.9 million, making for a net increase in population (ignoring immigration and emigration) of 1.7 million people. Evidently, then, we have not yet reached ZPG; but why not?

Part of the answer is that the replacement level must be maintained for a period of at least twenty-five years before ZPG is actually attained. The population of the United States has a great deal of "momentum" built into its age structure. There are currently many young people in their childbearing years, and comparatively few older people. The people born during the baby boom now represent a substantial portion of the total population, and they are just passing through the prime years of their reproductive lives. Even though they are having children at an all-time low rate, the mere fact of their numbers means that they will add significantly to the population.

A balance between deaths and births will be attained only when the baby-boom generation starts to reach retirement age—around the years 2010–2020—if nothing else changes. During that period the rate of population growth will begin to flatten out and will probably become stationary by about 2040 (see Figure 19.4). Thus if today's low birth rate persists, it *will* lead to zero population growth—not immediately, but in the reasonably near future. Of course, we should note here that all these projections depend on our assumption that neither the fertility rate nor the mortality rate will change significantly during the next half-century. The occurrence of the baby boom should serve to remind us that we should place only a cautious faith in such assumptions.

In addition, although we may attain a balance between births and deaths within the next three or four decades, we still may not reach absolute ZPG. This is because each year the United States receives about a half million legal immigrants, thousands of illegal immigrants (mainly from Latin America), and large numbers of refugees (in recent years primarily from Eastern Europe, Southeast Asia, and Latin America, notably Cuba). In the years ahead there is likely to be increasing pressure to take in an even larger number of immigrants from parts of the world where the rate of population growth is outstripping the rate of increased food production or economic growth.

THE 1980 CENSUS: PROBLEMS AND PROJECTIONS

Every decade, an unusual assortment of personalities—from first ladies and community leaders to athletes, entertainers, and cartoon characters—urge us to be counted in the census. They participate in a massive media campaign involving print, radio, and television—an extensive effort made not simply for reasons of good citizenship: the census has important ramifications. The 1980 census, for example, is expected to result in the shift of fourteen seats in the House of Representatives in response to the shift of population to the Sun Belt. Even greater impact is felt locally in the allocation, based on census figures, of $50-billion in federal funds: an undercount could be very costly to a community. The census is also important in confirming social trends and providing business and industry with information about the changing marketplace. So census data is important.

To collect it in 1980, the Census Bureau will have spent over $1 billion to deal with the 3.3 billion individual answers it receives—amassing, tabulating, recording, and then analyzing them, the latter a nine-month job for a battery of computers. Nearly 300,000 census workers will have been involved, 250,000 of them enumerators working from four to eight weeks and earning from $4 to $5 an hour. Around 83 percent of American households will have received the short form in the mail. It asks nineteen questions, such as each resident's name, sex, age, marital status, race (fifteen choices here), and whether the respondent is of Spanish/Hispanic origin. (Such specifics were requested by minority leaders who believe their numbers were previously overlooked.) The short form also asks about one's residence—number of rooms, owned or rented, shared or private entrance, partial or full plumbing. Seventeen percent of households will have received the long form, which asks forty-six additional questions about subjects such as education and income levels, physical and mental disability, level of English spoken, and type of heating used.

Thus the figures are important and great effort is involved in collecting them—but are they valid? Three factors compromise their accuracy, and have evolved into particularly salient issues concerning the 1980 census.

The accuracy of the census has always been controversial; even the original 1790 count was criticized on these grounds by George Washington, who railed against the "indolence of the mass" (who may have feared a census-based tax) and the "want of activity" by many census takers. In some ways, little has changed: some census takers still hesitate to venture deep into the crowded big-city neighborhoods where minority populations are densest. Yet these are the areas for which the most is at stake in the 1980 count. According to Maynard Jackson, Atlanta's mayor, in 1970 his city was "cheated out of $11.7-million in federal aid and almost 6,000 jobs" because of an undercount (*Time*, March 31, 1980, p. 25). Although an estimated 2.5 percent of the population as a whole

was missed in the 1970 census (5.3 million people), the undercount for blacks was around 7.7 percent; for whites, only 1.9 percent. (For young black men, the figure may be as high as 18 percent.) Thus big cities lost tens of millions in federal funds as the result of undercounting, a problem that has led some to suggest that modern sampling techniques such as those used in public-opinion polls would be better for the job.

The accuracy of the census has been questioned in two other areas: tax evaders and illegal aliens. Although the Census Bureau insists that their information is kept confidential, those who do not report their full income to the Internal Revenue Service (IRS) are unlikely to report it on their census forms. "When I tell people that the IRS can't get into the census files, they just smile," says a former Census Bureau offical (*Newsweek*, March 24, 1980, p. 40). Illegal aliens are also unlikely to put themselves on record, even though bureau officials "proudly cite their refusal during World War II to allow the War Department to have the names and addresses of Japanese Americans who had registered in the 1940 census" (*Time*, March 31, 1980, p. 25).

In spite of the controversy surrounding its accuracy, what can the 1980 census be expected to show? Based on projections from updates that the Census Bureau makes throughout the decade, the 1980 census will tell us the following:

The growth of population has slowed. At 9 percent, it is second only to the 7.2 percent of the Depression years.

The number of households grew by 25 percent, with the average number of household members decreasing from 3.1 to 2.7 persons.

People are staying single longer. More than half of women and two-thirds of men age twenty to twenty-four have never married. By age thirty-five, however, the percentage who have never married has remained stable.

People are moving to the Sun Belt. Nearly all the nation's population growth in the 1970s was in the South and West. New York, Pennsylvania, Rhode Island, and Washington, D.C., all lost population.

Americans are getting older. The median age is up from 28.1 in 1970 to 30.2. People over sixty-five will soon outnumber teenagers.

The black population is growing faster than that of whites (16 percent and 7.2 percent respectively), but the percentage of increase of "others" is greater than both: 73 percent. This is partly because of the influx of refugees. Still, whites represent 86 percent of the population, blacks 12 percent, and others, including Orientals, 2 percent.

More people—black and white—are moving to the suburbs.

Our incomes, in terms of buying power, haven't changed. But, though the proportion of Americans living below the poverty line decreased, the actual numbers of poor people increased, reversing a trend.

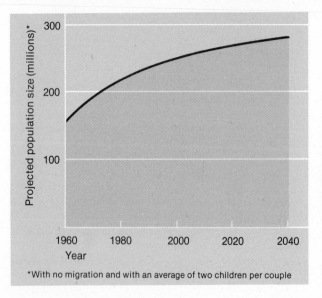

FIGURE 19.4

Because people born during the postwar baby boom are now at childbearing age, the population of the United States is likely to continue growing through 2020, even if most couples decide to have only two children. By 2040, however, it is projected that the rate of population growth will level off, leading eventually to zero population growth—if today's low birth rate continues. (Bogue, 1969)

In spite of a decreasing birth rate, the United States will probably not reach zero population growth because many immigrants and refugees enter the country annually. Here, Vietnamese immigrants arrive in Florida. (© Alex Webb/ Magnum)

Changes in age characteristics

One important consequence of reduced fertility is a change in the age structure of the population—most notably, an increasing proportion of older people. The age pyramids in Figure 19.5 show how an evolution of this type has occurred in the population of the United States over the past hundred years. The first pyramid shows the age composition of the United States in 1870, when, because of the high fertility and high mortality characteristic of the preindustrial nations of the past, the majority of people were young.

The pyramid for 1970 indicates some interesting changes. The decrease in the segment of the popula-

tion between ages twenty-five and forty-four reflects the low fertility of the 1930s, while the postwar baby boom is represented by the swell in the proportion of ten- to twenty-four-year-olds. The recent decline in fertility is shown by the indentation in the two age groups from birth to four years and from five to nine years.

The third pyramid shows the age structure of the population in the year 2000, projected by the Census Bureau on the basis of a replacement-level fertility rate. The major change from 1970 will be the reduced number of people under the age of forty—those born after the onset of lowered fertility during the 1960s. The baby boom itself will be visible as a bulge centered on the age brackets from thirty-five to fifty-four. There will

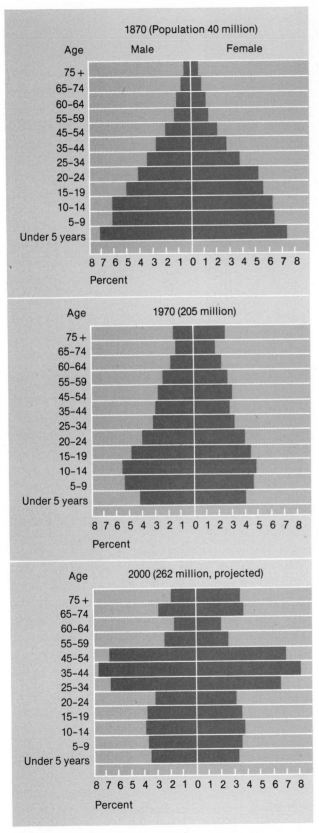

FIGURE 19.5

These three "age pyramids" show the age structure of the U.S. population in 1870 and 1970, and the Census Bureau's projection for 2000 at a replacement-level fertility rate. (1870 and 1970: Matras, 1977, pp. 60–61; 2000: Census Bureau, 1977, p. 60)

be a smaller bulge of five- to thirteen-year-olds, representing the children whose parents were part of the record baby-boom generation—a kind of "echo" of the boom.

These pyramids clearly show a trend toward a population with a higher median age and a greater proportion of people over retirement age. In 1870, for example, the median age in the United States was just slightly over twenty. By 1980 it had risen to thirty, and when (or perhaps we should say if) ZPG is achieved, the median age will be about thirty-seven. Similarly, people aged sixty-five and over, who now constitute 11 percent of the population in this country, will represent 19 percent by the year 2000. There will be 55 million more people over sixty-five than there are at present.

The age structure of a population affects both its potential productivity and its consumption demands. A society with very high fertility, and therefore a very youthful age structure, spends a large proportion of its total resources on infants and children who are not yet productive members of the society. By contrast, in a society whose age structure has a bulge in the middle, a larger fraction of the population is part of the productive work force, and productivity per capita tends to be high. Thus we may gain economically from changes in our age structure by being able to devote a significant proportion of our resources to further economic development or to programs aimed at improving the quality of life in our country.

But changes in the age structure may also bring problems. For example, the baby boom created a great need for more schools and teachers. The opportunities thus created led many people to train for a career in education—including many of the baby-boom children themselves as they reached college age in the 1960s and 1970s. Now these people are faced with the consequences of our lowered birth rate. School enrollments are leveling off or even declining, many teachers are

People aged sixty-five and over, who now constitute 11 percent of the U.S. population, will represent 19 percent by the year 2000. (Martin Adler Levick/Black Star)

finding it hard to get jobs, and others are being laid off. Retrenchment of programs and faculty has become an important issue in colleges and universities today.

The presence of more people at prime working age may also lead to difficulties. As most students are aware, the employment market has become glutted with qualified people, job advancement has slowed, and unemployment has increased. Early retirement may be one answer; but, given our society's emphasis on work, what will the retired then do with the rest of their lives? Senior citizens' and civil-rights organizations have begun to press for legislation against mandatory retirement at a specific age. Furthermore, early retirement combined with increased longevity have begun to put a strain on our social security system; more than 50 percent of social security recipients start collecting benefits at age sixty-two (*The New York Times*, January 28, 1979), and the majority receive benefits for many more years than Congress anticipated when it passed the Social Security Act of 1935. Though other factors, such as the pace of economic growth and technological change, may have a greater impact on employment patterns than changes in age structure do, the potential impact of age-structure changes is still likely to be considerable.

Another possible problem has to do with care of the increasing number of aged people. As *life expectancy*—the age to which a person now at a given age can, on the average, expect to live—increases, and the cost of medical care soars, more of the society's resources will obviously have to go toward meeting the needs of the elderly—who tend to be, at least in our present scheme of things, economically unproductive. Historically, the task of caring for the elderly has generally fallen to the individual family; but in Western societies today, more and more of the responsibility has been assumed by the state. Between 2010 and 2030, people born during the postwar baby boom will be in their retirement years, and the cost of supporting and caring for them will presumably be borne by the relatively smaller group of prime-age adults born after 1970. Resources may have to be poured into the training of medical and social-service personnel and into the construction of residential, recreational, and health-care facilities for an aging population. Yet not long after these facilities have been built and these people trained, the need for them (like the need for teachers in the 1970s) may lessen once again, as the numbers of the large baby-boom crop of adults diminish.

Now that we have examined some of the major population trends in the United States, let us consider the situation confronted by developing nations. What are the consequences of rapid population growth in these countries? What are the implications—demographic and political—of fertility-control programs in developing nations? We will examine these and other questions in the section that follows.

Population trends in the developing nations

Today, the developing nations have entered a phase that in some ways resembles the first phase of the demographic transition experienced by the industrialized nations of Western Europe: their mortality rates have sharply declined, and their birth rates have rocketed upward. In the developing areas of the world as a whole, the birth rate is nearly forty per 1,000 per year—more than two and a half times the rate of fifteen per 1,000 (Population Reference Bureau, 1978). In parts of Africa, it is even higher, reaching fifty-two per 1,000. The second phase, in which birth rates as well as death rates decline, is not yet in sight.

It is not at all clear whether there will even be a second phase, especially in view of the fact that the nations that are developing today are not comparable to Western Europe as it was several hundred years ago. First of all, the decline in mortality in industrialized societies occurred gradually over a period of several centuries. By contrast, in developing nations this decline has been much more rapid, occurring primarily during the twentieth century. Likewise, whereas the gradual decline in mortality that occurred in Western Europe and the United States was accompanied by considerable cultural and economic change, the sudden decline in mortality in today's developing countries has often been achieved without any major improvements in living conditions, without much increase in the average person's income, and without significant social change or major economic development. In fact, the causes of the decline in mortality did not, in most cases, themselves arise from changes *within* these societies; rather, they have been almost wholly the result of foreign assistance. For example, death rates have been affected by public-health programs run by international agencies. A well-known case is that of Sri Lanka (formerly called Ceylon). Prior to the mid-1940s, the death rate from malaria in Sri Lanka was extremely high; between 1934 and 1935, for example, about 100,000 persons died from this disease. Then, in 1946, under a cooperative program with the World Health Organization, DDT was sprayed throughout those areas that had a high incidence of malaria. This insecticide virtually eradicated the type of mosquito that carries malaria. Cases of the disease immediately declined, producing a *34 percent* drop in the death rate within a single year; by 1954, the death rate had been cut in half (Davis, 1956), and by 1960 there were only about five malaria cases per 100,000 population (Barlow, 1967). The experience of Sri Lanka is not unique; similar developments have taken place in nations throughout the developing world (see Figure 19.6).

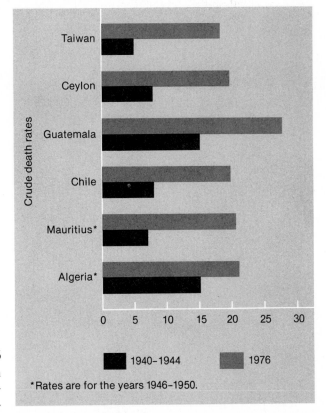

FIGURE 19.6

This chart shows changes in the crude death rates of six developing nations between 1940–1944 and 1976.

CONSEQUENCES OF RAPID POPULATION GROWTH

Age structure and economic development

The combination of high fertility and relatively low mortality that is now typical of the developing world tends to produce a population structure in which there is an extremely high proportion of young people: the decline in mortality occurs primarily among infants and young children, and most of the girls who survive to childbearing age will subsequently have children of their own, further increasing the ratio of young to old. In many areas, well over 40 percent of the population is under fifteen years of age. This high proportion of children puts the economics of developing countries under a special strain. In order for a society to achieve eco-

nomic growth, it must be productive enough to meet the future as well as the present needs of the people. That is, not all the economic resources can be consumed; there must be some savings for future investment. Children, however, consume much more than they produce. Thus, in a society with a young age structure, few resources are available for investment in economic expansion; most resources must be used simply to prevent the standard of living from falling below the subsistence level. Kingsley Davis (1976) estimates that "With a constant population, a rate of investment of 3

The typical population trends in developing countries such as India are high fertility and relatively low mortality. As a result, a very high proportion of the population—often more than 40 percent—is less than fifteen years old. (Ira Kirschenbrum/Stock, Boston)

to 5 percent of national income is required to produce a 1 percent increase in per capita income, and with a population growing at 3 percent, 12 to 20 percent of GNP is required."

Urbanization and urban control

Another problem connected with rapid population growth in developing societies is that of swift urbanization and urban growth, which take place without corresponding social change. According to a report issued in 1980 by the United Nations Fund for Population Activities, about a billion people will be added to the population of Asia within the next two decades, swelling the already overcrowded urban centers. By the year 2000, it is predicted, Bombay will have 17.1 million residents, Calcutta 16.7 million, Jakarta 16.6 million, and Cairo 13.1 million. Services and facilities in the cities of the poorer nations cannot possibly expand to keep pace with the growing number of people who need them. Kingsley Davis describes one of the problems created by this failure—poor housing:

It is not only Caracas [Venezuela] that has thousands of squatters living in self-constructed junk houses on land that does not belong to them. By whatever name they are called, the squatters are to be found in all major cities in the poorer countries. [In the outlying areas of Baghdad, Iraq] are the

Effects on world ZPG

All the specific problems we have been discussing are merely aspects of a larger, more fundamental, and graver problem: the threat posed by the continued high birth rate in the developing nations to these nations' survival, and to the resources and political stability of the world as a whole. The industrialized nations are already so close to zero population growth that it makes relatively little difference how soon they reach it. Precisely when the developing nations stabilize their populations will be the decisive factor in determining how many people inhabit our planet in the coming century.

As we saw earlier, even after the birth rate has been cut to replacement levels, population continues to grow for a long time before finally leveling off. Using different time schedules for achieving replacement fertility levels (that is, an average of one daughter for each woman of childbearing age), Thomas Frejka (1973) has made population projections for the world. Had replacement fertility been achieved in 1975, 5.7 billion people would inhabit the earth in 2100. With a delay in attaining replacement fertility of just five years, that number would increase to 6.4 billion. Achieving replacement fertility by 2000—perhaps the most realistic projection—would produce a stable population in 2100 of 8.4 billion, more than twice the present number. If replacement fertility were not achieved until 2040, the world's population would reach 15 billion before growth ceased.

It is clear, then, that time is crucial; each year that lowered fertility is postponed means additional hundreds of millions of people on this planet by the time

sarifa areas, characterized by self-built reed huts; these areas account for about 45 percent of the housing in the entire city and are devoid of amenities, including even latrines. (1965, p. 52)

In Caracas, Venezuela, as in many other major cities in developing countries, thousands of people migrate from the countryside to look for work. Because jobs are scarce, many of them cannot afford decent housing and must live in the streets or in shacks they build from boards, sheets of metal, bricks, cardboard, and any other makeshift materials they can find. (Ken Heyman)

the world population levels off. The underlying threat, it almost goes without saying, is that population growth puts skyrocketing demands on the finite supply of world resources. Minerals for metalworking, fossil fuels, above-ground resources such as wood and unpolluted water—all these (at least in the forms in which they are currently used) may run out, and scientists may not develop alternatives to our current technology, or may not be able to develop them in time. Most serious, perhaps, are the limitations on supplies of food. This is a problem that was first pointed out over 150 years ago by Thomas Malthus.

THE MALTHUSIAN FORMULATION AND FERTILITY-CONTROL PROGRAMS

The Reverend Thomas Robert Malthus (1766–1834) was an English clergyman and gentleman scholar whose ideas have cast a long and frightening shadow. Malthus was an amateur student of mathematics and economics. In 1798 he published the brief first version of an essay that, elaborated and expanded through several subsequent editions, was to become one of the most influential works of the nineteenth century. Its title was *An Essay on the Principle of Population, or a View of Its Past and Present Effects on Human Happiness, with an Inquiry into Our Prospects Respecting the Future Removal or Mitigation of the Evils Which It Occasions.* Its contents were grim.

Malthus pointed out that the human population increases geometrically—that is, by multiplication (2, 4, 8, 16, 32)—while the food supply increases arithmetically, by addition (2, 4, 6, 8, 10). Consequently, Malthus believed, the food supply serves as a check on the human population. Whenever the population exceeds the capacity of the land to feed it, the result is inevitably starvation, pestilence, and war. These calamities increase the mortality rate and thus serve to bring down the rate of population growth, or even reverse it, for a time. But as soon as the food supply catches up with the population, population growth always begins again, and the same dismal pattern inevitably repeats itself.

An unpleasant corollary of Malthus' theory is that measures taken to increase productivity or raise the standard of living for people are, according to the the-ory, ultimately doomed to failure. Reducing hunger and disease simply lowers the death rate and gives more people the opportunity to have children. As a result, the population will rise until it is again pressing against the subsistence level, and all the gains will be wiped out. Since Malthus rejected contraception and abortion on moral grounds, he saw celibacy, along with voluntary abstinence from sexual relations in marriage, as the only hope of escape from this vicious cycle. But it was a slim hope; Malthus realized that few people would or could accept these restraints.

Population growth in industrialized societies, as we have seen, has not followed the pattern that Malthusian theory predicts. With increases in the standard of living, the rate of population growth in these societies has dropped sharply, not risen. Today we explain this turn of events in terms of the demographic transition—a phenomenon that Malthus lacked the historical perspective to understand, for he lived in the midst of it. But the ghost of Malthus still hovers over the developing world. There we often find the combination of rapid population growth and widespread poverty and hunger that the Malthusian model projects. Does this mean that Malthus was right after all? Many observers believe so; they readily accept the idea that hunger found in developing societies is a natural and inevitable result of rapid population growth. Hence, they advocate attempts to curb the growth of these populations. They are, of course, interested in fostering economic development at the same time; but they argue that population control can itself aid the economic development of developing nations. Ansley J. Coale and Edgar M. Hoover (1958), for example, measuring population growth in relation to economic growth, estimate that in a country such as India, a 50 percent reduction in fertility over a period of twenty-five years would result in a 40 percent increase in per capita income over thirty years, and a doubling of per capita income within sixty years.

Although birth-control programs are generally very expensive to operate and difficult to administer, and there is a great deal of controversy about their effectiveness, estimates like these have convinced many government leaders that fertility-control programs are a worthwhile use of their resources. As a result, there has been an upsurge in family-planning programs in developing nations. It is not easy to assess the impact of these pro-

Family-planning information is distributed from a station in Bombay, India. In this program, men receive a reward for getting a vasectomy. (Raymond Darolle/Sygma)

grams. After all, they are very recent—the earliest ones, introduced in India, date only from the 1950s—and an undertaking as large, complicated, and innovative as a national fertility-control program cannot be expected to show results very quickly. So far, however, the results appear to be mixed. In certain areas of Asia, notably China, South Korea, Taiwan, and Hong Kong, fertility-control programs seem to have been quite successful. However, in much of Africa—an area in which few countries have any kind of population-control policy—there continue to be high birth rates despite the adoption of such programs. Morocco, which adopted a program in 1968, only reduced its birth rate from 48 per 1,000 in 1967 to 45 per 1,000 by 1977 (Population Reference Bureau, 1978).

Proponents of family planning programs claim that a well-administered program can substantially reduce the birth rate and simultaneously encourage social and economic change. Opponents, though, feel that the birth rate reduction is too small to justify the cost of such programs. The most vehement critics say that fertility-control programs are an unnecessary use of limited financial resources because the birth rate will decrease naturally in the wake of social and economic changes such as increased literacy, a higher standard of living, and greater industrialization. Investing in fertility-control programs diverts scarce resources from edu-

cation, transportation, technological development, and even agricultural production. Thus, instituting fertility-control programs, these observers argue, may actually *retard* the transition to low fertility.

Cultural obstacles to fertility-control programs

The greatest obstacle to fertility control has little to do with whether contraceptives are available or whether people understand their use. It is rather that many of the social, cultural, and economic features of developing societies continue to encourage *high* fertility, no matter how well informed people may be about contraceptive methods. As we have already mentioned, until very recently the developing nations have had enormously high mortality rates. Thus high birth rates have always been essential to their survival. Customs and traditions that contribute to high fertility, such as early marriage and large families, are characteristic of these societies, and such customs die out slowly, if at all. In fact, leaving aside the threat of overpopulation, large families are still advantageous in many ways to people of the developing world. Not only do large families counterbalance high death rates (and mortality is still considerably higher in these regions than in Europe or the United States), but children are a valuable source

Children provide a valuable source of labor in the developing world—one of the advantages of large families that serves as a great obstacle to the adoption of contraception methods. These children prepare food as their mother washes laundry in the delta village of El Bayad, Egypt. (© Bernard Pierre Wolff 1979/Photo Researchers)

of labor. As one Indian peasant observed, "A rich man has his machines, I have my children" (Mamdani, 1974, p. 17). In addition, parents depend on their children to care for them in old age. Since infant mortality is high, a couple might need to have six children in order to be assured of having one or two survive to adulthood.

Kingsley Davis (1955) has suggested that the extended families characteristic of developing societies also encourage high birth rates. Under this system, the costs of rearing children as well as child-care responsibilities are shared by all family members rather than falling on the parents' shoulders alone. Thus some of the strain of child rearing is removed, making it easier for couples to marry early and bear many children. Another factor that encourages high birth rates is the segregation of gender roles, which confines women largely to domestic duties and reproductive functions.

Yet another cultural obstacle to the reduction of fertility in developing countries is the growing resent-

ment of and resistance to the intrusion of Western technology on traditional ways. Government officials and individual citizens alike often feel that they are being exploited by Western multinational corporations that are more interested in making a profit by, for example, marketing infant formula (see Garson, 1977) or testing experimental contraceptive drugs than in helping these countries lower their birth rates.

These and other cultural obstacles lead many experts to believe that extensive social, economic, and institutional changes must take place in developing countries before their fertility can decline. For example, the developing societies may eventually evolve programs that provide financial support for the elderly, as our own social security system and medicare programs are intended to do. This would lessen the need to have many children as "insurance" against poverty and isolation in old age. Changes in marriage patterns and attitudes toward the roles of women, as well as increased educational opportunities, may also in time contribute to lower fertility. Delaying or forgoing marriage and childbirth, for example, would almost certainly result in a lower birth rate, and would give women the opportunity to pursue other interests. Expanding the role of women beyond motherhood tends to encourage them to want fewer children. There is some evidence of a relationship between increased literacy among women and their use of contraception. Not only does the ability to read enable women to learn about birth-control techniques and use them correctly, but it also makes them more suited to jobs outside the home and therefore more likely to want to limit the size of their families.

It is not known exactly which of these changes, if any, would be most likely to bring about a demographic transition in developing countries comparable to the one that took place in the Western world. As we have pointed out, sociologists are not even sure what the causes of the transition were in Europe itself—or what parts industrialization, urbanization, contraception, economic factors, and such social factors as environmental concerns and the women's movement have played in the process.

PROBLEMS OF ECONOMIC DISTRIBUTION

It has been suggested that the current focus on birth control in the developing world—with or without supportive institutional changes—is misdirected. The real issue, some social scientists claim, is economic progress, not contraception and family planning. A study by William Rich (1973), for example, shows that with more equitable distribution of economic benefits, birth rates tend to fall, even in countries with low per capita incomes and rudimentary family-planning programs.

Furthermore, many people have asked whether the Malthusian perspective is the right one to employ in

the first place. Is it really true that there is not enough food to go around? The all too familiar images of emaciated adults and children with the swollen bellies of malnutrition that we see in news magazines and on television are commonly taken as proof that there are already too many people in the developing world, and not enough food to sustain them. Certainly there is much hunger in developing nations. One recent estimate indicates that perhaps 70 million people are chronically malnourished, while less conservative sources have put the figure at several hundred million (Eberstadt, 1976). And there is no doubt that in recent years millions—especially the very old and the very young—have died of starvation or the diseases that afflict the undernourished. But these horrors are by no

Starving mother and child in Ethiopia. Is starvation the result of overpopulation—or inequality of the distribution of resources? (Taurus Photos)

means the inevitable result of overpopulation. In the words of one expert, Nick Eberstadt, "There is no . . . justification for hunger of any kind anywhere; enough food is produced each year to feed everyone on earth comfortably" (1976, p. 34). Eberstadt goes on to point out that food production per person is actually increasing, rather than declining as many imagine. To the question of why people nevertheless starve, he gives a very simple answer: "It is inequality and inequality alone that can be blamed for hunger today." This is, of course, an oversimplification of the problem. Consider Cambodia, once one of the great rice-producing countries of Southeast Asia: hundreds of thousands have died of starvation in that country in recent years, not because of inequality, but because agricultural production and distribution have been disrupted by continuous warfare in the region.

However, Eberstadt's basic point is valid. Socioeconomic inequality—both between nations and between classes within nations—does affect food availability and consumption. People in the wealthier nations consume approximately 50 percent more calories and protein than those in the developing world. The average American eats nearly seven times more fat—mainly from animal sources—than the average Indian.

To make matters worse, only a limited amount of the surplus food produced by the wealthier nations is redistributed to the poorer ones. The 1972–1973 "food crisis" provides a case in point. In 1972, bad weather caused per capita world grain production to drop for the first time in almost twenty years. One of the nations hardest hit was the Soviet Union, which suffered substantial crop failure. While no one was in danger of starvation there, the political leaders of the country had committed themselves to increasing meat production, and to do this grain was needed for livestock feed (Eberstadt, 1976). The U.S.S.R. therefore purchased enormous quantities of wheat on the world market—much of it from the United States. One result of this purchase was a sharp rise in food prices in the United States, as demand outpaced supply. While Americans were grumbling about paying more for their bread, however, more serious consequences were being felt in the developing world. The amount of food available from the rich nations for famine relief was diminished, and, according to one estimate, more than 1 million people in India alone may have died as a result (Douglas, 1976).

Socioeconomic inequality within developing nations also contributes to food scarcity, chronic ill health, and a high death rate. In one district of Bangladesh, about one-quarter of the people own no land at all. The annual death rate for this group is nearly 36 per 1,000—about four times that of the U.S. population. But among farmers who own at least three acres of land, the death rate is about 12 per 1,000—only slightly higher than in many industrialized nations (Douglas, 1976).

An interesting case history in this connection is that of the "green revolution"—the introduction of new crop varieties that have been specially developed for their high yields. The improved strains of corn, wheat, and rice that have been bred in laboratories and agricultural research stations over the past two decades are capable of increasing yields per hectare (one hundred acres) as much as fivefold (Kirk, 1980, p. 947). In theory, use of modern agricultural techniques, along with the new varieties of "miracle rice," could enable a nation like Bangladesh not only to feed its own population but actually to export food to other nations.

Yet the green revolution, which so many people hoped would be part of the solution to inequalities of food distribution, has in practice often become part of the problem. Ironically, there is evidence that in many cases the introduction of these new crop strains has actually increased the extent of inequality within developing nations. The reasons for this provide an interesting lesson in economics. Among the advantages of the high-yield varieties are their great responsiveness to fertilizer and water. But these very qualities tend to make them impractical for small farmers, who do not have the money to invest in costly synthetic fertilizers and irrigation systems. Similarly, many of the new strains have proven extremely susceptible to parasites and diseases, so pesticides too are frequently required. The energy crisis has made fertilizers and pesticides increasingly expensive (Kirk, 1980, pp. 947–948). Because of these factors, the green revolution—even though it has been very successful in increasing overall food production in some areas—has done little to help those who need help most: the small farmers. What typically happened was this:

Because farming was becoming more profitable for the large landholders and because they were increasing their use of machinery, these owners tended to enlarge their holdings at the expense of small farmers. The higher yields on the large farms also depressed grain prices as grain supplies increased. The small farmer, who was unable to afford the new seeds, fertilizers, and pesticides (and so whose yields remained the same), experienced a drop in income. An end result of these and other forces was often a decrease in the number of small farmers and sharecroppers and an increase both in the number of rural laborers without their own land and in the number of displaced farmers migrating to the already overcrowded cities, where they joined the ranks of the unemployed. Thus the first decade of the green revolution saw the gap between the richest and poorest in many countries increase by 10 to 20 percent. While the rich got richer, the poor remained poor. (Kirk, 1980, p. 948)

Despite these inequities, it is important to note that the green revolution has by no means been a failure. It has demonstrated the great potential that exists for increasing crop yields through selective plant breeding and improved farming methods. It has also demonstrated the importance of developing seeds that provide better yields under the financial and topographical limitations actually faced by the small farmer, not just under the ideal conditions of the experimental farm. Finally, the green revolution has stimulated the growth

of research institutes in developing countries, which are crucial to a new, "second-generation" attack on the world's food problems that is now getting under way (Kirk, 1980, p. 948).

In view of the enormous potential for increased agricultural productivity worldwide, many observers now believe that limited natural resources, rather than inadequate food supplies, are what will ultimately determine the population size that a given region can support. By the same token, the lack of natural resources in certain parts of the world makes it improbable that enough nonagricultural industry can ever be developed to employ the growing numbers of displaced farmers. For example, India is the only country in all of South Asia that is known to have sufficient iron ore and coal to support development of heavy industry (Myrdal, 1971, p. 67). The rapid depletion of the world's finite natural resources and the effects on the environment of

Small-scale farming at El Fayum oasis in Egypt. One ironic effect of the green revolution has been in many cases to force the small farmer off the land. (© Bernard Pierre Wolff 1979/ Photo Researchers)

the exploitation of those resources are the cause of increasing concern among population experts.

With all the issues we have described in this chapter, it is not surprising that population control is the subject of highly charged worldwide debate. Is world population growth a ticking time bomb, as some writers such as Paul R. Ehrlich (1968) have claimed? Or is it simply part of a huge process of social change whose ultimate shape and outcome we cannot envision? At this point, there is no way to tell for certain, and it is therefore difficult to determine the best ways of dealing with the situation. What we do know, however, is that bringing about basic alterations in people's reproductive attitudes and behavior—or in patterns of inequality—is not going to be easy. Any attempt to modify such basic cultural and economic patterns will encounter many obstacles—a subject that we will discuss further in Chapter 22.

Summary

During the seventeenth century, the Western nations entered a *demographic transition*, beginning with a high *birth rate* combined with a declining *death rate*; the next stage was marked by declining rates of both birth and death; in the third stage, birth and death rates were in virtual equilibrium at low levels—the situation that exists in these countries today.

In the post-transition United States, the death rate has been relatively low for some time, especially because of developments in medicine that have reduced the effects of disease. The birth rate has also been relatively low in recent decades, except for the "baby boom" of 1946-1957. Among the explanations that have been put forth for the decline in the U.S. birth rate are these: changing lifestyles and values, including changing attitudes toward childbearing and family size and concern about the effects of population pressure on the environment; economic factors, such as expectations of a high standard of living, which may induce couples to limit the number of children they have; and more widespread availability and use of contraceptive methods and abortion. As for the future, it is likely that the United States will eventually come very close to achieving *zero population growth* and that the age structure of the population will shift, with an increasing proportion of older people as *life expectancy* increases.

It cannot be predicted whether the developing nations will go through the same demographic transition as the United States and other Western industrialized countries. At present, they are experiencing dramatically high birth rates and declining death rates. These trends have profound implications for the age structure and economic development of these countries. Rapid population growth has also produced urbaniz ation and growth of cities, which have taken place so quickly that expansion of facilities and social services has not been able to keep up. The high birth rates of the developing nations threaten their survival and the resources and political stability of the world. In the Malthusian view, unchecked population inevitably increases faster than the food supply. Accordingly, many observers believe that fertility-control programs are the best solution. However, such programs face great cultural obstacles; their results have been mixed, and they have been widely criticized on practical and political grounds. Approaches that aim at increasing the food supply have also had only limited success, largely because of unequal distribution of food and agricultural resources within many developing countries.

Glossary

BIRTH RATE The proportion of the number of births per year to the total population in a society, usually expressed as the number of births per 1,000 population.

DEATH RATE The proportion of the number of deaths per year to the total population in a society, usually expressed as the number of deaths per 1,000 population.

DEMOGRAPHER A social scientist who specializes in the measurement and analysis of population changes.

FERTILITY RATE The number of births that 1,000 women would have in their lifetimes if, at each year of childbearing age, they experienced the birth rate occurring in the specified year. Thus, in 1977, the U.S. fertility rate was 1,857 births for the lifetimes of 1,000 women, or 1.8 births per woman.

LIFE EXPECTANCY The age to which a person now at a given age can, on the average, expect to live. In the United States, for example, a white male who is now twenty years old can expect to live fifty-one more years, to the age of seventy-one; a twenty-year-old white female can expect to live fifty-eight more years, to the age of seventy-eight.

MIGRATION The rate at which people move into (immigration) or out of (emigration) a society. The difference between immigration and emigration during a given period is the society's *net migration*.

MORTALITY RATE Same as *death rate*.

SEX RATIO The proportion of males to females in a society.

ZERO POPULATION GROWTH (ZPG) The state of equilibrium that results in a population when the number of births each year equals the number of deaths.

Recommended readings

Hauser, Phillip M. (ed.). *The Population Dilemma*. 2nd ed. Englewood Cliffs, N.J.: Prentice-Hall, 1973. Consists of discussions of the many facets of the world population problem, from population policy to fertility-control programs, natural resources, and economic development.

Matras, Judah. *An Introduction to Population: A Sociological Approach*. Englewood Cliffs, N.J.: Prentice-Hall, 1977. An exceptionally fine book that takes a distinctly social-structural view of the determinants of change in populations. It introduces the student to the sources, methods of measuring, and basic techniques for analyzing demographic data, and provides interesting illustrative case materials.

Petersen, William. *Population*, 3rd ed. New York: Macmillan, 1975. The most comprehensive and up-to-date text on population and society. The author analyzes both historical and contemporary population patterns.

Spengler, Joseph J. *Population and America's Future*. San Francisco: W.H. Freeman, 1975. A discussion by a noted economist of the prospects for various population patterns in the United States, focusing on the economic consequences of the alternative paths.

Tauber, Karl E., Larry L. Bumpass, and James A. Sweet (eds.). *Social Demography*. New York: Academic Press, 1978. This book reports the fruits of the 1975 conference on selected topics in social demography. Though difficult reading, the various papers convey an understanding of current work and knowledge in this field.

Westoff, Leslie, and Charles Westoff. *From Now to Zero: Fertility, Contraception, and Abortion in America*. Boston: Little, Brown, 1971. A review of fertility patterns in the United States. The authors present, in terms the lay reader can readily understand, the results of large sample surveys of reproductive behavior in the United States.

Wrigley, F. A. *Population and History*. New York: McGraw-Hill, 1969. An excellent, easy-to-read presentation of the social and economic determinants and consequences of historical population change.

The population of the Dobe Area !Kung

NANCY HOWELL

Since 1963, a group of anthropologists have been studying the !Kung people in the South African Republic of Botswana in order to compile a complete picture of their way of life. As can be seen by this excerpt, dangers to the existence of the population seem to arise from both physical and cultural factors.

. . . Detailed study of one contemporary hunting and gathering society, the !Kung, and consideration of the impact of various aspects of their way of life on demographic processes suggest that while we should expect some variation between different hunting and gathering populations, in general the hunters and gatherers are probably characterized by fertility and mortality levels that are relatively low by the standards of agricultural peoples, intermediate in level between agricultural and industrial peoples today. . . .

During the period 1963–1969, a total of 840 individuals who are linguistically and culturally !Kung (or Zhū/twāsi, as they call themselves) were encountered and registered as members of the study population in the Botswana side of the northern Kalahari Desert. . . . These 840 people were not all alive at any one period of time; instead, people were added as they were encountered by the investigators, as they moved into the area, or as they were born; and their numbers were reserved to them even if they died or left the area. . . .

The Crude Death Rates for the same period range from 6 per 1,000 in 1968 to 26 per 1,000 in 1965, with an overall rate of 16 per 1,000. For comparison, the CDR of the US in 1971 is approximately 9, and that of Botswana as a whole is 23. . . . The !Kung under study here, however, have no doctors or clinics to serve them in the Dobe Area and must travel long distances to receive western-type medicine. No doubt members of the expedition saved some lives with antibiotics, and perhaps the physician who worked with us in the field for a few weeks at a time on several occasions during the period had a substantial effect. More likely, the causes of death in the area have been reduced in the recent decades, and the age-composition of the population is such that the decline is very great in this population. Whatever the reason, the mortality of the population was extremely low during the period of observation. . . .

The second source of loss to the population is outmigration. The average rate over the period is 8 per 1,000. Total reductions to the population, then, in the period of observation, were 24 per 1,000. The growth rate based simply on births and deaths for the period is 2.5 percent per year, which would cause the population to double in 28 years. With migration included, the population grew at 3.9 percent per year, which doubles a population every 18 years. . . .

In order to study the process by which the population has been formed over the lifetime of living people, and in order to gain as much information as possible about this small population, all the adult women living in the Dobe Area were interviewed in detail about their marital and reproductive history. . . .

All of the women past the age of menarche who were resident in 1968 were interviewed. In addition, a few who had not yet had menarche but who were married were interviewed and are included in the final results. . . .

Now let us look briefly at the results of the interviews with the women of the Dobe Area. The mean age at menarche in recent years (estimated upon 11 women who have had their first menstruation since 1963) is 16.5. About half of the 165 women married before their first menstruation and about half after. In recent years, at least, it tends to be the women who menstruate early who marry after menarche. The curve of first marriage frequencies starts as low as 9 but involves few women until about 15 and is essentially complete by 20. The maximum number who will ever marry is essentially the same as the number married by 20. The phenomenon of failure to marry is rare among these people. Only two women in the Dobe population had never married a !Kung, and both of these women had borne one child to a Bantu who did not settle down into marriage with her. . . .

If the young woman does not care for her husband, she may simply leave him and go home to her family. Women's wishes are generally respected concerning marriage, and women commonly form and dissolve several very brief marriages in the early teen-age years. Both divorce and remarriage are simple and hold little handicaps for a woman at any age. Therefore while most of the women are married at any point of time during their reproductive years, the divorce rate throughout life is substantial.

The first live birth tends to occur around the age of 19.5. . . . At this point we might just indicate that the chance of death within the first year (and most of this occurs within the first few days) is about 20 percent for infants. If the baby dies, the mother may conceive again in as little as a few months, and probably within a year. . . .

The timing to the next birth depends to some extent

on age; younger women have their babies somewhat closer together than older women. Few of these intervals are less than 3 years long, and the modal length is about 4 years. . . . The variance of the number of live births is small for the !Kung; the maximum number of live births is only 9. This level of fertility is considerably lower than any other population known that is practicing natural fertility. . . .

In the !Kung population almost none of the difference between the maximum level of human fertility and the observed low level can be attributed to the marriage patterns. Women marry young and remarry relatively quickly when marriages end in divorce or widowhood.

Nor can the low observed fertility be attributed in any large part to high rates of fetal wastage or infanticide. The rates of miscarriage and spontaneous abortion reported are very low for remote periods in the past as women forget to report these events. . . .

The !Kung women do not claim knowledge of any method of abortion that seems to be effective, but infanticide is practiced by !Kung women when in their opinion it is necessary: in all cases of birth defects; one of each pair of twins; and sometimes when one birth follows another too closely, and the baby would drink the milk of his older brother or sister; or when the woman feels she is too old to produce milk for another baby. All in all, only 6 of 500 live births reported to me died through infanticide, which is not a large contribution to infant mortality. . . .

While in the field I received many requests for medicine to increase fertility and only one request from an overtired mother of four to help her stop having so many.

This raises the possibility that disease or malnutrition is the cause of the very low fertility. Many more women complained of the stinginess of god than felt that they had been troubled by venereal disease, but an increasing proportion with age do report that they have had venereal disease. The fertility of those 35 women who believe they have had gonorrhea is noticeably lower than those of the same age who say they have not had it. . . .

The current fertility among younger women seems to be slightly lower than normal for the older women, probably due to gonorrhea, so that the rate of growth in the current phase should be less than expected in the long run, although still positive. On the other hand, we have seen a run of lowered mortality in the six years of observation, which may be partially due to real changes in the environment the people live in, perhaps partially due to the occasional contact they have with public health, as in the case of smallpox vaccination or in part to the increasing control of epidemic diseases that is being established in the surrounding populations of Botswana. In either case the strictly demographic prospect for the population is good in that they are growing but not at a threatening level. Dangers to the existence of the population appear to come from the direction of assimilation and intermarriage with other groups, in other words, from the loss of their way of life and culture rather than from any predictable loss of the population itself.

CHAPTER TWENTY
THE URBAN COMMUNITY

The city has been called one of the human race's prime achievements and its worst mistake. In ancient times, cities such as Thebes, Babylon, Athens, and Rome were essential to the growth of great civilizations. Today, major cities like New York, Washington, Paris, London, Moscow, and Peking are central to the political, economic, and cultural life of their societies. With their concentration of resources and people, their crosscurrents of ideas, and their wide range of lifestyles and economic activities, cities provide environments uniquely conducive to achievement.

At the same time, cities are often regarded as uncomfortable, impersonal, and dangerous. Only in a city, for example, can one imagine a situation like the one in which Kitty Genovese, a young New York woman, was murdered in 1964 while at least thirty-eight neighbors listened and watched from their apartments, but could not (or would not) intervene or even call the police. The list of modern urban problems is long and familiar: poor housing, transportation, health care, and educational services; high crime rates; environmental deterioration caused by air and water pollution, noise, and poor sanitation; financial difficulties, and for some, feelings of isolation, frustration, and helplessness. In some cases these problems may be related to the same factors—diversity, large scale, and rapid pace of change—that lead to a city's achievements. In other cases, they stem from aspects of the city that offer no benefits in exchange.

Just how well cities function is a question that no longer concerns only a small proportion of the world's population. As we noted in Chapter 19, in the last forty years the distribution of population over the globe has shifted, so that for the first time in history the *majority* of people live in urban areas. Urban problems touch us all.

Analyzing urban life and urban societies

What the casual observer is likely to note in any city or urban area is a large population, a dense pattern of residential settlement, and a maze of buildings and streets. What he or she may not see—but just as important—is the complex social organization characteristic of the city. It is a form of organization that tends to differ from that of small towns or rural areas. First, in the city, economic roles as well as other roles are highly specialized and differentiated. A glance at the 1981 New York City Yellow Pages is instructive. The automobile section has separate listings for more than *ninety* types of automobile-related enterprises: automobile air-conditioning equipment, automobile auctions, automobile axle-servicing equipment, automobile axles, automobile batteries, automobile bearings, automobile body manufacturers, and so on. As for economic differentiation, the P section yields listings for paddle-tennis court manufacturers, paint-deodorant makers, parachute-jumping instruction, park-bench manufacturers, pickle makers, and pawnbrokers. Second, the city has a complex social-stratification system. And third, the city is likely to have a multitude of groups and organizations. It has economic groups and organizations such as manufacturing companies, banks, small businesses, and rings of professional thieves; political groups such as lobbying groups, local branches of the national political parties, and branches of the local government from the marriage-license bureau to the city mortuary; recreational groups such as karate schools, camera clubs, model-car builders' clubs; charitable organizations from foster homes to associations for the blind; religious organizations from satanism centers to the board of rabbis. Consequently, people in cities tend to have a wide range of potential loyalties; they can be attached not only to their families but also to a greater variety of non-kin groups.

TÖNNIES: GEMEINSCHAFT AND GESELLSCHAFT

Many of the social differences seen by early observers between a rural area and a modern city were summed up by the German sociologist Ferdinand Tönnies (1855–1936) with the contrasting terms *Gemeinschaft*, or "community," found in the small, intimate peasant village, and *Gesellschaft*, or "society," epitomized by the large, impersonal industrialized city (1957).

The *Gemeinschaft*, or rural community, was seen as a cohesive social unit organized on the basis of shared values and norms that commanded strong allegiance

The Ainu of northern Japan (*top*) live in what Tönnies would call a *Gemeinschaft*. Most of their social relationships are primary and are organized on the basis of commonly held values, norms, beliefs, and attitudes. Residents of industrialized cities like New York (*bottom*) are members of what Tönnies would call a *Gesellschaft*. They pursue individual goals and tend to have diverse values, norms, beliefs, and attitudes. (Courtesy, Japan National Tourist Organization; © Leonard Speier, 1981)

from its members. People in the *Gemeinschaft* type of society referred to themselves as "we," and they did not join the community by choice—they were born into it. In the *Gesellschaft*, by contrast, individual self-interest is more prevalent; there is less consensus on norms or values and less commitment to the group. Instead of adherence to time-honored traditions, there is a never-ending search for more rational and efficient ways of doing things; change, rather than stability, becomes an important norm.

DURKHEIM: ORGANIC AND MECHANICAL SOLIDARITY

This contrast between traditional and modern society, which in some ways parallels the contrast between rural and urban society, was also noticed by Emile Durkheim. Durkheim hypothesized that individuals in modern societies derived a kind of social cohesiveness pre-

cisely *from* their many different roles (1893). Though each individual might be trying to attain ends different from those of other individuals, he or she is dependent on others for the attainment of these ends: the clothing retailer, for example, cannot carry out business without fabric merchants and wholesale garment houses. The social solidarity of people in modern societies, which Durkheim called *organic solidarity*, was the exact opposite of the social solidarity found in traditional societies, which he called *mechanical solidarity*. People in traditional societies had similar roles and shared similar values and goals; people in modern societies had a pragmatic interdependence based on self-interest. Each needed the others simply to survive.

Today, almost all societies are touched in some way by urbanism. But in spite of the fact that urban society is particularly characteristic of our own age, there have been urban societies even long before the birth of Christ.

The evolution of cities

Archaeological research suggests that human forms of life emerged on earth 5 to 15 million years ago, and that *Homo sapiens*, the species to which modern humans belong, developed only within the past 50,000 to 60,000 years. In relation to this time span, the city as a human habitat is remarkably recent—only about 5,000 to 6,000 years old. In a sense this is not surprising, for cities could not appear until humans had reached a relatively high degree of technological and social development. As sociologist Leonard Reissman notes:

Consider first the sheer technical knowledge and skill required to keep a relatively large number of people alive under urban conditions: the provision of food, shelter, sanitation, and health at a level adequate to keep people alive and productive . . . even more important, the social organization required to keep those people safe, orderly, and willing to stay. The city could not flourish by the code of every man for himself, so the problems of economic distribution, of division of labor, and of government had to be settled and all sorts of rules had to be created. What is more, there had to be a reasonably high level of consensus about these arrangements. Not that the city depends upon democratic agreement, nor that it arose by social contract, but at the very least the city must rely on the acceptance of minimal

rules. The plan worked, for even ancient peoples had time to build temples, to fashion philosophies, and to create art, proving that man finally had advanced a good way beyond the persistent biological struggle to stay alive. (1964, p. 2)

THE URBAN REVOLUTION

The development of cities brought such crucial changes in human existence that archaeologist V. Gordon Childe (1892–1957) described it as the "urban revolution." Life in the earliest cities differed markedly from that of the rural hamlets, where the great majority of the populations of the ancient world continued to live. For one thing, the urban community did not grow its own food; the food supply came from the rural area around it. In addition to a large, densely settled population, a high division of labor, and complex stratification systems, all early cities had public buildings, commerce, relatively high rates of literacy, and sophisticated knowledge of mathematics and pictorial and plastic arts (Childe, 1950). As Childe noted, some of these features had existed in at least simple forms in previous agricultural communities. But in the cities they became central institutions.

THE PREINDUSTRIAL CITY

At first, the growth of cities was confined to the fertile valleys of the Tigris-Euphrates, Nile, and Indus rivers. Eventually, however, through trade and military conquest, the new skills and institutions were diffused to other areas. The Persian Empire brought cities to western central Asia; Greek city-states developed and in turn set up colonies along the Mediterranean; India brought city life to southeast Asia. The typical city of this era had a population of about 5,000 to 10,000 (Gist and Fava, 1974). But during the long classical period that extended until the end of the Roman Empire, several cities grew particularly strong. Athens in the Periclean age had 150,000 people, and Rome under Caesar Augustus reached a population of 1 million (Cousins and Nagpaul, 1970).

Cities declined in Europe during the medieval period, but by the fourteenth century, the pace of urban concentration had resumed under the influence of growing markets, foreign trade, and metal currency, which helped to create international financial networks and centers of capital. Accompanying these economic changes was an increase in centralized power through-

out Europe, which encouraged the growth of political capitals. After the sixteenth century, London had a population of 250,000, Naples 240,000, Milan over 200,000, and Paris about 180,000 (Mumford, 1961).

Preindustrial cities shared certain features with what anthropologist Robert Redfield (1947) called folk societies—small, homogeneous societies totally unaffected by contact with other societies. Preindustrial cit-

Preindustrial cities, like the fortress town of Arles, France, shown here, were characterized by compact organization and well-defined physical and social boundaries. The elite lived in the center of town; artisans and workers lived around this central district; and the poor lived near or outside the city walls. (The Bettmann Archive)

Tourists visit the Parthenon, built in the heyday of ancient Athens, one of the great preindustrial cities. (© Peter Menzel/Stock, Boston)

ies had a relatively stable social order, based largely on family ties and religious beliefs. Most of the work was done on a small scale by humans or animals; goods were retailed in small shops, and weights and measures were not standardized.

Yet preindustrial cities had more heterogeneity, stratification, and occupational differentiation than Redfield's true folk societies. They had a small literate segment, a priestly class, and a distinct government, dominated by a ruling class that jealously guarded its power and privileges. The rigid economic and social structure was reflected in physical layout: groups and classes were often segregated into quarters, wards, or ghettos. The city's rigid structure was also reflected in its formal, stylized norms of behavior: elaborate systems of protocol dictated the interactions between inferiors and superiors, and distinctive dress styles marked each stratum and occupational group (Sjoberg, 1955).

Growth of the metropolis

It was not until the next great technological and cultural "revolution"—the Industrial Revolution—that most cities began to grow to their present large size and large areas of the globe became urbanized. As we noted in Chapter 18, two major factors encouraged urbanization in the Western European and North American countries where the Industrial Revolution started: the "push" of changing agricultural technology, which removed the peasants' traditional livelihood, and the "pull" of jobs in the new factories, located in cities near reliable sources of energy. (In England, the first country to industrialize, the nobles responded to the growth of

FIGURE 20.1

This chart shows the development of world urbanization, 1950–2000 (by percent). Industrialization, which tends to be associated with a high concentration of people in urban areas, is responsible for the steady increase. (Population Reference Bureau, 1978)

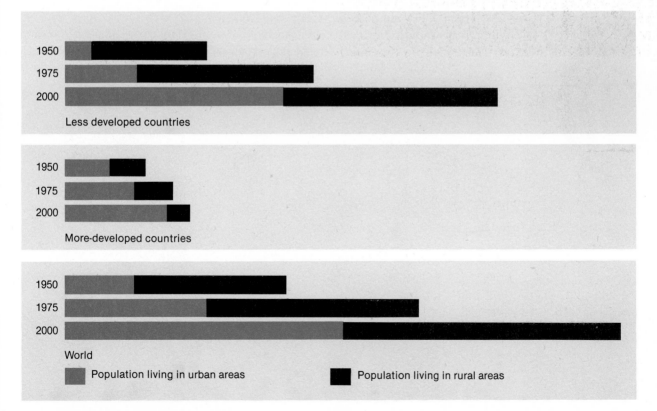

Less developed countries

More-developed countries

World

■ Population living in urban areas   ■ Population living in rural areas

the wool trade by "enclosure"—erecting fences to denote private ownership of pastures, thus keeping people from farming what had been common land.) In 1780 the first industrial city, Manchester, England, was a market town numbering only 25,000 people. Only forty years later, seventy-two textile mills had been constructed and the population had quadrupled. Within another thirty years, the number quadrupled again (Cousins and Nagpaul, 1970). Similar factory towns grew up throughout England and Wales, and other European nations and the United States soon followed the British example. The emergence of the factory combined with other factors to induce individuals to move to the cities. These included the growth of a middle class devoted to commerce, new opportunities for social mobility, and the spread of public education and literacy.

THE INDUSTRIAL CITY

The modern industrial city differed from the preindustrial city in certain crucial respects. First, along with mass production and the use of inanimate power sources unknown in preindustrial times, there was an explosion of new types of industry. The main part of the labor force shifted from primary industry (extracting raw materials) to secondary industry (processing these materials) and finally to tertiary industry (providing services rather than goods). There was also a "specializing out" of functions such as accounting, inventory control, selling, and distribution. Wool, for example, might now be spun in one factory, woven in another, and made into garments in a third; from there it might go to one or more wholesalers and then to many different retailers. Additional separate firms balanced the books, advertised the products, lent money to the entrepreneurs, and sold stock in companies to investors. In the city, even the functions of the household itself (personal services, housekeeping, repairs, shopping, recreation, education) were taken over by consumer-service industries. Likewise, industry and services in modern cities did not simply fill the needs of these cities' own populations. Each city became an administrative center that filled the educational, aesthetic, medical, financial, and governmental needs of the area around it. This process had begun in preindustrial times, but it speeded up as societies became increasingly industrialized.

THE METROPOLIS

These characteristics were even more conspicuous in the *metropolis*, a form of human settlement that new technology made possible. The metropolis developed

In the nineteenth century, the Industrial Revolution spurred the growth of cities such as Pittsburgh. The economies of these early industrial centers were characterized by secondary (processing) industries and specialization of functions. (International Museum of Photography at George Eastman House)

Chicago typifies the modern metropolis—a large area, with at least 500,000 people, whose economy is based on the large inventories, transportation facilities, and specialized services that today's businesses depend on. (Jean-Claude Lejeune/Stock, Boston)

from the city: as Hans Blumenfeld puts it, "the city burst its eggshell and emerged as a metropolis." Advances in transit and communications made possible settlements a hundred times larger in area than the biggest cities of former times. According to Blumenfeld (1973), a metropolis is "any area containing at least 500,000 people, in which the traveling time from the outskirts to the center is no more than about forty minutes." In general, a *metropolis* is a large city central to a country, state, or region, with adjacent, densely developed residential, industrial, commercial, educational, and recreational areas, and close-by satellite cities. The economy of the metropolis is based on the large inventories, transportation facilities, and specialized services essential to modern business. A metropolis often serves as an incubator for small, new, and experimental enterprises. Like other industrial cities, the metropolis serves the needs of the area around it; but on a larger scale, it often functions as a supply and administration center for a multistate region. Cities such as New York and Washington provide goods and services that are needed by the entire nation.

The modern industrial city and the metropolis, with their huge populations and intricate economic patterns, are forms of human settlement in which all inhabitants cannot possibly have characteristics in common. In such areas, close relationships may exist only within neighborhoods, ethnic subcultures, or friendship networks. How do people get along in the complex, confusing social setting the city can represent? What does living in a city do to one's personality? And in what way does the urban setting shape the social life that goes on within it? Sociologists have approached these questions from several different perspectives.

Urban social patterns

Why did the thirty-eight people who watched the assault on Kitty Genovese in 1964 fail to help her or to call the police—even though they had half an hour, during which she was repeatedly stabbed, to do so? Was it that they were numbed by the "apathy" or "moral callousness" of our times—as preachers, professors, and television specials exploring the incident have suggested? Or were they acting in accordance with a familiar stereotype, that of the cold, rushed, unfriendly city dweller? The social psychology of this particularly horrifying episode has been the subject of numerous investigations, among them an intriguing set of laboratory experiments set up by Bibb Latané and John M. Darley (see box). And, more generally speaking, the social psychology of city dwellers as a distinct "human type" has interested sociologists for over sixty years. The core of the debate concerns whether city dwellers really *are* different from their rural counterparts—and if so, how.

BYSTANDER APATHY IN URBAN EMERGENCIES: WHERE ARE THE GOOD SAMARITANS?

Was the inaction of the thirty-eight people who witnessed the murder of Kitty Genovese accurately diagnosed as "apathy" and "dehumanization"? Bibb Latané and John M. Darley, two researchers who were interested in this frightening incident, believe it was not. As they point out, the thirty-eight witnesses

did not merely look at the scene once and then ignore it. Instead they continued to stare out of their windows at what was going on. Caught, fascinated, distressed, unwilling to act but unable to turn away. . . . (1976, p. 310)

Latané and Darley set out to discover more about the process of individual reaction to an emergency. To begin with, they hypothesized that intervention in an emergency is a five-step process. A person must (1) notice something happening; (2) interpret the situation as an emergency; (3) decide whether he or she has a responsibility to intervene; (4) decide what form of assistance is needed; and (5) decide what method should be used to implement assistance. Failure to intervene in an emergency, then, may result from failure in any one of these five steps. Moreover, the most a person has to gain from intervention is a feeling of pride, perhaps even the feeling of being a hero; but worse things can happen: "he can be made to appear as a fool, he can be sued, or he can even be attacked and wounded. By leaving the situation, he has little to lose but his self-respect. There are strong pressures against deciding that an event is an emergency" (p. 312).

Furthermore, Latané and Darley realized that most emergencies first appear as ambiguous situations: black fog curling from a building, for example, may be rising from a dangerous fire or simply from a steam valve. How

the individual perceives such an event is likely to be influenced by the reactions of other bystanders. Just as a fearful crowd may pass panic from one person to another, indifference to a situation among a crowd may also be contagious. Even when an individual perceives a situation as an emergency, he or she may refrain from intervening for fear of being ridiculed by others who may interpret the situation differently.

In short, Latané and Darley argued, an individual's response to an emergency situation may vary with *social influence*: that is, under certain conditions, the presence of other people may inhibit an individual's response to the emergency. To pin down some of the variables in the process, they set up a series of five experiments—with striking results.

To test the strength of the social influencing process, Latané and Darley invited subjects to sit in a small room, where they were asked to fill out questionnaires. Smoke was then piped into the room, creating a situation that *could* have been interpreted as dangerous. Of persons tested while alone in the room, 75 percent reported the smoke. But among persons in groups of three, the proportion of reports dropped off sharply, to 15 percent. Each person was inhibited by the presence of the others from sounding an alarm, even when there was so much smoke in the room that they could hardly see.

The second experiment involved a victim. Subjects were tested for their reaction to the sound of a woman falling off a ladder in an adjoining room and apparently experiencing great pain. (The sounds actually came from a prepared tape recording.) Again, those subjects tested alone responded much more often than those tested in

SIMMEL'S APPROACH: THE URBAN PERSON

One of the first and most famous explorations of urban social psychology was in an essay, "The Metropolis and Mental Life," by the German sociologist Georg Simmel (1950). Simmel traced what he saw as the aloof, unfriendly, and preoccupied manner of the urban individual to the intense, ceaseless, nervous stimulation of urban life. To protect themselves from the confusing, disorienting onrush of sensations, urbanites develop certain defensive habits. The urbanite reacts, Simmel asserted, "with his head instead of his heart."

The metropolis was dominated by a monetary economy, and the value of all transactions—even the re-

spect accorded each person's individuality—was ultimately reduced to the question, "How much?" Though Simmel realized that individuals in the metropolis varied, he believed their preoccupation with money had a general tendency to transform intimate, emotional relations between persons into rational encounters in which "man is reckoned with like a number." One result, Simmel felt, was the creation of the blasé, matter-of-fact, and closed—perhaps even overintellectualized and somewhat antipathetic—personality that he thought characterized the city dweller. Yet there were benefits as well. As Simmel concluded, "This reserve with its overtones of hidden aversion appears in turn as the form or cloak of a more general mental phenomenon of the metropolis; it grants to the

groups. The response was greater in groups of friends than in groups of strangers; among friends, there is less fear of ridicule for responding in a way that may turn out to have been inappropriate.

The third experiment was a staged theft: a "villain" was observed stealing a case of beer from a store. Witnesses who were alone reported the "theft" to the store-owner 65 percent of the time—but only 34 percent of the witnesses who were in pairs informed the owner.

The presence of other persons also influences an individual's feeling of *responsibility* to intervene in an emergency. While a person who is alone will bear the entire guilt for inaction, in a group responsibility and potential blame may be diffused—with the result that a member of a group is less likely to intervene than a person alone. To prove this point, a fourth experiment was devised in which a person—actually a prerecorded voice heard through earphones—appeared to be suffering a seizure. Of persons who believed themselves to be the only one aware of the seizure, 85 percent responded. By contrast, of those persons who thought four other bystanders were present in separate rooms, only 31 percent responded, and took longer to do so. Nonintervenors were generally very concerned over the condition of the seizure victim— which demonstrates that their inaction was not born of indifference. Rather, what caused their inaction was an inability to decide which would be worse—letting the victim continue to suffer or rushing in to help and perhaps looking like a fool. Meanwhile, the responsibility for *not* taking action was diffused among all the members of the group.

In a fifth experiment, subjects watched a man who appeared to be receiving a severe electrical shock. Through a complicated system of communications, the researchers were able to determine that bystanders' nonintervention in this situation probably resulted from *both* a social influencing process and a diffusion of responsibility among group members. Again, those subjects who were alone reported that they felt much more responsibility to act than did those who were in groups.

Latané and Darley's results, which have been replicated by others, yielded evidence in support of their claim that specific social conditions, not apathy, are the cause of bystanders' nonintervention in emergencies like the rape-murder of Kitty Genovese. As they point out, these findings have particular relevance to the social conditions of city life. When a city dweller encounters an ambiguous and possibly dangerous situation, he or she is much more likely to be part of a collectivity of people than to be alone. And the others in the collectivity are much more likely to be strangers to him or her than friends. As Latané and Darley conclude:

We have become "indifferent," [some people claim,] "callous" to the fate of suffering others. Our society has become "dehumanized" as it has become urbanized. These glib phrases may contain some truth, since startling cases such as the Genovese murder often seem to occur in our large cities, but such terms may also be misleading. Our studies suggest a different conclusion. They suggest that situational factors—specifically, factors involving the immediate social environment—may be of greater importance in determining an individual's reaction to an emergency than such vague cultural or personality concepts as "apathy" or "alienation due to urbanization." (p. 330)

individual a kind and an amount of personal freedom which has no analogy whatsoever under other conditions" (Simmel, 1950).

WIRTH'S APPROACH: INTERACTION

Whereas Simmel's focus was primarily on the urban *person*, that of Louis Wirth, another pioneering observer, was on urban *interaction*. In his essay "Urbanism as a Way of Life" (1938), Wirth began by noting three large-scale aspects of the urban social setting that can be seen as *ecological* factors; that is, they had to do with the urban *environment*. These factors were popu-

lation size, density, and heterogeneity (see Figure 20.2). From them Wirth induced a number of principles that he felt underlay urban social behavior.

Size

It was the sheer *size* of the city's population, Wirth claimed, that rendered impossible the fully developed personal contacts of the small town or rural village. The more people in the social setting, the greater the range of variation among them, and the more varied their interaction. Each urbanite was likely to contact others in a variety of different groups, and in each group he or she was likely to display only a "segmental role," rather than his or her full personality. For example, Tom is

SIZE

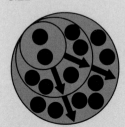

An increase in the number of inhabitants of a settlement beyond a certain limit brings about changes in the relations of people and changes in the character of the community.

Consequences: Dependence on a greater number of people, less dependence on particular persons.
Association with more people, knowledge of a smaller proportion, and, of these, less intimate knowledge.
More secondary rather than primary contacts; that is, increase in contacts that are face to face yet impersonal, superficial, transitory, and segmental.

DENSITY

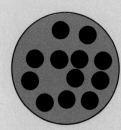

Reinforces the effect of size in diversifying people and their activities and in increasing the structural complexity of the society.

Consequences: Tendency to differentiation and specialization. Separation of residence from work place. Functional specialization of areas—segregation of functions.
Segregation of people: city becomes a mosaic of social worlds.

HETEROGENEITY

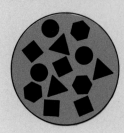

Cities are products of the migration of peoples of diverse origin. This heterogeneity of origin is matched by heterogeneity of occupations. Differentiation and specialization reinforce heterogeneity.

Consequences: Without common background and common activities, premium is placed on visual recognition: the uniform becomes symbolic of the role.
No common set of values, no common ethical system to sustain them: money tends to become the measure of all things for which there are no common standards. Formal controls as opposed to informal controls; necessity for adhering to predictable routines; the clock and the traffic signal are symbolic of the basis of the social order.
Mass production of goods and standardization of goods and facilities in terms of the average.

FIGURE 20.2

A schematic representation of Louis Wirth's sociological definition of the city in relation to size, density, and heterogeneity. Wirth concluded that the modern city was a *Gesellschaft,* and he analyzed what he thought were some of its negative consequences. Herbert J. Gans (1962), however, questioned Wirth's analysis because: (1) Wirth did not make distinctions among types of settlements within the city; (2) consistent evidence to prove that size, density, and heterogeneity result in the social consequences proposed by Wirth is lacking; (3) even if there were a causal relationship, a significant number of city dwellers would be shielded from those consequences by the social and cultural patterns developed within their relatively homogeneous groups. (Figure adapted from Shevky and Bell, 1955, pp. 7–8)

known to Harry only as a shop foreman, to John as a fellow member of a bowling team, and to Helen as an insurance client. This segmentalization of roles, according to Wirth, was the source of the supposedly blasé and indifferent manner of the city dweller.

Wirth also suggested connections between the numbers of people in the city and the types of social organization that grew up in it—and in modern society as a whole. A prime example was the emergence of the corporation. The corporation offered an efficient mechanism for organizing thousands of individuals into group enterprises. It was also the ideal institution for mobilizing segmented, impersonal relationships because, as Wirth put it, "the corporation has no soul." A second institutional manifestation of the city's numbers was the development of voluntary organizations. Since the individual counted for little, he or she had to team up with others to make his or her wishes felt. How effectively a group can fight for its interests depends at least in part on the numbers of people in it. And the group cannot fight *en masse;* it has to have a representative. Thus Wirth described a progression from a kind of social disintegration to new forms of integrated social patterning—the corporation, voluntary organizations, and representative government.

Density

Wirth believed population *density* offered ways of explaining certain specific ecological patterns in the city, namely, the selection and distribution of the population into settlements over a geographic area. Wirth argued that people living close to one another tend to segregate themselves into homogeneous clusters. In this way, the clash of incompatible norms and values is reduced, and the city resembles "a mosaic of social worlds in which the transition from one to the other is abrupt" (Wirth, 1938, p. 15). In New York City, for example, East 96th Street is the boundary between the upper- and middle-class East Side and the East Harlem slum.

Heterogeneity

A third aspect of urban society, in Wirth's view, is the *heterogeneous* makeup of the population. What are its implications? First, the variety of personalities and individual specialization greatly complicate the social structure. The rigid boundaries of caste and class tend to break down as individuals exercise their options and, in particular, choose different lifestyles and experience a more fluid system of social stratification than exists in rural areas. This social mobility, in turn, creates a rapid turnover in group membership and even neighborhood residence. Shifting to the level of individual experience, Wirth deduced that it was difficult to bind this changeable population into lasting associations or to create among its members long-term, intimate friendships. The result of this instability, he concluded, is urban alienation (see Figure 20.2).

Criticisms of Wirth's approach

Wirth's treatment of urban life has been challenged on the grounds that it does not explain how the three factors he focused on—size, density, and heterogeneity—interrelate. Even more damaging to his theory is empirical evidence that alienation and loss of common standards and values are not the sole, or even necessarily the dominant, patterns in urban social relationships. Industrial cities do not necessarily disrupt kinship, friendship, and neighborhood groups, but may instead cause them to be organized on new bases (Breese, 1966). The friendship group, for example, may now be physically dispersed throughout the urban area, and the neighborhood may be more a psychological than an ecological reality.

A study by Claude S. Fischer (1976) found "a small but real association" between urban residence and a

The extensive kinship and friendship networks that exist in large cities dispel the theory that alienation is the dominant urban social pattern. (© Eric A. Roth 1979/The Picture Cube)

sense of social isolation, which Fischer attributes to the high number of heterogeneous groups in the city. But this association was not large enough to suggest that city dwellers' sense of isolation outweighed their sense of security in their own social networks. In fact, other researchers have found that friendship networks grow stronger as a community *increases* in size. And Fischer found no relationship between urban residence and a sense of powerlessness. Responding to Wirth's statement about urban alienation, Fischer observes: "Fundamental personality dimensions—such as sense of control—are not affected directly by the gross ecological differences of town and country. . . . the attribution of 'urbanism as a way of life' seems incorrect" (Fischer, 1976, pp. 324–325).

For a long time, Wirth's second factor, density, was believed to be both an urban characteristic and a major cause of such typically urban problems as high crime rates, juvenile delinquency, and mental illness. But a recent review of the "density-pathology hypothesis" (Choldin, 1978) does not confirm that the city causes these problems just because too many people live in too small a space. The studies show that by itself, density—whether physical population density or household crowding—does not seem to produce social pathology. Rather, household crowding seems to be an indicator; it generally means neighborhoods characterized by miserable housing and poor families with young children. These may also be the neighborhoods with high crime and delinquency rates, but it is not the density that is necessarily causing the behavior (Choldin, 1978, pp. 91–113).

Another important criticism, put forward by Herbert Gans, is that Wirth did not distinguish between the ways of life in a "city" and those in more specifically defined settlements such as the inner city, the suburb, and the satellite town. Gans observed that Wirth's views on the heterogeneity of the population overlooked the fact that most of the city's population is bound into relatively homogeneous segments, "with social and cultural moorings that shield it fairly effectively from the suggested consequences of number" (Gans, 1962, p. 629).

SPATIAL PATTERNS

The ecological perspective, which formed the basis of Wirth's approach, has lent itself to a variety of other formulations. Robert Park, Wirth's teacher at the University of Chicago, proposed that the city should be viewed as "a kind of social organism," which could be studied in terms of processes such as competition, concentration, segregation, invasion, succession, and symbiosis—patterns like the biological processes observable among plants and animals (Park, 1916). Park's theory has been used to construct a variety of models of the city based on spatial patterns.

The concentric-circle model

Ernest W. Burgess (1925) and other members of the University of Chicago group studied the competition for land among various segments of the urban population. They noted that this competition was reflected in the development of five *concentric rings*. At the core, known as Zone I, was the "central business district," a high-rent inner circle where the most important stores, banks, and other economic enterprises were located. Zone II was labeled the "transition zone": it was a previously residential fringe around the city that had once housed the wealthy and then deteriorated. Here were the cheap taverns, flophouses, and "red-light" districts. The third concentric circle, Zone III, was called "the zone of workingmen's homes," a residential area of low-cost frame houses owned or rented by factory laborers. Zone IV embraced the "better residences," an

upper-middle-class area of good apartments and well-kept private homes. Finally, Zone V, "the commuters' zone," consisted of the suburbs, which existed either as integral parts of the city or as satellite communities attached to it.

The concentric-circle model was conceived as a dynamic model of a growing city, in which the tendency was for "each inner zone to extend its area by the invasion of the next outer zone" (Burgess, 1925). Not surprisingly, it best described Chicago, the city of its originators. It did not fully account for the physical configurations of other metropolises, particularly those that had evolved after the advent of the automobile.

The sector model

Homer Hoyt, an urban ecologist who was particularly interested in the changes introduced by the automobile, came to the conclusion that the pattern sketched by Burgess was no longer adequate, descriptively or conceptually (Hoyt, 1939). His *sector theory*, which he developed as a modification of Burgess' model, conceives of a central business district, with other areas of the city tending to develop in pie-shaped sectors that radiate outward along major transportation routes (see Figure 20.3). Hoyt's model was formulated as an ideal type, rather than as a description of the growth of any particular city. In actual fact, each city's own topographical pattern, including rivers and hills, shapes its land-use patterns in unique ways.

The multiple-nuclei model

Extending Hoyt's point about the connection between industrial land-use patterns and the unique topography of each city, Chauncy Harris and Edward I. Ullman (1951) suggested that a modern industrial city is characterized by a number of spatially separate nuclei around which differentiated activities grow.

The four factors that affect the rise of these differentiated districts are shown in Figure 20.3. First, certain activities require special facilities. Most retail districts are located at the point of maximum accessibility to intracity transportation, but manufacturing districts require large blocks of land together with adequate water or rail connections. Second, similar activities congregate because they profit from proximity. For example, retail establishments cluster together because they

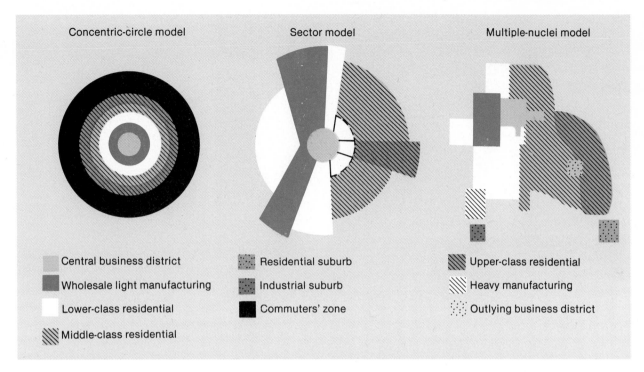

Concentric-circle model   Sector model   Multiple-nuclei model

Central business district

Wholesale light manufacturing

Lower-class residential

Middle-class residential

Residential suburb

Industrial suburb

Commuters' zone

Upper-class residential

Heavy manufacturing

Outlying business district

FIGURE 20.3

Three theories of urban ecology, each of which represents an attempt to describe patterns of land use in large cities during different periods of urban growth in the United States. *Left:* Ernest W. Burgess's concentric-zone model, which was applied to Chicago in the 1920s. *Center:* Homer Hoyt's sector model, which modified Burgess's model and accounted for changes brought about by the automobile. *Right:* The multiple-nuclei model of Chauncy Harris and Edward L. Ullman, which attempted to account for new land-use patterns resulting from differentiation of activities in modern industrialized cities. (From C. D. Harris and E. L. Ullman, 1951)

all benefit from the increased customer traffic made possible by such clustering; financial and office districts benefit from the ease of communication made possible by physical proximity. Third, certain dissimilar districts are inherently antagonistic to each other, such as a factory area close to a high-rent residential district. And fourth, certain people whose activities might benefit from a particular location may be unable to afford the rent for the most advantageous sites.

It is true that certain districts—wholesale and light manufacturing areas, heavy industrial areas, residential districts, retail shopping centers, and areas of cultural and educational activity—can be observed in all large cities, as Harris and Ullman's model suggests. But the multiple-nuclei model is less a theory than a description and attempt at explanation; its value in predicting patterns of urban growth has proved to be virtually nil. In many cities, for example, factory and manufacturing areas have now been partly converted to high-rent residential and commercial use. Shops and lofts coexist with small industries.

The ecological approach: an assessment

The ecological perspective is unlikely to produce an acceptable unifying theory of urban life, as its origina-

tors hoped. Every model based on it has drawn criticism because the focus is on physical and mechanistic patterns in the organization of the metropolis, with little regard for the culture of the inhabitants (Firey, 1947). At its worst, the ecological approach can lead to a fallacious determinism, in which behavior is interpreted primarily as a consequence of spatial properties rather than of the social and psychological characteristics of urban areas.

Recent studies of sub-areas within cities have shown

Neighborhood relationships are especially important to working-class urbanites. (Rick Smolan/Stock, Boston)

up the diversity of factors responsible for social activity within them. John Ottensmann's (1978) examination of eleven ethnographic studies of sections of cities—including such well-known works as Liebow's *Tally's Corner* and Whyte's *Streetcorner Society*—led him to suggest that the density of population of an area is not solely responsible for the degree of neighboring (social relationships restricted to the immediate area) that takes place: the relationship between social class and neighboring is nearly as telling—high degrees of neighboring tend to be associated with lower- or working-class areas, and moderate to low levels of neighboring with middle-class areas.

The racial makeup of the inhabitants and even their ages can also influence the way neighborhoods are used, according to Donald I. Warren (1977). He found that neighborhoods play a wider variety of roles in the lives of blacks than of whites in urban areas. Moreover, during two distinct stages in the life cycle—the early child-bearing years and old age—the neighborhood becomes highly important for social linkage.

The American city: problems and efforts at solutions

THE ANTIURBAN BIAS

The North American continent has a higher proportion of citizens living in cities than any other area on the globe. Yet despite this urban concentration, Americans have always been ambivalent—and often hostile—toward their metropolises. As J. J. Palen and K. H. Flaming point out,

American cities have frequently been the victims of ideological lag. While nineteenth-century America experienced rapid urban population growth, new forms of urban social organization, and the emergence of an industrial technology, its attitudes regarding the growing cities frequently reflected the rural ideology of an earlier age. Americans have never been neutral about their great cities. They have been either exalted as the vital commercial heart and soul of the nation or denounced as behavioral sinks of crime, vice, and moral corruption. Certainly the city was distrusted by many of the founding fathers, who contrasted the idealized life of the yeoman with the corruption of urban places. (1972, p. 23)

The anticity forces in American intellectual life have included such eminent figures as Ralph Waldo

Emerson, Henry David Thoreau, Henry Adams, and Henry James. Two of the nation's founders, Benjamin Franklin and Thomas Jefferson, exemplify particularly clearly the dichotomy in American attitudes toward cities. Franklin grew up and pursued his career in urban environments—Boston, Philadelphia, London, and Paris. Jefferson was repelled by what he saw as the mobs and the rabble of European cities, and—early in his career, at least—was vehemently antiurban. Jefferson initially opposed the introduction of manufacturing into the United States on the ground that it would spawn more cities. And in one famous letter, he even half-seriously considered the benefits of epidemics as checks upon urbanism: "The yellow fever," Jefferson wrote in 1800, "will discourage the growth of great cities in our nation and I view great cities as pestilential to the morals, the health, and the liberty of men" (quoted in Glaab and Brown, 1967, p. 55).

But great cities did grow as the United States industrialized and became a world power. Places such as San Francisco, Chicago, and New York became cultural as well as commercial centers, international cities whose inhabitants spoke many languages and followed many different customs. The antiurban bias, however, did not disappear: the functions of the cities were primarily commercial and governmental, and the urban way of life did not penetrate the towns and rural districts in which most people lived. Americans still tended to see the cities as "dens of vice and sin," a threat to the white, Anglo-Saxon Protestant way of life at the heart of American culture.

For a relatively brief period—hardly more than a century—the industrial city in the United States had well-defined boundaries, and thus its problems could be confined "within city limits." And the problems were appalling: in 1900 in such cities as Boston and Chicago, crime, disorder, vice, homeless people, alcoholism, mental illness, unemployment, poor housing, overcrowding, poor sanitation, health hazards, and inadequate city services were all causes for great concern. The cities did help launch many immigrants and their descendants on the path to upward social mobility and a better life— but that path usually led out of the city to the suburbs. To some extent, this antiurban bias remains today, though it is based on different reasons: now some of those concerned about ecology view cities as despoilers of the environment and as sources of pollution and destruction.

CENTRAL CITY VERSUS SUBURBIA

There is still a tendency for middle-class people to separate themselves, at least geographically, from the central cities. During and after World War II, the migration of rural American blacks and poor whites into the cities increased significantly. Today, urban centers are heavily populated by blacks, Spanish-speaking people, poor whites (as in Detroit and Chicago, which have many residents who moved north from Appalachia), and Native Americans. Meanwhile, people of Anglo-Saxon descent and the descendants of earlier European immigrants have tended to move out. One reason for this shift in residential patterns is the development of mass private ownership of the automobile, which has made it possible for workers to commute relatively long distances. Another reason is the postwar boom in the American economy, which, coupled with Federal Housing Authority and Veterans' Administration guarantees for low-interest, low-down-payment mortgage loans, made suburban home ownership a possibility for millions of Americans. Employment, shopping, and recreational opportunities have subsequently increased in the suburban areas—a pattern that tends to diminish middle-class involvement in and concern for the city.

A more recent exodus of whites from central cities has occurred in response to the desegregation of schools. Coleman, Kelly, and Moore (1975) have shown that in the first year of court-ordered desegregation, primarily in larger cities, white public school enrollment may decline at double or triple its normal rate, and may contribute to the phenomenon known as "white flight."

However, not all movement away from central cities is by whites. Blacks who can afford it leave for the same reasons as whites, including better schools and the tax benefits of home ownership as opposed to apartment rental.

Urban problems as a cause of population shifts

Since the 1920s, and particularly since 1950, the outlying portions of metropolitan areas in the United States have been growing much faster than the central cities, some of which have remained stable or even declined in population. What the migrants to suburbia are fleeing

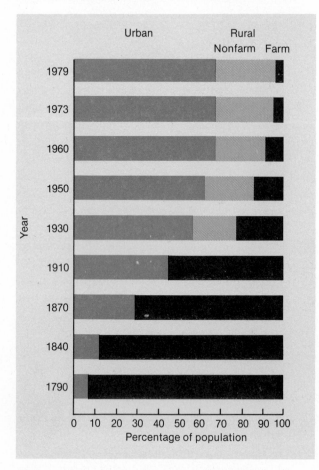

FIGURE 20.4
Since the beginning of this century, there has
been a steady migration from rural to urban
areas in the United States. Since 1950 a new
trend, suburbanization, has developed as more
people began to move out of the central cities
and into the surrounding communities.
(Adapted from Bogue, 1955, and Census Bureau, 1976, 1979)

is a physical and social environment with a host of interrelated problems.

One major problem is that many central-city buildings are dilapidated, and not enough new housing is
built. As a result, large, older properties are hastily converted to multiple-tenant occupancy, and central-city
dwellers must either accept these apartments or pay
relatively high sums for better housing. The National
Commission on Urban Problems found that nearly half
the residents of central cities either are ill-housed or pay
more than a fifth of their annual income in rent. The

average lower-income urban family pays between one-
fifth and one-quarter of its income for housing, and
urban blacks pay an average of 35 percent, far above the
percentage paid by the average middle-class suburban
family [Census Bureau, 1978, p. 494].

In addition, urban public services—education, mass
transportation, hospitals, police, sanitation—are often
inadequate, especially in poor neighborhoods. In New
York City's rich neighborhoods, there is one private
doctor for every 200 persons; in some poor inner-city
neighborhoods, there is one per 10,000 persons. Rates
of street crime, alcoholism, and mental illness are high.

Finally, central-city dwellers are relatively poor.
Whereas about 10 percent of city and suburban residents had an income that fell below the poverty line in
1977, 15 percent of inner-city dwellers were poor (Census Bureau, 1978, p. 471). And blacks, urban as well as
rural, are generally poorer than whites: median black
income averaged only 57 percent of median white income in 1977 (Census Bureau, 1978, p. 453). And rates
of unemployment and underemployment are disproportionately high for all races in the inner cities: in the
summer of 1979, the inner-city unemployment rate was
more than twice that of the nation as a whole.

Although a majority (75 percent) of Americans still
live in metropolitan areas, the trend of declining central-city population and suburban growth continues. In
the 1970s, the net growth in the nation's 285 metropolitan areas was in the suburbs (U.S. News & World Report, May 14, 1979). But this suburban growth was not
uniform across the nation: metropolitan areas of the
"sunbelt," the South and West, gained population
while Eastern and Midwestern areas such as New York,
Cleveland, and Pittsburgh had sizable declines.

This pattern of outward movement from the central city is no longer confined to whites; yet another
trend of the 1970s was the movement of blacks to the
suburbs. In the metropolitan areas examined in one recent study (Nelson), both blacks and whites have been
leaving for the suburbs, and in a few areas there is actually now a net outmigration of blacks. So far, those who
move are above average in education and income. If
this trend of outward movement continues, the pattern
may no longer be black central city versus white suburbs, but predominantly poor central city versus mid-
dle- and upper-class suburbs. Socioeconomic, in addition to racial, segregation compounds the cities'
problems.

The flight to the suburbs has been an important phenomenon in the United States since the 1920s and especially since 1950. (© Eric A. Roth 1979/The Picture Cube)

The double bind

The cities are caught in a two-way squeeze. On the one hand, their need for public services is greater than that of the suburbs. Rates of violent crime are higher, so the city needs more police; the population is poorer, so it needs more welfare services; its daytime population swells with the influx of commuters, so it needs more transport; its buildings are older and in worse repair, so it needs more fire protection. On the other hand, taxes cannot be raised too much. Many residents of the central city are poor, and industry is relocating to the suburbs as taxes rise. Higher property taxes also accelerate the process of deterioration and encourage the spread of slums, because property taxes fall most heavily on renovated property—a prospect that deters landlords from making improvements.

Why cannot some of the urban poor move to the suburbs? Because many suburbs have been able to use zoning regulations to exclude them. Undeveloped land in the suburbs can be zoned for large residential lots of several acres each. This means expensive houses that the poor cannot afford. These expensive houses may provide about as much tax revenue to the suburb as would a number of smaller, less expensive dwellings, but the zoning gives the suburb fewer and richer families and hence fewer children to educate and fewer poor people in need of public services.

Why cannot suburbanites, many of whom go into the city daily for work and entertainment, help to pay for some of the facilities and services they use? In some cases, they do: workers who live in New Jersey or Pennsylvania and travel to their jobs in New York City, for example, pay a small "commuter tax" on their incomes. But other measures, such as increasing toll fees on routes into the cities, risk commercial losses.

It has also proved difficult to streamline the finances and functioning of entire metropolitan areas by coordinating governmental operations. The governance and financial management of large cities have become difficult, chiefly because of their unprecedented scale. There is tremendous competition for scarce resources such as electricity, hot water, housing, clean air, and space for traffic, building, and recreation. But governance is also difficult because there is usually no one government with exclusive jurisdiction over the whole metropolitan area. Cities are often embedded in antiquated governmental structures that put them partly at the mercy of rural-dominated state legislatures and partly in the hands of many local, county, borough, and district governmental units that are rarely in a position to agree. (Not long ago there were over 1,400 different regulatory units in New York City alone.)

There is no single answer to the question of what is wrong with our cities, and there is no single best way of attacking urban problems. The urban planning and redevelopment programs of recent years have not always succeeded in meeting even limited goals.

CITY PLANNING AND REDEVELOPMENT

City planning is no recent innovation: Hippodamus, a Greek architect, laid out Athens' port, Piraeus, in the fifth century B.C. For the most part, however, city planning has been a spotty, partial exercise, directed mainly by the tastes and wishes of the elite classes. The "planned" dimension of the city has historically centered on such functions as city defense, the maintenance of governmental, religious, and commercial centers, the beautification and servicing of the elite's residential areas, the channeling of traffic, and the erection of amenities and monuments such as stadiums, tombs, baths, and churches. The design of Washington, D.C., actually created only a central, though beautiful, scheme for public buildings; the rest of the city was allowed to evolve into its current disarray of highly visible and ugly slums.

A rare exception to the urban-planning rule is Stockholm, Sweden, which for over three centuries has had a special and powerful office to guide the city's development. Stockholm's planning agency has emphasized the provision of housing and other public facilities, the integration of central-city and suburban growth, and the coordination of transportation with economic and residential development. All this has been done with an awareness of how demographic and economic trends are likely to affect a particular area's future growth.

American planners in recent years have had both successes and failures. The failures have reflected both a lack of appreciation for the social functioning of an area as well as a lack of funds. To many architects and planners, the design of the ghettos appeared to lend itself to easy remedial action. Most of the ghetto areas were overcrowded; buildings were small and run-down; streets were narrow and congested. Therefore, the obvious first step, it seemed, was to alter the structure of the ghetto through the construction of new housing. It was easier to do this than to tackle the more subtle, costly, and difficult issues of unemployment, poor schooling, and related social issues. Yet one of the first problems encountered in the drive to renovate the slums was lack of cash. Thousands of tenements were leveled, but only a fraction were replaced by new housing units. In one survey taken in the early 1960s, it was noted that

192,000 dwelling units had been razed for urban renewal projects, and only 28,000 new ones built (Gans, 1965)—and these were rented at rates that averaged about 25 percent higher than most tenants had paid for the old housing.

Moreover, the costs of providing housing for the urban poor have continually caused availability to lag behind need. Because of the expense of construction, the private sector is unable to build housing to rent at rates that poor people can afford. The government has in several major housing acts expressed a full commitment to provide decent housing for all Americans. After the ghetto riots in the 1960s, for example, the government committed itself, in 1968, to direct subsidy of 6 million new housing units in ten years. Yet by 1976, eight years later, only slightly over a third of that number had been built (Dackawich, 1979, p. 9).

The case of Pruitt-Igoe

Even where inexpensive public housing was completed, the effects were sometimes disastrous. One classic fiasco was the Pruitt-Igoe public housing project in St. Louis, a complex of forty-three buildings containing 2,800 low-rent apartments. It was completed in the mid-1950s at a cost of $30 million and was hailed as a model for improving the lot of the poor. Less than twenty years later, however, the apartments were vacated and the entire project was deliberately dynamited to the ground.

During its brief existence, Pruitt-Igoe became a nightmare of burglary, robbery, rape, and murder. What happened? For one thing, the apartments had been designed with almost jaillike efficiency. As an economy move, elevators stopped only at every third floor, making both elevators and stairways ideal areas for criminals. Residents locked themselves inside their apartments, afraid even to venture down the hall to socialize with neighbors. Tenants did not have even minimal control over their environment: all decisions were made by the housing authority, including the length of time visitors could stay, types of pets allowed, the kind of paint permitted, and the schedule for using the laundry rooms. The area had no economic base; almost everyone was subsidized by one governmental agency or another. The deterioration of Pruitt-Igoe was so thorough and swift that its sponsors believed the best and most reasonable solution was simply to destroy it.

It should be noted that publicly supported housing does not have to destroy a community; in fact, it can sometimes enhance it. In West Germany, for example, some form of direct subsidies support housing construction for 80 percent of the population, which means that blue-collar workers and manual workers can live side by side with professionals and business people, sharing schools and other neighborhood and community facilities (Dackawich, 1979, p. 25).

The case of Bedford-Stuyvesant

An important failing of many ghetto housing projects has been lack of appreciation for the cultural strengths of such enclaves. The ghetto—even with all its problems—can provide a powerful sense of community for its residents. To date, the most successful urban development projects have made use of such feelings about the community among its residents. One such project was initiated in the Bedford-Stuyvesant section of Brooklyn, New York.

In the 1960s this sprawling black ghetto had 450,000 inhabitants and the full roster of inner-city ills—unemployment, dilapidated buildings, and an angry, frustrated population. Local leaders rejected the bulldozer approach and refused to permit massive construction projects. Instead, they asked residents through interviews and questionnaires what they felt the area needed most. The respondents gave priority to jobs, improved housing, and education. Accordingly, a new development corporation called Restoration launched a series of small but multifaceted projects. With minimal financing, they offered homeowners and landlords exterior paint jobs and repairs at low cost, and they used the resulting contracts as a means of employing and training local laborers. Similar on-the-job training schemes were used in the full-scale rehabilitation of abandoned brownstone houses. New businesses were recruited to the area, and employment offices found 7,000 new jobs for residents by the mid-1970s. A community college was established and a cultural center opened, and television time was secured for regular broadcasting of events and news to residents. As one measure of Restoration's achievement, people who had moved out of Bedford-Stuyvesant began moving back.

A key element in the program's success, observers believe, was the granting of significant decision-making power to the ghetto residents. They understood, and applied their energies to, the area's resources, such as old but well-constructed buildings. Restoration also managed to keep all projects within practical limits: it would not start programs it could not complete. Ironically, Bedford-Stuyvesant's effort has been one of the cheapest yet launched: during a period when the United States committed $75 billion to urban-oriented projects, Restoration functioned on about $30 million in public and private capital. The Bedford-Stuyvesant program has been the model for development corporations in more than a score of other American cities.

Gentrification

A more recent form of urban renewal and redevelopment seems to be occurring not because of planning, but because of broader social and economic changes. One change is the growth of adult-oriented households: people are having fewer children, or none. Another is the shortages and skyrocketing costs of gasoline (for commuting to the city) and oil (for heating a large home in the suburbs). The combination has made the central city attractive again to substantial numbers of affluent people, particularly young professionals—the new "urban gentry." With new construction prohibitively expensive, landlords and developers have responded by renovating run-down neighborhoods into attractive high-rent districts. Good old brownstones are being bought and renovated; more and more rental buildings are being converted to tenant-owned "co-op" and condominium apartments; the solid nineteenth-century buildings of decaying factory areas are being turned into shopping and recreation centers. In Boston, for example, the hundred-year-old Quincy Market has been rebuilt into a shopping and restaurant complex in the heart of the downtown area. It has been immensely popular, attracting throngs of city dwellers and others eager for the excitement and bustle of humanity often lacking in the suburbs.

But although it may eventually solve some urban problems, this gentrification will probably create new ones. The working-class people displaced by renovation may be able to move to the suburbs, but the poor—the underclass—will again have nowhere to go.

GENTRIFICATION: MOVING TO THE INNER CITY

Washington, D.C.'s Capitol Hill area has, for many years, been a neighborhood of mostly black, low- and moderate-income families. They have lived on streets lined with stone row-houses, dating back to the late nineteenth and early twentieth centuries. But recently, the neighborhood has been changing.

According to Dennis E. Gale, a professor of urban planning at George Washington University, the new people on the block tend to be white, childless couples or singles in their late twenties or thirties, as in many other inner cities (July 1979, pp. 293-294). Most have professional or managerial jobs, with incomes above the national average. These "urban gentry" have not returned from the suburbs, but have moved to the inner-city from other parts of Washington. The same pattern holds for "resettlers" in Atlanta, Boston, and Cambridge, where over one-half "(and in some cases as many as 90 percent) . . . moved to the renovating area from somewhere within the city's municipal boundaries" (p. 296).

Why are these young people moving into neighborhoods that many were afraid to walk in only a short time ago? Part of the answer has to do with economics. With good jobs and no children, this group pays high personal income taxes. Home ownership has always been an avenue to tax relief, but what would people like these do in the suburbs? The new inner-city dwellers consider themselves quite different from suburbanites. With perhaps a touch of snobbery they see themselves as "more interesting" and "intellectual" than suburban dwellers. As one study concluded, these inner-city "young professionals identify themselves as part of an elite within the middle-class elite" (p. 297, quoted from the Parkman Center for Urban Affairs, 1977).

So, rejection of suburbia and the appeal of a good real estate investment combine to make the purchase of an inner-city house attractive. Living in the city also reduces the time spent commuting to work. Finally, the newcomers to the inner city like the architectural character of their houses and the historical significance of their neighborhoods.

Clearly, buying a well-built home in a formerly poor neighborhood represents a good investment for the "urban gentry." Neighborhood resettlement also benefits local governments. The new buyers renovate or restore their homes with an ensuing rise in real estate taxes and other revenues for the city's coffers. Simultaneously, pressure drops for social welfare and school services; neighborhood crime rates may go down; and neighborhood population density may drop.

So far, so good. But, for the poor people who live in the newly fashionable neighborhoods, there are problems. Many cannot pay the rents that rise along with property values and must move to other neighborhoods. One survey found that "significant dislocation was occurring in 82 percent of the neighborhoods undergoing middle-class renovation" (Clay 1978, p. 302). The racial composition of resettled neighborhoods is often also affected. In about one-half of the cities studied by Clay the minority group population had dropped, and in about one-third there was no change.

At the national level, the negative social effects of gentrification have not yet become severe. In part, this is because many people leave the resettled neighborhoods, not because they are forced to, but because of old age, illness, and family problems, thus making room for those who wish to move in. But, advises Gale, where dislocation rates become high, protection for and programs to assist the displaced are necessary.

Gentrification—the renovation of decaying urban areas, primarily by the affluent young—is solving some urban problems, but it is also displacing many poorer residents who have nowhere to go. (© Hazel Hankin 1980)

THE POST-URBAN AGE?

In the 1960s, when angry blacks and Puerto Ricans engaged in violent confrontations with police, there was much talk of the "urban crisis" and even of the impending destruction of American cities. In the 1970s, partly as a result of repression and partly as a result of small gains won for some and the failure of ghetto riots to produce large-scale change, mass urban violence has subsided, though the 1980 riots in Miami (see Chapter 12) show that it can easily happen again. Public concern for the cities has subsided as well. The 1970s saw national attention diverted to a new series of problems—energy shortages, inflation, pollution, women's rights.

Yet today the problems of the city are in a very real sense the problems of the country as a whole, for the political boundaries of cities no longer reflect the limits of their economic and social influence on the society. Residential, commercial, and industrial areas flow across such artificial boundaries, and newspapers, telephones, radio, and television have effectively extended the influence of the metropolis to areas well beyond the official suburbs. Rapid transit and expressways link the entire countryside to the central city. And the merchandising operations of the metropolis now constitute a single system that penetrates into the outermost reaches of exurbia.

In fact, many of the troubles of the cities have reached the suburbs as well. Real estate is expensive, and taxes continue to rise. The encroachment of industry and of high rises and shopping centers mars the countrified atmosphere that suburbanites have traditionally sought. And the suburbs confront serious problems of drug use, crime, and pollution.

Paradoxically, our society may actually be evolving toward what some sociologists have called a "post-urban" phase. Despite their continuing importance as centers of government and finance, as well as of cultural and social activity, cities have lost some of their major functions. Improvements in transportation and communication mean that much business and manufacturing need no longer be physically located in the city to maintain contacts or receive supplies. As a result, industry has been able to move away from the cities in search of more space and cheaper labor. Some manufacturing that makes intensive use of labor, such as garment production, has moved to other countries where manufac-

turing can be done even more cheaply because wage scales are lower. The emigration of the middle class, many of whom shop and work in the suburbs as well as live there, has also weakened the city as an economic center. In a controversial article titled "Are Big Cities Worth Saving?" (1970), George S. Sternlieb reaches the conclusion that they are not. "The problem of the city," Sternlieb states, "is a crisis of function. What is left to the city that it does better than someplace else?" (p. 42).

Suzanne Keller has suggested that the new mobility of humans, goods, and ideas seems to have obviated not only the traditional functions of the city but perhaps the very notion of permanent settlements altogether.

As mobility and diversity increase in the decades ahead, the mobility long characteristic of sailors, traveling salesmen, students, and the jet set will spread to ever wider sectors of the public. New patterns of domesticity, friendship, and vocation will then compel us to rethink the very idea of settled living and the assumption, still widespread, that human beings require a fixed territorial base for their round of daily life. Permanent residence in a fixed location may eventually become characteristic of particular groups or stages in the life cycle and be but one among several acceptable modes of habitation. (Keller, 1975, p. 292)

One product of such dispersal may be the continued growth of "new towns," specialized by function, which could replace the traditional urban centers. Thousands of such towns are now in the planning or construction stage throughout the world, in both industrialized and developing nations. One of the most successful new-town experiments is Columbia, Maryland, whose planners managed to achieve a balance of open, green space with residences and buildings over an 18,000-acre expanse that houses some 110,000 people. Since a key premise in Columbia's design was avoidance of the overwhelming "bigness" of the city, residential blocks and buildings in the community are kept to a small scale. Mailboxes are clustered in units of sixteen, to help ensure that neighbors meet one another; and each neighborhood unit of 900 houses is within walking distance of recreational facilities, schools, and community meeting rooms.

Is life more rewarding and less difficult in a new semiurban "utopia" such as Columbia? A survey of residents revealed that nearly twice as many were involved in Columbia civic affairs as had participated in the cities where they had previously lived—an involvement that attests to a feeling of community responsibility.

Yet many of the old problems existed even in this pleasant environment: Columbia still had drug abuse, teen-age vandalism, and crime (Eichler and Kaplan, 1967). New towns do not eliminate economic segregation, since factory workers and others who must work, and therefore live, in or near large cities, do not have the option of moving to them. Moreover, the planning that pervades every aspect of community life may actually inhibit the formation of a social structure that reflects the felt needs and concerns of the inhabitants. Whether future new-town planners can eliminate such problems remains an open question. But the example of Columbia does suggest that changing the physical surroundings of city dwellers will not solve all problems. And it also serves to remind students of urban patterns that even the most thoughtfully designed new town will inevitably be subject to some of the problems that trouble the larger society.

Summary

Modern cities are characterized by a complex social organization in which economic and other social roles are highly specialized and differentiated; in which the stratification system is likely to be more complex than in nonurban areas; and in which there are a great many groups and organizations. Ferdinand Tönnies observed that the *Gemeinschaft* ("community") was being replaced by the impersonal *Gesellschaft* ("society"). Emile Durkheim contrasted the *mechanical solidarity* of traditional societies with the *organic solidarity* of modern societies.

With the development of cities, most residents of a settlement for the first time no longer had to spend the majority of their time growing their own food. Ancient cities were also characterized by relatively large, densely settled populations, high division of labor, complex stratification systems, and such central institutions as public buildings, commerce, and art. Preindustrial cities were characterized by rigid economic, social, and even physical structures.

The industrialized city emerged with the technological and cultural changes of the Industrial Revolution. Workers moved from farms and villages to factory towns. Increasingly, the city—and the even larger and more complex *metropolis*—became a center for fulfilling the needs of its surrounding area.

Urban life has had an effect on the personalities of city dwellers. Georg Simmel offered the general observation that the city dweller's reserve functioned as a protection against the busier tempo of the city. Louis Wirth noted three ecological factors in urban interaction: size, density, and heterogeneity.

Social scientists have also studied the effects of urban spatial and demographic patterns on social life in the city. Many have made use of the ecological approach of Louis Wirth and Robert Park: Ernest W. Burgess (the concentric-circle model), Homer Hoyt (the sector model), and Chauncy Harris and Edward I. Ullman (the multiple-nuclei model).

Today's cities are beset by a variety of problems, for which many solutions have been offered. Many middle-class city dwellers have moved to the suburbs, leaving the central cities heavily populated by less affluent whites, blacks, Hispanics, and other minority-group members. Most big cities are burdened by such problems as poor housing, a diminishing tax base with which they must meet the increasing need for public services, high crime rates, and overlapping, diffused governmental jurisdiction and methods of financing. Solving any of these problems would contribute toward rescuing the cities from their plight. Some wholesale assaults on urban problems have been made by city planning and redevelopment programs, but their record is spotty, and some have even increased the problems they were supposed to solve. Gentrification, the return of affluent professionals, has improved some central-city areas, but will perhaps increase the problems of the poor who are displaced.

Some observers feel that cities have lost their basic functions, and that with a more dispersed and mobile population, we are entering a post-urban age. Planned "new towns" like Columbia, Maryland, are one such post-urban response. Yet ultimately most of the problems of the city in the United States are problems of the society as a whole.

Glossary

ECOLOGICAL Having to do with organisms and their relationship to their environment.

GEMEINSCHAFT "Community," the term used by Tönnies to describe a cohesive society organized on the basis of shared values and norms that commands strong allegiance from its members.

GESELLSCHAFT "Society," the term used by Tönnies to describe a society characterized by individual self-interest, little consensus on norms or values, little commitment to the group, and continual change.

HETEROGENEOUS SOCIETY A society made up of a variety of personalities and individuals.

MECHANICAL SOLIDARITY Durkheim's term for the binding together of human groups in a society through the similarity of their work roles and through the sharing of values and a moral consensus.

METROPOLIS A large city central to a country, state, or region, with adjacent, densely developed residential, industrial, commercial, educational, and recreational areas, and close-by satellite cities.

ORGANIC SOLIDARITY Durkheim's term for the binding together of human groups in a society through the interdependence that results from differentiation and specialization of work roles, and self-interest.

Recommended readings

Castells, Manuel. *The Urban Question: A Marxist Approach.* Translated by Alan Sheridan. Cambridge, Mass.: M.I.T. Press, 1977. An influential book stressing the broader political and economic factors with which urban issues must be considered.

Gist, Noel P., and Sylvia F. Fava. *Urban Society.* 6th ed. New York: Crowell, 1974. A comprehensive overview of the city—its growth, its organization, and the life of its people. This fundamental source on the city includes a valuable discussion of urban ecology.

Jacobs, Jane. *The Death and Life of Great American Cities.* New York: Vintage, 1961. In this now-famous work, the author describes life in the city and strongly argues for neighborhoods and against urban renewal that may destroy established communities.

Liebow, Elliot. *Tally's Corner: A Study of Negro Street-Corner Men.* Boston: Little, Brown, 1967. Liebow studies a group of black men that gather on Tally's Corner in inner-city Washington, D.C. Friendships among the men and the organization of their primary group leads Liebow to insights on personal reactions to urban life.

Reissman, Leonard. *The Urban Process.* New York: Free Press, 1964. A useful interpretive summary of major sociological efforts to understand the twin processes of urbanization and industrialization.

Suttles, Gerald D. *The Social Order of the Slum: Ethnicity and Territory in the Inner City.* Chicago: University of Chicago Press, 1968. In a study of Chicago's urban slum areas, Suttles examines interactions of ethnic groups as well as how they define their "turf." The tacit zoning and differences in behavior and values form a distinct social order out of seeming disorder.

Walton, John, and Donald Carns. *Cities in Change: Studies on the Urban Condition.* 2nd ed. Boston: Allyn & Bacon, 1977. A useful collection of articles on the origins of, and some possible solutions to, the problems facing modern cities.

CHAPTER TWENTY-ONE

COLLECTIVE BEHAVIOR AND SOCIAL MOVEMENTS

At certain times, great numbers of people take part in actions that are relatively goal-oriented, planned, and predictable. Thousands of slaves were forced to work together in the construction of the Egyptian pyramids; millions of soldiers were arrayed against one another in World Wars I and II; some 80 million Americans go to the polls every fourth year to elect a President. Such actions, however, are by no means the only kinds involving large numbers of people. Often mass actions emerge that are comparatively unplanned and unpredictable—spontaneous bursts of collective activity that energize and sweep along thousands or even millions of people without much conscious planning or central direction, at least in the beginning.

The storming of the Bastille, an infamous prison in Paris, at the start of the French Revolution is a familiar example of this second kind of activity. Other instances include the panic in 1938 after Orson Welles' *War of the Worlds* radio broadcast convinced a large number of people that Martians had actually landed in the United States, the behavior of the huge crowds at the Woodstock rock festival of 1969, and the outbreak of looting during the power blackout of July 1977, as well as the CB radio fad and the sudden popularity of disco dancing.

The nature of collective behavior

All these are examples of what sociologists call *collective behavior*. Logically, collective behavior could include any group behavior, whether institutionalized or not. However, the term is reserved in sociology for relatively *noninstitutionalized* mass behavior. Thus, *collective behavior* refers to *those similar actions of a multiplicity of individuals that are relatively spontaneous and transitory and are therefore in contrast to the more routine, predictable interactions of everyday life.* Thus defined, collective behavior may encompass a wide variety of phenomena, including fashions, fads, riots, revolutions, and social movements of all sorts. The term has also been used to describe the ebb and flow of public opinion and the effects of propaganda, rumor, and mass communications.

Collective actions may center harmlessly on trivial

objects, symbolic actions, vague goals such as hair and clothing styles, musical forms, or modes of consciousness; they may be destructive and seem irrational to observers, like the witch hunts of the sixteenth and seventeenth centuries; or they may change the course of political and social history, as did the Crusades in medieval Europe.

Incidents of collective behavior often involve some sort of new (although not necessarily enduring) pattern of behavior. It may be a new *norm*, with large numbers of people beginning to behave in similar ways—for example, shouting and running in a crowd. Or it may reflect a new *social relationship*, as when the "good guys" in an old-time Western movie form a posse to chase the villains. Many episodes embrace both (Weller and Quarantelli, 1973).

In order to see what actually happens, let us examine in some detail one specific incident—the killing of four students and the wounding of nine others by members of the Ohio National Guard on the campus of Kent State University in 1970.

The actual shooting at Kent State was the culmination of four days of escalating unrest and sporadic violence following then-President Richard Nixon's announcement on April 30, 1970, that American troops had been sent into Cambodia to destroy staging areas used by the North Vietnamese army. Even before this announcement that the scope of the Vietnam War had been widened, the Kent State campus—like many others across the nation—had been the scene of antiwar agitation. There had been a march at Kent State in October 1969, and a group from the university had participated in a mass antiwar rally in Washington, D.C., in November of that year. So emotions were already running high when the news of Nixon's action came— the more so because the American involvement in Southeast Asia and the war in Vietnam had seemed to be tapering off. The day after the announcement (Friday, May 1), there were two short and peaceful rallies

Although they are all in the same place at the same time, these office workers on Wall Street at lunchtime (top) are not engaging in what sociologists call collective behavior because their activities are relatively routine and predictable. The parade spectators (bottom), however, are involved in behavior that is transitory and not routine; sociologists would call this collective behavior. (Cornell Capa/Magnum; Roger Lubin/Jeroboam)

on campus, one concerning recent disturbances at Ohio State University and one directly concerning the war. By late evening, some less structured and more destructive crowd behavior began. Students started to gather in the streets of the town, where they were joined by patrons from local bars; there were antiwar chants, and bottles were thrown. When the city police arrived outfitted to deal with a riot, a crowd of about 500 began smashing store windows. The measures the police took were relatively firm (firmer, perhaps, than was wise, one bar owner suggested): they closed the bars, which put a lot of angry people on the streets, and used tear gas to disperse the crowd.

The next day, there was a good deal of general alarm. Rumors circulated among the townspeople that members of the Weathermen (a radical offshoot of Students for a Democratic Society, a leftist political group) were behind the disturbance, that there were weapons on campus, and that merchants had been threatened. On campus, at about 8 P.M., students began to gather on the University Commons, a central rallying point for student political activities. Within half an hour the milling crowd grew to perhaps a thousand persons. Many members of the crowd (though not all) threw matches, flares, and gasoline-soaked rags at the ROTC building, and some cut the hoses of the fire trucks that eventually arrived. Tear gas was again used on the crowd, this time by the campus police. Meanwhile, alarmed by the rumors that had spread throughout the day, the mayor asked the governor of Ohio to call out the National Guard. By about 9:30 P.M., the Guard had taken over the campus and was restricting movement, even of university officials.

Excitement was high the next day. Normal lines of communication and authority were further disrupted when the governor arrived and changed the Guard's orders from "protecting property and lives" to "breaking up any assembly on campus whether it was peaceful or violent" (Lewis, 1972, p. 89). That day saw a major confrontation between the National Guard and the students, without serious injuries on either side. Nevertheless, the Guard, armed with rifles and bayonets, remained on campus.

The following day, May 4, when a second confrontation took place, tensions were so high—and communication links so greatly weakened—that some members of the National Guard are said to have been afraid for their lives, which *may* be why a few of them disregarded orders and began to fire. It was one of the tragic paradoxes of the situation that the crowd the Guardsmen fired on was actually relatively small; a larger crowd had been dispersed, and when the shooting took place there were so few students present that, in less extreme circumstances, they might have presented very little threat to the Guard. Clearly, both sides were acting under the influence of spiraling misinformation, mounting tensions, and the breakdown of some traditional behavior patterns. A number of specific processes were involved, which will be discussed later in this chapter.

Collective behavior involving crowds

The Kent State events were characterized by many different kinds of collective behavior. First of all, there were several different types of behavior involving crowds. There were the peaceful rallies on Friday, involving what Herbert Blumer (1953) would call *expressive crowds*—people who came together mainly to express their feelings and interests. (The Woodstock rock festival is an example of this kind of crowd; for a short time, Woodstock and other music festivals became almost institutionalized vehicles for such expressive behavior.) There were also the incidents involving *acting crowds:* these included the window-smashing on Friday evening (when the behavior of the crowd was violent and destructive, but still relatively unstructured), and the more purposeful behavior on Saturday, when students set fire to the ROTC building, and on Monday, when the soldiers fired on the students. Meanwhile, throughout the four days, *casual crowds* of people who just happened to be there stood around, watching the events but not participating. Some students continued to attend classes, where they constituted what Blumer calls *conventional crowds*, whose behavior is guided by traditional norms, like the behavior of an audience at a concert. Thus there is no *one* phenomenon that can be thought of as "crowd behavior."

With these distinctions in mind, the next question

Many types of collective behavior were evident at Kent State University in May 1970. Here, tear gas hangs over the campus as National Guardsmen attempt to disperse rioting students. (Wide World Photos)

is, what are some of the dynamic processes that operate in many crowd situations? Gustave LeBon, a classic theorist of collective behavior, thought of a crowd as an aggregate of people behaving "irrationally" and "emotionally" and imitating each other's actions through an almost disease-like "contagion" (1895). LeBon thought of crowd members as held together by "mental unity"; he saw them as automatons, acting together without a conscious exercise of will. Sigmund Freud (1922) saw crowd members as regressing *en masse* to a state of infantile dependency on their leader. And Blumer (1953) thought of them as subject to a "circular reaction" process, which led them to copy one another's behavior without consciously considering what they were doing.

More recent approaches have called some of these ideas into question. Many misconceptions about

crowds arise partly because crowd behavior often takes place in political contexts (rallies and demonstrations, for example) that are threatening to many observers. It is thus all the more important to distinguish between the folklore and the facts about crowds. To see a crowd as a body of "herdlike" or "irrational" people is to see it as completely dissimilar to an aggregation of people in other social contexts, as a unique phenomenon that cannot be studied with the usual methods and assumptions of sociological investigation—in short, as alien. To look at a crowd in this way is often to ignore the significance of what its members are saying and doing, both within the immediate social surroundings and within the larger social and historical contexts. The Kent State incident, for example, took place within a social setting that included the town of Kent as well as the university campus, and also within the historical context of the highly controversial American foreign policy in Southeast Asia and the war in Vietnam. In this sense, the actions of both students and social-control agents at Kent State were far from meaningless or completely alien to the standards of the people in the surrounding society.

This is not to suggest, however, that crowds never behave irrationally. If people are acting on distorted information—as may be the case with crowds—their behavior may in some respects be irrational in relation to the reality of the situation. But there is only limited truth to the idea that people automatically act irrationally in collectivities, even under stress. The frequent cases of calm and purposeful behavior of people involved in airplane hijackings and disasters demonstrate this. On the other hand, people may act irrationally in non-crowd situations.

To what extent, then, does crowd behavior differ from social behavior in more institutionalized situations? In order to answer this question, it is helpful to break down what happens in a crowd into two aspects: what people know about their situation (or how they perceive it), and what they actually do.

RUMORS AND PERCEPTIONS

In one key respect, what happened in the crowds at Kent State (and in the town as a whole) was similar to what happens in a movie theater when there is an explosion, or what happened during the Cuban missile crisis of October 1962. Confronted with an ambiguous situation about which there was inadequate information, participants began to sense the presence of a threat. As Muzafer Sherif and O. J. Harvey (1952) point out, a situation such as this—without stable information "anchorages"—is one in which *rumors*, unverified reports passed along from one person to the next, are likely to develop. Rumors may be true, false, or a combination of the two; their origins are often hard to trace.

The rumor is typically based on some specific action or event that is not defined for those watching. For example, S. I. A. Marshall (1947, p. 146), who investigated the panic that occurred in battle during World War II, concluded that *in every case the "common denominator" was that "somebody failed to tell other men what he was doing."* Thus, in one case, a sergeant wounded during battle dashed back to a first-aid station without telling his squad why. Not aware that he was wounded, they ran after him, and the rumor spread throughout the line: "The order is to withdraw."

Sociologists have debated exactly what goes on in the rumor process—whether rumors become embroidered in the telling, whether they become enlarged like a rolling snowball, or even whether they come closer to the truth (Caplow, 1947). Gordon W. Allport and Leo Postman (1947), in a series of laboratory experiments

on the serial transmission of rumor, came up with data suggesting that the content of the rumor was increasingly distorted as it traveled farther from the original speaker. In their view, each individual's contribution to the rumor—that is, the details selected to be repeated and the extent and manner of distortion—depended on his or her own preexisting wishes or fears: what was wanted or expected to be true. In the Kent State incident, for example, the information received was distorted to reflect fears of dissident and violent groups such as the Weathermen, and it was on the strength of these rumors that the National Guard was called in.

According to Allport and Postman, two processes are involved in the spreading of a rumor: it becomes *sharpened*—certain details being selected from the larger context are exaggerated—and it also becomes *leveled*—shorter and more concise. These processes can be seen in operation at Kent State: various crowd incidents, both peaceful and violent, were merged in the rumors that spread throughout the town in such a way as to suggest a unified and planned action. In addition, people who were not on the campus to see what was happening passed along rumors that became more and more distorted. By the time these rumors reached Governor James Rhodes, he received the impression that officials were faced with what amounted to armed insurrection. When he came to Kent on Sunday, May 3, he said, "I think we are up against the strongest, well-trained militant group that has ever assembled in America," and he gave the National Guard orders that would be given in the face of armed rebellion (quoted in the Akron *Beacon Journal*, May 24, 1970).

BEHAVIOR IN DISASTERS

In disasters and other emergency situations—tornados, earthquakes, military invasions, fires—*panic* may develop. People may become intensely fearful, and each may try individually to escape without cooperating with others in the situation. For instance, if people stampede in a fire, many more die than would be the case if they left the building in an orderly, calm, and organized fashion. The result of panic behavior may therefore be increased confusion, danger, and even loss of life.

But research on eight actual disasters in the United States by the National Opinion Research Center, reported by Charles E. Fritz and Eli S. Marks (1954), did not support these traditional ideas of emotionalism and blind panic in every case of emergency. First of all, Fritz and Marks noted that panic flight and other highly uncontrolled forms of behavior occurred only among *some* people in any one disaster, and under certain limited conditions only in *some* disasters. Second, much depended on the participants' own definition of the situation and whether all participants perceived it the same way. Also important was the amount of warning participants received, for inadequate warning may lead to more injury and death than no warning at all, since people may be injured while rushing for safety. Panic was more likely when people were separated from family members or were in close contact with the dead and injured. And last, according to Fritz and Marks, panic occurred only when:

(1) the individual believed himself to be in a situation involving *immediate threat* of personal destruction, and (2) the individual believed escape was possible at the moment but might become impossible in the immediate future—i.e., that unless one got away, one would be trapped. (Fritz and Marks, 1954, p. 33)

Most social scientists now agree with these findings: behavior during disasters does not always involve panic or other disorganized, hysterical responses. E. I. Quarantelli (1975), for instance, holds that panic behavior—which he identifies with unchecked fear and with anticipated immediate danger to life—occurs in only a tiny fraction of disaster situations. Even in the Cocoanut Grove nightclub fire in Boston in 1942, often cited as an example of a panic, only about one-third of those involved may have engaged in this behavior, though nearly 500 people died and hundreds of others were seriously injured. Quarantelli reports that empirical investigations carried out since 1950 have produced a consensus among researchers around the world that "human behavior under stress is relatively controlled, rational, and adaptive" (1975, p. 6). He holds that if disaster behavior is compared with actual everyday behavior, rather than with some ideal of heroism, "there is not that much difference between the two" (p. 8).

THE EMERGENT NORM

Observers of crowd behavior often comment on what appears to be uniformity of the behavior. For example, if some members begin to throw rocks and bottles,

many others are likely to join in; if a few members start chanting a slogan, the chant is often taken up by all. Even though individuals in the crowd may have a different idea about the most appropriate behavior, they often end up behaving very similarly.

Ralph H. Turner and Lewis M. Killian (1972) attribute this phenomenon to the development of what they call an *emergent norm*. They argue that in the face of an ambiguous situation, members of the collectivity will seek not only a shared understanding of their situation but also an appropriate course of common action.

During an initial "milling" period, various alternatives and justifications may circulate through the group. Some of the possibilities for action that people suggest to one another may be of types from which they ordinarily would refrain. But everyday standards of judgment are weakened because the situation has lost many of its stable anchorages; thus people may commit acts generally considered deviant. Furthermore, the emerging pattern of behavior (such as the firing of guns or movement toward an exit) tends to be accepted, or at least tolerated, by most members of the collectivity, while contrary or dissenting behavior is inhibited or quashed by ridicule or coercion.

An alternative explanation for the uniformity of crowd behavior is the "convergence" theory, which holds that those drawn to the crowd already know what they want to do. Rather than focusing on how a shared definition of appropriate behavior may emerge out of interaction, this approach argues that people predisposed toward acting in a given way "converge" on the scene. This is often the case with protest demonstrations. Those concerned about a given issue may have a fairly clear idea of the actions they wish to take. They are drawn to the scene because they wish to march peacefully, occupy a building—or confront the National Guard.

CROWD STRUCTURE

Of course, not everyone in a crowd will be doing the same thing at the same time. In fact, many collectivities develop "divisions of labor." Within a crowd, for instance, people may circulate to exchange or compare rumors, in the process taking on various roles. Tamotsu Shibutani (1966) mentions the roles of messenger, interpreter, skeptic, protagonist (a person who supports one interpretation over others), auditor (one who merely listens but whose presence nevertheless influences the way a rumor is reported), and decision maker. Similarly, at Kent State, Jerry M. Lewis (1972) identified three separate categories of students involved in the incident on Monday: the "active core," who actually gestured, yelled, and threw things at the National Guard; the "cheerleaders," who showed support; and the "spectators." The emergent-norm theory offers a way of conceptualizing what happens within each small segment of a crowd, as well as within the crowd as a whole. Individuals in each segment may not be unanimous in their expectations and definitions of the situation, but they may *appear* so because dissenters are inhibited from expressing opposition.

Patterns of collective behavior

Sociologists have been more effective in describing and classifying the collective behavior of crowds than in explaining it. One reason for this is the enormous variability of crowd behavior. The standing ovation an audience gives a great orchestra, the fighting that breaks out among spectators at an athletic contest, the panic that causes patrons to jam the exits of a burning nightclub—all are examples of collective behavior. It is by no means easy to make generalizations or formulate theories that would explain all these kinds of behavior.

Sociologists do, nevertheless, recognize certain patterns that seem to appear in most incidents of collective behavior. First of all, the incident often involves an *ambiguous situation*, in which people lack reliable information; they may not know exactly what's going on. Norms may be lacking or inadequate, so that people don't know precisely what to do. In such a situation, a new norm often develops to fill the vacuum. Incidents of collective behavior often involve a good deal of *emotion*: people are afraid, angry, or excited. The emotional nature of the situation may be related to stress (such as fear of the effects of a disaster, of harm to one's family, of dissident elements in the society).

Sometimes the immediate precipitants of collective behavior are easy to identify. When a city is rocked by an earthquake, it is not surprising to find that many people immediately run into the streets. Sometimes the causes are more diffuse and remote, such as a rapid demographic shift, a marked transformation of values and norms, or a change in social conditions. At the same time, though, these phenomena can and often do occur without causing incidents of collective behavior. Sometimes, too, collective behavior appears to develop even in the absence of a visible dislocation or strain, as in the case of the "issueless riots" that have occurred when police have gone on strike, or when the home team has won the World Series (Marx, 1970).

Two problem areas illustrate the limits of present knowledge about it—methodology and labeling.

PROBLEMS OF METHODOLOGY

For research to be fruitful, there must be agreement on what is being studied. Although there has been a good deal of research on collective behavior, not all of it has been addressed to the same thing. This is not surprising, since the behavior of a crowd, or any other group of human beings, is not in fact one "thing," but many complex and disparate things occurring at the same time. As the variety of examples given in this chapter suggests, "collective behavior" is actually something of a catchall category encompassing many different kinds of actions. Although one definition of the term has been given in this chapter, others also have been offered. And no matter how the term is defined, it is often left with a meaning broad enough to be applicable to phenomena as diverse as the hula hoop craze and the civil-rights movement. The problem of definition is by no means trivial; knowledge is gained only when research builds on other research. When it is not based on the same assumptions, this cannot happen.

The study of collective behavior is also made difficult by its very nature: it is often short-lived, unpredictable, and complex, occurring here and there and in various manifestations. Often it is spread over a large geographical area, involves thousands (or even millions) of people, and is likely to change over time (Marx and Wood, 1975). The disorders following the assassination of Martin Luther King, Jr., for example, occurred at

TO OPEN, TEAR ALONG PERFORATION

"CONTAGIOUS" COLLECTIVE BEHAVIOR: FROM HYSTERIA TO FASHION

One interesting thing about collective behavior is that it can occur even among people who are separated from one another in time and space, a group of people that sociologists call a *diffuse collectivity*. In these cases, the novel behavior seems to travel from person to person almost as if it were a mysterious virus. Consider, for example, the following incident, which took place in Mattoon, Illinois, in the fall of 1944.

On September 1, a woman reported to local police that someone had opened her bedroom window and sprayed her with a sweet-smelling gas that had partially paralyzed her legs for about half an hour and made her ill. The local paper reported the story on page one under the headline: "ANESTHETIC PROWLER ON THE LOOSE." The following day three more people reported being gassed in a similar manner. By September 10, seventeen "attacks" had been reported, and that night, despite constant patrolling by police and local citizens, seven more were reported. After one more attack the next night, the incidents ceased. The "phantom anesthetist" was never caught—nor even seen. Officials said there was no gas with the properties described by the victims, and soon the press was filled with articles on the dynamics of this type of mass hysteria.

A similar occurrence took place in Enfield, Illinois, where a creature with "three legs and two pink eyes the size of flashlight lenses" was reported on April 25, 1973. After considerable media coverage that attracted "monster hunters" to Enfield, public preoccupation with the "monster" died. The mystery was never solved (Miller et al., 1978).

What lies behind such episodes? Smelser (1963) argues that strain may give rise to a generalized belief that relieves ambiguity by identifying the source of the strain. The generalized belief is passed from one person to another.

Hysteria

In cases such as the "phantom anesthetist" episode, *hysteria* transforms an ambiguous, anxiety-provoking situation into a potent generalized threat. Occurring as it did during World War II, this incident probably reflected anxiety over the war, worry about loved ones overseas, and perhaps fear of invasion. (Sexual fears may have been involved as well; the initial victim reported being attacked while in bed.) Related to hysteria is the *hostile belief*, a generalized belief that a particular agent is responsible for anxiety-producing conditions and that the strain will disappear as soon as the agent is removed. Overt acts of racism, anti-Semitism, and religious persecution are based on hostile beliefs.

roughly the same time in a number of widely separated cities. In some there were relatively mild disorders; in others, huge blocks of buildings burned for days as widespread looting and sniping continued. Some governors immediately responded by calling out the National Guard; some did not. Given the scale and complexity of these events, the study of the collective behavior poses an enormous task. Of course, a large nationwide event can be broken down into smaller parts and a sample of cities can be taken; a study might be made, for example, of the course of the disorders in several cities chosen because of their systematic differences.

Nevertheless, the sociologist who wishes to study even one circumscribed incident of collective behavior faces problems. The skills of a historian or reporter may be necessary simply to reconstruct what happened, people's memories of emotionally charged events being often unreliable. In addition, "what happened" occurred over time: that is, what is being studied is a *process*. As was suggested in the discussion of methodology in Chapter 2, a process is by its very nature more difficult to study than something static, such as a social structure at one point in time. In a process involving many people, the difficulties are multiplied. Of course, as the examples have shown, not only can collective behavior be studied, but useful generalizations about it can be drawn.

THE LABELING PROCESS

Because collective behavior can lead to change, it can be a challenge to the established order and seem to threaten the community or society in which it takes place. It is not surprising, then, that collective-behavior episodes are affected by the labeling process, just as deviant acts of individuals are (see Chapter 7).

In an analysis of the public perception of protest, Ralph H. Turner (1969) hypothesizes that when people in the larger society are faced by a collective disturbance, they "test" the incident in a number of ways before deciding how to define it. They can call it "pro-

Crazes, fads, and fashions

Another kind of collective behavior is the *craze*, in which a simplistic idea catches on as the solution to problems. The California Gold Rush of 1849 is a good example of a craze, as is the "South Sea Bubble" in England during the early 1880s, when many people rushed out to invest in glittering colonial trading ventures that never paid off. Elements of the craze can also be seen in political bandwagons and religious revivals, and indeed in any movement that seems to offer people a simple remedy for what ails them. Two closely related crazes that swept the country in the 1970s were jogging and the movement toward "natural" foods: both seemed to offer solutions to health problems.

Fads are examples of novel behavior that catch on for less obvious reasons (sometimes apparently for no reason), and that are adopted by large numbers of people for short periods of time. In the fifties, the hula hoop had its day; in the seventies, roller-skating suddenly blossomed among adults. Fads are particularly common among adolescents, who are in the process of establishing an identity and who may wish to stand out as a bit different from adults. Of course, when a fad becomes too widespread, it no longer marks its followers as "different" and may disappear as suddenly as it appeared.

Fashions are also temporary, but they are longer-lived and more highly regarded than fads and change gradually rather than abruptly. Often a fashion may have its roots in a fad, particularly one that began among the young. Long hair on men, for example, was first worn by young rock musicians and their followers, but eventually became the fashion that most men adopted, albeit with modifications. Perhaps the most striking example of a fad that became a fashion (and nearly a universal one at that) is the wearing of blue jeans. Worn for years by children, manual laborers, and cowboys, jeans became a fad in the 1960s, when they were worn by many young people, in part to show hostility toward the "establishment" and the war in Vietnam. By the seventies, the fad had become a fashion with a vengeance: not only were jeans worn by everyone from President Carter to Gloria Vanderbilt, they had become "status" garb and sported designer labels. In this case, a fad grew into a fashion that for many people is almost a way of life, and with hundreds of millions of pairs of jeans being manufactured each year, it shows no signs of dying. Such fads and fashions, with their unpredictability and light-hearted aspect, show that much "contagious" collective behavior is neither sinister nor ultimately harmful.

test," thus granting it a measure of legitimacy; or they can interpret it as "deviance" or "rebellion." The race riots in St. Louis in 1919 and in Detroit in 1943 were considered rebellions and were harshly suppressed; but beginning with Watts in 1965, mass violence by the black and Hispanic urban poor has come to be regarded as social protest by influential segments of the population. (A gang fight in the same urban area, however, is seen as deviance.)

What are some of the criteria people apply to an incident of collective behavior in the course of the labeling process? How do they judge it? Some key criteria, Turner suggests, include the credibility of the crowd's acts and goals in relation to traditional concepts of social protest and justice; the combination of appeal and threat the crowd communicates; and the possibility of avoiding full-scale conflict through gestures of conciliation, including labeling the incident "legitimate protest" instead of "rebellion." At Kent State, for example, authorities evidently saw no need to define the collective-behavior incident as "legitimate

protest," as a gesture of conciliation to the students. Instead, the National Guard was called out and deployed without any apparent attempts to sit down with demonstrating students and talk things over. An important point to bear in mind is that, as Turner suggests, the way third parties, authorities, or society define a collective disturbance has consequences not only for the specific incident but also for future manifestations:

A protest definition [of a disturbance] spurs efforts to make legitimate and nonviolent methods for promoting reform more available than they had been previously, while other definitions are followed by even more restricted access to legitimate means for promoting change. (Turner, 1969, p. 817; see also Turner and Killian, 1972)

The labor strike became an accepted—in fact, an institutionalized—means for emphasizing grievances in industrial relations; the McCarthy-era suppression of dissent appears to have significantly reduced all protest for a time by defining virtually *any* opposing viewpoint as treason or rebellion.

A related point is that the definition of *who* is involved in a collective-behavior incident has to do with the viewpoint of the observer. The violence at the 1968 Democratic convention in Chicago, for instance, had as much to do with police tactics as with the discontent of the antiwar groups. To those who felt no sympathy with the demonstrators, the police might not have seemed to be a part of the disturbance; they were simply doing their job and preserving order. But the opposite view is suggested by studies showing that during riots, police and rioters may be subject to the same crowd dynamics and pressures (Marx, 1970; Stark, 1972).

The relationship between the observer and the way collective behavior is defined became starkly apparent in the various reactions to the ghetto disorders in Newark, Detroit, and numerous other cities during the "long hot summer" of 1967 or more recently in Miami in May 1980. Were those disturbances simply incidents of mass violence and deviance—or were they protests, rich in political significance, against society's basic institutions? Discussing the civil disorders of the 1960s, the ninety-second president of the American Bar Association, William T. Gossett, remarked:

It is well known that mobs do not generate human progress; they retard it. It is known that mobs do not establish rights; they trample them. It is known that mobs do not inspire the advancement of civilization; they impede it. . . . Obviously, mob violence and destruction cannot be tolerated by any nation that calls itself civilized.

But, referring to the same disorders, civil-rights advocates Stokely Carmichael and Charles V. Hamilton commented in 1967:

This country, with its pervasive institutional racism, has created socially undesirable conditions; it merely perpetuates those conditions when it lays the blame on people who, through whatever means at their disposal, seek to strike out at the conditions. (p. 161)

Defining and categorizing incidents of collective behavior, then, is not merely an academic exercise. The language and labels used to characterize the individuals involved reflect deep political feelings and can have crucial consequences for society at large.

The nature of social movements

The kinds of collective behavior considered thus far are generally short-lived and do not lead to major changes in social structure. Crowds disperse; hysteria cools; fads and fashions come and go. But not all collective behavior is transitory. In some instances, people react to their grievances and dissatisfactions by uniting in more organized, longer-term efforts to bring about change—or, in some cases, to resist a change that they feel is disrupting their lives. Organized activities of this type, directed toward bringing about or preventing change, are termed *social movements.* (Those social movements aimed at resisting change are termed *countermovements.*)

Some sociologists argue that the collective behavior we have been considering is sufficiently distinct from social movements to justify its being treated as a separate area. Indeed, social movements can be distinguished from other kinds of collective behavior in several ways. Principally, social movements are more organized and more purposefully oriented. They involve sustained activities over a longer period of time. The civil-rights movement in this country, for example, encompassed many groups and organizations with a number of recognized leaders. Their activities were directed toward several goals: school desegregation, fair housing, equal employment opportunity, and so on. The movement as a whole extended over more than a decade—and it continues today, albeit generally out of the limelight.

Even though social movements can be distinguished from collective behavior, however, it is logical to study them together. The two are often intertwined (Marx, 1980). Social movements may include many episodes of collective behavior in the form of rallies, mass marches, and other demonstrations. And one particular incident of collective behavior can be important in directing the course of the social movement. The Kent State episode, for example, served to strengthen the resolve of the antiwar movement and engendered sympathy among many not previously involved. The same might be said of the famous civil-rights march on Washington in 1964.

In addition, collective behavior and social movements are similar insofar as they are both somewhat outside the realm of ordinary life; to a degree, they take place beyond the reach of conventional social institutions. Collective behavior, often occurring spontaneously in random groups of people, has been called *noninstitutional.* Social movements, on the other hand, organized to alter existing institutions, have been called *anti-institutional* (Traugott, 1978). They are alike, however, in being outside normal social structures.

There are many historical examples of far-reaching changes associated with social movements—the rise of Christianity, the Protestant Reformation, the French and American revolutions, the antislavery movement in the United States, the rise of communism, the emergence of fascism. Social movements have also brought about change in less sweeping but still significant ways, as has been the case with the civil-rights movement and the women's movement. Many aspects of our everyday life—the eight-hour workday, universal suffrage, the widespread use of birth control—were once the distant goal of social movements. Countermovements, too, are highly noticeable on the current American scene: witness the growth of various anti-homosexual organizations and the "right to life" movement, both of which have emerged in opposition to new trends that were considered to be threats. Even the growth of Christian fundamentalist sects outside the established churches, such as the Jesus people (see Chapter 16), is seen by some as a countermovement opposing the depersonalization and secularization of modern life.

Most social movements have one or more highly structured "core" organizations at their centers. Most also have a loosely structured body of members or fol-

Labeling a movement "legitimate" or "deviant" can have a strong effect on the treatment of that movement. Antiwar demonstrations at the 1968 Democratic convention in Chicago were seen as rebellious and, as seen here, were strongly suppressed by the police. (UPI)

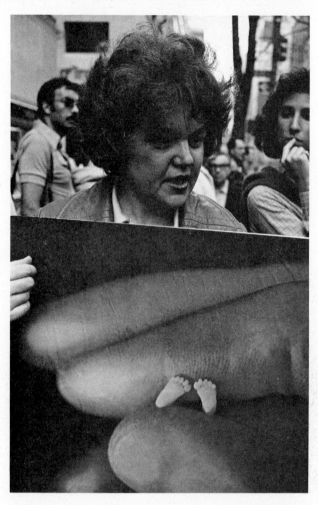

This anti-abortion protester is a member of a countermovement, a movement whose purpose is directly opposed to that of another group, in this case, those in favor of abortion rights. (© Lawrence Frank 1979)

lowers, not all of whom participate in all of the movement's activities.

A major factor that can unify the members is the movement's *ideology*—the set of beliefs that can spur members into action. (Smelser calls this a *generalized belief*.) The ideology offers a diagnosis and a prescription: it explains what may lie behind personal and social problems, and it sets forth a solution. Furthermore, it seeks to give its adherents a sense of worth and purpose. Some ideologies appeal to people who have been despised or disregarded, offering them a proud new identity—as in *transvaluational* religious ideologies that proclaim "the last shall be first."

An ideology can be liberating for those who embrace it. People driven by a powerful but unfocused discontent can, under the influence of an ideology, learn to see their grievances as part of a common pattern of wrongs that they believe they can do something about. Likewise, commitment to an ideology can carry with it the gratifying conviction that one is part of a select vanguard; it can provide the security of a meaningful, knowable world.

Types of social movements

Social movements vary tremendously, and researchers have put forward various ways of categorizing them. One relatively simple approach is that suggested by David Aberle (1966), in which he starts by determining whether it is the *social structure* or the *individual* that the social movement aims to change (or resist changes in), and then whether the change envisioned is *partial* or *total*.

In contrast to movements that strive for world-shaking renewals, there are *reformative* movements aiming at a partial change in the social structure. Movements of this type see the social order as basically good; they

object only to certain aspects of it that they believe can be rectified to make the system "work" better for all. Reformative movements of recent times have tried to change established legal and social attitudes (for example, the Gay Activist Alliance and the National Organization for the Reform of Marijuana Laws); have sought to alter defense and armament policies (for example, the Campaign for Nuclear Disarmament and the National Committee for a Sane Nuclear Policy); have striven to change discriminatory practices (for example, the National Association for the Advancement of Colored People, the National Organization for Women,

Antinuclear protesters at the Seabrook, New Hampshire nuclear power plant face police in riot gear. Reform movements such as this one frequently encounter strong opposition, but often triumph in the long run. (© Jim Anderson 1980)

holism and prostitution and on the need to gain redemption through Christ. The movement thus seeks to alter men and women and thereby alter the world" (1973, p. 24).

Movements that aim at total change in the individual (such as the Salvation Army, some of the Jesus-people groups, and the Hare Krishna movement) are what Aberle (1966) calls *redemptive:* they see the individual as needing to be completely redeemed from a wrong or evil inner state, converted and resocialized (topics that were discussed in Chapter 16), and then constantly protected from backsliding. Less all-encompassing are the aims of *alternative* movements, which attempt to change only certain specific character defects or learned behavior patterns in individuals considered fundamentally good—as in the programs of Weight Watchers and Alcoholics Anonymous.

Among movements focused on change in the social structure, there are, first of all, *transformative* movements, which aim at total change—usually cataclysmic and immediate. The Bolshevik party (whose 1917 revolution in Russia we discussed in Chapter 10) is a good example of a social movement of this type: the Bolsheviks participated in a sudden and complete overthrow of the existing order, giving power to new leaders who they argued were representatives of the common people. Judaism and Christianity, too, had some transformative themes, such as that of the imminent arrival or return of the Messiah, who will completely alter the social order of the world. Messianic beliefs have been the basis of numerous social movements in the past two millennia, including the Hasidic movement among European Jews—a movement which has followers among a small segment of American Jews—and the Jehovah's Witnesses sect.

Within specific movements, of course, there are often different ideological currents and groups of people, some advocating one approach, some another. Should the movement separate itself from the surrounding society, for example? One proponent of such separation was Marcus Garvey, a quasi-religious leader who, in the 1920s, elaborated a "back to Africa" philosophy for his fellow blacks. Similarly, the Black Muslims in the 1960s argued that blacks in America should establish a geographically separate society. Other black groups have encouraged modified separation within the framework of the larger society that would entail, for

and the Gray Panthers); and have aimed at protecting the natural environment (for example, the Sierra Club and the Friends of the Earth).

Parallel to these are movements focused on change in the individual, movements in which social problems are defined in terms of what is conceived to be the "inner state" of the members of the society taken one by one. For example, John Wilson points out that the Salvation Army "places extreme emphasis on individual guilt in its explanation of social problems such as alco-

A social movement may contain both moderate and radical factions. In the women's movement of the late nineteenth and early twentieth centuries, the moderate faction might be regarded as reformative, in that it focused on the attempt to get the vote for women and looked to existing institutions to accomplish its goals. The more radical faction might be seen as transformative, because its goal was a complete end to the oppression of women. Members of the latter group challenged the existing male-dominated institutions and thus were often subjected to criminal prosecution. (The Bettmann Archive, Inc.)

instance, maintaining ties with white-dominated business institutions while asserting a cultural separateness through the adoption of African religious practices and dress and natural hairstyles such as the "Afro." Still other black groups have pushed for the growth of black-owned capitalistic enterprises, to achieve leverage in dealing with the white economic community. Neil Smelser (1962) classifies movements according to whether they focus on changes in specific social *norms*, such as discriminatory hiring practices, or on the broad cultural *values* underlying them, such as the capitalistic ones that predominate in American society?

Norm-oriented movements, which might include the American Civil Liberties Union and the Save the Whales Foundation, limit the changes they advocate to some specific set of practices; value-oriented movements, which might include Castro's revolutionary

If a social movement appears to threaten a society's values, it may encounter repression and come to use extreme, often illegal, tactics in order to gain its ends. In the early stages of the black civil rights movement of the 1960s, for example, peaceful marches and sit-ins were met by a counter-movement of "white backlash." This perceived threat was one factor in the increased radicalization of segments of the movement, such as the Student Nonviolent Coordinating Committee and the Black Panther Party. (Norris McNamara/Nancy Palmer Agency)

movement in Cuba, offer a total reinterpretation of history in terms of its underlying value patterns and a total program for change. Often, however, norm-oriented and value-oriented currents of thought exist within a single movement. Many of today's Christian sects, for example, are involved in social-action programs aimed at dealing with specific community problems, such as the need for shelters for people with drug problems or runaways, while at the same time preaching fundamental changes in what they see as a loveless, spiritless, oversecularized society.

The difference between a value-oriented movement and a norm-oriented movement often lies in the eye of the beholder. Indeed, as with all labeling activities—including deviance (see Chapter 7)—how a movement is perceived and characterized reflects the values of the observer, and one person's orthodox social value may be another person's heresy. Thus, what one sees as moderate societal action to change a flaw in the normative pattern, another may see as an attack on everything the society stands for. The fact is that the dominant values of any society are diverse and often contradictory. "Freedom" and "equality"—to take examples that are particularly pertinent to our own society—are values that can conflict. From one point of view, measures to equalize opportunity enforce the true values of the society and thus can be norm-oriented; from another, they may restrict individual liberty (Williams, 1970), and thus can be seen as a threat to basic values.

To the extent a movement is (or is perceived to be) oriented toward a fundamental change in values, it runs the risk of being labeled "radical" or "revolutionary"—popular scare words that can provoke extreme reactions in the public and those in power. Ironically, however, a social movement may become radical partly as a result of being so defined. When a movement is outlawed as a danger to the social order, its activities suppressed by force, and its leaders harassed or imprisoned, it may react by adopting a more extreme position. The revolutionary label acts as a self-fulfilling prophecy, as seems to have been in part true in the case of the Black Panthers. But the process can also work in reverse. What started out as a radical movement, like the American labor movement, may end up as a moderate one if its militant tactics are eventually perceived as the expression of a legitimate grievance (Turner, 1969).

The origins of social movements

Under what conditions are social movements likely to arise? Contrary to what might be expected, they may *not* arise in a society oppressed by a despotic regime. Under a government that rigidly suppresses all political dissent, people may not even see their lives in political terms, let alone attempt to take action; many may turn to religion for solace. On the other hand, social movements may be more common in a relatively egalitarian society. When equality and individual freedom are valued by a society, deprivation may be perceived as an injustice rather than as a necessary condition of life. Thus in the United States, where dissent and vocal opposition to the status quo are considered inalienable rights, there has been a long history of reform movements aimed at altering (or preserving) norms in some delimited area. Opponents of nuclear energy hold a massive demonstration; a "right to life" organization campaigns against legalized abortion; the Amalga-mated Clothing and Textile Workers Union boycotts an antiunion employer. There have also, of course, been a number of radical movements in this country which have not been as tolerated by those in authority.

If we fully understood the origins of social movements, we might better able to predict their appearance than we are today. When political activism suddenly swept across colleges and universities in the 1960s, for example, it came as a shock to the writers and commentators who had been deploring student apathy. Similarly, the emergence of militant black movements—after years of quiet struggle—was generally unexpected. Predicting exactly when and where a given movement will appear is often beyond the scope of contemporary sociological theory. In tackling the problem, sociologists have taken two different but in some ways complementary perspectives: the *strain and deprivation* perspective and the *resource-mobilization* perspective.

THE STRAIN AND DEPRIVATION THEORY

Structural strain

Strain has been described by Smelser (1963) as the situation that arises when values, norms, or structures within a society cease to work smoothly together and give rise to ambiguities, tensions, conflicts, or deprivations. Strain, Smelser argues, may spur the development of a *generalized belief:* people sense that "something is wrong," and they develop a belief about what it is and what to do about it. This generalized belief is, in effect, the same thing as an ideology, or a series of connecting ideas that explain for its adherents the cause and nature of, and the solution to, one or more specific problems. Thus Smelser suggests that generalized beliefs are based on an "if only" mentality; for example, participants in a demonstration may believe that "if only" the war were ended or the city were more responsive to their needs, conditions would begin to improve.

Numerous studies have attempted to trace the connections between underlying structural strain and specific social movements. Talcott Parsons (1937), for example, traces the preconditions for Nazism to underlying strain. In his analysis, the seeds of Nazism

Talcott Parsons traces the preconditions of Nazism to the strain and deprivation experienced by Germany after its defeat in World War 1. Here, hungry Germans get horsemeat on a city street. (UPI)

lay in Germany's defeat in World War I and the strains that followed from it in the 1920s. The nation's humiliation had been compounded by heavy reparations levied by the victorious countries; the Great Depression of the 1930s had brought masses of unemployed people to the cities in search of work; disastrous inflation had destroyed the security of the middle class. In addition, the inexperienced democratic government seemed unable to act effectively. The stage was set for a movement that proposed strong measures to effect change. The National Socialists (Nazis) came to power in part because of their insistence on the notion that Germany was defeated in the war only because it was "stabbed in the back" by Jews and other internal enemies; this idea became a powerful generalized belief.

Objective versus relative deprivation

One form of strain that many observers feel can lead to the development of social movements is that resulting from *objective deprivation*—the denial of basic needs. People may rebel because they are hungry, as in the French Revolution, which was preceded by sharp increases in bread prices (Rude, 1964). In certain cases, they may rebel because they lack power. In their 1975 study of the industrialization of Europe, Charles, Louise, and Richard Tilly trace much of the violent conflict that occurred during the hundred years from 1830 to 1930 to realignments in political power. Industrialization, according to Marx, was likely to lead to increases in objective deprivation for the mass of workers. It has also been hypothesized more recently that while increasingly sophisticated technology demands more and more highly educated workers, it may also tend to frustrate the individual's need for autonomy that can be a by-product of education.

If people are suffering from hunger or a strong sense of powerlessness, will they inevitably develop a sense of deprivation and take collective action? One school of thought holds that there are no such "automatic" connections between the condition of the social structure and people's attitudes. Theories of *relative deprivation* hold that people are likely to become discontented not so much because they are objectively needy as because they see that they are deprived *relative to* or *in comparison with* other groups (or relative to their own condition in times past). Relative deprivation may be felt not only when production declines, or when taxes go up, or when people experience a loss of social status, but also when groups observe an improvement in the situation of others, but not in their own, or develop new beliefs about what is due them (Gurr, 1970).

Relative deprivation and revolution: Davies' J-Curve Theory

The theory of relative deprivation has been a focus of debate, particularly as to its predictions concerning revolutions. Some observers, for example, hold that much of the political unrest in the Third World countries, which are currently going through the process of modernization, is due not to objective deprivation but to rapid improvement in the lot of the average individual. James C. Davies, in a 1969 study of historical revolutions (such as the French Revolution as well as more recent ones), has corroborated this idea, showing that many did indeed occur after a prolonged period of rising expectations and gratifications, an observation de Tocqueville had made a century earlier. But, Davies noted, in many cases there had also been a short period of sharp economic reversal just before the revolution. (If "actual need satisfaction" is plotted on a graph, as in Figure 21.1, this period of reversal appears as a sharp downturn of the line representing need satisfaction, so that the curve of the graph resembles a letter "J" slanted down—whence the name "J-Curve Theory," by

which Davies' theory is known.) The important point about Davies' approach is that it brings together the objective-deprivation and relative-deprivation perspectives. Davies argues, as did Marx, that revolutions depend in part on the state of mind of groups of people within societies—that groups must develop class consciousness. This happens, in Davies' view, when "the

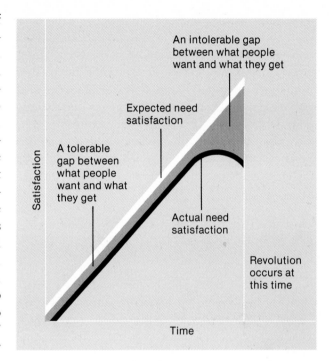

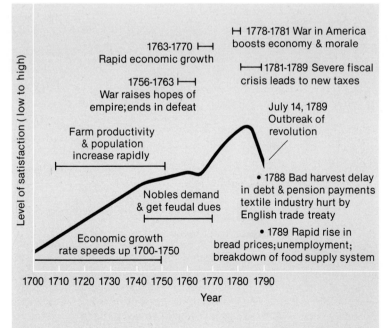

FIGURE 21.1

Top: Davies' J-Curve theory of revolutions states that during periods of improved conditions, people's expectations about the future tend to rise Although there may be a slight gap between what people want and what they can get, they consider the disparity tolerable. If there is a setback in the actual satisfaction of their needs without a corresponding reduction in their expectations, according to Davies, a revolution is likely to occur. *Bottom:* Davies' J-Curve theory of revolutions applied to the French Revolution of 1789. Following continued economic growth from the beginning of the eighteenth century, a severe fiscal crisis in the 1780s helped to create the conditions for revolution: the rising expectations of the French people could not be met by the faltering economy. The revolution broke out in July 1789. (Davies, 1969)

gap between expectations and gratifications quickly widens and becomes intolerable"—when people fear not simply that things will no longer continue to get better, but that they will actually get worse.

The J-Curve is not a complete theory of revolution, however. As Davies himself acknowledges, it does not predict when or why economic setbacks occur; it only says what may happen when they do occur. Furthermore, such setbacks may be necessary, but not sufficient, for revolutions to occur; they do not always result in revolutions. The Depression led to the Nazis' rise to power in Germany, but not to any revolution in Great Britain or the United States. It is true, however, that working-class consciousness and militancy did increase quite strikingly in all industrialized countries during the Depression. Even in modest business recessions American workers usually vote much more solidly for the Democratic party than they do in times of prosperity.

The resource-mobilization theory

It is true that many social movements have arisen against a background of shared grievances among the masses, of deprivation, and of generalized beliefs about what is to be done. However, as John D. McCarthy and Mayer N. Zald (1973) point out, it is important to bear in mind that such factors do not necessarily have to be present for a social movement to arise. Nor, if they are present, are they necessarily the most important preconditions. McCarthy and Zald, summarizing recent empirical work on this subject, note that

. . . a number of studies have shown little or no support for expected relationships between objective or subjective deprivation and the outbreak of movement phenomena and willingness to participate in collective action. . . . Other studies have failed to support the expectation of a generalized belief prior to outbreaks of collective behavior episodes or initial movement involvement. (1973, pp. 3-4)

In the view of McCarthy and Zald, it may be fruitful for sociologists investigating social movements

. . . to move from a *strong* assumption about the centrality of deprivation and grievances to a *weak* one, which makes them a component, indeed, *sometimes* a secondary component, in the generation of social movements. For instance, the senior citizens who were mobilized into groups to lobby

for Medicare were brought into groups only *after* legislation was before Congress. . . . Senior citizens were organized into groups through the efforts of a lobbying group created by the AFL-CIO. No doubt the elderly needed money for medical care. However, what is important is that the organization did not develop directly from that grievance, but very indirectly through the moves of actors in the political system. (1973, pp. 4-5)

The point McCarthy and Zald make is that there is *always* enough discontent in a society for a social movement to arise; there is no need to look for "special" deprivation or "special" strain. To them, the deciding factor is simply whether there are leaders present to organize the group effectively, and whether these leaders have some power and resources, especially those of an established elite, at their disposal for the mobilization of followers.

McCarthy and Zald go even further: in some instances, they claim, the people who provide the leadership and the resources do not actually share the values of their "grass-roots" followers; instead, they define, create, and manipulate grievances and discontent in the minds of these followers. In many cases, mass support is not even the crucial variable. As McCarthy and Zald point out, in an affluent society such as ours there are people with significant "discretionary resources," money and other wealth that they do not have to spend on basic material needs such as food and shelter. (Even time may be a discretionary resource in this sense.) People spend their discretionary resources on entertainment, voluntary associations, organized religion, and politics—so why not on social-movement organizations? Social-movement entrepreneurs may appear. They may resort to "social-movement organization advertising," in the form of "mailed material which demonstrates the good works of the organization." These entrepreneurs may also

. . . manipulate media coverage of their activities more or less successfully by staging events which will possibly be "newsworthy," by attending to the needs of news organizations, and by cultivating representatives of the media. . . . Another technique advertisers utilize to appeal to isolated adherents is the linking of names of important people to the organization, thereby developing and maintaining an image of credibility (Perrow, 1970). In the same way that famous actors, sports heroes, and retired politicians endorse consumer products, other well-known personalities are called upon to endorse social-movement products: Jane Fonda and

Dr. Spock were to the peace movement and Robert Redford is to the environmental movement what Joe Namath is to panty hose. . . . (1977, pp. 26–28)

If all this sounds extreme, McCarthy and Zald are the first to point out that it is not true of *all* social movements. And clearly there is nothing objectionable about any movement's concern with effective fund raising. The underlying point of their argument, however,

still holds: whether or not a particular strain or feeling of deprivation exists in a society, the emergence and developmental course of movements depend to an important extent on the leaders who are present, the followers they mobilize, and the resources they are able to command. We will take a closer look at these factors in the section that follows.

Leaders, followers, and the mobilization process

THE LEADERS OF MOVEMENTS

The leaders who set a social movement in motion are often the type Max Weber described as "charismatic" (see Chapter 16). They loom as figures of heroic proportions, a little larger than life—people whose self-confidence and authority inspire the loyalty and dispel the doubts of followers. In the earliest stages of a movement, several people often vie for the top leadership role, each with his or her own following (Killian, 1964, p. 440). Usually, when one succeeds in overshadowing the rest, often becoming the personal symbol of the movement, the others fall into place as lieutenants. Sometimes a disappointed contender will attempt to organize a competing group, especially when his or her interpretation of the basic ideology departs from the winning version; the formation of such splinter groups often occurs within a large, diverse movement.

But who are the leaders? What induces a talented individual to leave conventional paths and to lay his or her future—and sometimes life—on the line for a cause whose success is uncertain? Some leaders may be what McCarthy and Zald (1973, 1977) call "social-movement entrepreneurs"—a new category of professionals that has arisen in response to the increased availability of funding for social movements from foundations, churches, and the government. Why do these entrepreneurs and other types of people become social-movement leaders? One theory holds that in the case of many political protest movements the answer is simply self-interest (Oberschall, 1973, pp. 116–117). When society blocks their chances for a career, ambitious individuals from subordinate groups may come to feel that

they have little to lose and much to gain by overthrowing the system, or at least by attempting to make it more flexible. The risks may be high, but so are the rewards: not only the prestige and power that accompany the leadership of an important movement, but also the possibility of high position in the newly reorganized society if the movement is successful.

No doubt, some social-movement leaders are driven more by opportunism than by idealism, but it must also be said that some are motivated by a strong and sincere personal sense of moral indignation or commitment. In either case, from the standpoint of sociological theory, the kind of commitment that a leader brings to a movement is not a reliable basis on which to predict ultimate success or failure.

Indeed, there is considerable debate at this point over just how important any leader's role may be. Some commentators argue that leadership has been overemphasized, and that leaders are in fact constrained by the characteristics of their potential followers, who may at critical times move ahead on their own. For example, the massive peace demonstrations and student protests of the 1960s appear to have come about more in response to contemporary events than to the actions of leaders (Skolnick, 1969; McEvoy and Miller, 1969). Once again, we see the role that episodes of collective behavior can play within social movements. The Paris uprising of May 1968, as well as the Russian Revolution, were marked by intense independent activity, including discussion of the issues, circulation of pamphlets, and impromptu demonstrations. An in-

Leaders of social movements risk not only their careers in the old order, but often their lives. These youths recall the memory of one such leader, Martin Luther King Jr., the renowned leader of the civil rights movement. (Daniel S. Brody/Stock, Boston)

creasingly influential view focuses on the interaction between leader and follower: each influences the other, and both are important to the mobilization of a movement.

FOLLOWERS AND THE MOBILIZATION PROCESS

Not all movements actually have, or need to have, huge numbers of people involved in all their activities; illegal and conspiratorial movements, especially—such as the Bolshevik party in Russia between 1903 and 1917—are typically small, tightly organized, strictly disciplined, and highly restrictive of admission, even though they may seek and attract the support of a substantial number of sympathizers or "fellow travelers." But in times of crisis, such as revolutions, the sheer size of the movement's body of followers is likely to be important.

How followers are mobilized

How do leaders of movements mobilize followers? A major way is by gaining access to channels of communication. There are those in the United States today who hold the mass media primarily responsible for the rapid proliferation of both racial and student demonstrations since the mid-1960s. Other observers stress how the media may distort and even shape the popular image of a group (Gitlin, 1980). Even if the power of the media is exaggerated, it is true that radio and television communication can give coherence to a movement whose members are widely dispersed physically and who may never all come together at the same time or place. Publicity in the media can increase discontent as scattered individuals learn that others share their feelings. To avoid this, totalitarian regimes attempt to control all means of communication and to restrict individual freedom of expression in order to isolate and neutralize dissident members of the society. Of course, even in more open countries such as the United States, not all movement groups have sufficient resources to gain access to radio and television, nor do the news media give equal attention to all groups. Some get around this by making use of the communications channels of established organizations; many early civil-rights movements, for instance, spread word of their activities through the literature and personnel of the black churches.

Why people join

One of the most important and perplexing questions in the study of social movements is what makes people join—what the determinants of individual recruitment are. Some of the various psychological explanations of "participation proneness," such as those of Eric Hoffer, have the appeal of simplicity. Their central thrust is that personal maladjustment pushes people into membership; the most likely candidate is the misfit. Hoffer (1961) describes the fanatical members of social movements as "true believers," alike in their feelings of frustration and rejection—people whose conversion to a cause has little to do with its doctrines and everything to do with their emotional needs. In a similar vein, some researchers have attempted to link student activism to unresolved Oedipal conflicts, permissive child rearing, and social alienation. However, systematic evidence to support such theories is generally lacking.

Mass-society theory finds the answer to the recruitment question in the organization of the society itself. According to William Kornhauser (1959), the leading exponent of this theory, people may turn to mass movements when they lack attachments to intermediary groups, such as community organizations, labor unions, and professional associations; such groups would ordinarily enable large numbers of people to make their interests count in high places and, in addition, would provide them with a supportive and restraining interpersonal environment. In times of crisis and of rapid social change, according to this theory, ties with secondary associations tend to break down. During an economic depression, for example, the unemployed are likely to withdraw from their social circles into their separate family units. Mass-society theorists argue that people in this isolated situation—powerless in the face of a strong centralized government and outside the mainstream of society—are particularly vulnerable to the heady ideology of social movements, and of antidemocratic movements in particular.

Unfortunately, plausible as the theory may sound, it has not stood up under the test of evidence. In fact, numerous studies have found that socially isolated individuals are *less* likely to join social movements than are those who belong to secondary associations or have active social ties (Oberschall, 1973, pp. 103–107; Useem, 1973, p. 21).

Another recruitment hypothesis, based on a game-theory approach, starts from the simple premise that people try to do what is good for themselves. If they join a movement, particularly one of political protest, it is because the benefits offered by the movement promise to outweigh the disadvantages that accompany membership. According to this theory, certain economic, political, and social conditions can tip the scale, inducing the individual to join (Oberschall, 1973, pp. 114–115). One such condition is a fair degree of prosperity, which weakens the fear of economic reprisals. Another is a low risk of persecution from the government. Finally, organizational factors play a part: secondary associations that are segregated along class or ethnic lines tend to facilitate the mobilization of social movements (Oberschall, 1973, pp. 106–107, 112). People in this situation reinforce one another's grievances and are likely to perceive potential gains for themselves in collective action—a point, incidentally, that may help to account for the evidence contradicting mass-society theory.

A number of studies have found that personal influence is particularly important in inducing people to join social movements. For example, as a result of his study of the "Divine Precepts" movement (discussed in Chapter 2), known colloquially as the "Moonies," John Lofland (1979) has produced a model of mobilization that emphasizes processes of interaction as factors in recruitment. Contact with friends, relatives, or neighbors who belong seems to matter as much as—and perhaps more than—the ideology of the movement or the degree of strain the individual may be under at the time. Indeed, some individuals may develop an ideological commitment only after joining.

INFILTRATING SOCIAL MOVEMENTS: INFORMANTS AND SECRET AGENTS

For the student of social movements, as well as for sociological observers generally, things may not be what they appear to be. Spying, sabotage, and deception may be important parts of the operation of many organizations, and informants and secret agents who consciously project "false" selves may be participants in many social movements.

Since the Watergate investigation, which revealed a secret campaign of political espionage and "dirty tricks," there has been more public awareness of, and cynicism about, how political organizations operate. Some of that same cynicism may also be appropriate in probing how other institutions work. For instance, some prison riots have been instigated not just by inmates who are discontented with their conditions, but also by guards who engineer such events in order to embarrass their superiors or to sabotage plans for institutional reform.

Although sociologists have probed many aspects of social movements, relatively little attention has been paid to one of the most fascinating social actors in such movements, the *agent provocateur*. As Gary T. Marx defines the term in his article "A Neglected Category of Social Movement Participant: The *Agent Provocateur* and the Informant" (1974), an *agent provocateur* is a secret agent who infiltrates organizations in order to "create internal dissension, gain information, and/or provoke a group to illegal activities that would then justify official action and possibly turn public sentiment against them" (p. 403).

There are many historical examples of infiltrators, informants, and secret agents, both in this country and abroad. Stalin was suspected at one point of being a police spy. Anti-Nazi resistance groups in occupied Europe were heavily infiltrated. There are many instances of the use of *agents provocateurs* in the history of the American labor movement.

More recently, dozens of news items have appeared in the United States about secret agents who have been exposed. Each of the stories is a fascinating tale of deception. For example:

□ In 1970, during student demonstrations at the University of Alabama, an agent of the police reportedly urged violence, set fire to at least one campus building, and hurled fire bombs and other objects at the police. These actions led to a legal declaration of unlawful assembly and the arrest of 150 people.

□ Malcolm X's bodyguard, the man who administered mouth-to-mouth resuscitation to him when he was shot by an assassin in 1965, turned out to be a New York City detective who had been operating undercover for seven years.

□ An ex-Green Beret who was employed by the Los Angeles Police Department's intelligence squad, is reported to have delivered a box of hand grenades to two activists shortly before they were arrested for the possession of dangerous weapons.

□ A regional director of the Vietnam Veterans Against the War (VVAW) who had urged the necessity of "shooting and bombing"—and whose actions led to a bombing, an illegal demonstration at an Air Force base, and subsequent arrests—was an FBI informant. His testimony against VVAW leaders resulted in their indictment for planning to disrupt the 1972 Republican National Convention.

□ Jerry Rubin's bodyguard during the 1968 Democratic convention turned out to be a graduate of the FBI training school and the Chicago Police Academy, and a veteran of the Army counterintelligence service.

As such items suggest, the *agent provocateur* may be an employee of the police or the FBI. a foreign government or a rival social movement. Some agents are police officials who infiltrate a group; others are civilians who had been members of groups for years before they agreed to work as agents.

Their motives may vary as much as their roles within the movement do. Some are simply police officers who regard this activity as a normal part of their work. Others are civilians chosen because they can easily blend into the group they are asked to infiltrate. They may be disaffected idealists who turn informant out of a sense of

Dynamics of growth and change

The early days of a movement can be an intoxicating time, when a small vanguard, bonded by a common enthusiasm and the presence of a charismatic leader, forms a kind of intimate family. Later, norms of behavior may develop that can keep members' loyalty and commitment strong even when the group contains hundreds or even thousands of members. Prescribed positions on specific issues are spelled out, and expression of

"civic duty." Some take on the job because they need the money; others are coerced into the role by arrest or the threat of arrest.

How do such agents infiltrate a movement? Typically, infiltration of domestic organizations does not require preparations nearly as elaborate as those required of international spies. But cover stories must still be created and false identities constructed. In most cases, the agent simply appears on the scene, carries out routine tasks, offers stories of earlier victimization that serve to legitimize his or her alliance with the group, and often helps in procuring weapons or supplies. Especially when infiltrating loosely organized groups, such as the radical student groups of the 1960s, the agent often brings sorely needed resources and skills. During the 1960s, it was usually not difficult for an infiltrator to rise within the organization to a position of power, which allows access to the secret information that his or her employer wants.

But the *agent provocateur* can be much more than an informant. He or she can cause divisiveness within the organization, steer the movement away from its goals, plan activities that can lead to the arrest of fellow members, and otherwise entrap and frame the group's leaders. Even the suspicion that there may be an agent in their midst can be severely demoralizing to group members and can sap much of the group's energy.

All this presumes, of course, that the agent continues to identify with his or her employer and its interests, and is not converted to the cause he or she was hired to subvert. The secret agent's role is a fragile and complicated one, especially when the informant becomes a double agent who deceives everyone. Police and other agencies that hire secret agents often must proceed carefully because of the ever-present possibility that an agent is relaying false information or has become a double agent. Police may check on the reliability of their agents by planting *other* agents or by resorting to electronic surveillance of both their agents and the organizations they were hired to infiltrate.

As the Patty Hearst case suggests, an individual who is cut off from familiar social contacts for an extended period of time and interacts only with members of a cohesive group may well be converted to the group's beliefs. This can be a problem for the secret agent as well. To be effective, the agent has to be trusted by other members of the group. Gaining that trust means becoming immersed in the group's way of life and being isolated from familiar surroundings and friends. Therefore, the secret agent may experience severe cross-pressures that can lead both to doubts about whether the employer's instructions should be followed and to eventual conversion to the group's cause. This process was experienced, for example, by a student employed by the House Un-American Activities Committee to infiltrate a chapter of the Students for a Democratic Society (SDS). After a few months, he found that he was far more sympathetic to the goals of SDS and its members than he was to his employer. He gave up the secret agent role and became a dedicated SDS member.

Secret agents may be exposed when they surface as witnesses for the prosecution, when they take a public stand against the movement they had ostensibly been a part of, or when they are neither charged nor arrested after police raids on their organizations. Sometimes they are discovered after a faulty role performance, or when they are recognized by someone who knows their real identity. An organization may set up its own internal security system to detect undercover agents. One way of doing so is to overwhelm recruits with questions about their past, on the assumption that flaws can be spotted in even the most carefully constructed cover story. When the threat of secret agents is especially great, some organizations—such as the Black Panthers—have at times simply decided to stop accepting any new members.

An awareness of the *agent provocateur*'s role suggests that some of the most conventional organizations resort at times to illegitimate means. Secret agents and informants are among the most intriguing examples of individuals who perform what Everett Hughes calls the society's "dirty work."

these views becomes a mark of loyalty to the group. The norms may even suggest modes of dress (for example, the brown shirts of the early Nazis or the Mao peasant costume), styles of address (such as the salutation "Comrade" used by Communist party members), and forms of recreation deemed appropriate for members. A special language may develop, including terms and phrases that encapsulate the movement's stance on certain issues or attitude toward certain groups. All these norms are communicated to members through leaders' speeches, songs, printed propaganda, even buttons and bumper stickers, and a sense of solidarity is buttressed by meetings and rallies.

The resulting cohesion and "oneness" can have powerful consequences for the individual. Joining the movement may even acquire the significance of a "rite of passage" marking and dramatizing separation from the person's previous life and integration into a new order of existence. Some movements regulate almost every aspect of the member's life. In the "Divine Precepts" movement, for example, converts are expected to enter communal life, give all their money to the movement, and devote all their time to its goals—in short, to make the movement their whole concern (Lofland, 1979).

Meanwhile, however, certain changes are very likely to take place as time passes—changes that can even split or destroy the movement if they are sufficiently extreme.

CHANGES IN LEADERSHIP

Charisma and managerial skills rarely seem to go together. Even in the beginning, the figure whose personality dominates a movement will often be surrounded by lieutenants who handle organizational details and help translate ideology into practical terms. As a movement expands and the leadership roles become increasingly specialized, the administrative expert grows in importance. Often, a leader of the administrative type moves officially into the top spot after the charismatic founder has died. This new leader and his or her assistants will be able to pull together a complex assortment of activities—recruitment drives, fund-raising efforts, educational programs directed at the membership, and campaigns designed to influence decision makers and the larger public.

The new leadership is likely to be not only more practical but also more powerful and conservative than that heading the movement before its structure and membership expanded. In general, the model of organizational development advanced by Max Weber (1958) and Robert Michels (1915) seems to hold true. Weber and Michels maintained that, regardless of democratic principles to which members may adhere, the increasing size and complexity of an organization will result in a loss of local, grass-roots control and the concentration of responsibility in the hands of a few people. According to Michels, the central oligarchy will tend to push the movement into a more conservative and expediency-oriented position, because it is in their interest to do so. Nevertheless, Michels suggests, occasionally matters will take a different turn. A centralized leadership may in fact prove to be less conservative than the rank and file. Or, to avoid the development of a depersonal-

ized bureaucracy, a movement may organize its membership into small, autonomous units—a solution developed by the utopian Hutterite sect.

CHANGES IN MEMBERS' IDEOLOGICAL COMMITMENT

As time passes, the character and commitment of a movement's membership are also likely to change, and with them the ideology. New members will be recruited, perhaps attracted by some but not all of the movement's program. Old members may become disheartened as the goals that once inspired them fail to materialize. At this juncture, ideology may be de-emphasized, and new stress may be laid on the satisfactions of participation as a prime motivation for adherence. In some movements, however, failure to achieve reformist objectives works in the opposite direction, leading to a stronger emphasis on ideology. A shift to a radical ideology occurred, for example, among segments of the New Left, the women's liberation movement, and the black and Third World movements.

CHANGES INDUCED BY THE ENVIRONMENT

The way a movement develops and changes may be affected as much by outside influences as by its own internal growth processes. For better or worse, social movements are shaped by their environments. Public acceptance or opposition, as has been noted, can determine whether a movement adopts a moderate or a radical stance. The role played by the government through its agencies of social control can be especially crucial, even determining whether a movement continues to exist. The fates of some of the more radical black groups in the recent past, such as the Black Panthers, offer examples of this. Their failure was aided by the repressive and sometimes illegal actions of the local police and the FBI; among other tactics, these agencies sometimes made use of undercover agents who created dissension within the groups and provoked incidents that invited reprisals. It is also true, however, that a certain amount of opposition from the outside may serve to strengthen the movement by heightening the commitment of its members (Coser, 1968).

Consequences of social movements

Social movements that succeed do so in various ways. Their effects may range from the extensive transformation of a society through successful revolution (as in Russia in 1917, China in 1949, and Cuba in 1959) to small changes that are barely visible. Some movements have seen many of the major changes they desired in the structure of a society without ever seizing power. The American labor movement, for example, saw an important goal realized in 1934 with the passage of the National Labor Relations Act, which institutionalized collective bargaining and the rights of labor unions. And the goals and programs of American movements have sometimes been incorporated into the platforms of the major political parties. This was the ultimate fate of American Populism in the 1890s. Likewise, much of Norman Thomas' Socialist party platform of the 1920s found its way into Democratic and later into Republican party platforms.

Even when a social movement *seems* to have failed, it may have lasting, if subtle, effects. To cite one example, it was in 1866 that the National Labor Union called for an eight-hour workday, but it was not until 1938 that the proposal became federal law. In addition, influence may be exerted by example, in a kind of "spin-off" effect. Thus the civil-rights movement was influenced by Mahatma Gandhi's philosophy of passive resistance and by the labor movement of the 1930s. The civil-rights movement, in turn, had an effect on the student, antiwar, feminist, gay-liberation, and ecology movements.

An important question raised by these examples is, How should the success of a social movement be defined? This is a complex problem because, as we have seen, some movements succeed in attracting large numbers of followers and yet fail in the long run because they cannot follow through on their original ideologies. Access to power imposes new requirements on leaders. Those initially sympathetic to revolutionary movements promising freedom and justice may become disenchanted if such movements are followed by a reign of terror and the suppression of dissent. The program of a successful movement may have to be modified in the face of hard realities. Ideology may prove a better tool for obtaining power than for using it effectively.

During the 1960s, the dramatic appearance and sweep of social movements around the world stimulated sociologists, and others, to devote considerable effort to studying and understanding their origins, growth and development processes, and outcomes. Social movements are living laboratories in which the behavior of people in groups—the basic unit of sociological analysis—can be observed and recorded at first hand. Conflict can reveal aspects of group life that are often hidden or latent. The study of social movements offers one means of understanding how societies change or resist change.

Summary

Collective behavior is a term sociologists apply to a variety of different behavior patterns engaged in more or less spontaneously by large numbers of people; the term covers fads, fashions, crazes, panics, riots, and episodes of mass hysteria. Incidents of collective behavior often involve a new norm, a new social relationship, or both. Collective behavior has often been found to accompany ambiguous situations in which people are emotionally aroused.

Crowd behavior was one of the earliest types of collective behavior studied. Although LeBon and others thought of the crowd as "irrational," later research has questioned this belief. In disasters, for example, crowd behavior is often calm and purposeful. Blumer has classified crowds as *expressive, acting, casual,* or *conventional,* depending on their behavior.

Rumors often operate in crowds, becoming exaggerated and shortened in the retelling. Crowd behavior often shows considerable uniformity, attributed to the development of an *emergent norm,* which governs behavior in an ambiguous situation.

The study of collective behavior has been hampered by problems of methodology. There is disagreement about how the term should be defined, and there are inherent difficulties in studying such a complex process. In addition, the labels used to describe collective behavior, which invariably reflect a political viewpoint, may inhibit understanding.

Social movements are more organized, longer-term enterprises than are episodes of collective behavior, and they are more oriented toward a particular goal. Sometimes such movements spawn *countermovements*. Social movements may include episodes of collective behavior. Social movements are organized around a particular ideology. They can be *reformative* movements, seeking to change either individuals or the society, or *transformative* movements, seeking total change.

Social movements often arise in relatively open and egalitarian societies. Smelser has theorized that they are brought on by *structural strain*. McCarthy and Zald have argued that "entrepreneurs" may create social movements by tapping surplus time and money—the "resource-mobilization" theory.

Leaders are often important in recruiting participants in social movements. There are several theories as to why people join; some think "followers" are misfits, or people without strong social supports. Others believe that people join social movements simply because they see something to be gained by so doing.

As social movements continue over the years, charismatic leaders may be replaced by administrators. Ideology may change. Movements that are opposed or harassed may become more radical. Some reform movements—such as socialism and populism—have seen their programs adopted as mainstream policy, even though the movements do not gain power.

Glossary

COLLECTIVE BEHAVIOR Those similar actions of a multiplicity of individuals that are relatively spontaneous and transitory and are therefore in contrast to the relatively more routine, predictable interactions of everyday life.

COUNTERMOVEMENT A social movement aimed at resisting change.

CROWD An aggregate of people gathered in one place at one time.

DIFFUSE COLLECTIVITY Individuals separated from one another in space and time who nevertheless have a common concern or are involved in the same collective-behavior incident.

FAD A form of personal behavior adopted by large numbers of people for a short period of time.

FASHION Accepted, current styles of behavior or dress.

GENERALIZED BELIEF Smelser's term for a belief that locates responsibility for societal strain and suggests a solution.

HYSTERIA An uncontrollable outburst of emotion, such as fear.

PANIC Flight or escape behavior caused by sudden, intense fear.

RUMOR An unverified report passed along from one person to the next.

SOCIAL MOVEMENT An organized, relatively long-term type of collective behavior in which people unite to bring about or to prevent change.

STRUCTURAL STRAIN Defined by Smelser as the situation that arises when values, norms, or structures in a society cease to work smoothly together and give rise to ambiguities, tensions, conflicts, or deprivations.

Recommended readings

Ash, Roberta T. *Social Movements in America.* 2nd. ed. Chicago: Markham, 1977. An examination of social movements throughout American history, emphasizing the importance of economic factors.

Evans, Robert (ed.). *Readings in Collective Behavior.* Chicago: Rand McNally, 1975. A readable collection of articles on theories of collective behavior and empirical studies of protest movements.

Genevie, Louis E. (ed.). *Collective Behavior and Social Movements.* Itasca, Ill.: F. E. Peacock, 1978. A collection of readings illustrating the development and current state of collective behavior theory and research.

Lang, Kurt, and Gladys E. Lang. *Collective Dynamics.* New York: T. Y. Crowell, 1961. An introductory text focusing on collective behavior as an emergent phenomenon and one that is tied to social change.

LeBon, Gustave. *The Crowd: A Study of the Popular Mind* (1895). Dunwoody, Ga.: Berg, 1968. An important early effort to study crowds, using concepts that are now in limited currency.

Oberschall, Anthony. *Social Conflict and Social Movements.* Englewood Cliffs, N. J.: Prentice-Hall, 1973. Provides a historical, theoretical framework for the study of social conflict. Much of the book consists of valuable examples and case studies demonstrating the structural elements of social movements.

Perry, Joseph B., and M. D. Pugh. *Collective Behavior: Response to Social Stress.* St. Paul, Minn.: West, 1978. An eclectic approach to the topic. The book includes material on disasters, crowds, and social movements.

Roberts, Ron E., and Robert M. Kloss. *Social Movements between the Balcony and the Barricade.* St. Louis, Mo.: C. D. Mosby, 1979. An analysis that stresses the political and social change aspects of social movements.

Rudé, George. *The Crowd in History.* New York: Wiley, 1964. A historical approach to social movements that examines the history of mass movements in England and France from 1730 to 1848.

Smelser, Neil J. *Theory of Collective Behavior.* New York: Free Press, 1962. Offers a theory of collective behavior that seeks to explain where and when it will appear and what form it will take.

Turner, Ralph H., and Lewis M. Killian. *Collective Behavior.* 2nd. ed. Englewood Cliffs, N. J.: Prentice-Hall, 1972. In-depth readings and interesting case studies of the nature of collective behavior, the organization of crowds, publics, and movement participation.

Wilson, John. *Introduction to Social Movements.* New York: Basic Books, 1973. A useful introduction that draws on a wide array of empirical social-movement studies and stresses the organizational problems a movement confronts.

Prenez la ma
Use the hai

CHAPTER TWENTY-TWO

SOCIAL CHANGE AND MODERNIZATION

We need only look back a generation to grasp the significance of change in our own society. Modern life would be inconceivable without television, computers, and travel by jetliner, yet all these phenomena have existed only about twenty-five years. In the social realm, the relaxation of sexual mores, the widespread acceptance of divorce, the birth-control pill, and "living together" relationships have happened even more recently. Indeed, the pace of change has grown so rapidly that a best-selling book, *Future Shock* (1970) even suggested that changes now occur far faster than our ability to cope with them.

Of course, change is varied: not all is drastic and far-reaching. Change can occur with the abruptness of a military *coup d'état* or it can be continuous, like the long and varied process known as the Industrial Revolution. Change can be a simple interpersonal "readjustment," such as that which goes on in groups all the time—as when, for example, a leader emerges in a children's play group, or workers wiring circuits in a new electronics factory develop informal norms for the amount of work each one completes each day. Change can also mean fundamental modifications in a large social structure, as when a number of loosely connected tribes in an African country become unified politically into a centralized nation-state. Change can be obvious, as when a farming area becomes a vacation resort; or it can be more subtle, as when the spread of supermarkets in the United States helped modify norms for behavior in public markets, contributing to the elimination of informal bargaining between buyer and seller.

Change creates further change, and often a development in one realm of our society sends waves of change throughout the social structure as a whole. The first auto makers, for example, had little awareness of or interest in the thousands of different ways their new product would transform American life—from sexual behavior and child-parent relationships to the rise of the suburbs to the growth of a whole series of derivative industries, from insurance to concrete for building highways. Similarly, the development of birth-control devices has had a far-reaching influence not only on family size, but on women's participation in the work force, relationships between the sexes, and the economics of the family.

Defining social change

Understanding the process of social change, then, is vital to understanding our own society. Because of the complexity of the subject, it is helpful to begin with a definition: *social change* is the *significant* alteration of social structures, including the manifestations of such structures embodied in norms, values, and cultural products and symbols (Moore, 1963). This broad definition encompasses types of change as different as a homemaker's decision to go back to work and the violent overthrow of a government. Because the term includes so much, sociologists commonly draw some distinctions. A. R. Radcliffe-Brown, for example, has differentiated between "change within a structure" and "change of a structure." In change within a structure, for example, two people decide to marry, changing their individual status from "single" to "married" and changing their relationship to each other and to society as a whole. In change of a structure, a significant number of people in a society might decide to live permanently outside of conventional marriage, as cohabiting heterosexual and homosexual couples, singles, and so on. In this case, the *structure* of society would change: conventional marriage would no longer be the exclusive "unit" of which society is composed.

A second distinction is often made between social change and cultural change. Although this distinction is sometimes subtle because of the close connection between what people do and what they believe, think, and say, it can be said to divide actual human activities from their broader symbolic meanings. For example, the entry of blacks and women into new spheres of activity in recent years is an example of social change. An associated cultural change has been an alteration in our spoken and written language: "Negroes" and "colored people" have become "blacks"; "coeds" and "stewardesses" have become "female students" and "flight attendants." Manners have changed as well: for example, blacks and women are casually addressed by their first names less frequently now. Social and cultural change are obviously closely related, often occurring simultaneously.

A final distinction is made between small-scale and large-scale change. We speak of small-scale change

Change *within* a structure—here, a change in how women regard their role in society—can create the impetus for a change *of* structure. (© James R. Holland/Stock, Boston)

when we refer to change that occurs in limited groups of the population—for example, change within a political party. Large-scale change, in contrast, affects the society as a whole. In this chapter, we will move from a discussion of small-scale changes within structures (innovation) to a consideration of large-scale changes of structures (modernization).

How does change come about?

An enduring social structure, whether it is a small structure, like the staff of a university sociology department, or a large structure, like New York City, must change to some extent, if only because those who occupy its roles sooner or later give way to others. The newcomers will be different from their predecessors in their past socialization experiences and, often, in their stages of the life cycle; for these reasons alone, they are likely to perform their roles in slightly different ways. (We saw some instances of this sort of generational change in Chapter 6.)

When sociologists talk about social change, however, they usually have in mind not minor alterations like these, but broader, more fundamental changes—the kinds of changes, for example, wrought by a revolution or by a new development in technology. In Chapter 21, we discussed the types of broad change brought about by the actions of large collectivities of people and examined the complex relationship between social movements consisting of large numbers of people, and social change. Here, we will look at changes that originate with individuals—the types of change that are known as *innovations*.

INNOVATION

"An *innovation* is an idea for accomplishing some recognized social end in a new way or for a means of accomplishing some new social end" (LaPiere, 1965, p. 107). An innovation can be either a *discovery* of a thing or a phenomenon that already exists, such as Columbus' discovery of America (for Europeans) or Newton's discovery of the law of gravity, or an *invention*, the creation of something new out of existing materials, such as a new metal alloy, manufacturing technique, educational theory, or fashion in clothing.

As innovation theorist Richard LaPiere points out, even nonmaterial innovations are ultimately traceable to individuals. That is, individuals are the source not only of new technological inventions but also of "inventions" in music, painting, literature, and ideas, and even of "inventions" in social interaction, such as

worker ownership of factories. Even when an element of social organization develops so slowly and gradually that no one person can be identified as *the* innovator, it can be thought of as the result of the unconventional behavior of a number of individuals.

Are innovations the work of solitary geniuses appearing at random moments in history? Or are they "natural" occurrences that must inevitably arise, given particular historical conditions? Few scholars now believe that innovators merely "act out" predetermined laws of change or history. It is true that remarkable coincidences sometimes occur, with similar innovations cropping up at about the same time. But this should not be thought of as the result of some kind of historical predetermination; it merely reflects the fact that people working on a common problem will sometimes hit upon the same solution. Nor should innovations be thought of exclusively as radical breakthroughs or departures from the past. The component parts, in a sense, of an invention are often familiar ideas and existing techniques and materials that are combined in a novel way. In other words, innovations are very much products of their times. The discovery of the helical structure of DNA, for instance, did not happen by accident nor did it happen quickly. Rather, the discovery was the culmination of gradual developments stretching over a number of years in a variety of scientific disciplines, including physics, mathematics, X-ray crystallography, and biology.

The modern view of innovation is that it depends on the coming together of an individual, often with unique experiences or skills, with a set of particularly conducive societal conditions. Sociologists and psychologists have been studying the conditions that facilitate innovation by looking carefully, for example, at circumstances leading to outstanding scientific discoveries, or at the personality traits that characterize creative individuals.

The innovator as "outsider"

No innovation takes place in a vacuum. For a new idea to emerge, there must be a certain amount of interaction among thinkers and experimenters—some sharing of knowledge, opinions, and approaches. Yet the process of exploration undertaken by the individual innovator is crucial. Many innovations are the work of solitary individuals rather than institutional groups—which at first seems rather surprising, given the proliferation of research institutes (such as the Rand Corporation and other "think tanks") in recent decades. Yet these institutions function more to *develop* innovations—to refine and improve them—than to provide fertile ground for their genesis. One study of technological inventions made in the first half of the twentieth century shows that most inventions, except those in industrial chemistry, were made by individuals working outside the institutional context (Jewkes, Sawers, and Stillerman, 1958). For example, the development of rocketry took place in government-funded institutions, but the original idea was that of Robert Goddard, who worked by himself. Similarly, although the atomic bomb was developed during World War II within a highly institutionalized context, its development was possible only because the basic principles had already been discovered by individuals.

Who are these lone innovators? They tend to be nonconformists, at least intellectually, but they do not appear to be more intelligent than their noninnovating peers.

In any event, the innovators of the past have not, so far as evidence shows, been judged in childhood and youth as exceptionally bright; more often, they have been considered by their contemporaries as being a bit dull, if only because they have failed to grasp the fact that the world is flat, that two and two always make four, that an iron plow will poison the soil, or that the king can do no wrong. (LaPiere, 1965, p. 132)

Albert Einstein, for example, was a high school dropout who failed the entrance exam to polytechnic school; he worked for years as a minor official in a patent office, while at night working out the theory of relativity.

Innovators are also often newcomers to their fields, bringing to their work fresh views, nimbleness of mind, and no vested interest in the status quo. An innovator may also be a specialist in one field who is attracted to a problem in another field in which he or she has less or even no expertise. Ironically, a person who has extensive knowledge of a subject is more likely to be habituated to conventional ways than to look for new ones. This is the paradox of innovation: the more one familiarizes oneself with a subject (after a certain point), the

Physicist Albert Einstein is a classic example of the lone innovator who initiates social change. (Ernst Haas/Magnum)

less innovative one is likely to be. This problem of "knowing too much" retarded efforts to develop the internal combustion engine, for example. Leonardo da Vinci, observing the action of gunpowder in propelling a ball out of a cannon, sought to apply the same force to drive a piston. His efforts and those of several centuries of experimenters failed because, familiar with the cannon, they kept trying to use gunpowder as their fuel. Only when petroleum distillates were substituted—in the nineteenth century—did a real engine become feasible.

In one important respect, however, innovators apparently do differ significantly from most of their peers: they must be motivated enough to continue working in the face of failure and to cope with the penalties that may come from challenging established ways.

From the very nature of the innovative process it may be inferred that an innovator must have exceptional confidence in his own judgment and, conversely, subnormal regard for the judgment of others, for the power of authority, and for the evidence of the past. . . . Most men, including presumably most would-be innovators, are too sensitive to social pressures, too much concerned with their status, and too conventional regarding duties and social obligations to be able to concentrate their time and energies on tasks that are not sanctioned by society. (LaPiere, 1965, pp. 134–137)

Conditions conducive to innovation

Innovation, then, is a form of deviance, and deviance may be a result of "incomplete socialization," as we pointed out in Chapter 7. "Innovators," LaPiere writes, can be "but one of the human by-products of failure in socialization in a society that is undergoing change" (1965, p. 138). The less integrated and less stable the social system (short of complete chaos), the more likely are innovators to emerge. Societal conditions conducive to innovation arise frequently during periods of crisis, such as times of revolution, war, and economic depression (Kallen, 1937). Necessity, in these cases, does prove to be the mother of invention—a truth that is also borne out by the "premature" discoveries that sometimes lie fallow for generations, only to be exploited when the need arises. The parachute, for example, was sketched in the fifteenth century, but the idea was never used until the development of balloon flight in the 1780s.

Innovations are also likely to emerge in societies that have high access to infusions of new techniques and ideas from other cultures along with a general willingness to make use of these borrowed elements. (Cities, the meeting-places of cultures, are thus often places where innovations arise.) In addition, Robert Merton has pointed out that in some societies there may be significant social pressure *toward* deviance; some of this deviance will manifest itself in the form of innovation. Our culture, for example, may encourage deviance to the extent that it places a high premium on success but restricts opportunities to achieve it. Numerous innovative forms of deviance, such as new methods of swindling, have been the result. "The history of the great American fortunes is threaded with . . . institutionally dubious innovation, as is attested by many tributes to the Robber Barons" (Merton, 1967, p. 195). (See Chapter 7 for a more detailed discussion of Merton's theory of deviance.)

Although remarkably similar to modern parachutes, Leonardo's design, constructed around 1485, remained unknown for centuries and played no part in their development.

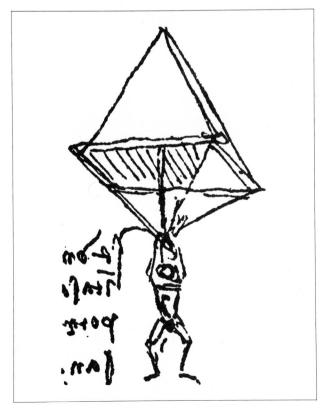

RESISTANCE AND DIFFUSION

In itself, an innovation has no effect if left to molder in the laboratory or desk drawer. If it is to result in actual social change, someone must *advocate* it, or induce society to accept it; and others must step forward and adopt it. In other words, a process of diffusion has to take place.

A particularly important factor in the diffusion process is *reinforcement*, defined as any stimulus that induces a positive or negative reaction in people (Hamblin and Miller, 1976). In a study of the adoption of a high-yielding strain of hybrid seed corn by farmers in the southern and midwestern United States, Robert Hamblin and Jerry Miller sought to explain why some areas adopted the hybrid corn before others. A mathematical and statistical analysis showed that between 60 and 90 percent of the variation in the speed of the diffusion process could be explained in terms of reinforcement factors that influenced either the behavior of the seed corn developers or the farmers.

The acceptance of change, or ease of diffusion, is of course also related to the alternatives offered by any given innovation, to the impact an innovation may have on established patterns of behavior and also, from a pragmatic point of view, to the power of the various parties or groups whose interests are most likely to be furthered or hindered by it.

Diffusion does not take place readily. Resistance to change is usually the norm, and acceptance of innovation the exception. Change threatens our sense of mastery over the environment in general and forces us to do the painful work of attending to something that formerly was an easy habit. Most people fear the unknown, and much of our sense of identity tends to be built up around familiar things. Of course, people's resistance to change has spared them some catastrophes,

From 1811 to 1816, bands of English workers organized under the name Luddites to destroy manufacturing machinery because they believed that it caused unemployment. This caricature of Ned Ludd, the Leicestershire worker for whom the movement was named, was published after one such "Luddite riot" in 1812. (The Granger Collection)

preventing them from "destroying themselves by adopting malfunctional devices or procedures" (LaPiere, 1965, p. 175). Nevertheless, as LaPiere points out, "the universal tendency for men to resist changes of any sort has often and for long prevented the adoption of functionally valuable innovations." Particular groups may resist change because of its incompatibility with their interests; thus, many utility companies have been reluctant to invest in solar power research and development because a commitment of this nature could ultimately lead to lower profits. Sometimes movements spring up in resistance to technological changes that are already taking place, as in the case of the nineteenth-century Luddites in England, who destroyed industrial machinery because they feared it would put people out of work. What appears as "progress" to some people is likely to appear to others as a step backward.

Who are the advocates?

Sometimes it is the innovators themselves who advocate their inventions. F. W. Woolworth, for example, pushed his own idea for the self-service store, Thomas Edison promoted his own inventions, and the English poet William Blake printed his own poems. Ordinarily, however, innovators are not their own advocates. The temperaments of the innovator and the "seller" of a new idea are usually different, and inventors rarely have the institutional positions to be successful advocates (LaPiere, 1965). Today, in the industrialized countries of the West, the primary advocates of material inventions are usually giant corporations, not individual peddlers. RCA, for example, kept its corporate ears open for news of inventions that could eventually lead to the development of television, and RCA executives tried to monopolize the appropriate ones as soon as they heard about them (Barnouw, 1975). A common pattern is for an individual inventor to market his or her product on a small scale, either alone or through a small business. Then, if the product proves successful, a large corporation buys out the whole operation and takes it over as its own. In capitalist countries, it is often argued, the advocacy of a material innovation is determined to a large extent not by the innovation's usefulness, but by its estimated profitability. If corporations see money in an invention, this argument holds, they will push it; if not, they won't.

Factors determining acceptance

Whether or not a population accepts an innovation depends on a number of factors: how the innovation "fits" with the values and norms of the receiving society, what kinds of resistance it has to overcome, how it is diffused, and how highly respected the advocates are. The last two factors merit further brief explanation.

THE MODE OF DIFFUSION. Some studies indicate that diffusion is connected with the extent to which potential adopters are integrated into a social network. For example, advertising is one of the most powerful tools available for stimulating demand for and acceptance of a new product, whether it be a household cleaner or a political candidate; yet while the mass media may be useful for stimulating initial awareness of an innovation, actual acceptance is much more effectively induced by interpersonal contact (Katz et al., 1963). In a study of the diffusion of a new variant of a common drug, for example, researchers found that the doctors most likely to adopt the drug initially were those who subscribed to many professional journals, attended specialized conferences, and had more contact with other doctors (Coleman, Menzel, and Katz, 1959). Knowledge of these and other factors involved in the diffusion-adoption process is critical to any effort to alter a social system through the deliberate introduction of new practices or processes, such as the many programs now underway in less developed nations to modernize agricultural methods or bring about changes in attitudes toward childbearing and personal health.

THE STATUS OF THE ADVOCATES. Acceptance is greatly aided when an innovation is legitimated by a person of high status, or adopted by a powerful advocate. The population's resistance to the use of anesthesia in Britain, for example, was dramatically reduced when Queen Victoria accepted chloroform during the birth of Prince Leopold (LaPiere, 1965).

The higher the class that originally accepts an innovation, the more likely it is to spread through all classes. As a general rule, innovations work their way downward in the class structure, in a process of adoption that has been termed "stratified diffusion" (Young and Willmott, 1973). This rule seems to hold true not primarily because the working classes are conservative, but because only through an improvement in living standards and cheaper methods of production can people at the bottom afford the innovation. If the lower classes are the first to adopt an innovation, the upper classes may be reluctant to copy them (Katz et al., 1963). There are, however, many exceptions, such as the transformation of blue jeans from a functional piece of laborer's clothing to a high-fashion status symbol sold in expensive boutiques, or the incorporation of spirituals or certain types of folk music into the repertoire of the dominant culture, or even the gradual adoption of cigarette smoking by the upper classes.

Although innovation and diffusion often lead to widespread social change, they are but two of the factors involved. The overall phenomenon of social change is thought to be the outcome of many interacting influences, and in the next section, we turn to some more ambitious theories that have been advanced to explain the movements of whole societies.

Theories of large-scale social change

Is there an overall direction in which societies move? People have been asking this question for thousands of years. Speculation that seemingly random social changes are actually moments in the unfolding of a predetermined grand historical design can be found in the writings of the earliest philosophers from Greece to China, and more recent theorists have continued to search for a master key to human events. The oldest theory of history is the idea that history follows a *cycli-* cal pattern. According to this view, either a particular course of events will endlessly repeat itself, or societies will go through a pattern of growth and decline analogous to the life cycle of individuals. Cyclical theorists point to the rise and fall of the great civilizations— ancient Greece, ancient Egypt, the Roman Empire, Imperial China. Oswald Spengler (1926), for example, argued that the West had already reached the zenith of its development and was soon to be superseded by the

East. One British historian, who did not adhere to the cyclical perspective, tartly remarked that current talk about the decline of civilization meant "only that university professors used to have domestic servants and now do their own washing-up" (Taylor, 1959). In other words, the cyclical conception often gains credibility when the thinker's own culture or subculture appears to be declining in some way.

Evolutionary theories, the philosophical opposite of the cyclical perspective, arise during periods of hope and progress, such as the Enlightenment and the late nineteenth century. Some of these evolutionary theories have seen history as an ascending line on a graph or an unfolding of progressively "higher" or "better" stages, culminating, say, in the perfection of the human race, national power, affluence for all, or political democracy.

PROCESSES OF CHANGE

Whatever the ultimate direction in which societies move, it has been argued by many sociologists that they move in that direction not because of any external master plan or destiny, but simply because of forces inherent in their own makeup. Many sociologists of the modern functionalist school have argued that it is impossible for change to take place in just one part of a social system; rather, they claim that even a minor modification in one institutional area may set in motion a series of changes and counterchanges felt throughout the society. Modern functionalists, such as Gerhard Lenski (whose theories are discussed in detail in Chapter 10), also see this internal process in terms of general trends in the direction of social evolution and increasing societal complexity, and they further depict the overall direction of change as being a positive movement toward the optimal functioning of the system. Functionalists argue that when there is a "maladjustment" or "disorganization" in one part of the social system, other parts of the system will tend to change in a compensatory manner, so that the whole system finally reaches equilibrium again. Conflict theorists, however, see no such inherent optimalizing mechanism at work. In their view, one change may set another in motion, but there is no reason to assume that the end result will be for the greater good of the whole society.

What kind of change comes first?

One debate connected with this idea of change and counterchange in the social system has to do with whether *technological* change causes *cultural* change, or vice versa. When the machine gun was developed, for example, it completely revolutionized the waging of war, making irrelevant the traditional notions of war as a test of will, ingenuity, honor, and courage (Ellis, 1975). In this case, material or technological change clearly brought cultural change. The sociologist William Ogburn (1922) argued that material change *generally* preceded nonmaterial change, and that there was often a gap in time—which he called *cultural lag*—between the two. Ogburn offered as an example the deforestation of certain areas of the United States. When industries began to make heavier use of trees, the forests began to diminish, and this eventually forced a change in social policy from one that favored exploitation of the forests to one that favored conservation.

The classic arguments on this issue are those of Karl Marx and Friedrich Engels on the one hand and Max Weber on the other. Weber asserted in *The Protestant Ethic and the Spirit of Capitalism* (1905) that ideas could play an independent role in determining social and economic structure. (We discussed this theory in more detail in Chapter 18.) Marx and Engels argued that the "final causes of all social changes are to be sought . . . in the modes of production and exchange" (Engels, quoted in Etzioni and Etzioni, 1964, p. 7). Marx is sometimes seen as the first technological determinist. Though he never defined technology as a force or abstract principle in its own right, he did suggest that capitalism gave a special impetus to technological change. In order for capitalists to survive as a class, he argued, they had to continually modify the conditions of production through technological innovation and changes in work organization (1867). But as they did so, they were actually hastening their own overthrow, in the view of Marx and Engels (1848). First of all, the capitalists were making possible a victory over material scarcity in the long run, so that the laws of supply and demand on which the free market was based would no longer operate; and second, they were undercutting the well-being of the people on whom their very profits were based—the laborers.

Sociologist William Ogburn believed that material or technological change—such as the development of the automobile—generally precedes and causes cultural change—for example, the geographic mobility Americans are accustomed to today. He termed this phenomenon *cultural lag*. (Ellis Herwig/Stock, Boston)

Robert Nisbet: a critique of the social-system approach

Meanwhile, other sociologists and historians argue that there is *no* overall direction or design to history. Robert Nisbet, for example, thinks that belief in the directionality of history is deeply embedded in Western culture, but that this is our imposition on events rather than something that is "in" history itself. "The direction," he says, "is in the mind of the beholder" (1972, p. 360). Nisbet argues that, contrary to evolutionary theories in general and functionalism in particular, it is erroneous to assume that "because internal strains and conflicts almost constantly exist in a social organization or group, change must be taking place" (p. 301). Random events—wars and other crises—impinging from outside a social system, Nisbet argues, have often been more important sources of change than internal strains. In direct contrast to the functionalist position, he asserts that "change cannot be deduced or empirically derived from the elements of social structure," nor is it sensible to view history or a society as having a "nature" to work out through change and counterchange.

BELIEFS ABOUT PURPOSIVE CHANGE

In the eighteenth century, the French philosopher Condorcet formulated what was at the time a radical and daring idea. He argued that through the use of systematic reason, people could discover the social laws that govern them and actually use those laws to design reforms. In this way, prejudice, poverty, and ignorance could be abolished and a new golden age inaugurated on earth. This notion—that human beings can apply the methods of natural science to the study of society and plan their futures in accordance with "scientific" laws—is termed *positivism*.

Such beliefs about grand designs of social change often carry implications concerning purposive social planning and action. If one does *not* believe that change is the result of forces inherent in the workings of a society, one may not expect to be able to influence the direction of change. Likewise, a belief in imminent apocalypse or in a cyclical model of change can breed a kind of fatalism that discourages human intervention. And there was even one branch of evolutionary theory, Social Darwinism, whose adherents—notably William Graham Sumner (1959)—argued that humans should not meddle with the processes of social differentiation and competitive struggle, on the ground that only the fittest *should* survive.

However, other evolutionary theorists, whose intellectual background included nineteenth-century liberal democratic beliefs and ideas of progress, believed optimistically that social problems could be solved and the "good" society attained—*if* humans actively took part in the process. Marx, too, advocated active intervention: in his view, because any ruling group or class develops vested interests in continuing its own domination, class struggle is essential if new forms of social structure are to develop.

The speed of social change is often jarring. Some observers fear that it will become catastrophic. As problems in one changing society come increasingly to affect other societies, the question of human intervention becomes more and more crucial. In the section that follows, we will consider social change in the countries of the Third World, which are under pressure from population growth, unemployment, hunger, internal and international strife, mushrooming urbanization, and numerous other strains.

Modernization in the Third World*

THE CONVERGENCE HYPOTHESIS: A LATTER-DAY EVOLUTIONARY PERSPECTIVE

Numerous functionalist theorists, in their study of the actions and reactions involved in changes within social systems, have been particularly interested in the period of change and readjustment that took place in Europe and America during the late nineteenth and early twentieth centuries as a consequence of the technological changes brought about by the Industrial Revolution. Particularly significant, in the functionalists' view, was the fact that there were certain similarities in the ways in which the United States and many European countries changed. Many attained an important degree of material wealth, as reflected in a high gross national product; all attained economic independence from other nations; in each, citizens' political allegiances tended to be transferred from the local to the national level, and citizens gained an increased sense of common national identity. Furthermore, these countries tended to develop democratic political values (*egalitarianism*—the notion that all citizens are equals regardless of their status or wealth—pluralism, a high level of mass participation) and an individualistic, capitalistic orientation. It was the functionalists' conclusion that industrialization would inevitably bring about these changes in *any* nation. Thus they developed a hypothesis that was applicable (in their view) to the Third World countries as well as to Europe, namely, that as industrialization proceeded, all industrialized countries would become more and more similar to one another, or would, in a word, *converge*.

Another aspect of the convergence hypothesis concerns the change in personal values that modernization is thought to entail. Some writers argue that in order for modernization to occur, the members of a society must have certain motivations and values. According to one definition, the values that characterize the "modern" individual are: (1) an openness to new experience; (2) loyalty to government leaders, rather than to parents or priests; (3) belief in the efficacy of science and medicine and in the possibility of change; (4) high occu-

---

* *Third World* is the term customarily—and rather chauvinistically—applied to the developing nations, especially in Africa and Asia, that are not aligned with or committed to the policies of either the United States and other democratic countries (the "First World") or the Soviet Union and other communist countries (the "Second World"). The term should be understood as being used here in a general descriptive sense and not a political one.

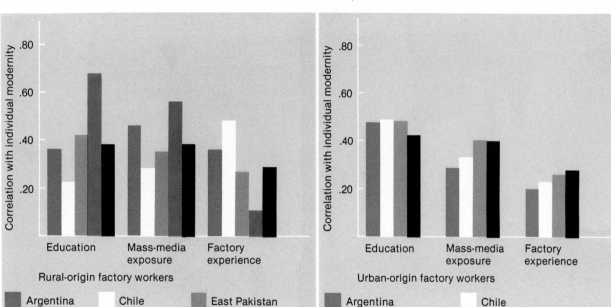

FIGURE 22.1

These two graphs show the correlation found in one study between the level of individual modernity among young male factory workers in six countries and the three variables of education, exposure to mass media, and experience in factory work. All three variables—especially education, in most countries—did have a significant effect on the level of modernity of both rural-origin factory workers (left) and urban-origin factory workers (right). (There were no rural-origin factory workers in the Israeli sample, and no urban-origin factory workers in the East Pakistani and Indian samples.) (Adapted from Inkeles, 1969, p. 266)

pational and educational ambitions; (5) an interest in planning one's affairs and being prompt; (6) readiness to take an active role in community affairs; and (7) an interest in attempting to keep abreast of national and world events. How do individuals learn such values, if they have not absorbed them in childhood? One study of young men in Argentina, Chile, India, Israel, Nigeria, and East Pakistan found that living in a city and working in industry were the experiences that seemed to help make individuals "modern" in the sense outlined above. An individual's schooling and factory experience, in particular, were closely correlated with this

level of "modernism," not because of their specific content, but because schools and factories were "rationalizing organizations" that emphasized and fostered the development of these values and attitudes (Inkeles, 1969, pp. 209–211). Exposure to mass media was also an important factor in individual modernization (see Figure 22.1).

The notion of convergence has come in for marked criticism. Some have pointed out that even in the nineteenth century, there was not really just one pattern of industrialization, but many. The industrialization of France, for example, in which the aristocracy did not begin commercial agriculture, and of England, where it did, led to quite different courses of development and political systems. Similarly, Germany and Japan industrialized in unique ways (Gortzel, 1976). Today, many differences among industrialized societies remain. For instance, the magnitude of inequality differs significantly from one society to the next, as does access to education, skilled jobs, and the like (Feldman, 1966). (In matters of family form, political structure, and religious patterns, the effect of industrialization per se is inconclusive.)

Despite such criticism, studies have continued to offer support for the convergence theory, at least in part

Views of Tokyo, Japan, and Hamburg, West Germany. No two countries have industrialized in precisely the same way. However, modern technology and urbanization have had many similar results throughout the world. (Wide World Photos; James R. Holland/Stock, Boston)

(Form, 1979). Although industrialized societies are by no means identical and no two countries have industrialized in exactly the same way, the introduction of technology and urbanization have had many similar effects. Even in countries with such "anti-modern" traditions as Japan and India, elements of Western industrialization have prevailed. In the rest of this chapter, we will look at modernization in the Third World in light of this hypothesis.

DEFINING MODERNIZATION IN THE THIRD WORLD

It is widely held that the Third World nations are—or should be—going through a process of social change known as *modernization*. But there is a political battle over the definition of the term *modernization* itself. One functionalist, applying the convergence hypothesis to Third World modernization, wrote:

What is involved in modernization is a "total" transformation of a traditional or pre-modern society into the types of technology and associated social organization that characterize the "advanced," economically prosperous, and relatively politically stable nations of the Western World (Moore, 1963, pp. 89–90)

But what exactly does (or should) *modernization* mean? Unquestionably, people of the Third World nations want the higher standard of living that they know people in industrialized societies enjoy. Unquestionably, too, the masses and the leaders in these countries want political and economic equality with the other nations of the world; and though tourism and improved agricultural methods can bring in some money, industrialization will have to be the major route to growth. But under what kind of government is all this to take place? Despite the prediction of the convergence hypothesis that Third World countries will evolve into capitalist democracies, in actuality many examples of successful modernization in the twentieth century have been seen in socialist countries

In many Third World countries, modernization has meant Westernization, as the Western dress of these Indian men suggests. (Toronto Star Syndicate)

France, Holland, Italy, and Germany all sought riches, raw materials, markets, and religious converts, and to get them, they sent colonists to pacify local populations and establish administrations to watch over their holdings. Money was introduced into the local economies, and transportation and communications systems were developed to connect areas of production with centers of export. The expansion of mining and agriculture, together with the development of some manufacturing, were facilitated by the introduction of Western religion (primarily Roman Catholicism), a selective educational system, and, where it suited the colonizers' ideological or practical ends, Westernized lifestyles. Such changes affected primarily the relatively small class of indigenous people who had fairly direct contact with the colonizers, either because they worked in the colonial administration or because they owned businesses that depended largely on such contact.

As more Third World nations gained their political independence, they began, more or less swiftly, to develop economically. There are two major schools of thought on what has happened and will continue to happen to the Third World countries. From the functionalist convergence hypothesis have arisen *diffusionist theories*, which hold that the industrialized capitalist nations have aided the less developed countries by serving as demonstration models of successful modernization and, more directly, by supplying economic and technical assistance. Adherents of *dependency theories*, by contrast, argue that the history of relations between the advanced capitalist countries and the Third World is not primarily a history of demonstration and assistance, but one of imperialism and exploitation.

(some exceptions would be those that have recently made their fortunes in oil exports). Likewise, will Third World people begin to think and act like Europeans and Americans? This too is debatable, as we shall see.

DIFFUSIONIST AND DEPENDENCY THEORIES OF THIRD WORLD ECONOMIC DEVELOPMENT

For more than 400 years the preindustrial areas of Latin America, Asia, and Africa were linked to the nations of Europe by colonialism. Spain, Portugal, England,

Economic neocolonialism

In the view of dependency theorists, even though the Third World nations are politically independent, they are still tied to their former mother countries by a pattern that may be thought of as *neocolonialism*. Most countries of the Third World originally developed as one-crop or one-commodity export economies, and they have remained so to the present day, dependent on the industrialized West for a market for their products and for the goods they need but cannot produce themselves. The Western industrialized countries need the Third World countries because they provide a steady supply of raw materials. Nevertheless, the Western industrialized countries usually have the economic and military power to keep their advantage, since the Third World countries risk economic disaster should their one crop fail or should technological change (such as the invention of synthetic rubber) lower the price of their primary product. Related to this notion of mutual dependence is the idea of a world system elaborated by Immanuel Wallerstein and more fully discussed in Chapters 10 and 18.

Other elements of Third World economic dependence include the import of capital, indebtedness, and conditional aid. In many cases, the owners of a Third World nation's primary product are corporations based in advanced capitalist countries (as we noted in the box on multinational firms in Chapter 18), and there is no guarantee that these corporations will invest the profits they *make* in the developing country in industries *based* in the developing country. In 1968, for example, U.S.-based corporations reaped nearly $1.4 billion in profits in Latin America, but they reinvested only $297 million (Mason, 1972). A salient aspect of this problem is that the profits that U.S.-based corporations make in the Third World are much higher than those they make in countries outside the Third World. Between 1950 and 1967, for example, for every dollar invested, American corporations made an average profit of $0.62 in Western Europe, $0.92 in Canada, but almost $3.00 in Latin America (Mason, 1972, pp. 32–33).

What about the foreign aid Third World countries receive from the developed countries—for example, the $22 billion that Third World countries received in 1973 (*U.N. Statistical Yearbook*, 1974)? Such aid is not seen by all parties as an unmitigated good, and there are often strings attached to it. A considerable proportion of foreign-aid funds goes for military hardware and training, and some pays for technicians from industrial centers. The aid may also increase the national debt— already high in many countries. It may be earmarked for industries that require heavy investments of capital (as opposed to industries that require intensive labor, a commodity likely to be in greater supply in Third World countries). And it may mean the introduction of an individualistic, profit-oriented emphasis in countries whose culture strongly emphasizes cooperation.

All this is not to say that Third World economies are completely stagnant as a result of economic neocolonialism. There has been some industrialization, and

TABLE 22.1

GROSS NATIONAL PRODUCT PER CAPITA (IN 1972 DOLLARS), 1963–1973

YEAR	DEVELOPED NATIONS*	UNDERDEVELOPED NATIONS*	WORLD
1963	$2,381	$185	$ 821
1964	2,509	194	857
1965	2,619	202	887
1966	2,742	207	917
1967	2,832	208	934
1968	2,967	212	967
1969	3,074	223	996
1970	3,164	236	1,020
1971	3,256	244	1,043
1972	3,378	251	1,071
1973	3,561	252	1,112
Average annual growth	3.9%	3.2%	2.9%

* "Developed nations" include: United States; Canada; all European NATO countries except Greece and Turkey; all Warsaw Pact countries except Bulgaria; and Austria, Finland, Ireland, Sweden, Switzerland, Australia, New Zealand, Japan, and South Africa. Twenty-eight countries were classified as developed. "Underdeveloped nations" include all those in Latin America; in the Near East including Egypt; in East Asia except Japan; in South Asia; in Africa except South Africa; and also Albania, Bulgaria, Greece, Malta, Spain, Turkey, and Yugoslavia. One hundred eight countries were classified as underdeveloped.

there has also been steady economic growth; in fact, many of the capital-intensive investments made by the neocolonialists have built hydroelectric plants, dams, communication networks, and other infrastructural elements that are critical to further development in an underindustrialized country. Nevertheless, as measured by gross national product per capita, world-scale inequality is increasing, as Table 22.1 shows. Underdeveloped countries have grown, but developed countries have grown even faster, and absolute inequality has increased enormously. The increasing disparity between less developed and advanced countries is a consequence, one economist believes, of Third World subjection to the economic market of capitalism: "the main obstacle to the development of Third World countries lies neither in a peculiarity of their own social structure nor in a deliberate strategy of the great powers or of big capital (although both of these factors may worsen the situation), but in the free working of market forces" (Emmanuel, 1974, pp. 71–72).

"Dual societies": contrasting interpretations

There are huge gaps between social strata in Third World countries—gaps so large that they create what is often thought of as a "dual society." The gap between peasant farmers and the urban elite, for example, is enormous: in many African nations, civil servants earn ten to twenty times the average wage (Marris, 1975). Diffusionists see such "dual societies" as made up of "advanced" segments, which are in contact with the West, and much larger "backward" segments, which live in quasi-feudal conditions because they have yet to move along the modernization road. In contrast, dependency theorists believe that it is precisely *because* the West intervened that the great masses of people in these societies are "backward." According to dependency theorists like André Gunder Frank (1969), the advance of capitalism penetrated into all but the most remote enclaves of the less developed nations, and capitalism is responsible for the appearance of "dual societies" within these nations:

Analogously to the relations between development and underdevelopment on the international level, the contemporary underdeveloped institutions of the so-called backward or feudal domestic areas of an underdeveloped country are . . . the product of the single historical process of capitalist developments . . . . (p. 6)

In other words, poor areas in Third World countries are not areas where modern trends have not arrived, but areas that are *exploited* by modern institutions. Frank envisions a kind of dependency "chain" linking the industrialized nations to the Third World nations, and in turn linking larger cities in Third World countries with their own satellite cities. The primary purpose of this chain, in his view, is to channel economic surplus out of satellite cities to the Third World metropolises, and "to channel part of this surplus to the world metropolis [Europe, the United States, or both] of which all are satellites" (p. 7). In direct contrast to the assertions of the diffusionists, Frank argues that those countries that have historically been *closest to the center* in this dependency chain now appear among the most *underdeveloped*, while countries with the weakest links to the Western industrialized countries are those most likely to experience development.

In sum, dependency theorists such as Frank argue that full industrialization and economic growth cannot take place unless the links with Europe and the United States are broken. As Frank points out, many Latin American countries experienced their most significant spurts of industrial development when they were the most cut off from the industrialized West—that is, during World War I, the Depression, and World War II. Likewise, they argue that the masses of people who live at rock-bottom poverty levels in Third World countries are not likely to gain economically unless they can avoid further exploitation by capitalist institutions.

TRENDS IN SOCIAL DEVELOPMENT IN THE THIRD WORLD

If the outlook for Third World countries is dismal in regard to economic equality, there have been some relative improvements in other factors associated with modernization. Between 1950 and 1970 (a period of economic expansion), Third World countries as a whole showed increases in regard to such indicators as electricity consumed per capita, percentage of males in the nonagricultural labor force, telephones and radios per capita, percentage of the young in all levels of schooling, urbanization, and physicians per million population (Meyer, Boli-Bennett, and Chase-Dunn, 1975). Table 22.2 shows the situation of various countries in regard to such overt indexes of modernization. More elusive factors often associated with modernization, such as social mobility, increased division of labor, ideas about the value of science and technology, belief in progress, and shift from an emphasis on ascribed to achieved status, have also been changing (Meyer, Boli-Bennett, and Chase-Dunn, 1975).

To what extent is the process of social modernization, as it is manifested in today's Third World countries, parallel to that which took place in Europe and the United States in the nineteenth century? In the Third World today, enormous social changes are being accomplished in a relatively short time, partly as a result of contact with the developed technologies of the West. This telescoping of time in the Third World has juxtaposed the computer and the digging stick, the technician and the camel herder. (The Indian city of Chandigarth, for example, was designed by the mod-

TABLE 22.2

SELECTED INDEXES OF MODERNIZATION IN THIRTY-ONE COUNTRIES*

	LITERACY	POPULATION 5–19 IN SCHOOL	POPULATION PER PHYSICIAN	DAILY NEWSPAPER CIRCULATION
AFRICA				
Algeria	26%	52%	6,535	17/1,000 pop.
Ethiopia	7%	12%	75,715	2.5/1,000 pop.
Morocco	20%	28%	12,503	21/1,000 pop.
Nigeria	25%	22%	23,341	613,000 ('75)/66,630,000 pop. ('77)
S. Africa	35%	59%	1,992	70/1,000 pop.
ASIA				
Bangladesh	25%	34%	9,896	356,000 ('75)/84,660,000 pop. ('78)
People's Republic of China	95%	62%	8,000	Not available
Australia	98%	78%	731	394/1,000 pop.
India	36%	40%	4,264	16/1,000 pop.
Iran	37%	45%	2,649	15/1,000 pop.
Israel	88%	63%	364	1,337,000 ('75)/3,690,000 pop. ('78)
Japan	99%	70%	867	60,780,000 ('76)/114,900,000 pop. ('78)
Korea, Rep. of	88%	66%	1,732 ('76)	6,010,000 ('75)/37,020,000 pop. ('78)
Lebanon	86%	72%	1,106	283,000 ('75)/3,060,000 pop. ('78)
New Zealand	98%	78%	739	Not available
Pakistan	25%	26%	3,894	358,000 ('75)/76,770,000 pop. ('78)
Turkey	55%	47%	1,900	Not available
U.S.S.R.	99%	61%	353	397/1,000 pop.
NORTH AMERICA				
Canada	95%	86%	593	4,872,000 ('75)/23,500,000 pop. ('78)
Mexico	82%	56%	1,410	Not available
U.S.	99%	85%	583	287/1,000 pop.
CENTRAL & SOUTH AMERICA				
Argentina	93%	58%	494	2,773,000 ('75)/26,390,000 pop. ('78)
Brazil	68%	50%	1,646	39/1,000 pop. ('73)
Chile	90%	73%	1,857	Not available
Cuba	83%	70%	941	53,000 ('75)/9,600,000 pop. ('78)
Ecuador	75%	57%	2,816	49/1,000 pop.
Guatemala	46%	29%	4,344	165,000 ('75)/6,620,000 pop. ('78)
Haiti	46%	29%	9,359	20/1,000 pop.
Jamaica	86%	68%	3,636	131,000 ('75)/2,090,000 pop. ('78)
Nicaragua	57%	44%	1,559	91,000 ('75)/2,400,000 pop. ('78)
Peru	72%	64%	1,780	95/1,000 pop. ('74)
Venezuela	82%	55%	950	1,067,000 ('75)/13,120,000 pop. ('78)

* All data is from the year 1975 unless otherwise indicated.

SOURCE: *The World Almanac & Book of Facts 1980.*

The Agra Road in Delhi, India. The rapidity with which industrialization proceeds in the Third World makes startling juxtapositions of the old and the new commonplace. (Ira Kirschenbaum/Stock, Boston)

ernist architect Le Corbusier but built by the age-old method of the "bucket brigade," with women moving stones by passing them along a human chain.) These changes are producing much social strain, as did industrialization and its associated changes in Europe in the nineteenth century. But they are not proceeding in the same way they did in countries that are now fully industrialized.

For one thing, the shift from local to national allegiance that took place in Western industrialized countries is proceeding unevenly in the Third World. At the same time, it should be noted that many industrialized countries now appear to be experiencing a shift from national to regional allegiances, as can be seen in the French separatist movement in Canada, the continuing "home rule" question in Ireland, ethnic fragmentation in the Soviet Union, and so on. The significance of these regional tendencies is not yet clear. Yet compared with what is nevertheless the relative homogeneity of the countries of Western Europe, where language and cultural identity are more likely to correspond to political affiliation, many Third World countries of Africa and Asia, because of the political boundaries imposed on them by the colonial powers, are composed of a mixture of peoples speaking different languages, with different cultural identities and unequal wealth. In the analysis of one sociologist, these differences have been exacerbated among many peoples because the jumble of traditional and modern ways has created confusion, and has led to a resurgence of tribalism as a means of reestablishing a solid identity (Marris, 1975).

Regional allegiances can be more powerful than national ties—even in Western industrialized countries. Here, a *oui* (yes) vote in the May 21, 1980, referendum (which did not pass) would have meant Quebec's independence from Canada. (Jean-Pierre Laffont/Sygma)

Another reason that national loyalties have been hard to focus in some Third World countries is the extreme inequalities mentioned earlier. Recent evidence suggests that the more dependent a country is on foreign markets and foreign economic penetration, the greater will be the inequality *within* that country. Thus, if we assume that dependence and inequality are problems produced by the presence of outsiders, those countries most in need of cohesion in their struggle against the influence of outsiders may, ironically, be those in the worst position to effect it.

PLANNING FOR MODERNIZATION

Diffusionist theory—despite its assumption of progress through the diffusion of technology, "modern" values, and capital from the industrialized West to the nations of the Third World—tends to view each society as a relatively autonomous entity that will inevitably move from an initial (backward) state to a final (modern) one. But, as we have just seen, the Third World countries are not self-contained societies that will converge by virtue of similar paths of development. They are not simply replicating the experience of developed countries, nor are they merely further behind in their development. The advanced capitalist countries were able to develop autonomously, but the Third World countries are dependent on the more developed countries and are even now becoming increasingly integrated into a capitalist world economy (Wallerstein, 1974).

Partly because of the need to gain more autonomy

on the global level, and partly because of other economic, social, and political pressures, the governments of the Third World are being forced to do a great deal of planning—unlike the governments of the countries that modernized more slowly and autonomously in the nineteenth and early twentieth centuries. A rough indicator of this is that before 1945, only eight nations had planning agencies, while by 1965, 136 did (Meyer, Boli-Bennett, and Chase-Dunn, 1975). Consensus is growing, one analyst has written, on the "need for decisive state intervention in initiating and sustaining a process of development. This applies to economic growth as well as to social redistribution and cultural transformation" (Portes, 1976, p. 59).

Some of the success stories of modernization in the contemporary world have been the result of deliberate national policies, begun by new ruling groups to promote national autonomy (Portes, 1976). The specific policies vary, but the need to reverse the traditional processes of the world market tends to underlie them all.

Three strategies of development through state intervention have become evident in the twentieth century. The first, exemplified by Brazil, entails active encouragement of foreign investment. But in order to attract this investment, wages have had to be kept down—during the period of high growth in recent years in Brazil, real wages actually declined substantially—which in turn requires a repressive and dictatorial regime. The second strategy is that of the so-called leftist military regimes, such as those in Peru and Ethiopia. These regimes are strongly nationalistic and place restrictions on "imports" of foreign capital, but close inspection indicates that they are more military than political or ideological and that in their own way, they too accept foreign investment (Quijano, 1971).

The third strategy is socialism—China and Cuba are prime examples—in which development rises on the tide of social revolution, the nationalization or elimination of foreign investment (i.e., investment from capitalist countries), and considerable central government control and planning. But countries moving in this direction often face enormous external constraints from the United States and other nations of the West. The United States, while ostensibly supporting the extension of liberal democracy, has in fact often supported dictatorships; and, as recent evidence shows, the United States has encouraged the overthrow of leftist

In a socialist government such as that of China, planners use posters to promote the objectives of the revolution. (© Georg Gerster/Rapho/Photo Researchers)

governments, regardless of their popularity. In Chile between 1970 and 1973, for example, the United States spent $8 million to help topple the democratically elected Marxist government of Salvador Allende (Church Committee Report, 1975, p. 1). The methods used were both direct and indirect: they included the machinations of the CIA and various forms of financial leverage, including a retraction of funds by the U.S. Agency for International Development and pressure by multinational corporations on countries that bought

Chilean copper. Factors such as these shape developments in many Third World countries seeking autonomy.

Social planners in the Third World, then, face difficult challenges on a number of fronts. There is little agreement either on the best methods of dealing with these challenges or on the proper goals for planning programs. Even if the Third World countries *could* replicate the Western model, it is not universally agreed that this would be desirable. Recently, discontent with the depersonalization and competitiveness of mass consumer society has created an interest in finding or developing alternatives to it (an issue discussed in Chapter 18). Moreover, if Third World countries were to develop the same consumption styles as the United States, Western Europe, and Japan, the natural resources of the planet might well disappear (Ward and Dubos, 1972). In view of this, it may be that ultimately all societies will diverge, to some extent, from the traditional Western model.

Summary

Social change has been defined as the significant alteration of social structures, including their manifestations in norms, values, and cultural products and symbols. Distinctions have been drawn between "change within a structure" and "change of a structure," between social change and cultural change, and between small-scale and large-scale change.

Innovations are new ideas or techniques that originate with individuals. Innovations are often inventions or discoveries that result from the common efforts of people to solve a problem. Although it is difficult to generalize about innovators, they often seem to be strongly independent, almost "deviant" figures, immune to peer pressure. Certain social conditions seem to encourage innovation: the less integrated and stable the society, the more likely it is that innovators will emerge. Times of crisis, such as war, revolution, and economic depression, also seem to spur innovation.

Most people, fearing the unknown, tend to resist innovations, and it often takes time for this resistance to change or break down. Innovation tends to spread gradually, through a process of diffusion. This process is helped along when the advocates of the new idea or product are wealthy or influential: most (though not all) innovations spread downward through the class structure.

Many theories have been advanced over the centuries to explain the changes that take place in whole societies. The oldest and most common theory is that history follows a cyclical pattern, with societies regularly rising and falling. The evolutionary perspective, on the other hand, holds that history shows a gradual progression of stages, each somewhat higher than the last.

There has been much debate on how social and cultural changes affect one another. One theory holds that technological change causes cultural change. In this view, culture is always a bit behind advancing technology—an idea known as *cultural lag*. The sociologist Max Weber argued that ideas could play an independent role in determining social and economic structure. Marx and Engels, on the other hand, argued that all social change is caused by developments in the modes of production and exchange.

In contrast to these theories, which ascribe some kind of understandable movement to the broad changes in history, Robert Nisbet has argued that there is no overall direction or design to history. This view stresses the role of random events, such as wars, in producing social change.

Positivism is the belief that human beings can apply the methods of natural science to the study of society and plan their futures in accordance with "scientific" laws. In this view, active intervention in the process of social change is justified in the interest of improving society.

The social changes that have been taking place in the modernizing nations of the Third World have given rise to the *convergence hypothesis*. According to this theory, industrialization in any country produces a typically Western kind of development, in which individualistic, "modern" values eventually prevail. Although this hypothesis has been challenged, certain similarities of development have been identified in a number of industrializing nations.

Debate continues inside and outside the countries of the Third World about what kind of "modernization" should be embraced there. Most of these countries have a colonial past, in which a developed country has played a role of helper or exploiter (depending on one's political perspective). According to diffusionist theories, the industrialized nations have helped encourage development in Third World countries; dependency theories hold that colonial exploitation and its aftermath have usually limited or hindered development. Although the Third World countries have made considerable progress in recent years, the industrial nations have progressed even faster, and absolute inequality has increased.

Uneven development in many Third World countries has produced "dual societies" in which huge gaps separate the social strata. In many countries, the introduction of developed technology from the West, with its relatively enormous prosperity for a few, has produced much social strain. Complicating matters are the diffuse populations of many of these countries, with conflicting ethnic and tribal loyalties. Whether development in the Third World countries follows a "free market" or socialist strategy, it is likely to diverge in some ways from the pattern of the industrialized West.

Glossary

ADVOCATE In social-change theory, an individual who induces other people in a population to accept an innovation.

DIFFUSION In social-change theory, the process by which an innovation is adopted by the members of a population.

INNOVATION Defined by Richard LaPiere as an idea for accomplishing some recognized social end in a new way or for a means of accomplishing some new social end.

POSITIVISM The belief that human beings can apply the methods of natural science to the study of society and plan their futures in accordance with "scientific" laws.

REINFORCEMENT Any stimulus that induces a positive or negative reaction in people.

Recommended Readings

Etzioni, Amitai, and Eva Etzioni (eds.). *Social Change: Sources, Patterns, and Consequences.* New York: Basic Books, 1964. One of the best collections of readings on the subject. Included are classical theories, modern theories, articles on modernization and levels and processes of change, all by recognized scholars in this field.

LaPiere, Richard T. *Social Change.* New York: McGraw-Hill, 1965. A comprehensive textbook that is an excellent introduction to the subject of social change.

Moore, Wilbert E. *Social Change.* 2nd ed. Englewood Cliffs, N.J.: Prentice-Hall, 1974. An introduction to change by a leading functionalist theorist. The book considers the nature of change and its theoretical aspects, particularly the results of industrialization and economic development.

Nisbet, Robert A. *Social Change and History.* New York: Oxford University Press, 1969. A critical assessment of theories of historical development that are riddled with value biases, and an argument against evolutionary theories of society.

Ogburn, William, *Social Change.* New York: Viking, 1950. The classic work (originally published in 1922) on social change, containing the first discussion of the theory of cultural lag.

The rich Arab states in trouble

ARNOLD HOTTINGER

The effect of sudden great wealth on a country is not necessarily beneficial. The oil-producing states on the Persian Gulf, caught between modernism, brought about largely by their vast oil revenues, and the old ways, may in fact be in for uneasy times as the writer, Arnold Hottinger, points out.

A careful analysis of the situation among the oil-producing states on the Persian Gulf reveals how simplistic is the view that the more money such a country earns the more "secure" it is. In reality the very opposite may be correct. During the first ten or twenty years after oil revenues have begun to flow, it is relatively easy to channel the funds in such a way that the population is satisfied and approves of the way government affairs are being managed. In a rich oil-producing country, government affairs consist largely of handing out the money. When this is done in a sensible manner, the government can be reasonably sure of popular support. Certain services are widely regarded as having priority and governing officials know that these must be provided: health and education, then housing, road construction, jobs. During the first generation of national prosperity it is much easier than it will be later to satisfy the needs and wishes of the populace, because the memory is still fresh in their minds of how living conditions were before the oil wealth began to flow. . . .

Certain governments, such as that of Kuwait, have made sure that most families in their realms have enjoyed at least something of the country's new wealth—though as always there are those who have profited enormously and others who have benefited to only a modest degree.

In most cases the popular distribution of a minimum of the oil wealth has had to do with real estate ownership and home building. The governments of these states have seen to it that all their citizens have their own home and a bit of land. This has enabled the common folk to profit from the fabulous boom which, in the course of just a few decades, has transformed what were once worthless pieces of desert on the edge of the oil towns into "parcels" now selling at prices close to those of New York real estate.

To the members of the first "oil generation" it was also a delight to be able to acquire an automobile, a refrigerator, an air conditioner, and a TV set. (For their sons and daughters, all these things have become absolute necessities of life. And indeed the new Kuwait and Abu Dhabi are so constructed that cars and air conditioners are virtually necessities.) For that first generation the fact that their children received a free primary education, then secondary-level schooling along with some pocket money, and finally university scholarships for those willing and able to use them, constituted an unprecedented privilege for which one had to be grateful—and was. Faced with all these sudden advantages, the people were prepared to accept and forgive the extravagances and more or less comprehensible ostentation of the ruling classes. . . .

Even in the first generation, of course, there was a clear difference between the broad though underpopulated Saudi Arabia and the ministates along the Gulf—Kuwait, Bahrain, Qatar, the Emirates. . . . The ruling class in these countries usually consists of a widely ramified family or clan, the chief figures of which hold the most important cabinet posts under an all-powerful ruler (emir or sheikh). The links between them and the citizens and subjects of the Gulf city-states have seldom been broken completely, no matter how rich the rulers have become. In Saudi Arabia, by contrast, the situation was different from the outset. Stretching over almost the entire Arabian Peninsula, this state was created on a foundation of the religious and tribal solidarity of the Wahabite tribes of eastern Arabia, under the leadership of its first monarch, Abdul Aziz Ibn Saud. . . . The Saudis' rule over their extensive kingdom is thus relatively young. In this huge territory there are many tribes, linked to the ruling class by complex political ties; there are also divergent religious movements, contrasts and conflicts of interest between urbanites and Bedouins, and extreme differences in mentality, such as those between internationally linked merchant families in the centers of pilgrimage and isolated oasis farmers.

When oil revenues began to flow into this broad, barren kingdom it was like rain in the desert, which quickly collects into rushing torrents that briefly fill the dry wadis with destructive masses of water. The money flowed in specific political and economic channels. It was very difficult to arrange for a broadly based distribution that would have benefited the country's approximately five million people with some degree of equity. Those who already had money and thus were in a position to make good deals became steadily richer, while the torrents of money flowed right past many Saudis, who experienced little more than their inflationary effects.

In former years, of course, some channels led from the Saudi court to the various tribal chieftains, who retained great power over their tribes to the extent that they were able to count on the financial and military support of the Riyadh regime. . . .

But with the influx of oil money that society began to

change. Its tribal structures are dissolving, the tribesmen and their families moving to the cities and the urban slums around them. The traditional tribal leaders, who themselves are moving into urban luxury housing, are losing their control over the people. Citizens with money now travel to Europe and elsewhere. On the surface many of these prosperous people continue to lead strictly traditional Muslim lives. But behind the walls of their villas and palaces the customary luxuries of the West are being cultivated. In time, of course, the former tribesmen now crowding the urban slums learn what is happening in the centers of opulence, and in many cases they may imagine it as even more sensational and vice-ridden than it really is. The religion which once bound these people together now becomes a divisive element, because the common folk are inclined to believe that the upper classes only pretend to be strict Muslims in order to ensure that the masses will remain bound to the strict Wahabite rules of behavior.

On the Arab side of the Persian Gulf the oil began to flow shortly after World War I. By the time oil revenues quadrupled in 1973, the second generation had just grown up and begun entering active economic and social life. This is a generation of people to whom the pre-oil days are known only from hearsay, who take for granted—or even regard as their natural right—all those things for which the former generation was so grateful. They no longer compare the old Kuwait or Qatar with the new; instead they measure today's Qatar or Bahrain against London, Zurich, or New York. Why should their cities, as rich as Zurich and richer than either London or New York, not be equally pleasant to live in? And if they are not, it is obviously the fault of the government. The ruling classes find it steadily more difficult to satisfy a population which has already attained a considerable level of prosperity without having had to earn it by their personal labors.

The governments of these Arab oil-producing states, often advised by foreigners who have an interest in selling them industrial equipment, have begun making provision for the time when their oil deposits will have run out by attempting to establish modern industries. In doing so they have found it necessary to call in two kinds of foreigner: highly trained specialists, and the more numerous workers required to undertake those labors which the now-prosperous native sons are no longer willing to carry out. Certain categories of experts have had to be brought in from other Arab lands, most notably (for linguistic reasons) teachers, instructors of all kinds, administrative spe-

cialists, communications experts in the mass media, officers, and to some extent physicians. Other specialists have been brought in from Europe, Japan, the US, the Arab world, and the Indian subcontinent. Large numbers of lower-level workers have come from Iran, Pakistan, some from India and Korea.

In Saudi Arabia the largest contingent of imported workers is from Yemen, a poor mountainous country with a significantly larger population than Saudi Arabia's. There are between one and two million Yemenite workers in Saudi Arabia today, which means that as many Yemenites as Saudis, if not more, are working in that country. . . .

As industrialization has progressed in the Arab oil-producing states, two fundamental difficulties have become increasingly evident. First, that the new industrial facilities are in general neither profitable nor competitive on world markets. Second, in many cases these industries must be headed by foreign specialists (because of a lack of qualified locals) and operated mainly by foreign workers (because unskilled locals prefer earning their living in such occupations as taxi driver). The relatively few well-educated native members of the younger generation prefer to work primarily as managers and businessmen, in the hope of joining the ranks of domestic millionaires. . . .

At the same time the big profits from industrial expansion are going to Saudi entrepreneurs, many of whom already have more money than they can ever spend and whose life style is patterned accordingly. Thus the cleft running through Saudi society grows steadily deeper and wider. The foreign buyers of Saudi oil as well as the big businessmen working closely with the country's ruling class are eager to see more and more of the oil money circulating, which in turn further promotes the social imbalance. In recent months the Saudi rulers appear to have begun to realize, although still only dimly, that the more money it spends the shorter the regime will last. As a result there have been demands from within the royal family for a reformulation of the kingdom's development plans. . . .

The ministates along the Persian Gulf are heavily dependent on the military and political power of Saudi Arabia. They know that they would inevitably be affected by any storms that might break out in the Saudi kingdom. The rulers and political observers of those tiny countries are therefore keeping a concerned, if not worried, eye on Saudi Arabia these days, wondering how much longer its present regime will be able to stay in power.

References

The numbers in brackets after each entry refer to the chapter or chapters in this book in which that work is cited.

Abbott, Edith. *Women in Industry.* New York: Appleton, 1909. [13]

Aberle, David. *The Peyote Religion Among the Navaho.* Chicago, Aldine, 1966. [21]

Abrahamson, Mark, Ephraim H. Mizruchi, and Carlton A. Hornung. *Stratification and Mobility.* New York: Macmillan, 1976. [11]

Acker, Joan R. "Women and Stratification: A Review of Recent Literature," *Contemporary Sociology,* 9 (1980), 25–39. [11]

Ackerman, Bruce A., *et al. The Uncertain Search for Environmental Quality.* New York: Free Press, 1974. [11]

Adams, Don. *Schooling and Social Change in Modern America.* New York: McKay, 1972. [15]

Adorno, Theodor W., Else Frenkel-Brunswik, Daniel J. Levinson, and R. Nevitt Sanford. *The Authoritarian Personality.* New York: Harper, 1950. [2]

Agger, R. E., D. Goldrich, and B. E. Swanson. *The Rulers and the Ruled.* New York: Wiley, 1964. [17]

Ahlstrom, W., and R. Havighurst. *Delinquent Boys in High School.* San Francisco: Jossey-Bass, 1971. [8]

Akers, Ronald L. "Socio-Economic Status and Delinquent Behavior: A Retest," *Journal of Research in Crime and Delinquency,* 1 (January 1964), 38–46. [7]

Akron Beacon Journal, May 24, 1970. [21]

Alba, Richard D. "Social Assimilation Among American Catholic National-Origin Groups," *American Sociological Review,* 41 (December 1976), 1030–1046. [12]

Aldrich, Howard E. *Organizations and Environments.* Englewood Cliffs, N.J.: Prentice-Hall, 1979. [9]

Alford, Robert R., and Roger Friedland. "Political Participation and Public Policy," *Annual Review of Sociology,* 1975, 429–479. [17]

Allport, Gordon W., and Leo Postman. *The Psychology of Humor.* New York: Holt, 1947. [21]

Antonovsky, Aaron. "Social Class, Life Expectancy and Overall Mortality." In Paul Blumberg (ed.), *The Impact of Social Class.* New York: Crowell, 1972. Pp. 467–491. [11]

Aronoff, Joel, and William D. Crano. "A Re-examination of the Cross-Cultural Principles of Task Segregation and Sex Role Differentiation in the Family," *American Sociological Review,* 40 (February 1975), 12–20. [13]

Asch, Solomon. *Social Psychology.* Englewood Cliffs, N.J.: Prentice-Hall, 1952. [8]

Ash, Roberta T. *Social Movements in America.* 2nd ed. Chicago: Markham, 1977. [21]

Atchley, Robert C. *The Social Forces in Later Life: An Introduction to Social Gerontology.* 3rd ed. Belmont, Calif.: Wadsworth, 1980. [13]

Babbie, Earl R. *The Practice of Social Research.* Belmont, Calif.: Wadsworth, 1975. [2]

_____. *The Practice of Social Research.* 2nd ed. Belmont, Calif.: Wadsworth, 1979. [2]

Bales, Robert F. *Interaction Process Analysis: A Method for the Study of Small Groups.* Reading, Mass : Addison-Wesley, 1950. [8]

Bales, Robert F., and Edgar F. Borgatta. "Size of Group as a Factor in the Interaction Profile." In A. Paul Hare, Edgar F. Borgatta, and Robert F. Bales

(eds.). *Small Groups: Studies in Social Interaction.* Rev. ed. New York: Knopf, 1955. Pp. 495–536. [8]

Bales, Robert F., Fred L. Strodtbeck, Theodore M. Mills, and Mary E. Roseborough. "Channels of Communication in Small Groups," *American Sociological Review,* 16 (1951), 461–468. [8]

Baltzell, E. Digby. *Philadelphia Gentlemen.* Glencoe, Ill.: Free Press, 1958. [15]

_____. *The Protestant Establishment: Aristocracy and Caste in America.* New York: Random House, 1964. [11]

_____. *Puritan Boston and Quaker Philadelphia: Two Protestant Ethics and the Spirit of Class Authority and Leadership.* New York: Free Press, 1980. [11, 17]

Bandura, A., D. Ross, and S. Ross. "Transmission of Aggression Through Imitation of Aggressive Models," *Journal of Abnormal Social Psychology,* 63 (1961), 575–582. [6]

Bane, Mary J. *Here to Stay: American Families in the 20th Century.* New York: Basic Books, 1978. [14]

Banks, J. S., and Olive Banks. *Feminism and Family Planning in Victorian England.* New York: Schocken, 1964. [19]

Barlow, Robin, "The Economic Effects of Malaria Eradication," *American Economic Review,* 57 (May 1967), 130–148. [19]

Barnet, Richard J. "Multinationals: A Dissenting View," *Saturday Review,* February 7, 1976, pp. 11, 58. [18]

Bates, Alan. *The Sociological Enterprise.* Boston: Houghton Mifflin, 1967. [1]

Bauman, K., and R. Wilson. "Sexual Behavior of Unmarried University Students in 1968 and 1972," *Journal of Sex Research,* 10 (1974), 327–333. [14]

Beauvoir, Simone de. *The Second Sex.* New York: Knopf, 1953. [13]

_____. *The Coming of Age.* Patrick O'Brian (tr.). New York: Putnam, 1972. [13]

Becker, Gary S. "An Economic Analysis of Fertility," *National Bureau of Economic Research,* 1960. [19]

Becker, Howard S. "Becoming a Marihuana User," *American Journal of Sociology,* 59 (November 1953), 235–242. [6]

_____. *The Outsiders.* 2nd ed. New York: Free Press, 1963. [7]

_____. "Personal Change in Adult Life," *Sociometry,* 27 (March 1964), 40–53. [6]

_____. "Whose Side Are We On?" *Social Problems,* 14 (Winter 1967), 239–248. [9]

Belkin, Gary S., and Norman Goodman. *Marriage, Family, and Intimate Relationships.* Chicago: Rand McNally, 1980. [6, 14]

Bell, Daniel. *The End of Ideology.* New York: Free Press, 1962. [7]

_____. *The Coming of Post-Industrial Society.* New York: Basic Books, 1973. [18]

Bell, Robert R., and Jay B. Chaskes. "Premarital Sexual Experience Among Coeds, 1958 and 1968," *Journal of Marriage and the Family,* 30 (February 1970), 81–84. [14]

Bellah, Robert N. "Civil Religion in America," *Daedalus,* 96 (Winter 1967), 1–21. [16]

_____. "The New Religious Consciousness and the Crisis of Modernity." In R. Glock and R. Bellah (eds.). *The New Religious Consciousness.* Berkeley: University of California Press, 1976. Pp. 335–352. [16]

Bellingrath, Geroge C. *Qualities Associated with Leadership in the Extra-Curricular Activities of the High School.* New York: AMS Prss, 1930. [8]

Bendix, Reinhard, and Frank W. Howton. "Social Mobility and the American Business Elite." In Reinhard Bendix and Seymour Martin Lipset (eds.). *Social Mobility in Industrial Society.* Berkeley: University of California Press, 1959. Pp. 114–143. [11]

Bendix, Reinhard, and Seymour Martin Lipset (eds.). *Class, Status, and Power.* New York: Free Press, 1966. [10]

Benedict, Ruth. *Patterns of Culture.* Boston: Houghton Mifflin, 1934. [5, 6]

_____. "Continuities and Discontinuities in Cultural Conditioning," *Psychiatry,* 1 (1938), 161–167. [6]

Bengston, Vern L., and Ron C. Manuel. "The Sociology of Aging." In Richard H. Davis (ed.). *Aging: Prospects and Issues.* Rev. ed. University Park, Calif.: University of Southern California Press, Andrus Gerontology Center, 1973. Pp. 41–57. [6]

Benson, Leonard. *Fatherhood: A Soctological Perspective.* New York: Random House, 1968. [6]

Benson, Margaret. "The Political Economy of Women's Liberation," *Monthly Review,* 21:4 (1969), 13–27. [14]

Berelson, Bernard R., Paul F. Lazarsfeld, and William N. McPhee. *Voting.* Chicago: University of Chicago Press, 1954. [17]

Berg, Ivar. *Education and Jobs: The Great Training Robbery.* Boston: Beacon Press, 1971. [15]

Berger, Joseph, Bernard P. Cohen, and Morris Zelditch, Jr. "Status Conceptions and Social Interaction," *American Sociological Review,* 37 (1972), 241–255. [8]

Berger, Peter L. *Invitation to Sociology: A Human Perspective.* Garden City, N.Y.: Doubleday/Anchor, 1963. [1, 4]

_____. *The Sacred Canopy: Elements of a Sociological Theory of Religion.* Garden City, N.Y.: Doubleday, 1967. [16]

Bernard, Jessie. "Sex Differences: An Overview." In Alexander G. Kaplan and Joan P. Bean (eds.). *Beyond Sex Role Stereotypes: Readings Toward a Psychology of Androgyny.* Boston: Little, Brown, 1976. Pp. 10–26. [13]

Berry, Brian J. L., and John D. Kasarda. *Contemporary Urban Ecology.* New York: Macmillan, 1977. [4]

Berscheid, Ellen, Karen Dion, Elaine Walster, and G. William Walster. "Physical Attractiveness and Dating Choice: A Test of the Matching Hypothesis," *Journal of Experimental Social Psychology,* 7 (March 1971), 173–189. [2]

Bibby, Reginald W., and Merlin B. Brinkerhoff. "The Circulation of the Saints: A Study of People Who Join Conservative Churches," *Journal for the Scientific Study of Religion,* 12:3 (September 1973), 273–283. [16]

Bierstedt, Robert (ed.). *A Design for Sociology: Scope, Objectives and Methods.* Philadelphia: The American Academy of Political and Social Sciences, 1969. [1]

Biraben, Jean-Noël. "L'évolution de la fécondité en Europe occidentale," *European Population Conference, 1966.* Vol. Cl. Strasbourg: Council for Europe, 1967. Pp. 1–29. [19]

Blackstone, Sir William. *Commentaries on the Laws of England.* Vol. 1. Thomas M. Cooley (ed.). Chicago: Bancroft, 1872. [13]

Blau, Francine. "Women in the Labor Force: The Situation at Present." In Ann Yates and Shirley Harkness (eds.). *Women and Their Work.* Palo Alto, Calif.: Mayfield, 1976. [13]

Blau, Peter M. "Social Mobility and Interpersonal Relations," *American Sociological Review,* 21 (June 1956), 290–295. [11]

Blau, Peter M., and Otis Dudley Duncan. *The American Occupational Structure.* New York: Wiley, 1967. [11]

Blau, Peter M., and W. Richard Scott. *Formal Organizations.* San Francisco: Chandler, 1962. [9]

Blauner, Robert. *Alienation and Freedom: The Factory Worker and His Industry.* Chicago: University of Chicago Press, 1964. [9]

———. *Racial Oppression in America.* New York: Harper & Row, 1972. [12]

Blood, Robert O., and Donald M. Wolfe. *Husbands and Wives: The Dynamics of Married Living.* Glencoe, Ill.: Free Press, 1960. [14]

Blumenfeld, Hans. "The Urban Pattern." In John Walton and Donald E. Carns (eds.). *Cities in Change: Studies on the Urban Condition.* Boston: Allyn and Bacon, 1973. Pp. 38–48. [20]

Blumer, Herbert. "Collective Behavior." In Alfred M. Lee (ed.). *Principles of Sociology.* New York: Barnes & Noble, 1953. [21]

———. "Society as Symbolic Interaction." In Arnold Rose (ed.). *Human Behavior and Symbolic Processes: An Interactionist Approach.* Boston: Houghton Mifflin, 1962. Pp. 179–192. [3]

———. "What Is Wrong with Social Theory." In Herbert Blumer (ed.). *Symbolic Interactionism.* Englewood Cliffs, N.J.: Prentice-Hall, 1969. Pp. 147–148. [7]

Bogue, Donald J., and Evelyn Kitagawa. *Suburbanization of Manufacutring Activity Within Standard Metropolitan Areas.* Chicago: University of Chicago with the Population Research and Training Center, 1955. [20]

Bonacich, Phillip. "Norms and Cohesion as Adaptive Responses to Potential Conflict: An Experimental Study," *Sociometry,* 35 (1972), 357–375. [8]

Bossard, James H. S., and Eleanor Boll. *The Sociology of Child Development.* 4th ed. New York: Harper & Row, 1966. [14]

Bott, Elizabeth. "The Concept of Class as a Reference Group," *Human Relations,* 7 (1954), 259–286. [11]

Bottomore, Tom. *Classes in Modern Society.* New York: Pantheon, 1966. [10]

Bottomore, Tom, and Robert Nisbet (eds.). *A History of Sociological Analysis.* New York: Basic Books, 1978. [3]

Botwinick, Jack. *Aging and Behavior: A Comprehensive Integration of Research Findings.* New York: Springer, 1973. [13]

Bowles, Samuel, and Herbert Gintis. *Schooling in Capitalist America: Educational Reform and the Contradictions of Economic Life.* New York: Basic Books, 1976. [15]

Braungart, Richard G. "Youth and Social Movement." In Sigmund E. Dragastin and Glen H. Elder, Jr. (eds.). *Adolescence in the Life Cycle: Psychological Change and Social Context.* New York: Halsted, 1975. [13]

———. *Society and Politics: Readings in Political Sociology.* Englewood Cliffs, N.J.: Prentice-Hall, 1976. [17]

———. "Changing Electoral Politics in America," *Journal of Political and Military Sociology,* 6 (Fall 1978), 261–269. [17]

———. "Multinational Corporations: New Dimensions in Community Power," *Sociological Symposium* (Fall 1978). [17]

Breese, Gerald. *Urbanization in Newly Developing Countries.* Englewood Cliffs, N.J.: Prentice-Hall, 1966. [20]

Brim, Orville G., Jr. "The Parent–Child Relation as a Social System. I. Parent and Child Roles," *Child Development,* 28:3 (September 1957), 343–364. [14]

———. "Family Structure and Sex Role Learning by Children: A Further Analysis of Helen Koch's Data," *Sociometry,* 21:1 (March 1958), 1–16. [6]

———. "Personality Development as Role-Learning." In Ira Iscoe and Harold Stevenson (eds.). *Personality Development in Children.* Austin: University of Texas Press, 1960. [6]

Brim, Orville G., Jr., and Stanton Wheeler. *Socialization After Childhood: Two Essays.* New York: Wiley, 1966. [6]

Bromley, David W., and Anson D. Shupe, Jr. *Moonies in America: Cult, Church, and Crusade.* Beverly Hills, Calif.: Sage Publications, 1979. [16]

Brookover, Wilbur B., and Edsel Erickson. *Sociology of Education.* Homewood, Ill.: Dorsey Press, 1975. [15]

Brower, Michael. "Experience with Self-Management and Participation in United States Industry," *Administration and Society,* 7:1 (May 1975), 65–84. [9]

Brown, Frank, and Madelon D. Stint. *Minorities in U.S. Institutions of Higher Education.* New York: Praeger, 1977. [15]

Brown, Roger, and H. Garland. "The Effects of Incompetency, Audience Acquaintanceship, and Anticipated Evaluative Feedback on Face-Saving Behavior," *Journal of Experimental Social Psychology,* 7 (1971), 490–502. [8]

Brownmiller, Susan. *Against Our Will: Men, Women, and Rape.* Simon and Schuster, 1975. [13]

Burgess, Ernest W. "The Growth of the City: An Introduction to a Research Project." In Robert E. Park, Ernest W. Burgess, and Roderick D. McKenzie. *The City.* Chicago: University of Chicago Press, 1925. Pp. 47–62. [20]

Burgess, Robert L., and Robert L. Akers. "A Differential Association–Reinforcement Theory of Criminal Behavior," *Social Problems,* 14 (Fall 1966), 128–147. [7]

Burnham, Walter Dean. "Jimmy Carter and the Democratic Crisis," *New Republic,* July 3 and 10, 1976, pp. 17–19. [17]

Burns, Beverly. "The Emergence of Socialization of Sex Differences in the Earliest Years," *Merrill-Palmer Quarterly,* 22 (1976), 229–254. [6]

Burr, Wesley R. "Satisfaction with Various Aspects of Marriage Over the Life Cycle: A Random Middle Class Sample," *Journal of Marriage and the Family,* 32 (February 1970), 129–137. [14]

Butler, Edgar W. *Traditional Marriage and Emerging Alternatives.* New York: Harper & Row, 1974. [14]

Butler, Robert N. "Age-Ism: Another Form of Bigotry," *Gerontologist,* 9 (Winter 1969), 243–246. [13]

Byrne, D. "Interpersonal Attraction and Attitude Similarity," *Journal of Abnormal and Social Psychology,* 62 (1961), 713–715. [8]

Byrne, D., C. R. Ervin, and J. Lamberth. "Continuity Between the Experimental Study of Attraction and Real-Life Computer Dating," *Journal of Personality and Social Psychology,* 16 (1970), 157–165. [8]

Caldwell, O. W., and B. L. Wellman. "Characteristics of School Leaders," *Journal of Educational Research,* 14 (1926), 1–13. [8]

Caplan, Nathan. "The New Ghetto Man: A Review of Recent Empirical Studies," *Journal of Social Issues,* 26:1 (Winter 1970), 59–73. [17]

Caplovitz, David, and Candace Rogers. *Swastika 1960: The Epidemic of Anti-Semitic Vandalism in America.* New York: Anti-Defamation League of B'nai B'rith, 1960. [2]

Caplow, Theodore. "Rumors in War," *Social Forces,* 25 (March 1947), 298–312. [21]

Carmichael, Stokely, and Charles V. Hamilton. *Black Power: The Politics of Liberation in America.* New York: Random House, 1967. [21]

Carpenter, Edmund. *They Became What They Beheld.* New York: Outerbridge and Dienstfrey, 1970. [5]

Carr-Saunders, Alexander Morris. *World Population: Past Growth and Present Trends.* New York: Oxford University Press, 1936. [19]

Cartwright, Dorwin. "The Nature of Group Cohesiveness." In Dorwin Cartwright and Alvin Zander (eds.). *Group Dynamics: Research and Theory.* 3rd ed. New York: Harper & Row, 1968. Pp. 91–109. [8]

———. "Risk Taking by Individuals and Groups: An Assessment of Research Employing Choice Dilemmas," *Journal of Personality and Social Psychology,* 20 (1971), 361–378. [8]

Cartwright, Dorwin, and Alvin Zander (eds.). *Group Dynamics: Research and Theory.* New York: Harper & Row, 1968. [8]

Casler, Lawrence. *Is Marriage Necessary?* New York: Human Sciences Press, 1974. [14]

Castells, Manuel. *The Urban Question: A Marxist Approach.* Alan Sheridan (tr.). Cambridge, Mass.: MIT Press, 1977. [20]

Catton, William R., Jr. "What Kind of People Does a Religious Cult Attract?" *American Sociological Review,* 22 (1957), 561–566. [16]

Catton, William R., Jr., and R. J. Smircich. "A Comparison of Mathematical Models for the Effects of Residential Propinquity on Mate Selection," *American Sociological Review,* 29 (August 1964), 522–529. [14]

Cavelli-Sforza, L. L., and A. W. F. Edwards, "Analysis of Human Evolution." In S. J. Geertz (ed.). *Genetics Today.* Vol. 3. Elmsford, N.Y.: Pergamon Press, 1963. [12]

Census Bureau. *Statistical Abstract of the United States, 1976.* Washington, D.C.: U.S. Government Printing Office, 1976. [7, 17, 18, 20]

———. *Current Population Reports,* Series P-20, No. 303, 1978, Figure 3. [13]

———. "Marital Status and Living Arrangements: March 1978," *Current Population Reports,* Series P-20, No. 338, 1979. [14]

———. "Voting and Registration in the Election of November 1978," Series P-20, No. 344, September 1979. [17]

Centers, Richard. *The Psychology of Social Classes.* New York: Russell & Russell, 1949. [11, 14]

Chafe, William H. *The American Woman: Her Changing Social, Economic, and Political Roles, 1920–1970.* New York: Oxford University Press, 1972. [13]

Champion, Dean J. *The Sociology of Organizations.* New York: McGraw-Hill, 1975. [9]

Chauncey, Henry. "The Use of the Selective Service Qualification Test on the Deferment of College Students," *Science,* 116 (July 1952), 75–85. [15]

Childe, V. Gordon. "The Urban Revolution," *Town Planning Review,* 21 (April 1950), 3–17. [20]

Choldin, H. "Urban Density and Pathology," *Annual Review of Sociology,* 4 (1978), 91–113. [20]

Chowdhry, K., and T. M. Newcomb. "The Relative Abilities of Leaders and Non-Leaders to Estimate Opinions of Their Own Groups," *Journal of Abnormal and Social Psychology,* 47 (1952), 51–57. [8]

Church Committee Report. *Covert Action.* Hearing Book 7. Washington, D.C.: Select Committee on Intelligence, December 4 and 5, 1975. [22]

Cicourel, Aaron V. *The Social Organization of Juvenile Justice.* New York: Wiley, 1968. [7]

Clark, Alice. *Working Life of Women in the Seventeenth Century.* London: Routledge, 1919. [13]

Clark, Burton R. *The Open Door College.* New York: McGraw-Hill, 1960. [15]

———. *Educating the Expert Society.* San Francisco: Chandler, 1962. [15]

Clausen, John (ed.). *Socialization and Society.* Boston: Little, Brown, 1968. [6]

Clayton, Richard R. *The Family, Marriage, and Social Change.* Lexington, Mass.: Heath, 1975. [14]

_____. *The Family, Marriage, and Social Change.* 2nd ed. Lexington, Mass.: Heath, 1978. [14]

Clegg, Stewart. *The Theory of Power and Organization.* Boston: Routledge & Kegan Paul, 1979. [9]

Clough, Shepard Bancroft, and Charles Woolsey Cole. *Economic History of Europe.* Lexington, Mass.: Heath, 1941. [10]

Cloward, Richard, and Lloyd Ohlin. *Delinquency and Opportunity.* Glencoe, Ill.: Free Press, 1961. [7]

Coale, Ansley J., and Edgar M. Hoover. *Population Growth and Economic Development in Low-Income Countries.* Princeton, N.J.: Princeton University Press, 1958. [19]

Cohen, Albert K. *Delinquent Boys.* Glencoe, Ill.: Free Press, 1955. [7]

_____. *Deviance and Social Control.* Englewood Cliffs, N.J.: Prentice-Hall, 1966. [7]

Cohn, Norman. *The Pursuit of the Millennium.* New York: Harper & Row, 1961. [3]

Cole, Jonathan R., and Stephen Cole. "The Reward System of the Social Sciences." In Charles Frankel (ed.). *Controversies and Decisions: The Social Sciences and Public Policy.* New York: Russell Sage Foundation, 1976. Pp. 55–88. [13]

Cole, Robert. "Structure Function Theory, the Dialectic, and Social Change." *Sociological Quarterly,* 7 (Winter 1966), 39–58. [3]

Cole, Stephen. *The Sociological Method.* 3rd ed. Chicago: Rand McNally, 1980. [2]

Coleman, James S., Sara D. Kelly, and John A. Moore. *Trends in School Segregation, 1968–73.* Washington, D.C.: Urban Institute, 1975. [20]

Coleman, James, Herbert Menzel, and Elihu Katz. "Social Processes in Physicians' Adoption of a New Drug," *Journal of Chronic Diseases,* 9:1 (1959), 1–19. [22]

Coleman, James S., *et al. Equality of Educational Opportunity.* Department of Health, Education, and Welfare. Washington, D.C.: Government Printing Office, 1966. [15]

Coleman, James S., *et al. Supplemental Appendix to the Survey on Equality of Educational Opportunity.* Washington, D.C.: U.S. Government Printing Office, 1966. [15]

Coleman, James S., *et al. Youth: Transition to Adulthood.* Chicago: University of Chicago Press, 1974. [6, 13]

Collins, Barry, and Bertram Raven. "Group Structure: Attraction, Coalition, Communication and Power." In Gardner Lindzey and Elliot Aronson (eds.). *Handbook of Social Psychology.* 2nd ed. Vol. 4. Reading, Mass.: Addison-Wesley, 1969. Pp. 119–185. [8]

Collins, Randall. "Functional and Conflict Theories of Educational Stratification," *American Sociological Review,* 36 (December 1971), 1002–1019. [15]

Comte, Auguste. *The Positive Philosophy of Auguste Comte.* 3 vols. Harriet Martineau (tr. and condensed). London: Bell, 1896. [3, 4]

Conklin, Kenneth R. "Why Compensatory Schooling Seems to Make 'No Difference,'" *Journal of Education,* 156:4 (May 1974), 34–42. [15]

Connor, Walker. "Nation-Building or Nation-Destroying?" *World Politics,* 24:3 (April 1972), 319–355. [12]

Constantine, L., and J. Constantine. *Group Marriage: A Study of Contemporary Multilateral Marriages.* New York: Macmillan, 1973. [14]

Conway, J. "Stereotypes of Femininity in a Theory of Sexual Evolution." In M. Vicinus (ed.). *Suffer and Be Still: Women in the Victorian Age.* Bloomington, Ind.: Indiana University Press, 1973. Pp. 140–154. [13]

Cooley, Charles Horton. *Human Nature and the Social Order.* New York: Scribners, 1902. [6, 8]

Corwin, Ronald G. *Education in Crisis: A Sociological Analysis of Schools and Universities in Transition.* New York: Wiley, 1974. [15]

Coser, Lewis A. *The Functions of Social Conflict.* Glencoe, Ill.: Free Press, 1956. [3, 4, 8, 21]

_____. "Some Functions of Deviant Behavior and Normative Flexibility," *American Journal of Sociology,* 68 (September 1962), 174–182. [7]

_____. *Continuities in the Study of Social Conflict.* New York: Free Press, 1967. [3, 4, 8]

_____. *Masters of Sociological Thought: Ideas in Historical and Social Context.* 2nd ed. New York: Harcourt Brace Jovanovich, 1977. [3]

Coser, Lewis A. (ed.). *Sociology Through Literature.* 2nd ed. Englewood Cliffs, N.J.: Prentice-Hall, 1972. [4]

Coser, Rose Laub, and Gerald Rokoff. "Women in the Occupational World: Social Disruption and Conflict," *Social Problems,* 18 (Spring 1971), 535–554. [13]

Cousins, Albert N., and Hans Nagpaul. *Urban Man and Society.* New York: Random House, 1970. [20]

Cox, Harvey. *The Secular City.* Rev. ed. New York: Macmillan, 1966. [16]

Crano, William D., and Joel Aronoff. "Expressive and Instrumental Role Complementarity in the Family," *American Sociological Review,* 43 (August 1978), 463–470. [13]

Cremin, Lawrence. *The Transformation of the School: Progressivism in American Education 1876–1957.* New York: Random House/Vintage, 1964. [15]

Crosbie, Paul. *Interaction in Small Groups.* New York: Macmillan, 1975. [8]

Cubberly, Ellwood P. *Changing Conceptions of Education.* Boston: Houghton Mifflin, 1909. [12]

Dackawich, S. John. "Housing in America: A Functional Comparison with Four Other Western Democracies." Paper presented at the annual meetings of the Western Social Sciences Association, 1979. [20]

Dahl, Robert A. *Who Governs?* New Haven, Conn.: Yale University Press, 1961. [17]

Dahrendorf, Ralf. "Toward a Theory of Social Conflict," *Journal of Conflict Resolution,* 2 (June 1958), 170–183. [3]

Danziger, Kurt. *Socialization.* Baltimore: Penguin Books, 1971. [6]

Darwin, Charles. *The Origin of Species* (1859). New York: Macmillan, 1962. [4, 12]

_____. *The Descent of Man* (1871). Philadelphia: Richard West, 1902. [5]

Davies, James C. "The J-Curve of Rising and Declining Satisfactions as a Cause of Some Great Revolutions and a Contained Rebellion." In Hugh Davies Graham and Ted Robert Gurr (eds.). *Violence in America: Historical and Comparative Perspectives.* New York: Bantam, 1969. Pp. 690–730. [21]

Davis, Kingsley. "Extreme Social Isolation of a Child," *American Sociological Review,* 45 (January 1940), 554–564. [6]

_____. "A Conceptual Analysis of Stratification," *American Sociological Review,* 7 (June 1942), 309–321. [10]

_____. "Final Note on a Case of Extreme Isolation," *American Journal of Sociology,* 50 (March 1947), 432–437. [6]

_____. *Human Society.* New York: Macmillan, 1948 and 1949. [4, 6, 8, 10]

_____. "Institutional Patterns Favoring High Fertility in Underdeveloped Areas," *Eugenics Quarterly,* 2:1 (March 1955), 33–39. [10, 19]

_____. "The Amazing Decline of Mortality in Underdeveloped Areas," *American Economic Review,* 46:2 (May 1956), 305–318. [19]

_____. "The Urbanization of the Human Population," *Scientific American,* 213:3 (September 1965), 41–53. [19]

_____. "World's Population Crisis." In Robert K. Merton and Robert A. Nisbet (eds.). *Contemporary Social Problems.* New York: Harcourt, Brace and World, 1966. P. 382. [19]

_____. "Population Policy: Will Current Programs Succeed?" *Science* (November 10, 1967), 730–739. [19]

Davis, Kingsley, and Wilbert E. Moore. "Some Principles of Stratification," *American Sociological Review,* 10 (April 1945), 242–249. [10, 15]

Davis, Wallace M., and George McGurn. "Occupational Education in the United States," International Conference on Education sponsored by Europe, Year 2000, Madrid, November 1975. [15]

Dawes, Robyn. "I.Q.: Methodological and Other Issues," *Science,* 178 (1972), 229–230. [15]

Deaux, George. *The Black Death: 1347.* New York: Weybright and Talley, 1969. [19]

Deck, Leland. "Short Workers of the World, Unite!" *Psychology Today,* 5 (August 1971), 102. [11]

Deckard, Barbara. *The Women's Movement: Political, Socioeconomic, and Psychological Issues.* New York: Harper & Row, 1975. [13]

DeJong, Peter Y., *et al.* "Patterns of Female Intergenerational Occupational Mobility: A Comparison with Male Patterns of Intergenerational Occupational Mobility," *American Sociological Review,* 36:6 (1971), 1033–1042. [11]

Denzin, Norman K. *Childhood Socialization.* San Francisco: Jossey-Bass, 1977. [6]

_____. *The Research Act: A Theoretical Introduction to Sociological Methods.* Chicago: Aldine, 1977. [2]

Dinitz, Simon, *et al.* (eds.). *Deviance: Studies in Definition, Management, and Treatment.* 2nd ed. New York: Oxford University Press, 1975. [7]

Dion, Karen. "Physical Attractiveness and Evaluations of Children's Transgressions," *Journal of Personality and Social Psychology* (1972). [2]

Dobzhansky, Theodosius. *Mankind Evolving.* New Haven, Conn.: Yale University Press, 1962. [12]

Domhoff, G. William. *Who Rules America?* Englewood Cliffs, N.J.: Prentice-Hall, 1967. [11, 17]

_____. *Higher Circles: The Governing Class in America.* New York: Random House, 1971. [17]

_____. *Who Really Rules?: New Haven and Community Power Reexamined.* New Brunswick, N.J.: Transaction Books, 1978. [11, 17]

Douglas, John H. "The Slowing Growth of World Population," *Science News* (November 13, 1976), 316–317. [19]

Dowse, R. E., and J. A. Hughes. *Political Sociology.* New York: Wiley, 1972. [10]

Dragastin, Sigmund E., and Glen H. Elder, Jr. (eds.). *Adolescence in the Life Cycle: Psychological Change and Social Context.* Washington, D.C.: Hemisphere Publishing, 1975. [6]

Drucker, Peter F. *The Age of Discontinuity: Guidelines to Our Changing Society.* New York: Harper & Row, 1969. [12]

Duberman, Lucile. *Reconstituted Family: A Study of Remarried Couples and Their Children.* Chicago: Nelson-Hall, 1975. [14]

_____. *Social Inequality: Class and Caste in America.* Philadelphia: Lippincott, 1976. [10, 11]

Duncan, Beverly. "Dropouts and the Unemployed," *Journal of Political Economy,* 73 (April 1964), 121–134. [15]

Dunham, Warren H. *Community and Schizophrenia: An Epidemiological Analysis.* Detroit: Wayne State University Press, 1965. [7]

Durkheim, Emile. *On the Division of Labor in Society* (1893). George Simpson (tr.). New York: Free Press, 1966. [4]

_____. *The Rules of Sociological Method* (1895). New York: Free Press, 1950. [4]

_____. *Suicide: A Study in Sociology* (1897). John A.

Spaulding and George Simpson (trs.). Glencoe, Ill.: Free Press, 1951. [1, 3, 7]

———. *The Elementary Forms of the Religious Life* (first published in English 1915). Joseph W. Swain (tr.). Glencoe, Ill.: Free Press, 1954. [7, 16]

Dye, Thomas R. *Who's Running America? Institutional Leadership in the United States.* Englewood Cliffs, N.J.: Prentice-Hall, 1976. [17]

Eberstadt, Nick. "Myths of the Food Crisis," *New York Review,* February 19, 1976, 32–37. [19]

Edmiston, Susan. "How to Write Your Own Marriage Contract," *Ms. Magazine,* Spring 1972, 66–72. [14]

Ehrenreich, Barbara, and Deirdre English. *Witches, Midwives, and Nurses: A History of Women Healers.* Old Westbury, N.Y.: Feminist Press, 1973. [13]

Ehrlich, Paul R. *The Population Bomb.* New York: Ballantine, 1968. [19]

Eichler, Edward P., and Marshall Kaplan. *The Community Builders.* California Studies in Urbanization and Environmental Design. Berkeley, Calif.: University of California Press, 1967. [20]

Eisenstadt, S. N. *From Generation to Generation: Age-Groups and Social Structure.* Glencoe, Ill.: Free Press, 1956. [15]

———. *Social Differentiation and Stratification.* Glenview, Ill.: Scott, Foresman, 1971. [10]

Eister, Allan W. "An Outline of a Structural Theory of Cults," *Journal for the Scientific Study of Religion,* 11:4 (December 1972), 319–333. [16]

Elder, Glen H., Jr. *Adolescent Socialization and Personality Development.* Chicago: Rand McNally, 1968. [6, 13]

———. "Adolescence in the Life Cycle: An Introduction." In Sigmund E. Dragastin and Glen H. Elder, Jr. (eds.). *Adolescence in the Life Cycle: Psychological Change and Social Context.* New York: Halsted, 1975. [6, 13]

Elkin, Frederick, and Gerald Handel. *The Child and Society: The Process of Socialization.* 3rd ed. New York: Random House, 1978. [6]

Ellis, Albert. "Group Marriage: A Possible Alternative?" In Herbert A. Otto (ed.). *The Family in Search of a Future: Alternate Models for Moderns.* New York: Appleton-Century-Crofts, 1970. Pp. 85–98. [14]

Ellis, John. *The Social History of the Machine Gun.* New York: Pantheon, 1975. [22]

Ember, Carol R., and Melvin Ember. *Anthropology.* New York: Appleton-Century-Crofts, 1973. [14]

Emmanuel, Arghiri. "Myths of Development Versus Myths of Underdevelopment," *New Left Review,* 85 (May–June 1974), 61–82. [22]

Engineering Manpower Commission of Engineers Joint Council. *Engineering Manpower Bulletin,* No. 31 (November 1976), 7. [15]

Epstein, Cynthia F. "Encountering the Male Establishment: Sex-Status Limits on Women's Careers in the Professions," *American Journal of Sociology,* 75:6 (1970), 965–982. [11]

Erikson, Erik H. *Identity: Youth and Crisis.* New York: Norton, 1968. [6]

Erikson, Kai T. *Wayward Puritans.* New York: Wiley, 1966. [7]

Essien-Udom, E. U. *Black Nationalism.* New York: Dell, 1962. [16]

Etzioni, Amitai. *A Comparative Analysis of Complex Organizations.* New York: Free Press, 1961. [9]

Etzioni, Amitai, and Eva Etzioni (eds.). *Social Change: Sources, Patterns, and Consequences.* New York: Basic Books, 1964. [22]

Evans, Robert (ed.). *Readings in Collective Behavior.* Chicago: Rand McNally, 1975. [21]

Faris, Robert E. L., and Warren H. Dunham. *Mental Disorders in Urban Areas.* Chicago: University of Chicago Press, 1939. [11]

Farley, Reynolds. "Trends in Racial Inequalities: Have the Gains of the 1960s Disappeared in the 1970s?" *American Sociological Review,* 42:2 (April 1977), 189–208. [12]

Featherman, David L., and Robert M. Hauser. *Opportunity and Change.* New York: Academic Press, 1978. [11]

Federal Bureau of Investigation. *Uniform Crime Reports.* Washington, D.C.: Government Printing Office, 1976, 1979. [7]

Feldman, Saul. "The Presentation of Shortness in Everyday Life: Height and Heightism in American Society: Toward a Sociology of Statures." Paper presented at the American Sociological Convention, Denver, 1971. [11]

Ferree, Mira. "A Woman for President? Changing Responses: 1958–1972," *Public Opinion Quarterly,* 38:3 (1974), 390–399. [13]

Feshbach, S. "The Drive Reducing Function of Fantasy Behavior," *Journal of Abnormal Social Psychology,* 50 (1955), 3–11. [6]

Festinger, Leon, Stanley Schachter, and Kurt Back. *Social Pressures in Informal Groups: A Study of Human Factors in Housing.* New York: Harper & Row, 1950. [8]

Fiedler, Fred. "A Contingency Model of Leadership Effectiveness." In Leonard Berkowitz (ed.). *Advances in Experimental Social Psychology,* Vol. 1. New York: Academic Press, 1964. [8]

———. *A Theory of Leadership Effectiveness.* New York: McGraw-Hill, 1967. [8]

———. "Validation and Extension of the Contingency Model of Leadership Effectiveness," *Psychological Bulletin,* 76 (1971), 128–148. [8]

Finn, Peter. "Teenage Drunkenness: Warning Signal, Transient Boisterousness, or Symptom of Social Change?" *Adolescence,* 14 (Winter 1979), 819–834. [7]

Firey, Walter. *Land Use in Central Boston.* Cambridge, Mass.: Harvard University Press, 1947. [20]

Fischer, Claude. *The Urban Experience.* New York: Harcourt Brace Jovanovich, 1976. [20]

Fischer, David Hackett. *Growing Old in America.* New York: Oxford University Press, 1977. [13]

Flacks, Richard. *Youth and Social Change.* Chicago: Markham, 1971. [18]

Fox, Thomas G., and S. M. Miller. "Economic, Political and Social Determinants of Mobility: An International Cross-Sectional Analysis," *Acta Sociologica,* 9 (1965), 76–93. [11]

Frank, André Gunder. *Latin America: Underdevelopment of Revolution.* New York: Monthly Review Press, 1969. [22]

Frazier, E. Franklin. *Black Bourgoisie.* Glencoe, Ill.: Free Press, 1957. [15]

Freeman, Jo. *The Politics of Women's Liberation.* New York: McKay, 1973. [13]

Frejka, Thomas. *The Future of Population Growth: Alternative Paths to Equilibrium.* New York: Wiley, 1973. [19]

French, J. R. P., and B. H. Raven. "The Bases of Social Power." In Dorwin Cartwright (ed.). *Studies on Social Power.* Ann Arbor, Mich.: University of Michigan Press, 1959. Pp. 150–167. [8]

Freud, Sigmund. *Group Psychology and the Analysis of the Ego.* James Strachey (tr.). London: Hogarth Press, 1922. [21]

———. *Civilization and Its Discontents.* James Strachey (tr. and ed.). New York: Norton, 1961. [6]

Friedan, Betty. *The Feminine Mystique.* New York: Norton, 1963. [13]

Friedl, Ernestine. *Women and Men.* New York: Holt, Rinehart and Winston, 1975. [10]

Frisch, Karl von. *The Dance Language and Orientation of Bees.* Cambridge, Mass.: Harvard University Press, 1967. [5]

Fritz, Charles E., and Eli S. Marks. "The NORC Studies of Human Behavior in Disaster," *Journal of Social Issues,* 10 (1954), 26–41. [21]

Fuller, Raymond G. "Child Labor." In Edwin R. A. Seligman (ed.). *Encyclopedia of the Social Sciences,* Vols. 3–4. New York: Macmillan, 1944. [13]

Gagnon, John H. *Human Sexualities.* Glenview, Ill.: Scott, Foresman, 1977. [13]

Gagnon, John H., and Cathy Greenblat. *Life Designs: Individuals, Marriages, and Families.* Glenview, Ill.: Scott, Foresman, 1978. [14]

Galbraith, John Kenneth. *The New Industrial State.* Boston: Houghton Mifflin, 1967. [10]

Gallup Opinion Index. *Religion in America.* Report No. 145, 1977–78. [16]

Gamson, William A. *Power and Discontent.* Homewood, Ill.: Dorsey Press, 1968. [17]

Gans, Herbert J. "Urbanism and Suburbanism as Ways of Life: A Reevaluation of Definitions." In Arnold Rose (ed.). *Human Behavior and Social Processes.* Boston: Houghton Mifflin, 1962. Pp. 184–200, 625–648. [20]

———. *The Urban Villagers.* New York: Free Press, 1965. [20]

Garfinkel, Harold. *Studies in Ethnomethodology.* Englewood Cliffs, N.J.: Prentice-Hall, 1967. [3]

Garson, Barbara. "The Bottle Baby Scandal," *Mother Jones* (December 1977). [19]

Gelles, Richard J. "An Exploratory Study of Intra-Family Violence." Durham, N.H.: Unpublished Ph.D. dissertation, 1973. [14]

———. "Power, Sex, and Violence: The Case of Marital Rape," *The Family Coordinator,* 26 (1977), 339–347. [14]

———. "Violence Toward Children in the United States," *The American Journal of Orthopsychiatry,* 48 (1978), 580–592. [14]

Genevie, Louis (ed.). *Collective Behavior and Social Movements.* Itasca, Ill.: F. E. Peacock, 1978. [21]

Gerard, Harold B., R. A. Wilhelmy, and E. S. Conolley. "Conformity and Group Size," *Journal of Personality and Social Psychology,* 8 (1968), 79–82. [8]

Gergen, Kenneth J. *The Concept of Self.* New York: Holt, Rinehart and Winston, 1971. [6]

Germani, Gino. "The Social Consequences of Mobility." Paper prepared for Social Science Research Council Conference of Social Structures and Social Mobility in Economic Development, January 30, 1964. [11]

Gibb, Cecil. "The Principles and Traits of Leadership," *Journal of Abnormal and Social Psychology,* 42 (1947), 267–284. [8]

Giddens, Anthony. *The Class Structure of the Advanced Societies.* New York: Barnes & Noble, 1973. [10]

Giles, Michael W., Douglas S. Garlin, and Everett F. Cataldo. "Racial and Class Prejudice: Their Relative Effects on Protest Against School Segregation," *American Sociological Review,* 41 (April 1976), 280–288. [15]

Gillespie, Dair L. "Who Has the Power? The Marital Struggle," *Journal of Marriage and the Family,* 33 (August 1971), 445–458. [14]

Gist, Noel P., and Sylvia Fleis Fava. *Urban Society.* 6th ed. New York: Crowell, 1974. [20]

Glaab, Charles N., and Theodore Brown. *A History of Urban America.* New York: Macmillan, 1967. [20]

Glazer, Nathan. "Slums and Ethnicity." In Thomas D. Sherrard (ed.). *Social Welfare and Urban Problems.* New York: Columbia University Press, 1968. [12]

Glazer, Nathan, and Daniel P. Moynihan. *Beyond the Melting Pot: The Negroes, Puerto Ricans, Jews, Italians, and Irish of New York City.* 2nd rev. ed. Cambridge, Mass.: MIT Press, 1963/1970. [4, 12]

Glock, Charles Y., Benjamin B. Ringer, and Earl R. Babbie. *To Comfort and to Challenge: A Dilemma of the Contemporary Church.* Berkeley, Calif.: University of California Press, 1967. [16]

Glock, Charles Y., and Rodney Stark. *Religion and Society in Tension.* Chicago: Rand McNally, 1965. [16]

_____. *Christian Beliefs and Anti-Semitism.* New York: Harper & Row, 1966. [2]

Goertzel, Ted. *Political Society.* Chicago: Rand McNally, 1976. [10]

Goffman, Erving. *The Presentation of Self in Everyday Life.* Garden City, N.Y.: Doubleday/Anchor, 1959. [3]

_____. *Asylums.* Chicago: Aldine, 1961. [6, 7]

_____. *Interaction Ritual: Essays in Face to Face Behavior.* Garden City, N.Y.: Doubleday/Anchor, 1967. [6]

_____. *Strategic Interaction.* New York: Ballantine, 1969. [6]

Goldschmidt, Walter. *Man's Way: A Preface to the Understanding of Human Society.* New York: Holt, 1959. [10]

Goode, Erich. "On Behalf of Labeling Theory," *Social Problems,* 22 (June 1975), 570–583. [7]

Goode, William J. "The Theoretical Importance of Love," *American Sociological Review,* 24 (February 1959), 38–47. [14]

_____. "A Theory of Role Strain," *American Sociological Review,* 25 (August 1960), 483–496. [4]

Goodenough, Florence L. "Interrelationships in the Behavior of Young Children," *Child Development,* 1 (1930), 29–47. [8]

Goodman, Norman. "Adolescent Norms and Behavior: Organization and Conformity," *Merrill-Palmer Quarterly,* 15 (April 1969), 199–211. [6]

_____. "Socialization I: A Systematic View" and "Socialization II: A Developmental View." In Harvey Farberman (ed.). *Symbolic Interaction: Original Essays in Interpretive Sociology.* New York: Harper & Row, 1982. [6, 14]

Goodman, Norman, Orville G. Brim, Jr., Leonard S. Cottrell, Jr., and Theodore D. Kemper. "Adolescent Personality as Self-Other Systems." Unpublished manuscript, n.d. [6]

Goodman, Norman, and Kenneth A. Feldman. "Expectations, Ideals, and Reality: Youth Enters College." In Sigmund E. Dragastin and Glen H. Elder, Jr. (eds.). *Adolescence in the Life Cycle: Psychological Change and Social Context.* New York: Halsted, 1975. [6]

Goodman, Norman, and Richard Ofshe. "Empathy, Communication Efficiency, and Marital Status," *Journal of Marriage and the Family,* 30:4 (November 1968), 597–603. [14]

Goodsell, Willystine. *A History of the Family as a Social and Educational Institution.* Norwood, Pa.: Norwood Editions, 1915. [14]

Gordon, David M. "Class and the Economics of Crime," *Review of Radical Political Economics* (Summer 1971), 51–75. [7]

Gordon, Michael (ed.). *The American Family in Social-Historical Perspective.* New York: St. Martin's, 1973. [14]

Gordon, Milton M. "Assimilation in America: Theory and Reality," *Daedalus,* 90:2 (Spring 1961), 263–285. [12]

_____. *Assimilation in American Life.* New York: Oxford University Press, 1964. [12]

Gortmaker, Steven L. "Poverty and Infant Mortality in the United States," *American Sociological Review,* 44 (1979), 280–297. [11]

Goslin, David A. *The School in Contemporary Society.* Glenview, Ill.: Scott, Foresman, 1965. [6]

_____. (ed.). *Handbook of Socialization Theory and Research.* Chicago: Rand McNally, 1969. [6]

Gough, Kathleen. "The Origin of the Family," *Journal of Marriage and the Family,* 33 (November 1971), 760–771. [13]

_____. "An Anthropologist Looks at Engels." In Nona Y. Glazer and Helen Y. Waehrer (eds.). *Woman in a Man-Made World.* 2nd ed. Chicago: Rand McNally, 1977. Pp. 156–168. [13]

Gouldner, Alvin W. "Cosmopolitans and Locals: Towards an Analysis of Latent Social Roles," *Administrative Science Quarterly,* 2 (December 1957), 281–292. [8]

_____. "Organizational Analysis." In Robert K. Merton *et al.* (eds.). *Sociology Today.* New York: Basic Books, 1959. Pp. 400–428. [9]

Gove, Walter R. (ed.). *The Labelling of Deviance.* Beverly Hills, Calif.: Sage Publications, 1980. [7]

Gracey, Harry L. "Learning the Student Role: Kindergarten as Academic Boot Camp." In Dennis H. Wrong and Harry L. Gracey (eds.). *Readings in Introductory Sociology.* New York: Macmillan, 1967. Pp. 288–299. [6]

Grambs, Jean, and Walter Waetjen. *Sex: Does It Make A Difference?* North Scituate, Mass.: Duxbury Press, 1975. [6, 13]

Gray, Francine du Plessix. Review of *Of Woman Born,* by Adrienne Rich. *New York Times Book Review,* October 10, 1976, p. 3. [13]

Greeley, Andrew. *Unsecular Man.* New York: Schocken, 1972. [16]

_____. *Ethnicity in the United States: A Preliminary Reconnaissance.* New York: Wiley, 1974. [12]

_____. "Ethnicity, Denomination, and Inequality." Unpublished paper. Center for the Study of American Pluralism, National Opinion Research Center, Chicago, 1975. [16]

_____. "Council or Encyclical?" *Review of Religious Research.* 18:1 (Fall 1976), 3–24. [16]

Greenblat, Cathy S., Peter J. Stein, and Norman F. Washburne. *The Marriage Game.* 2nd ed. New York: Random House, 1977. [14]

Greiff, Barrie S., and Preston K. Munter. *Tradeoffs: The Executive, Family and Organization.* New York: Simon and Schuster, 1979. [13]

Griffith, W., and R. Veitch. "Preacquaintance Attitude—Similarity and Attraction Revisited: Ten Days in a Fallout Shelter," *Sociometry,* 37 (June 1974), 163–173. [8]

Gross, Neal, Ward S. Mason, and Alexander W. McEachern. *Explorations in Role Analysis: Studies of the School Superintendency Role.* New York: Wiley, 1958. [6]

Gurin, Patricia, Arthur H. Miller, and Gerald Gurin. "Stratum Identification and Consciousness," *Social Psychology Quarterly,* 43 (1980), 30–47. [11]

Gurr, Ted. R. *Why Men Rebel.* Princeton, N.J.: Princeton University Press, 1970. [21]

Gusfield, Joseph R. "Social Structure and Moral Reform: A Study of the Women's Christian Temperance Union," *American Journal of Sociology,* 61 (November 1955), 221–232. [9]

Haas, J. Eugene, and Thomas E. Drabeck. *Complex Organization: A Sociological Perspective.* New York: Macmillan, 1973. [9]

Habbakuk, H. J. "English Population in the Eighteenth Century," *Economic History Review,* 2nd series, 6 (1953), 117–133. [19]

Hacker, Andrew. Quoted in *Time,* December 23, 1970, p. 35. [14]

Hacker, Helen M. "Women as a Minority Group," *Social Forces,* 30 (October 1951), 60–69. [13]

Hadden, Jeffrey K. *The Gathering Storm in the Churches.* Garden City, N.Y.: Doubleday, 1969. [16]

Hall, John R. "The Apocalypse at Jonestown," *Society* (September-October 1979), 52–61. [16]

Hamilton, M. L. *Fathers' Influence on Children.* Chicago: Nelson-Hall, 1977. [6]

Hammond, Phillip E. (ed.). *Sociologists at Work: Essays on the Craft of Social Research.* New York: Basic Books, 1964. [2]

Hare, A. Paul. *Handbook of Small Group Research.* New York: Free Press, 1962. [6]

Harris, Chauncy, and Edward L. Ullman. "The Nature of Cities." In Paul K. Hatt and Albert J. Reiss, Jr. (eds.). *Reader in Urban Sociology.* Glencoe, Ill.: Free Press, 1951. Pp. 222–232. [20]

Harris, Marvin. *Cows, Pigs, Wars, and Witches: The Riddles of Culture.* New York: Random House/Vintage, 1975. [5, 15]

_____. *Culture, People, Nature: An Introduction to General Anthropology.* 2nd ed. New York: Crowell, 1975. [5]

Hartley, Ruth E. "Sex-Role Pressures and the Socialization of the Male Child," *Psychological Reports,* 5 (1959), 457–468. [6]

Hartshorne, H., and M. A. May. *Studies in Deceit.* New York: Macmillan, 1928. [2]

Hauser, Philip M. "The Chaotic Society: Product of the Social Morphological Revolution," *American Sociological Review,* 34:1 (February 1969), 1–19. [4]

_____. (ed.). *The Population Dilemma.* 2nd ed. Englewood Cliffs, N.J.: Prentice-Hall, 1969. [19]

_____. *Social Statistics in Use.* New York: Russell Sage Foundation, 1975. [11]

Hauser, Robert M., and David L. Featherman. "Trends in Occupational Mobility of U.S. Men, 1962–1970," *American Sociological Review,* 38:3 (1973), 302–310. [11]

_____. *The Process of Stratification: Trends and Analyses.* New York: Academic Press, 1977. [11]

Havens, Elizabeth M., and Judy Corder Tully. "Female Intergenerational Occupational Mobility: Comparisons of Patterns," *American Sociological Review,* 37:6 (1972), 774–777. [11]

Hayes, Harold T. P. "The Pursuit of Reason," *New York Times Magazine,* June 12, 1977, pp. 21–23, 73–79. [5]

Hedges, J. N., and J. K. Barnett. "Working Women and the Division of Household Tasks," *Monthly Labor Review,* 95 (April 1972), 9–14. [13]

Henley, Nancy, and Jo Freeman. "The Sexual Politics of Interpersonal Behavior." In Jo Freeman (ed.). *Women: A Feminist Perspective.* Palo Alto, Calif.: Mayfield, 1975. Pp. 391–401. [13]

Hershovits, Melville J. *Cultural Relativism: Perspectives in Cultural Pluralism.* Frances Hershovits (ed.). New York: Random House/Vintage, 1973. [5]

Himmelweit, H. T., A. N. Oppenheim, and P. Vince. *Television and the Child.* Published for the Nuffield Foundation. New York: Oxford University Press, 1958. [6]

Hindelang, Michael J., Travis Hirschi, and Joseph G. Weis. "Correlates of Delinquency: The Illusions of Discrepancy Between Self-Report and Official Measures," *American Sociological Review,* 44 (December 1979), 955–1014. [7]

Hirsch, Jerry. "Behavior-Genetic Analysis and Its Biosocial Consequences," *Seminars in Psychiatry,* 2 (1970), 89–105. [15]

Hirschi, Travis. *Causes of Delinquency.* Berkeley: University of California Press, 1969. [7]

Hodge, Robert W., Paul M. Siegel, and Peter H. Rossi. "Occupational Prestige in the United States, 1925–1963," *American Journal of Sociology,* 70 (November 1964), 286–302. [11]

Hodgson, Godfrey. "Do Schools Make a Difference?" *Atlantic,* 231:3 (March 1973), 35–46. [15]

Hoffer, Eric. *The True Believer: Thoughts on the*

Nature of Mass Movements. New York: Harper & Row, 1951. [21]

Hoffman, Lois W. "Childhood Experiences and Achievement," *Journal of Social Issues,* 28 (1972), 129–156. [6]

Hoffman, Martin L., and Herbert D. Saltzstein. "Parent Discipline and the Child's Moral Development," *Journal of Personality and Social Psychology,* 5 (January 1967), 45–57. [6]

Holcombe, Lee. *Victorian Ladies at Work.* Hamden, Conn.: Shoe String Press, 1973. [13]

Hollander, Edwin P. "Competence and Conformity in the Acceptance of Influence," *Journal of Abnormal and Social Psychology,* 61 (1960), 365–369. [8]

Hollander, Edwin P., and J. W. Julian. "Studies in Leader Legitimacy, Influence, and Innovation." In Leonard Berkowitz (ed.). *Advances in Experimental Social Psychology.* Vol. 5. New York: Academic Press, 1970. Pp. 33–69. [8]

Hollingshead, August B. *Elmstown's Youth.* New York: Wiley, 1949. [15]

———. "Cultural Factors in the Selection of Marriage Mates," *American Sociological Review,* 15 (October 1950), 619–627. [14]

Hollingshead, August B., and Frederick C. Redlich. *Social Class and Mental Illness.* New York: Wiley, 1958. [7, 11]

Holtzman, W. H. "Adjustment and Leadership," *Journal of Social Psychology,* 36 (1952), 179–189. [8]

Homans, George C. *The Human Group.* New York: Harcourt, Brace, 1950. [3]

———. *The Nature of Social Sciences.* New York: Harcourt, Brace & World, 1967. [1, 3]

Hoyt, Homer. *The Structure and Growth of Residential Neighborhoods in American Cities.* Washington, D.C.: Government Printing Office, 1939. [20]

Huber, Joan. "Toward a Socio-technological Theory of the Women's Movement," *Social Problems,* 23 (April 1976), 371–388. [13]

Huber, Joan, and William H. Form. *Income and Ideology: An Analysis of the American Political Formula.* New York: Free Press, 1973. [17]

Hunt, Morton. "Sexual Behavior in the 1970's," *Playboy* (October 1973a), 84ff. [14]

———. "Sexual Behavior in the 1970's," *Playboy* (November 1973b), 74–75. [14]

Hunter, E.C., and A. M. Jordan. "An Analysis of Qualities Associated with Leadership Among College Students," *Journal of Educational Psychology,* 30 (1939), 497–509. [8]

Hunter, Floyd. *Community Power Structure.* Chapel Hill: University of North Carolina Press, 1953. [17]

Inciardi, James A. (ed.). *Radical Criminology: The Coming Crisis.* Beverly Hills, Calif.: Sage Publications, 1980. [7]

Inkeles, Alex. *What Is Sociology?* Englewood Cliffs, N.J.: Prentice-Hall, 1964. [1, 4]

Institute of Life Insurance. *The Life Cycle.* Trend Analysis Program Report No. 8. New York, 1974. [18]

Jacobs, Jane. *The Death and Life of Great American Cities.* New York: Vintage, 1961. [20]

Jaffe, C. L., and R. L. Lucas. "Effects of Rates in Talking and Correctness of Decisions on Leader Choice in Small Groups," *Journal of Social Psychology,* 79 (1969), 247–254. [8]

Jencks, Christopher. *Who Gets Ahead? The Determinants of Economic Success in America.* New York: Basic Books, 1979. [11, 15]

Jencks, Christopher, *et al. Inequality: A Reassessment of the Effect of Family and Schooling in America.* New York: Basic Books, 1972. [15]

Jennings, Helen Hall. *Leadership and Isolation.* New York: Longmans, Green, 1950. [8]

Jensen, Arthur. "How Much Can We Boost I.Q. and Scholastic Achievement?" *Harvard Educational Review,* 29 (1969), 1–123. [15]

Kaats, G. R., and K. E. Davis. "Dynamics of Sexual Behavior of College Students," *Journal of Marriage and the Family,* 32 (1970), 390–399. [14]

Kahl, Joseph Alan. *The American Class Structure.* New York: Rinehart, 1959. [11]

Kalleberg, Arne L. "Work Values and Job Rewards: A Theory of Job Satisfaction," *American Sociological Review,* 42 (February 1977), 124–143. [18]

Kallen, Horace M. "Innovation." In Edwin R. A. Seligman and Alvin Johnson (eds.). *The Encyclopedia of the Social Sciences.* Vol. 4. New York: Macmillan, 1937. [22]

Kandel, Denise B. "Race, Maternal Authority, and Adolescent Operations," *American Journal of Sociometry,* 76 (May 1971), 999–1009. [6]

Kanter, Rosabeth Moss. *Commitment and Community: Communes and Utopias in a Sociological Perspective.* Cambridge, Mass.: Harvard University Press, 1972. [4]

Kaplan, Alexander G., and Joan P. Bean (eds.). *Beyond Sex Role Stereotypes: Readings Toward a Psychology of Androgyny.* Boston: Little, Brown, 1976. [13]

Katz, Alvin M., and Reuben Hill. "Residential Propinquity and Marital Selection. A Review of Theory, Method, and Fact," *Marriage and Family Living,* 20 (February 1958), 27–34. [14]

Katz, Daniel, and Robert L. Kahn. *The Social Psychology of Organizations.* New York: Wiley, 1966. [9]

———. *The Social Psychology of Organizations.* 2nd ed. New York: Wiley, 1978. [9]

Katz, Elihu, Martin L. Levin, and Herbert Hamilton. "Traditions of Research on the Diffusion of Innovation," *American Sociological Review,* 28 (April 1963), 237–252. [22]

Katznelson, Ira, and Mark Kesselman. *The Politics of Power: A Critical Introduction to American Government.* New York: Harcourt Brace Jovanovich, 1975. [11, 17]

Kautsky, Karl. *Foundations of Christianity.* Henry F. Mins (tr.). New York: Russell and Russell, 1953. [16]

Keller, Mark, and Carol Gurioli. *Statistics on Consumption of Alcohol and on Alcoholism.* New Brunswick, N.J.: Rutgers Center of Alcohol Studies, 1976. [7]

Keller, Suzanne. "The Social Origins and Career Lines of Three Generations of American Business Leaders," Ph.D. dissertation, Columbia University, 1953. [11]

———. "The Planning of Communities." In Lewis Coser (ed.). *The Idea of Social Structure: Essays in Honor of Robert Merton.* New York: Harcourt Brace Jovanovich, 1975. Pp. 283–299. [20]

Kelley, Dean. *Why the Conservative Churches Are Growing: A Study in the Sociology of Religion.* New York: Harper & Row, 1972. [16]

Kemper, Theodore D. "Reference Groups, Socialization and Achievement," *American Sociological Review,* 33 (February 1968), 31–45. [8]

Kephart, William M. *The Family, Society and the Individual.* Boston: Houghton Mifflin, 1977. [14]

Kerner Commission (National Advisory Commission on Civil Disorders). *Report of the National Advisory Commission on Civil Disorders.* New York: Bantam, 1968. [12]

Kessler, Ronald C., and Paul D. Cleary. "Social Class and Psychological Distress," *American Sociological Review,* 45 (June 1980), 463–478. [11]

Key, V. O. *Public Opinion and American Democracy.* New York: Knopf, 1961. [17]

Killian, L. M. "Social Movements." In R. E. L. Faris (ed.). *Handbook of Modern Sociology.* Chicago: Rand McNally, 1964. Pp. 426–455. [21]

Kimmel, Douglas C. *Adulthood and Aging: An Interdisciplinary Developmental View.* New York: Wiley, 1974. [6, 13]

Kinloch, Graham C. *Sociological Theory: Its Development and Major Paradigms.* New York: McGraw-Hill, 1977. [3]

Kirk, David L., *et al. Biology Today.* 2nd ed. New York: CRM/Random House, 1975. [12, 15]

Kirk, David L., *et al. Biology Today.* 3rd ed. New York: Random House, 1980. P. 947. [19]

Kirkpatrick, Jeane. *The New Presidential Elite: Men and Women in National Politics.* New York: Russell Sage Foundation and The Twentieth Century Fund, 1976. [17]

Kluckhohn, Clyde. *Mirror for Man.* New York: McGraw-Hill, 1949. [3, 5]

Knight, Athelia. "Teacher Attitudes on Blacks Sparked Va. Dispute," *Washington Post,* May 9, 1978, p. C-1. [15]

Knoke, David. "A Causal Model for the Political Party Preferences of American Men," *American Sociological Review,* 37 (December 1972), 679–689. [17]

———. *Change and Continuity in American Politics: The Social Bases of Political Parties.* Baltimore: Johns Hopkins University Press, 1976. [17]

Kogan, N., and M. Wallach. *Risk Taking: A Study in Cognition and Personality.* New York: Holt, Rinehart and Winston, 1964. [8]

Kohn, Melvin. *Class and Conformity.* Homewood, Ill.: Dorsey Press, 1969. [6]

Komarovsky, Mirra. "Cultural Contradictions and Sex Roles: The Masculine Case," *American Journal of Sociology,* 78 (January 1973), 873–884. [13]

Kornhauser, William. "Conflict, Power and Relative Deprivation," *American Political Science Review,* 68 (December 1959), 1569–1578. [21]

Krause, Elliot. *Why Study Sociology?* New York: Random House, 1980. [1]

Krauss, Irving. *Stratification, Class, and Conflict.* New York: Free Press, 1976. [11, 13]

Krech, David, Richard S. Crutchfield, and Egerton L. Ballachey. *Individual in Society: A Textbook of Social Psychology.* New York: McGraw-Hill, 1962. [5]

Krech, David, *et al. Psychology: A Basic Course.* New York: Knopf, 1976. [15]

Kremen, Bennet. "Lordstown—Searching for a Better Way of Work," *New York Times,* September 9, 1973, Section 3, pp. 1, 4. [9]

Kroeber, A. L., and Clyde Kluckhohn. *Culture: A Critical Review of Concepts and Definitions.* New York: Random House/Vintage, 1952. [5]

Kuhn, M. H., and T. S. McPartland. "An Empirical Investigation of Self-Attitudes," *American Sociological Review,* 19 (January 1954), 68–76. [6]

LaBarre, Weston. "The Cultural Basis of Emotions and Gestures," *Journal of Personality,* 16 (September 1947), 49–68. [5]

Labor Department. Women's Bureau. *Handbook on Women Workers.* Bulletin 297. Washington, D.C.: Government Printing Office, 1975. [13]

Ladner, Joyce. *Tomorrow's Tomorrow: The Black Woman.* Garden City, N.Y.: Doubleday, 1971. [6]

Landis, Benson Y. (ed.). *Yearbook of American Churches for 1963.* New York: National Council of Churches of Christ in the U.S.A., 1963. [16]

Lang, Kurt, and Gladys E. Lang. *Collective Dynamics.* New York: Crowell, 1961. [21]

Langer, William L. "What Caused the Explosion?" *New York Review of Books,* April 28, 1977, pp. 3–4. [19]

LaPiere, Richard T. *Social Change.* New York: McGraw-Hill, 1965. [22]

Lasch, Christopher. "What the Doctor Ordered." Review of Edward Shorter, *The Making of the Modern Family* (New York: Basic Books, 1975), *New York Review of Books,* December 11, 1975, pp. 50–54. [14]

Latané, Bibb, and John M. Darley. "Help in a Crisis: Bystander Response to an Emergency." In John Thibault (ed.). *Contemporary Topics in Social Psychology.* Morristown, N.J.: General Learning Press, 1976. [20]

Laumann, Edward O. *Prestige and Association in an Urban Community.* New York: Bobbs-Merrill, 1966. [17]

Lebergott, Stanley. *The American Economy.* Princeton, N.J.: Princeton University Press, 1976. [12]

LeBon, Gustave. *The Crowd (La Psychologie des Foules)* (1895). Dunwoody, Ga.: Berg, 1968. [21]

Lee, R. B. "'!Kung Bushmen Subsistence: An Input-Output Analysis." In A. P. Vayda (ed.). *Environment and Cultural Behavior.* Garden City, N.Y.: Natural History Press, 1969. [10]

———. "The !Kung Bushmen of Botswana." In M. Bicchieri (ed.). *Hunters and Gatherers Today.* New York: Holt, Rinehart and Winston, 1972. [10]

Lenski, Gerhard. *Power and Privilege: The Theory of Social Stratification.* New York: McGraw-Hill, 1966. [10, 11]

Leslie, Gerald R. *The Family in a Social Context.* New York: Oxford University Press, 1973. [14]

Leuba, James H. *The Belief in God and Immortality.* Boston: Sherman French, 1916. [16]

Levison, Andrew. *The Working Class Majority.* New York: Coward, McCann and Geoghegan, 1974. [11]

Lewis, Jerry M. "A Study of the Kent State Incident Using Smelser's Theory of Collective Behavior," *Sociological Inquiry,* 42 (1972), 87–96. [21]

Libby, Roger W., and Robert N. Whitehurst (eds.). *Marriage and Alternatives: Exploring Intimate Relationships.* Glenview, Ill.: Scott, Foresman, 1977. [14]

Liebow, Elliot. *Tally's Corner: A Study of Negro Streetcorner Men.* Boston: Little, Brown, 1967. [20]

Lifton, Robert Jay. "Thought Reform: Psychological Steps in Death and Rebirth." In Alfred Lindesmith and Anselm Strauss (eds.). *Readings in Social Psychology.* New York: Holt, Rinehart and Winston, 1969. Pp. 324–340. [6]

Likert, Rensis. *The Human Organization.* New York: McGraw-Hill, 1967. [9]

Lindesmith, Alfred R., and Anselm L. Strauss. "Critique of Culture-Personality Writings," *American Sociological Review,* 15 (October 1950), 587–600. [6]

Lindesmith, Alfred R., Anselm L. Strauss, and Norman K. Denzin. *Social Psychology.* 4th ed. Hinsdale, Ill.: Dryden, 1975. [6, 8]

Lindzey, Gardner, and Elliot Aronson (eds.). *Handbook of Social Psychology.* 2nd ed. Vol. 4: *Group Psychology and Phenomena of Interaction.* Reading, Mass.: Addison-Wesley, 1968. [8]

Linton, Ralph. *The Study of Man.* New York: Appleton-Century, 1936. [5]

———. *The Cultural Background of Personality.* New York: Appleton-Century-Crofts, 1945. [5]

Lipman-Blumen, Jean, and Ann R. Tickameyer. "Sex Roles in Transition: A Ten-Year Perspective," *Annual Review of Sociology* (1975), 297–337. [13]

Lipset, Seymour Martin. *Political Man.* Garden City, N.Y.: Doubleday, 1960. [15, 16, 17]

———. "Equality and Inequality." In Robert K. Merton and Robert A. Nisbet (eds.). *Contemporary Social Problems.* 4th ed. New York: Harcourt Brace Jovanovich, 1976. Pp. 307–353. [11]

Lipset, Seymour Martin, and Reinhard Bendix. *Social Mobility in Industrial Society.* Berkeley: University of California Press, 1959. [11]

Lipset, Seymour Martin, and William Schneider. "Political Sociology." In Neil J. Smelser (ed.). *Sociology.* New York: Wiley, 1973. Pp. 399–491. [17]

Litwak, Eugene. "Occupational Mobility and Extended Family Cohesion," *American Sociological Review,* 25 (February 1960a), 9–21. [14]

———. "Geographical Mobility and Extended Family Cohesion," *American Sociological Review,* 25 (June 1960b), 385–394. [14]

Loehlen, John C., Gardner Lindzey, and J. N. Spuhler. *Race Differences in Intelligence.* San Francisco: W. H. Freeman, 1975. [15]

Lofland, John. *Doomsday Cult.* Englewood Cliffs, N.J.: Prentice-Hall, 1966. [2]

———. *Deviance and Identity.* Englewood Cliffs, N.J.: Prentice-Hall, 1969. [2]

———. *Analyzing Social Settings.* Belmont, Calif.: Wadsworth, 1971. [2]

———. "The Boom and Bust of a Millennarian Movement: Doomsday Cult Revisited." Preface to *Doomsday Cult.* Rev. ed. New York: Irvington, 1977. [2]

———. *Doomsday Cult: A Study of Conversion, Proselytization, and Maintenance of Faith.* Enl. ed. New York: Irvington, 1979. [21]

Lofland, John, and Rodney Stark. "On Becoming a World Saver: A Theory of Conversion to a Deviant Perspective," *American Sociological Review,* 30 (December 1965), 862–875. [2]

Lopreato, Joseph. "Upward Social Mobility and Political Orientation," *American Sociological Review,* 32 (1967), 586–592. [11, 14]

Lopreato, Joseph, and Lawrence E. Hazelrigg. *Class, Conflict, and Mobility.* San Francisco: Chandler, 1972. [11]

Lövaas, O. I. "Effect of Exposure to Symbolic Aggression on Aggressive Behavior," *Child Development,* 32 (1961), 37–44. [6]

Lowenthal, Leo. "Biographies in Popular Magazines: From Production Leaders to Consumption Idols." In William Petersen (ed.). *American Social Patterns.* Garden City, N.Y.: Doubleday, 1956. [2]

Lowie, Robert H. *Primitive Society* (1920). New York: Boni and Liveright, 1970. [14]

Lundberg, Ferdinand. *The Rich and the Super-Rich.* Eileen Brand (ed.). Secaucus, N.J.: Lyle Stuart, 1968. [11]

Lyell, R. G. "Adolescent and Adult Self-Esteem as Related to Cultural Values," *Adolescence,* 8 (1973), 85–92. [6]

Lyle, Jack. "Television in Social Life: Patterns of Use (Overview)." In Eli A. Rubinstein, George A. Comstock, and John P. Murray (eds.). *Television and Social Behavior, Reports and Papers. Vol. IV: Television in Day-to-Day Life: Patterns of Use.* Rockville, Md.: National Institute of Mental Health, Department of Health, Education, and Welfare, 1972. [6]

Lynd, Robert S., and Helen Merrell Lynd. *Middletown, A Study in American Culture.* New York: Harcourt, Brace, 1929. [4, 17]

———. *Middletown in Transition: A Study in Cultural Conflicts.* New York: Harcourt, Brace, 1937. [4, 17]

Maccoby, Eleanor E. "Effects of the Mass Media." In Martin Hoffman and Lois Hoffman (eds.). *Review of Child Development and Research. I.* New York: Russell Sage Foundation, 1964. Pp. 323–348. [6]

Maccoby, Eleanor E., and Carol Jacklin. *The Psychology of Sex Differences.* Stanford, Calif.: Stanford University Press, 1974. [6, 13]

Mack, Joanna. "What Makes a Good School?" *New Society,* March 22, 1979. [15]

Malinowski, Bronislaw. *Magic, Science and Religion.* Glencoe, Ill.: Free Press, 1948. [3]

Malthus, Thomas. *On Population* (1798). Gertrude Himmelfarb (ed.). New York: Modern Library, 1960. [19]

Mamdani, Mahmood. "The Ideology of Population Control," *Concerned Demography,* 4:2 (Winter 1974), 13–22. [19]

Mannheim, Hermann. *Comparative Criminology.* Boston: Houghton Mifflin, 1965. [7]

March, James G. (ed.). *Handbook of Organizations.* Chicago: Rand McNally, 1965. [9]

Mariani, John. "Television Evangelism: Milking the Flock," *Saturday Review,* February 3, 1979. [16]

Mariolis, Peter. "Interlocking Directorates and Control of Corporations: The Theory of Bank Control," *Social Science Quarterly,* 56 (December 1975), 425–439. [9]

Marland, S. P., Jr. "Career Education—More Than a Name." Speech delivered at annual meeting of the State Directors of Vocational Education. Washington, D.C., May 4, 1971. [15]

———. *Career Education: A Proposal for Reform.* New York: McGraw-Hill, 1974. [15]

Marlowe, David, and Kenneth J. Gergen. "Personality and Social Interaction." In Gardner Lindzey and Elliot Aronson (eds.). *Handbook of Social Psychology.* Rev. ed. Reading, Mass.: Addison-Wesley, 1968. Pp. 111, 590–665. [8]

Marrett, Cora Bagley. "The Precariousness of Social Class in Black America," *Contemporary Sociology* (January 1980), 16–19. [12]

Marris, Peter. *Loss and Change.* Garden City, N.Y.: Doubleday, 1975. [22]

Marshall, Joan E., and Richard Heslin. "Boys and Girls Together: Sex Composition and the Effect of Density and Group Size on Cohesiveness," *Journal of Personality and Social Psychology,* 31 (May 1975), 952–961. [8]

Marshall, S. L. A. *Men Against Fire.* New York: Morrow, 1947. [21]

Marshall, Thomas H. "Citizenship and Social Class." In *Sociology at the Cross Roads.* London: Heinemann, 1963. Pp. 67–127. [17]

———. *Class, Citizenship and Social Development.* Garden City, N.Y.: Doubleday, 1974. [10]

Marston, Linda L., and Richard Morse. "The Present Significance of Race: Findings from National Surveys, 1976–1978." Unpublished paper, 1978. [12]

Martin, William C. "The God Hucksters of Radio," *The Atlantic,* 1970. [16]

Marx, Gary T. "Religion: Opiate or Inspiration of Civil Rights Militancy Among Negroes?" *American Sociological Review,* 32:1 (February 1967), 64–72. [16]

———. "Civil Disorders and the Agents of Social Control," *Journal of Social Issues,* 26 (1970), 19–57. [21]

———. "Thoughts on a Neglected Category of Social Movement Participant: The *Agent Provocateur* and the Informant," *American Journal of Sociology,* 80 (September 1974), 402–442. [21]

———. "Conceptual Problems in the Field of Collective Behavior." In H. Blalock (ed.). *Social Theory and Research: A Critical Appraisal.* New York: Free Press, 1981. [21]

Marx, Gary T., and J. Wood. "Strands of Theory and Research in Collective Behavior," *Annual Review of Sociology,* 1 (1975). [21]

Marx, Karl. *Marx: Early Writings.* T. B. Bottomore (ed. and tr.). New York: McGraw-Hill, 1964. [9]

———. *Das Kapital* (1st vol. published 1867). Eden Paul and Cedar Paul (trs.). New York: Dutton, 1976. [10, 22]

Marx, Karl, and Friedrich Engels. *The Communist*

Manifesto (1848). Chicago: Regnery, 1960. [10, 11, 22]

———. *The German Ideology.* New York: International Publishers, 1947. [10]

Mason, Karen Oppenheim, John L. Czajka, and Sara Arber. "Change in U.S. Women's Sex-Role Attitudes, 1964–1974," *American Sociological Review,* 41 (August 1976), 573–596. [13]

Masters, William H., and Virginia E. Johnson. *Human Sexual Inadequacy.* Boston: Little, Brown, 1970. [14]

Matras, Judah. *Population and Societies.* Englewood Cliffs, N.J.: Prentice-Hall, 1973. [19]

———. *Introduction to Population: A Sociological Approach.* Englewood Cliffs, N.J.: Prentice-Hall, 1977. [19]

Mayo, Elton. *The Human Problem of Industrial Civilization.* New York: Macmillan, 1933. [9]

Mazur, Allan. "Effects of Testosterone on Status in Primate Groups," *Folia Primatologica,* 554 (1976), 278–290. [13]

Mazur, Allan, and Leon S. Robertson. *Biology and Social Behavior.* New York: Free Press, 1972. [12]

McCarthy, John D., and Mayer N. Zald. *The Trend of Social Movements in America: Professionalization and Resource Mobilization.* Morristown, N.J.: General Learning Press, 1973. [21]

———. "Resource Mobilization and Social Movements," *American Journal of Sociology,* 82:6 (May 1977), 1212–1241. [21]

McCloskey, Herbert, Paul J. Hoffman, and Rosemary O'Hara. "Issue Conflict and Consensus Among Party Leaders and Followers," *American Political Science Review,* 54 (June 1960), 406–427. [17]

McEvoy, J., and A. Miller (eds.). *Black Power and Student Rebellion.* Belmont, Calif.: Wadsworth, 1969. [21]

McGrath, Joseph E., and Irwin Altman. *Small Group Research: A Synthesis and Critique of the Field.* New York: Holt, Rinehart and Winston, 1966. [8]

Mead, George Herbert. *Mind, Self, and Society.* Chicago: University of Chicago Press, 1934. [2, 6]

Mead, Margaret. *Sex and Temperament in Three Primitive Societies.* New York: Morrow, 1935. [13]

———. "Marriage in Two Steps," *Redbook,* 127 (July 1966), 48–49. [14]

Melville, Keith. "Play's the Thing," *The Sciences* (January–February 1974), 12–14. [5]

———. *Marriage and Family Today.* 2nd ed. New York: Random House, 1980. [14]

Menninger, Karl. *The Human Mind.* New York: Knopf, 1946. [7]

Merton, Robert K. "Fact and Factitiousness in Ethnic Opinionnaires," *American Sociological Review* (February 1940), 13–28. [12]

———. *Social Theory and Social Structure.* Glencoe, Ill.: Free Press, 1957. [8]

———. *Social Theory and Social Structure.* Rev. and enl. ed. New York: Free Press, 1967. [3, 7]

Merton, Robert K., and Robert A. Nisbet. *Contemporary Social Problems.* 4th ed. New York: Harcourt Brace Jovanovich, 1976. [7]

Meyer, John W., John Boli-Bennett, and Christopher Chase-Dunn. "Convergence and Divergence in Development," *Annual Review of Sociology,* 1975. [22]

Michels, Robert. *Political Parties: A Sociological Study of the Oligarchical Tendencies of Modern Democracy* (1915). New York: Collier, 1962. [8, 9, 17, 21]

Michener, James A. *Sports in America.* New York: Random House, 1976. [13]

Middlebrook, Patricia Niles. *Social Psychology and Modern Life.* New York: Knopf, 1974. [8]

Milbrath, Lester W., and M. L. Goel. *Political Participation.* 2nd ed. Chicago: Rand McNally, 1977. [17]

Mills, C. Wright. *White Collar: American Middle Class.* New York: Oxford University Press, 1951. [18]

———. *The Power Elite.* New York: Oxford University Press, 1956. [11, 17]

———. *The Sociological Imagination.* New York: Oxford University Press, 1959. [1]

———. "The Sociology of Stratification." In Irving Louis Horowitz (ed.). *Power, Politics and People: The Collected Essays of C. Wright Mills.* New York: Oxford University Press/Galaxy Books, 1967. [11]

Mills, Theodore. *The Sociology of Small Groups.* Englewood Cliffs, N.J.: Prentice-Hall, 1967. [8]

Milner, Murray. *The Myth of Equality.* San Francisco: Jossey-Bass, 1972. [15]

Miyamoto, S. Frank, and Sanford Dornbusch. "A Test of the Symbolic Interactionist Hypothesis of Self-Conception," *American Journal of Sociology,* 61 (January 1956), 399–403. [6]

Monahan, Thomas P. "The Extent of Interdenominational Marriage in the United States," *Journal for the Scientific Study of Religion,* 10 (1971), 85–92. [14]

Money, John, and Anke A. Ehrhardt. *Man and Woman, Boy and Girl.* Baltimore: Johns Hopkins University Press, 1972. [13]

Moore, Barrington. *Terror and Progress, U.S.S.R.* Cambridge, Mass.: Harvard University Press, 1954. [10]

Moore, J. C. *A Further Test of the Interactionist Hypotheses of Self-Conception.* Stanford, Calif.: Stanford University Laboratory for Social Research, Tech. Dept. No. 6, May 1964. [6]

Moore, W. "Industrialization and Social Change." In B. F. Hoselitz and W. E. Moore (eds.). *Industrialization and Society.* Paris: UNESCO, 1963. [22]

———. *Social Change.* 2nd ed. Englewood Cliffs, N.J.: Prentice-Hall, 1974. [22]

Moreno, Jacob L. *Who Shall Survive?* New York: Beacon House, 1953. [8]

Morren, George. "Woman, the Hunter." *Concerned Demography,* 4:1 (Spring 1974), 16–20. [10]

Morrison, Denton E., and Ramon Henkel (eds.). *Significance Test Controversy: A Reader.* Chicago: Aldine, 1970. [2]

Mosca, Gaetano. *The Ruling Class.* New York: McGraw-Hill, 1939. [17]

Mumford, Louis. *The City in History: Its Transformations, and Its Prospects.* New York: Harcourt, Brace & World, 1961. [20]

Murdock, George Peter. *Our Primitive Contemporaries.* New York: Macmillan, 1934. [10]

———. "Comparative Data on the Division of Labor by Sex," *Social Forces,* 15 (May 1937), 551–553. [13]

———. "The Common Denominations of Cultures." In Ralph Linton (ed.). *The Science of Man in World Crisis.* New York: Columbia University Press, 1945. [5]

———. *Social Structure.* New York: Macmillan, 1949. [14]

Mussen, P., and E. Rutherford. "Effects of Aggressive Cartoons on Children's Aggressive Play," *Journal of Abnormal Social Psychology,* 62 (1961), 461–464. [6]

Myrdal, Gunnar. *Asian Drama: An Inquiry into the Poverty of Nations.* New York: Pantheon, 1971. [19]

Nam, Charles B. *Population and Society.* Boston: Houghton Mifflin, 1968. [19]

Nash, Dennison. "A Little Child Shall Lead Them: A Statistical Test of an Hypothesis That Children Were the Source of the American Religious Revival," *Journal for the Scientific Study of Religion,* 7:2 (1968), 238–240. [16]

Nash, John. "The Father in Contemporary Culture and Current Psychological Literature." In Marcia and Thomas Lasswell (eds.). *Love, Marriage, Family: A Developmental Approach.* Glenview, Ill.: Scott, Foresman, 1973. Pp. 352–364. [6]

National Academy of Education. "Education for Employment: Knowledge for Action." Report of the Task Force on Education and Employment, National Academy of Education. Washington, D.C.: Acropolis Press, 1979. [15]

National Commission on the Causes and Prevention of Violence. 13 vols. Staff Report. Washington, D.C.: Government Printing Office, 1969. [7]

National Education Association Research Division. *Status of American Public School Teachers, 1975–1976.* Washington, D.C.: National Education Association, 1977. [15]

Nelson, Kathryn P. "Recent Suburbanization of Blacks: How Much, Who, and Where." Prepared for the Office of Economic Affairs, the Office of Policy Development and Research, Department of Housing and Urban Development. Washington, D.C.: Department of Housing and Urban Development, 1979, vii–34. [20]

Neugarten, Bernice L. "Developmental Perspectives." In Alexander Simon and Leon J. Epstein (eds.). *Aging in Modern Society.* Psychiatric Research Report No. 23. Washington, D.C.: American Psychiatric Association, February 1968. [7]

New York Post, June 15, 1977, p. 2. [7]

New York Times, January 28, 1979. [19]

Newcomer, Mabel. *The Big Business Executive.* New York: Scientific American, 1964. [11]

Newman, Frank, *et al. Report on Higher Education.* Washington, D.C.: Office of Education, Department of Health, Education, and Welfare, March 1971. [15]

Newsday, October 19, 1976. [13]

———, Part II, October 23, 1979, p. 7. [14]

Newsweek, February 28, 1977. [13]

Nie, Norman H., Sidney Verba, and John R. Petrocik. *The Changing American Voter.* Enl. ed. Cambridge, Mass.: Harvard University Press, 1980. [17]

Niebuhr, H. Richard. *The Social Sources of Denominationalism.* New York: Holt, 1929. [16]

Nilson, Linda Burzotta. "The Social Standing of a Married Woman," *Social Problems,* 23:5 (June 1976), 581–592. [11]

Nisbet, Robert A. *Social Change and History.* New York: Oxford University Press, 1969. [22]

———. (ed.). *Social Change.* New York: Harper & Row, 1972. [22]

Nisbet, Robert A., and Robert G. Perrin. *The Social Bond: An Introduction to the Study of Society.* New York: Knopf, 1977. [11]

Noble, Ernest P. (ed.). *The Third Special Report to the U.S. Congress on Alcohol and Health.* Washington, D.C.: Department of Health, Education, and Welfare, June 1978. [7]

Noel, Donald. "A Theory of the Origins of Ethnic Stratification," *Social Problems,* 16 (Fall 1968), 157–172. [12]

Nye, F. Ivan, and Felix M. Berardo. *The Family: Its Structure and Interaction.* New York: Macmillan, 1973. [14]

Nye, F. Ivan, James F. Short, Jr., and Virgil J. Olson. "Socio-Economic Status and Delinquent Behavior," *American Journal of Sociology,* 63 (January 1958), 381–389. [7]

Oberschall, Anthony. *Social Conflict and Social Movements.* Englewood Cliffs, N.J.: Prentice-Hall, 1973. [21]

O'Connor, James. *The Fiscal Crisis of the State.* New York: St. Martin's, 1973. [17]

O'Faolain, Julia, and Lauro Martines (eds.). *Not in*

God's Image: A History of Women from the Greeks to the Nineteenth Century. New York: Harper & Row, 1973. [13]

Ofshe, Richard (ed.). *Interpersonal Behavior in Small Groups.* Englewood Cliffs, N.J.: Prentice-Hall, 1973. [8]

Ogburn, William Fielding. *Social Change.* New York: Viking, 1922. [22]

——. *Social Change with Respect to Culture and Original Nature.* New York: Viking, 1927. [13]

Ogburn, William Fielding, and Meyer F. Nimkoff. *Sociology.* 4th ed. Boston: Houghton Mifflin, 1964. [4]

Olmstead, Michael, and A. Paul Hare. *The Small Group.* 2nd ed. New York: Random House, 1978. [8]

O'Neill, Nena, and George O'Neill. *Open Marriage: A New Life Style for Couples.* New York: M. Evans, 1966. [14]

——. "Open Marriage: A Synergic Model," *Family Coordinator,* 21 (October 1972), 403–409. [14]

Oppenheimer, Valarie Kincade. "Demographic Influence on Female Employment and the Status of Women." In Joan Haber (ed.). *Changing Women in a Changing Society.* Chicago: University of Chicago Press, 1973. Pp. 184–199. [13]

Orden, Susan, and Norman M. Bradburn. "Dimensions of Marriage Happiness," *American Journal of Sociology,* 73 (May 1968), 715–731. [14]

Orlansky, Harold. "Infant Care and Personality," *Psychological Bulletin,* 46 (January 1949), 1–48. [6]

Orum, Anthony M. *Introduction to Political Sociology: The Social Anatomy of Body Politics.* Englewood Cliffs, N.J.: Prentice-Hall, 1978. [17]

Ossowski, Stanislaw. *Class Structure in the Social Consciousness.* New York: Free Press, 1963. [11]

Ottensmann, John. "Social Behavior in Urban Space," *Urban Life,* 7 (April 1978), 3–22. [20]

Paige, Jeffrey M. "Changing Patterns of Anti-White Attitudes Among Blacks," *Journal of Social Issues,* 26:4 (Autumn 1970), 69–86. [17]

Palen, J. J., and K. H. Flaming. *Urban America: Conflict and Change.* Hinsdale, Ill.: Dryden, 1972. [20]

Palmer, Francis H. "The Effects of Early Childhood Intervention." Paper read at the annual meeting of the American Association for the Advancement of Science, Denver, 1977. [15]

Panel on Youth, President's Science Advisory Commission. *Youth: Transition to Adulthood.* Chicago: University of Chicago Press, 1974. [13]

Pareto, Vilfredo. *Mind and Society.* New York: Harcourt, Brace, 1935. [15, 17]

Park, Robert E. *On Social Control and Collective Behavior: Selected Papers* (1916). Ralph H. Turner (ed.). Chicago: University of Chicago Press, 1967. [20]

——. *Race and Culture.* Glencoe, Ill.: Free Press, 1949. [12]

Park, Robert E., *et al. The City* (1925). Chicago: University of Chicago Press, 1968. [4]

Parsons, Talcott. *The Structure of Social Action.* New York: McGraw-Hill, 1937. [21]

——. *The Social System.* Glencoe, Ill.: Free Press, 1951. [6, 14]

——. "Family Structure and the Socialization of the Child." In Talcott Parsons and Robert F. Bales (eds.). *Family Socialization and Interaction Process.* Glencoe, Ill.: Free Press, 1955. Pp. 35–131. [6]

——. *Social Structure and Personality.* Chap. 2. New York: Free Press, 1964. [6]

Parsons, Talcott, Edward Shils, Kasper D. Naegeles, and Jesse R. Pitts (eds.). *Theories of Society: Foundations of Modern Sociological Theory.* 2 vols. New York: Free Press, 1961. [4]

Partridge, Ernest D. *Leadership Among Adolescent Boys.* New York: AMS Press, 1934. [8]

Payne, B., and F. Whittington. "Older Women: An Examination of Popular Stereotypes and Research Evidence," *Social Problems,* 23 (Spring 1976), 488–504. [13]

Pearlin, Leonard I., and Joyce S. Johnson. "Marital Status, Life-Strains and Depression," *American Sociological Review,* 42 (1977), 704–715. [14]

Pechman, Joseph A. "The Rich, the Poor and the Taxes They Pay," *Public Interest,* 17 (Fall 1969), 22. [11]

Perlman, Selig. *A History of Trade Unionism in the United States.* New York: Macmillan, 1923. [11, 18]

Perrow, Charles. *Organizational Analysis: A Sociological View.* Monterey, Calif.: Brooks-Cole, 1970. [21]

——. *Complex Organizations: A Critical Essay.* 2nd ed. Glenview, Ill.: Scott, Foresman, 1979. [9]

Perrucci, Robert. "The Significance of Intra-Occupational Mobility: Some Methodological and Theoretical Notes, Together with a Case Study of Engineers," *American Sociological Review,* 26 (December 1961), 874–883. [11]

Perry, Joseph B., and M. D. Pugh. *Collective Behavior: Response to Social Stress.* St. Paul, Minn.: West, 1978. [21]

Petersen, William. *Population.* 3rd ed. New York: Macmillan, 1975. [19]

Peterson, Richard. "Revitalizing the Culture Concept." In Alex Inkeles, James Coleman, and Ralph H. Turner (eds.). *Annual Review of Sociology* (1979), 137–166. [5]

Pettigrew, Thomas F. "The Changing—Not Declining—Significance of Race," *Contemporary Sociology* (January 1980), 19–21. [12]

Peyrefitte, Alain. *Le Mal Francais (The French Illness).* Paris: Plon, 1976. [9]

Pfeiffer, John E. *The Emergence of Society: A Prehistory of the Establishment.* New York: McGraw-Hill, 1977. [4]

Pfuetze, Paul E. *Self, Society, and Existence: Human Nature and Dialogue in the Thought of George Herbert Mead and Martin Buber.* New York: Harper & Bros., 1961. [6]

Phillips, David P., and Richard H. Conviser. "Measuring the Structure and Boundary Properties of Groups: Some Uses of Information Theory," *Sociometry,* 35 (June 1972), 235–254. [8]

Piaget, Jean. *The Psychology of Intelligence.* New York: Harcourt, Brace, 1950. [6]

——. *The Language and Thought of the Child.* 3rd ed. New York: Humanities Press, 1962. [6]

——. "Developmental Psychology: A Theory of Development." *The Encyclopedia of the Social Sciences.* New York: Macmillan, 1968. Pp. 140–147. [6]

Piore, Michael J. "Jobs and Training." In Samuel H. Beer and Richard E. Barringer (eds.). *The State and the Poor.* Englewood Cliffs, N.J.: Prentice-Hall/Winthrop, 1970. Pp. 53–83. [12]

Pitts, Jesse. "The Structural-Functional Approach." In Harold T. Christensen (ed.). *Handbook of Marriage and the Family.* Chicago: Rand McNally, 1964. Pp. 88–90. [14]

Plumb, J. H. "Do We Owe It All to Love or Money?" Review of Edward Shorter, *The Making of the Modern Family* (New York: Basic Books, 1975), *New York Times Book Review.* December 21, 1975, p. 3. [14]

Plunkett, M. "School and Early Work Experience of Youth," *Occupational Outlook Quarterly,* 4 (1960), 22–27. [15]

Polyani, Karl. *The Great Transformation.* Boston: Beacon Press, 1957. [18]

Pope, Liston. *Millhands and Preachers.* New Haven, Conn.: Yale University Press, 1942. [16]

Population Reference Bureau. *1978 World Population Data Sheet.* Washington, D.C., 1978. [19, 20]

Porter, L., and E. Lawler III. "Properties of Organizational Structure in Relation to Job Attitudes and Job Behavior," *Psychological Bulletin,* 64 (1965), 23–51. [8]

Public Opinion, May/March 1979, p. 34. [16]

Quarantelli, E. L. "Panic Behavior: Some Empirical Observations." Paper presented at the American Institute of Architects Conference on Human Response to Tall Buildings, Chicago, July 19, 1975. [21]

Quarantelli, E. L., and Joseph Cooper. "Self-Conceptions and Others: A Further Test of Median Hypotheses," *Sociological Quarterly,* 7:3 (Summer 1966), 281–297. [6]

Quijano, Anibal. *Nationalism and Capitalism in Peru: A Study in Neo-Imperialism.* New York: Monthly Review Press, 1971. [22]

Quinney, Richard. *The Social Reality of Crime.* Boston: Little, Brown, 1970. [7]

——. *Class, State, and Crime: On the Theory and Practice of Criminal Justice.* New York: McKay, 1977. [7]

Rabban, Meyer L. "Sex Role Identification in Young Children in Two Diverse Social Groups," *Genetic Psychological Monographs,* 42 (1950), 81–158. [6]

Radcliffe-Brown, Alfred Reginald. *The Andaman Islanders.* Glencoe, Ill.: Free Press, 1910. [10]

Rainwater, Lee. *Family Design: Marital Sexuality, Family Size and Contraception.* Chicago: Aldine, 1968. [14]

——. "The Lower Class: Health, Illness, and Medical Institutions." In Lee Rainwater (ed.). *Social Problems and Public Policy.* Chicago: Aldine, 1974. Pp. 179–187. [11]

Ramey, James W. "The Impact of Legal Regulations on Nontraditional Families." Unpublished paper, Center for Policy Research, New York, 1977. [14]

Raven, Bertram H. "Social Influence and Power." In Ivan D. Steiner and Morris Fishbein (eds.). *Current Studies in Social Psychology.* New York: Holt, Rinehart and Winston, 1965. Pp. 371–382. [8]

Reckless, Walter C. *The Crime Problem.* 4th ed. New York: Appleton-Century-Crofts, 1967. [7]

Reckless, Walter C., Simon Dinitz, and Ellen Murray. "Self Concept as an Insulator Against Delinquency," *American Sociological Review,* 21 (December 1956), 744–746. [7]

Redfield, Robert. "The Folk Society," *American Journal of Sociology,* 52:4 (January 1947), 293–308. [20]

Reisman, David. *The Lonely Crowd.* Garden City, N.Y.: Doubleday, 1953. [17]

Reiss, Albert J., Jr. "Police Brutality—Answers to Key Questions," *Trans-Action,* 5 (July 1968), 10–19. [1]

Reiss, Albert J., Jr., with Otis D. Duncan, Paul K. Hatt, and Cecil C. North. *Occupations and Social Status.* New York: Free Press, 1961. [11]

Reiss, Ira L. *The Social Context of Sexual Permissiveness.* New York: Holt, Rinehart and Winston, 1967. [6]

Reissman, Leonard. *The Urban Process.* New York: Free Press, 1964. [20]

Rele, J. R. *Fertility Analysis Through Extension of Stable Population Concepts.* Berkeley, Calif.: International Population and Urban Research, 1967. [19]

Renne, K. S. "Childlessness, Health, and Marital Satisfaction," *Social Biology,* 23 (1976), 183–197. [14]

Research Triangle Institute. "National Longitudinal Study of the High School Class of 1972: A Capsule

Description of First Follow-Up Survey Data." Washington, D.C.: U.S. Government Printing Office, 1976. [15]

Revelle, Roger. "Food and Population," *Scientific American,* September 1974, 163. [19]

Rich, William. *Smaller Families Through Social and Economic Progress.* Monograph No. 7, 1973. [19]

Rieken, Henry W., and George C. Homans. "Psychological Aspects of Social Structure." In G. Lindzey (ed.). *Handbook of Social Psychology.* Reading, Mass.: Addison-Wesley, 1954. Pp. 786–833. [8]

Riley, Matilda White, Ann Foner, and Marilyn Johnson, in association with others. *Aging and Society.* New York: Russell Sage Foundation, 1968 (Vol. 1, *Inventory of Findings),* 1969 (Vol. 2, *Aging and The Professions),* and 1972 (Vol. 3, *A Sociology of Age Stratification).* [13]

Rindfuss, Ronald, and Charles Westoff. "The Initiation of Contraception," *Demography,* 11 (February 1974), 75–87. [19]

Robbins, Thomas, Dick Anthony, M. Doucas, and T. Curtis. "The Last Civil Religion: Reverend Moon and the Unification Church," *Sociological Analysis,* 37 (Summer 1976), 111–125. [16]

Roberts, Ron E., and Robert M. Kloss. *Social Movements Between the Balcony and the Barricade.* St. Louis, Mo.: C. V. Mosby, 1979. [21]

Roethlisberger, Fritz J., and William J. Dickson. *Management and the Worker.* Cambridge, Mass.: Harvard University Press, 1939. [8]

Rollins, Boyd C., and Harold Feldman. "Marital Satisfaction Over the Family Cycle," *Journal of Marriage and the Family,* 32:11 (February 1970), 20–37. [14]

Rony, Vera. "Bogalusa: The Economics of Tragedy," *Dissent* (May/June 1966), 234–242. [9]

Rosaldo, Michelle Zimbalist. "Woman, Culture, and Society: A Theoretical Overview." In Michelle Zimbalist Rosaldo and Louise Lamphere (eds.). *Women, Culture and Society.* Stanford, Calif.: Stanford University Press, 1974. Pp. 17–42. [13]

Rose, Arnold. *The Power Structure: Political Process in American Society.* New York: Oxford University Press, 1967. [17]

Rose, R., P. Bourne, and R. Poe, *et al.* "Androgen Responses to Stress. II. Excretion of Testosterone, Epitestosterone, Androsterone and Etiocholanolene During Basic Combat Training and Under Threat of Attack," *Psychosomatic Medicine,* 31 (1969), 418–436. [13]

Rose, R., T. Gordon, and I. Bernstein. "Plasma Testosterone Levels in the Male Rhesus. Influences of Sexual and Social Stimuli," *Science,* 178 (1972), 643–645. [13]

Rose, R., J. Holaday, and I. Bernstein. "Plasma Testosterone, Dominance Rank and Aggressive Behavior in Male Rhesus Monkeys," *Nature,* 231 (1971), 366–368. [13]

Rose, R., R. Poe, and J. Mason. "Psychological State and Body Size as Determinants of 17-OHCS Excretion," *Archives of Internal Medicine,* 121 (1968), 406. [13]

Rosen, Lawrence. "Policemen." In Peter I. Rose, Stanley Rothman, and William J. Wilson (eds.). *Through Different Eyes: Black and White Perspectives on American Race Relations.* New York: Oxford University Press, 1973. Pp. 257–290. [7]

Rosenberg, Morris R. *Conceiving the Self.* New York: Basic Books, 1979. [6]

Rosenfeld, Rachel A. "Women's Intergenerational Occupational Mobility," *American Sociological Review,* 43 (1978), 36–46. [11]

Rosenthal, D. *Genetic Theory and Abnormal Behavior.* New York: McGraw-Hill, 1970. [7]

Rosenthal, Robert, and Lenore Jacobson. *Pygmalion in the Classroom: Teacher Expectations and Pupil's*

Intellectual Development. New York: Holt, Rinehart and Winston, 1968. [15]

Rosow, Jerome M. (ed.). *The Worker and the Job: Coping with Change.* Englewood Cliffs, N.J.: Prentice-Hall, 1974. [18]

Rossi, Alice S. "Sex Equality: The Beginnings of Ideology," *The Humanist* (September/October 1969). [13]

———. "A Biosocial Perspective on Parenting," *Daedalus* (Spring 1977), 1–31. [13]

Rothschild-Whitt, Joyce. "The Collectivist Organization: An Alternative to Rational-Bureaucratic Models," *American Sociological Review,* 44 (1979), 509–527. [9]

Rubington, Earl (ed.). *Deviance: The Interactionist Perspective.* 3rd ed. New York: Macmillan, 1978. [7]

Rudé, G. *The Crowd in History: A Study of Popular Disturbances in France and England 1730–1848.* New York: Wiley, 1964. [21]

Runcie, John F. *Experiencing Social Research.* Homewood, Ill.: Dorsey Press, 1976. [2]

Rushing, William A., and Suzanne T. Ortega. "Socioeconomic Status and Mental Disorder: New Evidence and a Sociomedical Formulation," *American Journal of Sociology,* 84 (1979), 1175–1196. [11]

Rutter, Michael, *et al. Fifteen Thousand Hours: Secondary Schools and Their Effects on Children.* Cambridge, Mass.: Harvard University Press, 1979. [15]

Ryan, William. *Blaming the Victim.* New York: Random House, 1976. [12]

Sager, Clifford, *et al.* "The Marriage Contract," *Family Process,* 10 (September 1971), 311–326. [14]

Salpukas, Agis. "Jobs Rotated to Fight Boredom," *New York Times,* February 3, 1973. [9]

Sapir, Edward. "The Status of Linguistics as a Science," *Language,* 5 (1929), 207–214. [5]

Scanzoni, Letha, and John Scanzoni. *Men, Women and Change: A Sociology of Marriage and Family.* New York: McGraw-Hill, 1976. [8, 14]

Schein, Edgar H., *et al. Coercive Persuasion.* New York: Norton, 1971. [6]

Schneider, David J. *Social Psychology.* Reading, Mass.: Addison-Wesley, 1976. [8]

Schramm, Wilbur, Jack Lyle, and Edwin B. Parker. *Television in the Lives of Our Children.* Stanford, Calif.: Stanford University Press, 1961. [6]

Schultz, David A. *The Changing Family.* Englewood Cliffs, N.J.: Prentice-Hall, 1972. [14]

Schur, Edwin M. *Crimes Without Victims.* Englewood Cliffs, N.J.: Prentice-Hall, 1965. [7]

———. *Labeling Deviant Behavior: Its Sociological Implications.* New York: Harper & Row, 1971. [7]

Schutz, Alfred. *Collected Papers, I: The Problem of Social Reality.* M. Natanson (ed.). The Hague: Nijhoff, 1962. [3]

———. *Collected Papers, II: Studies in Social Theory.* A. Brodersen (ed.). The Hague: Nijhoff, 1964. [3]

Scott, Robert A. *The Making of Blind Men.* New York: Russell Sage Foundation, 1969. [7]

Scott, W. Richard. *Social Processes and Social Structures: An Introduction to Sociology.* New York: Holt, Rinehart and Winston, 1970. [4]

Seaman, Barbara. *Free and Female.* New York: Coward, McCann and Geoghegan, 1972. [14]

Sears, Robert, Eleanor Maccoby, and Harry Levin, in collaboration with Edgar Lowell, Pauline Sears, and John W. M. Whiting. *Patterns of Child Rearing.* Evanston, Ill.: Row, Peterson, 1957. [6]

Sebald, Hans. *Adolescence: A Sociological Analysis.* New York: Appleton-Century-Crofts, 1968. [6, 13]

Seeman, Melvin. "Some Real and Imaginary Consequences of Social Mobility: A French-American Comparison," *American Journal of Sociology,* 82 (January 1977), 757–782. [11]

Selvin, Hanan C. "A Critique of Tests of Significance in Survey Research," *The American Sociological Review,* 22 (October 1957), 519–527. [2]

Selznick, Gertrude, and Stephen Steinberg. *The Tenacity of Prejudice.* New York: Harper & Row, 1969. [2]

Sennett, Richard. "The Boss's New Clothes," *The New York Review,* February 22, 1979. [18]

Sennett, Richard, and Jonathan Cobb. *The Hidden Injuries of Class.* New York: Knopf, 1972. [11]

Severy, Larry, John Brigham, and Barry Schlenker. "Brainwashing: Comply or Else." *A Contemporary Introduction to Social Psychology.* New York: McGraw-Hill, 1976. Pp. 315–317. [6]

Sewell, William H. "Infant Training and the Personality of the Child," *American Journal of Sociology,* 58 (July 1952–May 1953), 150–159. [6]

———. "Inequality of Opportunity for Higher Education," *American Sociological Review,* 36 (October 1971), 793–809. [11, 15]

Sexton, Patricia, and Brendan Sexton. *Blue Collars and Hard Hats: The Working Class and the Future of American Politics.* New York: Random House, 1971. [11]

Shanas, Ethel. "The Family as a Social Support System in Old Age," *Gerontologist,* 19 (1979), 169–174. [13]

Shaw, Marvin E. (ed.). *Group Dynamics.* 2nd ed. New York: McGraw-Hill, 1976. [8]

Sheehy, Gail. *Passages.* New York: Dutton, 1976. [6]

Shepherd, Clovis R. *Small Groups: Some Sociological Perspectives.* San Francisco: Chandler, 1964. [8]

Sherif, Muzafer. *The Psychology of Social Norms.* New York: Harper & Row, 1966. Pp. vii–xiii. [8]

Sherif, Muzafer, and O. J. Harvey. "A Study in Ego-Functioning: Elimination of Stable Anchorages in Individual and Group Situations," *Sociometry,* 15 (1952), 272–305. [21]

Sherif, Muzafer, and Carolyn W. Sherif. *Groups in Harmony and Tension.* New York: Harper, 1953. [8]

———. *Reference Groups: Exploration into Conformity and Deviation of Adolescents.* New York: Harper & Row, 1964. [8]

———. *Social Psychology.* 3rd ed. New York: Harper & Row, 1969. [8]

Sherif, Muzafer, B. Jack White, and O. J. Harvey. "Status in Experimentally Produced Groups," *American Journal of Sociology,* 60 (1955), 370–379, [8]

Sherman, Howard J., and James L. Wood. *Sociology: Traditional and Radical Perspectives.* New York: Harper & Row, 1979. [12]

Shevky, Eshref, and Wendell Bell. *Social Area Analysis.* Stanford Sociological Series No. 1. Stanford, Calif.: Stanford University Press, 1955. [20]

Shibutani, Tamotsu. "Reference Groups as Perspectives," *American Journal of Sociology,* 60 (May 1955), 562–569. [8]

———. *Improvised News.* Indianapolis: Bobbs-Merrill, 1966. [21]

Shibutani, Tamotsu, and Kian M. Kwan. *Ethnic Stratification: A Comparative Approach.* New York: Macmillan, 1965. [12]

Shils, Edward. *Center and Periphery: Essays in Macrosociology.* Chicago: University of Chicago Press, 1975. [4]

Shorter, Edward. *The Making of the Modern Family.* New York: Basic Books, 1975. [14]

Shrewsbury, J. F. D. *A History of the Bubonic Plague in the British Isles.* Cambridge, Eng.: Cambridge University Press, 1970. [19]

Siegel, A. E. "Film-mediated Fantasy Aggression and Strengths of Aggressive Drive," *Child Development,* 27 (1956), 365–378. [6]

Silberman, Charles. *Crisis in the Classroom.* New York: Random House, 1970. [15]

Sills, David E. (ed.). "Sociology," *International Ency-*

clopedia of the Social Sciences. Vol. 15. New York: Macmillan and Free Press, 1968. Pp. 1–53. [1]

Silver, Allan. "The Demand for Order in Civil Society: A Review of Some Themes in the History of Urban Crime, Police, and Riot." In D. J. Bordua (ed.). *The Police: Six Sociological Essays*. New York: Wiley, 1967. Pp. 152–169. [17]

Simmel, Georg. "The Metropolis and Mental Life." Kurt H. Wolff (tr.). In *The Sociology of Georg Simmel*. New York: Free Press, 1950. Pp. 635–640. [8, 20]

———. *The Sociology of Georg Simmel*. Kurt H. Wolff (ed.). New York: Free Press, 1950. [3, 4]

Simpson, George E., and J. Milton Yinger. *Racial and Cultural Minorities: An Analysis of Prejudice and Discrimination*. 4th ed. New York: Harper & Row, 1972. [12]

Sjoberg, Gideon. "The Preindustrial City," *American Journal of Sociology*, 60 (March 1955), 438–445. [20]

Skinner, B. F. *Walden II*. New York: Macmillan, 1948. [14]

———. *Beyond Freedom and Dignity*. New York: Knopf, 1971. [6]

Skolnick, Arlene. *The Intimate Environment*. Boston: Little, Brown, 1973. [14]

———. *The Intimate Environment*. 2nd ed. Boston: Little, Brown, 1978. [14]

Skolnick, J. *The Politics of Protest*. New York: Ballantine, 1969. [21]

Slater, Philip E. "Role Differentiation in Small Groups." In A. Paul Hare, Edgar F. Borgatta, and Robert F. Bales (eds.). *Small Groups: Studies in Social Interaction*. New York: Knopf, 1955. Pp. 498–515. [8]

———. "Parental Role Differentiation," *American Journal of Sociology*, 47 (November 1961), 296–333. [6]

Smelser, Neil J. *The Theory of Collective Behavior*. New York: Free Press, 1963. [21]

———. *The Sociology of Economic Life*. 2nd ed. Englewood Cliffs, N.J.: Prentice-Hall, 1976. [18]

Smith, Adam. *Wealth of Nations* (1776). New York: Penguin, 1970. [18]

Sobel, Dava. "Researcher Challenges Conclusion That Apes Can Learn Language," *New York Times*, October 21, 1979. [5]

Solari, Aldo. "Secondary Education and the Development of Elites." In Seymour Martin Lipset and Aldo Solari (eds.). *Elites in Latin America*. New York: Oxford University Press, 1967. Pp. 457–483. [15]

Sowell, Thomas. "New Light on Black I.Q." *New York Times Magazine*, March 27, 1977. [15]

Spencer, Herbert. *First Principles*. New York: Appleton, 1898. [4]

Spengler, Joseph. "The Aging of Individuals and Populations: Its Macroeconomic Aspects." In John C. McKinney and Frank T. DeVyver (eds.). *Aging and Social Policy*. New York: Appleton-Century-Crofts, 1966. Pp. 42–76. [13]

———. *Population and America's Future*. San Francisco: W. H. Freeman, 1975. [19]

Spengler, Oswald. *The Decline of the West*. New York: Knopf, 1926. [22]

Spiro, Melford E. "Is the Family Universal?—The Israeli Case." In Norman W. Bell and Ezra F. Vogel (eds.). *A Modern Introduction to the Family*. Rev. ed. New York: Free Press, 1968. Pp. 68–79. [14]

Srole, Lee, Thomas S. Langer, Stanley T. Michael, Marvin K. Opler, and Thomas A. C. Rennie. *Mental Health in the Metropolis*. New York: McGraw-Hill, 1962. [7, 11]

Stanfiel, J. D., and F. P. Watts. "Freshman Expectations and Perceptions of the Howard University Environment," *Journal of Negro Education*, 39:2 (Spring 1970), 132–138. [6]

Stark, Rodney. *Police Riots*. Belmont, Calif.: Wadsworth/Focus Books, 1972. [21]

Stark, Rodney, and James McEvoy. "Middle Class Violence," *Psychology Today*, 4 (November 1970), 52–65. [14]

Stearns, Marion S. *Report on Preschool Programs: The Effectiveness of Preschool Programs on Disadvantaged Children and Their Families*. Department of Health, Education, and Welfare. Washington, D.C.: U.S. Government Printing Office, 1971. [15]

Steiner, I. *Group Process and Productivity*. New York: Academic Press, 1972. [8]

Steinmetz, Suzanne K., and Murray A. Straus (eds.). *Violence in the Family*. New York: Dodd, Mead, 1974. [14]

Stephens, William N. *The Family in Cross-Cultural Perspectives*. New York: Holt, Rinehart and Winston, 1963. [14]

Stern, Bernhard J. "Woman, Position in Society: Historical." In Edwin R. A. Seligman (ed.). *Encyclopedia of the Social Sciences*, Vol. 15. New York: Macmillan, 1944. Pp. 442–451. [13]

Sternlieb, George S. "Are Big Cities Worth Saving?" *U.S. News and World Report*, July 26, 1971, pp. 42–49. [20]

Steward, Julian, and Louis Faron. *Native Peoples of South America*. New York: McGraw-Hill, 1959. [10]

Stinchcombe, Arthur L. *Constructing Social Theory*. New York: Harcourt Brace Jovanovich, 1968. [3]

Stockard, Jean, and Mariam M. Johnson. *Sex Roles: Sex Inequality and Sex Role Development*. Englewood Cliffs, N.J.: Prentice-Hall, 1980. [13]

Stogdill, R. M., and A. E. Coons (eds.). *Leader Behavior: Its Description and Measurement*. Columbus, Ohio: Bureau of Business Research, 1957. [9]

Stoll, Clarice Stasz. *Female and Male: Socialization, Social Roles, and Social Structure*. Dubuque, Iowa: William C. Brown, 1974. [13]

Stoller, Frederick H. "The Intimate Network of Families as a New Structure." In Herbert A. Otto (ed.). *The Family in Search of a Future: Alternate Models for Moderns*. New York: Appleton-Century-Crofts, 1970. Pp. 145–160. [14]

Stoner, J. A. F. "Comparison of Individual and Group Decisions Involving Risk." Unpublished Master's thesis, Massachusetts Institute of Technology, School of Industrial Management, 1961. [8]

Strauss, Anselm L. *Mirrors and Masks: The Search for Identity*. San Francisco: Sociology Press, 1969. [6]

Strodtbeck, Fred L., Rita M. James, and Charles Hawkins. "Social Status in Jury Deliberations," *American Sociological Review*, 22 (1957), 713–719. [8]

Stuart, Reginald. "Schools in Louisville are Calmer in 2d Year of Desegregation Plan," *New York Times*, September 10, 1976, p. 60. [15]

Sumner, William Graham. *Folkways: A Study of the Sociological Importance of Usages, Manners, Customs, Mores, and Morals*. New York: Dover, 1959. [7, 22]

Sussman, Marvin B. "The Isolated Nuclear Family: Fact or Fiction." In Marvin B. Sussman (ed.). *Sourcebook in Marriage and the Family*. Boston: Houghton Mifflin, 1963. Pp. 48–53. [14]

Suter, Larry E., and Herman P. Miller. "Income Differentials Between Men and Career Women," *American Journal of Sociology*, 78 (January 1973), 962–974. [13]

Sutherland, Edwin H. *Principles of Criminology*. 4th ed. Chicago: Lippincott, 1974. [7]

———. *Criminology*. 10th ed. New York: Harper & Row, 1978. [7]

Suttles, Gerald D. *The Social Order of the Slum: Ethnicity and Territory in the Inner City*. Chicago: University of Chicago Press, 1968. [20]

Sutton-Smith, Brian, and B. G. Rosenberg. *The Sibling*. New York: Holt, Rinehart and Winston, 1970. [6]

Swerdloff, Peter, and the Editors of Time-Life Books. *Men and Women*. New York: Time-Life, 1975. [13]

Sykes, Gresham M. "New Crimes for Old," *American Scholar*, 40:4 (Autumn 1971). [7]

———. *Social Problems in America*. Glenview, Ill.: Scott, Foresman, 1971. [10]

Syzmanski, Albert. *The Capitalist State and the Politics of Class*. Cambridge, Mass.: Winthrop, 1978. [17]

Tar, Zoltan. *The Frankfurt School: The Critical Theories of Max Horkheimer and Theodor W. Adorno*. New York: Wiley, 1977. [3]

Taylor, A. J. P. *The Observer*, June 21, 1959. [22]

Tedeschi, J. T., B. R. Schlenker III, and T. V. Bonoma. *Conflict, Power and Games*. Chicago: Aldine, 1973. [8]

Teger, Allan L., and Dean G. Pruitt. "Components of Group Risk Taking," *Journal of Experimental Social Psychology*, 3 (1967), 189–205. [8]

Terborg, J. R., C. Castore, and J. A. DeNinno. "A Longitudinal Field Investigation of the Impact of Group Composition on Group Performance and Cohesion," *Journal of Personality and Social Psychology*, 34 (1976), 782–790. [8]

Terkel, Studs. *Working*. New York: Random House, 1974. [18]

Terry, Robert M. "Discrimination in the Handling of Juvenile Offenders by Social Control Agencies," *Journal of Research in Crime and Delinquency*, 4 (July 1967), 218–230. [7]

Thamm, Robert. *Beyond Marriage and the Nuclear Family*. San Francisco: Canfield Press, 1975. [14]

Thernstrom, Stephan. "Class and Mobility in a Nineteenth Century City." In Reinhard Bendix and Seymour Martin Lipset (eds.). *Class, Status and Power*. 2nd ed. New York: Free Press, 1966. Pp. 602–615. [11]

Thibaut, John A., and Harold H. Kelley. *The Social Psychology of Groups*. New York: Wiley, 1959. [8]

Thomas, Keith. "Age and Authority in Early Modern England," *Proceedings of the British Academy*, 62 (1977). [13]

Thomlinson, Ralph. *Population Dynamics: Causes and Consequences of World Demographic Change*. 2nd ed. New York: Random House, 1976. [19]

Thompson, E. P. *The Making of the English Working Class*. New York: Vintage, 1963. [11]

Thornten, Arland, and Deborah Freedman. "Changes in the Sex Role Attitudes of Women 1962–1977: Evidence from a Panel Study," *American Sociological Review*, 44 (October 1979), 831–842. [13]

Tilly, Charles, Louise Tilly, and Richard Tilly. *The Rebellious Century: 1830–1930*. Cambridge, Mass.: Harvard University Press, 1975. [2, 17]

Time, Inc. "America's most important, fastest growing market," 1979. [11]

Tocqueville, Alexis de. *Democracy in America*. Phillips Bradley (tr. and ed.). New York: Random House, 1954. [17]

Toffler, Alvin. *Future Shock*. New York: Random House, 1970. [22]

Tönnies, Ferdinand. *Community and Society—Gemeinschaft and Gesellschaft*. Charles P. Loomis (ed. and tr.). East Lansing, Mich.: Michigan State University Press, 1957. [20]

Traugott, Mark. "Reconceiving Social Movements," *Social Problems*, 26 (October 1978), 38–49. [21]

Treiman, Donald J. *Occupational Prestige in Comparative Perspective*. New York: Academic Press, 1977. [11]

Treiman, Donald J., and Kermit Terrell. "Sex and the Process of Status Attainment," *American Sociological Review*, 40 (April 1975), 174–200. [13]

Troeltsch, Ernst. *Social Teachings of the Christian*

Churches. New York: Macmillan, 1949. Chap. 1, pp. 331–343. [16]

Trow, Martin. "The Second Transformation of American Secondary Education," *International Journal of Comparative Sociology,* 2 (September 1961), 146–166. [15]

———. "The Democratization of Higher Education in America," *European Journal of Sociology (Archives Européenes de sociologie),* 3 (1962), 231–263. [15]

———. "Two Problems in American Public Education." In Howard S. Becker (ed.). *Social Problems: A Modern Approach.* New York: Wiley, 1966. Pp. 76–116. [15]

Tsuchigane, Robert, and Norton Dodge. *Economic Discrimination Against Women in the United States.* Lexington, Mass.: Lexington, 1974. [13]

Tuchman, Gaye, *et al.* (eds.). *Hearth and Home: Images of Women in the Mass Media.* New York: Oxford University Press, 1978. [6]

Tumin, Melvin M. *Social Stratification: The Forms and Functions of Inequality.* Englewood Cliffs, N.J.: Prentice-Hall, 1967. [11]

Turner, Jonathan H. *The Structure of Sociological Theory.* Homewood, Ill.: Dorsey Press, 1974. [3]

Turner, Jonathan H., and Charles E. Starnes. *Inequality: Privilege and Poverty in America.* Pacific Palisades, Calif.: Goodyear, 1976. [11]

Turner, Ralph H. *The Social Context of Ambition.* San Francisco: Chandler, 1964. [6]

———. "The Public Perception of Protest," *American Sociological Review,* 34:6 (December 1969), 815–831. [21]

———. *Family Interaction.* New York: Wiley, 1970. [14]

Turner, Ralph H., and Lewis M. Killian. *Collective Behavior.* Englewood Cliffs, N.J.: Prentice-Hall, 1972. [21]

Tyler, Robert L. "The Two–Marriage Revolving–Mate Generation—Bringing Plan to Save Marriage." In Jack R. DeLora and Joann DeLora (eds.). *Intimate Life Styles,* 2nd ed. Pacific Palisades, Calif.: Goodyear, 1975. Pp. 406–410. [14]

Tylor, Edward B. *Primitive Culture.* 2 vols. London: Murray, 1871. [5]

Tyree, Andrea, and Judith Treas. "The Occupational and Marital Mobility of Women," *American Sociological Review,* 39:3 (1974), 293–302. [11]

Udry, J. Richard. *The Social Context of Marriage.* 3rd ed. Philadelphia: Lippincott, 1974. [13, 14]

United Nations. *Determinants and Consequences of Population Trends.* 2nd ed. New York: United Nations, 1973. [19]

Useem, Michael. *Conscription, Protest, and Social Conflict.* New York: Wiley, 1973. [21]

———. "The Social Organization of the American Business Elite and Participation of Corporation Directors in the Governance of American Institutions," *American Sociological Review,* 44 (1979), 553–572. [17]

———. "Corporations and the Corporate Elite," *American Review of Sociology* (1980). [11]

U.S. News and World Report, May 14, 1979. [20]

U.S. Public Health Service. *XYY Chromosome Abnormality.* Publication No. 2103. Washington, D.C.: Government Printing Office, 1970. [7]

van den Berghe, Pierre L. *Race and Racism: A Comparative Perspective.* New York: Wiley, 1967. [12]

Vander Zanden, James W. *American Minority Relations.* 3rd ed. New York: Ronald, 1972. [12]

Vanfossen, Beth E. *The Structure of Social Inequality.* Boston: Little, Brown, 1979. [11]

Vanneman, Reeve. "The Occupational Composition of American Classes: Results from Cluster Analy-

sis," *American Journal of Sociology,* 82:4 (1977), 783–807. [11]

Veblen, Thorstein. *The Theory of the Leisure Class* (1899). Garden City, N.Y.: Doubleday/Mentor, 1953. [11]

von Hagen, Victor W. *The Ancient Sun, Kingdom of the Americas: Aztec, Maya, Inca.* Cleveland: World, 1961. [10]

Voss, Harwin L. "Socio-Economic Status and Reported Delinquent Behavior," *Social Problems,* 13 (Winter 1966), 314–324. [7]

Wade, Nicholas. "IQ and Heredity: Suspicion of Fraud Beclouds Classic Experiment," *Science,* 194 (November 26, 1976), 916–919. [15]

Wagley, Charles, and Marvin Harris. *Minorities in the New World.* New York: Columbia University Press, 1958. [12]

Wallace, Walter L. (ed.). *Sociological Theory: An Introduction.* Chicago: Aldine, 1969. [3]

Wallach, M. A., and N. Kogan. "The Roles of Information, Discussion, and Consensus in Group Risk Taking," *Journal of Experimental Social Psychology,* 1 (1965), 1–19. [8]

Wallerstein, Immanuel. *The Modern World System: Capitalist Agriculture and the Origins of the European World Economy in the 16th Century.* New York: Academic Press, 1974. [4, 10, 17, 18]

Walster, Elaine, Vera Aronson, Darcy Abrahams, and Leon Rottman. "Importance of Physical Attractiveness in Dating Behavior," *Journal of Personality and Social Psychology,* 4 (1966), 508–516. [2]

Walton, John, and Donald Carns. *Cities in Change: Studies on the Urban Condition.* 2nd ed. Boston: Allyn & Bacon, 1977. [20]

Walum, Laura Richardson. *The Dynamics of Sex and Gender: A Sociological Perspective.* Chicago: Rand McNally, 1977. [13]

Ward, Barbara, and Rene Dubos. *Only One Earth: The Care and Maintenance of a Small Planet.* New York: Norton, 1972. [22]

Warner, W. Lloyd, *et al. Social Class in America.* New York: Harper & Row, 1960. [11]

Warren, Donald I. "Urban Neighborhoods," *Urban Affairs Quarterly* (December 1977), 168–180. [20]

Warshay, Leon H. *The Current State of Sociological Theory: A Critical Interpretation.* New York: McKay, 1975. [3]

Weber, Max. *The Protestant Ethic and the Spirit of Capitalism* (1905). Talcott Parsons (tr.). Glencoe, Ill.: Scribners, 1930. [1, 2, 16, 22]

———. "Authority and Legitimacy." *The Theory of Social and Economic Organization* (1922). New York: Free Press, 1947. Pp. 324–333, 341–345, 358–363. [17]

———. *The Theory of Social and Economic Organization* (1925). A. M. Henderson and Talcott Parsons (trs.). Talcott Parsons (ed. and introd.). Glencoe, Ill.: Free Press, 1947. [3, 4, 9]

———. *The Methodology of the Social Sciences.* E. A. Shils and H. A. Finch (trs. and eds.). New York: Free Press, 1949. [3, 4]

———. *The Religion of China.* Hans H. Gerth (tr.). Glencoe, Ill.: Free Press, 1951. [2]

———. *Ancient Judaism.* Glencoe, Ill.: Free Press, 1952. [2]

———. *The Religion of India.* Glencoe, Ill.: Free Press, 1958. [2]

———. "Class, Status, and Party." In H. H. Gerth and C. Wright Mills (eds. and trs.). *From Max Weber: Essays in Sociology.* New York: Oxford University Press/Galaxy Books, 1958. [10, 11, 21]

———. *The Sociology of Religion.* Ephraim Fischoffs (tr.). Boston: Beacon Press, 1964. [16]

Webster, Murray, Jr. *Actions and Actors.* Cambridge, Mass.: Winthrop, 1975. [6]

Weiss, Jane A., Francisco O. Ramirez, and Terry

Tracy. "Female Participation in the Occupational System: A Comparative Institutional Analysis," *Social Problems,* 23 (June 1976), 593–608. [13]

Weiss, Robert S., Edwin Harwood, and David Riesman. "The World of Work." In Robert K. Merton and Robert A. Nisbet (eds.). *Contemporary Social Problems.* 4th ed. New York: Harcourt Brace Jovanovich, 1976. [18]

Weitman, Sasha R. "National Flags: A Sociological Overview," *Semiotica,* 8:4 (1973), 328–367. [5]

Weitzman, Lenore J. "Legal Regulation of Marriage: Traditions and Change," *California Law Review,* 62 (July–September 1974), 1169–1288. [14]

Weller, Jack M., and E. L. Quarantelli. "Neglected Characteristics of Collective Behavior," *American Journal of Sociology,* 79:3 (1973), 665–685. [21]

Wellford, Charles. "Labelling Theory and Criminology: An Assessment," *Social Problems* (February 1975), 332–345. [7]

Westoff, Charles F. "Trends in Contraceptive Practice, 1965–1973," *Family Planning Perspectives,* 8:2 (March–April 1976), 54–57. [19]

Westoff, Charles F., and Larry Bumpass. "The Revolution in Birth Control Practices of U.S. Roman Catholics," *Science,* 179:4068 (January 5, 1973), 41–44. [16]

Westoff, Leslie, and Charles F. Westoff. *From Now to Zero: Fertility, Contraception, and Abortion in America.* Boston: Little, Brown, 1971. [19]

Wheeler, Stanton. "Socialization in Correctional Communities," *American Sociological Review,* 26 (October 1961), 697–712. [6]

White, Leslie. *The Concept of Cultural Systems.* New York: Columbia University Press, 1977. [5]

Whorf, Benjamin Lee. *Language, Thought and Reality: Selected Writings of Benjamin Lee Whorf.* John B. Carroll (ed.). Cambridge, Mass.: MIT Press, 1956. [5]

Willhelm, Sidney. *Who Needs the Negro?* Cambridge, Mass.: Schenkman, 1970. [12]

Williams, Raymond. *Culture and Society, 1780–1950.* New York: Harper & Row/Torchbook, 1966. [11]

Williams, Robin M., Jr. *American Society.* New York: Knopf, 1970. [5, 21]

Wilson, Everett K., and Hanan C. Selvin. *Why Study Sociology: A Note to Undergraduates.* Belmont, Calif.: Wadsworth, 1980. [1]

Wilson, John. *Introduction to Social Movements.* New York: Basic Books, 1973. [21]

———. *Religion in American Society: The Effective Presence.* Englewood Cliffs, N.J.: Prentice-Hall, 1978. [16]

Wilson, William J. *Power, Racism, and Privilege.* New York: Macmillan, 1973. [12]

———. *The Declining Significance of Race.* Chicago: University of Chicago Press, 1978. [12]

———. "A Response to Marrett and Pettigrew," *Contemporary Sociology* (January 1980), 21–24. [12]

Wirth, Louis. "Urbanism as a Way of Life," *American Journal of Sociology,* 44 (July 1938), 1–24. [20]

Wohl, Richard R. "The Rags to Riches Story: An Episode of Secular Idealism." In Reinhard Bendix and Seymour Martin Lipset (eds.). *Class, Status and Power.* Glencoe, Ill.: Free Press, 1953. Pp. 388–395. [14]

Wolfenstein, Martha. "Fun Morality: An Analysis of Recent American Child-Training Literature." In Margaret Mead and Martha Wolfenstein (eds.). *Childhood in Contemporary Cultures.* Chicago: University of Chicago Press, 1955. Pp. 168–178. [14]

Wolfinger, R. E., *et al. Dynamics of American Politics.* Englewood Cliffs, N.J.: Prentice-Hall, 1976. [17]

Work in America: Report of a Special Task Force to the Secretary of Health, Education, and Welfare. U.S.

Department of Health, Education, and Welfare. Cambridge, Mass.: MIT Press, 1973. [13, 18]

Wright, Erik Olin, and Luca Perrone. "Marxist Class Categories and Income Inequality," *American Sociological Review,* 42 (February 1977), 32–55. [11]

Wright, James D. *The Dissent of the Governed: Alienation and Democracy in America.* New York: Academic Press, 1976. [17]

Wrigley, F. A. *Population and History.* New York: McGraw-Hill, 1969. [19]

Wuthnow, Robert. "Recent Patterns of Secularization: A Problem of Generations?" *American Sociological Review,* 41 (October 1976), 850–867. [16]

_____. *Experimentation in American Religion: The New Mysticisms and Their Implications for the Churches.* Berkeley: University of California Press, 1978. [16]

Wuthnow, Robert, and Charles Y. Glock. "God in the Gut," *Psychology Today,* 8 (November 1974), 131–136. [16]

Wynder, Ernest L., and Marvin M. Kristein, "Suppose We Died Young, Late in Life . . . ?" *Journal of the American Medical Association,* 238 (1977), 1507. [13]

Yankelovich, Daniel. "The Meaning of Work." In Jerome M. Rosow (ed.). *The Worker and the Job.* Englewood Cliffs, N.J.: Prentice-Hall, 1974. [18]

_____. "The New Psychological Contract at Work," *Psychology Today* (May 1978). [5, 18]

Yarrow, Marion Radke, J. D. Campbell, and R. V. Burton. *Child Rearing: An Inquiry into Research and Methods.* San Francisco: Jossey-Bass, 1968. [6]

Yearbook of American and Canadian Churches. Constant H. Jacquet (ed.). Nashville, Tenn.: Abingdon, 1975, 1976. [16]

Yetman, Norman R., and C. Hoy Steele. *Majority and Minority: The Dynamics of Racial Ethnic Relations.* 2nd ed. Boston: Allyn and Bacon, 1975. [12]

Yinger, J. Milton. *The Scientific Study of Religion.* New York: Macmillan, 1970. [16]

Young, Michael, and Peter Willmott. *The Symmetrical Family: A Study of Work and Leisure in the London Region.* London: Routledge & Kegan Paul, 1973. [22]

Zeitlin, Maurice. "Corporate Ownership and Control: The Large Corporation and the Capitalist Class," *The American Journal of Sociology,* 79 (March 1974), 1073–1119. [9]

Zelditch, Morris, Jr. "Role Differentiation in the Nuclear Family: A Comparative Study." In Talcott Parsons and Robert F. Bales (eds.). *Family, Socialization, and Interaction Process.* Glencoe, Ill.: Free Press, 1955. Pp. 307–352. [13]

Zelnik, Melvin, and John F. Kantner. "Sexual Contraceptive Experiences of Young Unmarried Women in the United States, 1976 and 1971," *Family Planning Perspectives,* 9 (March–April 1977), 55–71. [14]

Zey-Ferrell. *Dimensions of Organizations.* Santa Monica, Calif.: Goodyear, 1979. [9]

Zigler, Edward, and Irwin L. Child. "Socialization." In Gardner Lindzey and Elliot Aronson (eds.). *The Handbook of Social Psychology,* 2nd ed. Vol. 3. *The Individual in a Social Context.* Reading, Mass.: Addison-Wesley, 1969. Pp. 450–589. [6]

Zito, George V. *Methodology and Meanings: Varieties of Sociological Inquiry.* New York: Praeger, 1975. [2]

Name index

Subject index